21 世纪法学规划教材

国际商法

International Business Law

|第四版|

姜作利　著

法律出版社
——北　京——
始创于 1954 年

好书，同好老师和好学生分享

图书在版编目(CIP)数据

国际商法 / 姜作利著. -- 4 版. -- 北京 : 法律出版社, 2020(2025.7 重印)
ISBN 978-7-5197-4341-3

Ⅰ. ①国… Ⅱ. ①姜… Ⅲ. ①国际商法-教材 Ⅳ. ①D996.1

中国版本图书馆 CIP 数据核字(2020)第 048390 号

国际商法(第四版)
GUOJI SHANGFA(DI-SI BAN)

姜作利 著

责任编辑 郑怡萍
装帧设计 凌点工作室

出版发行 法律出版社
编辑统筹 法律教育出版分社
责任校对 宋丽娜
责任印制 刘晓伟
经　　销 新华书店

开本 720 毫米×960 毫米 1/16
印张 28　字数 524 千
版本 2020 年 5 月第 4 版
印次 2025 年 7 月第 4 次印刷
印刷 三河市龙大印装有限公司

地址:北京市丰台区莲花池西里 7 号(100073)
网址:www.lawpress.com.cn
投稿邮箱:info@lawpress.com.cn
举报盗版邮箱:jbwq@lawpress.com.cn
销售电话:010-83938349
客服电话:010-83938350
咨询电话:010-63939796

书号:ISBN 978-7-5197-4341-3　定价:49.00 元
凡购买本社图书,如有印装错误,我社负责退换。电话:010-83938349

出版说明

法律出版社作为中国历史最悠久、品牌积淀最深厚的法律专业出版社，素来重视法学教育图书之出版。

原“21世纪法学规划教材”系列作为本社法学教育出版的重心，延续至今已有十余年。该系列一直以打造新世纪新经典教材为己任，遍揽名家新秀，因其卓越品质而颇受瞩目并广受肯定。当前，根据法学教育发展变化的客观需要，本社将原有教材系列调整重组，形成新编“21世纪法学系列教材”，以便更好地为法学师生服务。

中国的法学教育正面临深刻变革，未来的法学教育势必以培养高素质法律人才为目标，以知识教育与应用教育相结合、职业教育与素质教育相结合、精英教育与大众教育相结合为导向，法学教育图书的编写与出版也将由此进入变革与创新的时代。

为顺应未来法学教育的改革方向和发展趋势，本社将应时而动，为不同学科、不同层次、不同阶段、不同需求的法学师生量身打造法学教材及教学辅助用书。在教材方面，将推出课堂教学系列、实训课程系列、通识课程系列、简明本系列、双语教学系列等；在教学辅助用书方面，将推出案例教程系列、法规教程系列、练习与测验系列、法学讲座系列、专业培训系列等。或革新，或全新，以厚基础、宽口径、多元化、开放性为基调，力求从品种、内容和形式上呈现崭新风采，为法学师生提供更好教本与读本，同享规划教材之盛。

“好书，同好老师和好学生分享。”本社在法学教育图书出版上必将继往开来，以精益求精的专业态度，打造全新“21世纪法学系列教材”，传播法学知识，传承法学理念，辅拂法律教育事业，积累法律教育财富，服务于万千法学师生和明日法治英才。

法律出版社

作者简介

姜作利 男,生于1956年2月,山东蓬莱人,山东大学法学院教授,法学博士,博士研究生导师。任联合国国际贸易法委员会(UNCITRAL)专家、WTO争端解决机构专家小组(Panel)专家、世界知识产权组织(WIPO)专家、教育部双语示范课程专家、司法部项目评审专家、山东省调解委员会调解员及山东济南市国际贸易法学会副会长等。意大利罗马大学法学院访问学者(1995~1998年),巴斯大学访问学者(2004~2005年)。曾多次应联合国、WTO总部、世界知识产权组织邀请参会和演讲。曾赴美国、英国、加拿大、瑞典、瑞士、意大利、荷兰、奥地利、前南斯拉夫、日本及韩国等国家的高校参会和讲学。精通英语、意大利语、法语、拉丁语等多门外语,使用英语讲授国际商法近30年,承担教育部的双语示范课程,积累了较丰富的使用英语讲授法律的经验。在(Journal of International Economic Law, Oxford University Press)、(Tsinghua China Law Review)、(China and WTO Law Review)、《现代法学》、《当代法学》、《比较法研究》、《政治与法律》、《法学论坛》、《国际经济法学刊》及《国际贸易问题》等刊物发表中英文论文近百篇。出版著作和教材多部。主持完成国家社科、教育部、司法部、山东社科及山东大学等重大及一般科研项目多项。

第四版说明

本教材自2004年出版以来,有幸博得了法律出版社及广大读者朋友的厚爱与呵护,已被100多所高等院校选为国际商法或法律英语教材,印刷了18次之多,着实远超我的初始设想。更令我欣喜不已的是,不少老师和同学在使用本教材过程中,不顾工作和学业之繁忙,给我提出了不少修订建议。这非但没有使我沾沾自喜,而是更鞭策着我不敢有丝毫懈怠,时刻准备着对本教材进行适时修订。另外,随着我国对外开放的快速发展,特别是“一带一路”倡议的广泛实施,国际国内新法目不暇接,也催促我加快修订的步伐。

本次修订是本教材出版以来最大范围的一次,主要本着“与时俱进”和“切实可行”的原则展开。

1.“与时俱进”是本次修订的最大特点。近年来,随着经济及法律全球化的快速发展,我国建设更高水平开放性经济新体制的步伐突飞猛进,“一带一路”倡议迅速展开,建设“人类命运共同体”的理念正逐步获得联合国和各国的共识。这样一来,越来越多的国际规定及国内新法频频出台,致使本教材第三版中的一些内容老旧滞后,修订工作刻不容缓!为此,这方面的修订主要包括:

(1)增补了一些新法律,大大拓展了本教材的覆盖面,同时,参考了国际国内最新的资料,最大限度地使其“与时俱进”。例如,为了适应我国国际电子商务发展的需要,增加了“国际电子商务”一章。再如,在“国际金融贸易”一章中增补了“福费廷统一规则”一节,填补了我国相关教材的空白。特别是,本次修订也纳入了于2020年生效的《外商投资法》及《外商投资法实施条例》,有助于读者及时研习我国的外商投资法。此外,由于《跟单信用证统一惯例》(UCP600)在信用证实务中已经取代了UCP500,本次修订也做了适时调整。

(2)重新改写了第三版中的“合伙法”、“公司法”和“中国外资企业法”,更好地适应我国对外投资和招商引资的需要。第三版中的“合伙法”、“公司法”主要介绍的是外国法,难以适应中国企业在“一带一路”下的对外投资需要,也不利于我国企业宣传我国的法治理念和传统文化;我国新《外商投资法》及《外商投资法实施条例》是我国加快对外开放步伐的重要标志,必然有助于促进我国的招商引资工作。

2.“切实可行”原则旨在提高本教材指导国际商事实务的作用,也是本次修订的特点之一。

(1)删去了一些实务性不强或与我国相关法律重复的内容。由于我国《合同法》中的不少规则已经接近于国外相关规定,本次修订删去了一些内容,如第三版教材第四章合同法中的“误述”、“错误”、“欺诈”、“胁迫”及“不当得利”等。

(2)增补了十几个实际案例。不少教师和学生反映第三版教材中的案例太少,覆盖面窄,且没有涉及中国企业的案例。为此,本次修订增补了一些案例,也包括几个我国法院和仲裁院审理的案例,以提高我国商人及律师在国际商务中参考相关案例的针对性。

此外,本次修订在提高本教材“实用性”的基础上,也适当兼顾了一定的学术性,为志在攻读硕士乃至博士学位的学生提供些许参考。

需要强调的是,虽然这次修订尽了最大努力,大大提高了教材的“适应性”,使她更加与时俱进,但是由于我的能力有限,可能难以满足所有读者朋友的良好期盼,只能寄希望于以后的修订。敬请广大读者朋友一如既往地谅解,并义无反顾地呵护和提携她,不断提出宝贵意见,使她早日破茧成蝶,切实为我国对外开放宏伟大业作出更大的贡献。

姜作利

2020 年 1 月 13 日于山东大学青岛校区

第三版说明

本书自第二版以来，受到越来越多读者的关怀和厚爱，连续印刷了7次，使我欣喜不已。法律出版社的丁小宣先生和吴昉编辑考虑到本书在我国法学教材中较高的认知度，多次建议将本书纳入法律出版社的“21世纪法学规划教材”系列，同时进行第三版修订。

我在第三版中主要做了以下修订：

一、再一次纠正了第二版中存在的拼写及语法错误。虽然第二版对存在的拼写及语法错误进行了仔细修改，但在使用中发现仍存在个别错误。本次修订中，我仔细将本书通读一遍，进一步改正了一些错误。

二、增加了部分新的内容，提高了本书的实践价值。近年来，随着经济全球化的快速发展，国际商会等国际组织陆续出台了一些规范，很快得到了各国商人的广泛承认和适用。因此，本次修订增加了UCP 600、Incoterms 2010等内容，为提高我国的国际贸易实务水平提供些建议。此外，我通过多年对WTO与发展中国家专题的研究，尤其是2012年7月我作为中国唯一学者应WTO总部的邀请赴日内瓦参加学术会议，对广大发展中国家如何充分利用WTO来赢得合理的利益，有了不少体悟，在本次修订中也增加了这方面的内容，以督促中国作为最大发展中国家与其他发展中国家加强协作，对WTO进行必要的改革。

我衷心感谢法律出版社把本书纳入“21世纪法学规划教材”系列，也希望广大的读者一如既往地呵护和关爱本书，助她为中国的法治建设和促进国际贸易的发展作出更大的贡献。

姜作利

2012年9月10日于山东大学洪家楼校区

第二版说明

本书自出版以来,受到了广大读者的热情欢迎,不少院校的法学院、经济学院、管理学院等纷纷用她作为国际商法的双语教材,第一次印刷很快售完。同时,不少读者向法律出版社和我表示祝贺和鼓励,也提出了一些建议。为满足读者的要求,法律出版社进行了第二次印刷。针对读者的建议,法律出版社的丁小宣先生多次向我提议能否出版第二版,对第一版进行修订。因此,按照读者的建议和丁先生的提议,我在第二版中做了如下修改:

一、纠正了第一版中的拼写、语法及排版方面的错误。第一版为了应付教学上的需要,仓促成书,书中存在不少拼写等方面的错误,给读者们阅读带来了诸多不便。我在此表示深深的歉意。在第二版中,我和我的研究生对本书进行了反复修改,纠正了所发现的所有错误。当然,错误肯定在所难免,我会不停地修改下去。

二、在每一章的前面增加了汉语的内容提示。有些读者反映说,在学习每一章前,面对大篇的英文,常常感觉有些茫然,即使阅读几遍,也很难准确把握整章内容。为了帮助读者解决这一困难,我在每一章前增加了汉语的内容提示,帮助读者在阅读前就对本章内容有了宏观的了解,有助于掌握整章的内容。

三、增加了对难点的注释。国际商法是地道的欧美文化的产物,对中国学生来说,肯定存在许多难点。如果不进行适当注释,可能影响读者准确地理解原汁原味的法律。但是,我增加的注释重点在法律学生不熟悉的领域,如古代法、经济学等,对法律学生比较熟悉的领域,限于篇幅及鼓励学生阅读英文法律文献的考虑,恕不一一注释。

四、增加了对法律英语中同义词的辨析,以提高学生阅读和使用法律英语的能力。不少读者反映,他们院不开设法律英语课,他们的法律英语词汇量太小,尤其是对如何区别法律英语中的同义词,常常茫然无知。他们希望阅读本书既能学到法律知识,又能提高法律英语水平。我对读者的这一要求十分赞赏,欣然翻阅了不少英语同义词的书籍,将常用的法律英语中的同义词分成组,逐一辨析,并挑选了一些法律中常用的句子作为例句。这样,希望读者能收到一石双鸟的效果。

本书自出版以来,一直受到如此多读者的厚爱,着实超出了我的预料。值此受宠若惊之际,我在第二版中对本书做了以上修改,期望读者喜欢。我期盼广大读者继续关怀本书,和我一起爱抚她,扶助她,使她早日成熟起来,成为广大读者的良师益友。

姜作利
2005 年 11 月于山东大学新校区

前　言

我编著这部英文版的专著性国际商法教材，主要基于以下原因：

1. 适应我国高校法学专业学生学习国际商法之需要。根据国家教育部2001年颁发的《关于加强高等学校本科教学工作，提高教学质量的若干意见》的要求，法律专业要先行一步，力争在三年内，使用外语教学课程达到所开课程的5% ~10%。为此，许多高校相继尝试使用英语开设部分法律专业课。在讲授国际商法时，由于缺乏合适的教材，不少学校直接采用国外英文原版教材。我在多年使用国外原版教材的过程中发现，由于法律与政治之间存在微妙复杂的关系，国外教材中常常近一半的内容是直接为维护自己国家和商人利益而编写的。如果中国学生不分青红皂白使用国外教材，必然会出现中国学生为维护外国人利益而学习国际商法的可笑现象。可见，中国学生使用国外教材学习国际商法，是不合适的。因此，中国人必须有自己的国际商法教材，这无疑已经成为当务之急！

2. 为把中国相关法律推向国际市场，扩大我国在国际社会的影响贡献力量。传统法理认为，国际商法与中国法律无关，是地地道道的舶来品。中国只有被动地继受，别无选择。该观点有失偏颇。从理论上讲，国际商法虽然主要产生于欧洲发达国家，但随着经济全球化快速发展，各国法律日趋相同，各国的国内法已成为国际商法的重要渊源之一。另外，在经济全球化的强劲推动下，随着我国的法律日趋与国际接轨，立法水平也相应有了较大提高，越来越多的外商愿意适用中国法律来保护自己的合法权益。如果使用英文将中国相关法律编写进国际商法教材，既为外商来华投资经商提供了了解中国法律的机会，也有助于中国学生向外商介绍中国法律。这无疑有利于我国招商引资工作，促进我国经济的发展，扩大我国在国际社会的影响。

为此，本书具有以下特点：

1. 吸收了多部国外国际商法教材的优点，尽量将原汁原味的法律知识奉献给读者。多数国外教材具有结构条理分明，理论浅显易懂，语言通顺流畅的优点，但是，缺点也是很明显：内容庞杂，重点不够突出。因此，我对多部国外教材进行反复对比，筛选出最重要的内容，剔除不适合中国学生的章节。

我虽然多年来一直使用英语讲授国际商法，但一旦使用英语著书立说，深感自己英语语言的驾驭能力欠佳。为了使本书语言地道、流畅，我借鉴了多部国外原版教材语言通顺易懂的特点，在介绍国外著名判例时，也引用了不少国外学者及法官的评论。这既有利于中国学生研读原文的法律英语，也有助于读者在今后的法律工作中予以引用,以增强说服力。

2. 尽量体现中国的特色。本书在介绍国外相关法律的同时,适当考虑了中国政治、经济、法律、文化方面的特色,主要体现在以下几个方面:

(1) 注重对相关理论的探讨。国外原版教材的内容之所以浅显易懂,主要是因为教材是供学生自己读的,教师上课绝不照本宣科,而是在教材的基本框架下进行研究性讲授。此外,国外相关资料齐全,学生很容易阅读到大量补充材料。考虑到中国学生自学能力较差,资料又缺乏,我在本书中采用了国际国内学者的最新研究成果,并进行了深入的探讨。这样,节省了学生收集资料的时间,有利于学生掌握系统的法律知识,提高其研究、思考问题的能力。

(2)将中国相关法律,如"三资企业法"、"仲裁法"等吸收进来,丰富了国际商法的内容,将中国相关法律介绍到国际社会。

(3)补充了一些基本的经济学常识,如"经济全球化"、"自由经济"、"绝对优势"、"机会成本"等理论。这可以弥补我国法学专业学生不开设经济学课程之不足,有利于学生从经济学的角度理解国际商法。

(4)将本书中一些重要的法律术语译成准确的汉语,有助于中国学生正确理解法律概念。众所周知,中国人学习英文时,常常要求教师译成准确的汉语。由于国外法律中不少概念深奥难懂,学生往往产生坠入云山雾海之感。如果将准确的汉语告诉学生,常会收到事半功倍之效。

本书作为中国大陆第一本由中国人编著的英文版的国际商法教材,我深感荣幸!法律出版社丁小宣先生毅然决定将本书纳入新近推出的"高等学校法学教材",这种无私的鼎力支持使我铭记在心。山东大学法学院孙新强教授在百忙之中对本书大力举荐,使我感激不尽。在此向他们表示衷心的谢意!由于时间仓促,本人的水平所限,不足之处在所难免,谨请读者提出修改意见,我不胜感激。

姜作利

2004年2月于泉城

目录 CONTENTS

Chapter 1 Introduction to International Business Law 1

I. What is International Business Law? 1

II. History of International Business Law 3

III. Sources of International Business Law 3

IV. International Organizations 6

V. Comparison of Municipal Legal Systems 9

VI. International Business Law and China 16

Chapter 2 Forms of International Business 21

I. Some International Trade Theories 21

II. Exporting 24

III. Government Controls over Trade 25

IV. International Licensing Agreement 27

Chapter 3 Legal System of International Business 31

I. United Nations Convention on Contracts for the International Sale of Goods (CISG) 31

II. UNIDROIT Principles of International Commercial Contracts (PICC) 41

III. International Rules for the Interpretation of Trade Terms (Incoterms 2010) 52

Chapter 4 Contract Law for the International Sale of Goods 73

I. Definition and Form of Contract 73

II. Validity and Formation of International Sale of Contracts 76

III. Remedies for Breach of Contract 90

IV. Anticipatory Breach of Contract and Exceptio non Adimpleti Contractus in Civil Law 103

V. Liquidated Damages 106

VI. Obligations of the Seller and the Buyer 114

VII. Passing of Risk 124

VIII. Passing of Property 128

IX. Excuses for Non-performance 129

Chapter 5 International Regulation of Electronic Commerce 162
I. Definition of Electronic Commerce 163
II. The Effects of E-Commerce on Commercial Relationships 164
III. The Challenges of E-commerce to the Traditional Legal Systems 165
IV. International Measures to Harmonize the Legal Issues Relating to E-Commerce 171

Chapter 6 Carriage of Goods by Sea and Marine Cargo Insurance 189
I. Charterparties 189
II. Bills of Lading 191
III. Marine Cargo Insurance 207

Chapter 7 Finance of International Trade 213
I. The Bill of Exchange 213
II. Collection of Documentary Bills through Banks 220
III. Letters of Credit (L/C) 221
IV. UCP 600 231
V. Uniform Rules for Forfaiting 231
VI. International Factoring 242

Chapter 8 China Partnership Enterprise Law 249
I. Definition and Creation of a Partnership 249
II. Property of a Partnership Enterprise 252
Ⅲ. Partners' Rights and Duties 252
IV. Profits and Loss 253
V. Admission to and Withdrawal from a Partnership Enterprise 253
VI. Limited Partnership Enterprises 254
VII. Dissolution and Liquidation 255
VIII. Legal Liabilities 256

Chapter 9 China Company Law 261
I. History and Nature of Corporations 261
II. Purposes of China Company Law 263
III. Basic Categories of Company Organs 263

IV. Abuse of Shareholder Rights and Piercing the Corporate Veil 269
V. Special Provisions on Single Shareholder Limited Liability Company 271
VI. Limitations on Third Party Loans and Guarantees 272
VII. Corporate Combination and Division; Increase and Reduction of Registered Capital 272
VIII. Company Dissolutions and Liquidations 274

Chapter 10 Foreign Investment Law of China 282
I. Sources of Foreign Investment Law of China 283
II. Major Forms of Foreign Investment 284
III. Chinese Preferences Drawing Foreign Investment 288
IV. Chinese Domestic Laws Protecting Foreign Investors 291
V. Dispute Settlement for Foreign Investors 294
VI. Defects of the Chinese Legal System of Foreign Investment 301
VII. The Foreign Investment Law of the People's Republic of China 307

Chapter 11 Intellectual Property Right Law 314
I. The Creation of Intellectual Property Rights 314
II. International Provisions 322
III. International Licensing Agreement 329

Chapter 12 GATT and WTO Law 336
I. The Founding of GATT 336
II. Major Principles of GATT 1994 339
III. The World Trade Organization (WTO) 342
IV. WTO Dispute Settlement Procedures 348

Chapter 13 The Law of Agency 361
I. Creation of Agency 362
II. Duties of Agent and Principal 362
III. Termination of an Agency 367
IV. Third Party Relations of the Principal and the Agent 369

Chapter 14 International Commercial Dispute Settlement 384
I. Settlement of Disputes through Municipal Courts 384
II. International Tribunals 392

III. Alternative Dispute Resolution 394
IV. Commercial Arbitration 402

Bibliography 426

1 Chapter One Introduction to International Business Law

■ 导读

本章讲授的是国际商法概述,包括国际商法的渊源、历史发展、英美法系和大陆法系介绍、国际商法与我国法的关系。由于国际商法产生和发展的背景与我国有较大差异,我国法律学生对此可能有些陌生。因此,如果要学好国际商法,首先要对本章内容比较熟悉。在对国际商法产生和发展的背景有了大概了解后,阅读后面的内容,就会有高屋建瓴之感,自然就顺理成章了。考虑到有的读者刚接触英语法学教材可能遇到的语言上的困难,本章内容力求简明扼要,所用英语力求通顺易懂,以便让读者收获开卷见喜之成就感,满怀信心地阅读下一章的内容。

I. What Is International Business Law?

Economic globalization, in recent years, particularly, as the Cold War and its threat of major disaster seems to have receded, has been one of the hottest focuses in the world. Although it is extremely difficult to define economic globalization, many economists and business experts believe that no business can be purely domestic, and the realities of the modern world make all business international. The causes of these developments are numerous: incredible advances in efficiency of communication, extraordinary reductions in transport costs, growing prevalence of instant tele-and-cyber-transactions, treaty and other norms causing reduction of governmental barriers to trade, and economic climate more favorable to principles of market economics, cross-border influences of competition which have driven increases in production and service efficiencies, and, last but not least, the blessing of relative peace in the world. As a result, scholarly efforts and governmental policy studies have also been giving increased attention to international trade, legislative initiatives relating to trade, the activity of financial institutions such as the World Bank or the International Monetary Fund (IMF) and many other economic subjects relating to investment, competition policy, etc.

Economic policies which are based on market principles are the best approach for maximizing human satisfaction is, of course, controversial, but it is mostly believed that markets can be very beneficial to the peoples involved though not absolutely equal to all.

However, what is the role of law in the economic globalization? The Nobel Prize-winning economist Ronald Coase has stated: "It is evident that, for their operation, markets... requires the establishment of legal rules governing the rights and duties of those carrying out transaction ...To realize all the gains from trade...there has to be a legal system and political order...Economic policy consists of choosing those legal rules, procedures and administrative structures which will maximize the value of production." Another Nobel-Prize-winning economist said: "That institutions affect the performance of economics is hardly controversial...Institutions reduce uncertainty by providing a structure to everyday life...Institutions affect the performance of the economy by their effect on the costs of exchange and production."[1]

Human institutions embrace many structures and take many forms, but it is very clear that law and legal norms play the most important part of the institutions which are essential to make markets work. In today's world, there are economically two systems of law: the public international law which includes the Bretton Wood systems, the General Agreement on Tariffs and Trade, GATT, the WTO, and the private international law including law merchant, international model law, etc.

International business law is the body of rules and norms that regulates activities carried out outside the legal boundaries of states. In particular, it regulates the business transactions of private persons internationally, and the international relationships of international commercial organizations.

In comparison with the traditional international business law, contemporary international business law covers much more extensively, such as law for the international trading of goods, company law, negotiable instrument law, maritime law, insurance law, law of international technology transfer, industrial property law, international investment law, international financial law, international tax law, and law of international dispute settlement.

In sum, the author firmly believes that the current economic globalization which will not be possibly prevented by anyone (as commented by Xi Jinping and confirmed by his proposal of "One Belt and One Road") creates the best time in Chinese history for Chinese youth to seize this fleeting opportunity to study international business law. Therefore the author kindly suggests that Chinese youth work hard on this course and get fully-prepared for the greater contributions to China's rejuvenation.

---

[1] John H. Jackson, The Jurisprudence of GATT & the WTO, Higher Education Press, 2002, p. 7.

II. History of International Business Law

Many law scholars in western counties believe that the Hammurabi Codes (c. 18th c. B. C) in Babylon, the earliest known comprehensive codes of law in the world, is the origin of international business law, as considered to be applied most properly in business affairs. The Hammurabi Codes covers a wide range of business areas such as sale of goods, prices, tariffs, various contracts. In the course of trading outside their boundaries, Babylon merchants brought business law to the Phoenicians in Mediterranean areas. Rome began to be more and prosperous economically in 450 B. C., and as a result the law there was in quick development. The Roman law then was known as Ius Civil (civil law) which regulated the relationships of Romans and Ius Gentium (public international law) which regulated mostly the business affairs of Romans and foreigners. Romans conquered Greece in 146 B. C., and received the Rhode law which was popular in a Greek colony.

During the mid and late Middle Ages, along with the rapid development of economy, there in Europe developed a system of customary law known as law merchant, which regulated the dealings of mariners and merchants in all the commercial countries of the world until 17th century. Many of the law merchant's principles came to be incorporated into the common law, and modern international business law.

III. Sources of International Business Law

Sources (fantes iuris) in legal sense refer to something such as a constitution, treaty, statute, or custom that provide authority for legislation and for judicial decisions. [1] The sources of international business law are what international tribunals rely upon in determining the content of international business law, and they include national law, international model law, international commercial customs and usages, etc.

A. National Law

National law is usually the most extensive way of law-making, and one of the most important sources of international business law. It refers to all rules and norms made by a state. National law in China includes The Contract Law of the People's Republic of China, Trademark Law of the People's Republic of China, The Law of the People's Republic of China on Chinese-Foreign Joint Ventures, The Civil Procedure Law of the People's Republic of China, Arbitration Rules of China International Economic and Trade Arbitration Commission, etc.

National law will, in the long run, still be important source of international business

---

[1] Bryan A. Garner, Black's Law Dictionary, ST Paul, Minn., 1999, p. 1401.

law, chiefly because, though international business is universally recognized, it is not accepted by all the countries in the world; on the other hand, many rules in international business law are customarily developed, and state legislature is needed necessarily to assure efficient enforcement and authority to the rules.

B. International Treaties and Conventions

Legally, treaties are binding agreements between two or more states, and conventions are legally binding agreements between states sponsored by internationalorganizations, such as the United Nations. Both are binding upon states because of a shared sense of commitment, and because one state fears that if it does not respect its promises, other states will not respect their promises. Article 2(1)(a) of the Vienna Convention states that "Treaty" means an international agreement concluded between states in written form and governed by international law, whether embodied in a single instrument or two or more related instruments and whatever its particular designation.

Economically, the following are the most important international conventions: The United Nations Convention on Contract for the International sale of Goods in 1980 (hereafter called CISG) (《联合国国际货物销售合同公约》) in the area of the international sale of goods, Convention for the Unification of Certain Rules of Law Relating to Bills of Lading in 1924 (hereafter called the Hague Rules) (《海牙规则》) in the area of carriage of goods by sea, The Paris Convention on the Protection of Industrial Property in 1883 and revised in 1979 (hereafter called the Paris Convention) in the field of technical trade, WTO's Understanding of Rules and Procedures Governing the Settlement of Disputes in 1995 (hereafter called WTO's DSU) and Convention on the Recognition and Enforcement of Foreign Arbitral Awards in 1958 (hereafter called the New York Convention), etc.

C. International Model Law

International model law means the rules and norms worked out and passed by some international organizations for the free choice by individual nations. The most important international model laws are the UNCITRAL Model Law on International Commercial Arbitration by the United Nations Commission on International Trade Law in 1985 (hereafter called UNCITRAL Model Law), Principles of International Commercial Contract by the International Institute for the Unification of Private Law (UNIDROIT) in 1994 (hereafter called UNIDROIT PICC) (国际统一私法协会的国际商事合同通

则). [1] International model law differs from international treaties and conventions in that it is not passed in international conference and open to all nations for signature, and it is applied in practice only because of its persuasive value. The Article 1(1) of UNCITRAL Model Law points out: "This law applies to international commercial arbitration, subject to any agreement in force between this State or any other States or State." In the Preamble the UNIDROIT PICC provides: "These Principles set forth general rules for international commercial contracts. They shall be applied when the parties have agreed that their contract be governed by them".

Yet, the model law has a considerable role to play in at least five different contexts. The most important ways in which it can be used are as a model for national and international legislators; as a means of interpreting and supplementing existing uniform law; as rules governing the contract; as a substitute for the domestic law otherwise applicable.

International model law is not international treaties or conventions and is of no certain legal validity; however, it incorporates many general principles of law from various legal systems and also most well-known customs and usages in international business practices. Therefore, many countries like to use it as a means of interpreting international business customs, and as model for their national legislature. So, international model law is an important source for international business law.

D. International Trade Customs and Usages

International trade customs and usages mean the general rules and practices in international trade activities that have become generally adopted through unvarying habit and common use. [2] "The existence and scope of a usage of trade are to be determined as questions of fact. If a usage is embodied in a written trade code or similar writing the interpretation of the writing is to be determined by the court as a question of law. Unless otherwise agreed, a usage of trade in the vocation or trade in which the parties are engaged or a usage of trade of which they know or have reason to know gives meaning to

---

[1] The International Institute for the Unification of Private Law (UNIDROIT) is an intergovernmental organization with its seat in the Villa Aldobrandi in Rome. Its purpose is to examine ways of harmonizing and coordinating the private law of States and of groups of States and to prepare gradually for the adoption by States of uniform rules of private law. It was set up in 1926 as an auxiliary organ of the League of Nations, and it was, following the demise of the League, reestablished in 1940 on the basis of a multilateral agreement, the UNIDROIT Statute. UNIDROIT is financed by annual contribution from its member States as well as a basic annual contribution from the Italian Government. Now, UNIDROIT has 63 member States.

[2] Bryan A. Garner, Black's Law Dictionary, ST Paul, Minn., 1999, p. 391.

or supplements or qualities to their agreement."[1]

International trade customs and usages used to be oral rather than in writing among mostly European merchants. Years later, some non-governmental organizations compiled them into written rules of which some of the most worldly recognized are the Warsaw-Oxford Rules by the International Chamber of Commerce in 1932, the International Rules for the Interpretation of Trade Terms revised in 2010 by International Chamber of Commerce (hereafter called Incoterms 2010), the Uniform Customs and Practice for Commercial Documentary Credits revised in 2007 by the International Chamber of Commerce(hereafter called UCP 600). These international trade customs and usages now are widely recognized and accepted in international business areas.

International trade customs and usages are not law, yet, they play an important role in international business practices. For example, if a buyer sues a seller for delivery of defective goods. The seller points to a guarantee in the contract that the goods "will be of average and acceptable quality for the kind and type of goods sold in the trade." How would a court interpret this provision? It could look to testimony and evidence attesting to what the trade considers "average and acceptable." The CISG provisions of Article 9 more closely resemble the way trade usages are handled under the law of its members. The only trade usages that can be used to interpret or fill in the gaps in a contract are those to which the parties agree to be bound or that derive from their past dealings, or those usages of which the parties knew or ought to have known and that are regularly observed in the industry or trade involved.

IV. International Organizations

International organizations, both governmental and nongovernmental (NGO) play an increasingly important role in today's global society as forums for legal, political, and economic issues. The part of this chapter examines the structures and functions of several of these organizations, and pays particular attention to how they impact on international business.

A. Organizations Affiliated With the United Nations

The United Nations is an important organization that will also be discussed in other chapters. A number of organizations affiliated with the United Nations undertake activities affecting the international business environment. The United Nations Economic and Social Council consists of members elected by the General Assembly for three-year terms and coordinates the efforts of all specialized agencies "established by Governmental agreement

---

[1] Restatement(Second) of Contract §222 (1981).

and having wide international responsibilities...in economic, social, cultural, educational, health, and related fields."

Numerous commissions have also been established to deal with special issues. For example, the United Nations Commission on International Trade Law (UNCITRAL) (联合国国际贸易法委员会) promotes international trade through the harmonization of trade law among nations. This agency includes members from many nations. One of its major achievements has been the entry into force of the CISG which is discussed in a separate chapter. In 1976, UNCITRAL adopted arbitration rules, which have been widely used. Other projects involve the drafting of model laws to be used by countries, such as the model law on Electronic Funds Transfer.

1. International Monetary Fund

After World War I, a confluence of economic conditions resulted in many countries facing dramatically similar problems, including inflation, high unemployment, and currency fluctuations. Many nations turned toward protectionism as a way to deal with these problems. Although these measures were largely unsuccessful, the onset of World War II absorbed the world's attention. While World War II was still in progress, several major meetings were held laying the groundwork to prevent future economic and military catastrophes. A multinational conference was convened at Bretton Woods, New Hampshire, in 1944 to focus on short-term financial problems, ways to promote free trade, and the creation of a bank that would help finance the necessary rebuilding after the war. The conference culminated in the creation of the International Monetary Fund (IMF) and the International Bank for Reconstruction and Development (World Bank).

In general, the objectives of the IMF are "to promote international monetary cooperation, to facilitate the expansion and balanced growth of international trade and to promote stability in foreign exchange." The fund lends money to developing countries to assist them with fundamental problems blocking development, such as high interest rates and inflated oil prices. The fund works closely with commercial banks in this process.

The fund has a board of governors, 22 executive directors, and managing director. Quota subscriptions (dues) constitute the basic resource of the IMF. Each member's quota is related to its national income, monetary reserves, trade balance, and other economic criteria. A country's subscription influences its voting power and allotment of SDRs(特别提款权), although no SDRs have been assigned since 1981, Asian countries have only nine percent of the quotas when by equity they should have double that amount.

2. International Bank for Reconstruction and Development

The "World Bank" encompasses two institutions, the International Bank for

Reconstruction and Development (IBRD)(世界银行) and the International Development Association (IDA). The IBRD does not make high-risk loans, and the loans it makes are generally at market terms. Thus, it cannot achieve its goals as much as it might hope. The IDA was created in 1960 to bridge this gap between IBRD objectives and reality. The IDA makes loans to poor countries with average per capita GNP of less than $410 on more favorable terms than the IBRD. Loans can be made only to government, however, which stifles some private initiatives. The IDA and the IBRD usually share staffs.

A separate entity, the International Finance Corporation (IFC), was created in 1956 to address the issue of loans to private enterprises in developing countries. The IFC works jointly with commercial banks and also advises countries on developing capital markets. The IFC does not have the backing of a governmental guarantee when it borrows.

The idea behind the IBRD and IDA is that countries should "graduate," moving first from the assistance of the IDA to the assistance of the IBRD and then eventually becoming a contributor to the IBRD.

B. Other International Organizations

Numerous other organizations with countries as members impact on international business.

1. GATT and WTO

In the aftermath of World War II, many nations reflected on recent history and tried to devise ways to avoid repeating past mistakes. The 1930s had brought a wave of protectionism and high tariff rates to keep foreign goods out. The United States jointed this trend by passing the Smoot Hawley Tariff Act of 1930, thereby exacerbating the Depression. As part of the postwar examination, in 1947 – 48, fifty-three nations negotiated the Havana Charter, which established the International Trade Organization (ITO). The United States, although a participant in the conference, changed its mind about signing as a result of ensuing Cold War tensions. The GATT (General Agreement on Tariffs and Trade) was signed on January 1, 1948, as a temporary measure to salvage some of the principles of the ITO.

The purpose of GATT was to commit member countries to the principles of nondiscrimination and reciprocity, meaning that if a bilateral trade treaty is negotiated between two GATT members, those provisions will be extended to other members. Countries that are members are granted "most favored nation" (MFN) status. All member nations must harmonize their laws with GATT of face sanctions.

GATT members bargain in multiyear rounds of discussion on tariff reduction, quantitative restrictions, and settlement of disputes. Although it has delivered dramatic reduction in tariffs, promoted the international trade, the GATT process has been criticized for its leisurely pace and, indeed, the group has been said to be so slow to agree that it should be called the "gentlemen's agreement to talk and talk." The GATT became the World Trade Organization (WTO) in 1995 which will be discussed in Chapter 12.

2. The Organization for European Economic Cooperation

The Organization for European Economic Cooperation (OECD), born out General Marshall's plan to aid recovery of Europe after World War II, was formed in 1948 by the Western European nations, with the United States and Canada as associate members. The purposes of the OECD are to establish the principle of "national treatment" for corporations, meaning treatment consistent with international law and no less favorable than domestic corporations receive. Other principles include disclosure of information, competition policy, financing, taxation, employment and industrial relations, support of trade unions nondiscrimination, and the goal of utilizing "reasonable terms" when transferring technology.

3. International Chamber of Commerce

The International Chamber of Commerce (ICC)(国际商会) is a worldwide organization that draws its members from all sectors of the business community. The basic purposes of the organization are stated in its brochure:

(1) Permanently represent business vis-à-vis the major intergovernmental institutions and conferences.

(2) Harmonize, codify, and standardize international business practices.

(3) Provide practical services for its members and for the international business community.

(4) Provide a link between countries with different economic systems, or a meeting place for sectors of economic activity with different interests.

The ICC can point to many achievements that have facilitated the development of multinational business. It developed the Uniform Customs and Practice for Documentary Credits, which are used in financing, and Incoterms, the uniform definitions used in trade. The ICC also created a forum for the settlement of disputes, the International Court of Arbitration. The ICC serves as a liaison with the United Nations and its agencies to help advocate the views of the private sector.[1]

V. Comparison of Municipal Legal Systems

Each of the more than 190 nations in the world today has a different set of laws

[1] Richard Schaffer, Bverley Earle, Filiberto Agusti, International Business Law and Its Environment, West Publishing Company, 1996, p. 73.

governing its people and its relations with the rest of the world. Whereas international law governs relations between states, institutions, and individuals across national boundaries, municipal law governs these same persons within the boundaries of a particular state. Although it would be impossible to describe the legal system of every nation, it is possible to describe basic systems or "family-groupings." The study, analysis, and comparison of the different municipal law systems are known as comparative law.

Scholars and lawyers of comparative law classify countries into legal families. The two most widely distributed families are the Romano-Germanic Civil Law and the Anglo-American Common Law. Another family that has become important internationally in recent years is Islamic Law.

Each of these families has many subfamilies; for example, within the Romano-Germanic family there are the Romanist, Germanic, and Latin American subfamilies. Additionally, many legal systems are hybrids: The Japanese and the South African legal systems thus have elements of both the civil and the common law. The Chinese legal system used to be based on the Romano-Germanic family, but ever since China has opened its door to the outside world, elements of common law began to be introduced into the Chinese legal system. Finally, some legal practices are truly unique to a particular country, especially in some African countries that use varying degrees of tribal customary law.

A. The Romano-Germanic Civil Law System

The oldest and most influential of the legal families is the Romano-Germanic legal system, commonly called the civil law(大陆法). [1] Historically, the civil law dates to 450 B. C, the traditional date when Rome adopted its Twelve Tables. The most significant historical event in the development of the civil law, however, was the compilation and codification of all Roman law done under the direction of Byzantine Emperor Justinian (A. D. 483 – 565). This code, known as the *Corpus Juris Civilis*, [2] was compiled between A. D. 528 and 534. It was important because it preserved the ancient legal system in written forms. The Roman law was displaced to some extent by the rules of the Germanic tribes when they overran the Western Empire. Germanic tribal law, however, recognized the principle of personal (as opposed to territorial) law, so the former Roman subjects and their descendants were allowed to follow the Roman law. The medieval Roman Catholic Church also played an important role in preserving the ancient

---

[1] Civil law: (1) the legal system derived from Roman and Germanic practice and set out in national law codes; (2) As distinguished from public law, the body of law dealing with the rights of private citizens.

[2] Corpus Juris Civilis: (Latin: "body of civil law") Codification of Roman law completed about A. D. 534 at the order of Emperor Justinian, which selected, arranged, and condensed the ancient laws.

law because its Canon law, the law used in church courts, was based on Roman law.

With the revival of interest in classical culture in Western Europe in the eleventh and twelfth centuries, accompanied by the discovery of a copy of the long lost *Corpus Juris Civilis*(国法大全), active study of the ancient Roman law began in earnest. At universities in northern Italy—especially Bologna—the *Corpus Juris Civilis* was systematically analyzed, first by glossators (who added notes—annotations—explaining its meaning) and later by commentators (who attempted to adapt it to the needs of their time). Students from throughout Europe, who traveled to Italy to study, returned to their own countries to start the new profession of lawyers. They not only set up new universities in Paris, Oxford, Prague, Heidelburg, Cracow, and Coperhagen, but also found work both in the Church and as advisors to princes and municipalities. Their common background led to the creation of a new civil law, one based on the Roman law, canon law, and the huge body of writings created by the glossators and commentators. This was called the jus commune,[1] or the common law of Europe.

At the same time, Europe was emerging from a long period of economic stagnation. The newly founded towns gave rise to markets, fairs, and banks, and the rapid development of maritime and overland trade eventually led to large commercial centers, which needed laws to govern their business transactions. The Germanic law, which had initially been adequate for the general needs of a rural agrarian society, did not contain legal concepts that suited the commercial community's needs. Nor did the Roman law, which presumed the presence of an extensive imperial government that no longer existed. The guilds and merchants' associations began to follow their own practices and set up their own courts. These courts worked out practical and fair rules and procedures based on the merchants' customs. Soon these same rules were being applied both in governmental and church courts, and eventually the lex mercatoria[2] became an international body of generally accepted commercial rules that transcended national boundaries. It also proved to be more influential than even the civil law, spreading to England where the Roman law tradition was resisted by the local legal community. Today, many of the concepts contained in the law merchant are incorporated in modern commercial law codes, such as the United Nations Convention on Contracts for the International Sale of Goods.

---

[1] Jus commune: (Latin: "the common right") Law based on Roman law, canon law, and the interpretations of glossators and commentators, and common to Europe at the beginning of the Renaissance.

[2] Lex mercatoria: (Latin: "law merchant") Common commercial rules and procedures used throughout Europe in the Renaissance period.

In the sixteenth and seventeenth centuries, the centers of European legal scholarship moved to France and Holland, where the new study of the Jus commune was carried on by French Humanists and Dutch Naturalists. Using historical analysis and philology (i. e., the tracing out of the development of the usage of words), the Humanists came to believe that the jus commune was only a product of history and the Corpus Juris Civilis was merely an ancient text (rather than a holy encapsulation of the "living law"). This desanctification of Roman law was continued by the Dutch Naturalists, who developed the theory that law was based on a universal law of nature and not on the contents of an ancient sacred book.

Along with the development of a theory of law, other events then taking place would eventually lead to the disappearance of the jus commune as the common law of Europe. The appearance of national states, with national literatures written in national languages (rather than Latin, as had been the case before), led to aspirations for systems of national law. In many of the states of continental Europe, legal nationalism found its embodiment in national codes, with the first such codes appearing in Scandinavia in the seventeenth century. In the eighteenth century, the codes of France, Prussia, and Austria were the product of "enlightened" monarchs like Frederick the Great Prussia (1712 - 1786) and Joseph II of Austria (1741 - 1790). As such, they attempted not only to bring about legal unity within a single kingdom but also to express the political and philosophical ideals of the time.

Two national codes have had such widespread and lasting influence that they are now regarded as the very basis of the modern civil law: the French Civil Code of 1804 and the German Civil Code of 1896. The French Civil Code is often referred to as the Code Napoléon, because of the extensive involvement of Napoleon Bonaparte (1769 - 1821) in its writing. It is rightfully regarded by most scholars as the first modern code. Although organized structurally like the Corpus Juris Civilis, it was not merely a restatement of prior law. It incorporated the principal ideas of the French Revolution, including the right to possess private property, the freedom to contract, and the autonomy of the patriarchal family. With regard to private property, the Code's authors consciously attempted to break up the old aristocratic feudal estates by prohibiting restraints on the sale of land as well as on its transfer in a will. The style and form of the French Code are straightforward, easy to read, and understandable to everyone—in many respects it is similar to the US Constitution. The authors of the French Code realized that they could not foresee every possible legal eventuality, so they set out flexible general rules rather than detailed provisions. Jean Portalis (1746 - 1807), one of the authors, said: "We have equally avoided the dangerous ambition to regulate and foresee everything.... The function of law is to fix in broad outline the general maxims of justice, to establish principles rich in implications, and not to descend into the details of the questions that can arise in each subject."[1]

The German Civil Code was enacted almost a century later, partly because Germany first had to take shape as a nation, and partly because of the influence of a group of German scholars known as Pandectists.[2] The leader of the Pandectists, Friedrich Karl von Savigny (1779 – 1861), argued that a German code could not be adopted until extensive study of Germany's legal institutions had been made. Rather than studying German legal materials, however, the Pandectists concentrated on the text of *Corpus Juris Civilis*, with the aim of discovering its "latent" or underlying principles and organization. From these studies a highly structured and technically precise system was eventually devised for use in Germany. Unlike the French Code, the elaborate cross-references keep the German Code reasonably brief and make it a logical and unified system. Unlike the French Code, which was intended to be a handbook for the citizen, the German Code is for the use of trained experts. Yet, these two codes are more similar than dissimilar. Both are based on the jus commune, especially in their approach to the law of obligations and in their overall structure. They also rely on many of the same political and philosophical ideas, notably laissez-faire economics and the autonomous rights of individuals.

In the twentieth century, especially in the years since World War II, changes in France and Germany—as well as the other civil law countries—have profoundly affected the civil law. There has been a movement away from relying only on the civil code, with special legislation and judicial interpretations becoming more influential. There has also been some revision of the codes themselves, especially in Germany. Also, with the advent of the European Union, there is now a move toward harmonizing the laws of the Union's member states.

B. The Anglo-American Common Law System

The origins of the Anglo-American Common Law(普通法)[3] System can be traced back to the year 1066, when the Normans conquered England and William the Conqueror began to centralize his new kingdom's governmental administration. The name "common law" is derived from the theory that the king's courts represented the common

---

[1] Ray August, Don Mayer and Michael Bixby, International Business Law, Six Edition, Pearson Education Limited, 2013, p. 67.

[2] Pandectists: (From Latin *pandect*: "all receiving") Scholars who attempted to prepare a pandect, or complete and comprehensive treatise or digest of the law.

[3] Common law: The legal system of England and countries that were once English colonies. It is based primarily on court-made rules or precedent.

custom of the realm, as opposed to the local customary law practiced in the county and manorial courts.

Development of the enduring principles of the common law was largely the product of three courts created by Henry II (1133 – 1189). The Court of Exchequer settled tax disputes; the Court of Common Pleas dealt with matters that did not involve the king's direct interest, such as title to land, enforcement of promises, and payment of debts; and the Court of King's Bench handled cases of a direct royal interest, such as the issuance of "writs" (written decrees) to control unruly public officials. Eventually, the jurisdiction of the King's Bench was used to control abuses of power by the king himself, establishing a fundamental doctrine of the common law: the supremacy of the law. [1] Also, when the Court of Common Pleas began to charge large fees to hear cases, much of its jurisdiction was taken over by the King's Bench. The judges of the King's Bench did this by broadly interpreting the writ of trespass so that it took in virtually every kink of tort, and by expanding the meaning of the writ of assumpsit [2] so that it applied to most forms of contracts.

An important aspect of the common law is its basis in the customary practice of the courts, and the term itself is often used to describe that part of English law that is not based on statutory law or legislation. In its narrow sense, the common law must also be distinguished from the law that evolved out equity [3] and out of admiralty, and other jurisdictions. The common law's basis in court decisions or precedent is also the principal factor distinguishing it from the Romano-Germanic civil law, where the grounds for deciding cases are found in codes, statutes, and prescribed texts.

One limitation of early common law practice was its inflexibility. In 1285, the Statute of Westminster curtailed the creation of new writs that the courts had been devising up until then in an attempt to expand their jurisdiction. As a consequence, the courts soon could hear only cases that fit precisely within the parameters of the traditional writs. Also, as the scope of the courts' jurisdiction narrowed, the procedural rules they followed became more complex. Finally, with the exception of a few kinds of suits that involved

---

〔1〕 Supremacy of the law: Doctrine that all persons, including the sovereign, are subordinate to the rule of law. Today, the doctrine of supremacy means not only that the king is subject to the law but also that the acts of ordinary government agencies can be reviewed in the courts.

〔2〕 Assumpsit: Latin: "he promised." At early common law, a cause of action to recover damages for the nonperformance of a simple contract that was neither of record nor under seal.

〔3〕 Equity: (From Latin *acquitas*: "even" or "fair") Being just, impartial, and fair. Justice applied in circumstances not covered by rules of law. In common law, it means principles of justice developed by the king's chaplain, or chancellor, to provide parties with a remedy when none was available in the king's courts.

the recovery of real or personal property, the only remedy the court could give was money for damages actually done. In part, the courts of equity—which had the power to order an injunction, restitution, or specific performance—were created to overcome these limitations.

A sharp division between the common law and equity continued until the nineteenth century. Then New York enacted a code of civil procedure in 1848, drafted by David Dudly Field (1805 - 1894) that merged law and equity into one jurisdiction. This "Field Code" required lawsuits to be tried in a single class of courts, using a single procedure. It was soon adopted by most of the American states, by the American federal government, by England in the Judicature Acts of 1873 and 1875, and eventually in many British colonies.

The way in which the common law spread around the world is different from how the civil law was distributed. In each of the principal nations in which the common law developed—Australia, Canada, India, Ireland, New Zealand, and the United States—there was a direct political linkage to England. Although there was a tie of sorts with Rome for the European and Latin American civil law countries, the connection with other civil law countries is more tenuous. Also, the civil law is the easier of the two legal traditions to be received, as it is encapsulated in convenient codes and it deals primarily with private law that is of little threat to the local political system. Common law, on the other hand, is a matrix of case law and statutes; it uses the jury system and the doctrine of supremacy to limit the actions of the government; and it encompasses a complex terminology.

It is clear that the civil law and common law are two different legal systems, and one author summarized the difference as follows: "If we may generalize, the European is given to making plans, to regulating things in advance and therefore in terms of drawing up rules and systematizing them. He approaches life with fixed ideas and operates deductively. The Englishman improvises, never making a decision until he has to ... and so he is not given to abstract rules of law.... But recently the attitudes of common law and continental (civil) law have been drawing closer. On the continent statute law is losing something of its primacy; lawyers no longer see decision-making as a merely technical and automatic process, but accept the comprehensive principles laid down by statute call for broad interpretation.... At the same time, the need for large scale planning and ordering of social affairs has forced Anglo-American law into using abstract norms."

The chief principles of the civil law and the common law have been coming so close, particularly in recent years, that some legal doctrines can hardly be distinguished from each other. The numerous causes for this are the growing similarity of political, cultural, economic systems of all nations, a long period of peace time in the world, as brought chiefly by economic and legal globalization. However, we must not ignore the fact that the civil law, in the international business areas, is gaining more and more primacy though elements of common law are still being incorporated into international business law.

VI. International Business Law and China

China has a legal history of several thousands of years, but unfortunately, little business rules and norms can be found in the Chinese legal systems. China started to introduce international business law during the late period of Qing Dynasty, and enacted in the period of Kuomintang some business law such as Company Law, Negotiable Instrument Law, Maritime Law, Insurance Law, Trade-Mark Law, Bankruptcy Law, etc. The Chinese government, after the founding of the People's Republic of China, though in a winding course, began to adopt open-door policies, has pushed forward the Chinese economy. The Chinese communist party at its 14th congress pointed out definitely that China is undertaking socialist market economy, and this has significantly encouraged its law-making work, and resulted in the promulgation of a number of business rules and norms, including the well-known Contract Law of the People's Republic of China. A variety of principles and reasonable contents in international business law are during this time incorporated into Chinese business law, and till then the Chinese business law is on the whole developing along with the international business law. Internationally, the dramatic changes in Eastern Europe and the breakup of the Soviet Union demonstrate that more and more nations are involved in economic globalization and legal reforms. Nationally, China's entry into WTO in 2001 has undoubtedly created the best opportunity in the history of China for the application of international business law. And this will certainly help China develop its foreign trade, and push forward China's progress to a modern socialist country.

■ Notes

cold war 冷战,外交术语,主要指第二次世界大战以后,东西方尤其是苏联与美国之间利用非战争的方式来赢得各自的政治及经济方面的优势地位所呈现的状态。

economic globalization 经济全球化。至今学者对此尚未形成一致的定义。一般来说,它是指随着国际经济的迅速发展,物、资金、技术及人员等在全世界范围的快速流动,形成世界性的大市场。经济全球化的出现大大推进了各国经济贸易的发展,使各国的政治、法律及经济制度趋向统一。同时,它也带来了一系列问题,如各国之间贫富悬殊的拉大、对环境造成了不可忽视的破坏等。

International Monetary Fund 国际货币基金组织。该组织于1945年12月27日依据《国际货币基金协定》正式成立,1947年3月开始活动,同年11月15日成为联合国的专门机构。我国是该组织创始会员国之一,于1980年4月17日恢复合法代表席位。该组织的主要任务是:促进国际货币合作;促进国际贸易的扩大和均衡增长;促进汇率的稳定。该组织资金主要由会员国按额交纳,投票权及借款权的大小均由份额的多少来确定。

Bretton Woods System 布雷顿森林体系,指第二次世界大战后成立的以美元为中心的国际货币体系。根据1944年7月在美国新罕布什尔金融会议通过的《国际货币基金协定》而形成。该协定确认美国1934年1月规定的0.888671克的美元含金量,即35美元等于1盎司黄金,并规定其他成员国货币的平价按一定数量的黄金或美元来表示;市场汇率的波动幅度如超过平价上下的1%,各国政府有义务进行干预;平价变动幅度如超过10%时,须得到基金组织的同意。美国则承担接受各国政府或其中央银行用美元向美国兑换黄金的义务。这样,其他成员国的货币就与美元建立了固定的比价。但从20世纪60年代起,多次发生美元危机,西方主要货币相继实行浮动。自此,由于美元不能兑换黄金,这个以美元为中心的国际货币体系遂告瓦解。

Jus Civil (拉丁语)市民法,指早期罗马法中调整罗马公民之间关系的法律。与此相对的是Jus Gentium(拉丁语:万民法),指调整罗马公民与外国人之间关系的法律,学者通常认为这是现代国际公法的最早的渊源。随着罗马经济的扩展,罗马人与外国人的交往增多,市民法和万民法逐渐合一,统称为罗马法。

Lex Mercatoria (拉丁语。英语为:Law Merchant)商人法,也可译成商人习惯法。最早产生于中世纪公元11~13世纪,当时在地中海沿岸的一些城邦国家和法国、意大利、德国的某些自治城市从事航运和国际贸易的商人阶层中,曾经形成过一些有关国际货物买卖、代理、合伙合同的统一的习惯法规则。15世纪后,随着欧洲国家主权思想的产生发展和近代民族国家的兴起,欧洲各国政府先后开始采取不同的方式将商人法纳入各自的国内法范畴。18~19世纪,欧洲进入了商事法典化时期,许多欧洲国家的商法典都吸收了不少商人法的原则和内容。商人法具有以下几个特点:(1)普遍适用于各国商人,具有较大的广泛性。(2)较好地体现了公平、合理的原则。由于商人法建立在商品经济之上,必然要求商人之间在法律上享有平等的地位,为了调整具有不同社会背景、不同法律制度的商人之间的利益,商人法必然成为所有商人自觉妥协的产物,照顾到各国商人的利益。因此,一方面,商人法与国内法相比,较好地体现了公平、合理的原则。但是,另一方面,由于商人法主要产生于欧洲国家尤其是西欧各国商人之间,自然对那些发展中国家商人的利益考虑不够,发展中国家在借鉴中应加以分析和合理利用。(3)主要由商人选择的法官来掌握,在国际商事仲裁中采用较多。(4)它特别强调效率。因此,与国内法相比,其在适用时程序简便,时间性强,效率较高。(5)体系庞杂,相互冲突的规则较多,在适用中容易引起争议。

international model law 国际示范法,指第二次世界大战以后出现的一些由国际组织或民间性的国际组织制定的,没有法律效力,仅供各国在立法或司法时参考的规范。其中,最有代表性的是国际统一私法协会于1994年公布的《国际商事合同通则》。

Corpus Juris Civilis 国法大全,指由罗马皇帝优士丁尼于公元6世纪主持编撰的罗马法法典,是近两千年罗马法的集大成法典,其重要的法律原则对世界各国的民法产生了重大的影响。

laissez-faire economics (法语)自由(经济),指由市场供求规律(law of supply and demand)来决定商品价格的经济,最大限度地减小政府干预。

SDR(Special Drawing Rights) 特别提款权,是国际货币基金组织创设的一种储备资产和记账单位,代表会员国的一种特别使用资金的权利。1969 年 9 月为解决国际清偿力的不足而决定采用。按成员国的基金组织的任缴份额比例分配,分配到的特别提款权可通过基金组织换取外汇,故可同黄金、外汇一起作为成员国的国际储备,因此又称为"纸黄金"。

glossators 注释派,指早期研究罗马法的学者,其主张探究和讲授罗马法的原意,采取的方法是对优士丁尼的《国法大全》的各种文本进行解释。

■ Important Legal English Usages

norms 标准,规范,法则,规则,准则。由此可见,该词一般指组织或惯例中的准则或规则,不指立法机关所制定的法律。

请注意下列同义词之间的区别及不同用法:

(1)law:法律,法令。这是一个常用词,主要指由最高当局制定、由立法机构通过或由习惯认可而由法院执行的法律。例如,All are supposed to be equal before the law (法律面前人人平等); The Law of the People's Republic of China on Chinese-Foreign Joint Ventures (《中华人民共和国中外合资经营企业法》)。

(2)code:法典,法规。该词着重指集体的法规,例如,civil code(民法典), criminal code(刑法典)。

(3)regulation:条例,规则,规章。该词主要表示用以指导,管理或控制某系统或某组织的规则或原则。例如,traffic regulations(交通规则); Regulations for the Implementation of the Law of the People's Republic of China on Chinese-Foreign Joint Ventures (《中华人民共和国中外合资经营企业法实施细则》)。

(4)rules:规则,规章。指某团体的规章,条例或比赛规则,常与 regulation 互换使用。例如,Every student must obey the rules of the school (每个学生都必须遵守校规); Rules for the Implementation of the Registration and Administration of Enterprises in the Shenzhen Special Economic Zone (《深圳经济特区企业登记管理施行细则》)。

(5) provision:规定,规范。指具体部门所制订的规定。例如,Provisions of the People's Republic of China for Labour Management in Chinese-Foreign Joint Ventures (《中华人民共和国中外合资经营企业劳动管理规定》)。

(6)procedures:程序,办法。主要指具体部门或行业为实施某法律制订的具体步骤。例如,Procedures of the People's Republic of China for the Registration and Administration of Chinese-Foreign Joint Ventures (《中华人民共和国中外合资经营企业登记管理办法》)。

institutions 制度,法律,法令;公共机构。该词主要表示制度、公共机构或诉讼的提起,例如,institution of law (法律制度), institution of petition(情愿的提起)。

rule of law 法治。最权威的《布莱克法律词典》认为,该词具有至少四方面的意义:(1)实体法律原则;(2)与专制相对的法律至上原则;(3)任何人都必须遵守法律的原则;(4)由法院来决定个人权利的宪法原则。显然,该词的主要意义是法律至上,反对专制。

legal doctrines 法律理论。主要表示具体的法律理论,例如,doctrine of estoppel(禁止反比言理论), doctrine of stare decisis(先例约束力原则)。

注意下列几个词的用法:

(1)theory:理论。这是一个通常词,在法律中使用的不频繁。

(2)jurisprudence:法学理论,法学。该词通常专指法学理论,例如,jurisprudence(法理学), faculty of jurisprudence(法学院)(大陆法国家的用法。英美法国家一般采用 school of law 或 law school)。

(3)principle:原则,法理。一般指普遍承认的重要的原则,例如,principle of good faith(诚信原则),principle of justice and equality(公正平等原则)。

regulate 调整,管理,控制。主要表示法律或规则调整某些特定的关系,例如,This law is to regulate the unified supervision and administration of inspection work of import and export commodities throughout the county(本法调整全国所有关于进出口商品检验的监督及管理工作)。

注意该词与 govern 的区别。govern 主要用于合同的适用法律方面,例如,This contract is to be governed by the United Nations Convention on Contract for the International Sale of Goods(本合同受联合国国际货物销售合同公约调整)。

apply 应用,适用,提出申请。例如,These regulations shall apply to all enterprises, institutions, operators and individuals engaged in offshore oil exploration and development within the sea areas under the jurisdiction of the People's Republic of China, and to the fixed and mobile platforms and other relevant facilities used by them(本条例适用于中华人民共和国管辖海域从事石油勘探开发的企业、事业单位、作业者和个人,以及他们所使用的固定式和移动式平台及其他有关设施)。

legal validity 法律效力。例如,the formation and legal validity of contract for international sale of goods(国际货物买卖合同的成立和有效性)。

注意与下列词的区别:

(1)effect:效力。例如, These regulations shall come into effect from the day of their promulgation(本法于公布之日起生效)。

(2)force:效力。例如, This law shall enter into force as of the date of its promulgation(本法于公布之日起生效)。

■ Review Questions

1. What is meant by the term 'International Model Law'? Briefly list three of its main features.

2. Explain international treaties, using two examples.
3. Outline three circumstances in which international trade customs and usages are effective to the parties to a contract.
4. Compare and contrast the Roman-Germanic Civil Law System and the Anglo-American Common Law System.
5. Briefly describe how and why China came to accept international business law.
6. The CISG contains no provisions that a contract for the sale of goods be supported by consideration. Further, the CISG does not address questions related to the validity of the contract, including legality, mistake, fraud, duress, or undue influence. How will national courts handle these issues in cases that they might be called upon to decide under the CISG? In common law countries? In civil law countries? How has this been addressed by courts in China?

2 Chapter Two Forms of International Business

■ **导读**

本章讲授的是国际商事方式,包括最基础的国际贸易理论、进出口、国家对国际贸易的管理及国际许可证协议等内容。国际商法是国际贸易发展的必然结果,而绝不仅仅是几个国际贸易惯例或法条,如果不了解国际贸易的基本理论,根本不可能对国际商法有深刻的理解。由于国际贸易理论体系极为庞杂,有些理论深奥难懂,本书只能用通俗的英语介绍最基本的几个理论,目的是让法律学生对国际贸易理论略知一二,启发他们进一步了解法律与经济的关系,进而阅读相关的书籍。读者在阅读本章时还可参考本章的"注释"。另外,自我国对外开放以来,国际许可证协议成为我国充分利用外国先进技术的主要方式之一,希望读者认真阅读。

Trade as the most important form of business is as old as the oldest civilization. Throughout history, countries traded to obtain needed items that were not readily available in their country. The marketplaces of Europe, Africa, Asia, and the Middle East had been the scene of trade for hundreds of years before seaborne trade became established. By the sixteenth century, the first international sea trade routes were established by the Europeans. With the advent of great naval power, Portugal and Spain opened the Americas, India, and the Pacific to trade. By the eighteenth century the Dutch had created a great trading empire based on pepper and spices, and England relied on America for tobacco, corn, and cotton. Since World War II, the U. S. trade has increased dramatically and become the biggest trader in the world. The creation of GATT and WTO helps to push international trade develop significantly faster.

This chapter focuses essentially on the forms of international business, including important free trade theories.

I. Some International Trade Theories

We do not often stop to ponder all the ways in which imported goods enrich our lives and improve the material well-being of all nations of the world. But why nations trade? We are going to discuss some important free trade theories.

A. Specialization

Why nations trade? Economists in western countries believe that the reason is that all nations benefit from specialization. All nations have particular talents and resources; like individuals, whole nations are able to specialize in one or many activities. For example, the islands of the Caribbean have abundant sunshine and good weather year round, and so the islands specialize in tourism. Specialization here means that each nation should specialize by applying the law of comparative advantages to its resource endowment. It enables nations to emphasize the activities at which they are most efficient and at the same time gain certain advantages through trade. Nation A will specialize in X, if that is where its comparative advantage lies, and produce all X demanded by itself and Nation B. It will obtain from B since B produces enough for both. If costs rise as outputs increase, specialization will not be complete; trade will be carried to the point where costs are equalized in the countries.

B. Absolute Advantage

Adam Smith said trade between nations would increase real wealth via the division of labor. He assumed an absolute advantage(绝对优势)necessary, in that an exporting industry must be able to produce, with given inputs, a larger output than any rival. Assume that two nations use the same composite input mix of land, labor, and capital with the result that nation A produces twice as much of two commodities as nation B. Nation A has absolute advantage with respect to both commodities; therefore, B cannot produce for export trade.

C. Comparative Advantage

Absolute advantage explains that trade between two countries will likely emerge because each can specialize at what it does best—emphasizing the production at which it is most efficient—and with the other country for its requirements of the other goods. So, both countries will be better off because specialization and trade lead to increases in production and there to increases in the attainable consumption levels of both goods in both countries. However, this trade theory does not explain why a country with the ability to produce two or more goods but at higher input cost trade with other countries with the same ability. That's to say, neither countries have absolute advantage in production of any goods.

Comparative advantage means that countries will specialize in producing several products and services in which they have lower opportunity costs than their trading partners. For example, a hilly, rocky country will not be able to raise as many sheep per acre as a country with fertile grasslands, but the rocky land cannot support any production other than sheep raising, whereas the grassland will support more lucrative cattle production. Even though the grassland is absolutely more efficient at producing both sheep and cattle, the rocky land has a comparative advantage in sheep growing because the opportunities forgone are nearly worthless. The rocky country will therefore tend to specialize in sheep, the grassy country in cattle.

It is clear that comparative advantage explains that even a country that does not have any absolute advantage in producing several goods, can benefit from trading with other countries.

D. Opportunity Cost

Opportunity cost theory is one of the most important theories in international trade and the well-known concept of sustainable development of world economy. Opportunity cost means the value of the benefit that is given up to produce one economic good as opposed to another.

The concept of opportunity cost is crucial to all economic activities, because all resources are limited. Steel used to product girders cannot be used to produce locomotives; labor services used to product shoes cannot be used to build houses. Therefore, in order to ascertain the cost of choosing one alternative use of a given set of limited resources rather than another, the economist uses the opportunity cost concept. He measures the "real" cost of doing business by its opportunity cost, not by its explicit, or outlay, cost. The real cost of producing nails, for example, is the value of another product, say rails, that might have been produced from the same amount or resources.

In utilizing the opportunity cost concept, however, it is not sufficient simply to compare the values of different products that can be produced by utilizing a given set of resources in more or less the same manner. To illustrate, assume that a man has a farm and has invested his life savings in land and equipment, with all of which he grows alfalfa. The opportunity cost of such economic activity might be the difference between the value of alfalfa and the value of some other crop that he could also produce. He could have put his self-owned, self-employed resources to entirely different uses, however. By using his resources as he has, he has forgone the opportunities of (1) lending his savings and receiving interest on that investment, (2) renting his land and receiving income therefrom, (3) working for someone else for wages. If the total return from such alternative uses of his resources were greater than the return from the production of any other crop that he might grow, it is that return that is the measure of the opportunity cost to him of growing alfalfa.

From the point of view of economics, the most rational use of resources is that use which produces the greatest return. Although opportunity cost is the true measure of the cost of one use of a given set of resources as compared with any other use, the most rational use is that which produces the greatest return. Therefore, the economically relevant opportunity cost of a given activity is the difference between the value of the benefit that would have been produced by the most rational alternative use of the resources concerned.

II. Exporting

Trade is often a firm's first step into international business. Compared to the other forms of international business (licensing and investment) trade is relatively uncomplicated. It provides the inexperienced or smaller firms with an opportunity to penetrate a new market, or at least to explore foreign market potential, without significant capital investment and the risks of becoming a full-fledged player (i. e., citizen) in the foreign country. For many larger firms, including multinational corporations, exporting may be an important portion of their business operations. In today's world, almost all the well-known multinational corporations in developed countries rely heavily on exports for significant revenues. Happily, more and more Chinese firms have started to take international market as their main targets, and resulted tremendous increases of their exports.

Exporting is generally divided into two types: direct and indirect.

A. Direct Exporting

At first glance, direct exporting seems similar to selling goods to a domestic buyer. A prospective foreign customer may have seen a firm's products at a trade show, located a particular company in an industrial directory, or been recommended by another customer. A firm that receives a request for product and pricing information from a foreign customer may be able to handle it routinely and export directly to the buyer. With some assistance a form can overcome most hurdles, get the goods properly packaged and shipped, and receive payment as anticipated. While many of these one-time sales are turned into long-term business success stories, many more are not. A firm hopes to develop a regular business relationship with its new foreign customer. However, the problems that can be encountered even in direct exporting are considerable.

Many foreign firms engaged in direct exporting on a regular basis reach the point at which they must hire their own full-time export managers and international sales specialists. These people participate in making export marketing decisions, including product development, pricing, packaging, and labeling for export. They should take primary responsibility for dealing with foreign buyers, for attending foreign trade show, for complying with government export and import regulations, for shipping, and for handling the movement of goods and money in the transaction.

Due to the possible differences of political, economic, cultural, legal systems in different countries, almost all foreign firms export to other countries, especially to developing countries, through foreign sales agents who work on commission. They also export by selling directly to foreign distributors. Foreign distributors are independent firms, usually located in the country to which a firm is exporting, that purchase goods for resale to their customers. They assume the risks of buying and warehousing goods in their market and provide additional product support services. The distributor usually services the products they sell, thus relieving the exporter of that responsibility. They often train end users to use the product, extend credit to their customers, and bear responsibility for local advertising and promotion.

B. Indirect Exporting

Indirect exporting is used by companies seeking to minimize their involvement abroad. Lacking experience, personnel, or capital, they may be unable to locate foreign buyers or are not yet ready to be handling the mechanics of a transaction on their own. There are several different types of indirect exporting. *Export trading companies*, commonly called ETCs, are companies that market the products of other manufacturers in foreign markets. They usually have extensive sales contacts overseas and experience in air and sea shipping. They often operate with the assistance and financial backing of large banks, thus making the resources and international contacts of the bank's foreign branches available to the manufacturers whose products they market.

Export management companies, or EMCs, on the other hand, are really consultants that advise manufacturers and other exporters. They are used by firms that cannot justify their own in-house export managers. They engage in foreign market research, identify overseas sales agents, exhibit goods at foreign trade shows, prepare documentation for export, and handle language translations and shipping arrangements. As in direct exporting, all forms of indirect exporting can involve sales through agents or to distributors.

Today, most Chinese manufacturers are granted the authority to do import and export. The inexperienced companies can conduct their exports through specific import and export companies working on commission. Under the leadership of the Chinese Communist Party headed by Xi Jinping, China will stick to the all-round opening-up policy, and continue to liberalize and facilitate trade and investment. Therefore, we can reasonably foresee a considerable increase of China's exports in a shortest possible time.

III. Government Controls over Trade

Importing and exporting is governed by the law and regulations of the countries through which goods or services pass. Nations regulate trade in many ways. The most common methods are tariffs, nontariff barriers and export restrictions.

A. Tariffs

Tariffs are taxes placed on imports either by value (ad valorem duty)(从价税)or per unit of quantity (specific duty)(从量税). They are imposed for many reasons, including (1) the collection of revenue, (2) the protection of domestic industries from foreign competition, and (3) political control (e. g., to provide incentives to import products from politically friendly countries and to discourage importing products from unfriendly countries.)

B. Nontariff Barriers to Trade

Nontariff barriers are all barriers to importing or exporting other than tariffs. Nontariff barriers are generally a greater barrier to trade than are tariffs, because they are more insidious. Unlike tariffs, nontariff barriers are often disguised in the form of government rules or industry regulations and are often mot understood by foreign companies. Countries impose nontariff barriers to protect their national economic, social, and political interests. Imports might be banned for health and safety reasons. Imported goods usually have to be market with the country-of-origin and labeled in the local language so that consumers know what they're buying. One form of nontariff barrier is the technical barrier to trade, or product standard. Examples of products standards include safety standards, electrical standards, and environmental standards. A quota is a restriction imposed by law on the numbers or quantities of goods, or of a particular type of good, allowed to be imported. Unlike tariffs, quotas are not internationally accepted as a lawful means of regulating trade except in some special cases. An embargo is a total or near total ban on trade with a particular country, sometimes enforced by military action and usually imposed for political purposes. An internationally orchestrated embargo was used against Iraq after its invasion if Kuwait in 1990, and this embargo was strengthened by the U. S. invasion on Iraq in the spring of 2003. A boycott is a refusal to trade or do business with certain firms, usually from a particular country, on political or other grounds.

Tariffs and nontariff barriers have a tremendous influence on how firms make their trade and investment decisions. These decisions in turn are reflected in the patterns of world trade and the flows of investment capital. For example, when Japanese firms learned that Mexican-made products could be traded in North America with lowered tariffs and nontariff barriers, companies from Japan quickly sought to establish manufacturing facilities in Mexcio to take advantage of changes in trade laws. Chinese firms who wish to invest abroad have to pay due attention to the means of trade controls by foreign countries, and take quick measures to penetrate foreign markets.

C. Export Restrictions

Export restrictions are another important type of control over trade by government. An export restriction limits the type of product that may be shipped to any particular country. They are usually imposed for economic or political purposes. For instances, high-tech computers might not be allowed to be shipped from the United States or Canada to another country without a license from the U. S. or Canadian governments. Also, Chinese government does not allow some valuable traditional Chinese medicines to be exported. Before signing a contract for the sale of these valuable goods, Chinese exporter must consider whether they will be able to obtain licensing for the shipment.

IV. International Licensing Agreement

Intellectual property rights are a grant from a government to an individual or firm of the exclusive legal right to use a copyright, patent, or trademark for a specified time. Copyrights are legal rights to an artistic or written work, including books, software, films, music, or to a layout design of a computer chip. Trademarks include the legal right to use a name or symbol that identifies a firm or its product. Patents are governmental grants to inventors assuring them of the exclusive legal right to produce and sell their inventions for a period of years. Copyrights, trademarks, and patents compose substantial assets of many domestic and international firms. And as valuable assets, intellectual property can be sold or licensed for use to others through a licensing agreement(许可协议).

International licensing agreements are contracts by which the holder of intellectual property will grant certain rights in that property to a foreign firm under specified conditions and for a specified time. Licensing agreements represent an important foreign market entry method for firms with marketable intellectual property. For example, a firm might license the right to manufacture and distribute a certain type of computer chip or the right to use a trademark on apparel such as bluejeans or designer clothing. It might license the right to distribute Hollywood movies or to reproduce and market word-processing software in a foreign market, or it might license its patent rights to produce and sell a high-tech product or pharmaceutical.

Licensing is considered a more important method than exporting in western countries to gain entry into foreign markets. When exporting to a foreign market, the firm must overcome obstacles such as long-distance shipping and the resulting delay in filling orders. Exporting requires a familiarity with the local culture. Redesign of products or technology for the foreign market may be necessary. And importantly, an exporter may have to overcome trade restrictions such as quotas or tariffs set by the foreign government.

Licensing to a foreign firm allows the licensor to circumvent trade restrictions by having the products produced locally, and it allows entrance to the foreign market with minimal initial start-up costs. In return, the licensor might choose to receive a guaranteed return based on a percentage of gross revenues. This arrangement insures payment to the licensor whether or not the licensee earns a profit. Even though licensing agreements give the licensor some control over how the licensee utilizes its intellectual property, problems can arise. For example, the licensor may find that it cannot police the licensee's manufacturing or quality control process.

A. Technology Transfer

The exchange of technology and manufacturing know-how(专有技术)between firms in different countries through arrangements such as licensing agreements is known as technology transfer. Transfer of technology and know-how are regulated by government control in some countries. This control is more common when the licensor is from a highly industrialized country such as the United States and the licensee is located in a developing country such as those in Latin America, the Middle East, or Asia. The licensee may, in a manner to benefit his own country to industrialize, modernize, and develop a self-sufficiency in technology and production methods, require the licensor to transfer most modern technology to its country, or train workers in its use, while the licensor may be reluctant to do so.

B. International Franchising

Franchising is a form of licensing that is gaining in popularity worldwide. The most common form of franchising is known as a business operations franchise, usually used in retailing. Under a typical franchising agreement, the franchisee is allowed to use a trade name or trademark in offering royalty based on a percentage of sales or other fee structure. The franchisee will usually obtain the franchiser's know-how in operating and managing a profitable business and its other "secrets of success". For example, franchising in the United States accounts for a large proportion of total retail sales. In foreign markets as well, franchising has been successful in fast-food retailing, hotels, video rentals, convenience stores, photocopying services, and real estate services, to name but a few.

■ Notes

comparative advantage 比较优势。资产阶级的一种国际贸易理论。英国古典经济学家大卫·李嘉图(David Ricardo, 1772 ~ 1823)所提出。从生产成本的相对差别出发,认为两个国家生产力不同,一国即使生产不出成本绝对低的商品,只要能生产出成本相对低的商品,就可以同另一国进行贸易,并使贸易双方都得到好处。

opportunity cost 机会成本,也称为“择机代价”。在生产要素的供应有限的情况下,生产一种产品就不能生产另一种产品。这样,生产一种产品的实际或机会成本就等于生产另一种产品的代价。

import quota 进口配额。限制外国商品输入的一种办法。对于某种商品在一定期间的进口数量或金额加以规定,超过部分不准进口。有的国家为了实行差别待遇,除规定总的进口配额外,还对各出口国分别规定不同的国别配额。有的国家还将征收关税与进口配额结合起来,在配额以内征收较低的关税,超过配额征收较高的关税,称为“关税配额”。配额属于非关税壁垒。

embargo 禁运。一国或数国禁止对某国输出或从某国输入全部或部分商品。禁运往往被某些经济大国用来作为对其他国家实行政治讹诈和经济封锁的一种手段。如20世纪50年代初,美国操纵联合国大会通过一项对我国和朝鲜民主主义人民共和国实行禁运的非法决议。

sustainable development 可持续性发展。一项重要的经济理论,其定义尚不统一,但一般认为,指经济发展要有长远目标,不能为了现时的发展而以破坏环境、浪费有限的自然资源为代价。

■ Important Legal English Usages

essential 重要的,根本性的。例如,essential rights(基本权利),essential provisions(主要规定)。

注意该词与下列词的不同用法:

(1)substantial:重大的,严重的。例如,The seller's breach of contract substantially deprives of the buyer's interest that he is entitled to expect under the contract(卖方的违约行为严重地剥夺了买方依据合同有权期望得到的利益)。

(2)fundamental:根本性的。例如,fundamental breach of contract(根本性违约)。

(3)material:重要的,严重的。例如,material injury(严重损害),material difference(重大区别)。

obligation 义务。例如,The seller has contractual obligation to deliver the goods in conformity with the contract(卖方有交付符合合同规定的货物的义务)。

注意该词与下列词的区别:

(1)duty:义务。该词常与obligation互换使用,例如,The seller has duties as follows(卖方具有下列义务)。

(2)responsibility:责任。例如,If this constitutes a crime, he shall be investigated for the criminal responsibility according to law(如果构成犯罪,将依法追究其刑事责任)。

■ Review Questions

1. Briefly describe, giving two examples, how 'comparative advantage' is applied to

promote international economics.

2. Explain the differences between ‘comparative advantage’ and ‘absolute advantage’, giving three examples.
3. Define ‘opportunity cost’ and identify its main features.
4. Outline three reasons why a state imposes tariffs.
5. List and explain three basic forms of international business.
6. What industries in your province are the leading exporters? Who are the leading export firms? What do you think is the impact of exports on your province's economy? What role does your provincial government play in promoting exports?

3 Chapter Three Legal System of International Business

■ 导读

本章讲授的是国际商事法律体系，包括了本体系中最重要的法律和国际贸易惯例，例如，《联合国国际货物销售合同公约》(CISG)，罗马国际私法统一协会的《国际商事合同通则》及《国际贸易术语解释通则》(Incoterms 2010)等。本章是本书中的核心内容之一，希望读者认真阅读。其中最重要的是CISG和Incoterms 2010。CISG是联合国体系下唯一的具有法律拘束力的关于国际货物销售的国际合同公约，目前有七十多个国家批准通过。我国商人所签订的大多数国际贸易合同都采用CISG来调整，读者必须认真学习。Incoterms 2010是国际商会制定的文本，虽不是法律，却是国际商事中最重要的国际惯例，已成为当前错综复杂的国际贸易术语的最权威的解释，几乎所有的国家都承认它的权威性，愿意选择它来解释合同中的贸易术语。因此，我国法律学生必须将其作为重点来学习。

The legal system of international business is an extremely complex and tremendous system, and this chapter discusses only its most important rules and norms.

I. United Nations Convention on Contracts for the International Sale of Goods (CISG)

A. The Development of International Business Law

In the twelfth century, medieval Europe experienced a renaissance of trade and commerce. Merchants from the cities, many traveling by caravan, met at trade fairs and city markets to exchange goods such as wool, salted fish, cotton cloth, wine, fruit, and oils. Trade routes to the East were opening, with access to silk and new spices. Rudimentary banking systems were founded so that money could be used as payment in long-distance transactions. New legal instruments—the forerunners of today's bank checks—were created. Over time the merchants developed a set of customs for exchanging goods—unwritten codes of how to bargain, barter, and sell goods at market. For instance, merchants decided that if one bought goods at a city market and later discovered that the goods had been stolen, then the innocent buyer took ownership of the goods anyway. By relying on customs, they knew what was expected of both parties to a transaction and how to avoid or resolve a disagreement. These customs of the marketplace became known as the lex mercatoria or law merchant, and they were "enforced" by the merchants themselves. Similar customs were developing in the maritime trade. In the centuries to follow, the local courts recognized the law merchant and used juries made up of other merchants to decide cases. As trade spanned greater distances, and nations created colonies, merchants took on greater risks, and transactions required more complex legal rules. In England, by the eighteenth century, the law merchant became a part of the common law of England when a famous English judge, Lord Mansfield, ruled that it was up to the English courts to say what the law merchant was and not merely what merchants thought it to be.

More than 100 years later, in 1894, England enacted its *Sale of Goods Act* (《英国货物买卖法》) that codified many rules for merchants, thus adapting the common law to business needs of the time. In Europe, the law merchant gave way to stricter legal codes enacted by local lawmakers and legislatures, based on legal concepts dating to the Roman period. In 1906, in the United States the *Uniform Sales Act* (although no longer in effect) was passed in many states codifying the law of sales. The result, by the dawn of the twentieth century, was that nations had developed very different commercial codes. As the business world became more complex, and with the dawn of air travel and worldwide communications, there was a need for a clearer set of modern rules, and for more uniformity in the application of commercial laws around the world. Virtually all trading nations of the world today have modern commercial codes governing the sale of goods. For instance, in 1951 a new commercial law was proposed in the United States. Known as the *Uniform Commercial Code* (UCC) (《美国统一商法典》), it is the primary body of commercial law for domestic transactions in the United States. The purposes of the UCC are (1) to simplify, clarify, and modernize the law governing commercial transactions, (2) to permit the continued expansion of commercial practices through custom, usage, and agreement of the parties, (3) to make uniform the law among the various jurisdictions (states). The UCC has been adopted in all fifty states (only partially in Louisiana). It covers many areas of commercial law, ranging from bank deposits to secured transactions. It does not, however, cover the sale or real estate or services, insurance, intellectual property, bankruptcy, or many other areas.

B. The Drafting of the CISG

The sales contract is universally recognized as the legal mechanism for conducting trade in goods. It is essential to trade because an international agreement to buy and sell goods, like many domestic agreements, takes time to perform. If buyer and seller could fully perform the contract at the moment the agreement was reached, or if every seller handed over the goods when the purchase price was paid, they would not need binding agreements. But few merchants or traders, from any country, would risk entering a potentially risky long-term transaction without a contract. Thus the contract's importance stems from its embodiment of the agreement of the parties, which provides assurances that each party will perform its part of the bargain. If the agreement breaks down, and a court must resolve a dispute, the rights and obligations of the parties will be based on the law applicable to the case.

In an international transaction, at least one party is likely to have its rights decided under the law of a foreign country because two parties to the sales contract must be governed by the law of only one country. What is more important, there are many differences between national laws. Some differences date back to the time when the law merchant was incorporated into English common law, while the European countries moved toward Roman civil law. Even greater differences occurred in those countries whose legal codes were based on Islamic religious beliefs or on planned economy. As a result, the function and nature of sales law are viewed differently in different legal systems. Each system has its individual rules for deciding the validity of a contract for interpreting its terms, and for defining the remedies available to a party upon a breach. Thus, when a firm enters a contract governed by foreign law, it is undertaking an added risk. Obviously, the conflicts of laws of different countries are a big impediment to both parties to a sales contract.

In the late 1920s, the *International Institute for the Unification of Private Law* (UNIDROIT) began early attempts at constructing an international law of sales. UNIDROIT successfully developed two conventions in 1964. However, the conventions never received wide acceptance because, the United States and many other common law countries did not participate in drafting these documents, and the conventions were primarily a European one.

In 1966 the United Nations created the *U. N. Commission on International Trade Law* (UNCITRAL). UNCITRAL consists of 36 representatives from nations in every region of the world. Supported by a highly respected staff of lawyers, it is headquartered at the U. N. 's Vienna International Center in Austria. UNCITRAL has drafted several widely accepted legal codes for international business, including the Convention on Contracts for the International Sale of Goods (CISG). Unlike many other U. N. codes that are not binding, the CISG is a convention or agreement among nations that is binding once the legislature of a country adopts it. It then becomes a part of the country's domestic law.

The CISG has already been adopted by many countries and is being considered by still others. [1] Translations are available in Arabic, Chinese, English, French, Russian, Spanish, and other languages. Students of law are encouraged to refer to it often in this book.

C. Applicability of the CISG

1. Applicability

The CISG applies if the following three conditions are met:

(1) The contract is for the commercial sale of goods.

(2) It is between parties whose places of business are in different countries (nationality or citizenship of individuals is not a determining factor).

(3) The places of business are located in countries that have ratified the convention.

This is called place of business requirement. In the case of buyers or seller with places of business in more than one country, such as a multinational corporation, its "place of business" would be considered to be in the country that has the closest relationship to the contract and is closest to where it will be performed. This could mean that if two Chinese companies negotiated a contract entirely within China, but one of them had a place of business outside China and the contract was to be performed outside China, then the CISG might govern the transaction.

Students are required to note that CISG may apply even if the buyer's and seller's places of business are not in a contracting state. For example, assume that seller has a place of business in State A (a noncontracting state) and buyer a place of business in State B (also a noncontracting state). They enter into a contract in State C (a contracting state) and the seller breaches performance in State C. Buyer brings an action in State B, whose choice of law rules point to the laws of State C as applying to the contract. Because State C is a contracting party, and the transaction is international, CISG would apply.

This possibility—that the CISG could apply in situations where neither the seller nor the buyer had a place of business in a contracting state—was a cause of concern for some of the participants involved in its drafting. They feared that the choice of law rules might lead to the application of one state's laws for the formation of a contract and to another state's laws for its performance. This could mean that only parts of CISG might apply, when CISG was meant to apply as a unified whole. As a consequence, CISG's final provisions allow a ratifying state, if it wishes, to declare that it will apply CISG only when

---

[1] Upon to August, 2019, 83 countries have ratified or acceded to CISG (http//www. cisg, org, 11/15/2019).

the buyer and seller are both from contracting states. [1]

2. Sales and Issues Excluded

The following types of sales have been specifically excluded from the convention:

(1) Consumer goods sold for personal, family, or household use

(2) Goods bought at auction

(3) Stocks, securities, negotiable instruments, or money

(4) Ships, vessels, or aircraft

(5) Electricity

(6) Assembly contracts for the supply of goods to be manufactured or produced wherein the buyer provides a "substantial part of the materials necessary for such manufacture or production"

(7) Contracts that are in "preponderant part" for the supply of labor or other services

(8) Liability of the seller for death or personal injury caused by the goods

(9) Contracts where the parties specifically agree to "opt out" of the convention or where they choose to be bound by some other law.

Note that the parties to a sales contract are free to negotiate other terms that might differ from the CISG. If they feel unsure about the code, they may "opt out" entirely, simply by specifying that the Contract Law of the People's Republic of China (or the law of some other nation) will apply. Article 6 of the CISG states, "The parties may exclude the application of this Convention or ... derogate from or vary the effect of any of its provisions."

The legality of the contract, the competency of the parties and the rights of third parties are excluded from the coverage of CISG. Domestic laws vary greatly in determining when a contract is illegal and when it is void or voidable because one or both of the parties are incompetent. Contraband, for example, cannot be legally sold. However, what is contraband in one country may not be in another; for example, alcohol, drugs, pornography, religious tracts, political tracts, and so on. Similarly, the extent to which a contract can be avoided because it was fraudulently obtained varies greatly. And domestic rules on insanity, infancy, and other contractual disabilities are equally diverse.

The drafters of the Convention recognized that the sensitive issues of legality and

---

[1] CISG Article 95 states: "Any state may declare at the time of the deposit of its instrument of ratification, acceptance, approval or accession that it will not be bound by subparagraph (1) (b) of Article 1 of this Convention." China, for one, has so declared.

competency reflect the morals and social values of particular cultures. To avoid a disagreement that might have jeopardized the adoption of CISG, these questions were left for settlement by domestic law. Also, diverse domestic laws apply to the matters of third-party claims differently, and the drafters left them out.

D. Interpreting CISG

The underlying goal of CISG is the creation of a uniform body of international commercial sales law. In deciding questions governed by the Convention, Article 7(2) directs a court to look to the following sources, in this order: (1) the Convention, (2) the general principles on which the Convention is based, and (3) the rules of private international law.

1. The Convention

When the words of CISG itself require interpretation, Article 7(1) directs a court to consider (a) the international character of the Convention, (b) the need to promote uniformity in the Convention's application, and (c) the observance of good faith. Article 7(1), however, does not describe the sources the Court may—or—must—use in making its interpretation.

On its face, CISG implies that a court may use only the plain meaning of the language in the Convention. The plain meaning rule is common to countries whose judicial practices follow those of England. In England, at least until very recently, courts may deduce the meaning of legislation only from the words contained in a statute. In most other countries, however, including the United States and the civil law countries, the courts also look to a statute's legislative history—the *travaux préparatoires* (French: "preparatory work")—to determine its intent. Additionally, when an international tribunal interprets a treaty, its legislative history is commonly used both to confirm the meaning derived from treaty's terms, and to determine the treaty's meaning when the terms are ambiguous or obscure. [1] Considering the widespread general use of *travaux préparatoire*, it seems likely that most courts will turn to it in interpreting CISG's provisions, especially as the record of the Convention's preparation is now widely available.

---

[1] Article 31(1) of the Vienna Convention on the Law of Treaties (1969) provides: "A treaty shall be interpreted in good faith in accordance with the ordinary meaning to be given to the terms of the treaty in their context and in the light of its object and purpose." Articles 32 adds: "Recourse may be had to supplementary means of interpretation including the preparatory work of the treaty and the circumstances of its conclusion, in order to confirm the meaning resulting from the application of Article 31, or to determine the meaning when the interpretation according to Article 31: (a) leaves the meaning ambiguous or obscure; or (b) leads to a result which is manifestly absurd or unreasonable."

In addition to *travaux préparatoire*, courts in most countries use case law to interpret statutes and treaties. At present, the number of cases that have interpreted CISG is small, but undoubtedly this will change quickly. As it does, the courts will have to keep in mind the Convention's admonitions: that CISG is an international treaty, that its purpose is to establish uniform international rules, and that the courts are bound by the principle of good faith in interpreting the Convention. Because CISG is an international treaty, it will be interpreted by the courts of many countries. The directive that it be interpreted to promote uniformity in its application compels courts to examine and follow the decisions of the courts in other contracting states. The requirement to use good faith means that courts must accept foreign decisions as precedents and depart from them only when they are clearly distinguishable, clearly erroneous, or no longer applicable to changed international circumstances.

2. General Principles

CISG calls for courts to look to the general principles on which the Convention is based when interpreting its provisions, but it gives no list of general principles. It is for the courts to divine those principles. Two that have been suggested are (a) a party to a contract has the duty to communicate information needed by the other party, and (b) parties have the obligation to mitigate damages resulting from a breach. Both concepts appear, in varying forms, throughout the Convention. [1]

Although CISG does not give a list of general principles, it does set out the mechanism for determining them. They must be derived from particular sections within the Convention, and then extended, by analogy, to the case at hand. In choosing this particular mechanism the drafters rejected the adoption of general principles derived from public or private international law, as well as from domestic law codes. This limitation on the sources that the courts may turn to in creating general principles was consciously made, and reflects the drafters' concern for uniformity and consistency, both in the drafting and in the evolution of the Convention.

3. Rules of Private International Law

The rules of private international law are the third and final source for interpreting the Convention. They may be used, however, only when CISG itself does not directly settle a matter, or when the matter cannot be resolved by the application of a general principle derived from the Convention itself.

Private international law rules vary from country to country. Some states—notably in

---

[1] The general duty to communicate is in the CISG Articles 19(2), 21(2), 26, 39(1), 48(2), 65, 71(3), 72(2), 79(4), and 88(1). The duty to mitigate is in the CISG Articles 77, 85, and 86.

Central and Eastern Europe—have enacted private international law codes, while others—such as the English common law countries—rely on case law. This will undoubtedly produce inconsistent holdings. Nevertheless, these rules are much more harmonious internationally than other rules of domestic law and adoption of their use represents a pragmatic decision by the authors of the Convention. By allowing courts to turn to the rules of private international law, the convention avoids the possibility that courts will adopt interpretive aids on an entirely ad hoc basis.

4. Statements and Conduct of the Parties

A contract is sometimes said to be formed only when the parties have a "meeting of minds" or a "common intent". This comes from the idea, commonly accepted in many civil law countries, that parties are bound by a contract only when they subject their "will" to its terms. This theory is called subjective intent approach.〔1〕This obviously has a problem. If a dispute arises about the meaning of the contract, the parties are hardly impartial witnesses about what was in their minds at the time they made the contract. This shortcoming has led some courts, notably those in the common law countries, to reject completely the use of subjective intent in the interpretation of a contract. As Oliver Wendell Holmes, a noted American judge, once wrote: "The law has nothing to do with the actual state of the parties' minds. In contract, as elsewhere, it must go by the externals, and judge parties by their conduct."〔2〕

Of course, the subjective intent of the parties is the best evidence for interpreting a contract—if it can be fairly ascertained—and CISG allows courts to turn to it first. Thus, courts are to use the subjective intent of a speaker but only if "the other party knew or could not have been unaware" of the speaker's intent. When a speaker's intent is not clear, CISG directs the court to look at objective intent.〔3〕In that case, a party's statements and other conduct "are to be interpreted according to the understanding that a reasonable person of the same kind as the other party would have had in the same circumstances."

The most famous common law case dealing with the intent of the parties in the formation of a contract is *Raffles v. Wichelhaus and Another*. In it, both parties meant different things when they made a contract for the shipment of cotton. The court was unwilling to accept their expressions of subjective intent, and instead looked at their objective conduct.

---

〔1〕This doctrine means the rule that contracts should be interpreted according to the actual intent and understanding of the parties at the time they made their agreement.

〔2〕See Ray August, International Business Law, Prentice Hall New Jersey, 1997, p. 503.

〔3〕This means the rule that contracts should be interpreted according to the understanding that a reasonable person would have had at the time the agreement was made.

Case 3 – 1 Raffles v. Wichelhaus and Another

England. Court of Exchequer, 1864

English Reports, Vol. 159, p.375 (1864)

Facts: For that it was agreed between the plaintiff and the defendants, to wit, at Liverpool, that the plaintiff should sell to the defendants, and the defendants buy of the plaintiff certain foods, to wit, 125 bales of Surat cotton, guaranteed middling fair merchant's Dhollorah, to arrive ex "Peerlees" from Bombay; and that the cotton should be taken to the quay, and that the defendants would pay the plaintiff for the same at a certain rate, to wit, at the rate of 171/4 d. per pound, within a certain time then agreed upon after the arrival of the said goods in England. The said goods did arrive by the said ship from Bombay in England, to wit, at Liverpool, and the plaintiff was then and there ready, and willing and offered to deliver the said goods to the defendants, & c. Breach: that the defendants refused to accept the said goods or pay the plaintiff for them.

Issue: Is there a binding contract?

Decision: No. That the said ship mentioned in the said agreement was meant and intended by the defendants to be the ship called the "Peerless," which sailed from Bombay, to wit, in October; and that the plaintiff was not ready and willing and did not offer to deliver to the defendants any bales of cotton which arrived by the mentioned ship, but instead thereof was only ready and willing to deliver to the defendants 125 bales of Surat cotton which arrived by another and different ship, which was also called the "Peerless," and which sailed from Bombay, to wit, in December....

There is nothing onthe face of the contract to show that any particular ship called the "Peerless" was meant; but the moment it appears that two ships called the "Peerless" were about to sail from Bombay there is a latent ambiguity, and parol evidence may be given for the purpose of showing that the defendant meant one "Peerless" the plaintiff another. That being so, there was no consensus *ad idm*, [1] and therefore no binding contract. [2]

5. Negotiations

When a court is to determine intent—be it the party's subjective intent or a reasonable person's objective understanding—Article 8 (3) of CISC directs that " due

[1] Latin: "to the same point."

[2] Ray August, International Business Law, Prentice Hall New Jersey, 1997, p. 504.

consideration" be given "to all relevant circumstances," including (1) the negotiations leading up to the contract, (2) the practices which the parties have established between themselves, and (3) the parties' conduct after they agree to the contract.

The purpose of Article 8(3) is to do away with the technical rules that domestic courts sometimes use to interpret contracts. One notable example is the common law's parol evidences rule.[1] The parol evidence rule(口头证据原则)forbids a court from considering any "prior" or any "contemporaneous oral understanding" when it is interpreting a writing that the parties intended as a "final expression of their agreement." Article 8(3) specifically allows courts to consider the parties' preliminary negotiations when they interpret a contract.

Nevertheless, while Article 8(3) gives court the flexibility to consider all relevant evidence, Article 6 allows the parties to "derogate from or vary the effect of" any of the provisions of the Convention. Thus, if the parties include a contract term (often called an "integration clause") that directs a court to ignore all prior or contemporaneous agreements, the court will have to give effect to that term. In other words, if the parties choose to adopt the parol evidence rule, they can do so. However, unless they specifically do so, the court will look at all the relevant circumstances of the case.

In addition to considering prior and contemporaneous conducts, CISG lets a court consider the parties' subsequent conduct. Again, this is contrary to the practice in some domestic tribunals. CISG, however, does reflect the most widely followed practice, and as is the case for parol evidence, the parties are free to insert a provision in their contract excluding its consideration.

6. Practices and Usages

Both Article 8(3) and Article 9(1) of CISG state that parties are bound by "any practices which they have established between themselves." Article 9(1) also allows a court to consider any usages which the parties agreed to, and Article 9(2) lets it consider "a usage of which the parties knew or ought to have known and which in international trade is widely known to, and regularly observed by parties to contracts of the type involved in the particular trade concerned."

Article 9(2) was a compromise between the capitalist and communist delegates who participated in the drafting of CISG. Trade usages are not considered unless a contract specifically adopted them and they did not violate statutory rules. In the Western world, on the other hand, flexibility and freedom of contract are more important than certainty. In

---

[1] This rule means that when a contract describes itself as being complete and final, preliminary or informal agreements made prior to or at the same time the contract was made will be ignored when interpreting it.

some circumstances, trade usages apply in the West even when they contradict a statutory provision or the contract is silent. [1] The delegates ultimately agreed to let a court consider international trade usages, but only if they are "widely known" and "regularly observed."

II. UNIDROIT Principles of International Commercial Contracts (PICC)

The International Institute for the Unification of Private Law (UNIDROIT), set up in 1926 as an auxiliary organ of the League of Nations, is an independent intergovernmental organization with its seat in Rome, Italy. Its purpose is to study needs and methods for modernizing, harmonizing and coordinating private and in particular commercial law as between States and groups of States. It' Principles of International Commercial Contracts (UNIDROIT PICC) have been hailed as one of the most important model laws of international commerce.

A. Origin and Preparation of UNIDROIT PICC

1. Background

UNIDROIT PICC is a non-legislative means of unification or harmonization of law in the area of international commerce. The great French comparativist Edouard Lambert, at the beginning of 20th century, stressed the fact that legislation was only one, and perhaps not even the most important channel to arrive at the establishment of such a supranational law. [2] The ancient *ius commune* which had for centuries constituted a uniform legal framework in medieval Europe, notwithstanding its division into a myriad of distinct political entities each of which had its own particular statutes, is as old as the movement for unification itself.

Yet, while such a common legal framework was long considered to be little more than a utopia, its realization has recently been advocated as a veritable necessity in the far from satisfactory present situation of uniform law. A first attempt in this direction may be seen in the Restatements of the Law in the United States, prepared and periodically brought up

---

[1] The U. S. Uniform Commercial Code Section 1 – 205(4) states: "The express terms of an agreement and an applicable course of dealing or usage of trade shall be construed wherever reasonable as consistent with each other, but when such construction is unreasonable express terms control both course of dealing and usage of trade and course of dealing controls usage of trade." Section 1 – 205 (5) states: "An applicable usage of trade in the place where any part of performance is to occur shall be used in interpreting the agreement as to that part of the performance." Section 1 – 205(6) states: "Evidence of a relevant usage of trade offered by one party is not admissible unless and until he had given the other party such notice as the court finds sufficient to prevent unfair surprise to the latter." Section 2 – 208 has the similar provisions.

[2] Michael Joachim Bonell, An International Restatement of Contract Law, 2nd ed., Irvington-on-Hudson, New York, 1997, p. 1.

to date by academics and practitioners under the auspices of the American Law Institute. These Restatements deal with a variety of subjects, such as contract, tort, agency, restitution, conflict of laws, etc. which traditionally fall within the competence of the common law of each State. Their success is shown by the fact that there now already exists a second, or even a third, "generation" of the various Restatements.

UNIDROIT's initiative for the elaboration of "Principles of International Commercial Contracts" goes in the same direction, but is even more ambitious since the UNIDROIT PICC are intended to be applied globally and to meet the needs of international trade relationships, including those between developed and less developed countries.

The coexistence of different domestic laws governinginternational contracts inevitably raises a problem of conflict of laws, in the sense that in each case it is necessary to establish which of the various legal systems having contacts with the given contract will ultimately govern it. The uncertainties and inconveniences that derive from this are only too evident. Because of the different national rules of private international law, parties risk remaining uncertain as to the law applicable to their contract until the competent forum is established; and even then, depending on the conflict-of-laws-rules of the forum chosen, the same contract may well be subject to the law of State X or to the law of State Y.

It is true that in recent times States have adopted an increasing number of international conventions in the fields of both private international law and substantive law, with a view to eliminating the uncertainties arising out of the coexistence of different national legal systems.

Yet, international conventions are normally rather fragmentary in character. Thus, most of them deal exclusively with the effects of the respective types of contract covered (e.g., agency, leasing, factoring, etc.) Finally, international conventions are likely to be interpreted differently in different countries and, in the case of lacunae, will be supplemented by rules taken from non-unified domestic law. In addition, they have by their very nature a very limited capacity for growth, if any. As has been observed, "The inflexibility of many international conventions may be too heavy price to pay. The need to revise the law arises constantly, and international procedures sometimes slow the process of necessary law reform to an unacceptable extent." [1]

Parties are of course free to lay down in their contract a detailed and possibly exhaustive regulation of their rights and obligations so as to avoid to the greatest possible extent any recourse to external sources. Yet, apart from the fact that such supposedly

---

〔1〕 Michael Joachim Bonell, An International Restatement of Contract Law, 2nd ed., Irvington-on-Hudson, New York, 1997, p. 12.

"self-regulatory" contracts equally cannot do without a general legal framework within which to operate—in so doing the parties often encounter insurmountable difficulties arising from the language barriers between them and the absence of internationally uniform legal terminology on which they can rely.

Even the parties' use of their right to choose the applicable law does not always provide an entirely satisfactory solution. This is especially true in cases where, for reasons of prestige or political imperative, a party is not willing to choose the law of a foreign country, although perfectly aware that its own national law is clearly inadequate to regulate the kind of transaction at hand.

2. Preparation of the UNIDROIT PICC

In 1968 to celebrate the 40th anniversary of the foundation of UNIDROIT, President of UNIDROIT proposed to undertake a similar initiative as "Restatements of the Law" in the United States of America, at the international level. The UNIDROIT Governing Council—the Institute's highest scientific organ—decided in 1971 to include in the Work Programme of the Institute the initiative. After the new Work Programme was approved by the Member States of UNIDROIT, the President set up a small Steering Committee, composed of Professors Rene David (University of Aix-en-Provence), Clive M. Schmitthoff (City University of London) and Tudor Popescu (University of Bucharest), in representation of the civil law, the common law and the former socialist systems, was set up with the task of making preliminary inquiries. In 1980 a special Working Group set up with the task of preparing the various draft chapters of the PICC. The members of the Group, which included representatives of all the major legal and socio-economic systems of the world, were leading experts in the field of contract law and international trade law. Most of the members were academics, some high ranking judges or civil servants; they all sat, however, in a personal capacity and did not express the views of their governments.

The Working Group concluded the last reading of the different draft chapters in February 1994, after which the text was submitted to a special Editorial Committee, chaired by E. Allan Farnsworth and composed of Rapporteurs on the various chapters. In May 1994 the Governing Council gave its formal imprimatur to the UNIDROIT PICC and recommended their widest possible distribution in practice.

B. General Principles of the UNIDROIT PICC

There are a number of principles underlying the UNIDROIT PICC, and it is highlighting at least the most significant of these.

1. Freedom of Contract

One of the most fundamental ideas underlying the UNIDROIT PICC is that of freedom of contract. This principle is expressly stated in Article 1. 1 ("Freedom of contract") which reads: "The parties are free to enter a contract and to determine its content." As pointed out in the Comment, "The right of business people to decide freely to whom they will offer their goods or services and by whom they wish to be supplied, as well as the possibility for them freely to agree on the terms of individual transactions, are the cornerstones of an open, market-oriented and competitive international economic order."

The first of the two aspects of the principle of freedom of contract, i. e. the possibility of concluding contracts with any other person, irrespective of their legal status and their nationality, evidently falls outside the scope of the UNIDROIT PICC. Whether, and if so, to what extent a system of free movement of goods and services is established at both the domestic and international level is entirely dependent on the particular trade policy adopted by each single state and/or by the community of states.

With respect to the second aspect, i. e. the freedom of the parties to determine the content of their contract, the principle as expressed in Article 1.1 is further confirmed in Article 1.5 ("*Exclusion or modification by parties*") which states that "the parties may exclude the application of these Principles or derogate from or vary the effect of any of their provisions, except as otherwise provided in the Principles."

It is clear that the parties enjoy the widest possible autonomy, in the sense that they may in each individual case either exclude the application of the UNIDROIT PICC in whole or in part or modify their content so as to adapt them to the specific needs of the kind of transaction involved.[1]

2. Openness to Usages

Another essential element of the UNIDROIT PICC is its marked openness to usages. In other words, like other legal instruments specifically dealing with international commercial transactions, in particular CISG, the UNIDROIT PICC accords usages and practices developing within the different trade sectors a central role in the determination of the rights and duties of the parties to each individual contract. The reason for this is to be found in the general objective pursued by the UNIDROIT PICC to provide a regulation sufficiently flexible to permit of its constantly adapting to the ever-changing technical and economic conditions of cross-border trade.

The relevance of trade usages and practices within the system of the UNIDROIT PICC is stated in general terms in Article 1.8 ("Usages and practices") according to which parties are bound not only by "any usage to which they have agreed and ... any practices which they have established between themselves," (paragraph 1), but also by

[1] See Comment 1 to Article 1.5.

"a usage that is widely known to and regularly observed in international trade by parties in the particular trade concerned, except where the application of such a usage would be unreasonable" (paragraph 2)

Apart from the last proviso, the importance of this article lies in the fact that it expressly recognizes that usages may be binding not only when they have been agreed upon between the parties, but even in the absence of any such intention, provided that they meet certain objective requirements.

On the hand, it is important to note that the UNIDROIT PICC, like CISG, restrict the range of relevant trade usages to those "which are widely known to and regularly observed in international trade by parties in the particular trade concerned." As a consequence, usages of a purely local or national origin are applicable only exceptionally without any reference thereto by the parties.

Even more important are the references to usages contained in Articles 4.3 ("Relevant circumstances") and 5.2 ("Implied obligations"). Indeed, according to the first of the two provisions usages are one of the means of interpretation of single statements or the conduct of a party or of the contract as a whole, i. e. they have to be taken into account to establish the intention of the parties or the meaning that reasonable persons of the same kind as the parties would give to the statement or conduct or to the contract in question. The second, in indicating usages as a possible source of implied obligations, makes even clearer what already follows from the general statement in Article 1.8, i. e. that in the system of the UNIDROIT PICC the rights and obligations of the parties to a particular contract are determined, among other things, by the applicable usages.

3. Favor Contractus

Another principle underlying the UNIDROIT PICC is the so called *favor contractus*, i. e. the aim of preserving the contract whenever possible, thus limiting the number of cases in which its existence or validity may be questioned or in which it may be terminated before time. The reason behind this is the acknowledgement that despite shortcomings which might arise in the course of the formation or performance of the contract it is normally in the interest of both parties to do all possible to keep their original bargain alive than to renounce it and to look for alternative goods or services elsewhere on the market. [1]

One example of a provision based on this assumption may be seen in Article 2.1 ("Manner of formation"), according to which a contract may be concluded either by the

---

[1] Michael Joachim Bonell, An International Restatement of Contract Law, 2nd ed., Irvington-on-Hudson, New York, 1997, p. 118.

acceptance of an offer or by conduct of the parties that is sufficient to show agreement. As stated in the Comment, in commercial practice contracts, particularly when related to complex transactions, are often concluded after prolonged negotiations without an identifiable sequence of offer and acceptance. Since in such cases it may be difficult to determine if and when a binding agreement has been reached, it is important to admit that a contract may be considered to be concluded even though the moment of its formation cannot be determined provided that the conduct of the parties is sufficient to show agreement.

Other provisions of this kind are Articles 2.11(2) ("Modified acceptance") and 2.12 ("Writings in confirmation"). According to paragraph 2 of Article 2.11, a reply to an offer which purports to be an acceptance but contains additions or modifications may nonetheless lead to the conclusion of a contract, if the additional or different terms do not materially alter the terms of the offer and the offeror does not object to the discrepancy without undue delay: moreover, if the offeror does not object, the terms of the contract are the terms of the offer with the modifications contained in the acceptance.[1]

4. Observance of Good Faith and Fair Dealing in International Trade

Paragraph 1 of Article 1.7. clearly states: "each party must act in accordance with good faith and fair dealing in international trade," and this clearly indicates that under the system of the UNIDROIT PICC it is throughout the life of the contract, including the negotiation process, that the parties' behaviour must conform to good faith and fair dealing. In this respect the UNIDROIT PICC follow an approach familiar to the generality of civil law systems, but not necessarily to common law systems which, even where admitting good faith and fair dealing as a general principle, confine its operation basically to the performance of contracts.

Secondly, although no definition is given of what is meant by "good faith", the fact that the term is coupled with "fair dealing" makes it clear that it is to be understood in an objective sense, as synonymous with what in the same UNIDROIT PICC is elsewhere referred to as "reasonable commercial standards of fair dealing, and not in a subjective sense, as a state of mind or just acting honestly."[2]

Finally, the reference to "good faith and fair dealing in international trade" makes it clear that in the context of the UNIDROIT PICC the two concepts are not to be applied according to the standards originally adopted within the different national legal systems. In

---

〔1〕 The provision corresponds almost literally to Article 19 (2) CISG.

〔2〕 Michael Joachim Bonell, An International Restatement of Contract Law, 2nd ed., Irvington-on-Hudson, New York, 1997, p. 138.

other words, as pointed out in the Comment, such domestic standards may be taken into account only to the extent that they are shown to be generally accepted among the various legal systems. Moreover, since standards of business practice may vary considerably from one trade sector to another, and even within a given trade sector they may be more or less stringent depending on the socio-economic environment in which the enterprises operate, their size and technical skill, etc., a further implication of the language used is that good faith and fair dealing must be construed in the light of the special conditions of international trade.

Something very innovative, at least for some legal systems, is Article 2.16 ("Duty of confidentiality") stating that "where information is given as confidential by one party in the course of negotiations, the other party is under a duty not to disclose that information or to use it improperly for its own purpose, whether or not a contract is subsequently concluded ..."

Article 2.15 ("Negotiations in bad faith") which in paragraph 2 lays down the general rule according to which "... a party who negotiates or breaks off negotiations in bad faith is liable for the losses caused to the other party ..." [1] and in paragraph 3 specifies "It is bad faith, in particular, for a party to enter into or continue negotiations when intending not to reach an agreement with the other party."

This last provision especially, which by imposing on the parties in general terms a precontractual liability for negotiating in bad faith, aims at reconciling freedom of negotiation with the principle of good faith and fair dealing laid down in Article 1.7, may even be considered revolutionary in some parts of the world.

According to professor Bonell, precontractual liability for negotiating in bad faith ("culpa in contrahendo") as corollary of the general duty of good faith and fair dealing in the bargaining process is a well known principle only in the civil law systems, where the

---

[1] Professor Bonell at the Faculty of Law of the University of Rome in Italy, and the Chairman of the working group for the preparation of the UNIDROINT PICC, believes that the use of the word "losses" (as contrasted to the word "harm as used in Article 7.4.2 dealing with damages for non-performance") is intentional. It stresses the fact that the aggrieved party may in principle only recover the expenses incurred in the negotiations and, at best, be compensated for the lost opportunity to conclude another contract with a third person (so-called reliance or negative interest), but may not recover the profit which would have resulted if the original contract had been concluded and properly performed (so-called expectation or positive interest) This solution corresponds to what is generally provided for in domestic law, even though there are instances where the amount of damages awarded was in effect equal to the amount that would have been due for non-performance of the contract; for an ample comparative survey. See Michael Joachim Bonell, An International Restatement of Contract Law, 2nd ed., Irvington-on-Hudson, New York, 1997, p. 140.

entering into negotiations with no serious intention to contract or the abusive rupture of negotiations are generally viewed as among the most significant, though not exclusive, instances of negotiating in bad faith. By contrast, common law systems are traditionally reluctant to restrict the freedom of negotiation and favour a view of negotiations according to which parties are at risk until a contract is actually formed, although the absence of a general obligation of fair dealing does not necessarily mean that specific claims for precontractual liability may not be based on other grounds, such as unjust enrichment, misrepresentation or specific promise.

The most significant example, however, is Article 4.8 ("Supplying an omitted term") which refers to good faith and fair dealing as one of the criteria to be used whenever it becomes necessary to supply a term on which the parties have failed to agree but which is important for determining their rights and duties.

The chapter on non-performance also contains a number of specific applications of the general principle of good faith and fair dealing. For instance, Article 7.1.2 ("Interference by the other party") states: "a party may not rely on the non-performance of the other party to the extent that such non-performance was caused by the first party's act or omission or by another event as to which the first party bears the risk." and of Article 7.1.7 ("*force Majeure*") which in paragraph 1 excludes a party's liability for its non-performance due to an impediment beyond that party's control and that it could not reasonably be expected to have taken the impediment into account at the time of the conclusion of the contract or to have avoided or overcome it or its consequences.

C. The Purposes of the UNDROIT PICC

Even though the UNIDROIT PICC will be applied in practice only because of their persuasive value, they may still have a considerable role to play in at least five different contexts. The most important ways in which the UNIDROIT PICC can be used as a model for national and international legislators; as a means of interpreting and supplementing existing uniform law; as rules governing the contract; as a substitute for the domestic law otherwise applicable—are set out in the Preamble. As stated in the Introduction, there may well be other uses for the UNIDROIT PICC, first and foremost that of constituting a guide for drafting international contracts.

1. A Model for National and International Legislators

The UNIDROINT PICC may in the first place serve as a model to both national and international legislators for the elaboration or drafting of new legislation in the field of general contract law or with respect to special types of transactions. The UNIDROIT PICC may be particularly useful to the countries in which a sufficiently developed body of legal rules relating to contracts in general has so far been lacking and which intend to proceed to update their law, at least with respect to foreign economic relationships, so as to meet current international standards.

2. A Means of Interpreting and Supplementing Existing International Instruments

The UNIDROIT PICC may also play a role in interpreting and supplementing international instruments.

Any legislation, whether of international or national origin, raises questions concerning the precise meaning or its individual provisions. Moreover, such legislation is by its very nature unable to anticipate all of the problems to which it will be applied.

Traditionally, principles and criteria provided in domestic law are usually used to interpret and supplement international instruments. Yet, as a result of the economic and legal globalization, international principles are becoming more and more fair and justice, and nowadays judges and arbitrators tend to interpret and supplement the international instruments according to international uniform principles.

3. A Guide for Drafting Contracts

The UNIDROIT PICC may moreover serve as a guide for the drafting of international commercial contracts. In drafting the Contract Law of the People's Republic of China (hereafter called "China Contract Law") that came into force in 1999, the Chinese legislators referred extensively to the UNIDROIT PICC. Many articles of the China Contract Law, in particular those in the Chapter on General Provisions, are similar in spirit to the UNIDROIT PICC. For instance, Articles 3 – 7 of the China Contract Law set forth its basic principles, i. e. equality (Article 3), party autonomy (Article 4), fairness (Article 5), good faith (Article 6), public interest (Article 7). Such basic principles are likewise embodied in UNIDROIT PICC, albeit in different words. For example, Article 4 of the China Contract Law states: "The parties shall have the right voluntary to enter into a contract in accordance with the law. No entity or individual may illegally interfere with such right."

The same applies to the principle of good faith. Article 6 of China Contract Law says: "(1) the parties must act in accordance with good faith and fairing dealing in international trade, (2) the parties may not exclude or limit this duty."

Clearly, the basic principle in the China Contract Law and the UNIDROIT PICC are much alike.

4. The UNIDROIT PICC as Rules Governing the Contract

One of the most important features of the UNIDROIT PICC is that its principles are common to the existing legal systems and/or best adapted to the special requirements of international commercial contracts, and this is usually the chief reason why the UNIDROIT PICC are considered a sort of "*ius commune*", to which the parties themselves or, in case of dispute, arbitrators and, to a certain extent at least, also State courts may refer as the rules of law governing the contract.

According to the research by Prof. Bonell, several State courts and arbitral tribunals have already applied the UNIDROINT PICC as the governing law of contract. [1]

D. Comparison of the UNIDROINT PICC and CISG

The CISG that was unanimously adopted in 1980 by adiplomatic Conference held in Vienna with the participation of representatives from 62 States and 8 international organizations represents a landmark in the process of international unification of law. The importance of CISG is further demonstrated by the fact that the number of decisions rendered by both State courts and arbitral tribunals in its application is rapidly increasing.

Yet, CISG has some obvious shortcomings, due to the differences in legal tradition and at times, even more significantly, in the social and economic structures prevalent in the States participating in the negotiations some issues had to be excluded at the outset from the scope of the envisaged instrument, while with respect to a number of other items the conflicting views could only be overcome by compromise solutions leaving matters more or less undecided.

1. Some Shortcomings of CISG

In comparison with UNIDROIT PICC, CISG has at least the following shortcomings:

(1) CISG is less comprehensive in contents than UNIDROIT PICC.

Since the UNIDROIT PICC were not intended to become a binding instrument aimed at unifying national laws relating to international contracts, they were much less conditioned by the differences existing between the various legal systems. As a result, it was possible for them to address a number of matters which are either completely excluded or not sufficiently regulated by CISG. For instance, some categories of sale—among which are also transactions of considerable importance in international trade practice, such as sales of shares and other securities, of negotiable instruments and money, of ships and aircraft—are expressly excluded from its scope. But also in regard to ordinary sales contracts a number of important issues have not been taken into consideration such as the validity of the contract, the effect of the contract on the property in the goods and the liability of the seller for death or personal injury caused by the goods to the buyer or any other person.

An emphasis must be made to the fact that UNIDROIT PICC impose upon the

---

[1] Michael Joachim Bonell, An International Restatement of Contract Law, 2nd ed., Irvington-on-Hudson, New York, 1997, pp. 192 – 220.

parties a duty to act in good faith throughout the life of the contract, including the negotiation process, while CISG, in contrast, expressly refers to good faith only in the context and for the purpose of the interpretation of the Convention as such. UNIDROIT PICC lays greater stress on the importance to the principle of good faith, and this fits in with the tendency of emphasis on good faith in the contract laws of all over the world. This is also considered by experts both in China and abroad as UNIDROIT PICC 's most well-known feature. [1]

(2) Some provisions in UNIDROIT PICC are more reasonable and suitable to international trade practices

Article 9(2) of CISG states: "The parties are considered, unless otherwise agreed, to have impliedly made applicable to their contract or its formation a usage of which the parties knew or ought to have known and which in international trade is widely known to, and regularly observed by, parties to contracts of the type involved in the particular trade concerned." While Article 1.8(2) provides: "The parties are bound by a usage that is widely known to and regularly observed in international trade by parties in the particular trade concerned except where the application of such a usage would be unreasonable." As stated in the Comment of UNIDROIT PICC, the reason for this limitation is that the application of a particular usage, though regularly observed by the generality of business people in a particular trade sector, may nevertheless be unreasonable in a given case, because of the special conditions in which one or both parties operate and/or the typical nature of the transaction.

Another example is the adoption of the "receipt" principle for every kind of notice, including the notice a party must give in order to preserve its rights in case of the other party's non-performance, while according to CISG in the latter cases a delay of error in the transmission or the failure of the notice to arrive does not deprive the notifying party of the right to rely on that notice, or the provisions allowing the valid conclusion of a contract even without the determination of the price, a possibility which seems to be excluded under CISG. [2]

(3) The trade-encouraging principle is better embodied in UNIDROIT PICC

Article 19(3) of CISG states that any modifying term contained in the purported acceptance, relating to the price, payment, quality and quantity of the goods, place and time of delivery, extent of one party's liability to the other or the settlement of disputes, is

---

[1] Charles L. Knapp & Nathen M. Crystal: Problems in Contract Law. New York: Little, Brown and Company, 1999, p. 978.

[2] CF. Articles 14 and 55 CISG.

considered to be a material modification of the terms of the offer and therefore transforms the acceptance into a counteroffer, no such list is provided for in Article 2. 11 of the UNIDROIT PICC. [1] It is clear that the provision in CISG is so strict that almost any modifications will amount to counteroffer, which will certainly be taken as excuse for avoidance of contract by bad faith parties.

Also, while under CISG a court, notwithstanding the fact that the right to require performance is expressly stated in Articles 46 and 62, is not bound to enter a judgment for specific performance unless it would do so under its own domestic law,[2] according to the UNIDROIT PICC specific performance is not a discretionary remedy, i. e. a court must order performance, unless one of the exceptions laid down in Article 7. 2. 2 applies.

2. UNIDROIT PICC as a means of interpreting and supplementing CISG

Prof. Bonell held that UNIDROIT PICC may be used as a means of interpreting and supplementing CISG. [3] For example, the criteria laid down in Article 7. 3. 1 ("*right to terminate the contract*") for the determination of whether or not there has been a fundamental breach of contract, may be used for a better understanding of the rather cryptic manner in which this important concept is defined in CISG. According to Article 25 of CISG, the non-performance that substantially deprives the aggrieved party of what it was entitled to expect under the contract, provided the other party could not reasonably have foreseen such result, amounts to fundamental breach of contract, and the defaulting party have the right to terminate the contract. However, how to determine the fundamental breach of contract remains to be a problem. Article 7. 3. 1 of UNIDROIT PICC indicates as further factors to be taken into account in each single case whether strict compliance with the non-fulfilled obligation is of essence under the contract, whether the aggrieved party has reason to believe that it cannot rely on the other party's future performance, and finally whether the defaulting party would suffer disproportionate loss as a result of the preparation or performance if the contract is terminated.

III. International Rules for the Interpretation of Trade Terms (Incoterms 2010)

In today's international trade practices, most of the transactions are carried out by means of trade terms. This part discusses some important trade terms and related

[1] CF. Article 2. 11 of the UNIDROIT PICC.

[2] CF. Article 28 CISG.

[3] Michael Joachim Bonell, An International Restatement of Contract Law, 2nd ed., Irvington-on-Hudson, New York, 1997, pp. 75 – 76.

problems.

A. Concept and Role of Trade Terms

International trade is, in contrast to national trade, characterized by long distance between parties, more comprehensive scope, more complex links, more risks, etc. If parties in every transaction have to allocate the rights and obligations and risks in negotiation, this must undoubtedly prove to be not only time consuming, but also expensive. In order to save time and reduce trade costs, merchants in European countries began gradually to use trade terms as a shorthand method of expressing shipping terms as well as allocating the risk of loss. Trade terms are usually expressed in the form of abbreviated symbols, such as FOB or CIF. They permit the parties to express their agreement quickly, with little confusion, and with few language problems. If the parties use a trade term in their contract, they must define it. If it is not defined in the contract a court would have to look to the applicable law, such as the UCC or the ICC's International Rules for the Interpretation of Trade Terms (hereafter called "Incoterms 2010").

Incoterms is the most important set of trade term definitions published by the Paris-based International Chamber of Commerce. These definitions have the support of important business groups, including manufacturing, shipping, and banking industries worldwide. In order to establish commonly accepted definitions and rules related to the delivery of goods between trading partners worldwide to provide certainty and clarity to business and traders, ICC published the first edition in 1936, and then has periodically revised the Incoterms rules to reflect changes in the international trade system in 1953, 1967, 1976, 1980, 1990, 2000, 2010 and 2020. The newest revision was released in 2019.

More accessible and easier to use, Incoterms 2020 includes more detailed explanatory notes with enhanced graphics to illustrate the responsibilities of importers and exporters for each Incoterms rule. The introduction to Incoterms 2020 also includes a more detailed explanation on how to choose the most appropriate Incoterms rule for a given transaction, or how a sales contract interacts with ancillary contracts.

On the release of Incoterms ® 2020, ICC Secretary General John W. H. Denton AO said: "Incoterms 2020 rules make business work for everyone by facilitating trillions of dollars in global trade annually. Because they help importers and exporters around the world to understand their responsibilities and avoid costly misunderstandings, the rules form the language of international sales transactions, and help build confidence in our valuable global trading system."

Incoterms is an acronym for international trade terms, provides rules or determining the obligations of both seller and buyer when different trade terms are used. They state what acts seller must do to deliver, what acts buyer must do to accommodate delivery, what costs each party must bear, and at what point in the delivery process the risk of loss passes from seller to buyer. Each of these obligations may be different for different trade terms.

Since the ICC is a non-governmental entity, Incoterms is neither a national legislation nor an international treaty. Thus, it cannot be "the governing law" of any contract. Instead, it is a written form of custom and usage in the trade, which can be, can often be, expressly incorporated by a party or the parties to an international contract for the sale of goods. Alternatively, if it is not expressly incorporated in the contract, Incoterms could be made an implicit term of the contract as part of international custom.

B. Contents of Incoterms 2010

In consideration of Incoterms 2010 being the most frequently used edition, this part focuses on this edition. Incoterms 2010 defines 11 rules, reducing the 13 used in Incoterms 2000 by introducing two new rules ("Delivered at Terminal", DAT; "Delivered at Place", DAP) that replace four rules of the prior version ("Delivered at Frontier", DAF; "Delivered Ex Ship", DES; "Delivered Ex Quay", DEQ; "Delivered Duty Unpaid", DDU). In the prior version, the rules were divided into four categories, but the 11 pre-defined terms of Incoterms 2010 are subdivided into two categories based only on method of delivery. The larger group of seven rules applies regardless of the method of transport, including CIP (Carriage and Insurance Paid), CPT (Carriage Paid to), DAP (Delivered at Place), DAT (Delivered at Terminal), DDP (Delivered Duty Paid), EXW (Ex Works), FCA (Free Carrier), and the smaller group of four being applicable only to sales that solely involve transportation over water, including CFR (Cost and Freight), CIF (Cost, Insurance and Freight), FAS (Free Alongside Ship) and FOB (Free on Board). In comparison with the Incoterms 2000, a few changes have been made to the specific trade terms within the two groups.

Another feature of the Incoterms 2010 is that, in addition to the 11 rules, it includes extensive guidance notes and illustrative graphics to help users efficiently choose the right rule for each transaction, new classification to help choosing the most suitable rule in relation to the mode of transport, advice for the use of electronic procedures, information on security-related clearances for shipments, and advice for the use of Incoterms 2010 in domestic trade. Although this interpretation is provided as a guide only, it is certainly important to new users in their correct understanding and application in their business practices.

C. FOB (free on board) (port of shipment)

This rule is to be used only for sea or inland waterway transport. "Free on Board" means that the seller delivers the goods on board the vessel nominated by the buyer at the named port of shipment or procures the goods already so delivered. The risk of loss of or damage to the goods passes when the goods are on board the vessel, and the buyer bears all costs from that moment onwards. The seller is required either to deliver the goods on board the vessel or to procure goods already so delivered for shipment. The reference to "procure" here caters for multiple sales down a chain ('string sales'), particularly common in the commodity trades.

FOB may not be appropriate where goods are handed over to the carrier before they are on board the vessel, for example goods in containers, which are typically delivered at a terminal. In such situations, the FCA rule should be used. FOB requires the seller to clear the goods for export, where applicable. However, the seller has no obligation to clear the goods for import, pay any import duty or carry out any import customs formalities.

1. Obligations of the Seller

The seller must provide the goods and the commercial invoice in conformity with the contract of sale and any other evidence of conformity that may be required by the contract. The seller must deliver the goods either by placing them on board the vessel nominated by the buyer at the loading point, if any, indicated by the buyer at the named port of shipment or by procuring the goods so delivered. In either case, the seller must deliver the goods on the agreed date or within the agreed period and in the manner customary at the port. The seller must provide the buyer, at the seller's expense, with the usual proof that the goods have been delivered.

If no specific loading point has been indicated by the buyer, the seller may select the point within the named port of shipment that best suits its purpose.

Where applicable, the seller must obtain, at its own risk and expense, any export license or other official authorization and carry out all customs formalities necessary for the export of the goods.

The seller must, at the buyer's risk and expense, give the buyer sufficient notice either that the goods have been delivered or that the vessel has failed to take the goods within the time agreed.

Unless such proof is a transport document, the seller must provide assistance to the buyer, at the buyer's request, risk and expense, in obtaining a transport document.

The seller must pay the costs of those checking operations (such as checking quality, measuring, weighing, and counting) that are necessary for the purpose of delivering the goods, as well as the costs of any pre-shipment inspection mandated by the authority of the country of export. The seller must, at its own expense, package the goods, unless it is usual for the particular trade to transport the type of goods sold unpackaged. The seller may package the goods in the manner appropriate for their transport, unless the buyer has notified the seller of specific packaging requirements before the contract of sale is concluded. Packaging is to be marked appropriately.

The seller must, where applicable, in a timely manner, provide to or render assistance in obtaining for the buyer, at the buyer's request, risk and expense, any documents and information, including security-related information, that the buyer needs for the import of the goods and/or for their transport to the final destination.

The seller must reimburse the buyer for all costs and charges incurred by the buyer in providing or rendering assistance in obtaining documents and information.

2. The Obligations of the Buyer

The buyer must give the seller sufficient notice of the vessel name, loading point and, where necessary, the selected delivery time within the agreed period.

The buyer must pay the price of the goods as provided in the contract of sale. Any document referred to in this edition may be an equivalent electronic record or procedure if agreed between the parties or customary.

Where applicable, it is up to the buyer to obtain, at its own risk and expense, any import license or other official authorization and carry out all customs formalities for the import of the goods and for their transport through any country.

The buyer must take delivery of the goods when they have been delivered as envisaged here.

The buyer must contract, at its own expense for the carriage of the goods from the named port of shipment, except where the contract of carriage is made by the seller as provided for here.

The buyer must pay (a) all costs relating to the goods from the time they have been delivered as envisaged here, except, where applicable, the costs of customs formalities necessary for export, as well as all duties, taxes and other charges payable upon export; (b) any additional costs incurred, either because: (i) the buyer has failed to give appropriate notice, or (ii) the vessel nominated by the buyer fails to arrive on time, is unable to take the goods, or closes for cargo earlier than the time notified, provided that the goods have been clearly identified as the contract goods; and (c) where applicable, all duties, taxes and other charges, as well as the costs of carrying out customs formalities payable upon import of the goods and the costs for their transport through any country.

The buyer must reimburse the seller for all costs and charges incurred by the seller in providing or rendering assistance in obtaining documents and information as envisaged here. The buyer must, where applicable, in a timely manner, provide to or render assistance in obtaining for the seller, at the seller's request, risk and expense, any documents and information, including security-related information, that the seller needs for the transport and export of the goods and for their transport through any country.

3. Some Important Issues

Problems often arise of the application of FOB in the practices of international trade:

(1) Dispute may arise of the class of the carrying ship assigned by the buyer. If the buyer charters carrying ship in low class after the conclusion of contract, he can reduce the expenses, while the seller may require him to charter carrying ship in higher class. In order to avoid possible dispute, the best choice for both the seller and buyer is to make detailed provisions as to the classification, age etc. in the contract.

(2) The timing of the arrival of the carrying ship is also an important issue. If the arrival of the ship is well in advance of the stipulated date of shipment, the buyer may well be placed in an awkward position as the goods may not be ready for shipment, then who is going to pay the shipowner for the idle time, i. e, the demurrage? Conversely if it is far behind the stipulated time, the warehousing expenses thus incurred should be borne by the buyer who is responsible for chartering the ship. Occasionally, the buyer may entrust the seller with chartering business, however in case he fails to charter a ship as required owing to some unforeseen circumstances, the seller is not liable for any expenses arising therefrom.

(3) A FOB contract with additional services are sometimes applied in international trade practices. Clearly, in a FOB contract it is the duty of the seller to place the goods on board the vessel. The contract of carriage by sea has to be made by, or on behalf of the buyer, and the cost of freight and likewise of insurance has to be borne by the buyer if the buyer wishes to insure the goods. However, in a FOB contract with additional services, the parties have agreed that the arrangements for the carriage by sea and insurance shall be made by the seller, but for and on behalf of the buyer and for his account. If after the conclusion of the contract of sale these charges are increased, the buyer has to bear the increase. If the seller has paid the increased charges, he is entitled to have them refunded by the buyer.

(4) Who should bear the loading expense is also a possible issue. FOB (free on board) seems literally to indicate that all the expenses before the goods on board the vessel should be borne by the seller. But, due to the fact that different countries and regions may interpret the term "on board the vessel" differently, there often arises the problem that who should bear the expense of carrying the goods alongside the ship, of crane lifting the goods on board the ship, of stowing the goods in ship's hold, of trimming a ship? Customarily, in order to avoid the possible dispute on this problem, the parties should

make detailed provisions in the contract: (a) FOB liner terms. This means that the seller does not bear the loading expenses as the practices of liner vessel; (b) FOB stowed. This means that the loading expenses including the expense of stowing the goods in ship's hold should be borne by the seller; (c) FOB trimmed. This means that the loading expenses including the expense of trimming a ship should be borne by the seller.

D. CIF (cost, insurance and freight) (port of destination)

This rule is to be used only for sea or inland waterway transport. "Cost, Insurance and Freight" means that the seller delivers the goods on board the vessel or procures the goods already so delivered. The risk of loss of or damage to the goods passes when the goods are on board the vessel. The seller must contract for and pay the costs and freight necessary to bring the goods to the named port of destination.

The seller also contracts for insurance cover against the buyer's risk of loss of or damage to the goods during the carriage. The buyer should note that under CIF the seller is required to obtain insurance only on minimum cover. Should the buyer wish to have more insurance protection, it will need either to agree as much expressly with the seller or to make its own extra insurance arrangements.

1. Obligations of the Seller

The seller must provide the goods and the commercial invoice in conformity with the contract of sale and any other evidence of conformity that may be required by the contract. Any document here may be an equivalent electronic record or procedure if agreed between the parties or customary.

Where applicable, the seller must obtain, at its own risk and expense, any export license or other official authorization and carry out all customs formalities necessary for the export of the goods.

The seller must contract or procure a contract for the carriage of the goods from the agreed point of delivery, if any, at the place of delivery to the named port of destination or, if agreed, any point at that port. The contract of carriage must be made on usual terms at the seller's expense and provide for carriage by the usual route in a vessel of the type normally used for the transport of the type of goods sold.

The seller must obtain, at its own expense, cargo insurance complying at least with the minimum cover provided by Clauses (C) of the Institute Cargo Clauses (LMA/IUA) or any similar clauses. The insurance shall be contracted with underwriters or an insurance company of good reputes and entitle the buyer, or any other person having an insurable interest in the goods, to claim directly from the insurer. When required by the buyer, the seller shall, subject to the buyer providing any necessary information requested by the seller, provide at the buyer's expense any additional cover, if procurable, such as cover as provided by Clauses (A) or (B) of the Institute Cargo Clauses (LMA/IUA) or any similar clauses and/or cover complying with the Institute War Clauses and/or Institute Strikes Clauses (LMA/IUA) or any similar clauses.

The insurance shall cover, at a minimum, the price provided in the contract plus 10% (i. e., 110%) and shall be in the currency of the contract. The insurance shall cover the goods from the point of delivery to at least the named port of destination. The seller must provide the buyer with the insurance policy or other evidence of insurance cover. Moreover, the seller must provide the buyer, at the buyer's request, risk, and expense (if any), with information that the buyer needs to procure any additional insurance.

2. Obligations of the Buyer

The buyer must pay the price of the goods as provided in the contract of sale and take delivery of the goods when they have been delivered as envisaged here and receive them from the carrier at the named port of destination.

Any document here may be an equivalent electronic record or procedure if agreed between the parties or customary. The buyer must accept the transport document provided as envisaged here if it is in conformity with the contract.

Where applicable, it is up to the buyer to obtain, at its own risk and expense, any import license or other official authorization and carry out all customs formalities for the import of the goods and for their transport through any country.

The buyer has no obligation to the seller to make a contract of carriage.

The buyer has no obligation to the seller to make a contract of insurance. However, the buyer must provide the seller, upon request, with any information necessary for the seller to procure any additional insurance requested by the buyer as envisaged here.

If the buyer fails to give notice, then it bears all risks of loss of or damage to the goods from the agreed date or the expiry date of the agreed period for shipment, provided that the goods have been clearly identified as the contract goods.

The buyer must pay (a) all costs relating to the goods from the time they have been delivered as envisaged here, except, where applicable, the costs of customs formalities necessary for export, as well as all duties, taxes and other charges payable upon export as referred to; (b) all costs and charges relating to the goods while in transit until their arrival at the port of destination, unless such costs and charges were for the seller's account under the contract of carriage; (c) unloading costs including lighterage and wharfage charges, unless such costs and charges were for the seller's account under the contract of carriage; (d) any additional costs incurred if it fails to give notice, from the agreed date or the expiry date of the agreed period for shipment, provided that the goods have been clearly identified as the contract goods; (e) where applicable, all duties, taxes and other charges, as well as the costs of carrying out customs formalities payable upon import of the goods and the costs for their transport through any country, unless included within the cost of the contract of carriage; and (f) the costs of any additional insurance procured at the buyer's request.

The buyer must, whenever it is entitled to determine the time for shipping the goods and/or the point of receiving the goods within the named port of destination, give the seller sufficient notice thereof.

The buyer must reimburse the seller for all costs and charges incurred by the seller in providing or rendering assistance in obtaining documents and information as envisaged here.

The buyer must, where applicable, in a timely manner, provide to or render assistance in obtaining for the seller, at the seller's request, risk and expense, any documents and information, including security-related information, that the seller needs for the transport and export of the goods and for their transport through any country.

3. Some Important Problems

(1) This rule has two critical points, because risk passes and costs are transferred at different places. While the contract will always specify a destination port, it might not specify the port of shipment, which is where risk passes to the buyer. If the shipment port is of particular interest to the buyer, the parties are well advised to identify it as precisely as possible in the contract.

The parties are well advised to identify as precisely as possible the point at the agreed port of destination, as the costs to that point are for the account of the seller. The seller is advised to procure contracts of carriage that match this choice precisely. If the seller incurs costs under its contract of carriage related to unloading at the specified point at the port of destination, the seller is not entitled to recover such costs from the buyer unless otherwise agreed between the parties. The seller is required either to deliver the goods on board the vessel or to procure goods already so delivered for shipment to the destination. In addition the seller is required either to make a contract of carriage or to procure such a contract. The reference to "procure" here caters for multiple sales down a chain ('string sales'), particularly common in the commodity trades.

(2) Under CIF terms, the seller is obligated to arrange insurance and pay insurance premium. It is provided for in Incoterms that the goods should be covered on FPA terms at 110% of the invoice value. However, sometimes, the buyers request WPA insurance instead of FPA and occasionally demand inclusion of war risks or other special risks in insurance coverage. There are times when the buyers in some Asian countries intend to better protect his cost and profit, they require the insured value to be 150% or anywhere

more than 110% of the invoice value. How to cope with such a situation?

In view of the limited protection offered by FPA terms, it is deemed necessary that the CIF buyer, when the contract is made, requires the seller to get more extensive cover; but it must be made clear in the contract that the additional expenses thus incurred shall be for the buyer's account.

(3) Under CIF terms, it is the seller's responsibility to book shipping space in the case of relatively small consignment, i. e., less than shipload, or to charter a tramp vessel in the case of shipload cargo, and pay the freight up to destination. If the buyer requests the seller to ship his goods on board of a designated vessel of certain type, nationality, class, age etc., how does he cope with this request? From the legal point of view, the seller has the right to decline the buyer's request as such. Notwithstanding that, the seller may accommodate the buyer's request provided that this arrangement is entirely feasible from the seller's point of view and does not add anything to his transportation cost.

(4) Under CIF terms, the seller shall pay the freight, but whose responsibility it is to pay unloading expenses at the port of destination is to be decided according to the custom of the port. At some ports, it is the responsibility of the shipowner to pay unloading expenses; at some others, the seller has to pay the additional expenses incurred for moving the cargo from ship to wharf; but sometimes the situation is quite different, those expenses should be borne by the buyer alone. Therefore it is equivocal which party shall pay the unloading expense under CIF terms the seller or the buyer. For this reason, the following CIF variants are introduced to clarify the doubtful point: (a) CIF Liner terms. The unloading expenses will be for the account of the party who pays the freight, i. e. the seller under CIF terms; (b) CIF Ship's Hold. The buyer is to pay all unloading expenses when the goods are discharged from the ship's hold to the wharf. These CIF variants clarify the division of expenses between buyer and seller. The risks pass from seller to buyer in the same manner as under CIF terms, i. e. at the time when the goods have effectively passed the ship's rail.

(5) The central feature of CIF term is the symbolic delivery. This means that under CIF term the seller does by delivery of the shipping documents to the buyer, and not by physical delivery of the goods. So long as the seller deposits the goods on board the ship at contracted time and place, and provides the required documents including the bill of lading, the insurance policy or certificate, the invoice, etc., the seller is said to have already fulfilled his obligation, and he is not obligated to assure the arrival of the goods. Even if the seller knows that the goods have been lost at the time the shipping documents are tendered, he can still compel the buyer to take and pay for them. Conversely, in the case of the fact that the seller has delivered the documents not in conformity with the

contract, even the goods have arrived in perfect and complete condition, the buyer still has the right to reject payment.

E. Modification of Trade Terms

As is discussed above, the occurrence of trade terms frauds is chiefly due to the symbolic delivery feature of some terms, mostly the CIF term, under which the seller can be paid without providing assurance of the arrival of the goods at the port of destination, and quiet often the buyer has to pay the price without seeing the goods first. On occasion in western countries, the parties may be tempted to alter the meaning of a trade term in their contract to meet their own business requirements. This is especially important to the Chinese merchants, because many Chinese merchants customarily favor the mode of transaction where the seller makes physical delivery of the goods face to face to the buyer in exchange for the payment by the buyer, for fear that they would be cheated by foreign merchants. Comparatively, Chinese merchants tend to more often alter trade terms as a method to avoid trade frauds.

The International Chamber of Commerce and many experienced lawyers usually recommend that buyer and seller do not attempt to add to, explain, or change the meaning of any trade term without legal advice. This only causes needless confusion. The problem usually arises in CIF contract cases. The general rule is that if the additional shipping terms added by the parties to a CIF contract do not contradict the usual terms of a CIF contract, then the contract will still be considered a CIF contract.

Case 3 - 2 Kumar Corporation v. Nopal Lines, Ltd.

462 So. 2d 1178 (1985)

District Court of Appeals of Florida, Third District

Facts: Kumar sold 700 television sets to one of its largest customers, Nava, in Venezuela. The contract was on CIF terms, Maracaibo. However, they agreed that Nava would not pay Kumar until Nava actually sold the merchandise. Kumar obtained the televisions from its supplier, received them in a Miami warehouse, loaded them on a trailer, delivered the trailer to its freight forwarder, Maduro, in Florida, and obtained the shipping documents. The trailer was stolen from the Maduro lot and found abandoned and empty. Kumar had failed to obtain marine insurance on the cargo. Kumar sued Maduro and the carrier. The defendants argued that, since the risk of loss had passed from Kumar to Nava, Kumar did not have standing to sue. The trial court agreed with the defendants and dismissed Kumar's case. Kumar appealed.

Issue: Does the seller have the standing to sue the carrier for the cargo loss?

Decision: Yes. Kumar's argument that it is the real party in interest proceeds... from the premise that its agreement to postpone Nava's obligation to pay for the goods modified the ordinary consequence of the CIF contract the risk of loss shifts of the buyer. A CIF contract is a recognized and established form of contract, the incidents of which are well known. Thus, if a buyer and seller adopt such a contract, "they will be presumed, in the absence of any express term to the contrary, to have adopted all the normal incidents of that type of contract," one of which is that the buyer, not the seller, bears the risk of loss when the goods are delivered to the carrier and the seller's other contractual obligations are fulfilled. A CIF contract is not a contract "that goods shall arrive, but a contract to ship goods complying with the contract of sale, to obtain, unless the contract otherwise provides, the ordinary contract of carriage to the place of destination, and the ordinary contract of insurance of the goods on that voyage, and to tender these documents against payment of the contract price."

It is clear, however, that parties may vary the terms of a CIF contract to meet their own requirements. But where the agreed upon variation is such that it removes a vital ingredient of a CIF contract, then the contract ceases to be a CIF contract. Thus, "if according to the intention of the parties the actual delivery of the goods\[to the buyer\] is an essential condition of performance, the contract is not a CIF contract."

In the present case, Kumar and Nava agreed to payment upon Nava's sale of the goods in Venezuela... \[thereby negating an essential ingredient of the CIF contract\]... The use of the term CIF does not ipso facto make the contract a CIF contract if the contract has been altered in a manner that is repugnant to the very nature of a CIF contract. Therefore, because the record before us does not ... conclusively show that the contract remained a true CIF contract despite the agreement between Kumar and Nava concerning the payment for the goods, it was improper for the trial court to conclude as a matter of law that the risk of loss passed to Nava when Kumar delivered the goods to the shipper.

But even assuming, arguendo, that we were to conclude, as did the trial court, that the risk of loss passed to Nava merely by virtue of the label CIF on the contract, Kumar must still prevail. Under the CIF contract, Kumar was obliged to procure insurance, and by not doing so, acted, intentionally or unintentionally, as the insurer of the shipment. As the insurer of the shipment, Kumar was obliged to pay Nava, the risk bearer, for the loss when the goods were stolen. Being legally obliged to pay Nava's loss, Kumar would thus be subrogated to Nava's claims against the appellees. Since a subrogee is the real party in interest and may sue in its own name, Kumar would have standing to sue under this theory.

Reversed and remanded for further proceedings.

The court held that where, under a CIF contract, the seller fails to obtain marine cargo insurance on behalf of the buyer, the risk of loss remains with the seller, who becomes a self-insurer of the property. As such, the seller has standing to sue the carrier for the cargo loss. [1]

Case 3-3 St. Paul Guardian Insurance Company v. Neuromed Medical Systems & Support, GmbH

Cases, no. 5096 (2002) United States District Court for the Southern District of New York

LEXIS United States District Court

District Judge Sidney H. Stein

Facts: Plaintiffs St. Paul Guardian Insurance Company and Travelers Property Casualty Insurance Company have brought this action as subrogees of Shared Imaging, Inc., to recover $285,000 they paid to Shared Imaging for damage to a mobile magnetic resonance imaging system ("MRI") purchased by Shared Imaging from defendant Neuromed Medical Systems & Support GmbH ("Neuromed"). Neuromed has moved to dismiss the complaint ... [It contends that] the complaint fails to state a claim for relief.... The crux of Neuromed's argument is that it had no further obligations regarding the risk of loss once it delivered the MRI to the vessel at the port of shipment due to a "CIF" clause included in the underlying contract. Plaintiffs respond that ... the generally understood definition of the "CIF" term as defined by the International Chamber of Commerce's publication, INCOTERMS 1990, is inapplicable here ... Pursuant to the applicable German law—the U. N. Convention on Contracts for the International Sale of Goods (CISG)—the "CIF" term in the contract operated to pass the risk of loss to Shared Imaging at the port of shipment, at which time, the parties agree, the MRI was undamaged and in good working order. Accordingly, Neuromed's motion to dismiss the complaint should be

---

[1] Richard Schaffer, Beverley Earle and Filiberto Agusti, International Business Law and Its Environment, West Publishing Company 1996, p. 222.

granted and the complaint dismissed.

Shared Imaging, an American corporation, and Neuromed, a German corporation, entered into a contract of sale for a Siemens Harmony 1.0 Tesla mobile MRI. Thereafter, both parties engaged various entities to transport, insure, and provide customs entry service for the MRI. Plaintiffs originally named those entities as defendants, but the action has been discontinued against them by agreement of the parties. Neuromed is the sole remaining defendant.

According to the complaint, the MRI was loaded aboard the vessel "Atlantic Carrier" undamaged and in good working order. When it reached its destination of Calmut City, Illinois, it had been damaged and was in need of extensive repair, which led plaintiffs to conclude that the MRI had been damaged in transit.

The one-page contract of sale contains nine headings, including: "Product," "Delivery Terms," "Payment Terms," "Disclaimer," and "Applicable Law." Under "Product" the contract provides, the "system will be delivered cold and fully functional." Under "Delivery Terms" it provides, "CIF New York Seaport, the buyer will arrange and pay for customs clearance as well as transport to Calmut City."

Under "Payment Terms" it states, "By money transfer to one of our accounts, with following payment terms: U.S. $93,000—downpayment to secure the system; U.S. $744,000—prior to shipping; U.S. $93,000—upon acceptance by Siemens of the MRI system within three business days after arrival in Calmut City." In addition, under "Disclaimer" it states, "system including all accessories and options remain the property of Neuromed till complete payment has been received." Preceding this clause is a handwritten note, allegedly initialed by Raymond Stachowiak of Shared Imaging, stating, "Acceptance subject to Inspection."

Issue: What are the unexpected results of the parties' failure to use any trade term at all?

Neuromed contends that because the delivery terms were "CIF New York Seaport," its contractual obligation, with regard to risk of loss or damage, ended when it delivered the MRI to the vessel at the port of shipment and therefore the action must be dismissed because plaintiffs have failed to state a claim for which relief can be granted. Plaintiffs respond that the generally accepted definition of the "CIF" term, as defined in INCOTERMS 1990, is inapplicable. Moreover, plaintiffs suggest that other provisions of the contract are inconsistent with the "CIF" term because Neuromed, pursuant to the contract, retained title subsequent to delivery to the vessel at the port of shipment and thus, Neuromed manifestly retained the risk of loss.

...

1. Applicable Law

The parties have each submitted relevant opinions of German legal experts and the Court has independently researched the applicable foreign law. On the basis of those submissions and analysis, the Court finds the expert opinion of Karl-Ulrich Werkmeister for the defendants to be an accurate statement of German law.

The parties concede that pursuant to German law, the UN Convention on Contracts for the International Sale of Goods ("CISG") governs this transaction because (1) both the U. S. and Germany are Contracting States to that Convention, and (2) neither party chose, by express provision in the contract, to opt out of the application of the CISG.

The CISG aims to bring uniformity to international business transactions, using simple, non-nation specific language. To that end, it is comprised of rules applicable to the conclusion of contracts of sale of international goods. In its application regard is to be paid to comity and interpretations grounded in its underlying principles rather than in specific national conventions.

Germany has been a Contracting State since 1991, and the CISG is an integral part of German law. Where parties, as here, designate a choice of law clause in their contract—selecting the law of a Contracting State without expressly excluding application of the CISG—German courts uphold application of the Convention as the law of the designated Contracting state. To hold otherwise would undermine the objectives of the Convention which Germany has agreed to uphold.

2. CISG, Incoterms and "CIF"

"CIF," which stands for "cost, insurance and freight," is a commercial trade term that is defined in INCOTERMS 1990, published by the International Chamber of Commerce ("ICC"). The aim of INCOTERMS, which stands for international commercial terms, is "to provide a set of international rules for the interpretation of the most commonly used trade terms in foreign trade." These "trade terms are used to allocate the costs of freight and insurance" in addition to designating the point in time when the risk of loss passes to the purchaser. INCOTERMS are incorporated into the CISG through Article 9(2) which provides that.

The parties are considered, unless otherwise agreed, to have impliedly made applicable to their contract or its formation a usage of which the parties knew or ought to have known and which in international trade is widely known to, and regularly observed by, parties to contracts of the type involved in the particular trade concerned.

At the time the contract was entered into, INCOTERMS 1990 was applicable. INCOTERMS define "CIF" (named port of destination) to mean [that] the seller delivers when the goods pass "the ship's rail in the port of shipment." The seller is responsible for paying the cost, freight and insurance coverage necessary to bring the goods to the named port of destination, but the risk of loss or damage to the goods passes from seller to buyer upon delivery to the port of shipment. Further, "CIF" requires the seller to obtain insurance only on minimum cover.

Plaintiffs' legal expert contends that INCOTERMS are inapplicable here because the contract fails to specifically incorporate them. Nonetheless, he cites and acknowledges that the German Supreme Court—the court of last resort in the Federal Republic of Germany for civil matters—concluded that a clause "fob" without specific reference to INCOTERMS was to be interpreted according to INCOTERMS "simply because the [INCOTERMS] include a clause 'fob.'"

Conceding that commercial practice attains the force of law under section 346 of the German Commercial Code, plaintiffs' expert concludes that the opinion of the BGH "amounts to saying that the [INCOTERMS] definitions in Germany have the force of law as trade custom." As encapsulated by defendant's legal expert, "It is accepted under German law that in case a contract refers to CIF-delivery, the parties refer to the INCOTERMS rules...." The use of the "CIF" term in the contract demonstrates that the parties "agreed to the detailed oriented [INCOTERMS] in order to enhance the Convention." Thus, pursuant to CISG Article 9(2), INCOTERMS definitions should be applied to the contract despite the lack of an explicit INCOTERMS reference in the contract.

3. Incoterms, the CISG and the Passage of Risk of Loss and Title

Plaintiffs argue that Neuromed's explicit retention of title in the contract to the MRI machine modified the "CIF" term, such that Neuromed retained title and assumed the risk of loss. INCOTERMS, however, only address passage of risk, not transfer of title. Under the CISG, the passage of risk is likewise independent of the transfer of title. Plaintiffs' legal expert mistakenly asserts that the moment of "passing of risk" has not been defined in the CISG. Chapter IV of that Convention, entitled "Passing of Risk," explicitly defines the time at which risk passes from seller to buyer pursuant to Article 67(1).

If the contract of sale involves carriage of the goods and seller is not bound to hand them over at a particular place, the risk passes to the buyer when the goods are handed over to the first carrier for transmission to the buyer in accordance with the contract of sale. If the seller is bound to hand the goods over to a carrier at a particular place, the risk does not pass to the buyer until the goods are handed over to the carrier at that place.

Pursuant to the CISG, "the risk passes without taking into account who owns the goods. The passing of ownership is not regulated by the CISG according to Article 4 (b)." Article 4(b) provides that the Convention is not concerned with "the effect which the contract may have on the property in the goods sold." Moreover, according to Article 67(1), the passage of risk and transfer of title need not occur at the same time, as the seller's retention of "documents controlling the disposition of the goods does not affect the passage of risk."

Had the CISG been silent, as plaintiffs' expert claimed, the Court would have been required to turn to German law as a "gap filler." There again, plaintiffs' assertions falter. German law also recognizes passage of risk and transfer of title as two independent legal acts. In fact, it is standard "practice under German law to agree that the transfer of title will only occur upon payment of the entire purchase price, well after the date of passing of risk and after receipt of the goods by the buyer." Support for this proposition of German law is cited by both experts. They each refer to section 447 of the German Civil Code, a provision dealing with long distance sales, providing in part—as translated by plaintiff's expert—that "the risk of loss passes to the buyer at the moment when the seller has handed the matter to the forwarder, the carrier or to the otherwise determined person or institution for the transport."

Accordingly, pursuant to INCOTERMS, the CISG and specific German law, Neuromed's retention of title did not thereby implicate retention of the risk of loss or damage.

4. Conclusion

For the foregoing reasons, Neuromed's motion to dismiss for failure to state a claim is granted and the complaint is dismissed.

5. Casepoint

This case involves the sale of an expensive piece of medical equipment (an MRI scanner) by a seller in Germany to a buyer in the United States. The scanner was damaged when it arrived at the buyer's place of business. It was thus important to determine when the risk of loss passed. The contract shipping terms were "CIF, New York Seaport." The court stated that the CISG incorporated therelevant Incoterms, unless the parties had specified otherwise, and found that the term "CIF, New York" meant that the risk of loss effectively moved from seller to buyer when the goods were loaded onto the carrier in Germany for the trip to New York. The Incoterms regarding risk of loss are not tied to the passage of title, as the buyer claimed, so here the loss must fall upon the buyer.[1]

■ Notes

Roman law 罗马法。古罗马奴隶制国家的法律的总称。其中最为完备、对后世影响最大的是私法。罗马法对简单商品生产的各种法律关系,如所有权、债、契约等,都作了详尽的规定。罗马法成为古代法律中反映商品生产和商品交换最完备、最典型的法律,对后世资本主义私法的发展起到极其重要的作用,成为许多国家立法的依据。中国从清末开始的民律草案以及中华民国时期国民党政府的民法五编,也都深受罗马法的影响。

Islamic law 伊斯兰法。中世纪信奉伊斯兰教的阿拉伯国家与其他伊斯兰国家的法律。公元7世纪伊斯兰教产生后逐渐形成,8世纪初随阿拉伯的扩张日趋完备。以《古兰经》与"圣训"《穆罕默德言行汇录》为基本渊源。从9世纪起,各教法学派开始编撰本派法典,作为法院判决的主要依据。随着阿拉伯帝国的崩溃以及穆斯林国家中资本主义的发展,世俗法律已在大多数伊斯兰国家中取代伊斯兰法,但伊斯兰法对穆斯林的行为仍具有不同程度的约束力。

Restatement of Law 法律重述。早在19世纪初,美国法学会成立伊始,就决心开展一项宏伟的计划——编撰法律重述(restatements),以解决当时美国法律所存在的不确定性和复杂性问题。1923年关于成立美国法学会的报告指出:"美国法中两个缺陷是其不确定性和复杂性。这两个缺陷引起毫无用处的争议,阻碍着当事人通过诉诸法院来实施权利,常常使法院难以向当事人提供权利性的建议,争议开始时,造成迟延和增加费用。"

由于美国当时的48个州和联邦政府都是独立的法源,自然使各自的法律相互之间存在差异。上述报告指出:"这些法律上的差异本身构成了不确定性和复杂性的原因……交易不仅在两个或多个州之间进行,而且也在州内部进行。"因此,美国产生了法律重述的想法,以便将法律进行系统性的重述,动员法官、学者和律师一起改变美国法律所面对的混乱状态。"本重述的目的不仅在于使不确定性变为确定,使复杂的法律简单化,还要提高法律适应生活需要的实用性。""重述的基本目的是阐明法律。""重述不只是法规和决定的汇集和比较……不止是对现存法律的讲解……它还应该考虑法院或立法者尚未讨论,但在将来可能引起争议的情事……它应该将具体法规讲解清楚……它所提出的变化应该符合简化法律的方向……或符合将详尽的法律更好地适用于法律总目的。"[2]

美国法学会采用非立法的方式(non legislative means)统一和调和法律的做法,对各

---

〔1〕 Ray August, Don Mayer and Michael Bixby, International Business Law, Six Edition, Pearson Education Limited, 2013, p. 613.

〔2〕 Report of the Committee on the Establishment of a Permanent Organization for the Improvement of the Law, pp. 17-23.

国统一国内法和国际组织统一国际商事合同的工作产生了重要影响。

precontractual liability 合同前责任。主要指不遵守诚信原则的一方在谈判中故意拖延时间,耽误了对方交易的机会。虽然最终没有达成合同,双方没有合同义务,但是由于不诚信的一方给另一方造成了损失,本着诚信原则的要求,也应承担相应的责任。

the Institute Cargo Clauses(LMA/IUA) 英国伦敦保险业协会货物保险条款(LMA/IUA)。LMA(Lloyd's Market Association)和IUA(International Underwriting Association of London)分别指劳埃德市场协会和伦敦国际保险协会。劳埃德市场协会是由一个名叫Edward Lloyd的英国商人于1688年在伦敦泰晤士河畔塔街开设的咖啡馆演变发展而来的,现在已经成为世界上著名的航海保险机构。伦敦国际保险协会是经营海上保险的保险人公众组织。该组织1884年建立于伦敦,由英国各海上保险公司共同组成,主要研究制定通用的海上保险条款。该协会制定的保险条款为国际上广泛采用,通称协会条款。

■ Important Legal English Usages

enact 制定法律(特指议会制定法),颁布(法令),通过(法案)等。

注意该词与下列词在用法上的区别:

(1)formulate:制定法律、法规、条例等。例如,This law is formulated to strengthen the administration of trademarks, protect the right to exclusive use of trademarks, and encourage producers to guarantee the quality of their goods and safeguard the reputation of consumers and promote the development of the socialist commodity economy(为了加强商标管理,保护商标专用权,促使生产者保证商品质量和维护商标信誉,以保障消费者的利益,促进社会主义商品经济的发展,特制定本法)。

(2)promulgate:公布。例如,These regulations shall be implemented as of the date of its promulgation(本条例自公布之日起实施)。

transaction (具体的)交易。例如,to conclude a transaction(达成一笔交易)。

注意该词与下列词在用法上的区别:

(1)deal:(具体的)交易,与transaction相比,更口语化和通俗化。

(2)business:商业,行业,生意(一般用语)。例如,We are ready to do business with all countries on a basis of equality and mutual benefit(我们愿意和一切国家在平等互利的基础上做生意)。

(3)commerce:商业(常指海外通商或与"工业"相对)。例如,This trading company carries on commerce with western countries(这家贸易公司和西方各国有商业来往)。

(4)trade:贸易,行业(特别指手工业)。例如,He is a baker by trade(他是面包师)。

enter into 缔结条约、合同等。例如,enter into a treaty(缔结一项条约)。

注意下列同义词的用法:

(1)conclude:签订合同(常用于一般性合同)。例如,Such damages may not exceed the loss which the party in breach foresaw or ought to have foreseen at the time of the conclusion of the contract(这种损害赔偿不得超过违反合同一方在订立合同时,已经预见

或理应预见到的事实和情况）。

（2）sign：签（名），署（名）。例如，sign a legislative bill into a law（签字批准法案使其成为法律）。

treaty 条约。普通用词，指按照国际法规定，经过外交谈判而正式签订的协约。例如，the Treaty of Versailles（凡尔赛和约）。

注意该词与下列同义词的区别：

（1）pact：协定，公约，指与 treaty 所表示的相比，较不重要及约束力较弱的协定。例如，the Warsaw Pact（华沙条约）。

（2）convention：公约，指在联合国等重要的国际组织主持下缔结的多边条约。例如，the United Nations Convention on Contract for the International Sale of Goods（联合国国际货物买卖销售合同公约）。

applicable law 适用法，主要指合同所应适用的法律。proper law，指准据法，也包括合同所应适用的法律，但与 applicable law 相比，proper law 多用于国际私法中所指的准据法，实践中用得不多。

must 必须，语气很强。例如，The seller must bear all costs and risks of the goods until the goods pass the ship's rail（卖方必须承担货物越过船舷前的所有费用和风险）。需要指出的是，法律中多用 shall 来表示依据法律必须做某事。例如，In handling economic contract dispute cases within the scope of their functions and powers, the arbitration authorities shall implement a single instance adjudication system（仲裁机关在其职权范围内处理经济合同纠纷案件，应实行一次裁决制度）。

■ Review Questions

1. Outline three reasons that helped the international business law develop, giving examples if possible.
2. Under what circumstances arise the conflicts between the applicability of the CISG and national law of a CISG member state?
3. State three ways in which the UNIDROIT PICC was prepared.
4. Briefly describe the differences and similarities between the CISG and the UNIDROIT PICC.
5. What are the main principles of the UNIDROIT PICC?
6. How is the principle of "good faith" defined in UNIDROIT PICC? Do you agree with it?
7. List and explain the roles of trade terms in international trade practices.
8. Compare and contrast "FOB" and "CIF", and list the main differences between them.
9. Seller agreed to ship 10,000 tons of potatoes FOB Tacoma, Washington, to Buyer in Japan. Buyer designated the SS Russet to take delivery at pier 7 in Tacoma. On the

agreed date for delivery, Seller delivered the potatoes to pier 7, but the ship was not at the pier. Because another ship using the pier was slow in loading, the Russet had to anchor at a mooring buoy in the harbor and Seller had to arrange for a lighter to transport the potatoes in containers to the ship. The lighter tied up alongside the Russet and a cable from the ship's boom was attached to the first container. As the container began to cross the ship's rail the cable snapped. The container then fell on the rail, teetered back and forth for awhile, and finally crashed down the side of the ship and capsized the lighter. All of the potatoes were dumped into the sea. Buyer now sues Seller for failure to make delivery. Is Seller liable?

10. Buyer and seller entered into a contract for the sale of sugar from the Philippines to New York on CIF terms. They added language to the contract that delivery was to be "at a customary safe wharf or refinery at New York, Philadelphia, or Baltimore to be designated by the buyer." Before the sugar arrived, the United States placed a quota on sugar imports. The sugar was not allowed to be imported and was placed in a customs warehouse. The buyer refused the documents and the seller sued, claiming that the import restriction was no excuse for the buyer's nonpayment. The buyer argued that the language calling for delivery to a U. S. port converted a shipment contract into a destination contract. Was this a CIF contract or a destination contract? What was the effect of the additional shipping language used by the parties? Why should the parties not attempt to modify a trade term or add other delivery language?

4 Chapter Four Contract Law for the International Sale of Goods

■ 导读

本章讲授的是国际货物销售合同,包括国际货物销售合同的定义、合同的形式、合同的有效及构成、违约补救、损失赔偿、买卖双方各自的义务、风险转移及免责事由等。其中如何索赔及索赔的范围、买卖双方的具体权利和义务、风险转移及不可抗力等是重中之重的内容。因此,合同是国际商事交易的基础,是保护合同双方当事人权益的依据。如果双方没有能力签订一个好的合同,要做好一笔国际商事交易是不可想象的。我国国际商事的实践也表明,国际商事方面的纠纷大多与合同有关。因此,国际货物买卖合同是本书中的核心,读者必须倍加努力,真正掌握合同法的相关理论和规定。可见,学好本章内容,可在国际商事实践中出现纠纷时从容镇定,有条有理地据理力争,切实保护好自己的合法权益。

Contract is playing a more and more important role in today's international sale of goods, and considered as basic tool for international business transaction. [1] For instance, a successful business transaction has to be based on at least sales contract that provides the transfer of title and risk of the goods and the obligations of parties, transportation contract that states the transfer of possession of the goods, contract of payment that stipulates the effective payment, and insurance contract that provides the transfer of the insured risk to the insurance company, etc. Therefore, a successful business transaction is chiefly decided by a good contract. The students of law in China are required to pay due attention to this chapter.

I. Definition and Form of Contract

A. Definition of Contract

In common law countries, contract under English law means a promise or set of promises, for breach of which the law gives a remedy, or the performance of which the law in some way recognizes as a duty. Sir Frederick Pollok pointed out: "A contract is a

[1] Shen Sibao, Wang Jun, Jiao Junhong, International Business Law, Publishing House of the University of International Economic and Business, 2002, p. 192.

promise or set of promises which the law will enforce." [1] Under American law, a contract is a promise, or a set of promises that the law will enforce or at least recognize in some way. [2] The Restatement Second of Contracts §1 in the United States defines a contract as "a promise or a set of promises for the breach of which the law gives a remedy, or the performance of which the law in some way recognizes as a duty." [3]

Black's Law Dictionary defines a contract "an agreement between two or more parties creating obligations that are enforceable or otherwise recognizable at law 'a binding contract'; the writing that sets forth such an agreement 'a contract is valid if valid under the law of the residence of the party wishing to enforce the contract'." [4]

The nature of contract, under civil law, is a"meeting of minds" or "mutual assent". Article 1101 of "French Civil Code" states: "Contract is a mutual assent with which one person or more is obligated to give a thing, to do or not to do a thing to one person or more persons."

In modern practices, most countries even including the United States do not have requirement of consideration to the formation of contract. For instance, UCC 2 - 209 states: "An agreement modifying a contract within this Article needs no consideration to be binding". The UNIDROIT PICC 3. 2, one of the best achievements of modern contract law of international business, states: "A contract is concluded, modified or terminated by the mere agreement of the parties, without any further requirement" Its comment of the Article says: "In common law systems, consideration is traditionally seen as a prerequisite for the validity or enforceability of a contract as well as for its modification or termination by the parties. However, in commercial dealings this requirement is of minimal practical importance since in that context obligations are almost

---

[1] He Baoyu, Contract Law of the United Kingdom, Publishing House of the China University of Politics and Law, 1999, p. 38.

[2] E. Allan Farnsworth, Contracts, Little, Brown and Company, Boston, 1990, p. 3.

[3] The American Law Institute, formed in 1923 with a select membership of practitioners, judges, and law professors, began to make Restatement of the Law to reduce the mass of case law to a body of readily accessible rules. The Restatement of Contracts was completed in 1932. Williston acted as Reporter, with responsibility for preparing drafts, and Corbin served as Special Adviser and Reporter for the chapter on Remedies. However, the original Restatement of Contracts is characterized by what has been described as a "staccato" style, which seemed suitable when its authors thought that it would be orchestrated by accompanying treaties. In 1952, the American Law Institute began the process of revising the Restatement to produce a "Restatement Second," and in 1962 it started such a revision of the Restatement of Contracts. The Restatement Second of Contracts was published in 1981. Its major changes in substance include an increased recognition of a party's reliance on the contract and the introduction of a number of innovations by analogy to the UCC.

[4] Bryan A. Garner, Black's Law Dictionary, ST. PAUL, MINN., 1999, p. 319.

always undertaken by both parties. It is for this reason that Article 29(1) CISG dispenses with the requirement of consideration in relation to the modification and termination by the parties of contracts for the international sale of goods. The fact that the present article extends this approach to the conclusion, modification and termination by the parties of international commercial contracts in general can only bring about greater certainty and reduce litigation."

China Contract Law has the similar provision, and Article 2 states: "A contract in this Law refers to an agreement establishing, modifying and terminating the civil rights and obligations between subjects of equal footing, that is, between natural persons, legal persons or other organizations."

B. Form of Contract

Form in contract law means whether a contract is made in writing or orally. Traditionally, many countries have required that a contract be in writing. The English Statute of Frauds of 1677 required a signed writing to enforce a wide variety of contracts, including contracts for the sale of goods. The same requirement reappears in the UK *Sale of Goods Act* of 1893, the US *Uniform Sales Act* of 1906. In 1954, however, the United Kingdom repealed the writing requirement when it revised its Sale of Goods Act, and this revision was adopted by many former colonies that had inherited the British Act. [1] Under UCC, American law requires that contracts for sale of goods or $500 or that more must in writing. Today, however, many exceptions to this UCC rule make most oral sales contracts quite enforceable.

The civil countries of Europe for the most part never had any writing requirement at all. Under the CISG, contracts for the sale of goods need not be in writing. Article 11 states: "A contract of sale need not be concluded in or evidenced by writing and is not subject to any other requirements as to form. It may be proved by any means, including witnesses." Article 1.2 in the UNIDROIT PICC Article provides: "Nothing in these Principles requires a contract to be concluded in or evidenced by writing. It may be proved by any means, including witness."

The China Contract Law that came into effect in 1999 provides that a contract in writing is also effective.

Clearly, the provision of the China Contract Law on the form of contract is already similar to the stipulations of other countries, and international conventions and customs.

---

[1] Ray August, Don Mayer and Michael Bixby, International Business Law, Six Edition, Pearson Education Limited, 2013, p. 579.

II. Validity and Formation of International Sale of Contracts

Under the common law, a valid contract is an agreement that contains all of the essential elements of a contract. As students of business law well know, a contract contains a number of elements: (1) It is an agreement between the parties entered into by their mutual assent (e, g. , an offer and acceptance of the contract's material terms). (2) The contract must be supported by legally sufficient consideration (e. g. , the exchange in the contract as bargained for by the parties). (3) The parties must have legal capacity (e. g. , that the parties are not minors, legally incompetent, or under the influence of drugs or alcohol). (4) The contract must not be for illegal purposes or to carry on an activity that is illegal or contrary to public policy.

The civil law countries have similar stipulations to that except for the legally sufficient consideration.

If a contract is missing any one of these essential elements, it is a void contract. It will not be enforced by the courts. The CISG only governs the forming of a contract and the rights and obligations of the seller and buyer. The CISG does not provide rules for determining whether a contract is valid, for determining whether a party to a contract is legally competent, nor for determining whether a party is guilty of fraud or misrepresentation. These rules are left to individual state or national laws.

The contract laws of all countries require that the parties reach a mutual agreement and understanding about the essential terms of a contract. This agreement is reached through the bargaining process, between offeror and offeree. The offeror, by making the offer, creates in the offeree the power of acceptance, or the power to form a contract. The negotiations between the parties need not always lead to a contract. Inquires may be made or offers invited but no offer may be made or, if one is made, it need not be accepted.

Before the concepts of offer and acceptance can be considered in detail, it is necessary to distinguish certain statements preliminary to the offer from the offer itself.

A. Invitation Offer

An invitation offer (邀请要约) is not capable of being turned into a contract by acceptance. It is used to invite others to make offer. An advertisement is normally only intended to be an invitation to treat, i. e. , to negotiate. In the United Kingdom, a shopkeeper who displays goods in his window with a ticket on them stating a price, does not make an offer, but merely invites the public to make an offer to buy the goods at the price stated. Therefore, if a customer enters the shop, tenders the price and demands the article, the shopkeeper is not bound to sell it to him. The demand of the customer is the offer which the shopkeeper is free to accept or reject as he pleases. [1]

B. The Offer

An offer is a proposal by one person to another indicating an intention to enter into a contract under specified terms. In the words of the Restatement Second of Contracts § 24, an offer must be a "manifestation of willingness to enter into a bargain, so made as to justify another person in understanding that his assent to that bargain is invited and will conclude it." Thus, the first element of an offer is a manifestation of an intention to be presently bound subject only to an appropriate acceptance.

1. Requirements of Offer

(1) The contract law of most nations holds that an offer must be addressed to one or more specific persons. In those countries, an advertisement can never create the power of acceptance in a member of the public who reads the ad. In Germany, for instance, advertisements addressed to the public in general are mere invitations to deal. Other countries, such as the United States, recognize that if an advertisement is specific enough in describing the goods, their quantity, and price, it may be considered an offer. The CISG takes a middle position by creating a presumption that an advertisement or circular is not an offer "unless the contrary is clearly indicated by the person, making the proposal." Nevertheless, a seller may want to include in all of its price sheets and literature a notice that the material does not constitute an offer.

(2) Under Article 11 of the CISG an offer must be sufficiently definite and indicates the intention of the offeror to be bound. An offer is considered sufficiently definite if it (a) indicates or describes the goods; (b) expressly or implicitly specifies the quantity, and (c) expressly or implicitly specifies the price for the goods. The criteria for judging definiteness are somewhat ambiguous. The offer is definite enough if the goods are "indicated," which does not seem to require that they be described with any particularity. Similarly, an offer is definite if it "expressly or impliedly fixes or makes provision for determining the quantity and the price," but it is not clear whether failure to meet that criterion requires a finding of indefiniteness.

However, one should not think that the presence of these three terms always indicate a contract. In many international contracts involving a great deal of money, no firm would make a commitment without reaching an agreement on many other terms, such as methods of payment, delivery dates, quality standards, etc. In this case, the court will try to find whether the parties had the intention to be bound, if the court finds the parties did have the intention to be bound, it can supply many of the missing terms by looking at

---

[1] CF. Pharmaceutical Society v. Boots Cash Chemists (Southern) [1953] 1 Q. B. 401.

the past dealings of the parties, and at customs in the trade or industry, or by referring to the applicable provisions of the CISG.

CISG seems similar to those of U. S. state law. Article 55 states that where price is not fixed, the price will be that charged " for such goods sold under comparable circumstances in the trade concerned." Accordingly, if the buyer and seller fail to specify the price of the goods, a court might be able to look to the trade to make its own determination of price, and the contract and all its other provisions will remain in effect.

(3) An offer becomes valid when it arrives at the offeree.

2. The Binding of an Offer

As a general rule, an offer isn't binding on the offeree. If the offeree doesn't accept it, he has no obligation to give a notice to the offeror. Whether or not an offer is binding on the offeror is rather complex.

In Common Law countries an offer generally isn't binding on the offeror, due to the lack of consideration not being signed and sealed, and the offeror can withdraw the offer at any time before the offeree's acceptance.

Obviously, the above stipulation doesn't meet the development of modern economic life. UCC (2 - 205) has improved this and holds that an offer can't be revoked if (a) the offeror is merchant (b) if has a period of validity (c) the offer must be in writing and the offeror must sign on it.

Under Germany law an offer is binding on the offeror, while under French law the offeror can revoke the offer before the acceptance of the offeree. Article 14 of the CISG states: (1) Until a contract is concluded an offer may be revoked if the revocation reaches offeree before he has dispatched an acceptance; (2) However, an offer can't be revoked, (a) if it indicates, whether by stating a fixed time for acceptance or otherwise, that it is irrevocable or (b) if it was reasonable for the offeree to rely on the offer as being irrevocable and the offeree has acted in reliance on the offer.

3. Lapse of Offer

Under the United Kingdom law an offer lapses: (1) On the death either of the offeror or the offeree before acceptance. Death after acceptance does not affect the obligations arising from a contract unless they are of a personal nature. (2) By non-acceptance within the time prescribed for acceptance by the offeror. (3) When no time for acceptance is prescribed, by non-acceptance within a reasonable time. What is a reasonable time depends on the nature of the contract and the circumstances of the case.

The reason why the offer lapses is that the offeree is regarded as having refused it if he has not accepted it within a reasonable time. If the offeree indicates within a reasonable time that he accepts the offer but sends a formal letter of acceptance later, the offeror cannot claim that his offer has lapsed byeffluxion of time. [1]

4. Revocation of Offer

Revocation of offer means that the offeror notifies the offeree before acceptance of the invalidity of the offer so as to be free from it. Common Law countries and civil law countries still differ to whether the offeror is entitled to the revocation of offer before acceptance, though those two legal families are getting more and closer.

Under English common law, (1) an offer may be revoked at any time before acceptance. Under Companies Act 1948, there is, however, a statutory exception to this rule, when an application for shares in or debentures of a company is made in pursuance of a prospectus issued generally. Such an application cannot be revoked until after the third day after the opening of the subscription lists. (2) Revocation does not take effect until it is actually communicated to the offeree. Communication for this purpose means that the revocation must actually have reached the offeree. Under the UCC, as between merchants, an offer may not be revoked if it is made in a signed writing that gives assurance that it will remain open for a stated period of time, not to exceed three months.

Some civil law countries, such as inGermany, France, Italy, and Japan, go even further in limiting the offeror's power to revoke during the period of time normally needed for the offeree's acceptance to arrive.

Article 16 of the CISG states: (1) Until a contract is concluded an offer may be revoked if the revocation reaches the offeree before he has dispatched an acceptance. (2) However, an offer cannot be revoked: (a) if it indicates, whether by stating a fixed time for acceptance or otherwise, that it is irrevocable; or (b) if it was reasonable for the offeree to rely on the offer as being irrevocable and the offeree has acted in reliance on the offer. The UNIDROIT PICC takes a middle position between the two legal families and makes similar provisions to the CISG.

Articles 18 and 19 of China Contract Law adopts the provisions of the CISG and the UNIDROIT PICC, only with different words.

C. The Acceptance

A contract isn't formed until the offer is accepted by the offeree. The acceptance is the offeree's manifestation of the intention to be bound to the terms of the offer. In all legal systems, the offeree may accept at any time until the offer is revoked by the offeror, until the offer expires due to the passage of time, until it is rejected by the offeree, until the offeree makes a counteroffer, or until termination in some other manner. Under the CISG, an acceptance may take the form of a statement or any other conduct by the offeree

[1] Clive M. Schmitthoff, David A. G. Sarre, Mercantile Law, London Stevens & Sons, 1984, p. 14.

that indicates the offeree's intention to be bound to the contract.

1. Requirements of Acceptance

(1) An acceptance must be made by the offeree.

(2) An acceptance must be made within the period of validity. (late acceptance is a counteroffer only)

(3) An acceptance must match the terms of the offer exactly and unequivocally. Otherwise it is considered a counteroffer and thus a rejection of the original offer.

2. Time of Acceptance

Under the common law, a contract is formed when the acceptance is dispatched by the offeree. In the case of an acceptance by letter, the time of dispatch is the time the letter is put into the hands of the postal authorities. This is known as "Mail-box rule". This rule assumes that the correct mode of transmission is used, i. e., one that the offeror specifies or, if none, one that is reasonable under the circumstances. This assumption makes sense, for if a fax arrives offering to sell fresh roses sitting on the tarmac in Columbia, one does not accept by letter and expect a contract to be formed on dispatch. Hence, if a buyer submits a purchase order to a seller, a contract is formed upon the dispatch of the seller's order confirmation. The buyer's power to withdraw the purchase order ended at that time. Furthermore, the effect of this rule is that the seller is also bound to the contract upon dispatch and may no longer withdraw the offer after that time.

Under most civil law countries, the receipt theory is used. For example, a buyer sends a seller an acceptance through the mails and the acceptance is lost. If the dispatch theory were applied, a contract would have come into existence at the time the acceptance was mailed, and the seller would be required to perform. Under the receipt rule, however, no contract would exist, and a perception that it more fairly allocates responsibility for loss or delay. The CISG opted for the receipt theory used in civil law countries. Article 2.6(2) of the UNIDROIT PICC and Article 26 of China Contract Law also adopted the receipt theory.

D. Battle of the Forms

The mirror image rule(镜像原则) requires that an acceptance be unconditional and that it not attempt to change any of the terms proposed in the offer. These requirements present special problems when both parties, buyer and seller, negotiate back and forth via "standard" business forms. The seller might rely on an order confirmation form or sales form. The buyer might make use of a preprinted purchase order form used to place orders with all vendors. Typically, these forms leave room on the front so the parties may insert important contract terms such as price, quality, or ship date. The reverse side often contains detailed provisions or standard clauses, often called terms and conditions, or general conditions of sale. They are often drafted by attorneys to protect their client's rights, placing greater liability on the other party.

In international trade practices, both parties may not even be aware of the legal significance of these seldom read provisions on the reverse side, because they usually read carefully the crucial terms. Usually the preprinted terms on these forms differ, sometimes in significant ways. Here are several examples of how they might differ: (1) Buyer's purchase order might call for disputes to be resolved in the buyer's country. Seller's confirmation calls for disputes to be heard in the courts of the seller's country. (2) Buyer's purchase order requires shipment by a certain date named in the order. Seller's confirmation allows a grace period for late shipping or provides for excuses for late shipment.

This potential for conflict is almost endless. When this occurs, lawyers call it a battle of forms.

1. The Battle of the Forms under the Common Law

In the United States the mirror image rule has been modified by statute to deal with modern business practices and to avoid the problems. Under UCC (2 – 207):

(1) "A written confirmation which is sent within a reasonable time operates as an acceptance even though it states terms additional to or different from those" in the purchase order, unless the confirmation "is expressly made conditional on assent to the additional or different terms."

(2) If both parties are merchants, any additional terms contained in the seller's confirmation automatically become a part of the contract unless:

(a) The buyer's purchase order "expressly limits acceptance" to the terms in that order;

(b) The additional terms in the confirmation "materially alter" the terms of the order, or

(c) The buyer notifies the seller of an objection to the additional terms within a reasonable time after receiving the confirmation containing the new terms.

A careful reading of UCC 2 – 207 shows that the UCC attempts to uphold the intentions of the parties by keeping the contract in existence where there are only minor differences between the forms used by the parties. The UCC states that, between merchants, an acceptance by confirmation that contains additional terms that reflect only minor changes from the buyer's order will be effective to produce a contract, and the *minor terms* become a part of it unless the buyer notifies the seller of an objection to the new term. A minor term might be one that is in usual and customary usage in the trade.

The situation is different in the case of new terms in the acceptance that attempt to *materially alter* the offer. A material term is generally considered to be one that is not commonly accepted in the trade and that would result in surprise hardship to one party if unilaterally included in the contract by the party. Such new terms do not become a part of the contract unless accepted by the other party.

2. The Battle of the Forms under the CISG

The CISG rules fall somewhere between the rules set out by the common and civil law and the UCC. In an international sales transaction governed by the CISG, an acceptance containing new terms that do not materially alter the terms of the offer becomes a part of the contract, unless the offeror promptly objects to the change. However, an acceptance that contains additional or different terms that do materially alter the terms of the offer would constitute a rejection of the offer and a counteroffer. No contract would arise at all unless the offeror in return accepts all of the terms of the counteroffer (recall that under the UCC a contract would arise, but without the new terms.)

In the following case, *Filanto v. Chilewich International Corporation*, a U. S court discussed the battle of the forms under the CISG. As you read, consider the importance of knowing the rules for forming a contract if you are a businessperson. Also consider the need for the parties to communicate clearly during the negotiating process and to object to contract proposals that they do not want to be a part of their agreement.

Under the CISG, an acceptance of the counteroffer may arise by assent or by performance. In other words, if the original offeror takes some steps toward performing the contract, after having received a counteroffer, the offeror will be deemed to have accepted the counteroffer and a contract will be created on the new terms.

Unlike the UCC, the CISG states those key elements of a contract that will materially alter a contract: price, payment, quality and quantity of goods, place and time of delivery, extent of one party's liability to the other, and settlement of disputes. Thus, under the CISG, almost any new or different term in the acceptance could constitute a counteroffer. The effect is that many businesspeople may believe that they are "under contract" when they really are not.

It is clear that the provisions of the CISG, in comparison with the UCC, are less flexible and do not meet the requirement of the trade-encouraging principle on the international business transaction, as considered one of the shortcomings in the CISG.

Article 2.11 of the UNIDROIT PICC states:

"(1) A reply to an offer which purports to be an acceptance but contains additions, limitations or other modifications is a rejection of the offer and constitutes a counter-offer. (2) However, a reply to an offer which purports to be an acceptance but contains additional or different terms which do not materially alter the terms of the offer constitutes an acceptance, unless the offeror, without undue delay, objects to the discrepancy. If the offeror does not object, the terms of the contract are the terms of the offer with the modifications contained in the acceptance." [1]

A careful reading of this stipulation in the UNIDROIT PICC shows that the UNIDROIT PICC attempts to keep the contract in existence where an offer purports to be an acceptance but contain additional or different terms which do not materially alter the terms of the offer. This obviously will help produce more contracts and promote international business transactions.

In the following case, a U. S. court discussed the battle of the forms under the CISG.

Case 4-1 Filanto v. Chilewich International Corporation

789 F. Supp. 1229 (1992)
United States District Court
(S. D. N. Y.)

Facts: Chilewich, a New York company, entered a contract for the sale of shoes to Raznoexport, a foreign trade agency of the Soviet Union. The contract provided that all disputes were to be settled by arbitration in Moscow. Chilewich then negotiated with Filanto, an Italian company that manufactures footwear, offering to purchase the boots needed to fulfill its contract with Raznoexport. In March 1990, Chilewich prepared and sent to Filanto a signed "Memorandum Agreement" for signature by Filanto. It contained price, payment, and delivery terms. It called for Chilewich to open a letter of credit at its bank to assure payment to Filanto. This offer also incorporated the arbitration agreement of the original Russian contract. Filanto did not sign and return this memo at this time. In May, Chilewich had its bank issue the letter of credit to Filanto. Some boots were shipped and paid for. In August, Filanto signed and returned the memo. It appended a cover letter stating that although it agreed to supply the boots, it excluded the arbitration clause. Chilewich never accepted the balance of the boots

---

[1] The comment of the UNIDROIT PICC on the "material" states: "What amounts to a 'material' modification cannot be determined in the abstract but will depend on the circumstances of each case. Additional or different terms relating to the price or mode of payment, place and time of performance of a non-monetary obligation, the extent of one party's liability to the other or the settlement of disputes, will normally, but need not necessarily, constitute a material modification of the offer. An important factor to be taken into account in this respect is whether the additional or different terms are commonly used in the trade sector concerned and therefore do not come as a surprise to the offeror."

it had ordered. Filanto brought this action to enforce the balance of the contract. Defendant Chilewich claims that the case must be arbitrated in Moscow.

Issue: Must the case be arbitrated in Moscow?

Decision: Yes. ...[A]s plaintiff correctly notes, the "general principles of contract law" relevant to this action, do not include the Uniform Commercial Code; rather, the "federal law of contracts" to be applied in this case is found in the United Nations Convention on Contracts for the International Sale of Goods (the "Sale of Goods Convention")....

Defendant Chilewich contends that the Memorandum Agreement dated March which it signed and sent to Filanto was an offer. It then argues that Filanto's retention of the letter, along with its subsequent acceptance of Chilewich's performance under the Agreement—the furnishing of the letter of credit—estops it from denying its acceptance of the contract...[T]his is... and acceptance by conduct argument, e. g., that in light of the parties' course of dealing, Filanto had a duty timely to inform Chilewich that it objected to the incorporation by reference of all the terms of the Russian Contract. Under this view, the return of the Memorandum Agreement along with the covering letter purporting to exclude parts of the Russian contract, was ineffective as a matter of law as a rejection of the March offer, because this occurred some five months after Filanto received the Memorandum Agreement and two months after Chilewich furnished the Letter of Credit. Instead, in Chilewich's view, this action was a proposal for modification of the March Agreement. Chilewich rejected this proposal... Accordingly, Filanto under this interpretation is bound by the written terms of the March Memorandum Agreement; since that agreement incorporates by reference the Russian Contract containing the arbitration provision, Filanto is bound to arbitrate....

The Court is satisfied on this record that there was indeed an agreement to arbitrate between these parties. There is simply no satisfactory explanation as to why Filanto failed to object to the incorporation by reference of the Russian Contract in a timely fashion. As noted above, Chilewich had in the meantime commenced its performance under the Agreement, and the Letter of Credit it furnished Filanto on May 11 itself mentioned the Russian Contract. An offeree who, knowing that the offeror has commenced performance, fails to notify the offeror of its objection to the terms of the contract within a reasonable time will, under certain circumstances, be deemed to have assented to those terms. The *Sale of Goods Convention* itself recognizes this rule: Article 18 (1), provides that "A statement made by or other conduct of the offeree indicating assent to an offer is an acceptance." Although mere "silence or inactivity" does not constitute acceptance, *Sale of Goods Convention Article* 18 (1), the Court may consider previous relations between the parties in assessing whether a party's conduct constituted acceptance, *Sale of Goods Convention Article* 8 (3). In this case, in light of the extensive course of prior dealing between these parties, Filanto was certainly under a duty to alert Chilewich in timely fashion to its objections to the terms of the March Memorandum Agreement—particularly since Chilewich had repeatedly referred it to the Russian Contract and Filanto had had a copy of that document for some time....

Lastly, the plaintiff contends that if this Court does order arbitration, the Court should take judicial notice of the unsettled conditions inMoscow and order arbitration to proceed in this judicial district.... These parties, though, did agree to arbitrate their disputes in Moscow. Whatever the applicability of these cases in the arbitration context, the chosen forum in this case does have a reasonable relation to the contract at issues, as the ultimate purchaser of the boots was a Russian concern and the Russian Contract was incorporated by reference into Filanto's Memorandum Agreement with Chilewich. Furthermore, though conditions in the Republic of Russian are unsettled, they continue to improve and there is no reason to believe that the Chamber of Commerce in Moscow cannot provide fair and impartial justice to these litigants.

Judgment for the defendant, Chilewich. The parties were referred to arbitration in Moscow. According to the CISG, Filanto's failure to object to the arbitration term in Chilewich's offer in a timely fashion, and its willingness to accept Chilewich's performance, amounted to an acceptance. Filanto was under a duty to alert Chilewich in a timely fashion to its objections to the terms of the Memorandum Agreement. [1]

E. Consideration in Common Law

Consideration is one of the three elements of contract formation in common law, the other two being offer and acceptance. Consideration is not present in other legal systems. Civil law including the CISG and the UNIDROIT PICC emphasize the agreement process, and does not include a "consideration" requirement. An examination of most commercial transactions will show that there is no real issue concerning consideration in

[1] Richard Schaffer, Beverley Earle and Filiberto Agusti, International Business Law and its Environment, West Publishing Company New York, 1996, p. 168.

most of them. So, this part discusses briefly "consideration".

1. Definition

Consideration is some benefit received by a party who gives a promise or performs an act, or some detriment suffered by a party who receives a promise. It may also be defined as "that which is actually given or accepted in return for a promise." It was defined by the court in Currie v. Misa (1875) L. R. 10 Ex 153 as "some right, interest, profit or benefit accruing to one party, or some forbearance, detriment, loss, or responsibility given, suffered or undertaken by the other," but to this definition there should be added that the benefit accruing or the detriment sustained was in return for a promise given or received. Put in plain English, consideration is the price you pay to purchase another person's promise. Under common law, something must be given in return for the promise of the promisor. Often, consideration is payment of money, but it can also be doing something or promising to do or not do something. The consideration paid could be as little as $1. It could be a promise to do something or to give to the other party an item which others might regard as worthless.

2. General Rules on Consideration

(1) Consideration required for all simple contracts. Consideration is necessary for the validity of every contract not under seal. Even contracts in writing require it. "A promise without consideration is a gift; one made for consideration is a bargain." [1]

(2) Consideration must have a value that is recognized by the law but need not be equal to the promise. This principle is sometimes explained as "consideration need not be equal to the promise" or "consideration may not be adequate but it must be sufficient." In other words, the consideration is not adequate in terms of market value but it has a value that is recognized by the law; that is, it has some sufficient value. If, for example, A engages B as his clerk at a salary of £80 a week it would be a difficult, if not impossible, task in most cases for the courts to ascertain whether the salary was adequate to B's work, or whether B's services were worth the salary. In all cases, therefore, the courts only concern themselves with the presence of consideration, and assume that the parties themselves have attended to its value.

(3) Consideration must be present or future and cannot be past. Past consideration is no consideration at all because it happens after an act has already been performed. For instance, when a person returns a lost dog and the gleeful owner promises a reward, that promise cannot be enforced by law because the act of returning the dog occurred before the reward was promised and was therefore not based on the offer of a reward. Another

---

[1] Clive M. Schmitthoff, Mercantile Law, London Stevens & Sons, 1984, p. 51.

example, after a man had sold his horse, he promised the new owner that the horse was healthy and not vicious. The horse turned out to be quite vicious, so the new owner sued for breach of contract. The court held that the promise that the horse was not vicious was not binding, since the sale transaction had been completed prior to the promise. Thus, no consideration was given for this promise. [1]

(4) Consideration must be possible to perform. A promise to do the impossible would not be accepted as consideration.

(5) Consideration must be legal. An illegal consideration makes the whole contract invalid.

(6) Consideration must move from the promisee. This means that the person to whom the promise is made must furnish the consideration. In cases where a promise is made to more than one person and only one of those persons has provided the consideration, all the promisees have acquired rights under the contract. This rule is based on the principle that a stranger to the contract cannot sue on it, a rule known as the doctrine of privity of contract. [2]

(7) Consideration must not be too vague. Consideration must not be so vague that value cannot be placed on it. A sense of moral obligation out of natural love and affection is no longer accepted as valuable consideration. That is to say, moral obligation isn't consideration. Shane's uncle, out of the goodness of his heart, pays higher education fees to help Shane through college. Shane promises to repay his uncle when he gets a decent paying job. After Shane has been working for five years, his uncle gets tired of waiting and sues, claiming that Shane has a moral obligation to pay the amount claimed. The court held that the claim would fail, since a moral obligation is not consideration. [3]

(8) Performance of an existing contractual duty is not valuable consideration. The captain of a ship hired a crew in London. Two of the crew deserted during the trip. The captain promised the remaining crew members a share of the deserters' wages if they would get the ship safely back to London. When they arrived in London, the owners of the ship refused to pay the extra amount, claiming that there was no new consideration because the crew members were hired in the first place to do all they could to bring the

---

[1] Roscorla v. Thomas (1842), Q. B. 234.

[2] This means in common law that there be privity of contract between the parties. Consequently a contract cannot impose liabilities upon one who is not a party to the contract. Also, a contract for the benefit of a third party, giving the latter an actionable right to sue the promiser, is not admitted. For instance, if A validly contracts with B to pay C £ 100, B's obligation can only be enforced by A, but it cannot be enforced by C. the technical reason for this antiquated rule is that no consideration has moved from C to B.

[3] Wayne Pendleton, Roger Vickery, Australian Business Law, Prentice Hall Sydney, 1998, p. 180.

ship safely back to port. The court held that the desertion of the two crew members did not add to the existing contractual duty of each remaining crew member and therefore there was no new consideration. The crew members lost their case. [1]

3. Exceptions to the Consideration Requirement

The consideration requirement is a classic example of a traditional contract law rule. It is precise, abstract, and capable of almost mechanical application. It can also, in some instances, result in significant injustice. Modern courts and legislatures have responded to this potential for injustice by carving out numerous exceptions to the requirement of consideration. Some of these exceptions, for example, are Code firm offer, contract modification rules, contract under seal, estoppel, etc.

(1) Contract under seal does not need consideration.

(2) Promissory Estoppel. Traditional contract law is basically designed to protect bargains that people make and that satisfy all the legal requirements for a binding contract. Around the turn of this century, however, the courts were confronted with cases in which persons relied on promises made by others that did not amount to contracts because they lacked consideration required for a contract. Allowing the person who made such a promise (the promisor) to argue that no contract was created could, in some cases, work an injustice on the person who relied on the promise (the promisee).

In cases where denying enforcement would produce a serious injustice, some courts began to protect pormisees by saying that the promisors were estopped (prevented) from raising any legal defense they might have to the enforcement of the promise. For example, John's parents told him that they would give the family farm to him when they died. Relying on this promise John stayed at home and worked on the farm for several years. When they died, John's parents left the farm to his sister Martha. Should Martha and parents' estate be allowed to defeat John's claim to the farm by arguing that the parents' promise was unenforceable because John gave no consideration for the promise (since the parents did not request that John stay home and work on the farm in exchange for their promise?) Many courts began to say that Martha and the parents' estate were estopped from raising this defense because of the unfairness to John that would result. Out of such cases grew the doctrine of promissory estoppel.

The Restatement Second of Contracts § 90 says: "A promise which that promisor should reasonably expect to induce action or forbearance on the part of the promisee or a third person and which does induce such action or forbearance is binding if injustice can be avoided only by enforcement of the promise. The remedy granted for breach may be

---

[1] Wayne Pendleton, Roger Vickery, Australian Business Law, Prentice Hall Sydney, 1998, p. 180.

limited as justice requires."

While the Restatement does not have the force of law, most courts follow the requirements for promissory estoppel stated in it. Thus, they require: a promise that the promisor should foresee is likely to induce reliance; significant reliance on the promise by the promisee; and injustice as a result of reliance. So, promissory estoppel is used to enforce promises that are not supported by consideration. [1]

Lord Denning made memorable remarks on the case *Central London Property Trust Ltd. v. High Trees House Ltd.* (1947) *KB* 130: "At this time of day, however, when law and equity have been joined together of over seventy years, principles must be reconsidered in the light of their combined effect. It is to be noticed that in the Sixth Interim Report of the Law Revision Committee, it is recommended that such a promise as that to which I have referred, should be enforceable in law even though no consideration for it has been given by the promise. It seems to me that, to the extent I have mentioned, that result has now been achieved by the decisions of the courts." [2]

Case 4-2 FIEGE v. BOEHM

Court of Appeals of Maryland, 1956.
210Md. 352, 123 A. 2d 316.

Facts: This suit was in the Superior Court of Baltimore City by Hilda Louise Boehm against Louis Gail Fiege to recover for breach of a contract to pay the expenses incident to the birth of his bastard child and to provide for its support upon condition that she would refrain from prosecuting him for bastardy. In 1951 defendant had sexual intercourse with the plaintiff although she was unmarried, and as a result thereof she became pregnant, and defendant acknowledged that he was responsible for her pregnancy. On September 29, 1951, she gave birth to a female child, and defendant acknowledged on many occasions that he is its father. Before the child was born, defendant agreed to pay all her medical and miscellaneous expenses and to compensate her for the loss of her salary caused by the child's birth, and also to pay her ten dollars per week for its support until it reached the age of 21, upon condition that she would not institute bastardy proceedings against him as long as he made the payments in accordance with the agreement. After defendant

[1] A. James Barnes, Terry Morehead Dworkin, and Eric L. Richards, Law for Business, IRWIN Chicago, 1997, p. 119.

[2] Yang Liangyi, Game of Rules in International Commercial Pracitces, Publishing House of the China University of Politics and Law, 2000, p. 419.

found through a medical blood test that he could not have been the father of the child, he refused to perform the contract.

Issue: Was the contract valid?

Decision: Forbearance to sue for a lawful claim or demand is sufficient consideration for a promise to pay for the forbearance if the party forbearing had an honest intention to prosecute litigation which is not frivolous, vexatious, or unlawful, and which he believed to be well founded. Defendant lost the suit. [1]

III. Remedies for Breach of Contract

Usually, both parties to a contract for the sale of goods perform the obligations they agreed to in the contract. Occasionally, however, one of the parties to a contract fails to perform his obligations. When this happens, the injured party has a variety of remedies for breach of contract. The objective of these remedies is to put the injured person in the same position as if the contract has been performed.

Prof. Treitel (1999) has defined a breach of contract in the following: "a breach of contract is committed when a party without lawful excuse fails or refuses to perform what is due from him under the contract, or performs defectively or incapacitates himself from performing." [2] It should be noted that in all cases the failure to provide the promised performance must be 'without lawful excuse'. Thus, where the contract has been frustrated there is no liability for breach of contract because both parties have been provided with a "lawful excuse" for their non-performance. Similarly, where one party has breached the contract and the breach has given to the other party the right to terminate performance of the contract. That party is not in breach of contract in refusing to continue with performance because he is given "lawful excuse" for his non-performance.

A. General Principles of Remedies

For what is it that the claimant is entitled to be compensated? How to measure damages for the injured party? Theoretically, a claimant could claim compensation on one of a number of different grounds.

1. The Doctrines of Compensation

(1) The doctrine of expectation interest. This doctrine means that both parties at the time of the conclusion of a contract have expectation interest over the contract, and the

---

[1] John D. Calamari, Joseph M. Perillo, and Helen Hadjiyannakis Bender, Contracts, West Publishing Co. St. Paul, Minn, 1989, p. 156.

[2] Evan McKendrick, Contract Law, Law Press China, 2003, p. 381.

injured party is entitled to his expectation interest lost by the party in breach. Therefore, courts ordinarily protect the expectation that the injured party had when making the contract by attempting to put the injured party in as good a position as that party would have been in had the contract been performed, that is, had there been no breach. The interest measured in this way is called expectation interest and is said to give the injured party the "benefit of the bargain". The expectation interest is based not on the injured party's hopes at the time of making the contract, but on the actual value that the contract would have had to the injured party had it been performed.

In contract of sale of goods the measure of damages according to the doctrine of expectation interest when there is an available market for the goods is the difference between the market price at the date of the breach and the contract price. If, therefore, the market price is equal to or below the contract price the plaintiff will be in the same financial position as if the contract had been performed, and so will only be entitled to nominal damages. A sale to a merchant who has bought for resale makes no difference to the measure of damages where there is a market. If goods of special manufacture are sold and it is known they are to be resold and cannot be bought in the market, loss of profit is the measure of damages.

(2) The doctrine of reliance interest. This means that when the defendant's promise to perform his contractual obligations, the claimant has acted to his detriment in entering into the contract and the award of damages should compensate the defendant. The aim here is to put the claimant in as good a position as he was in before the defendant's promise was made.

(3) The doctrine of restitution interest. A claimant who claims the protection of his restitution interest does not wish to be compensated for the loss which he has suffered; rather, he wishes to deprive the defendant of a gain which he has made at the claimant's expense.

Clearly, there are three doctrines for the claimant to claim damages, but which of these can be used by a claimant? A very simple example will help us to answer this question. Let us suppose that a person enters into a contract to purchase a computer for $ 2000. Let us make the further assumption that the market value of such a computer is, in fact, $ 2000. In breach of contract the seller provides with a defective computer which is worth only $ 1000. He fulfils his side of the bargain and pays $ 2000. If the doctrine of expectation interest is applied, he should be put in the position which he would have been in had the contract been performed according to its terms. Had the contract been performed according to its terms, he would have obtained a computer worth $ 2000, whereas he has obtained a computer which is worth only $ 1000. Therefore, the expectation measure is calculated by deducting the value of what he has actually received (\$1000) from the value of what he expected to receive (\$2000). Damages would therefore be assessed at \$1000.

Under the doctrine of reliance interest, he would be put in the position which he would have been in had he not entered into the contract. Had he not entered into the contract, he would not have parted with his \$2000 and he would not have received a computer worth \$1000. So the reliance measure is calculated by deducting the value of what he has received (\$1000) from the amount which he has paid out (\$2000). Damages would, once again, be assessed at \$1000 so that, on the facts of this case, the expectation measure and the reliance measure would be exactly the same. An award which sought to protect his restitution interest would restore to him the benefit which he had conferred upon the seller. So he would be entitled to the return of the \$2000 and the seller would be entitled to the return of the computer. [1]

2. The Doctrine of Limitations on Damages

A person may not recover for all losses flowing from a breach. There must be limitations on damages.

(1) Non-breaching party has the duty to mitigate damages. This "duty to mitigate" is a commonsense requirement that forbids persons from sitting idly back and allowing losses to pile up.

(2) Damages must be established with a reasonable degree of certainty. This certainty limitation does not demand calculations that are mathematically precise. Damages from the breach of an output contract, for example, can be recovered although they are not mathematically certain. Nevertheless, damages may not be awarded on a purely speculative basis. This certainty limitation has, therefore, often been used to deny recovery for the lost profits of a new business resulting from a breach, since these losses would be too uncertain.

(3) Damages must be either foreseeable to the breaching party or would naturally flow from the breach. This limitation is often referred to as the rule in *Hadley v. Baxendale*, for it was this 1854 English decision that laid down this limitation. The rule in *Hadley v. Baxendale* may be divided into two parts. First, the injured party may recover those damages that "may fairly and reasonably be considered ...to arise naturally ... from such breach of contract itself." Thus, if a machine part for a lathe is not delivered on time, the injured party can naturally be expected to have to rent a lathe and thus lose the rental value of the lathe for the period of delay. Second, in addition, damages may be recovered

---

[1] Evan McKendrick, Contract Law, Law Press. China, 2003, p. 397.

if the breaching party had reason to know of any additional damages that might flow as a probable result of the breach. Using the prior illustration, if the breaching party had reason to know that no substitute machine was available, that party would be liable in addition for the lost profits resulting from the delay. The following case applies the rule of *Hadley v. Baxendale* to a modern setting.

Case 4-3 PRUTCH v. FORD MOTOR COMPANY

618 P. 2d 657 (colo. 1980)

Facts: Carl and Sam Prutch, the plaintiffs, purchased a tractor, plow, disc harrow, and hay baler from Baldridge Implement Company. The Prutches contend that they suffered crop damages as a result of defects in those farm implements.

The Prutches sued Baldridge and the manufacturer of the farm equipment, Ford Motor Company, for breach of express and implied warranties. The trial resulted in a verdict in favor of the Prutches against Ford Moter Co. in the mount of $ 60,200. Ford appealed. The court of appeals overturned the jury verdict. The Prutches appealed to the Supreme Court of Colorado.

Issue: Can the manufacturer be expected to foresee the defects of its products?

Decision: Yes. Ford contends that it cannot be charged with the crop damages incurred by the Prutches. Colorado law authorizes consequential damages for "any loss resulting from general or particular requirements and needs of which the seller at the time of contracting had reason to know and which could not reasonably be prevented ... " The court of appeals noted that the Colorado statutory scheme rejects the "tacit agreement" test that would permit consequential damages only if the seller specifically contemplated or actually assumed the risk of such damages ...Rather, as the court of appeals observed, recovery of consequential damages is determined by the test of "foreseeability" of consequence.

Ford would have us construe "foreseeability" to generate liability only if a manufacturer had some prior actual knowledge as a basis for anticipating damage. But the defendant, in trying to add the ingredient of "prior knowledge" to the "foreseeability" concept, confuses "foreseeable" with "actually foreseen." A standard that would require actual "prior knowledge" by defendant would impose liability only upon proof that the defendant actually foresaw consequential damages. Such a test would be excessively restrictive. The statutory "reason to know" standard, in our view, triggers liability for consequences that may not have been actually foreseen but which were foreseeable.

A manufacturer knowing that its products will be used for crop production reasonably can be expected to foresee that defects in those products may cause crop losses. In such circumstances, therefore, the manufacturer should not escape liability by arguing that it did not actually foresee probable consequences which it should have foreseen. [The court of appeals judgment is reversed and the jury verdict reinstated.][1]

B. Buyer's Remedies

A seller may breach a contract in a number of different ways: the most common are: (1) failing to make an agreed delivery, (2) delivering goods that do not conform to the contract, and (3) indicating an intention not to fulfill the obligations under the contract.

Under CISG, the remedies that are unique to the buyer are (1) to compel specific performance, (2) to avoid the contract for fundamental breach or nondelivery, (3) to reduce the price, (4) to refuse early delivery, and (5) to refuse excess quantities.

1. Specific Performance

(1) Common law and civil law

Specific performance is used when a court requires a party to the contract to perform, or carry out its part of the bargain. The usual remedy in civil law countries is that of specific performance, while the usual legal remedy in contract cases in common law countries is an award for money damages. Therefore, courts in the United States and other common law countries hesitate to require parties to specifically perform. It is considered a harsh remedy to be used only where money damages cannot be calculated or are inadequate, which may occur when the subject matter of the contract is unique. For example, in a dispute over the sale of a famous work of art, a common law court may specifically require a seller to deliver the item to the buyer because of the "unique" nature of the goods. Money damages would not have been sufficient to remedy the buyer in such a case; the buyer wants the goods contracted for. But in civil law countries, the use of specific performance is not only more common, it is preferred.

(2) The CISG

The CISG draws strongly on the civil law's acceptance of specific performance as a remedy in contract cases. This is based on the idea that the buyer wants what was ordered and not just the right to sue for those injuries that the seller's nondelivery may have caused. Under Article 46, a court may grant specific performance only if the following

---

[1] Elliot I. Klayman, John W. Bagby and Nan S. Ellis, IRWIN's Business Law, Irwin Burr Ridge Boston, 1994, p. 346.

conditions are met: (1) the buyer had not resorted to another remedy, such as avoidance or price reduction; (2) the seller had failed to deliver or, in the case of nonconforming goods, the nonconformity was so serious that it constituted a fundamental breach; (3) the buyer gave timely notice to the seller that the goods were nonconforming; and (4) the buyer had made a timely request that the seller provide substitute goods.

(3) The UNIDROIT PICC

The UNIDROIT PICC permits specific performance, but there are exceptions. Article 7.2.2 of the UNIDROIT PICC states:

"Where a party who owes an obligation other than one to pay money does not perform, the other party may require performance, unless

(a) performance is impossible in law or in fact ;

(b) performance or, where relevant, enforcement is unreasonably burdensome or expensive ;

(c) the party entitled to performance may reasonably obtain performance from another source ;

(d) performance is of an exclusively personal character; or

(e) the party entitled to performance does not require performance within a reasonable time after it has, or ought to have, become aware of the non-performance."

According to Article 7.2.4. (1) Where the court orders a party to perform, it may also direct that this party pay a penalty if it does not comply with the order. (2) The penalty shall be paid to the aggrieved party unless mandatory provisions of the law of the forum provide otherwise. Payment of the penalty to the aggrieved party does not exclude any claim for damages.

(4) China Contract Law

Under Article 110 of China Contract Law, if one party to a contract fails to perform the non-monetary debt or its performance of non-monetary debt fails to satisfy the terms of the contract, the other party may request it to perform it except under any of the following circumstances: (1) It is unable to be performed in law or in fact; (2) The object of the debt is unfit for compulsory performance or the performance expenses are excessively high; or (3) The creditor fails to request for the performance within a reasonable time period.

The debt is unfit for compulsory performance means that compulsory performance of the debt may be against the statute, or due to the special feature of object, specific performance cannot be fulfilled. For example, a painter who refuses to paint as contracted cannot be forced to paint because this may break the law for the protection of human dignity and personal freedom. Also, if an actress is injured in a car accident on the way to a theater, she cannot be requested to act on the stage.

2. Avoidance

(1) Common law and civil law

Under common law and civil law, if the breach is material or fundamental, the buyer need not take delivery nor pay for the goods, nor find a buyer to take them. A buyer may simply cancel the contract by notifying the seller of avoidance of the contract, take care that the goods are temporarily protected and preserved, and return them for a full refund of monies already paid. When the goods can rapidly deteriorate or decay, such as with certain foods, the buyer may notify the seller and then take steps to sell them.

(2) The CISG

Under the CISG, a buyer may avoid a contract if either (a) the seller commits a fundamental breach of (b) the buyer gives the seller a *Nachfrist* notice and the seller rejects it or does not perform within the period it specifies. [1] A buyer's notice is the fixing of "an additional period of time of reasonable length for performance by the seller of his obligations." [2] The period must be definite and the obligation to perform within that period must be clear. Once the *Nachfrist* period has run, or once the fundamental breach becomes clear, the buyer has a reasonable time in which to avoid the contract. [3] Obviously, during the *Nachfrist* period, the seller is entitled to correct (i. e., cure) the nonconformity at his own expense. Even if there has been a breach, the seller is entitled to make a cure, unless the circumstances-including the circumstance of the offer to make the cure-indicate that the breach is fundamental and the buyer chooses to avoid the contract. [4]

(3) The UNIDROIT PICC

Article 7.3.1. (1) of the UNIDROIT PICC provides: "A party may terminate the contract where the failure of the other party to perform an obligation under the contract amounts to fundamental non-performance." Article 7. 3. 1. (2) further states: "In determining whether a failure to perform an obligation amounts to a fundamental non-performance regard shall be had, in particular, to whether

(a) the non -performance substantially deprives the aggrieved party of what it was entitled to expect under the contract unless the other party did not foresee and could not reasonably have foreseen such result;

(b) strict compliance with the obligation which has not been performed is of essence

---

〔1〕 CF. Article 49(1) of the CISG.

〔2〕 Id. Article 47(1).

〔3〕 Id. Article 49(2).

〔4〕 Id. Article 48.

under the contract ;

(c) the non-performance is intentional or reckless;

(d) the non-performance gives the aggrieved party reason to believe that it cannot rely on the other party's future performance ;

(e) the non-performance party will suffer disproportionate loss as a result of the preparation or performance if the contract is terminated.

Article 7.3.1. (3) stipulates the relationship between the delay in performance and the termination of contract: "In the case of delay the aggrieved party may also terminate the contract if the other party fails to perform before the time allowed it under Article 7.1.5 has expired."

(4) China Contract Law

Article 94 of China Contract Law provides: "The parties to a contract may rescind the contract under any of the following circumstances:

The purpose of the contract is not able to be realized because of force majeure;

One party to the contract expresses explicitly or indicates through its acts, before the expiry of the performance period, that it will not perform the principal debt obligations;

One party to the contract delays in performing the principal debt obligations and fails, after being urged, to perform them within a reasonable time period;

One party to the contract delays in performing the debt obligations or commits other acts in breach of the contract so that the purpose of the contract is not able to be realized; or other circumstances as stipulated by law."

3. Price Reduction

Price reduction for the buyer is used when the seller makes only a partial shipment, or if the goods are nonconforming. A buyer who would like to retain the goods may adjust the amount paid by withholding a proportionate part of the purchase price in order to offset the shortage or to reflect the reduced value of the nonconfoming goods. If the buyer can repair the goods, or to bring them up to contract specifications, the buyer may adjust the price paid accordingly. If the goods have already been paid for, the buyer may ask that the seller return a portion of the amount paid. Obviously, the amount of price reduction is far easier to calculate when the seller delivers less than the promised amount when the goods are damaged or of inferior quality. The amount of reduction, then, is within the discretion of the buyer. A seller who disputes the buyer's calculation can only resort to legal action.[1]

4. Refusing Early Delivery and Excess Quantity

Article 52 of the CISG provides: "(1) If the seller delivers the goods before the date fixed, the buyer may take delivery or refuse to take delivery. (2) If the seller delivers a quantity of goods greater than that provided for in the contract, the buyer may take delivery or refuse to take delivery of the excess quantity. If the buyer takes delivery of all or part of the excess quantity, he must pay for it at the contract rate."

C. Seller's Remedies

The remedies that are unique to the seller are (1) to compel specific performance, (2) to avoid the contract for a fundamental breach or failure to cure a defect, and (3) to obtain missing specifications. Clearly, the seller's remedies are rather similar to those of the buyer.

D. Remedies Available to Both Buyers and Sellers

The remedies available to both buyers and sellers are (1) suspension of performance, (2) avoidance in anticipation of a fundamental breach, (3) avoidance of an installment contract, (4) avoidance, and (5) damages.

1. Damages

In breach of contract cases, the usual remedy granted by common law courts to both buyers and sellers is the legal remedy of money damages. Article 74 of the CISG provides: "Damages for breach of contract by one party consist of a sum equal to the loss, including loss of profit, suffered by the other party as a consequence of the breach. Such damages may not exceed the loss which the party in breach foresaw or ought to have foreseen at the time of the conclusion of the contract, in the light of the facts and matters of which he then knew or ought to have known, as a possible consequence of the breach of contract."

The method of measuring money damages due to a buyer in the event of the seller's breach, depends on whether the buyer has been able to purchase substitute goods, the buyer may claim damages if the substitute goods cost more than contract price. If the buyer has not purchased substitute goods, damages are measured by the difference between the contract price and the current market price. As under English common law

---

[1] Article 50 of the CISG states: "If the goods do not conform with the contract and whether or not the price has already been paid, the buyer may reduce the price in the same proportion as the value that the goods actually delivered had at the time of the delivery bears to the value that conforming goods would have had at that time. However, if the seller remedies any failure to perform his obligations in accordance with Article 37 or Article 48 or if the buyer refuses to accept performance by the seller in accordance with those articles, the buyer may not reduce the price."

and the UCC, damages under the CISG may also include an amount for *lost profits* and other consequential damages as a "reasonably foreseeable" consequential of the breach. These consequential damages are limited under Article 74 to those that the parties "foresaw or ought to have foreseen at the time of the conclusion of the contract." [1]

An emphasis must be made on the provision of the UNITROIT PICC. It's Article 7.4.1 states: "Any non-performance gives the aggrieved party a right to damages either exclusively or in conjunction with any other remedies except where the non-performance is excused under these Principles." Article 7.4.2 further provides: "(1) The aggrieved party is entitled to full compensation for harm sustained as a result of the non-performance. Such harm includes both any loss which it suffered and any gain of which it was deprived, taking into account any gain to the aggrieved party resulting from its avoidance of cost or harm. (2) Such harm may be non-pecuniary and includes, for instance, physical suffering or emotional distress." The above full compensation must be also limited, according to Article 7.4.3 that provides: "(1) Compensation is due only for harm, including future harm, that is established with a reasonable degree of certainty. (2) Compensation may be due for the loss of a chance in proportion to the probability of its occurrence. (3) Where the amount of damages cannot be established with a sufficient degree of certainty, the assessment is at the discretion of the court." Article 7.4.4 states: "The non-performing party is liable only for harm which it foresaw or could reasonably have foreseen at the time of the conclusion of the contract as being likely to result from its non-performance. (1) The non-performance party is not liable for harm suffered by the aggrieved party to the extent that the harm could have been reduced by the latter party's taking reasonable steps. (2) The aggrieved party is entitled to recover any expenses reasonably incurred in attempting to reduce the harm."

After reading these provisions of the UNIDROIT PICC, you will easily find that although they are based on the common law, civil law, and especially the CISG, they have their own characteristics. For instance, under the UNIDROIT PICC, the right to damages may arise not only in the context of non-performance of the contract, but also

---

[1] Consequential damages refers to losses that do not flow directly and immediately from an injurious act, but that result indirectly from the act. (Bryan A. Garner, Black's Law Dictionary, West Group S. Paul, Minn., 1999, p. 394.) Suppose David promises to deliver 15,000 yards of a special fabric to Dorsey by September 1. David knows that Dorsey wants to acquire the material to make garments suitable for the Christmas season. David also knows that in reliance on the contract with it, Dorsey will enter into contracts with department stores to deliver the finished garments by October 1. If David fails to deliver the fabric or delivers the fabric after September 1, it may be liable to Dorsey for any consequential damages that she sustains if she is unable to acquire the same material elsewhere in time to fufill her October 1 contract.

during the pre-contractual period. (See Article 2. 15 in case of negotiations in bad faith, Article 2. 16 in the event of breach of the duty of confidentiality, or Article 3. 18 in the case of mistake, fraud, threat or gross disparity). Also, the full compensation includes non-pecuniary harm. According to its comment, this may be pain and suffering, loss of certain amenities of life, aesthetic prejudice, etc. as well as harm resulting from attacks on honor or reputation. This rule might find application, in international commerce, in regard to contracts concluded by artists, outstanding sportsmen or women and consultants engaged by a company or by an organization.

Under Article 112 of China Contract Law, if one party fails to perform the contract obligations or its performance fails to satisfy the terms of the contract, the party shall compensate for the losses. Article 113 further affirms that the amount of compensation for losses shall be equal to the losses caused by the breach of contract, including the interests receivable after the performance of the contract, provided not exceeding the probable losses caused by the breach of contract which has been foreseen or ought to be foreseen when the party in breach concludes the contract. Article 119 stipulates that the innocent party has the duty to take proper measures to prevent from the enlargement of losses; otherwise, the party may not claim any compensation as to the enlarged losses.

2. Avoidance of Installment Contracts

Under Article 73 of the CISG, if there was a fundamental breach with respect to a particular installment, then the other party may declare the contract avoided with respect to that installment. Also, if the breach of one installment gives a party "good grounds" to believe that a fundamental breach of later installments "will occur," then those later installments may be anticipatorily avoided. Finally, if the installments are interdependent, a fundamental breach of one installment will allow a party to avoid the entire contract (past and future installments included). [1]

The following case discussed that the injured party must mitigate damages.

Case 4-4 Delchi Carrier, SpA v. Rotorex Coroiration

United States, District Court, Northern District of New York, 1994.

Lexis-nixies, 1994 US District Courts file, Case No. 12820

Facts: In January 1988, Rotorex Corporation (Rotorex), a New York corporation, agreed to sell Delchi Carrier, SpA (Delchi), an Italian corporation, 10,800 Rotorex model K39A593A compressors, to be delivered in three

〔1〕 Ray August, Don Mayer and Michael Bixby, International Business Law, Six Edition, Pearson Education Limited, 2013, p. 605.

installments by May 15, 1988. Delchi told rotorex at that time that it was ordering the compressors for use in the production of its "Ariele" line of portable room air conditioners that it planned to sell during the summer of 1988.

Rotorex's delivered its first installment of 2,438 compressors to an ocean carrier for shipment to Delchi on March 26, 1988 and Delchi paid for the installment with a letter of credit shortly thereafter. These compressors arrived at Delchi's place of business in Villasanta, Italy on April 20, 1988. On May 9, 1988, Rotorex shipped a second installment of 1, 680 compressors to Delchi, and again Delchi paid $ 129,985.60 in the form of letters of credit for the second shipment. While Rotorex's second installment of compressors was en route to Italy, Delchi discovered that the Rotorex compressors from the first lot were nonconforming, and it therefore rejected the compressors and cancelled the contract.

Delchi attempted to help Rotorex cure the defects by paying for the shipment of substitute Rotorex grommets and connecters and by employing its workers to rework, inspect, and test the compressors. When this proved unsuccessful, it paid to store the Rotorex compressors in Italy.

Because Delchi had no compressors with which to manufacture its Ariele air conditioners, it shut down its assembly line for four days in May, 1988. Because it was unable to obtain substitute compressors from other sources in time for the 1988 selling season for air conditioners, Delchi suffered a loss in the volume of Ariele it was able to manufacture for the 1988 selling season.

Delchi was able to expedite a shipment of Sanyo compressors it already had on order bypaying for priority shipping. It was then able to partially fill the void resulting from Rotorex's breach. However, because of the breach, Delchi was unable to completely fill orders it had from carrier, White—Westingthouse, and other companies in Europe. Having sustained a substantial loss, Delchi sued Rotorex in a United States court to obtain damages.

Issue: Was Delchi entitled to compensation?

Decision: Yes! According to Judge Howard G. Munson, Sr., the court has jurisdiction over this action.... The governing law of the instant case is the United Nations Convention on Contracts for the International sale of Goods (UNCCISG).

Rotorex breached its contract with Delchi by failing to supply 10, 800 conforming compressors. Under UNCCISG [Article 74], Delchi is entitled to collect monetary damages for Rotorex's breach in "a sum equal to the loss, including loss of profit," although not in excess of the amount reasonably envisioned by the parties. This provision seeks to provide the injured party with the benefit of the bargain, including both its expectation interest and its reliance expenditures.

1. Consequential Damages

Delchi is entitled to recover damages incurred as result of its attempts to remedy thenonconformity of Rotorex's compressors. These were not anticipated costs of production, but were costs that would not have been incurred without Rotorex's breach. Further, such damages were a foreseeable result of Rotorex's breach. Hence Delchi is entitled to recover:

(1) 183,170 lire for unreimbursed expenses relating to the shipment of connectors;

(2) 1,309,851 lire for unreimbursed expenses relatingto the shipment of substitute Rotorex grommets;

(3) 15,874,030 lire for labor costs relatingto replacing original, problematic grommets with substitutes;

(4) 11,687,142 lire for extraordinary reinspection and testingof units after installation of the substitute grommets and connectors.

Delchi is further entitled to collect costs incurred for handling and storage of nonconforming compressors, including 11,096,400 lire related to Rotorex's first shipment. Further, although Delchi failed to establish the precise cost of storage of second shipment of Rotorex compressors, the court holds that Delchi is entitled to 2,103,683 lire as a reasonable expanse for that purpose. Thus, delchi is entitled to recover 13,200,083 lire expenses incurred for handling and storage of Rotorex's nonconforming compressors.

2. Lost Profit

UNCCISG permits recovery of lost profit resulting from a diminished volume of sales. In conformity with the common law and with the law of New York, to recover a claim for lost profit under UNCCISG, a party must provide the finder of fact with sufficient evidence to estimate the amount of damages with reasonable certainty.

Delchi proved with sufficient certainty that it incurred as a foreseeable and direct result of Rotorex's breach, the following lost profit damages:

(1) 421,187,095 lire from lost sales of 2,395 Ariele to Carrier-affiliated companies throughout Europe;

(2) 31,310,200 lire fromlost sales of 100 Ariele to White-Westinghouse Company;

(3) 266,057,772 [lire] from lost sales of 604 Delchi Brand Ariele in Italy, and 280,319,840 [lire] from lost sales of 653 White- Westinghouse brand Ariele in Italy, for a total of 546,377,612 lire in lost profit from lost salesin Italy.

Delchi did not prove with sufficient certainty any lost sales from "indicated orders" in Italy. Delchi's claim of 4,000 additional lost sales in Italy is supported only by the speculative testimony of Italian sales agents Renato Comolla, Georgia Viale, Luigi Diblase, and Angelo Calaciura, who averred that they would have ordered more Arieles had they been available. The number of additional units they might have ordered, although specified in Delchi's Post-Trial Brief, is not in evidence, as the court sustained Rotorex's timely objections to the speculative nature of such testimony. Delchi provides no documentation of additional lost sales in Italy, and no evidence that if any such lost sales did exist, that Delchi's inability to fill those orders was directly attributable to Rotorex's breach. Delchi can not recover on its claim for additional lost profits in Italy because the amount of damages, if any, can not be established with reasonable certainty.

...

Defendant Rotorex Corporation is liable to plaintiff Delchi Carrier SpA in the amount of [US] $ 1,248,331.87 [1,545,434,848 lire] in principal, in satisfaction of Rotorex's breach of contract... [1]

IV. Anticipatory Breach of Contract and Exceptio non Adimpleti Contractus in Civil Law

A. Anticipatory Breach in Common Law

One contracting party may inform the other party, before the time fixed for performance under the contract, that he will not perform his obligations under the contract. This is called an anticipatory breach of contract, which entitles the innocent party to terminate performance of the contract immediately. The novel feature of anticipatory breach is that acceptance of the breach entitles the innocent party to claim damages at the date of the acceptance of the breach. He does not have to wait until the date fixed for performance, even though this has the effect of accelerating the obligations of the party in breach. It does seem somewhat illogical to say that a party can be in breach of contract before the time fixed for performance under the contract. The doctrine of anticipatory breach can best be rationalized as a breach of an implied term of the contract

[1] Ray August, International Business Law, Prentice Hall New Jersey, 1997, pp. 534 - 535.

that neither party will, without just cause, repudiate his obligations under the contract before the time fixed for performance.

The operation of the doctrine of anticipatory breach can be illustrated by reference to the case of *hochster v. De La Tour* (1853) 2 E & B 678. In April of 1852 the defendant agreed to employ the claimant to act as his courier for 3 months from 1 June. But on 11 May the defendant wrote to the claimant informing him that his services would no longer be required. The claimant commenced his action on 22 May and it was held that he was entitled to commence his action for damages at that date; he did not have to wait until 1 June when performance was due.

Once again the innocent party is not obliged to exercise his right to terminate performance of the contract; he can elect to affirm the contract and demand performance from the other party at the time stipulated in the contract. But where the innocent party doesdecide to terminate performance of the contract he must give notice to the party in breach that he is accepting the anticipatory breach and he must not act inconsistently with his decision to accept the breach.

B. Exceptio non Adimpleti Contractus in Civil Law

Exceptio non Adimpleti Contractus[1] in Civil Law means that one party is entitled to reject performance unless the other party performs his obligations according to the contract. Article 321 of the "German Civil Code" provides: "if one party to a bilateral contract is obligated to give first, he may reject his obligation in the case where the other party's property becomes so obviously less that his right is injured, and before he provides guarantee."

The UNIDROIT PICC Article 7. 1. 3 provides: "(1) Where the parties are to perform simultaneously, either party may withhold performance until the other party tenders its performance. (2) Where the parties are to perform consecutively, the party that is to perform later may withhold its performance until the first party has performed." Article 7. 3. 4. further states: "A party who reasonably believes that there will be a fundamental non-performance by the other party may demand adequate assurance of due performance and may meanwhile withhold its own performance. Where this assurance is not provided within a reasonable time the party demanding it may terminate the contract." This article is undoubtedly based on the Exceptio non adimpleti Contractus in Civil Law."

Articles 71 and 72 of the CISG provide the requirements of anticipatory breach and remedies. The requirements are (1) anticipatory beach takes place after the conclusion of

---

[1] Latin: exemption of one party's obligation in case of the other party's failure of performance.

the contract, or prior to the date for performance of the contract; (2) it becomes apparent that the other party will not perform a substantial part of his obligations as a result of: (a) a serious deficiency in his ability of perform or in his creditworthiness; or (b) his conduct in preparing to perform or in performing the contract.

The remedies for anticipatory breach of contract are: to suspend the performance of his obligations or to prevent the handing over of the goods to the buyer even though the buyer holds a document which entitles him to obtain them. The injured party can also resort to anticipatory avoidance. However, the anticipatory avoidance is different from the avoidance remedies that apply specifically by buyers and sellers. The difference is that those remedies apply only after an offending party has committed a fundamental breach and anticipatory avoidance arises as soon as "it is clear" that the other party "will commit a fundamental breach." If time allows, the party intending to declare the contract avoided must give reasonable notice to the other party in order to permit him to provide adequate assurance of his performance.

There seem to be only a few cases where this remedy can be invoked. These include (1) the specific goods promised to the buyer are wrongfully sold to a third party; (2) the seller's only employee capable of producing the goods dies or is fired; and (3) the seller's manufacturing plant is sold. In most other cases the breach will already have occurred, or the circumstances will be such that a suspension of performance is the appropriate remedy.[1]

China Contract Law has successfully put together the anticipatory breach of contract and Exceptio non adimpleti Contractus. Article 66 provides: "If both parties have obligations towards each other and there is no order of priority in respect of the performance of obligations, the parties shall perform the obligations simultaneously. One party has the right to reject the other party's request for performance before the other party's performance. One party has the right to reject the other party's corresponding request for performance if the other party's performance does not meet the terms of the contract." Article 69 has the effect of the Exceptio non adimpleti Contractus which states: "One party to a contract which suspends its performance of the contract in accordance with the provisions of Article 68 of this Law, shall promptly inform the other party of such suspension. It shall resume its performance of the contract when the other party provides a sure guarantee. After the suspension of the performance, if the other party does not reinstate its capacity of performance and does not provide with a sure guarantee,

[1] Ray August, Don Mayer and Michael Bixby, International Business Law, Six Edition, Pearson Education Limited, 2013, p. 605.

the party suspending performance of the contract may rescind the contract."

V. Liquidated Damages

A. Common Law

Liquidated damages refer to the amount of money which shall be payable in the event of a breach of contract. Such a clause in a contract helps to eliminate uncertainty because it enables the parties to know in advance the extent of their potential liability and to plan accordingly (for example, in relation to the calculation of the price and the allocation of responsibility for insurance). However, in common law countries, the courts have retained a jurisdiction to control the content of such clauses. The basic rules which the courts have established may be stated in the following terms. If the clause represents a genuine pre-estimate of the loss which is likely to be occasioned by the breach, then it is a "liquidated damages clause" and is enforceable. The function of such a clause is to fix the sum which is to be paid irrespective of the actual damage suffered by reason of the breach. So, for example, if the loss suffered is greater than the sum stipulated, the innocent party cannot ignore the clause and sue for his actual loss. The sum stipulated in the liquidated damages clause is the sum recoverable, even though that sum is greater or smaller than the loss which has actually been suffered.

But if the sum stated in the clause is not a genuine pre-estimate of loss, it is a "penalty clause" and is unenforceable. The aim of such a clause is to punish the party in breach and the courts held that such an aim is impermissible. A clause which is held to be a penalty clause is not struck out of the contract, but it will not be enforced by the court beyond the actual loss of the party seeking to rely on the clause. The court is not required to consider whether the party in breach is entitled to relief; the court often automatically relegates the party seeking to rely on the penalty clause to a claim in damages.

The distinction between a liquidated damages clause and penalty clause rests ultimately on the intention of the parties at the time of entry into the contract: that is to say, was the clause a genuine or bona fide attempt to assess the loss likely to be occasioned by the breach or was it designed to punish the party in breach? The fact that the parties have described the clause as a "liquidated damages clause" or a "penalty clause" is a relevant factor but it is not conclusive. The difference between a liquidated damages clause and a penalty clause is in fact a question of construction and the courts have established a number of rules of construction which they apply in deciding whether a particular clause is penalty clause or a liquidated damages clause:

(1) A clause will be held to be a penalty clause, if the sum stipulated for is extravagant and unconscionable in amount in comparison with the greatest loss that could

conceivably be proved to have followed from the breach.

(2) A clause will be held to be a penalty clause, if the sum stipulated is a sum greater than the sum which ought to have been paid.

(3) There is a presumption (but no more) that it is penalty when a single lump sum is made payable by way of compensation, on the occurrence of one or more or all of several events, some of which may occasion serious and others but trifling damage.

This presumption can act as a trap for the unwary. Contract draftsmen must seek to distinguish between serious and trifling breaches of contract because a failure to distinguish between the two may result in the clause being held to be a penalty clause.

Clearly, a penalty clause is invalid and unenforceable, however, this leads to a potential anomaly where the loss which the innocent party has suffered is greater than the sum stipulatedin the contract. In such a case, can the innocent party argue that the clause is a penalty clause so that it can be ignored and he can recover his actual loss? In *Wall v. Rederiaktiebogalet Luggude* (1915) 3 KB 66, it was held that the innocent party could do this and recover his actual loss, although the decision was only at first instance, the reasoning is not at all clear and the issue has been the subject of vigorous debate among academic lawyers. [1]

An emphasis should be made to Chinese merchants doing business with those from common law countries. Chinese merchants must take care in stipulating a proper sum in contract governed by common law, otherwise, this clause may be regarded by the courts as "penalty clause" and such a clause is invalid and unenforceable.

B. Civil Law

Under French law, the stipulation of liquidated damages, as a result of freedom of contract, is valid and enforceable. According to Article 1152 of the "French Civil Code", courts in principle cannot adjust such a stipulation by the parties to a contract.

German law provides that liquidated damages even if characterized by punitive role is valid and enforceable. For instance, under Article 340 (2) of the "German Civil Code", if the innocent party suffers a loss greater than the liquidated damages stipulated, he is entitled to not only the liquidated damages, but also the sum exceeded.

C. The UNIDROIT PICC

The liquidated damages clause in a contract is also valid and enforceable under the UNIDROIT PICC. Article 7.4.13 provides:

"(1) Where the contract provides that a party who does not perform is to pay a specified sum to the aggrieved party for such non-performance, the aggrieved party is

---

[1] Evan McKendrick, Contract Law, Law Press. China, 2003, p. 432.

entitled to that sum irrespective of its actual harm.

However, notwithstanding any agreement to the contrary the specified sum may be reduced to a reasonable amount where it is grossly excessive in relation to the harm resulting from the non-performance and to the other circumstances."

Here "the agreed payment for non-performance" is defined broadly as a specified sum in case of non-performance, whether such agreements be intended to facilitate the recovery of damages (liquidated damages according to the common law) or to operate as a deterrent against non-performance (penalty clauses proper), or both.

In view of the frequency in international contract practice, this article in principle acknowledges the validity of any clauses providing that a party who does not perform is to pay a specified sum to the innocent party for such non-performance, with the consequence that the latter is entitled to the agreed sum irrespective of the harm actually suffered by it. The non-performing party may not allege that the innocent party sustained less harm or none at all.

In order to prevent the possibility of abuse to which such clauses may give rise, this article permits the reduction of the agreed sum if it is grossly excessive "in relation to the harm resulting from the non-performance and to the other circumstances". The same paragraph makes it clear that the parties may under no circumstances exclude such a possibility of reduction.

The agreed sum may only be reduced, but not entirely disregarded as would be the case were the judge, notwithstanding the agreement of the parties, to award damages corresponding to the exact amount of the harm. However, it may not be increased, at least under this article, where the agreed sum is lower than the harm actually sustained (see Comment 4 on Article 7.1.6.).

D. China Contract Law

Article 114 of China Contract Law makes similar provisions to that of the UNIDROIT PICC, but with slight difference that Article 114 states that if the agreed breach of contract damages are lower than the losses caused, any party may request the people's court or an arbitration institution to increase it, and this article also emphases that if the parties to a contract agree upon breach of contract damages in respect to the delay in performance, the party in breach shall perform the debt obligations after paying the breach of contract damages.

Case 4-5 China International Economic and Trade Arbitration Commission

Industrial raw materials case (4 June 1999)

Facts: On 20 April 1998, [Seller] and [Buyer] signed Contract (hereinafter: the Contract) which provides for the purchase by [Buyer] from [Seller] of 17 tons of industrial raw materials for a contract price of US $239,761.46, with payment by Letter of Credit (hereinafter: L/C).

Issue: What damages shall [Buyer] recover in this case?

Seller's claim: After signing the Contract, [Buyer] issued the L/C. [Seller] shipped the goods according to the Contract. However, when [Seller] submitted the L/C to the paying bank for negotiation, the bank dishonored the L/C because the carrier mistakenly wrote 1999 as 1998 in the Bill of Lading (hereinafter: B/L). [Seller] notified [Buyer] about this disparity, and requested [Buyer] to perform the Contract, accept the disparity and redeem the B/L. However, [Buyer] did not redeem the B/L, but requested [Seller] to reduce the price due to this disparity. When [Seller] refused [Buyer]'s request, [Buyer] refused to make the payment. In order to mitigate the loss, [Seller] had to resell the goods to another company for US $204,719.40. [Seller]'s loss due to the price difference is US $35,042.06.

[Seller] applied for arbitration and made the following claims:

1. [Buyer] should pay [Seller] the loss of price, US $35,042.06;
2. [Buyer] should pay [Seller] the loss of interest until the day [Buyer] makes the payment (to the end of 1998, the interest should be US $4,616.71);
3. [Buyer] should pay the demurrage, US $1,245.91 and bank interest, RMB 1,330;
4. [Buyer] should bear the entire arbitration fee of this case.

Buyer's reply: 1. [Buyer] issued the L/C in accordance with the Contract, but [Seller] did not deliver a complete set of documents as required by the L/C. This constitutes a breach of contract. [Buyer] has no duty to accept the disparity with the Contract, and did not breach the Contract. According to Article 34 of the United Nations Convention on Contracts for the International Sale of Goods (1980) (hereinafter: CISG), it is an important duty for [Seller] to deliver the documents to [Buyer]. [Seller] did not deliver the documents required by the L/C. Therefore, [Seller] breached the Contract. [Seller], in its correspondence, admitted that there was an "error" with respect to the year on the L/C, and this shows that the disparity was caused by [Seller]'s fault and that [Buyer] was not liable. When the documents do not comply with the L/C, the bank has sufficient reason to dishonor the L/C.

2. As to the disparity of the documents, [Seller] should revise it in order for the bank's negotiation, but [Seller] did not make the revision in a timely manner. Although, in its correspondence, [Seller] stated that the shipping company had taken some measures to deal with the disparity, [Seller] did not provide the revised B/L to the bank or [Buyer]. [Buyer], as a trader, signed this Contract in order to resell the goods to gain profits out of the price difference. Most international sales of goods are documentary transactions. [Seller] mistakenly wrote 1999 in the B/L, and this would cause severe trouble for [Buyer] to resell the documents and would also cause a large expense by [Buyer]. On 8 June 1998, [Buyer] wrote to [Seller], stating that because the year in the B/L was mistakenly written, [Buyer]'s client could not resell the goods to its downstream buyer, and [Buyer]'s client refused to accept all of the goods. Accordingly, [Buyer] proposed to reduce the price, and [Seller] has no right to make any claim on this basis.

3. [Buyer] never stated that it would refuse to accept the goods. However, without notifying [Buyer], [Seller] unilaterally avoided the Contract and resold the goods. This constitutes a fundamental breach of contract. [Buyer] tried to negotiate with [Seller] to mitigate the loss as much as possible. [Buyer] never expressed or implied that it would refuse to accept the goods or avoid the Contract. And [Seller] did not provide any evidence to prove that [Buyer] made such statement. According to the CISG, if one party wants to avoid the contract, he must send notice to the other party, and then the avoidance can take effect. [Seller] completely deprived [Buyer] of its economic interest because [Seller] avoided the Contract unilaterally without giving [Buyer] any notice. [Seller] fundamentally breached the Contract, and has no right to claim for damages against [Buyer].

After the hearing, [Buyer] made the following supplementary reply:

1. In international sales of goods, the seller's duty to deliver the documents is a key to the performance of its duty of "delivery". This is because the B/L, one of the documents delivered by [Seller], is the certificate of ownership of the goods, and possession of the B/L represents possession of and control over the goods. In addition, from a commercial perspective, [Buyer], as a trader, cannot resell the goods after taking physical possession of the goods, but resells the relevant documents after obtaining the documents. Also, the documents are the basis for [Buyer] to claim against any third parties for damages. Because the shipping documents are very important to [Buyer], the documents delivered by [Seller]

must be in strict compliance with the Contract. Although scholars have different opinions on strict compliance, the principle of strict compliance stipulated in the UCP 500 is binding. [Seller] did not provide the documents in strict compliance with the L/C, so it breached the Contract. [Buyer] may suffer loss if it is requested to accept the non-compliance or make payment.

2. [Seller] asserts that if payment by the L/C is impossible, [Seller] still has the right to deliver the goods directly to [Buyer] instead of delivering the documents and that [Buyer] should pay [Seller] by other means. It is [Buyer]'s position that [Seller] is not entitled to require [Buyer] to make the payment directly to [Seller] except where (a) the bank is bankrupt; or (b) the bank wrongfully refused the documents. In this case, no such situations exist. Thus, [Seller] is not entitled to require [Buyer] to make the payment directly.

3. As stated above, because the documents submitted by [Seller] and the L/C are not in compliance, payment by L/C is impossible. [Seller] fundamentally breached the Contract, and [Buyer] has the right to avoid the Contract. Even if acts of [Seller] do not constitute fundamental breach and [Buyer] still has a duty to make the payment, according to the CISG, [Buyer] has no duty to make the payment before it has a reasonable opportunity to inspect the goods. [Buyer] may suffer unforeseeable losses, if it accepts the disparity of the relevant documents. Therefore, [Buyer]'s request to reduce the price is reasonable. A businessman's judgment is always based on his concern on profitability. [Buyer]'s action in response of the market price is therefore reasonable.

4. The payment term stipulated in the Contract is by L/C. However, because the documents submitted by [Seller] are not in compliance, the payment by L/C is impossible. This shows that the payment clause in the Contract automatically terminated. The parties did not reach a new agreement on the payment term, so the original contract lacked a basic clause and was not validly established.

5. Moreover, [Seller]'s resale price is unreasonable. *First*, the resale price is lower than the reduced price which [Buyer] suggested. *Second*, in July 1998, the high and low floating prices of the goods were US $6.407/LB and US $5.983/LB, respectively, and the average price was US $6.047/LB. However, on 30 July 1998, [Seller]'s resale price was US $5.55/LB, which differs greatly from the average market price. The difference is US $0.497/LB [i.e., 6.047 – 5.55]. The total price difference is US $18,626.83438. In addition, [Seller]'s calculation of loss of interest is unreasonable. The date of [Seller]'s evidence for

demurrage is later than the day when the goods were resold, so the evidence should not be admissible.

Opinion of the Arbitration Tribunal:

1. The disparity in the documents. Both [Seller] and [Buyer] acknowledge that the documents submitted by [Seller] for negotiation are not in compliance with the L/C, and that the disparity is the date of the B/L, which should be 1998 but was mistakenly typed as 1999. [Seller] asserts that [Buyer] should accept this lack of compliance and redeem the documents, but [Buyer] refused to do this and asked [Seller] to reduce the price. The Arbitration Tribunal holds that: (1) The payment term stipulated in this Contract is by L/C, so after delivering the goods, [Seller] should deliver documents that are in compliance with the L/C in order to get the payment. Under the usual circumstances, the documents must strictly comply with the L/C, but not every non-compliance constitutes a breach. According to the facts acknowledged by both parties, the lack of compliance in this case is that the date of the B/L, which should be 1998, was mistakenly printed as 1999. The Contract in this case was signed and performed in 1998, and [Seller] presented the documents to the bank for negotiation in 1998, so it is easy for [Seller], [Buyer] or any person with international trade knowledge to know that this was obviously a typing error. (2) In contracts for the international sales of goods, it is the seller's duty to deliver the documents. However, in this case, the typing mistake of the date in the B/L would not affect [Buyer]'s taking delivery of the goods. [Buyer] should have given up its lack of compliance complaint, gotten the documents from the bank, and taken delivery of the goods. (3) The documents submitted by [Seller] have no other non-compliance, except for the typing mistake of the date in the B/L. On the basis of the documents, no one can conclude that the goods delivered by [Seller] are not those under the Contract, or that the goods are seriously defective. [Buyer], as a businessman, should perform its duty in good faith. Its assertion that the disparity between the documents submitted by [Seller] and the L/C constitutes a fundamental breach and therefore [Buyer] is entitled to avoid the Contract and refuse to take delivery of the goods cannot be upheld. The Arbitration Tribunal holds that [Buyer] should give up the disparity and accept the goods, and has no right to request a price reduction. In other words, when payment by L/C is impossible, [Buyer] should pay directly to [Seller] with its own credit, rather than the credit of the bank. (4) [Buyer] asserts that the disparity affects [Buyer]'s resale and financing. The Arbitration Tribunal holds that merely this typing mistake regarding the date in the B/L cannot

constitute a barrier to [Buyer]'s resale.

To sum up, the Arbitration Tribunal holds that [Buyer] should accept the goods and has no right to request a price reduction.

2. [Seller]'s resale. [Seller] delivered the goods in accordance with the Contract and fulfilled its duty to deliver the goods. As stated above, [Buyer] should have accepted the goods and had no right to request a price reduction. [Buyer], however, requested a price reduction on the basis that the documents and the B/L were not in compliance. When [Seller] refused to reduce the price, [Buyer] did not, within a reasonable time, show its intention to accept the goods. The Arbitration Tribunal holds that such acts of [Buyer] constitute an abandonment of the Contract, and accordingly [Seller] had the right to resell the goods in order to mitigate its losses. Because [Buyer] abandoned the Contract, [Seller] was not obliged to send a written notice of avoidance to [Buyer] before [Seller] exercised its right [to resell].

3. [Seller]'s claims. As found by the Arbitration Tribunal, the total amount of the goods delivered by [Seller] is 17 tons (1 ton = 2,204.62 pounds), the content of V205 is 98.42%, the unit price under the Contract is US $6.5/pound, and the total contract price is US $6.5/pound 2204.62 pounds 17 98.42% = US $239,761.46. [Seller] resold the goods at US $5.55/pound. The total resale price is US $5.55/pound 2,204.62 pounds 17 98.42% = US $204,719.40. Accordingly, the loss caused by the price difference is US $239,761.46 – US $204,719.40 = US $35,042.06.

[Buyer]'s assertion that [Seller]'s resale price was lower than the then-current market price is unreasonable. The Arbitration Tribunal finds that, according to the evidence submitted by [Seller], the average then-current market price was US $6.047/pound, which only differs with [Seller]'s resale price by US $0.479/pound. The Arbitration Tribunal holds that because of [Buyer]'s refusal to accept the goods, [Seller]'s goods became goods backlogged at the port and were at a disadvantageous position to be resold. Accordingly, it is reasonable for the resale price to be slightly lower than the then-current market price. The Arbitration Tribunal upholds [Seller]'s claim for its loss caused by the price difference, in the amount of US $35,042.06. [Buyer] shall also pay interest on this amount at the annual rate of 8% from 16 May 1998 to the day when the payment is made. [Buyer] shall pay for the demurrage caused by [Buyer]'s refusal to take the goods. Accordingly, the Arbitration Tribunal upholds [Seller]'s claim for the demurrage in the amount of US $1,245.91. [Seller] also claims for its bank expenses in the amount of RMB 1,330. The Arbitration Tribunal finds that the delivery term in this Contract is C&F and [Seller] is liable for loading the goods. Because the shipping company arranged by [Seller] mistakenly typed the date in the B/L and this mistake caused the bank's refusal to pay, [Seller] shall bear the bank expenses RMB 1,330.

Award: The Arbitration Tribunal makes following award:

1. [Buyer] shall compensate [Seller] for the loss caused by the price difference, US $35,042.06, and the interest on this amount at the annual rate of 8% from 16 May 1998 to the day when the payment is made.

2. [Buyer] shall compensate [Seller] for the demurrage, US $1,245.91.

3. [Buyer] shall bear the entire arbitration fee. [Seller] has paid the arbitration fee in advance. Thus, [Buyer] shall pay [Seller] RMB ×××.

4. [Seller]'s other claims are dismissed.

[Buyer] shall pay the above amount within 45 days after the date of this award. Otherwise, [Buyer] shall pay additional interests at an annual rate of 9%.

This is the final award. [1]

VI. Obligations of the Seller and the Buyer

The discussion on the obligations of the seller and the buyer is to be based on principally the CISG because it usually governs most of the international business transactions in China.

A. Seller's Obligations

Under the CISG a seller is required to (a) deliver the goods, (b) hand over any documents relating to them, and (c) ensure that the goods conform with the contract.

1. Delivery of the Goods

The seller's basic obligation is to deliver the goods called for by the contract. Delivery is the voluntary transfer of possession from one person to another. It may be actual or constructive. Delivery is constructive when the goods themselves are not delivered, but the means of obtaining possession of the goods is delivered.

(1) Place for delivery. According to Article 31 of the CISG, If the seller is not bound to deliver the goods at any other particular place, his obligation to deliver consists:

(a) if the contract of sale involves carriage of the goods--in handing the goods over

---

[1] https://www.uncitral.org/clout/clout/data/chn/clout_case_808_leg-2205.html, visit on 30 December, 2019.

to the first carrier for transmission to the buyer;

(b) if, in cases not within the preceding subparagraph, the contract relates to specific goods, or unidentified goods to be drawn from a specific stock or to be manufactured or produced, and at the time of the conclusion of the contract the parties knew that the goods were at, or were to be manufactured or produced at, a particular place--in placing the goods at the buyer's disposal at that place;

(c) in other cases—in placing the goods at the buyer's disposal at the place where the seller had his place of business at the time of the conclusion of the contract.

Article 32 provides that if the seller, in accordance with the contract or this Convention, hands the goods over to a carrier and if the goods are not clearly identified to the contract by markings on the goods, by shipping documents or otherwise, the seller must give the buyer notice of the consignment specifying the goods. If the seller is bound to arrange for carriage of the goods, he must make such contracts as are necessary for carriage to the place fixed by means of transportation appropriate in the circumstances and according to the usual terms for such transportation. And, if the seller is not bound to effect insurance in respect of the carriage of the goods, he must, at the buyer's request, provide him with all available information necessary to enable him to effect such insurance.

In addition to providing insurance information when requested, the seller must, at the time he delivers the goods to a carrier, either (a) identify to the carrier both the goods and the buyer "by markings on the goods, by shipping documents or otherwise," or (b) "give the buyer notice of the consignment of the specifying goods." [Article 32 (3)]. Failure to comply with this requirement is a breach of the contract, and the seller will be liable for any damages that may result. (Articles 45, 49, and 74)

(2) Time for delivery. Article 33 states that if a date is fixed by or determinable from the contract, the seller is to delivery the goods on that date, or if a period of time is fixed by or determinable from the contract, at any time within that period unless circumstances indicate that the buyer is to choose a date; or in any other case, within a reasonable time after the conclusion of the contract.

2. The Turning Over of Documents

If the seller is bound to hand over documents relating to the goods, he must hand them over at the time and place and in the form required by the contract. If the seller has handed over documents before that time, he may, up to that time, cure any lack of conformity in the documents, if the exercise of this right does not cause the buyer unreasonable inconvenience or unreasonable expense. However, the buyer retains any right to claim damages as provided for in this Convention.

3. The Seller's Assurance of the Quality of Goods

The laws of almost all countries have detailed provisions of seller's assurance of the quality of goods, the most important of which are the English Sales of Goods Act 1973, the UCC and the CISG.

(1) Sales of Goods Act 1973 (Articles 12 – 15) provide that seller's goods must be in conformity with the following implied conditions: for the sale of goods by description, there is an implied term that the goods will correspond with the description; When the seller sells goods in the course of a business, there is an implied term that the goods supplied under the contract are of satisfactory quality. Satisfactory quality means: (a) fitness for all the purposes for which goods of the kind in question are commonly supplied; (b) appearance and finish; (c) freedom from minor defects, (d) safety, and (e) durability.

Satisfactory quality doesn't extend to the following situation: (a) the quality of goods is specifically drawn to the buyer's attention before the contract is made; (b) where the buyer examines the goods before the contract is made, which that examination ought to reveal, or (c) in the case of a contract for sale by sample, which would have been apparent on a reasonable examination of the sample.

When the seller sells goods in the course of a business and the buyer, expressly or by implication, makes known to the seller any particular purpose for the goods, there is an implied term that the goods supplied under the contract are reasonably fit for that purpose, except where the circumstances show that the buyer does not rely, or that it is unreasonable for him to rely, on the skill or judgment of the seller or credit-broker.

In the case of a contract for sale by sample there is an implied term (a) the bulk will correspond with the sample in quality; (b) the buyer should be given reasonable time for comparison of the goods and sample; (c) the goods will be free from any defect, making their quality unsatisfactory which would not be apparent on reasonable examination of the sample.

(2) The UCC. Sales of Goods Act calls seller's assurance of quality of the goods as implied conditions, while UCC calls it warranties, and further divides it into express warranties and implied warranties.

Express Warranties (2 – 313) are created as follows: If the seller makes to the buyer any affirmation of fact or promise which relates to the goods and becomes part of the basis of the bargain, the goods shall conform to the affirmation or promise. If the seller makes any description of the goods which is made part of the basis of the bargain, the goods shall conform to the description. If any sample or model which is made part of the basis of the bargain, the whole of the goods shall conform to the sample and the model.

UCC holds that it isn't necessary that the seller use formal words such as "warranty" or "guarantee" or that he have a specific intention to make a warranty, any one of the above three creates a warranty.

Implied Warranty (2 – 314) includes merchantability and fitness for particular purpose. If the seller is a merchant, there shall be an implied warranty that the goods shall be merchantable. Merchantability must at least such as (a) pass without objection in the trade under the contract description; and (b) in the case of fungible goods, are of fair average quality within the description; and (c) are fit for the ordinary purposes for which such goods are used; and (d) run, within the variations permitted by the agreement, of even kind, quality and quantity within each unit and among all units involved; and (e) are adequately contained, packaged, and labeled as the agreement may require; and (f) conform to the promises or affirmations of fact made on the container of label if any.

Fitness for particular purposes (2 – 315) include (a) if the seller at the time of contracting has reason to know any particular purpose for which the goods are required, and (b) the buyer is relying on the seller's skill or judgment to select or furnish suitable goods.

There is an implied warranty that the goods shall be fit for such a purpose.

UCC (2 – 316) holds that if the parties want to exclude or modify the implied warranty of merchantability or any part of it, the language must mention merchantability and the writing must be conspicuous.

(3) CISG. CISG (Article 35, 36) states that the seller must deliver goods which are of the quantity, quality and description required by the contract and which are contained or packaged in the manner required by the contract. The goods are fit for the purposes for which goods of the same description would ordinarily be used; The goods fit for any particular purpose expressly or impliedly made known to the seller at the time of the conclusion of the contract, except where the circumstances show that the buyer did not rely, or that it was unreasonable for him to rely, on the seller's skill and judgment; The goods possess the qualities of goods which the seller has held out to the buyer as a sample or model; The goods are contained or packaged in the manner usual for such goods or, where there is no such manner, in a manner adequate to preserve and protect the goods.

4. The Seller's Assurance of Ownership of the Goods

Under the Article 12 of Sales of Goods Act (1979), the seller shall have the obligation of implied undertaking: the goods are free, and will remain free until the time when the property is to pass, from any charge or encumbrance not disclosed or known to the buyer before the contract is made, and the buyer will enjoy quiet possession of the goods.

Article 55 states that the seller shall not exclude the above implied undertaking.

According to the UCC 2 - 312, there is in a contract for sale a warranty by the seller that (a) the title conveyed shall be good, and its transfer rightful; and (b) the goods shall be delivered free from any security interest or other lien or encumbrance of which the buyer at the time of contracting has no knowledge.

Unless otherwise agreed a seller who is a merchant regularly dealing in goods of the kind warrants that the goods shall be delivered free of the rightful claim of any third person by way of infringement or the like but a buyer who furnishes specifications to the seller must hold the seller harmless against any such claim which arises out of compliance with the specifications.

Article 41 of the CISG provides that the seller must deliver goods which are free from any right or claim of a third party, unless the buyer agreed to take the goods subject to that right or claim. However, if such right or claim is based on industrial property or other intellectual property, the seller's obligation is governed by Article 42.

Article 42 further states that the seller must deliver goods which are free from any right or claim of a third party based on industrial property or other intellectual property, or which at the time of the conclusion of the contract the seller knew or could not have been unaware, provided that the right or claim is based on industrial property or other intellectual property: (a) under the law of the State where the goods will be resold or otherwise used, if it was contemplated by the parties at the time of the conclusion of the contract that the goods would be resold or otherwise used in that State; or (b) in any other case, under the law of the State where the buyer has his place of business.

The obligation of the seller under the preceding paragraph does not extend to cases where: (a) at the time of the conclusion of the contract the buyer knew or could not have been unaware of the right or claim; or (b) the right or claim results from the seller's compliance with technical drawings, designs, formulas or other such specifications furnished by the buyer.

Clearly, the seller's obligation under CISG concerning title to the goods under CISG is to deliver the goods not only free from any encumbrances on their title, but also free from any claim of a third party. Thus, like UCC § 2 - 312, seller is obligated to transfer 'quiet possession' of the goods. Although the obligation is very broad, it probably is not breached by claims which are frivolous on their face or by state restrictions on use of the goods.

What is more important is that CISG emphasizes the seller's obligation to deliver the goods free from patent, trademark and copyright claims assertable under the law of the buyer's "place of business" or the place where both parties expect the goods to be used or resold. This obligation is however, subject to multiple qualifications. First, the seller's obligations arise only with respect to claims of which "seller knew or could not have been unaware." Second, seller has no obligation with respect to intellectual property rights or claims of which buyer had knowledge when the contract was formed. Third, seller is not liable for claims which arise out of its use of technical drawings, designs or other specifications furnished by the buyer, if the seller's action is in "compliance with" the buyer's specifications. It is clear that this provision applies when seller is following specifications required by the contract, but its application is not clear when the seller is merely following "suggestions" of buyer as to how best to meet more general contract provisions. Fourth, seller is excused from these obligations if buyer does not give notice of breach under Article 42, unless seller knew of the claim, which knowledge may be required under Article 41 (1) in order to create liability initially.

B. Buyer's Obligations

The buyer has two primary obligations under CISG in a sale contract: to pay the price, and to take delivery of the goods. The former duty is the more important of the two.

1. Payment of the Price

Under Sales of Goods Act, buyer's obligation to accept the goods is integrated with his right to examine the goods. Article 27 states that it is the duty of the buyer to accept the goods and pay for them, in accordance with the terms of the contract of sale. If the buyer is not given an opportunity to examine the goods, the buyer has the right to reject the goods until he has reasonable time to examine the goods. But if the buyer is given such opportunity but refuses to examine, the buyer will lose his right to examine the goods and the right to reject the goods.

According to the UCC (2 – 513), buyer's obligation to pay is integrated with his obligation to accept the goods and to examine the goods. Unless otherwise agreed, the buyer has a right before payment or acceptance to inspect them at any reasonable place and time and in any reasonable manner. When the seller is required or authorized to send the goods to the buyer, the inspection may be after their arrival.

In terms of buyer's obligation to pay the price, CISG states that the buyer shall comply with steps or formalities to enable payment to be made; determine the price; and refers to the price generally charged at the time of the conclusion of the contract. The price is fixed by the net weight.

With regard to the place of payment, Article 57 states: if the buyer is not bound to pay the price at any other particular place, he must pay it to the seller: (a) at the seller's place of business; or (b) if the payment is to be made against the handing-over of the goods or of documents, at the place where the handing-over takes place. The seller must bear any increase in the expenses incidental to payment which is caused by a change in his place of business subsequent to the conclusion of the contract.

2. Taking Delivery

Article 60 of the CISG provides: "The buyer's obligation to take delivery consists: (a) in doing all the acts which could reasonably be expected of him in order to enable the seller to make delivery; and (b) in taking over the goods." In addition, the buyer is obligated to cooperate with the seller to facilitate the transfer and to actually "take over the goods", if the buyer fails to cooperate, he will be responsible for any resulting costs, and if he fails to take delivery he assumes the risk for any damage to the goods after that time.

Case 4 – 6 The Natural Gas Case

Austria Supreme Court, 1996.

Case No. 518/95. Osterreichische Zeitschrift fur Rechtsvergleichung.

Vol. 1996, p.248 (1996)

Facts: In the fall of 1990, the plaintiff, a German company, negotiated to buy natural gas from the defendant, an Austrian partnership. After a series of proposals and counterproposals, the plaintiff faxed the defendant on December 18, 1990, offering to buy 700 to 800 metric tons of propane gas from the defendant. The defendant responded the next morning that it could ship the propane from the United States for delivery to the plaintiff in Belgium for $376 per ton. At 2:16 p.m. on December 19, the plaintiff sent a confirming fax agreeing to this price and confirming the other terms of contract, including that the propane would be shipped by a tanker from the United States on January 2, 1991. Because the parties had not dealt with each other before, the plaintiff agreed to secure its purchase with a letter of credit. In the 2:16 p.m. fax, the plaintiff asked the defendant to identify the place in the United States where the gas would be loaded aboard a tanker, because the plaintiff's bank needed this information before it would issue a letter of credit. At 3:19 p.m. the defendant responded by fax stating that it was waiting to get the information from the United States as to the place of loading.

While this exchange of faxes was taking place, the parties were talking to each other on the telephone. The defendant wanted the plaintiff to order a larger quantity of propane to make the transaction more worth its time. The plaintiff, in response to this request, contracted a Dutch natural gas reseller that agreed to buy 3,000 tons of propane at $381 per ton. The plaintiff then increased its order by 3,000 tons.

On January 2, 1991, [not having heard if the propane had been loaded for shipment as the parties had agreed,] the plaintiff sent a fax to the defendant asking to be notified of the place where the propane would be loaded. The next day the plaintiff sent another fax to tell the defendant that its bank would not process the letter of credit until the bank received the place of loading information.

On January 7, 1991, the defendant informed the plaintiff by fax that its United States supplier would not agree to let the propane gas be exported to Belgium, and therefore that the defendant could not deliver the propane.

The next day the plaintiff notified the defendant that, because of the defendant's breach, the Dutch natural gas reseller had had to make a substitute purchase at a price above what the defendant had promised. On January 15, 1991, the plaintiff sent a letter to the defendant forwarding the Dutch natural gas reseller's claim of $ 141,131 arising out of the substitute purchase. The defendant rejected this claim.

Later, after the Dutch natural gas reseller sued the plaintiff in a separate proceeding for $ 141,131 compensation due the reseller and for the loss of its own profits of $ 15,000. The trial court held in favor of the plaintiff and the court of appeals affirmed its decision. The defendant then appealed to the Supreme Court.

Issue: Was the plaintiff entitled to the compensation?

Decision:

[The Breach]

[Following the making of the contract,] the plaintiff did not open a letter of credit and the plaintiff did not deliver the agreed goods (the natural gas).

[The United Nations Convention on Contracts for the International Sale of Goods (CISG),] Article 54, provides that "the buyer's obligation to pay the price includes taking such steps and complying with such formalities as may be required under the contract or any laws and regulations to enable payment to be made." In light of this, a buyer in a sale of goods contract who has agreed to open a letter of credit must do so in a timely manner. In the case at hand, however, the plaintiff did not open the letter of credit because the defendant failed to notify it of the place where the natural gas would be loaded. And this was so, even though the defendant had expressly promised to do so in its fax of December 19, 1990.... The defendant cannot complain that the plaintiff did not fulfill its obligation [to open a letter of credit,] as the defendant's own obligation to notify the plaintiff as to the place where the goods were to be loaded had to happen first. The defendant knew that the plaintiff had to know the place of loading in order to open the letter, and it was the defendant's failure to notify the plaintiff of the place of loading that led to the plaintiff's failure to open the letter of credit.... In other words, the failure of the plaintiff to open the letter of credit was caused by the defendant's own failure to act. And, as stated in CISG, Article 80, "a party may not rely on a failure of the other party to perform, to the extent that such failure was caused by the first party's act or omission."

More significantly, the failure of the plaintiff to open a letter of credit was not the reason for the breach of this contract. As the lower courts have held, it was the defendant's failure to obtain the appropriate clearances ... needed to export the propane gas to Belgium that was the cause of the breach. According to CISG, Article 30, "the seller must deliver the goods, hand over any documents relating to them and transfer the property in the goods, as required by the contract...." The defendant's argument (first made in this appeal) that it was the buyer that was obliged to obtain the appropriate authorization for the goods to be imported into Belgium is without merit.... A buyer is not obliged to ask a seller if there are any unusual restrictions that may keep the seller from performing. If the seller does not inform the buyer of such restrictions, the seller may reasonably assume that such circumstances do not exist. CISG, Article 41, says that "the seller must deliver goods which are free from any right or claim of a third party" unless the buyer had agreed to accept such goods. If the seller's supplier will not allow the goods to be exported, then the goods are subject to a restriction. The buyer, of course, may agree to accept the goods anyway, but it doesn't have to. And, if the buyer doesn't agree to accept the goods, and the seller is then unable to deliver them because of the restriction, it is the seller that has breached the contract.

[Indemnification]

Because the seller breached the contract, the buyer is entitled to be fully indemnified for its losses. In other words, the non-breaching party is to be put in the position that it would have been had the breaching party performed as promised. The breaching party, moreover, does not have to be at fault or to have acted illegally to be liable in such a case. [The parties sought to apply CISG, Articles 75 and 76, in ascertaining the damages due the plaintiff.] The provisions in the CISG, Articles 75 and 76, deal with the awarding of damages when one party avoids the contract because of a breach by the other party. However, because there has been a breach, does not necessarily mean that there will be avoidance. The CISG does not provide for avoidance as a matter of law, even if the non-breaching party is deprived of what it expected to receive. 123 Avoidance, under the CISG, can only come about by a unilateral declaration of the non-breaching party. Such a declaration, however, does not have to be in any particular form, nor [with the exception of certain cases set out in CISG, Article 49(2) which are inapplicable here] is it subject to any time limit. The parties to this case argued over whether the declaration of avoidance described in CISG, Article 49(1), had to be made expressly or whether it could be implied from the non-breaching party's conduct. This argument, however, is irrelevant, because it is not the mere giving of notice that constitutes avoidance, but the non-breaching party's intention not to adhere to the contract that is important. This intention, moreover, must be clear to the breach party. The findings of fact in the lower courts suggest that the plaintiff never actually notified the defendant that it was avoiding the contract. Indeed, the plaintiff never claimed that it had given such notice. Nor can one imply that such notice was given merely from the fact that the plaintiff gave the defendant a list of the losses suffered by its customer [the Dutch natural gas reseller]. Because the contract was not avoided, the damages [are not to be determined in accordance with CISG, Articles 75 and 76, but rather] are to be determined in accordance with CISG, Article 74. Article 74 applies to those cases when the damages come about because of delay in delivery or because of some defect in the goods.

[Loss of Profits]

When, as the case here, the non-breaching party is claiming a loss of profits from an expected resale of the goods to a third party, the loss of profits will only be considered if the breaching party had reason to know of this expected resale. Of course, when merchantable goods are sold to a merchant, the expected resale can be presumed. The defendant does not challenge this. Indeed, it has conceded that it knew that the plaintiff intended to resell the goods. [The plaintiff, accordingly, is entitled to the $15,000 claimed in lost profits.]

[Duty to Mitigate]

A non-breaching party may not claim damages, including a loss of profits, if it fails to make reasonable efforts to mitigate its losses. Such efforts are reasonable if a reasonable person in the position of the non-breaching party would have undertaken them in good faith. The defendant argues that the plaintiff breached this obligation. However, the burden of proving such a breach is on the defendant, and the defendant has failed to meet its burden.... It has not shown what the plaintiff did to breach this obligation, it has not shown that the plaintiff had other alternatives to what it did, nor has it shown how much the damages would have been lessened if the plaintiff had engaged in some alternative conduct. [In addition to lost profits, therefore, the plaintiff is entitled to recoup the $141,131 due the Dutch natural gas reseller.]

The decision of the Court of Appeals is affirmed.

Casepoint

In this case, the court considered whether a seller of propane gas had breached its contractual duties by failing to deliver the gas as promised and, if so, what damages were appropriate. First, the court looked at each party's duties under the CISG and found that the buyer was supposed to open a letter of credit. But here, the buyer could not do so because the seller never supplied the necessary information for the letter. Also, the breach was really due to the seller's failure to make proper arrangements to ship the gas, not because of the letter of credit. So, the court concluded that the seller had breached the contract and the buyer was entitled to damages. [1]

VII. Passing of Risk

The loss of goods through fire, theft, or other means can occur at any time: prior to delivery, during transit or inspection, or after delivery. The parties to a contract must know when they are responsible for damage or loss to goods and when they are not. Clearly, the seller is responsible if the goods are destroyed by fire during production at the seller's plant. Likewise, if the goods are destroyed after they have been moved into the buyer's warehouse, then the buyer is responsible. But when does the risk pass from one party to the other? In some countries, including the United Kingdom, the party who bears the risk of loss is the party who has "title" to the goods—the party who owns them at that moment. However, since the document of title does not move physically with the goods, a determination of who owned the goods at the exact time of their destruction is often difficult. This "title" method was employed in the United States until the adoption of the UCC.

Passing of risk is defined as the shifting of responsibility for loss or damage from the seller to the buyer. This means that once the risk passes, the buyer must pay the agreed-upon price for the goods involved. The buyer must then absorb the cost of the loss or lodge a claim against his insurer. Only if he can show that the loss or damage was due to an act or omission of the seller is he excused from paying the price. [2]

---

[1] Ray August, Don Mayer and Michael Bixby, International Business Law, Six Edition, Pearson Education Limited, 2013, p. 591.

[2] Ray August, Don Mayer and Michael Bixby, International Business Law, Six Edition, Pearson Education Limited, 2013, p. 594.

In most cases, the loss will be covered by insurance. Even so, it is important to determine whether the buyer or seller is responsible for obtaining the insurance.

A. Common Law

1. Sales of Goods Act

Article 20 of Sales of Goods Act states: "(1) Unless otherwise agreed, the goods remain at the seller's risk until the property in them is transferred to the buyer, but when the property in them is transferred to the buyer the goods are at the buyer's risk whether delivery has been made or not. (2) But where delivery has been delayed through the fault of either buyer or seller the goods are at the risk of the party at fault as regards any loss which might not have occurred but for such fault."

2. The UCC

Under the UCC 2 – 509, the risk passes to the buyer when the goods are delivered to the buyer. (1) Both parties may decide the line of risk through contract, and also through some international trade terms such as FOB, CIF, CFR. (2) If both parties fail to stipulate the line of risk in the contract, the passing of risk can be decided by the following:

The goods need to be moved. If it does require him to deliver them at a particular destination, the risk of loss passes to the buyer when the goods are duly delivered to the carrier even though the shipment is under reservation; if it does require him to deliver them at a particular destination and the goods are there duly tendered while in the possession of the carrier, the risk of loss passes to the buyer when the goods are there duly so tendered as to enable the buyer to take delivery.

Where the goods are held by a bailee to be delivered without being moved, the risk of loss passes to the buyer (a) on his receipt of a negotiable document of title covering the goods; or (b) on acknowledgment by the bailee of the buyer's right to possession of the goods; or (c) after his receipt of a non-negotiable document of title or other written direction to deliver.

The breach of one party has effect on risk of loss:

(1) Seller's breach: (a) where a tender or delivery of goods so fails to conform to the contract as to give a right of rejection the risk of their loss remains on the seller until cure or acceptance. (b) Where the buyer rightfully revokes acceptance he may to the extent of any deficiency in his effective insurance coverage treat the risk of loss as having rested on the seller from the beginning.

(2) Buyer's breach: where the buyer as to conforming goods already identified to the contract for sale repudiates or is otherwise in breach before risk of their loss has passed to him, the seller may to the extent of any deficiency in his effective insurance coverage treat the risk of loss as resting on the buyer for a commercially reasonable time. In this case,

the buyer must bear the risk, the conditions are (a) the goods delivered by the seller must be conforming with the contract; (b) the buyer breaches the contract before the risk passes to him; (c) the goods are already identified to the contract for sale; (d) the risk of loss rests on the buyer for a commercially reasonable time.

B. The CISG

The CISG contains provisions that allocate the risk of loss in Articles 66 – 70. Like the UCC, CISG gives up the idea of the United Kingdom that the one who has the title of the goods bears the risk, and determines the passing of risk through in principle time of delivery of the goods.

1. CISG Allows the Parties to Decide the Time of Passing of Risk

Clearly, the agreement of both parties is prior to the CISG, so the CISG provisions apply only if the parties do not specify by agreement when the risk shifts from the seller to the buyer.

2. The Effect of Passing of Risk.

Article 66 states that loss of or damage to the goods after the risk has passed to the buyer does not discharge him from his obligation to pay the price, unless the loss or damage is due to an act or omission of the seller. Therefore, after the risk has already passed from the seller to the buyer, the buyer should be responsible for the loss and pay the price even if the goods are lost.

3. Where the Goods Need to be Moved

Under Article 67, if the contract of sale involves carriage of the goods and the seller is not bound to hand them over at a particular place, the risk passes to the buyer when the goods are handed over to the first carrier for transmission to the buyer in accordance with the contract of sale. If the seller is bound to hand the goods over to a carrier at a particular place, the risk does not pass to the buyer until the goods are handed over to the carrier at that place. The fact that the seller is authorized to retain documents controlling the disposition of the goods does not affect the passage of the risk.

Also, the risk does not pass to the buyer until the goods are clearly identified to the contract, whether by markings on the goods, by shipping documents, by notice given to the buyer or otherwise.

4. The Passing of Risk of the Goods in Transit

Usually, the determination of time of passing of risk of the goods in transit is extremely difficult, because nether the seller or the buyer knows anything about the goods at the disposal of the carrier. Article 67 of the CISG provides three solutions to solve this problem. (1) The risk in respect of goods sold in transit passes to the buyer from the time of the conclusion of the contract. (2) If the circumstances so indicate, the risk is assumed by the buyer from the time the goods were handed over to the carrier who issued the documents embodying the contract of carriage. As to the correct understanding of "If the circumstances so indicate", regard should be had to the particular case and its circumstances. (3) If at the time of the conclusion of the contract of sale the seller knew or ought to have known that the goods had been lost or damaged and did not disclose this to the buyer, the loss or damage is at the risk of the seller.

5. Fundamental Breach of Contract's Effect on the Passing of Risk

According to Article 70 of the CISG, if the seller has committed a fundamental breach of contract (see Article 25 of the CISG), the above stipulations do not impair the remedies available to the buyer on account of the breach. This means that if the seller commits a fundamental breach of contract in accordance with the CISG, it in due course of the trade does not effect the passing of the risk to the buyer, but the buyer has the remedies available to the damages caused by the seller's fundamental breach.

C. China Contract Law

China contract law contains detailed provisions of the passing of risk of goods from Articles 142 – 149. The basic principles are (1) the parties to a contract have the right to reach agreement to the time of passing of risk. (2) In the case of no agreement by the parties, the risk of damage to or missing of an object shall be borne by the seller before the delivery of the object and by the buyer after the delivery. (3) Where there is no agreement as to the place of delivery or such agreement is unclear, and the object needs carriage, the risk shall be borne by the buyer after the seller has delivered the object to the first carrier. (4) In the case of the goods en route of carriage, the risk shall be borne by the buyer as of the time of establishment of the contract, except as otherwise agreed upon by the parties. (5) If the goods delivered have not satisfied the quality requirements, and the buyer is entitled to refuse to accept the goods or may rescind the contract, the seller shall bear the risk. (6) Where the goods cannot be delivered due to causes of the buyer, the buyer shall bear the risk. For example, if the vessel by the buyer fails to arrive in time, and the seller cannot deliver the goods according to the contract, the risk shall pass from the seller to the buyer as of the date of the delivery by the contract. (7) Where the seller has put the goods at the place of delivery according to the contract, but the buyer fails to take delivery of the goods, the risk shall be borne by the buyer as of the date of breach. (8) Even if the risk has already passed to the buyer, the buyer's right may not be affected to claim damages for the seller's breach of contract.

In international business practices in China, most of the contracts allocate risk through trade terms such as FOB, CIF, CFR. Under these trade terms, the risk passes to the buyer at the time when the goods are over on board the ship in the port of shipment.

Clearly, the provisions of China contract law are consistent with international trade customs and stipulations of most countries.

VIII. Passing of Property

The property in the goods means the ownership of the goods, as distinguished from their possession. In international trade it is extremely important to know the precise moment of time at which the property in the goods passes from the seller to the buyer. In case of the destruction of the goods by fire or other accidental cause it is necessary to know which party has to bear the loss.

Internationally, however, different countries have different provisions to this problem.

A. Common Law

Sales of Goods Act of the United Kingdom contains provisions on specific goods and unascertained goods.

1. Specific Goods

Under Sales of Goods Act, specific goods are goods identified and agreed upon at the time the contract is made. The property of specific goods passes to the buyer at the time when the parties intend it to pass. Unless a contrary intention appears, the following rules are applicable for ascertaining the intention of the parties: (1) Where there is an unconditional contract for the sale of specific goods in a deliverable state, the property passes to the buyer when the contract is made (Article 18). (2) Where there is a contract for the sale of specific goods not in a deliverable state, i. e. the seller has to do something to the goods to put them in a deliverable state, the property does not pass until that thing is done and the buyer has notice of it. (3) Where there is a contract for the sale of specific goods in a deliverable state, but the seller is bound to weigh, measure, test or do something with reference to the goods for the purpose of ascertaining the price, the property does not pass until that thing is done and the buyer has notice of it (Article 18). (4) When goods are delivered to the buyer on approval or "on sale or return," the property therein passes to the buyer.

2. Unascertained Goods

Sales of Goods Act provides that the property in unascertained goods does not pass until the goods are ascertained. Unascertained goods are goods defined by description only, e. g. 100 tons of coal, and not goods identified and agreed upon when the contract is made. The property in unascertained or future goods sold by description passes to the buyer when goods of that description and in a deliverable state are unconditionally appropriated to the contract, either by the seller with the assent of the buyer or by the buyer with the assent of the seller. The buyer's assent may be either express or implied and be given either before or after appropriation is made.

The UCC 2 - 401 states to the effect: (1) Title to goods cannot pass under a contract for sale prior to their identification to the contract. (2) In case of the goods to be moved, if the contract requires or authorizes the seller to send the goods to the buyer but does not require him to deliver them at destination, title passes to the buyer at the time and place of shipment, but (3) if the contract requires delivery at destination, title passes on tender there. (4) In case of the goods without being moved, if the seller is to deliver a document of title, title passes at the time when he delivers such documents; or (5) if the goods are at the time of contracting already identified and no documents are to be delivered, title passes at the time and place of contracting.

B. The CISG

Article 4 of the CISG provides that this Convention governs only the formation of the contract of sale and the rights and obligations of the seller and the buyer arising from such a contract. In particular, except as otherwise expressly provided in this Convention, it is not concerned with: (a) the validity of the contract or of any of its provisions or of any usage; (b) the effect which the contract may have on the property in the goods sold.

However, the CISG provides in principle that the seller is obligated to transfer the title to the buyer and make assurance to deliver the goods of which the third party cannot make any claims.

The reason for the CISG's failure to make provisions to the passing of property is that there are considerable differences between the provisions of different countries and it is extremely difficult to unify them.

C. China Contract Law

Under Article 133 of China Contract law, the parties to a contract can agree upon the time of transferring the ownership of the goods. Except as otherwise stipulated by law or agreed upon by the parties, the ownership of goods shall be transferred upon the delivery of the goods.

IX. Excuses for Non-performance

A. Common Law

Occasionally, a party will find that circumstances make carrying out its part of the contract difficult, unprofitable, or even impossible. As a defense to an action for breach of contract, it may claim that it has been excused because intervening events beyond its control have made performance impossible or financially impracticable. But it will have a difficult time convincing a court. Courts generally do not allow a party to escape contractual obligations merely because it becomes unable to perform, even though inability to perform was through no fault of its own. When a seller's employees are on strike, when suppliers fail to deliver raw materials on time, when equipment breaks down, when crops are destroyed due to bad weather, or when a party simply becomes financially distressed, its failure to deliver on time will generally not be excused. This common ruling is in keeping with generally accepted legal principles, which hold that contracts are binding. The famous lawyer John Uff in his book "Construction Law" says: "As a general rule contractual obligations are absolute in that a party is not absolved merely because performance becomes more expensive or even proves to be impossible. A party who contracts to do the impossible is liable for failing to do it, unless he excludes such liability."

Yet, in the real world in which international transactions are conducted, the parties are liable to find many roadblocks in their path to performance.

Whether an intervening event will cause a party to be excused and discharged from its contractual promise depends on the reasoning used by the court. Some courts reason that a party's performance is excused (1) if performance of the contract has been rendered physically or legally impossible; (2) if the underlying purposes of the contract no longer exist; or (3) if a change in circumstances has rendered the contract commercially or financially impracticable.

1. Impossibility of Performance

Under the strict English view of impossibility, dating back to the case Paradine v. Jane (1647), a party will not be excused from performing its part of an agreement, even if it becomes impossible for it to do so. This doctrine was gradually weakened in the late 1800s by English courts as some excuses began to be recognized. Under the concept of impossibility, a court may excuse a party's nonperformance where it becomes objectively impossible for it to perform. The courts hold that it must be impossible for anyone to perform, not just this particular party, and that the parties did not expressly assume such risk. Impossibility would therefore excuse nonperformance in cases involving (1) the death of one of the parties; (2) the destruction of the specific subject matter of the contract; (3) when performance of the contract has been rendered illegal or made impossible due to the fault of the other party.

In the case "The Molton" (1938) (a vessel was hired to carry some Spanish refugees to France, but soon was seized by some enemy.) The well-known judge Goddard said: "if the foundation of the contract goes, either by the destruction of the subject—matter or by reason of such long interruption or delay that the performance is really in effect that of a different contract, then the performance of the contract is regarded as frustrated." [1]

2. Supervening Illegality

A contract becomes impossible to perform and the parties excused when performance becomes illegal. For instance, suppose that a company is under contract to ship computers to Iraq. After Iraq's invasion of Kuwait, the U. S. government declared that conducting business with Iraq or shipping goods there was illegal. Since the contract has been rendered illegal, performance is discharged.

3. Frustration of Purpose

Under the English common law, a party's performance could be excused if some unforeseen event occurred that frustrated the purposes of the contract. This event would have to destroy totally the value of the contract to the party relying on the excuse.

In a leading English case, Knell v. Henry (1903), a party leased a room overlooking the coronation route of the king. When the king took ill and the coronation canceled, the court ruled that the party was excused form paying rent on the room, because the coronation was essential to the purposes of the contract. Although it had been possible to perform the party would have realized no value in doing so.

In the case Davis Contractors Ltd. v. Fareham U. D. C (1956), Lord Radcliffe said: "frustration occurs whenever the law recognizes that, without default of either party, a contractual obligation has become incapable of being performed because the circumstances in which performance is called for would render it a thing radically different from that which was undertaken by the contract. Lord Radcliffe also said: "it was not hardship or inconvenience or material loss itself which calls the principle of frustration into play. There must be as well such a change in the significance of the obligation that the thing undertaken would, if performed, be a different thing from that contracted for."

In the case National Carriers v. Panalpina (1981), Lord Simon said: "Frustration of a contract takes place when there supervenes an event (without default of either party and for which the contact makes no sufficient provision) which so significantly changes the nature (not merely the expense) of the outstanding contractual rights and/or obligations from what the parties could reasonably have contemplated at the time of its execution that it would be unjust to hold them to the literal sense of its stipulations in the new circumstances; in such case the law declares both parties to be discharged from further performance."

According to case practices in the United Kingdom, the following circumstances will

[1] Yang Liangyi, Game of Rules of International Business Practices, The Publishing House of the China University of Politics and Law, p. 477.

not create frustration:

(1) Where a party gives an absolute undertaking. A contract to perform something that is obviously impossible, e. g. , to build in the air, is void because there is no real consideration for the contract, but an absolute undertaking is binding though it might be difficult or even impossible to perform.

(2) Where the change is not fundamental.

(3) Strikes and outbreak of hostilities between foreign nations, in which the United Kingdom is not involved, may affect the performance of the contract but these events do not automatically operate as frustration.

In the United Kingdom, examples of frustration of purposes are, however, extremely rare. The reason for this is that the courts do not wish to provide an escape route for a party for whom the contract has simply become a bad bargain.

Frustration of purpose is not widely recognized in the United States today.

4. Commercial Impracticability

A party to a contract that is prevented from performing may attempt to be excused under the doctrine of commercial impracticability. This modern doctrine is used in the United States today. It dates back to 1916 when a court stated, "A thing is impossible in legal contemplation when it is not practicable; and a thing is impracticable when it can be done only at an excessive and unreasonable cost." Today, impracticability in the United States has been codified in the UCC (2-615) and CISG.

Remember, courts hesitate to excuse parties from contracts. Accordingly, the non-breaching party will be excused only if performance would result in extreme hardship, difficulty, or unreasonable expense as a result of an unforeseen event.

The courts have experienced some difficulty in determining what is a "hardship" and how much additional cost is "unreasonable." If the cost of performing the contract becomes so excessive that performance is rendered unrealistic and senseless, and threatens the viability of the business itself, performance may be excused. Of course, what is a lot of money to one company may be a drop in the bucket to another. Thus, if a large multinational corporation contracts to deliver goods at a contract price, and discovers that wage increases or an increase in the price or raw materials will cause it to loose millions of dollars on the deal, the courts still may not release the company from its obligation.

Courts also look to see whether the party claiming the excuse should have foreseen the likelihood of its occurrence. If the event was foreseeable, the non-performing party will not be released from its obligations, which does not mean that the parties had to foresee the specific event that actually occurred. Rather, the parties should have foreseen that an event of this kind could occur. Thus, if a party is a sophisticated business, experienced and familiar with the risks of entering into this kind of contract, they might have difficulty in proving that they should not have foreseen a particular risk. Consider the following examples:

(a) A mining company should foresee the possibility of a cave-in.

(b) A farming conglomerate should foresee the possibility of bad weather.

(c) An oil company should foresee the possibility of oil price increases in the Middle East.

The next case explains how the court keeps a contract and how difficult it is to employ commercial impracticability as an excuse for non-performance.

Case 4 -7 Transatlantic Financing Corporation v. United States (1966)

363 F. 2d. 312 (1996) U. S. Court of Appeals (D. C. Cir.)

Facts: The United States contracted with Transatlantic Financing operator of a steamship, under a voyage charter to ship a cargo of wheat from Texas to Iran in 1956. Six days after Transatlantic's ship sailed from Texas, the government of Egypt was at war with Israel and had blocked the Suez Canal to shipping. As a result, the ship had to sail around the Cape of Good Hope on the tip of the African continent. Transatlantic sued for the added expense of thee longer journey, claiming that it had contracted only to travel the "usual and customary" route to Iran. The lower court ruled in favor of the United States and the plaintiff appealed.

Issue: Was the performance of this contract rendered legally impossible?

Decision: No. If anything, the circumstances surrounding this contract indicate that the risk of the Canal's closure may be deemed to have been allocated to Transatlantic. We know or may safely assume that the parties were aware, as were most commercial men with interest affected by the Suez situation that the Canal might become a dangerous area. No doubt the tension affected freight rates, and it is arguable that the risk of closure became part of the dickered terms. We do not deem the risk of closure so allocated, however. Foreseeability or even recognition of a risk does not necessarily prove its allocation. Parties to a contract are not always able to provide for all the possibilities of which they are aware, sometimes because they cannot agree, often simply because they are too busy. Moreover, that some abnormal risk was contemplated is probative but doer not necessarily established an allocation of the risk of the contingency which actually occurs. In this case, for example, nationalization by Egypt of the Canal Corporation and formation of the Suez Users Group did not necessarily indicate that the Canal would be blocked even if a confrontation resulted. The surrounding circumstances do indicate, however, willingness by Transatlantic to assume abnormal risks, and this fact should legitimately cause us to judge the impracticability of performance by an alternative route in stricter terms than we would were the contingency unforeseen.

We turn then to the question whether occurrence of the contingency rendered performance commercially impracticable under the circumstances of this case. The goods shipped were not subject to harm from the longer, less temperate southern route. The vessel and crew were fit to proceed around the Cape. Transatlantic was no less able than the United States to purchase insurance to cover the contingency's occurrence. If anything, it is more reasonable to expect owner operators of vessels to insure against the hazards of war. They are in the best position to calculate the cost of performance by alternative routes (and therefore to estimate the amount of insurance required), and are undoubtedly sensitive to international troubles which uniquely affect the demand for and cost of their services. The only factor operating here in appellant's favor is the added expense, allegedly $ 43,972,00 above and beyond the contract price of $ 305,842,92, of extending a 10,000 mile voyage by approximately 3,000 miles. While it may be an overstatement to say that increased cost and difficulty of performance never constitute impracticability, to justify relief there must be more of a variation between expected cost and the cost of performing by an available alternative than is present in this case where the promisor can legitimately be presumed to have accepted some degree of abnormal risk, and where impracticability is urged on the basis of added expense along.

We conclude, therefore, as have most other courts considering related issues arising out of the Suez closure, that performance of this contract was not rendered legally impossible.

The judgment was affirmed for the United States. Under a voyage charter, the risks of the journey are on the shipowner, and an increase in expense due to a change in routes did not excuse its performance under the contract. [1]

B. The UNIDROIT PICC

The UNIDROIT PICC uses the term "hardship" in replace of "impossibility of performance", "frustration of purpose", "force majeure", "impediment beyond control", etc. Article 6.2.2 defines hardship as "There is hardship where the occurrence of events fundamentally alters the equilibrium of the contract either because the cost of a

[1] Richard Schaffer, Beverley Earle and Filiberto Agusti, International Business Law and Its Environment, West Publishing Company, pp. 184 – 185.

party's performance has increased or because the value of the performance a party receives has diminished, and (1) the events occur or become known to the disadvantaged party after the conclusion of the contract; (2) the events could not reasonably have been taken into account by the disadvantaged party at the time of the conclusion of the contract; (3) the events are beyond the control of the disadvantaged party; and (4) the risk of the events was not assumed by the disadvantaged party."

Article 6. 2. 3 provides the effects of hardship: (1) In case of hardship the disadvantaged party is entitled to request renegotiations. The request shall be made without undue delay and shall indicate the grounds on which it is based. (2) The request for renegotiation does not in itself entitle the disadvantaged party to withhold performance. (3) Upon failure to reach agreement within a reasonable time either party may resort to the court. (4) If the court finds hardship it may, if reasonable, (a) terminate the contract at a date and on terms to be fixed; or (b) adapt the contract with a view to restoring its equilibrium.

C. The CISG

In order to maintain an impartial position, the CISG uses the term "Impediments beyond Control". Article 79 provides that a party is not liable for a failure to perform any obligations if (1) it was due to an impediment beyond control; (2) the impediment was not reasonably foreseeable at the time the contract was concluded; (3) the impediment was unavoidable or beyond his control; and (4) notice was given to the other party of the impediment and of its effect on the contract.

An impediment does not entirely excuse performance, but merely suspends it during the time that the impediment exists.

D. Force Majeure Clauses

Courts do not like to release parties to a contract on the basis of an excuse. Under the rule of commercial impracticability, a party will not be excused if the risk was foreseeable, because the party is assumed to have provided for that excuse in the contract itself. As a result, lawyers frequently advise their clients to incorporate a force majeure clause into a contract.

The term force majeure means "superior force." A force majeure clause in a contract is an exculpatory clause, it excuses a party from failing to perform on the occurrence of an event specified in the clause itself—a force majeure. These usually list, specifically, those events that will excuse nonperformance. These events might include war, blockades, fire, acts of governments, inability to obtain export licenses, acts of God, acts of public enemies, failure of transportation, quarantine restrictions, strikes and others. In major contracts, the drafting of a force majeure clause requires skilled lawyers. Language that is too narrow may not provide sufficient protection and language that is too broad may leave too many outs in the contract. In practice, most force majeure clauses do not excuse a party's nonperformance entirely, but only suspend it for the duration of the force majeure.

Merchants in common law countries often use the following model as force majeure clause in a contract:

"Seller shall not be liable for loss or damage due to delay in manufacture, shipment, or delivery resulting from any cause beyond seller's direct control or due to compliance with any regulations, orders, acts, instructions, or priority requests of any government authority, acts of God, acts or omissions of the purchaser, fires, floods, epidemics, weather, strikes, factory shutdowns, embargoes, wars, riots, delays in transportation, delay in receiving materials from seller's usual sources, and any delay resulting from any such cause shall extend shipment or delivery date to the extent caused thereby and seller shall be reimbursed its additional expenses resulting from such delay. In the case of delay lasting more than eight weeks, seller has the right to cancel contract. Receipt of merchandise by the buyer shall constitute a waiver of any claims for delay."

A model also is recommended to Chinese merchants:

1. A Model of Generality

Force Majeure: If the shipment of the contracted goods is prevented or delayed in whole or in part due to Force Majeure, the seller shall not be liable for nonshipment or late shipment of the goods of this contract. However, the seller shall notify the buyer by cable or telex and furnish the latter within 15 days by registered airmail with a certificate issued by the China Council for the Promotion of International Trade attesting such event or events.

2. A Model of Listing

Force Majeure: If the shipment of the contracted goods is prevented or delayed in whole or in part by reason of war, earthquake, flood, fire, storm, heavy snow, the seller shall not be liable for non-shipment or late shipment of the goods of this contract. However the seller shall notify the buyer by cable or telex and furnish the latter within 15 days by registered airmail with a certificate issued by the China Council for the Promotion of International Trade attesting such event or events.

3. A Model of Comprehensiveness

Force Majeure: If the shipment of the contracted goods is prevented or delayed in whole or in part by reason of war, earthquake, flood, fire, storm, heavy snow or other causes of Force Majeure, the seller shall not be liable for non-shipment or late shipment of the goods of this contract. However the seller shall notify the buyer by cable or telex and furnish the latter within 15 days by registered airmail with a certificate issued by the China Council for the Promotion of International Trade attesting such event or events.

In drafting force majeure clauses, attention should not be paid only to standard contingencies such as those listed, but also to the special nature of the contract and the type of business involved. Also, a model of comprehensiveness is better recommended because this form leaves the least outs in the contract.

Case 4-8 China International Economic & Trade Arbitration Commission Steel Case (4 February 2002)

Facts: On 2 February 1999, the [Buyer] and the [Seller] signed Contract (hereafter, the "Contract") with the following terms:

— *Goods*: 7,600 tons deformed steel bars, origin: Russia;

— *Price*: US $185 per ton;

— *Transport*: CNF Shantou;

— *Payment*: US $175 by L/C (The L/C should be issued before 11 February 1999) and US $10 per ton remitted to the account appointed by Seller;

— *Shipment*: The [Seller] should load all steel before 5 March 1999;

— *Other provisions*: The expiry date of the L/C shall 26 March 1999.

On 5 February 1999, the [Seller] faxed to the [Buyer] and urged the [Buyer] to remit the US $10 per ton, total US $80,000 to the account appointed by the [Seller]. On 10 February 1999, the opening bank issued the L/C.

— Item 44C of the L/C stipulated that the [Seller] should ship the goods before 5 March 1999;

— Item 31D of the L/C stipulated that the expiry date of the L/C is 26 March 1999 in Singapore.

On 12 February 1999, the [Buyer] received the invoice from the [Seller]. On 22 February 1999, the [Seller] faxed to the [Buyer] that it had not received the payment of US $80,000 and advised that immediate shipment is not possible. In its fax, the [Seller] urged the [Buyer] to remit the $80,000 payment and asked for three modifications to the L/C, modifications to the beneficiary in Item 59. to the loading port in Item 44A, and to the name of manufacturer in Item 45A. On 22 February 1999, the [Buyer] stated by fax that, according to the contract, the US $10 per ton should be paid to the [Seller] within seven working days after the contract is signed. The [Buyer] received the original invoice from the [Seller] on 12 February 1999. However, due to the Spring Festival, the bank did not work until 23 February 1999. Therefore, the [Buyer] was not able to remit the US $80,000 payment aforesaid. The [Buyer] advised that it would remit "this week".

On 23 February 1999, in accordance with the request of the [Seller], the [Buyer] asked the opening bank to modify the L/C. There were modifications requested by the [Buyer] (the name of beneficiary and manufacturer) and modifications requested by the [Seller]. On 25 February 1999, the [Seller] faxed to the [Buyer] thanking the [Buyer] for the fax on the modification of the L/C, and urged the [Buyer] to fax the remittance receipt of US $80,000 to the [Seller]. On 25 February 1999, the [Seller] asked the [Buyer] to modify the L/C again, including the modification of: Item 44B on the description of the port of destination; Item 46A (5) on the description of the issuing institute of "Certificate of Chinese Origin", and to cancel Item 46A(7).

On 26 February 1999, the [Buyer] faxed to the [Seller] that payment of US $80,000 will be remitted that day and that the remittance receipt will be faxed to the [Seller] in the afternoon. The [Buyer] agreed to modify the L/C; and asked the [Seller] to be sure to arrange for the carrying ship as soon as possible.

On 2 March 1999, the [Seller] faxed to the [Buyer] and informed that it had not received the payment of US $80,000 and asked the [Buyer] to fax the remittance receipt in order to inquire about it. On 3 March 1999, the [Seller] received the information from the receiving bank that the payment of US $80,000 has been transferred. After deducting the bank fees, the balance was US $79,995. On 5 March 1999, the [Seller] informed the [Buyer] of the name of the carrying ship and the berthing time of the port of departure (10 to 14 March), and asked the [Buyer] to modify the shipping time (before 16 March 1999) on the L/C. On 8 March 1999, without any response from the [Buyer], the [Seller] faxed to the [Buyer] and pointed out that according to the contract, the [Buyer] should have paid the US $80,000 before 11 February, but this payment was not remitted to the [Seller] until 2 March leading to the delay of the sailing date. As per the fax to the [Buyer] on 5 March, the carrying ship has been found, please postpone the shipping period and the period of validity of the L/C.

In a telephone call on 10 March 1999, the [Buyer] asked the [Seller] to postpone the shipping period for a period of time. The [Seller] faxed to the [Buyer] on that day and stated that "... it is to our surprise to hear from you today that you wish to delay the shipment to a much later date to be advised," stating that, of course the [Seller] will try its best to persuade its supplier to agree to your request, but if the [Seller]'s supplier does not cooperate, the [Seller] has no choice but to require the [Buyer] to take full responsibility for the [Seller]'s loss and pay for compensation based on the contract.

On 30 March 1999, the [Seller] asked the [Buyer] to modify the L/C, including:

— Postponement of the period of validity of the L/C to 6 May 1999;

— Setting the shipping time as before 15 April;

— Increasing the total amount of goods from 7,600 tons to 8,000 tons; and

— Setting forth the specification of the goods more concretely.

On 30 March 1999, the [Buyer] faxed to the [Seller] and stated that "... because the match ratio of deformed steel bar provided by your Co. is very different from the former and less than 8,000 tons, now our Co. asked to change deformed steel bar 7,600 (8,000) tons to rod bundle 7,600 (8,000) tons ..."

On 9 April 1999, the [Seller] faxed to the [Buyer] and stated that the goods have been prepared for a long time, the goods should be dispatched to the [Buyer] at the latest before 14 April 1999 and, if that cannot be done, the [Seller] has to sell the goods to other buyers and claim as compensation the difference between the price in the contract and the price of resale. In response to import license difficulties alleged by the [Buyer] over the telephone phone (see comments on that subject below), the [Seller] pointed out that if the [Buyer] is not able to receive the import license before 14 April 1999, the [Buyer] should resell the goods to other buyers in order to carry out this deal. On 12 April 1999, the [Seller] faxed to the [Buyer] again and restated the points expressed in the fax of 9 April.

Issues: How to allocate the responsibilities of [Seller] and [Buyer] fairly and reasonably?

[Buyer]'s position

The [Buyer] claimed that the important fact of this case is that after the contract was signed, the [Buyer] issued the L/C in good time, and that the amount of the L/C accounted for 94.6% of the total payment. 1. Because of Chinese foreign exchange controls, for the [Buyer] to pay US $76,000 via telegraphic transfer according to the contract, it is required that the [Seller] provide an original invoice in order for [Buyer] to purchase the foreign exchange. 2. After the [Buyer] informed the [Seller] of this, the [Seller] sent the original invoice to the [Buyer], but this was delayed until 12 February 1999. That is a Friday, the next day is Saturday and the day after that is Sunday. The following Monday is 15 February. Because of the Chinese Spring Festival, the bank did not resume work until 22 February. On 22 February, the [Buyer] immediately contacted the bank and remitted US $80,000 to the [Seller] on Thursday.

Although the [Buyer] did not remit the US $76,000 within seven working days, the [Buyer] did not delay any time in remitting the US $76,000 due to the Chinese foreign exchange controls known by the [Buyer] and the [Seller]. On 22 February 1999, the [Seller] asked the [Buyer] to extend the shipment date stipulated in the L/C from 5 March 1999 to 10 March 1999, under the condition that the [Seller] knew clearly that the [Buyer] had not remitted the US $76,000 according to the contract. The period of validity of L/C was postponed from 26 March 1999 to 1 April 1999. The behavior of the [Seller] indicated clearly that under the premise of not having received the US $76,000, the [Seller] nevertheless accepted that it would ship and deliver before 10 March 1999. On 24 March 1999, the [Buyer] amended the L/C. But the [Seller] had not actively searched for a loading ship in a timely manner. Although the [Buyer] had urged [Seller] to arrange for the shipment two times on 26 February and 1 March, the [Seller] still refused to find the loading ship. It was not until 3 March, that the [Seller] began to look for the loading ship after the [Seller] received the US $80,000 via telegraphic transfer from the [Buyer]. On 5 March, the [Seller] found a loading ship, but this ship was not able to ship within the shipment date stipulated in the L/C.

From the process aforesaid, it is not difficult to see that the [Seller] did not fulfill the obligation of supplier to actively arrange for the loading ship in good faith. The [Seller] asked the [Buyer] to amend the shipment date in the L/C under the condition that the [Seller] did not receive the payment of US $76,000, it is actually that the [Seller] made the acceptance that the shipment would be before 10 March under the condition of without receiving the payment of US $76,000. Due to this acceptance, the [Seller] has abandoned the right of defense about delivery after receiving the payment; the [Seller] was still amenable to shipment on 10 March 1999, although the [Seller] had not received the payment of US $76,000 which is authorized by the United Nations Convention on Contracts for the International Sales of Goods (CISG).

It is a pity that the [Seller] did not fulfill its acceptance to deliver on the shipment date stipulated on the L/C after amendment, although the [Buyer] urged the [Seller] to arrange for the shipment as quickly as possible by written form twice. Although the [Buyer] informed the [Seller] that the payment of US $76,000 has been remitted and faxed the telegraphic remittance receipt, the

[Seller] did not do anything. It was not until 3 March that the [Seller] began contact with the ship after the [Seller] received the payment. But at that time there was no suitable ship available for loading before 10 March; the ship which the [Seller] contacted was only able to arrive at the port between 10 March and 14 March.

The [Seller] then put forward to amend the L/C again. But at that time, the Chinese government had noted that the < Specific imports of goods registration certificate > held by the [Buyer] would expire due to invalidity on 31 March 1999. Considering the voyage from the Russian port to the Chinese Shantou Port and the fact that the ship found by the [Seller] was not suitable to anchor at the Shantou East Seaport, it was not possible to extend the validity of the < Specific imports of goods registration certificate > held by the [Buyer], so after explaining the circumstance aforesaid, the [Buyer] refused the application for amendment to the L/C from the [Seller] and revoked the contract.

In fact, in the fax of 30 March 1999, the [Seller] asked to amend the L/C again with the big alteration of supplying amount, specification and match ratio. It is not difficult to see that the [Seller] had not prepared the goods at all before 30 March 1999, because the goods supplied by the [Seller] on 30 March are different from the goods the [Seller] contracted to provide to the [Buyer] in amount, specification and match ratio.

After this, the [Seller] faxed to the [Buyer] many times and put forward to amend L/C again. But the [Buyer] refused all of these requests, because it was not possible for the [Buyer] to obtain the import license. As the contract has been revoked, the application for amendment to the L/C sent to the [Buyer] was actually a new offer, but this offer was not accepted by the [Buyer]. The new contract has not been concluded; there was no new legal relationship between the parties.

To sum up, the fault and liability for not performing the contract is due to the failure to perform the new acceptance that the [Seller] should load the ship before 10 March. The [Seller], for the sake of 5.4% of the payment, abandoned its obligation to act in good faith in actively searching for the loading ship to assure the shipment before the deadline stipulated on the amended L/C — so much that at the time of shipment and delivery, the [Seller] had not prepared the goods at all. Therefore, the fault and liability for the failure to perform the contract is attributed to the [Seller]. The [Seller] did not deliver in accordance with the contract. The [Seller] fundamentally breached the contract.

The [Buyer] applied for arbitration according to the arbitration clause in the contract, and filed claims requesting that:

(1) The [Seller] should immediately return the US $80,000 paid by the [Buyer];

(2) The [Seller] should pay interest of US $8,946.85 on that amount (temporarily calculated to 15 December 2000 until the day of actual payment);

(3) The [Seller] should compensate the [Buyer] for attorneys' fees of US $1,067.40 (converted into renminbi [RMB] 8,859.42), traveling expenses [RMB] 2,000 incurred by the arbitration process;

(4) The [Seller] should bear the entire arbitration fee.

[Seller]'s position

In response, the [Seller] submitted a statement of defense and filed a counterclaim alleging that: In this case, it is clear that until 30 March 1999, although the shipment of the goods was delayed for various reasons, the [Seller] still expected to deliver and the [Buyer] still wanted to receive the goods, and the obligations of the two parties under the contract were not released. On 30 March 1999, the [Buyer], via fax, asked the [Seller] to change the goods from deformed steel bar to rod bundle. The reasons for this request are: (1) the deformed steel bar provided by the [Seller] is very different from the former; (2) the amount is less than 8,000 tons. Because the second reason did not stand solidly (the contract stipulated 7,600 tons, the [Seller] expected to deliver 8,000 tons in the fax sent on 30 March 1999), the only one problem which should be resolved is whether a change of the match ratio of the deformed steel bar would be a fundamental breach of contract and whether that would give the [Buyer] the right to revoke the contract and respond with a new offer to purchase rod bundle.

The clause regarding the "diameter/weight" of the goods stipulated that the diameter of the goods was 12 to 25 millimeters, in at least five specifications approximately equal in amount, except that, for the 25 millimeter specifications, the amount would be at the most 1,000 tons. On 30 March 1999, the only difference in the fax from the [Seller] to the [Buyer] was that the goods of 25 millimeter amounted to 1,500 tons. This was not a reason to enable the [Buyer] to cancel the contract. Article 52(2) CISG stipulates that: "If the seller delivers a quantity of goods greater than that provided for in the contract, the buyer may take delivery or refuse to take delivery of the excess quantity." According to this regulation, the [Buyer] was entitled to refuse to take delivery of the excess part under the condition that the [Seller] delivered 500 excessive tons of goods of 25 millimeter, but the [Buyer] had no right to cancel the contract and refuse to accept delivery of the goods. If the [Buyer] refused to accept delivery of the added 500 tons of 25 millimeter goods, the remaining part was 7,500 tons.

According to the quantity clause of the contract, the [Seller] was entitled to deliver less than 10% of the stipulated amount, at least 6,840 tons (7,600 - 7,600 * 10%); therefore, the [Seller] was still in accord with the requirements of the contract, though the [Seller] delivered 7,500 tons. And in the fax of 30 March 1999, the [Seller] did not express that the [Buyer] had no choice in accepting delivery of the goods according to specification written in the fax. If the [Buyer] did not wish to receive the goods of this specification, the [Buyer] should have informed the [Seller] and given the [Seller] a chance to change the goods. The [Buyer]'s behavior of refusal to accept delivery of the goods without any negotiation was not in good faith. The [Buyer] breached the contract. Moreover, the [Buyer]'s refusal to extend the L/C was a fundamental breach of contract.

The [Seller] was not at fault in the delay of dispatch. According to the contract, the [Buyer] should have remitted the US $80,000 to the account appointed by the [Seller] within seven working days after the contract; it was impossible to attach the condition that the [Seller] should issue the original invoice and mail it to the [Buyer] before the remittance. Afterward, the [Buyer] asked the [Seller] to mail the original invoice before the remittance which led to a series of subsequent delays. It was more important that the two parties agreed to perform the contract under the condition that the dispatch of the goods has been delayed. In this circumstance, the delay of dispatch was not a valid basis for the [Buyer] to refuse to extend the validity time of the L/C and the shipment period. The [Buyer] did not extend the L/C after 5 March 1999; this was actually a refusal to accept delivery, and the [Buyer] breached the contract fundamentally.

Because of this, the [Seller] suffered economic loss.

According to Article 75 CISG, the [Seller] was entitled to ask the [Buyer] to compensate for the balance between the contract price and resale price. In this case, the concrete amount and calculating process were as follows: (1) The unit price of the goods under the contract was US $185 per ton CNF Shantou; (2) The first resale contract (hereafter, Resale Contract I) signed on 20 May 1999 stipulated that the unit price of the goods was US $178 per ton CIF Kampongsom; it is necessary to subtract the balance of insurance fees and freight in order to compare the contract price with the resale price in this case. The insurance fees for the transport of steel from Russia to Asian areas was 1‰ - 3‰, and calculated on 2‰,

Resale Contract I contained the insurance fees US $0.36 per ton (US $178 per ton * 2‰), otherwise the freight from the port of Nakhodka in Russia to Cambodia was US $27 per ton, but the freight under the contract (from Russia to China) was only US $13 per ton; the balance of both was US $14 per ton (27 minus 13). Therefore, after adjustment for the insurance fees and freight, the price was US $163.64 per ton (178 minus 0.36 minus 14). (3) The second resale contract (hereafter, Resale Contract II) signed on 14 October 1999 stipulated that the unit price was US $150 per ton CFR Singapore, it contained the freight US $25 per ton which was US $12 per ton more than the freight to China (25 minus 13). Therefore, after Resale Contract II price subtracts the balance of freight under the contract price in this case, the price (the match price of the contract of this case) was US $138 per ton (150 minus 12). (4) The average price of Resale Contract I and Resale Contract II was US $150.82 per ton CNF [(163.64 + 138)/2]. The [Seller]'s loss by reselling the goods was US $34.18 per ton (185 minus 150.82), so the [Seller]'s total loss of balance was US $259,768 (US $34.18 per ton * 7,600 tons).

There was also an interest loss due to the delay of resale of the goods. In this case, if the [Buyer] had not violated the contract and had extended the L/C according to the request from the [Seller] via fax on 30 March 1999, the goods could have been dispatched before 14 April 1999, and the [Seller] could have received the payment before 30 April 1999. Therefore, the [Seller] was entitled to have the [Buyer] compensate the interest loss incurred by delay of receiving the resale payment.

The goods under Resale Contract I were shipped on 6 June 1999, the contract stipulated the payment should be made within 120 days after the shipment date, so the date of receiving the payment should be 4 October 1999. The goods under Resale Contract II were shipped on 9 November 1999. According to the general custom in the trade, the [Seller] should receive the remittance on 24 November (15 days after the bill of lading date). The middle date under the two contracts was 29 October 1999, the time of delay on receiving payment was six months (from 30 April 1999 to 29 October). Under the two resale contracts, the average resale price was US $150.82 per ton; the total resale price under the contract of this case was US $1,146,232 (US $150.82 per ton 7,600). If the base amount for calculating interest was US 1,146,232 and the period for calculating interest was six months and the interest rate was 8% per year, the [Seller]'s interest loss because of the delay on resale of the goods was US $45,849.28 (US $1,146,232 *

6 months * 8% / 12).

The interest loss on the balance. The [Seller]'s loss of balance aforesaid was US $259,768. Because the [Seller] did not receive this balance, the [Seller] was entitled to claim compensation for the interest on the balance. This interest should be calculated from 1 May 1999 (if the [Buyer] had not violated the contract, this payment would have been received before 30 April 1999). The interest should apply to the balance due to the [Seller], US $259,768. The interest rate was 8%. The interest should be calculated until the date when the arbitral award is been executed.

The [Buyer] should bear the [Seller]'s attorneys' fee of renminbi [RMB] 90,000 incurred by this arbitration.

The [Seller] had received the balance payment US $80,000 from the [Buyer]. Therefore, the [Buyer] should pay the compensation (not contain the interest of the balance loss) US $225,617.28 (259,768 + 45,849.28 - 80,000) and renminbi [RMB] 90,000 after subtracted the US $80,000.

Thereafter, the parties filed supplementary statements and evidence with the Arbitral Tribunal many times. The responses were as follows:

[Buyer]'s supplementary response

The [Buyer] claimed that: (1) The [Seller] did not prepare the goods within the period under the contract. The [Seller] alleged that "on 5 March 1999 10,000 tons of goods had been prepared in Hai Shenwei, then the [Seller] allocated the goods according to the measure and match and faxed to the [Buyer] on 30 March 1999, and asked the [Buyer] to amend the L/C according to the measure and match of the goods." This indicated that the [Seller] had not prepared the goods under the L/C, the 10,000 tons of goods in Hai Shenwei were not supplied for the [Buyer].

However, there were no goods of the last two kinds under the contract and L/C. Among these goods, there were no goods of the specification of 16 millimeter stipulated in the contract and L/C.

From the above comparison, it is clear that among the goods received by the [Seller] on 5 March 1999, some specifications were decreased by 2,354.06 tons in all, and other specifications were increased by 4,718.83 tons. This means that among the 7,600 tons of goods under the contract, there were 7,072.89 tons of goods (take up 93%) that were not in accord with the specification. It was obvious that it could not be negotiated because of the loading goods not in accord with the specification stipulated in the contract and L/C.

The [Seller] faxed to the [Buyer] on 30 March 1999 and suggested that the [Buyer] should amend the L/C; it was indicated that the [Seller] did not intend to supply the [Buyer] with the goods in Hai Shenwei. These goods were not the [Buyer]'s goods; therefore the [Seller] dealt with the goods on 30 March 1999, the [Seller] did not prepare the goods needed by the [Buyer] on 5 March 1999. (2) The [Seller] altered the specifications of the goods many times without agreement from the [Buyer], and the goods sold to the third-party were not the ones under the contract signed by the [Buyer] and the [Seller]. Even according to the [Seller]'s allegations:

— The [Seller] has prepared the [Buyer]'s goods, but under the condition that the shipment could not be within the period stipulated in the L/C;

— The [Seller] changed the specifications of the goods without agreement from the [Buyer] and sold the changed goods to the third-party; these goods were not the ones under the contract.

To sum up:

— The [Seller] did not prepare the goods supplied for the [Buyer] within the period stipulated in the contract and L/C and did not rent the ship in time.

— The [Seller] by now still could not prove the economic loss because of this case, the request for the compensation for [Seller]'s economic loss is not supported by reasonable evidence and should be rejected according to the law.

— The fault and liability for failure to perform the contract is that of the [Seller]. By its failure to perform the supplying obligation, [Seller] breached the contract fundamentally. The US $80,000 should be returned to the [Buyer], and the [Seller] should compensate for the loss of the interest.

— The [Seller] also should also compensate the [Buyer] for the traveling fees renminbi [RMB] 30,000 and lawyer fees [RMB] 178,594.20.

[Seller]'s supplementary response

The [Seller] pointed out that: (1) There was no obligation to deliver before receiving the balance payment of US $80,000. (2) *The [Seller] prepared the goods within the period set forth in the contract.* To sum up, based on the contract, the [Seller] was entitled to adjust the measure of the goods according to the goods supplied by the former seller before delivery; the [Seller] had prepared the goods before the delivery was possible, the [Seller] adjusted and ascertained the measure of the goods prepared for the [Buyer] according to the goods which had been prepared. However, the [Buyer] refused to receive the entire goods without putting forward the details of the goods' measure in advance and putting forward the request for modification after the event, therefore the [Buyer] breached the contract fundamentally. (3) *The goods resold by the [Seller] were the goods under the contract.* The [Seller] had stated in the oral hearing that the good resold by the [Seller] were the goods under the contract, and filed comprehensive evidence to support this. The evidence indicated that the measure proportion of the 8,000 tons of goods resold to Cambodia Co. and Singapore Co. was the same as the measure proportion with the [Buyer]. (4) *The invalidity of the [Buyer]'s < Specific import of goods registration certificate > is the [Buyer]'s fault.* The [Buyer] did not file the import license with the Arbitral Tribunal. If the [Buyer] did not submit this license, the [Buyer] was not entitled to claim that it could not receive the goods due to expiration of the license, because the [Buyer] could not prove that [Buyer] had held it.

Supposing that the [Buyer] indeed held the license, which party should be responsible for the fault of not using the license? If the reason of Chinese foreign exchange control indeed existed, the [Buyer] should have told the [Seller] this when the contract was signed. In this way, the two parties could have stipulated that "the [Buyer] should remit US $80,000 to the account appointed by the [Seller] within seven days after the [Buyer] received the original invoice from the [Seller]." If the contract contained this stipulation, the [Seller] would mail out the original invoice immediately after the contract was signed in order to save time. Until 5 February 1999, the [Seller] still urged the [Buyer] to remit the US $80,000 as soon as possible. This indicated that the [Buyer] still did not mention the matter about the original invoice. The time of delay of delivery caused by this was at least five days. Suppose that on 6 February 1999, the [Buyer] had asked the [Seller] to mail the original invoice, there were five days between 2 February and 6 February. If not for this delay, the [Buyer] would have been able to remit the US $80,000 before the Spring Festival, and the dispute in this case would not have arisen.

The [Buyer] received the original invoice on 12 February 1999. Because the original invoice must be mailed instead of sent by fax, the [Seller] had no unreasonable delay in mailing the original invoice. Nor did the [Seller] have any fault in renting the ship. The [Buyer]'s claim that the ship rented by the [Seller] was not suitable to anchor at Shantou East Port could not be supported. The [Buyer] did not demur that the ship was not suitable to anchor. If the ship discharged at other ports, when it arrived at Shantou port, the sea gauge was shoal, it was possible to anchor.

The [Seller] had contacted for a ship on 2 or 3 March 1999 and found a ship on 5 March. This was the earliest ship the [Seller] could find under that condition. The ship would finish the shipment by 13 March. The amended L/C in this case stipulated that the latest shipment date was 10 March 1999. If the L/C was not extended, and the goods were dispatched from Russia port after 10 March, the L/C would not be negotiated. Had the [Buyer] faxed the remittance receipt to the [Seller] according to the [Seller]'s request on 2 March 1999, and the [Seller] found a ship on 3 March, there would not have been any unreasonable delay or violation of an obligation of goodwill.

To sum up, assuming that the real reason why the [Buyer] did not receive the goods is that the "import license" could not be used within the period of invalidity, it was because of the [Buyer]'s fault of delay. Moreover, an inability to use the import license is not a "force majeure" event that would exempt the [Buyer] from liability. According to Article 79 CISG, if the [Buyer] claimed for exemption for force majeure-type reasons, certain conditions must be satisfied: (1) *An impediment must have occurred.* (2) *The impediment must have been unpredictable.* Assume that the [Buyer] had obtained an "import license" that expired on 31 March 1999. When the [Buyer] concluded the contract in this case, it was predictable that the license will be invalid after expiration. (3) *The impediment or its consequences could not be overcome or avoided.* (4) *The [Buyer] must inform the [Seller] of the impediment in a timely manner.* In this case, the reason why the [Buyer] did not receive the goods was that the match ratio of the deformed steel bar provided by the [Seller] were far from the former, not that the behavior of Chinese government. In other words, the [Buyer] still expressed to the [Seller] that it was doing its best to apply for the "import license" after 31 March 1999. In a word, the [Buyer] never declared to the [Seller] that it could not perform the obligation of receiving the goods because of force majeure. Moreover, the contract stipulated that "the [Seller] is not responsible for the delay on delivery or shipment because of common acceptable events of force majeure, but the [Seller] must inform the [Buyer] of the event by phone immediately and airmail to the [Buyer] the certification issued by the official government or chamber of commerce at the place where the disaster occurs to the [Buyer] within fifteen days after the disaster occurs." According to the principle of equality, this clause is applicable to the [Buyer] as well as the [Seller]. The [Buyer] submitted to the Arbitral Tribunal a certification issued by Economic Committee of Shantou on 12 June 2001. If the [Buyer] had provided a valid certification of force majeure to the [Seller], the

[Seller] could have used it to exempt itself from liability to its supplier according to the force majeure clause in the contract the [Seller] had entered into with its supplier. In that case, the [Seller]'s loss would not have occurred, and the dispute between the [Seller] and the [Buyer] could have been solved that way.

Since the [Buyer] did not send the clear information to the [Seller] about the occurrence of the force majeure event in time and did not provide a valid certification of force majeure, the [Buyer] should be responsible for all the loss that occurred.

Opinion of the Arbitration Tribunal

1. Whether the [Buyer] is liable for the delay in the payment of US $ 80,000 and whether the [Seller] has justifiable reason to postpone the delivery. According to the stipulation of the contract, the [Buyer] should remit US $ 80,000 calculated as US $ 10 per ton to the account appointed by the [Seller] before 9 February 1999. The [Seller] informed the [Buyer] of its bank account on 6 February 1999. But the [Buyer] did not give the US $ 80,000 to Industrial and Commercial Bank of China until 6 February 1999. The [Seller] did not receive it until 3 March.

The two parties had no dispute on the fact of the [Buyer]'s delay on payment. The dispute between two parties is:

The [Seller] alleged it was the [Buyer]'s breach of contract; whereas the [Buyer] alleged that, because of Chinese foreign exchange controls, the [Buyer] must get the [Seller]'s original invoice, but the [Buyer] did not receive the original invoice from the [Seller] until 12 February, and that, due to the Spring Festival, the [Buyer]'s bank did not remit until 26 February. Therefore, the [Buyer] alleged that it was not responsible for the delay.

The Arbitral Tribunal concluded that:

— The contract, did not stipulate that [Seller] must submit the original invoice before receiving payment of the US $ 80,000).

— The [Buyer] should know the requirement that the Chinese foreign exchange control asks for the original invoice, but the [Seller] did not know this regulation (and the [Buyer] did not submit any evidence to prove that the [Seller] should have known of it).

— Therefore, the delay on remittance concerned with the original invoice is the [Buyer]'s fault. Because the [Buyer] did not stipulate it in the contract, it has nothing to do with the [Seller].

— As to the holiday of Spring Festival, it is not caused by the [Seller].

Therefore, as the [Buyer] is liable for the delay in the remittance of US $80,000, it is deemed that the [Buyer] breached the contract.

As the [Buyer] is liable for breach of contract concerning the delay on payment of US $80,000, the next question is:

2. *Was the [Seller] entitled to postpone the delivery?* As to this, the [Seller] stated that it had no obligation to dispatch the goods before receiving the US $80,000. The Arbitral Tribunal deems that according to the contract, the [Buyer] should remit the payment calculated as US $10 per ton before 9 February 1999 and issue the L/C calculated as US $175 per ton on 11 February. The Arbitral Tribunal notes that Industrial and Commercial Bank of China branch in Shantou issued the L/C on 10 February 1999. This means that the [Buyer] issued the L/C on time. In this case, even though the [Buyer] did not pay the money calculated as US $10 per ton (total US $80,000), as long as the [Seller] delivers on time, and the bill submitted by the [Seller] is in accord with the condition of L/C, and it is credible to receive the 95% of the payment.

3. About the amendment to the L/C in the last ten-day of February 1999. The [Seller] asked to amend the L/C many times, especially to amend the delivery time on the L/C. The [Buyer] alleged that this should be regarded as evidence that the [Seller] had not prepared the goods in time, and therefore the [Seller] was not able to deliver in time. The amendment to the L/C was from 22 to 25 February 1999. For [Seller]'s request of 22 February 1999, the amended content mainly had to do with specifications and quantity of the goods except for some spelling of some words, and the delivery time was changed from 5 March 1999 to 11 March 1999. The [Buyer] applied for amendment to the issuing bank on 23 February, and the issuing bank modified the specification and quantity of the goods on 25 February, but the amended delivery time was 10 March 1999.

The Arbitral Tribunal notes that in international sales of goods, it is common for parties to make modifications to Letters of Credit: One party may put forward a request for amendment, the other party may (1) refuse, i. e., not agree to amend; (2) the parties negotiate to amend it, with the party who requests providing some compensation; (3) the parties agree to amend, but reserve the right to claim for compensation; or (4) the parties may agree to amend unconditionally.

From 22 to 25 February 1999, four days in all, the [Buyer] agreed to amend unconditionally. It should be deemed that the amendment of the issuing bank on 25 February 1999 resulted from making more concrete the specification, quantity and match ratio of the goods and amendments to the delivery period agreed to by both parties. Since the two parties amended the L/C unconditionally, it is not necessary to investigate the reasons for the amendments to the L/C (There may be many reasons, not certainly the preparation of the goods).

4. Regarding the correspondence from the [Seller] on 5 March 1999 to inform of the name of the ship and the correspondence from the [Buyer] on 29 March 1999 (remark: instead the two parties both mistakenly said that the date was 30 March.) The [Buyer] alleged that on 26 February 1999 and 1 March 1999, the [Buyer] had asked the [Seller] to arrange for the ship and for shipment many times, but the [Seller] did not do it actively. The [Buyer] alleged that the [Seller] began to search for the ship after receiving US $80,000 and delayed the time, so the [Seller] should be held liable. The [Seller]'s correspondence about the name of the ship had been sent out on 5 March 1999, i. e., the [Seller] sent it out within two days of receipt of the US $80,000. Was this an unreasonable delay? The Arbitral Tribunal rules that it was not. The Tribunal noted that the [Buyer] had written that it would fax the remittance receipt to the [Seller] "this afternoon" in the correspondence on 26 February. But it can be shown from the correspondence from the [Seller] on 2 March that by 2 March, the [Buyer] still had not faxed the remittance receipt to the [Seller]. So the fault is ascribed to the [Buyer], because although it had answered, it had not faxed the remittance receipt to the [Seller] at that time. The liability for delay on the time should therefore not be laid upon the [Seller]; it was caused by the [Buyer]'s fault. In fact, considering that the [Seller] only received the US $80,000 from its own issuing bank on 3 March, the correspondence sent to the [Buyer] on 5 March was in time and reasonable.

The correspondence from the [Seller] on 5 March 1999, in addition to providing the ship's name and tonnage also asked to change the delivery period to before 16 March 1999. The [Seller] asked the [Buyer] to affirm that. The [Seller] faxed to the [Buyer] and urged [Buyer] again on 8 March and 10 March, but the [Buyer] did not reply to any of these communications. The Arbitral Tribunal notes that there was the following text in the fax from the [Seller] to the [Buyer] on 10 March 1999: "... it is to our surprise to hear from you today that you wish to delay the shipment to a much later date to be advised." "This indicates that it was the [Buyer], not the [Seller], that asked to delay the shipment. The [Buyer] did not send any correspondence to the [Seller] until 29 March, and wrote that: "... because the match ratio of deformed steel bar provided by your Co. is very different from the former and less than 8,000 tons, now our Co. asked to change deformed steel bar 7,600 (8,000) ton to rod bundle 7,600 (8,000) ton ..."

It is difficult to understand the expression in the correspondence from the [Buyer] to the [Seller] on 29 March. As to the requirement of the specification and quantity of deformed steel bar under the contract, the contract stipulated that "diameter 12 to 25 millimeter, at least five specifications, the quantity is equal approximately, if there was the specification of 25 millimeter, 1,000 tons at the most". The L/C was issued in accord with that. When the [Seller] asked to amend the L/C on 22 February 1999, the goods' specification put forward by the [Seller] was: 12 millimeter—1, 800 tons, 14 millimeter—1, 600 tons, 16 millimeter—1,800 tons, 22 millimeter—1,800 tons, 25 millimeter—1000 tons, total 8,000 tons in all. When the [Buyer] applied for the issuing bank to amend the L/C on 23 February 1999 and the issuing bank amended the L/C, the match ratio of the goods was: 12 millimeter—1,700 tons, 14 millimeter 1,500 tons, 16 millimeter 1,700 tons, 22 millimeter 1,700 tons, 25 millimeter 1,000 tons, total 7,600 tons in all. There was not any change until 29 March 1999. It means that the match ratio of the deformed steel bar and the quantity of 7,600 tons is decided by the [Buyer] itself. According to this, the sentence "the match ratio of the deformed steel bar is very different from the former and less than 8,000 tons" was the [Buyer]'s own idea, but the [Buyer] blamed the [Seller] in the correspondence which is difficult to understand.

In terms of the content of the correspondence from the [Buyer] on 29 March 1999, the essence of the [Buyer]'s conduct is that the [Buyer] revoked the contract unilaterally for a nonexistent reason. Because rod bundle and deformed steel bar are two different kinds of steel goods, if there is a change to provide rod bundle, the modification of the contract cannot solve the problem unless it can lead to a new contract.

5. About the < Specific import of goods registration certificate >. The [Buyer] stated that on 10 March 1999, it had faxed to the [Seller] and alleged that "the [Buyer]'s import license < Specific import of goods registration certificate > may be invalidated because of the [Seller]'s delay in renting ship.... and told the [Seller] that if the [Seller] could not load the ship on time, the [Buyer] would terminate the contract." However, in the materials submitted by the [Buyer] and the [Seller], there was no evidence to indicate that the [Buyer] had sent such a fax. The fact that could be relevant to this is the correspondence

from the [Seller] stating: "... it is to our surprise to hear from you today that you wish to delay the shipment to a much later date to be advised" in the correspondence from the [Seller] to the [Buyer] on 10 March. But from that sentence, we cannot find information about the [Buyer]'s import license (Specific import of goods registration certificate) and its possible invalidation.

The Arbitral Tribunal notes that the certification from Shantou economic committee on 12 July 2001 proved that a (Specific import of goods registration certificate) indeed existed. Then, there is an issue whether the matter of (Specific import of goods registration certificate) can be regarded as an act of the government that would exempt the [Buyer] from liability according to force majeure. The contract clause on "manpower force majeure" is for the benefit of the [Seller]. Supposing that the stipulation of force majeure under the contract is also applied to the [Buyer], then, the [Buyer] needs to: (1) inform timely; (2) submit the certification from the government or chamber of commerce within 15 days, if the [Buyer] indeed faxed (maybe by phone) the problem about the (Specific import of goods registration certificate) on 10 March 1999, but it did not submit the certification from the government or chamber of commerce within 15 days. The certification from Shantou economic committee seen was issued on 12 July 2001; it was not submitted by the [Buyer] within 15 days but 825 days! Moreover, in the correspondence from the [Buyer] on 29 March, the reason why the [Buyer] did not want deformed steel bar was said to be the problem of specification and match ratio and the quantity less than 8,000 tons, rather than the invalidation of the (Specific import of goods registration certificate). Therefore, the Tribunal concludes that the [Buyer] terminated the contract unilaterally and breached the contract fundamentally.

6. Resolution of the [Buyer]'s arbitration claims and the [Seller]'s counterclaim. The [Buyer] filed four claims; the [Seller] filed three counterclaims.

The [Buyer]'s first claim and the [Seller]'s first counterclaim

The [Buyer]'s first claim seeks to have the [Seller] return the US $80,000 paid by the [Buyer]. The [Seller]'s first counterclaim seeks to have the [Buyer] compensate US $225,617.28. The [Seller] has deducted the US $80,000 paid by the [Buyer] when the [Seller] calculated this compensation. With respect to the US $80,000, the [Buyer]'s claims and the [Seller]'s counterclaim are complementary. The decision on supporting the [Buyer]'s claims or the [Seller]'s counterclaim depends on whether it was the [Buyer] or the [Seller] who breached the contract.

According to the investigation, analysis and hearing by the Arbitral Tribunal, the Tribunal has affirmed that the reason why the contract had not been performed and why the [Seller] did not deliver is that the [Buyer] terminated the contract unilaterally and breached the contract fundamentally. According to the CISG, the [Buyer] should compensate the [Seller] for the loss that occurred because of this. The [Seller] resold the contract goods. According to the CISG, the [Seller] is entitled to have the [Buyer] compensate the loss. However, the [Buyer] demurred with respect to the [Seller]'s resale of 4,000 tons of deformed steel bars on 20 May 1999 and 4000 tons again on 14 October, alleging that the specifications and quantities are different from the specifications and quantity stipulated by the two parties on 25 February 1999, and also different from the specifications and quantities stipulated by the two parties on 30 March 1999. The [Buyer] alleged that the [Seller] did not file evidence to support that the two resales of deformed steel bars were of the goods the [Seller] had prepared to sell to the [Buyer]. The [Seller]'s response was:

The contract stipulated that "diameter 12 to 25, at least 5 specifications, the quantity is equal approximately, if there is the specification of 25 millimeter, the quantity is at the most 1,000 tons; the quantity 7,600 metric tons (+/-10%)", as long as accord with this stipulation, it is the goods under the contract. The [Seller] alleged that the goods resold by it were in accord with the scope under the contract.

The Arbitral Tribunal notes that the [Buyer] offered the following statement in rebuttal:

The deformed steel bars resold by the [Seller] were not the goods the [Seller] purchased from its supplier and intended to sell to the [Buyer]. The [Buyer] made a graph in order to compare the "stipulation on 25 February 1999", the "stipulation on 30 March 1999" and "the [Seller]'s way of resale".

The Arbitral Tribunal deems that the defense of the [Buyer] is actually about what is the "contract goods". Concerning on the character of the relation on the supply and demand such as deformed steel bar, the Arbitral Tribunal deems that the contract only stipulated the scope of the specification and the principle of quantity match ratio, did not specially stipulate concrete specifications and quantity, and did not stipulate how to make sure of the concrete specifications and quantity match ratio. This stipulation has its own special meaning. "The stipulation on 25 February 1999" and/or "the stipulation on 30 March 1999", specified the match ratio of specification and quantity, which is the concrete performance of the contract; it did not modify/replace the stipulation of the contract. Therefore, whether it is the "contract goods" is not based on the negotiation or "stipulation", but is inferred from whether it is in accordance with the description of the goods. From the graph made by the [Buyer], it can be indicated that in fact, whether the "stipulation on 25 February 1999", the "stipulation on 30 March 1999" or "the [Seller]'s way of resale" are all in accord with the description of the goods. Therefore, the Tribunal concludes that the deformed steel bar resold by the [Seller] was in accord with the stipulation under the contract.

Therefore, according to the CISG, the [Seller] is entitled to have the [Buyer] compensate for the loss of price balance.

The Arbitral Tribunal checked the [Seller]'s first counterclaim about the calculation on the loss of the compensation. The Tribunal deems that the [Seller] considered the price difference between the CNF price of the contract of this case and the CIF price of the First Resale Contract; and considered the deduction of the US $80,000; moreover, although the [Seller] resold 4,000 + 4,000 = 8,000 ton, the compensation was calculated on 7,600 tons under the contract, so this calculation is reasonable.

In its compensation claim, the [Seller] had also calculated interest due to delay in receiving the payment. The Arbitral Tribunal deems that according to the CISG, the [Seller] should resell the good within a reasonable period. In fact, the resale time was very late. Although it relates to the demand of the deformed steel bar's specification in the market, the delay on resale was not caused by the [Buyer]. Therefore, the Arbitral Tribunal does not support the claim for interest in the [Seller]'s first counterclaim. The Arbitral Tribunal deems that the [Buyer] shall pay the compensation US $179,768.

In fact, the [Buyer]'s first claim has been covered by the [Seller]'s first counterclaim, so the Arbitral Tribunal does not support the [Buyer]'s first claim.

The [Buyer]'s second claim and the [Seller]'s second counterclaim

The [Buyer]'s second claim seeks to have the [Seller] pay the interest on US $80,000; The [Seller]'s third counterclaim seeks to have the [Buyer] pay the interest of the compensation. The Arbitral Tribunal deems that either the return of US $80,000 or compensation for the resale price balance is decided after the award has been handed down. It means the debt relation between the [Buyer] and the [Seller] occurs after the award has been made. Therefore the Arbitral Tribunal does not support the request for interest from the [Buyer] or the [Seller].

The remaining claims of the parties

The [Buyer]'s third and fourth claim and the [Seller]'s second counterclaim all concern the arbitration fee and claims for other case fees. The Arbitral Tribunal deems that the arbitration fees for the [Buyer]'s claims shall be borne by the [Buyer]. The arbitration fees for the [Seller]'s counterclaims shall be borne by the [Buyer] (90%) and the [Seller] (10%). The [Buyer]'s attorneys' fees and traveling fees shall be borne by the [Buyer]; the [Seller]'s attorneys' fees, renminbi [RMB] 90,000. should be compensated by the [Buyer].

Award

According to the investigation, analysis, hearing and cognizance by the Arbitral Tribunal, the Arbitration Tribunal:

(1) Reject all claims of the [Buyer] and rules that;

(2) The [Buyer] shall pay the [Seller] US $179,768 to compensate the [Seller] for the loss of price difference by reselling the goods;

(3) The [Buyer] shall pay the [Seller] renminbi [RMB] 90,000 to compensate for the attorneys' fees paid by the [Seller] because of this case;

(4) The [Seller]'s third counterclaim is rejected;

(5) The arbitration fee for the [Buyer]'s claims in the amount of renminbi [RMB] 39,640 shall be borne by the [Buyer] entirely. The [Buyer] has paid the aforesaid amount in advance. The counterclaim arbitration fee of this case is US $7,116, of which the [Buyer] shall bear US $6,404.40 and the [Seller] shall bear US $7,116. The [Seller] has paid the aforesaid amount in advance, therefore the [Buyer] shall pay US $6,404.60 to the [Seller];

(6) The [Buyer] shall pay the above amount, totaling US $186,172.40 and renminbi [RMB] 90,000, within thirty days after the date of this award; otherwise, a yearly interest rate of 4% shall be added.

This is the final award. [1]

■ Notes

purchase order 购买订单。一般认为一项完整的订单构成一项要约,一旦对方接受,合同即告成立。订单应包括货物的名字、价格、数量、交货期、付款方式及有效期等。

consideration 对价。这是英美合同法中最难理解、争议最多的理论之一。多数国家的法律

---

[1] https://www.uncitral.org/clout/clout/data/chn/clout_case_1042_leg-2205.html, visit on 26 December, 2019.

规定,如果一项合同具有合法的要约和接受,该合同就具有拘束力。然而,英美法中则把合同分成两类:一类是签字蜡封合同(deed contract under seal),这种合同是由当事人签字、加盖印鉴并把它交给对方而做成(signed, sealed, and delivered)的,这种合同只要具有上述形式,不要求任何对价,即具有法律拘束力。另一类是简式合同(simple contracts),它包括口头合同和非以签字蜡封式做成的一般书面合同,这类合同必须要有对价,否则就没有拘束力,即对价是一种将当事人黏结在合同上的胶合剂(consideration is the glue that binds the parties to a contract together)。

据考证,英美法的对价制度已经有400多年的历史,法院在司法实践中也发展了一系列规则,但对对价的定义却一直争论不休,至今没有一个令人满意的定义。一直被广泛引用的定义是Luch J在Currie v. Misa(1875)案中所下的定义:"从法律上看,一项有价值的对价就是一方当事人得到某种权利、利益、利润或好处,或者对方当事人做出某种容忍(forbearance)、承受某种程度损害(detriment)、损失,或者承担某种责任。" Sir Frederick Pollock 在 Dunlop Pneumatic Tyre Co. Ltd. v. Selfridge & Co. Ltd.(1915)案中则把对价定义为:"一方的行为或容忍,或者他的这种许诺,是为了换取对方的许诺所支付的价格。"(An act or forbearance of one party, or the promise thereof, is the price for which the promise of the other is bought; and the promise thus given for value is enforceable)

上述定义是英国法官在众多判例中为对价归纳的定义,有些玄妙难懂。实际上,英国合同法将许诺分为两类:一类是可以得到强制执行的,另一类是不可以得到强制执行的。对价就是法官用来判断某项许诺是否可以得到强制执行的条件。例如,某人许诺支付一定数额来购买某物,但对方(卖方)对买方上述许诺没给予任何东西作为回报。那么,如果卖方认为付款时间已到,要求买方履行合同付款。买方就可能诉诸法院要求判他们彼此没有合同关系。法官就会认为,买方的许诺无法律效力,不能得到强制执行,因为卖方没有为买方所做的许诺支付任何对价,而没有对价的许诺是没有拘束力的。因此,法官就会判决他们中无合同关系,双方自然都没有任何合同义务。

美国合同法在这方面继承了英国合同法的基本观念,但美国合同法更强调对价必须经过一个讨价还价的过程。该规定的基本作用是供法院将"赠予"与合同区别开来。这里的讨价还价与商事交易中的要约、承诺的过程不同。根据《合同法重述》第71条(2),讨价还价,是指诺言人将许诺与受诺人的履约行为(performance)或回报许诺(return promise)进行交换。《合同法重述》第81条(2)规定:"如果一项许诺本身不能诱引履约行为或回报许诺,该许诺并不妨碍受诺人的履约行为或回报许诺成为有效的对价。"可见,美国合同法在解决对价纠纷时通常并不关心许诺本身的真正动机或诱引作用。

总之,英美合同法中的对价理论的目的是区别"赠予"和合同,一直受到不少学者的质疑,成为英美合同法中争议最大的问题之一。

promissory estoppel 许诺性禁反言理论。指由英国著名法官丹宁勋爵创立,旨在纠正对价理论所产生的不公平现象的理论。该理论认为,如果受要约人出于对要约的信赖,而实施了行为,即使没有对价,合同也应成立。要约人对自己的违约行为应承担责任。

restitution interest(返还利益),**reliance interest**(信赖利益)及 **expectation interest**(期望利益)。关于合同法中的损害赔偿目的的理论比较复杂,根据美国学者的观点,合同损害赔偿应追求三种目的,即期望利益、信赖利益和返还利益。首先,返还利益,是指法院迫使被告交出他从原告接受的价值,其目的是防止违约的许诺人从受诺人所支出的费用中获益,也就是说,防止被告获得不当得利。其次,信赖利益。基于对被告的信赖,原告改变了自己的处境,例如,依据货物买卖合同,买方在调查卖方的所有权上支付了费用,或者错过了订立其他合同的机会。原告(买方)可以要求法院判决被告赔偿原告因信赖被告(卖方)所受的损失,其目的是要使原告恢复到与被告许诺作出前一样的处境。最后,期望利益,指为寻求给予受诺人对许诺的期望价值,原告在一个损害赔偿中,可以要求法院判决被告支付这种履行的金钱价值,其目的是使原告处于假若被告履行其许诺时其所应处的处境。

一般地说,合同约定的价格(期望利益)不仅包括当事人为次支出的费用和成本(信赖利益),而且,还应包括扣除了这些费用和成本后的利润。因此,一种盈利的交易的信赖利益是不会大于期望利益的。如果信赖利益等于期望利益,则说明这一交易是不赔不赚的。而如果信赖利益大于期望利益,说明这一交易是亏本的。

reasonable person 理性人。这是欧美法学界假设的一个人,作为一种标准,主要用来确定一个人的行为是否构成疏忽。一般认为,一个理性人的行为和责任应该与社会中的普通人相符,遇事冷静,一般不会失去理性,习惯适中、性情温和、举止得体。例如,做事不会过分迟延,行为谨慎但不会过分,等等。

unique 独特的,无可匹敌的。根据英美法院的判例,该词主要指在当事人生活的区域,很难找到能够予以替代的物。

emotional distress 精神损失。

■ Important Legal English Usages

bind 有拘束力。例如,An offer generally is not binding on the offeree(一项要约通常对受要约人没有拘束力)。有时,也会使用该词的过去分词形式,例如,An offer shall indicate the intention to be bound(一项要约应表明要约人愿意受其拘束的意旨)。

provide 规定。例如,The law provides that it is the duty of the seller to deliver the goods, and of the buyer to accept and pay for them, in accordance with the terms of the contract of sale(法律规定卖方有义务依据买卖合同的条款交付货物,买方有义务依据买卖合同的条款支付货款)。

与 provide 同义的词还有 state, stipulate 等,它们一般可以互换使用。

revoke 撤销,废除。例如,Until a contract is concluded an offer may be revoked if the revocation reaches the offeree before he has dispatched an acceptance(在未订立合同之前,如果撤销的通知于受要约人发出接受通知之前送达要约人,要约得予撤销)。

与该词相近的词还有 cancel, avoid, rescind 等,注意他们在用法上的区别:

(1) cancel:删去,取消。该词在用法上与 void, abrogate, invalidate 可以互换。例如,He canceled his order(他取消了订货);A faulty signature may invalidate a cheque(签名出错就会使支票作废)。

(2) rescind:指废止一条法律或一项规章制度,并通过剥夺它们的权威性使之失去效力。例如，When issuing new regulations, a military headquarter may rescind earlier regulations governing the same subject（司令部在颁布新规定的同时，可以宣布以前的有关规定立即废止）。

该词可以与 repeal 互换使用。例如，He voted for the repeal of that law（他投票赞成废除那条法律）。

（3）avoid：也指撤销或废止合同，但用法有所不同。常用的短语是：to declare a contract avoided 或 to declare the avoidance of a contract（宣布撤销合同）。

constitute 构成，达到。例如，If it constitutes a crime, he shall be investigated for criminal responsibility according to law（构成犯罪的，依法追究其刑事责任）。

与该词意义相近的是 amount to，但是这个词的程度低一些，例如，If the seller's breach amounts to fundamental breach of contract, the buyer can declare the contract avoided（如果卖方的违约构成根本性违约，买方可以宣布撤销合同）。

be entitled to something 对某事享有权利。该词在法律英语中使用较多。例如，If the seller delivers the goods non-conforming with the contract, the buyer is entitled to money damages（如果卖方所交付的货物与合同不符，买方有权得到金钱赔偿）。

remedies 补救措施。例如，These remedies are available to both sellers and buyers（卖方和买方都有权使用这些补救措施）。

注意该词与下列词的区别：

（1）damages：损失。例如，money damages（金钱损失）。

（2）compensation：赔偿。例如，compensation for nominal damages（名义损失赔偿）。

ability 能力，合同法中主要指履约的能力。例如，ability to perform a contract（履行一个合同的能力）。

与此相关的词是 capacity，但意义不同。该词主要指行为方面的能力或资格。例如，capacity of marriage（结婚资格），capacity of action（诉讼能力），civil capacity of party（当事人的民事能力），capacity to contract（合同能力）。

correspond with 与……一致或相符。该词可与 conform to，in conformity with 等短语可以互换使用。例如，There is an implied term that the goods will correspond with the sample in quality（有一条默示的条款，即货物应与样品的质量相符）。The seller must deliver the goods in conformity with the contract（卖方必须交付符合合同的货物）。

■ Review Questions

1. What is meant by the term 'contract' in common law?
2. Explain the differences between an offer and an invitation offer, giving examples.
3. Briefly describe how the CISG attempts to resolve problems of 'battle of forms'.
4. Compare and contrast the provisions of the UCC and of the CISG on 'battle of forms'.

5. Outline main theories of the validity of ‘acceptance’.
6. List and explain, giving examples where possible, the general principles of remedies.
7. Briefly outline the remedies of the buyer and the seller respectively.
8. Under what circumstances will a court be reluctant to award specific performance? Why?
9. What criteria will be used to determine if a party has breached?
10. If nothing is said in the contract, where must the seller deliver the goods? When must delivery be made? Where and when must documents of title be turned over?
11. How does a court determine the amount of damages to be awarded in accordance with the CISG?
12. Outline and discuss the differences and similarities between ‘anticipatory breach of contract’ and ‘Exceptio non Adimpleti Contractus’.
13. How is ‘fundamental breach of contract’ defined in the CISG? Give two examples.
14. Define the term ‘liquidated damages’ and identify its main features.
15. What are the obligations of the buyer and the seller under the CISG?
16. Explain the rules of ‘passing of risk’ under the CISG, giving examples.
17. Compare and contrast the ‘excuses for non-performance’ systems of the common law and civil law.
18. Julie is moving to a better job in a different city and offers to sell her ‘surround-sound’ stereo system to Marcia for $900. Marcia says she will pay $800 for it. Julie says that is not enough. Marcia then says she will pay the original asking price of $900. Julie has since discovered that similar systems are selling for a lot more and asks you whether she has to sell to Marcia for $900. What would your advice to Julie be?
19. A (an American company) entered into a contract with B (a Japanese company). The contract provided that A delivers 1,000 personal computer housings by December 1 to B in Tokyo, for a total price of $50,000. On July 1, A faxed B that due to a rise in prices they could not deliver for less than $60,000. B replied that it would insist that A deliver at the $50,000 price. From July 1 through September, B could have bought the housings from other suppliers for $55,000 for December 1 delivery. On December 1, B covered and purchased the housings for $64,000 for delivery on February 1. Because of the delay until February 1 B suffered additional damages $2,000. What is the measure of B's damages? Was B under any duty to mitigate damages? Why or why not? (the answers must be done under the CISG)
20. X (a Chinese company) concluded, acting as an agent of Z (a Chinese factory), a contract with Y (an American company) to purchase ten machines. Upon the arrival

of the machines in Qingdao, the carrier handed over the machine to Z who showed a certificate by a municipal organ, failing to make the delivery to X who held the bill of lading but (the relevant businessman) was away in Guangzhou at a meeting. X sued Z for damages. Who should X sue for damages? Has the Property of the goods passed to Z? Was the carrier liable for the damages? What liabilities of X?

5 Chapter Five International Regulation of Electronic Commerce

■ **导读**

近年来,经济全球化和信息化的快速发展催生了电子商务的快速成长,成为推动当前世界经济增长的主要动力之一。同时,电子商务大大改变了传统的贸易方式,传统的相关法律制度面临着前所未有的挑战。本章简要介绍了电子商务的发展过程,对电子商务的主要法律问题和国际组织统一电子商务的工作进行了分析。从电子商务对日常生活的影响方面来看,我国的电子商务在世界上首屈一指,大大加快了我国的经济发展,释放发展活力,增进民生福祉。建议读者朋友认真阅读,为合理利用或有效规制如火如荼的电子商务做好准备。

The mid-1990s was heralded by politicians, economists, law makers and commercial entities as groundbreaking for the rapid worldwide development of the electronic commerce (hereafter 'E-commerce'). Information could now be freely circulated globally through computer networks provided people had the necessary skills and access to computer hardware and software and even mobile-phones. Creation of this open network imparted a new sense of living within a global community or a global village where people could be in constant touch regardless of spatial and temporal differences. The internet provides a ready platform for commerce to flourish—sellers could advertise their wares and services globally and buyers, businesses and consumers alike had access to products at competitive prices. Sellers could provide product information, prices, delivery terms, and interested parties could negotiate terms and conclude contracts electronically. Direct access to a potentially large customer base meant that sellers did not have to opt for the traditional methods for selling their products-for example, use of agents to market their products in distant lands. Equally, buyers did not have to go through agents to find suitable manufacturers of products they required.

E-commerce as one of the greatest emergences of new technology in recent decade raises new issues for policy makers, law makers and other stakeholders. This new technology is expected to have a wide and enormous economic impact due to its radical character such as its lack of geographic containment and national boundaries. Therefore, the worldwide use of E-commerce has to be regulated to keep a fine balance between the expected risks of the new technology and the opportunities created by it.

This chapter highlights some of the US, EU and China policies in respect of E-commerce and the legal harmonization of specific issues relating to E-commerce at the UNCITRAL, EU and ICC levels. It must be noted that the Internet raises a whole host of legal issues-for instance, the posting of pornographic and racist materials, data protection and intellectual property-related issues. These are not considered here since they are outside the scope of this book.

I. Definition of Electronic Commerce

E-commerce is the buying and selling of goods and services, or the transmitting of funds or data, over an electronic network, primarily the internet. These business transactions occur either as business-to-business, business-to-consumer, consumer-to-consumer or consumer-to-business. "UNCITRAL Model Law on Electronic Commerce with Guide to Enactment 1996" does not define E-commerce, but indicates that it includes "Data message" and "Electronic data interchange (EDI)." The former refers to information generated, sent, received or stored by electronic, optical or similar means including, but not limited to, electronic data interchange (EDI), electronic mail, telegram, telex or telecopy, and the latter means the electronic transfer from computer to computer of information using an agreed standard to structure the information. However, "UNCITRAL Model Law on Electronic Commerce" defines the term "commercial" widely to cover matters arising from all relationships of a commercial nature, whether contractual or not. Relationships of a commercial nature include, but are not limited to, the following transactions: any trade transaction for the supply or exchange of goods or services; distribution agreement; commercial representation or agency; factoring; leasing; construction of works; consulting; engineering; licensing; investment; financing; banking; insurance; exploitation agreement or concession; joint venture and other forms of industrial or business cooperation; carriage of goods or passengers by air, sea, rail or road.

E-commerce improves commercial efficiency, reduces the transaction cost greatly and also has changed tremendously the traditional business mode. First, transactional mode has changed revolutionarily. The intention of the parties involved in E-commerce is usually expressed by data messages rather than writing form in traditional business and the data messages transfer through electronic pathways in internet by computers instead of traditional post service. In addition, parts of trading performance in E-commerce can be fulfilled through internet, such as electronic payment, supply and delivery of virtual goods that replace traditional channels. Second, business activities become globalized more rapidly. E-commerce promotes, by resorting to international internet, trade activities globally, and link the traditional market and international market closely. Besides, the technology standards of E-commerce become more compatible and globalized. E-commerce has changed traditional writing documents into standard electronic data being transferred between all parties and result in an open business platform on which all parties contact on the basis of unified internet agreement (TCP/IP). And also identity authentication of parties and

Security is set up on this platform.

II. The Effects of E-Commerce on Commercial Relationships

A. Restructuring of Business Practices

The use of electronic technologies to organize, communicate, store, and process data is fundamentally changing the way in which companies transact business. Computer-to-computer linkages are not simply replacements for paper communications; they are contributing to internal the reorganization of a company's operations and the restructuring of its relationships with its trading partners.

For example, a manufacturer's computer may be programmed to monitor inventory needs during the manufacturing process and to issue purchase orders electronically when inventory levels decline to a certain level. This electronic purchase order is transmitted electronically to the supplier, whose computer can in turn immediately generate an electronic shipping order which is immediately filled by the supplier's warehouse. No individual need monitor or approve the transaction. Contracts are being entered into - and executed by computer. In a slightly different scenario, that of "quick response," a supplier's computer can be programmed to monitor its customers' inventory and generate an electronic shipping order for prompt shipment when the inventory dips below certain preestablished levels. No specific contract for the purchase of the goods will have been negotiated. Indeed in many respects, the boundaries between the computer systems of the supplier and the customer will become irrelevant as the operations of the supplier and customer become electronically integrated. Thus, the introduction of electronic communications technologies into the commercial sphere is drastically changing the way companies transact business and may call into question our legal framework for analyzing the creation and nature of enforceable commercial transactions.

B. Emergence of a New Industry

The second effect that the growth of electronic communications technologies has brought with it a new service industry composed of third party providers or value added networks. These providers or networks do more than merely transmit data. They "add value" by performing a wide variety of sophisticated functions such as protocol conversion; storage, transmission, and retrieval; format translation; message tracing, delivery notification and integration reports; record retention; implementation training and consultation; security enhancement; and database development. In turn, these companies move information among themselves for the benefit of their customers, creating an infrastructure or "electronic roadway" which is integral to an effective system of international electronic communications.

C. Emergence of a New Property

The third major impact of the advent and growth in the use of electronic media is the emergence of a new type of property with commercial value. In the past, the main types of international commercial transactions involved the sale, financing, transport, and payment for goods and services. Over the past few decades, we have seen a decline in the prominence of the goods-based contract in international commerce and a rise in the predominance of service contracts. In addition, we are beginning to see another change; the evolution of transactions in which the subject of the transaction is neither goods nor services, but rather, information. Today, virtually all of the information which is the subject of commerce is electronically processed, stored, and transmitted. Since information has become a highly prized and valuable commercial commodity in the information age, a reexamination of the nature of property rights and their application to this new species of property in the future is warranted.

Unfortunately, our law today lacks a coherent analysis of the rights in information as property. The recognition that information deserves protection will undoubtedly lead to additional administrative or legal controls, yet care must be taken so that the administrative or legal controls do not ultimately interfere with the use of electronic communications technologies as a means of transacting business internationally.

III. The Challenges of E-commerce to the Traditional Legal Systems

A. The Challenges

E-commerce presents at least the following tremendous challenges:

1. New Types of Legal Relations

The forms of transaction under traditional writing forms are comparatively simple. However, the substantive legal issues are most resolved by traditional legal branches, and the legal procedures become the core of E-commerce. More specifically, a variety of legal relations in terms of rights and obligations of the parties involved in E-commerce cannot be resolved by traditional legal branches such as whether the relevant data messages and electronic signatures are valid, the qualification and liability of authentication body in its issue and management of certificates. All these legal issues can hardly be solved by traditional legal branches.

2. Breakthroughs on Substantive Rules of Traditional Business

E-commerce as a means of expression exerts effects on forms of legal acts, but more one xecution of rights, fulfillment of obligations and undertake of liabilities. For instance, some civil acts of gross misunderstanding are revocable under circumstance of traditional business, but this is not possible in E-commerce. Generally, declaration of civil intentions should be regulated by the principles and systems of E-commerce rather than the legal requirements of traditional writing environment.

3. Close Integration of Science and Technology and Business Laws

Science and technology in E-commerce refers to modern information technology. Historically, the integration of science and technology issues and legal issues have never been more close than today. In E-commerce, the validity and force of more and more technical specifications are confirmed by laws, or directly become legal norms. For example, data signatures are accepted as electronic signatures in E-commerce. On the other hand, data messages and other technologies become more diverse in forms and will naturally be promoted and upgraded along with the rapid development of computing communication technology.

4. New Demands for the Unification of Business Norms and Rules

E-commerce is a product of the current economic and information globalization and also a driving force to promote the economic globalization and unification of international business law. Comparatively, legal globalization under the current international political conditions proves to be so complicated, but the realization of the unification of global norms and rules in E-commerce is feasible and necessary.

Internet is borderless. The legal issues of E-commerce are after all international business issues. As a result, the realization of the unification of global norms and rules in E-commerce is the natural requirements of E-commerce to the traditional legal systems. In other words, E-commerce calls for the creation of new legal rules for regulating E-commerce which inevitably leads to globalization.

5. Elimination of Boundaries between National Law and International Law in the E-commerce Legislature

E-commerce in the current world is mainly regulated by national laws though international law also is actively responsive to E-commerce. Most countries had a legal regime in place which governed such transactions on the national (as opposed to international) level. Because of their divergent legal cultures, these countries' legal regimes were at times contradictory. Thus, the challenge was to reconcile these existing divergent legal systems and develop an international framework which harmonized and uniformed the laws of the various nations. Because of their divergent legal cultures, these countries' legal regimes were at times contradictory. Thus, the challenge in the area of international electronic commerce is much more demanding. As of yet, none of the developing and developed countries, common law and civil law countries, and countries of different cultural and legal heritages, have developed a comprehensive legal structure governing electronic commerce. Accordingly, the challenge is to take countries of divergent economic capabilities, legal heritage, telecommunications infrastructures, and needs, and bring them together to develop common analyses of, and approaches to, problems never encountered previously. And the boundaries between national laws and international laws shall be gradually eliminated. The world of electronic commerce has moved and will continue to move ahead. The international law reform process needs to recognize these important commercial practices and facilitate international trade by providing a legal framework according to which parties may structure their contemporary business transactions.

B. The Fundamental Issues of E-commerce

1. Contracts

Three fundamental issues of E-commerce affecting a business are various but the most important are the validity and enforceability of its contracts, its rights and obligations in transactions (sales) and signatures. As mentioned, the Internet has expanded the potential geographic business market while reducing the cost of access. Contract formation and performance can be conducted over electronic media and can occur without using a single sheet of paper or a drop of ink. Since existing law rests upon a more limited business scope, physical documentation, and transactions involving more than electronic signals, an urgent need exists to adapt the law to reflect new business practices while retaining the predictability and authority of legislation and common law. E-commerce does not alter the substance of business contracts so much as it alters the process of agreement. For example, a magazine subscription purchase agreement will have the same terms regardless of whether it is made on a slip of paper, over the telephone, or on the Internet. The real issue is whether contract law will recognize that each process produces an equally enforceable agreement. In other words, will agreements made via the Internet receive the same protection under commercial and contract law as other types of contracts?

The Internet provides four principal processes by which parties may enter a contract: (1) e-mail, (2) listserv, (3) World Wide Web interfaces, and (4) electronic data interchange. While each process is similar to the others, subtle differences require that each receive separate legal attention. Additionally, many contracts will utilize a combination of these processes during negotiations and in the formation of a contract. A discussion of basic processes is the most rewarding approach for conceptualizing the electronic tools of commerce. First, electronic mail, or e-mail, is the most basic process used to form agreements. Simply stated, e-mail permits an individual to send an electronic message to another individual or group of individuals. Underlying the simple definition, however, is a complex mechanical process. To create an e-mail message, an individual writes a message and the computer breaks it down into a digital stream that is further disassembled by the computer's modem into analog tones. The tones are carried over communications links (usually telephone lines) to a computer network where the tones are reassembled into several digital "packets" that are each individually stamped with information concerning the content of the message, its level of confidentiality, time, and the identity of the sender and receiver. The packets are then transformed back into analog form. They are sent independently over the communications link and eventually arrive at the recipient's computer network, where they are reassembled and switched to a digital form readable by the recipient. Similar to letters sent through the postal system, e-mail is usually written and distributed by a person for another specific person or group. The contents of a message generally are personal and communication includes only the sender and recipient. E-mail messages can be "digitally signed" for authentication and verification purposes. Additionally, senders may "attach" other electronic files to an e-mail message that the recipient can view or use after opening the e-mail. The advantages of e-mail include ease of use, insignificant costs, direct communication, and ubiquity. Parties can use e-mail for business or commerce in a number of ways. Second, individuals may use listservs to form transactions. Listservs, or electronic bulletin boards, provide a forum for individuals to discuss particular topics by "posting" messages for others to read. A listserv provides a public forum for persons to communicate on a wide variety of subjects. By typing a message or attaching files, an individual creates a "post" for a listserv. The post is broken down by the individual's computer into analog pieces and transferred over communications lines to the listserv network. The listserv network computer reassembles the message and "posts" it to an electronic bulletin board with other messages from individuals. The posts are public and can be read by anyone who uses the listserv until the messages are purged after a given amount of time.

The third tool for Internet communications, including contract formation, is the World Wide Web. The Web is a graphical user interface (GUI) for intercommunication between a Web page and an individual who visits that page. On a basic level, an individual uses an Internet browser to type in a Web page address, and the browser displays the Web page. The individual can then "navigate" the site through links and buttons to access additional text and graphical material. On a technical level, the individual types in a Web page address, or uniform resource locator (URL), which the computer transforms into a binary code that is unique for a particular Web page. Using the URL to find where the Web page is located, the individual's computer contacts the Web page server over communications lines. Once contacted, the Web page's server transforms the page, written in hypertext mark-up language (HTML), into binary code "packets" that are transferred to the individual's computer to be reassembled. Web pages combine multimedia and the ability to intercommunicate. These characteristics not only permit a seller to provide product and service information, but also to communicate directly with potential buyers. Many electronic commercial Web sites include on-line purchase forms and permit payment over the Internet. The individual need only type personal information into specified fields and click on a "return" or "accept" button to complete the transaction. Transactions may include the purchase of physical goods such as luggage or clothing, or may involve the purchase of software or electronic files that are downloaded to the individual's computer immediately upon payment. For these transactions, negotiations are not common. Finally, transactions may occur electronically using EDI.

Having examined the processes by which electronic contracts operate, several conclusions emerge: (1) all communication is paperless and without a physical signature; (2) the identity of the parties to an electronic agreement is observable only by the information that each party provides about itself; (3) the mechanics of electronic contracts are all similar insofar as electronic communication disassembles messages into analog packets for transfer over communications lines.

2. Digital Signatures and Authentication

Just as writing contracts, parties should sign a contract with their full legal names to identify the parties and their intent to enter the contract that the writing purports to establish, an electronic contract also require (digital) signatures which serve to verify and authenticate messages.

The process of creating a digital signature is briefly as follows: to begin, assume that Buyer types a message on her computer that she will send to Seller. Buyer could send the message as it is, but a third party could intercept the message or even change its contents before Seller received it. Alternatively, Buyer could encrypt the message before she sends it to keep its contents secret and unchanged until Seller receives the message. To encrypt the message, Buyer's computer will use a complex mathematical formula (algorithm or "hash function"), or "key" to change the content of the message into an unintelligible string of symbols ("hash string"). Anyone attempting to intervene before Seller reads

Buyer's message will find only the incomprehensible hash string. Once Seller receives the message, he will decode or "unlock" the message using the same "key." This process is called "symmetric cryptosystem" or "private-key" encryption. Each party has both a "private-key," which is used only by a single individual, and a "public-key," which is available to others. The keys are mathematically related, but it is mathematically improbable to derive the private key from the public key that others can access.

Digital signatures promote authentication of sender identity, data integrity, and non-repudiation. First, digital signatures provide a process to determine who sends a communication and determine the identity of the sender. Second, digital signatures provide information about whether the message has been altered. Third, if a digital signature demonstrates that a message has not been altered and identifies the sender, the sender is unable to repudiate either the contents of the message or that it was sent by her. Essentially, these processes restrain problems of verifying and authenticating electronic communications.

Moving to international business transactions, the technological revolution has expanded the ability to communicate and interact across the globe. Problems arising domestically regarding electronic contracts (such as validity and signatures) are also of critical importance for international parties. The Internet and related electronic components are parts of a global media that spin an intricate web of connections useful for inducing and entering business deals. A potential solution to these dilemmas is the CISG. Promoting uniformity and "good faith in international trade," the CISG provides a substantial body of regulation for international sales contracts. A notable highlight is the CISG's permissive stance toward contracts not evidenced by writing. The CISG, however, applies only to goods and, moreover, presumes the parties are somewhat knowledgeable of the customs and practices of international law. Whereas the CISG abandons rigid rules by reliance on the strength of international custom and the presumption of sophistication of international traders, this reliance may not translate into a viable system of law to govern a vast subset of electronic contracts entered by everyday persons who have access to the entire world at their fingertips.

In conclusion, the growth in the use of electronic commerce in business transactions is picking up speed, and the urgent need for further new or revamped rules in contract law to cope with new electronic technologies is evident. UNCITRAL understood this challenge early on and is now in the forefront of work on the unification of rules in respect of formation of contracts and online arbitration. In this, it is fully supported by ICC, the European Union, WIPO, the Hague Conference on Private International Law and many professional circles.

It is also a fact that electronic commerce is rapidly gaining acceptance all over the world due to the many advantages it offers. That is why international legislation is needed to assist and facilitate its use. It should nevertheless be emphasized that both paper-based and electronic contracting will continue to be used side-by-side for quite some time to come. Since many developing countries still lack basic electronic facilities, the technological divide in the international community will not disappear overnight. In order to shorten the interval and narrow the gap, the developed countries and international organizations active in this area should consider ways and means of helping the developing countries (especially the least developed) to acquire the new technology (both appliances and know-how). Although this is obviously not a legal issue, it is very important and will benefit not only the developing countries but the developed world as well. It will naturally take time, but only once it is achieved may we expect true world-wide unification in the field of electronic commerce.

IV. International Measures to Harmonize the Legal Issues Relating to E-Commerce

The E-commerce has an enormous impact on the means of conducting international business in the last decade of the last century. As a result, the commercial world had direct access to a global marketplace and they could exploit it in an efficient and economically advantageous manner. Although politicians, policy makers and non-governmental organizations welcomed the E-commerce with open arms as providing an opportunity for raising the standards of living and providing a means of reducing the levels of poverty worldwide, the use of the information technology (IT) for conducting business and concluding contracts raises a number of legal issues-among them the formation of contracts. A number of international organizations set out to iron out the legal uncertainties and difficulties with the intention to promote E-commerce.

This part considers in brief the legislative measures of major trading partners-EU-in respect of E-commerce and the legal harmonization brought about through by models laws formulated by the well-known international organization UNCITRAL and the initiatives from other organizations such as the ICC.

A. UNCITRAL Legislative Measures

In order to bring about unification of any kind in the field of electronic commerce, certain obstacles must be removed with a view to achieving the legal validity of information sent by electronic means, typically through the Internet. UNCITRAL has played an important role in the contribution of the unification of E-commerce contract law.

1. The UNCITRAL Model Law on the Electronic Commerce

The increasing prominence of international E-commerce, and the need to establish rules for its conduct, has begun to attract considerable attention from the international legal community. National efforts to examine the issues have led to the development of numerous model interchange agreements to use in establishing electronic trading relations; current attempts are also underway to develop truly international model interchange agreements. One of the first attempts by the international organizations to harmonize and unify the practices resulted in the 1996 adoption of the UNCITRAL Model Law on the E-commerce. Originally, UNCITAL considered a report in 1985 (Recommendation on the Legal Value of Computer Records) which highlighted the legal problems associated with the use of computer-to-computer communications. The report focused on the writing requirement and signatures for the purposes of validity and enforceability of contract and recommended that governments review existing legal rules that required paper documentation or signatures as conditions for the validity or enforceability of a transaction with a view to amending them suitably to permit documents in computer-readable form. Then, UNCITRAL changed the Working Group on International Payments in 1988 into the Working Group on EDI and published UNCITRAL Model Law on International Credit Transfer in 1992. This Working Group aimed to form common legal framework facilitating EDI and also to include more modern methods of communication alongside EDI. Their work resulted in what we now know as the Model Law on Electronic Commerce (EC Model Law) which was published along with a Guide to the Enactment to be used as an aid to interpretation. In November 2005, UNCITRAL published the United Nations Convention on the Use of Electronic Communications in Electronic Contracts aiming to provide a practical framework for dealing effectively with electronic communications in international contracts. In 2017, UNCITRAL also issued the Model Law on Electronic Transferable Records which constitutes a useful addition to existing UNCITRAL texts in the area of electronic commerce by significantly assisting States in enhancing their legislation governing the use of electronic transferable records, or in formulating such legislation where none currently exists.

It must be noted that a model law does not have the same legislative weight as a convention and perhaps does not bring the same level of unification. But it has had worldwide impact and many legislations have either adopted it or drawn inspiration for their own law from it. The guiding principles of functional equivalence,[1] party autonomy and uniformity under the EC Model Law have been recognized and accepted by so many legislations. Let us take the principle of uniformity for an example: in order to achieve the stated objective of legal certainty, it is important that the EC Model Law is interpreted in a uniform fashion across jurisdictions. Inspired by Article 7 of the CISG, Article 3(1) of the EC Model Law provides that in its interpretation regard is to be had to its international origin and to the need to promote uniformity in its application and the observance of good faith.

The EC Model Law consists of two parts—Part I on E-commerce on general provisions such as definitions, interpretation, party autonomy, writing, signature, originals to data messages, and validity of messages, and Part II on carriage of goods.

The EC Model Law defines some important terms such as "Data message" as information generated, sent, received or stored by electronic optical or similar means including, but not limited to, EDI, electronic mail, telegram, telex or telecopy [Article 2 (a)]. Article 6(1) addresses the requirement of writing and provides that a data message where the information is accessible so as to be usable for subsequent reference would meet the requirement of writing.

Article 11 offers recognition of formation of contract by electronic means and its validity and states that contracts formed using messages shall not be denied validity or enforceability. Article 12 (1) provides that these messages be treated in the same manner as other conventional means of communication. In other words, parties can transact electronically with the certain belief that the transaction will not be denied legal effect or validity purely on the basis of nature of communication medium used. It must be noted that the EC Model Law gives freedom to the parties to agree otherwise in respect of Articles 11 and 12.

Practically the EC Model Law does at least two contributions to the development of E-commerce. First, it provides a series of international recognized norms of E-commerce to help remove legal barriers of E-commerce. Second, it offers "the Functional-equivalent Approach" as a simple and feasible legislative technique to national legislatures for E-commerce. This technique attempts to compare the functions of traditional legal regimes and E-commerce norms so as to bring it into the scope of traditional legal regimes.

---

[1] The "functional equivalent approach" means that electronic records can provide the same degree of security as paper and, in most cases, a much higher degree of reliability and speed, especially with respect to the identification of the source and content of the data, provided that a number of technical and legal requirements are met. (the Guide to Enactment appended to the EC Model Law)

2. UNCITRAL Model Law on Electronic Signatures

It is recognized extensively that the ability of the E-commerce can shrink space and time, bring people together without traversing long distances and create new marketplaces and to contribute to global economic growth. On the other hand, the E-commerce poses problems. Among them: can the electronic message be trusted? Does it originate from the person claiming to send it? Can the message be relied upon? How secure is the message, given that electronic documents can be easily manipulated? Is the received message the same as the message sent? What legal status does an electronically signed message have? Can a sender be held to his electronically communicated message should a dispute arise? Do electronic messages and electronic signatures meet the legal requirements of writing and signature?

Vulnerability of the electronic medium from external threats such as hacking, the introduction of viruses and worms, the use of computers for committing fraud and blackmail, and manipulation of computer-held material causes untold economic harm and adds a further layer of uncertainty. It has the potential to undermine the effectiveness and reliability of medium. There is no doubt that commercial transactions are fraught with risks, more so when they involve an international element. These vulnerabilities and legal uncertainties are sufficiently potent to act as a barrier to E-commerce with the result that policy makers both at the regional and international level have tried to address the problems through legislation. Therefore, a brief account is provided of the UNCITRAL Model Law on Electronic Signatures (ES Model Law) in 2001 relating to establishing the authenticity of the message and authentication of a message.

The professionals, as far back as the 1970s, were working on the confidentiality/integrity problems associated with electronic communications. The technology hailed as a digital signature is available and legislators rushed to pass legislation authorizing the use of this technology to meet the signature requirements prescribed by law. It was against this backdrop that UNCITRAL set out to work on its ES Model Law with the intention of harmonizing the law without resorting to the promotion of a specific technology. The following sections set out the founding principles of the ES Model Law and examine the main provisions.

(1) Founding principles

The ES Model Law presented four founding principles: harmonization and certainty, party autonomy, technology neutrality and non-discrimination and functional equivalence. The principle of harmonization and certainty is at the heart of the ES Model Law. Due to the shortcomings of international convention for achieving harmonization, UNCITRAL drafted the ES Model Law as a model law made by a body composed of government representatives and experts such as practitioners, and academics. Model laws do not share bureaucratic nightmares or rigidity, do not require the requisite numbers of ratification to come into force and states, while free to adopt the model law verbatim, may amend it to suit their needs, or use it as a framework for drafting their legislation. This level of flexibility increases the chance for widespread adoption, albeit at the cost of high degree of harmonization.

The ES Model Law preserves the principle of party autonomy to allow parties, in the absence of legal solutions to uncertainties, to a business transaction to agree to solutions in the contract. This principle is embodied in Art 5 which states that "... the provisions of this law may be derogated from or their effect may be varied by agreement, unless that agreement would not be valid or effective under applicable law." Articles 3, 6 and 12 specifically further reinforce the principle of party autonomy expressed by Article 5.

The ES Model Law is founded on the principle of technology neutrality as indicated by Article 3 which states that "... nothing in this law ... shall be applied so as to exclude, restrict or deprive of legal effect any method of creating an electronic signature that satisfies the requirements referred to in Article 6 (1) or otherwise meets the requirements of applicable law." The explanatory memorandum also makes clear that Article 3 "embodies the fundamental principle that no method of electronic signature should be discriminated against ... [and] ... the fundamental principle of non-discrimination is of general application" subject of course to the principle of party autonomy.

The ES Model Law adopts also a "functional equivalence approach" in drafting its legislation-an approach that extrapolates the functions of a paper document to create the criteria that need to be met by the paperless document for attaining a status equivalent to that of the paper document. [1]

(2) Interpretation

All laws need interpretation. The ES Model Law as part of the current drive towards harmonization and certainty includes also an interpretation provision inspired by Article 7 of the CISG. According Article 4, in interpreting the ES Model Law "regard is to be had to its international character and to the need to promote uniformity in its application and the observance of good faith". While the provision is rational in a global world promoting transnational law, it is difficult to assess what exactly is expected of a court or tribunal under Article 4. If legislation based on the ES Model Law become part of domestic law, are the courts expected to disregard rules of interpretation formulated and developed in

[1] Indira Carr, Peter Stone, International Trade Law, fourth Edition, Routledge Cavendish, New York, 2010, p. 129.

their legal system? Are they to disregard the interpretation of identical words in other domestic legislation? Are they to explore how courts in other jurisdictions interpret the provisions? Are the judgers expected to rid themselves of the conceptual framework derived from their own domestic law? In an ideal world, in aiming towards harmonization, it makes sense to leave the shackles created by sovereignty. There is however a gap between theory and practice as experience with the CISG. As a result, there is reluctance on the part of courts, regardless of the legal background, to refer to opinions from other jurisdictions as an aid to interpretation. In other words, arbitral tribunals and national courts naturally tend to interpret international norms and rules with resort to national legal traditions and interpretation methods (known as "Homeward Trend") which harms the goal of the CISG to attempt to achieve and even possibly ruin the CISG. [1]

(3) Nature and reliability of an electronic signature

As stated earlier, the UNCITRAL followed a "functional equivalence approach" for formulating both the Model Law for Electronic Commerce and ES Model Law. Article 2 (a) defines electronic signature as "data in an electronic form in, affixed to or logically associated with, a data message and indicate the signatory's approval of information contained in the data message." Data message refers to information that is sent, generated, received or stored by electronic, optical or similar means. It includes, but is not limited to, electronic data interchange, electronic mail, telegram, telex or telecopy.

The electronic signature could be a digital signature, a digitized image of a handwritten signature or based on biometrics such as a fingerprint or iris scan. For an electronic signature to be legally effective, the ES Model Law requires that electronic signatures meet the requirements of reliability in the light of all the circumstances including any agreement there might be between the parties. Reliability requirements for a legally effective electronic signature are stated in Article 6(3). First, the signature creation date must be linked to a signatory and no other person. Secondly, the signature creation data at the time of signing must be under the control of the signatory and of no other person, any alteration to the electronic signature after the time of signing is detectable, and where the legal requirement for a signature is for ensuring the integrity of the information to which it relates, any alteration made after signing is detectable. Issues such as whether the signature creation data is uniquely linked to or under the control of the signatory, or for

---

[1] Philip Hackney, "Is the United Nations Convention on the International Sale of Goods Achieving Uniformity"? 61 *La. L. Rev.*, 2001, p. 476; Paul B. Stephan, "The Futility of Unification and Harmonization in International Commercial Law", 39 *Va. J. In'l L.*, 1999, p. 760.

that matter, the question of whether any alteration is detectable after signing are technical issues and will depend on the technology and the mechanisms that have been put in place by the signatory and the certification service provider.

The ES Model Law makes room, in its Article 7, for the enacting state to designate a public or private authority to specify the types of electronic signatures that would meet the reliability criteria set out in Article 6, subject to the proviso that the recommended technology meets recognized international standards. The explanatory memorandum makes clear that the standard is not to be interpreted restrictively and is not confined to standards set by relevant international organizations. It includes trade usages, industry practices, recommendations from international organizations such as the International Chamber of Commerce (ICC) and UNCITRAL. [1]

Realising that the form of signature is very important for the development of electronic commerce, some international, regional and many national rules have been adopted on electronic signature. Thus, in 1999, the European Union adopted Directive 1999/93/EC on a Community framework for electronic signatures. Article 2 of this Directive provides that "electronic signature" means data in electronic form, which are attached to or logically associated with other electronic data and serve as a method of authentication. Article 5 contains a provision on the legal effect of electronic signatures. Many national laws have been adopted in recent years on electronic signatures. Most of these take into consideration pre-existing provisions contained either in UNCITRAL or European Community laws. The country that first started regulating electronic commerce was the United States of America, and it will come as no surprise that its Uniform Electronic Transactions Act (UETA) adopted in 1999 was seized upon as a basis for much international, regional and national unification of electronic commerce and, more specifically, of electronic signature. It is interesting to note, for instance, that, according to UETA, "electronic signature" means an electronic sound, symbol or process attached to or logically associated with a record and executed or adopted by a person with the intent to sign a record. Similarly, UETA provides a definition on "security procedure" employed for the purpose of verifying that an electronic signature, record or performance is that of a specific person or for determining changes or errors in the information in an electronic record. It further points out that: "the term includes a procedure that requires the use of algorithms or other codes, identifying words or numbers, encryption, or callback or other acknowledgment procedures."

Digital signatures promote authentication of sender identity, data integrity, and non-

[1] A/CN9/WG IV/WP 88, para. 130.

repudiation. First, digital signatures provide a process to determine who sends a communication and determine the identity of the sender. Second, digital signatures provide information about whether the message has been altered. Third, if a digital signature demonstrates that a message has not been altered and identifies the sender, the sender is unable to repudiate either the contents of the message or that it was sent by her. Essentially, these processes restrain problems of verifying and authenticating electronic communications.

The security that digital signatures provide has led to growing interest by numerous commercial industries seeking to exploit technology. A majority of states have adopted digital signature laws and others probably will follow suit upon introduction of UCITA, which "legitimizes" digital signatures for commercial contracts. The United States Congress has become involved, as well. The American Bar Association has published guidelines and promoted a national public-key system. Private companies, such as Verisign, Inc., are stepping forward as certification authorities to hasten the widespread use of E-commerce. Additionally, Intel has developed the Pentium microchips with embedded serial numbers that can be used in conjunction with digital signatures not only to authenticate communications, but also to determine the specific computer that sent the communication. Moreover, governmental agencies and industries are beginning to recognize the value of digital signature technology.

(4) Responsibilities of the parties

Article 2 of the ES Model Law envisages three parties taking part in the use and creation of an electronic signature: the signatory, who is the holder of the signature creation device; the third party (known as the certificate service provider) who plays a central role in adding integrity to the electronic signature by issuing certificates that confirm the link between the signatory and the signature creation date; and the relying party isa person that may act on the basis of a certificate or an electronic signature.

Article 8 provides the responsibilities of the signatory: (a) to exercise reasonable care to avoid unauthorized use of its signature creation data; (b) without undue delay, to utilize means made available by the certification service provider pursuant to Article 9 of this Law, or otherwise use reasonable efforts, to notify any person that may reasonably be expected by the signatory to rely on or to provide services in support of the electronic signature if: (i) the signatory knows that the signature creation data have been compromised; or (ii) the circumstances known to the signatory give rise to a substantial risk that the signature creation data may have been compromised; (c) where a certificate is used to support the electronic signature, to exercise reasonable care to ensure the accuracy and completeness of all material representations made by the signatory that are relevant to the certificate throughout its life cycle or that are to be included in the certificate.

From the explanatory memorandum, it appears that the life cycle of a certificate runs from the application to the revocation or expiry of a certificate. Applying the interpretation provision, it could be said that the signatory is expected to exercise good faith in making his material representations on the basis of which the certificate is issued.

Similarly, the certificate service provider has to meet a list of obligations under the provisions of Article 9(1) where the electronic signature used has a legal effect: (a) to act in accordance with representations made by it with respect to its policies and practices; (b) to exercise reasonable care to ensure the accuracy and completeness of all material representations made by it that are relevant to the certificate throughout its life cycle or that are included in the certificate; (c) to provide reasonably accessible means that enable a relying party to ascertain from the certificate: (i) the identity of the certification service provider; (ii) that the signatory that is identified in the certificate had control of the signature creation data at the time when the certificate was issued; (iii) that signature creation data were valid at or before the time when the certificate was issued; (d) to provide reasonably accessible means that enable a relying party to ascertain, where relevant, from the certificate or otherwise: (i) the method used to identify the signatory; (ii) any limitation on the purpose or value for which the signature creation data or the certificate may be used; (iii) that the signature creation data are valid and have not been compromised; (iv) any limitation on the scope or extent of liability stipulated by the certification service provider; (v) whether means exist for the signatory to give notice pursuant to Article 8, paragraph 1 (b), of this Law; (vi) whether a timely revocation service is offered; (e) where services under subparagraph (d) (v) are offered, provide a means for a signatory to give notice pursuant to Article 8, paragraph 1 (b), of this Law and, where services under subparagraph (d) (vi) are offered, ensure the availability of a timely revocation service; (f) to utilize trustworthy systems, procedures and human resources in performing its services.

As for the relying party, Article 11(a) places him under an obligation to verify the reliability of an electronic signature. Where it is supported by a certificate, he is to take "reasonable steps to verify the validity, suspension or revocation of the certificate and to observe any limitation with respect to the certificate" [Article 11(b)].

What happens if the actors do not meet the obligations set out in the ES Model Law? In Articles 8(2), 9(2) and 11, the ES Model Law provides that they will bear the legal consequences of their failure to exercise their respective obligations. While it is reasonable to impose obligations on the signatory and the certification service provider and expect them to bear the legal consequences, it is debatable whether this should extend to all members who fall within the class termed "relying party". Relying party could include not only big businesses but also small to medium sized enterprises and consumers. It is questionable whether small to medium sized enterprises, especially in developing countries, will have the expertise and personnel to take the necessary steps to verify the signatures. Given the ES Model Law is designed for global adoption, it is a pity that it has been drafted taking into account circumstances prevailing in developed countries. Therefore, regard should be had by the Working Group of UNCITRAL to the possibility of differential treatment for small to medium sized enterprises in developing countries.

Unfortunately, the ES Model Law failed to define what kind of consequences a breaching party will have to bear. Legal consequence could be criminal or civil liability, and the nature of liability could, for instance, be fines or damages. This open-ended attitude towards legal consequences introduces an element of surprise and uncertainty given the promotion of cross-border recognition of certificates and electronic signatures by the ES Model Law. A certification service provider might find that he is suddenly subject to unexpected liabilities of a foreign jurisdiction. Actually, the Working Group had initially planned to draft detailed rules in respect of the obligations of the various parties involved in an electronic signature. In the end, the Working Group did not persist in arriving at detailed rules since not all countries have the infrastructure or the capacity in the IT industry for adopting a self-regulatory scheme.

3. The United Nations Convention on the Use of Electronic Communications in Electronic Contracts

The modernization of contract law (sales, banking) now and in the near future is inconceivable without taking into account electronic commerce and its use in concluding sales contracts (business-to-business and business-to-consumers) and handling banking transactions, both domestic and international. Ten years ago in New York, at the 1992 UNCITRAL Congress devoted to "Uniform Commercial Law in the Twenty-first Century", there were many papers dealing with electronic data interchange. The familiar scenario of international transactions had changed dramatically, traditional types of international transaction such as sale, financing, and transport of goods were being transformed and services were overtaking international business transactions in importance. As one author stressed, electronic interchange now stood in the forefront of business transactions. The world had entered into the "information age" in which electronic information itself is the subject of commerce. These citations were expressed ten years ago and have proved over-modest in light of the almost unbelievable development of electronic technology and its practical application by the business community. Speaking of unification, the view was expressed at the UNCITRAL Congress that the "universal system may be built ... before the laws and attitudes of individual nations are too far developed and crystallized." This has turned out to be correct in much of UNCITRAL's unification work, since countries are far more readily persuaded to adopt new rules for new activities than to change the legal practices they established and used over long periods of time. It should not, however, be forgotten that electronic technologies affect not only contract law but many other areas of law as well, especially administrative law (raising issues of protection of privacy, for instance) as well as customs, taxation, etc. All this brings us to the conclusion that electronic commerce is emerging rapidly and the vision of very able scholars as expressed in 1992 is already being overtaken by the rapid development of electronic technologies and their application in all fields, especially in business transactions, both domestic and international.

The United Nations Convention on the Use of Electronic Communications in Electronic Contracts (The EC Convention) was adopted in November 2005 but it is not yet in force. The purpose of the EC Convention is to provide a practical framework for dealing effectively with electronic communications in international contracts. It adopts the functional equivalence approach adopted by the EC Model Law and includes a few substantive rules to ensure that electronic communications are effective. This Convention applies to the use of electronic communications in connection with the formation or performance of a contract between parties whose places of business are in different States. However, this Convention does not apply to electronic communications relating to any of the following: (a) contracts concluded for personal, family or household purposes; (b) transactions on a regulated exchange; foreign exchange transactions; inter-bank payment systems, inter-bank payment agreements or clearance and settlement systems relating to securities or other financial assets or instruments; the transfer of security rights in sale, loan or holding of or agreement to repurchase securities or other financial assets or instruments held with an intermediary. This Convention does not apply to bills of exchange, promissory notes, consignment notes, bills of lading, warehouse receipts or any transferable document or instrument that entitles the bearer or beneficiary to claim the delivery of goods or the payment of a sum of money.

The functional equivalence approach is also adopted by the EC Convention and in this it is no different from the EC Model Law. So contracts cannot be denied validity or enforceability on the basis that electronic communications were used. Further, the EC Convention allows for the possibility of electronic communications carried out by electronic agents (automated messages systems). Where such systems are used for electronic communications they are not to be denied validity or enforceability on the basis that no natural person reviewed them (Article 12).

Article 20 of the EC Convention tries to remedy the lack of specific provisions on electronic communications in contract formation or contract performance in other international conventions such as Convention on the Recognition and Enforcement of Foreign Arbitral Awards (New York, 10 June 1958), Convention on the Limitation Period in the International Sale of Goods (New York, 14 June 1974) and Protocol thereto (Vienna, 11 April 1980), the CISG, United Nations Convention on the Liability of Operators of Transport Terminals in International Trade (Vienna, 19 April 1991), United Nations Convention on Independent Guarantees and Stand-by Letters of Credit (New York, 11 December 1995), United Nations Convention on the Assignment of Receivables in International Trade (New York, 12 December 2001).

The provisions of this Convention apply further to electronic communications in connection with the formation or performance of a contract to which another international convention, treaty or agreement not specifically referred to in paragraph 1 of this article, and to which a Contracting State to this Convention is or may become a Contracting State, applies, unless the State has declared, in accordance with Article 21, that it will not be bound by this paragraph.

Where a state has ratified the EC Convention and is a contracting state, or is to become a contracting state to the listed conventions, the expectation is that the courts of the state will apply the EC Convention in relation to the electronic communications used in dealings that attract the application of the listed conventions. For instance, if two parties have entered an agreement to which the Vienna Convention applies and they enter into electronic communications in respect of, let's say, failure to deliver, and the forum state is also a party to the EC Convention, then Article 20 enables its application to those electronic communications. [1]

In conclusion, the global significance of E-commerce is a fact, and it is important that divergent approaches to legislation and the resulting uncertainties do not curtail the growth of E-commerce. One way to achieve legal certainty and predictability is to harmonize the laws, and undoubtedly UNCITRAL has played a central role in formulating model laws and conventions for both electronic commerce and electronic signatures, but it is not sufficiently comprehensive to achieve the desired level of harmonization. What may be core provisions such as the issue of liability and burden of proof are left to be addressed by national law.

---

〔1〕 Indira Carr, Peter Stone, International Trade Law, fourth Edition, Routledge Cavendish, New York, 2010, p. 123.

B. The EU Directive on E-Commerce

The EU Directive on E-Commerce (E-Commerce Directive) was adopted on 8 June 2000. Compared with the EC Model Law, some provisions deal with contractual matters, but its major focus is the free movement of information society services amongst member states and the protection of online consumer. It states "... the first objective is to build trust and confidence ... both consumers and businesses must be confident that their transaction will not be intercepted or modified, that the seller and buyer are who they say they are and that transaction mechanisms are available, legal and secure ... The second objective is to ensure full access for electronic commerce to the single marketplace" (at paras 35 – 38).

As with the EC Model Law, the E-Commerce Directive does not provide a definition of E-commerce because it is unlikely to be sufficiently progressive to accommodate new developments to the electronic marketplace. However, Article 1(3) does indicate the kind of information society services that would fall outside its scope: the activities of notaries or equivalent professions to the extent that they involve a direct and specific connection with the exercise of public authority, the representation of a client and defense of his interests before the courts, and gambling activities which involve wagering a stake with monetary value in games of chance, including lotteries and betting transactions.

It is clear from the above exclusions that the E-Commerce Directive includes a wide range of activities-from sale of goods, accountancy services, and medical services to legal services-that would be on offer, for instance, on the Internet.

Since the information service provider is likely to market his services or goods on the Internet in a variety of ways-for example, advertisements-the provider is required to meet certain transparency requirements set out in Article 6. The commercial communication[1] has to be clearly identifiable as such and the natural or legal person on whose behalf the commercial communication is made shall be clearly identifiable as such. Where promotional offers or promotional competitions are the subject matter of the communication, then they should be clearly identifiable as such and the conditions must be easily accessible, and presented clearly and unambiguously.

Article 9 addresses the issue of legal recognition of electronic transactions. It requires member states to ensure that "legal requirements applicable to the contractual process neither create obstacles for the use of electronic contracts nor result in such contracts being

[1] Defined in Article 2(f) as: ... any form of communication designed to promote, directly or indirectly, the goods services or image of a company, organization or pursuing a commercial, industrial or craft activity or exercising a regulated profession.

deprived of legal effectiveness and validity on account of their being made by electronic means".

The E-Commerce Directive confirms that the Internet Service Providers play an important role by providing access to communication networks and also in hosting of web pages, but it also emphasizes the liability of the Internet Service Providers for the content of the messages that travels through their networks or are hosted on their website. In other words, the Internet Service Provider should be liable for the illegal content of the information if the intention is to ensure the growth of E-commerce. On the other hand, Article 12 makes clear that mere conduits are not liable for the information transmitted as long as the provider does not initiate the transmission, does not select the receiver of the transmission or does not select or modify the information contained in the transmission. Article 15 states clearly that a provider is not under a general obligation to monitor information that is transmitted or store by them. Neither is there an obligation to positively seek facts or circumstances indicating illegal activity. The provider, under Article 14 (3), however, is subject to injunctive relief that may be ordered by a court or administrative authority.

C. The International Chamber of Commerce Initiatives

The first attempt by the international electronic data interchange community to harmonize and unify its practices resulted in the 1987 adoption of the Uniform Rules of Conduct for Interchange of Trade Data by Tele-transmission (UNCID) by the International Chamber of Commerce. Set forth in the form of non-mandatory rules which users of electronic communications technology and suppliers of network services can by reference incorporate into their communication agreements, UNCID covers such issues as: the required care for transferring and receiving messages; identification of the parties throughout the communications process; acknowledgement of receipt of a message, if requested; verification of the completeness of a received message; protection of commercial information exchanged; and, the maintenance of records on the transmission and storage of data. The ICC's activity has provided guidance for a number of other groups. For example, the Commission of the European Communities, through its Trade Electronic Data Interchange Systems ("TEDIS") programme established in 1987, has conducted research into the legal issues inhibiting the development of EDI trade in the European Community. It has identified three principal legal impediments to the development of EDI: (1) requirements of paper documents; (2) problems of evidence; and, (3) problems determining when a transaction is effected through the use of EDI. In its second phase of operations, the TEDIS programme is concentrating on the appropriate response to these legal problems.

The International Chamber of Commerce is also a keen participator in the promotion of E-commerce. The Uniform Rules on Conduct for Interchange of Trade Data by Teletransmission (UNCID) published in 1987 was widely accepted. UNCID however was specifically designed for closed networks and was insufficient for establishing trust and reliability in open networks. The ICC therefore set out to work on international guidelines for E-commerce on the open network. This resulted in the publication of General Usage for International Digitally Ensured Commerce (GUIDEC) in 1997 and a subsequent document GUIDEC II in 2001. It provides a statement of best practices for adoption by businesses to promote trust in E-commerce by focusing on issues such as authentication devices, certification policies, public key certificates and record keeping. Besides, ICC set up Electronic Trade Practices Working Group (ETP) which aims at drafting basic rules of E-commerce and creating solutions accordingly, and work to provide E-terms service to promote simplified trade terms for E-commerce.

In conclusion, many international and national organizations are engaged in drafting legal rules with a view to helping electronically conducted international business transactions to be recognized as valid. A key role in the international regulation of commercial (contract) matters is played by UNCITRAL, but there are many others that have contributed to the unification of rules relating to electronic commerce (especially to digital signature and recognition of electronic messages as valid evidence in any proceeding, provided that certain rules and conditions are observed): the European Union, the International Chamber of Commerce (ICC), the Comité Maritime International (CMI) and the UN Economic Commission for Europe (ECE). A special body exists within the ECE (CEFACT— the erstwhile Center for Facilitation of Procedures and Practices for Administration, Commerce and Transport, now renamed Center for Trade Facilitation and Electronic Business) which co-operates successfully with WTO, the World Customs Organization (WCO), Organization for Economic Co-operation and Development (OECD) and the World Intellectual Property Organization (WIPO). Obviously, under the legal governance and with the extensive hard-workings by those national and international organizations, the E-commerce will contribute more to the development of the welfares of the whole world.

Case 5 – 1 Khoury v. Tomlinson

United States of America: Texas: Court of Appeals,

1st Dist. No. 01 – 16 – 00006 – CV, 30 March 2017

Relating to the UNCITRAL Model Law on Electronic Signatures (2001) (MLES)

Facts: An investor and a president of a company entered into an oral agreement relating to the repayment of money invested in the company. One week after the conclusion of the agreement, the investor sent an email to the president listing the terms of their agreement and requesting confirmation of those terms. The president replied with an email writing "We are in agreement". The name of the president did not appear in the body of that email, but it appeared in the "from" field. As the repayments were not made, the investor sued the president of the company for violations of the Securities Act, common law fraud and breach of contract due to the failure to repay the loan pursuant to the terms of the e-mail exchange between the parties. The first instance decision was partially favourable to the president of the company. The investor appealed.

Issue: Does the name of email address in the "from" field constitute a signature?

The Statute of Frauds, enacted in the Business and Commerce Code of Texas, requires a promise to answer for a debt to be signed by the debtor in order to be enforceable. The Court of Appeal had to decide whether the name or email address in the "from" field constitutes a signature for purposes of the Statute of Frauds.

The Court identified the Texas Uniform Electronic Transactions Act, which is an enactment of the Uniform Electronic Transactions Act ("UETA"), as the law applicable to the case. UETA is a piece of uniform legislation influenced by the UNCITRAL Model Law on Electronic Commerce ("MLEC") and the principles on which it is based. The Court made reference to the general principle of non-discrimination against the use of electronic means contained in the Texas UETA [§ 322.007(a) of the Business and Commerce Code of Texas, similar to art. 5 MLEC]. The Court also made reference to the definition of electronic signature as "an electronic sound, symbol, or process attached to or logically associated with a record and executed or adopted by a person with the intent to sign the record" [§ 322.002(8) of the Business and Commerce Code of Texas; compare art. 2(a) MLES]. The court explained that a name or email address in a "from" field is a symbol logically associated with the email. Moreover, the Court noted that emails were a common and legitimate practice for exchanging commercial documents, including settlements.

Decision: The court concluded that a "from" field performed the same authenticating function as a signature block in an email and that both signature methods satisfied the requirement of a signature under the Texas UETA. After additional consideration of the fact that, by sending the email with the "from" field, the sender intended to authenticate the email, the Court concluded that the evidence was sufficient to establish that the president of the company had signed the email and that the signed email satisfied the Statute of Frauds. [1]

■ Notes

Electronic commerce 电子商务。含义接近的英文词语还有 Electronic Business, Electronic Trade, Electronic Transaction, Cybershoping 等。电子商务指利用现代计算机技术通过电子信息网络所进行的商务活动。由于电子商务越来越深刻地改变着传统商务模式,对建立在纸面形式基础之上的传统法律制度构成多方面挑战,自然产生了诸多法律问题。其中主要的是,如何确定一条电子信息是否构成要约或承诺?当事人之间因电子交易形式的使用是否引起的权利义务关系?有关数据电文是否有效?电子签名是否有效?认证机构的资格如何确定及它在证书的颁发与管理中应承担何种责任问题,等等。

One-Key or Symmetric cryptosystem 单钥或对称密码体制或单钥。一般认为,这是指加密密钥和解密密钥为同一密钥的密码算法。因此,信息的发送者和信息的接受者在进行信息的传输与处理时,必须共同持有该密码(称为对称密码)。通常,使用的加密算法比较简便高效,密钥简短,破译极其困难。由于系统的保密性主要取决于密钥的安全性,在公开的计算机网络上安全地传送和保管密钥是一个严峻的问题。

■ Important Legal English Usages

Interpretation 解释。该词在法律英语中使用十分广泛。例如,The Catholic interpretation of the Bible is slightly different(天主教对圣经的解释略微有些不同),legal interpretation(法律解释)。一般地说,虽然该词可以用于多个方面,但主要用于法律解释。

主要与下列近义词在用法上的不同:

(1) construe:指在正式场合下的解释。例如,Please do not construe this as any criticism of yourself(请别把这理解为对你的批评)。该词也可以用在法律解释方面,但并不多见。

(2) explain:多指在日常生活中对某些事情做的说明和解释,极少用于法律解释方面。例如,The doctor explained the risks to me before the operation(手术前医生向我说明了手术前的风险);I will try to explain how a car engine works(我会试着解释一下汽车引擎的工作原理);You'll have to explain yourself more clearly(你得把自己的意思表达得更清楚一些)。

(3) account for:主要指对自己应该负责的事情予以解释。例如,You will be brought

---

[1] https://documents-dds-ny.un.org/doc/UNDOC/GEN/V19/104/22/PDF/V1910422.pdf? OpenElement, visit on 31 December, 2019.

before the disciplinary panel to account for your behavior (你将被带到纪律委员会面前对你的行为做出解释)。

Review Questions

1. Briefly define "E-commerce" and state its main characteristics compared with traditional trade based on paper documents.
2. What is meant by the term "authentication"? And outline its relevant legal issues.
3. Explain the functional equivalence approach, giving examples where possible
4. Briefly describe the challenges of E-commerce to the Traditional Legal Systems, giving examples.
5. What are the responsibilities of the parties under Article 2 of the ES Model Law? Giving examples.
6. Please make a brief comment on the United Nations Convention on the Use of Electronic Communications in Electronic Contracts (The EC Convention).

6 Chapter Six Carriage of Goods by Sea and Marine Cargo Insurance

■ 导读

本章讲授的是货物海上运输及保险，主要包括航次租船合同、定期租船合同、光船租船合同、提单及其法律问题、海上货物保险等内容。当前的国际货物买卖中的大多数货物还是依靠海上运输，由于这方面的法律及国际惯例十分复杂和混乱，读者必须认真学习。其中最重要的内容是提单及其相关法律问题。在国际货物运输及保险中，提单是最重要的文件，其涉及的问题最多、最复杂，自然成为纠纷最多的领域。因此，希望读者在这方面多下工夫。

The last chapter examined the legal relationship between the seller and buyer in a contract for the international sale of goods. We introduced some basic concepts about contracts of sale of goods. This chapter discusses the liability of the carrier for damage or loss to cargo while it is in transit. Due to the fact that most of the goods in today's international business practices are transported by ocean vessels, this chapter addresses the following subjects: (1) the liability of international sea carrier, (2) bills of lading, and (3) selected issues in maritime and marine cargo insurance law.

I. Charterparties

There are two types of contract of carriage by sea. They are: contracts contained in a charterparty; and contracts evidenced by a bill of lading.

The charterparty is a contract whereby the charterer hires a ship from the shipowner. Three types of charterparties are in use: the voyage charterparty, the time charterparty, and the charterparty by demise.

A. Voyage Charterparties

When a charterer hires a ship and its crew for the carriage of goods from one place to another, the charterer and shipowner have entered into a voyage charterparty. Under the terms most commonly used in such a contract, the owner agrees to provide the ship at a named port at a specified time and to carry the goods to the contracted destination. The charterer agrees to provide a full cargo and to arrange for its loading at an agreed-upon time.

In the charterparty both the port of loading and the port of discharge must be mentioned, although the charterer may be given power to order the ship to proceed to any port within the limits named in the charterparty.

1. The Implied Terms

The law implies the following three terms into every voyage charter: that the ship is seaworthy; it shall proceed with reasonable dispatch; and that there should be no unjustifiable deviation.

2. Lay Days and Demurrage

When the ship is an arrived ship and the shipowner gives the charterer notice of readiness, the lay days begin to run. Notice of readiness to load must always be given, though it may be given orally, but notice of readiness to discharge is not required unless so stated in the charterparty.

The lay days are the time specified in the charterparty for loading or unloading. If the charterparty does not fix the lay days, the charterer must load and unload the cargo within a reasonable time. The charterparty sometimes specifies as lay days "working days" or "weather working days."

If the lay days are exceeded and the ship is detained longer in the port of loading or unloading than agreed in the charterparty, demurrage is payable by the charterer to the shipowner.[1]

B. Time Charterparties

Under a time charterparty the charterer engages the use of a vessel for a stated period of time. The charterer normally pays "hire" monthly, and the shipowner will be entitled to withdraw the ship from the charterer's use if a monthly installment is not paid promptly.

The charterer has the right to direct the ship to proceed to wherever it is needed. Ordinarily, the only limitation on this right is the charterer's promise to engage only in lawful trades, to carry only lawful goods, and to only direct the vessel to safe ports. If the shipowner attempts to interfere with the charterer's use of the vessel, he will be in breach of the charterparty.

C. Charterparties by Demise

Under this type of charterparty, known in American law as bare boat charterparty, the charterer obtains possession and control of the ship and puts in his own master and crew, who are his employees. Such charterparties are not frequently used in the ordinary

---

[1] Demurrage: A charge made by a shipowner when a charterer keeps a ship idle for more than the agreed-upon lay days.

trade, but they are often used in the oil tanker trade.

II. Bills of Lading

A bill of lading is an instrument issued by an ocean carrier to a shipper with whom the carrier has entered into a contract for the carriage of goods,[1] which states that certain goods have been shipped on a particular ship or have been received for shipment. It sets out the terms on which those goods have been delivered to and received by the shipowner. On being signed by or on behalf of the carrier, it is handed to the shipper.

A. Laws of Bills of Lading

The law regarding an ocean carrier's liability for damage or loss to cargo is rooted in the history of transportation and trade. As goods moved across the high seas on sailing ships, they were under the exclusive control of the ship's captain for months at a time. Shippers had no way of proving that goods were lost or destroyed as a result of a natural disaster, the pilferage of theft. As a result, the maritime laws of both England and the United States held carriers to be absolutely liable for all loss or damage to cargo in their possession. With the growth of trade and the advent of steamships, carriers became more economically powerful. They began to include provisions in their bills of lading that would limit their liability. These limitation-of-liability clauses attempted to free the carrier from all responsibility, including liability for its own negligence or even for providing an unfit vessel. The small shippers were at the mercy of the steamship companies. The result was a period of great uncertainty over the liability of ocean carriers.

1. The Harter Act

In order to remove the uncertainty over the liability of ocean carriers, the U. S. Congress in 1892 first addressed the problem in the *Harter Act*, a federal law still in effect today. This act set out the liability of a carrier for the care of its cargo, and imposed restrictions on the use of exculpatory clauses in bills of lading. Subsequent developments in the law have resulted in the Harter Act's limited application. Today, the Harter Act remains applicable to contracts for the carriage of goods only from one U. S. port to another U. S. port.

2. The Hague Rules

At the end of the first World War, other nations attempted to develop similar rules.

---

[1] Article 71 of China Maritime Code defines a bill of lading as a document which serves as an evidence of the contract of carriage of goods by sea and the taking over or loading of the goods by the carrier, and based on which the carrier undertakes to deliver the goods against surrendering the same. A provision in the document stating that the goods are to be delivered to the order of a named person, or to order, or to bearer, constitutes such an undertaking.

The result was the near universal acceptance of a 1924 international convention on bills of lading known as the *Hague Rules* (the International Convention for the Unification of Certain Rules of Law Relating to Bills of Lading). This is an international regulation which aimed at reconciling the interests of the shipowners, cargo owners and insurers promoted with the assistance of the Maritime Law Committee of the International Law Association. This treaty is known both as the 1921 Hague Rules—because they were originally proposed by the International Law Association at a meeting at The Hague in 1921—and the Brussels Convention of 1924—because they were recommended for adoption at a diplomatic conference held in Brussels in 1924.

3. The Hague-Visby Rules

Ever since the Hague Rules came into force, many shippers especially smaller shippers from developing counties began to complain the Hague Rules about its excessive limitations to carrier's liability. This resulted extensive revision on the Hague Rules in 1968, known as the Hague-Visby Rules. Up till now, only a few countries have adopted the Hague-Visby Rules.

4. The Hamburg Rules

Chiefly because many shippers and cargo owners still complain the Hague-Visby Rules about its partiality to the interests of carriers, the United Nations in 1978 completed drafting a new Convention on the Carriage of Goods by Sea, known as the Hamburg Rules. These rules are different from the Hague Rules. They do not relieve the carrier for errors in navigation or in the management of the ship, and they make ocean carriers liable for losses resulting from negligence. They also make it easier for cargo owners to win their cases against carriers. These rules were drafted by the United Nations to serve the interests of cargo owners and shippers in developing countries that do not have large carrier fleets. As a result, these rules have been ignored by all of major maritime states. Only a few countries have adopted these rules.

5. Maritime Code of the People's Republic of China

Maritime Code of the People's Republic of China (hereafter called China Maritime Code) was, after more 40 years of revisions and modifications, adopted at the 28th Meeting of the Standing Committee of the Seventh National People's Congress on November 7, 1992, and came into force on July 1, 1993. China maritime code has transplanted into it a number of important international conventions. For example, Chapter IV (Contract of Carriage of Goods by Sea) is in principle based on the Hague-Visby Rules and the Hamburg Rules, and Chapter X (General Average) has adopted some rules from the *York-Antwerp Rules*. Thus, China maritime code is one of the best maritime laws in the world.

B. Characteristics of the Bills of Lading

The bill of lading has three characteristics: (a) it is a receipt issued by or on behalf of the carrier whereby he acknowledges that he has shipped the goods or received them for shipment; (b) it evidences the terms of the contract of carriage which is normally concluded earlier; (c) it is a document of title.

1. The Receipt Character

The receipt which the carrier gives the shipper may either acknowledge that he has "shipped" the goods in a named ship, or it may acknowledge that he has "shipped" the goods in a named ship, or it may acknowledge that he has "received the goods for shipment." The carrier can issue a "shipped" bill only if he has actually loaded the goods on board the vessel. Bills certifying that the goods have been properly loaded on board are known as "on board bills of lading," or clean bills. [1]

Should there be a discrepancy between the goods loaded and the goods listed, the statement on the bill is considered *prima facie* evidence that the goods were received in the condition shown in any dispute between the shipper and the carrier. Nevertheless, the carrier can, if it is able, introduce evidence to rebut this evidence. However, once the bill is endorsed and negotiated to a third party, this is no longer the case. An endorsee's knowledge of the goods is limited to what is on the bill of lading. For this reason, the Hague and Hague-Visby Rules hold that the bill is conclusive evidence as to the goods loaded once the bill has been negotiated in good faith to a third party. The carrier is then barred from introducing evidence to contradict the bill of lading.

From the point of view of the buyer, a "shipped" bill of lading is more valuable than a "received for shipment" bill of lading because, if he receives the former type of bill, he knows that the goods are in transit to their destination.

If payment has to be made under a letter of credit, the nominated bank will refuse to accept a "received for shipment" bill of lading, unless expressly instructed by the applicant of the credit to accept such a bill.

2. Evidence of the Contract of Carriage by Sea

The contract of carriage by sea is normally concluded before the carrier issues the bill of lading. The contract is made when the goods are accepted by agents of the carrier for loading or even earlier, when shipping space is reserved. The bill of lading is issued only when the ship leaves port. But the bill normally contains the terms of the contract of carriage. It is the evidence of those terms.

---

[1] Clean bill of lading is a bill of lading indicating that the goods have been properly loaded on board the carrier's ship.

3. The Bill of Lading as a Document of Title

This is the most important characteristic of the bill of lading. Its significance is that the carrier need deliver the goods only if an original bill of lading is presented to him. The bill of lading is thus "the key to the goods." If on arrival of the vessel there is nobody to tender an original bill of lading, the master would be entitled to unload the goods into a warehouse and to sail away. [1]

Special emphasis must be made to the fact that the term "document of title" in China is traditionally translated as "document of property" (物权凭证). This incorrect Chinese translation easily has confused in China a correct understanding of the term "document of title." Benjamin said in his "Sale of Goods" that there is no authoritative definition of "document of title to goods" at common law, but it is submitted that it means a document relating to goods the transfer of which operates as a transfer of the constructive possession of the goods, and may operate to transfer the property in them. The English Factors Act 1889 defined that the expression "document of title" shall include any bill of lading, dock warrant, warehouse-keeper's certificate, and warrant or order for the delivery of goods, and any other document used in the ordinary course of business as proof of the possession or control of goods, or authorizing or purporting to authorize, either by endorsement or by delivery, the possessor of the document to transfer or receive goods thereby represented. [2] Clearly, a bill of lading is "document of possession" rather than "document of property."

The view that a bill of lading is document of possession accords with the practices of the carriage of goods by sea, and helps reduce transportation costs and promote international trade. For example, a carrier is usually concerned about whether the consignee is the holder of original bill of lading, rather than the owner of the goods. Even if two or more holders tender the bill of lading to the carrier, the carrier has the right to deposit the goods for the court to decide the real holder, and he does need to determine who is the owner of the goods.

The bill of lading differs from the bill of exchange. The bill of lading is the representation or symbol of the goods to which it refers. Strictly speaking, the bill of lading is not a negotiable instrument. Unlike transferees of bills of exchange, a transferee who obtains an order bill of lading in good faith and for value paid is not a holder in due course who is entitled to claim the goods from the carrier "free of equities" or "free of

---

[1] Clive M. Schmitthoff, Mercantile Law, London Stevens & Sons, 1984, p. 576.

[2] Yang Liangyi, Bill of Lading and Documents, the Publishing House of the China University of Politics and Law, p. 7.

personal defenses." This is a significant difference. In practice, it means that should an order bill of lading be obtained by fraud and endorsed to a bona fide purchaser for value, the recipient will not acquire title to the goods described in the bill. On the other hand, if the same thing were to happen with a bill of exchange that was neither overdue nor dishonored, the recipient (who would be a holder in due course) would be entitled to the money or property described in that bill. Because of this difference, an order bill of lading is sometimes described as only a "quasi-negotiable" instrument. [1]

C. Transfer of Property under a Bill of Lading

As we discussed above, the transfer of the bill of lading does not mean the transfer of the property in the goods in transit. There are usually two ways to transfer the property in the goods under a bill of lading.

1. The Intention of the Parties

Whether transfer of the bill of lading also transfers property in the goods, depends on the intention of the parties. Where the seller of goods transfers the bill of lading to the buyer, the intention of the parties will normally be that the title to the goods shall pass to the buyer. If the bill is negotiable, the buyer may then further transfer the bill to a repurchaser, and so forth, and the title to the goods which are in transit, may thus pass from hand to hand by transfer of the bill of lading. But the intention of the parties may also be not to pass property in the goods. For example, a seller may endorse a bill of lading to his agent in the port where the goods are to be discharged so that the agent can deal directly with a particular buyer. Because the seller did not intend to pass property to the agent by his endorsement, property would not pass. A negotiable bill of lading is a bankable document. It may be accepted by a bank as collateral security for a loan. In this case the intention of the parties, when transferring the bill of lading to the bank, is only to create a pledge or lien on the goods in favor of the bank.

2. Lex loci (The Law of the Place Where the Goods Are Located)

If the parties fail to agree upon the transfer of the property in the goods, many countries usually determine the transfer of the property through Lex loci, mostly *lexfori* (the law of the place where court is situated).

D. Carrier's Duties under A Bill of Lading

A carrier transporting goods under a bill of lading is required by the Hague and Hague-Visby Rules to bear many duties, of which the most important two are (a) to exercise due diligence to the ship seaworthy, before and at the beginning of the voyage,

---

[1] Ray August, Don Mayer and Michael Bixby, International Business Law, Six Edition, Pearson Education Limited, 2013, p. 633.

and (b) to exercise due diligence to properly and carefully loading, handling, stowing, carrying, keeping, caring for, and discharging the goods carried.

1. To Exercise Due Diligence to the Ship Seaworthy, before and at the Beginning of the Voyage

Two important terms here must be explained:

(1) Due diligence. Diligence (diligentia in Roman law) originates from Roman law where diligence is divided briefly into two types: diligentia exactissima (Latin: extraordinary diligence) and diligentia quam suis rebus (Latin: ordinary diligence). "The texts distinguish two standards of diligence, a higher and a lower. The higher is the diligence which the good father of a family habitually exhibits in his own affairs (diligentia exactissima). The lower is the diligence which the person in question exhibits in his own affairs (diligentia quam suis rebus). This may, in fact, reach a high degree of diligence or it may not. But, at least, where this standard is applied nothing extraordinary is expected. It is a concrete standard. It is enough that the person in question pursues his normal course. According to a traditional terminology, there the first standard is applied, there is said to be liability for culpa levis in abstracto (Latin: slight negligence in the abstract); in the second case there is liability for culpa levis in concreto—slight negligence in the concrete."[1]

Generally, due diligence refers to the diligence reasonably expected from, and ordinarily exercised by, a person who seeks to satisfy a legal requirement or to discharge an obligation. A failure to exercise due diligence may sometimes result in liability, as when a broker recommends a security without first investigating it adequately. However, there is no in maritime law an authoritative definition to due diligence. We can grasp the main idea of this term from the well-known cases: in the case G. E. Dobell &. v. Steamship Rossmore Company Ltd. (1895) 2 Q. B. 408, the Lord Esher said: "It is obvious to my mind ... that the words of the 3rd section which limit the owner's liability if he shall exercise due diligence to make the ship in all respects seaworthy, must mean that this is to be done by the owner by himself or the agents whom he employs to see to the seaworthiness of the ship before she starts out of that port ..." Kay also said: "... It seems to me to be plain on the face of this contract that what was intended was that the owner should, if not with his own eyes, at any rate by the eyes of proper competent agents, ensure that the ship was in a seaworthy condition before she left port, and that it is not

[1] R. W. Lee, The Elements of Roman Law, 4th ed, 1956, p. 288.

enough to say that he appointed a proper and competent agent."[1]

The "Amstelslot" (1963) 2 Lloyd's Rep. 223 is an important case to show that the carrier has already exercised his due diligence. The lord Eventide said: "It is clear on the evidence that the examination made in fact of the 'Amstelslot' was in all respects in accordance with the standard generally applied to ships of the same kind on a continuing survey and was founded on the skill and experience of Lloyd's Register of shipment. If, therefore, there was no lack of care in so examining the ship ... it would appear to follow that the appellants (shipowner) satisfy the burden of proving that due diligence was taken by them, unless it can be shown that upon the facts and in the circumstances of the case the duty of diligence required the appellants to apply some higher standard ..."[2]

Clearly, the Hague and Hague-Visby Rules' requirement to the carrier to exercise due diligence in making the ship seaworthy is extremely strict.

(2) Seaworthiness of the ship. This assurance has been called the "warranty of seaworthiness." One definition of the "seaworthiness" is "Seaworthiness may be defined as the state of a vessel in such a condition, with such equipment, and manned by such a master and crew, that normally the cargo will be loaded, carried, cared for and discharged properly and safely on the contemplated voyage."[3]

A vessel is seaworthy if it is reasonably fit to carry the cargo it has undertaken to carry on the intended journey. In other words, the carrier must not only use due diligence to inspect the vessel for repair, but it must be sure the vessel is the proper type for carrying this specific type of cargo on this particular voyage. The standard of seaworthiness includes a number of factors, including the type of ship and the condition and suitability of its equipment, the competence of its crew, the type of cargo being carried and the manner in which it is stowed, the weather (e. g., was the ship prepared for the type of weather expected?), and the nature of the voyage. In addition, the carrier is responsible for properly manning, equipping, and supplying the ship, and making the refrigerating and cooling chambers, and all other parts of the ship in which goods are carried, fit and safe for receiving, carrying, and preserving the goods.

2. To Exercise Due Diligence to Properly and Carefully Loading, Handling, Stowing, Carrying, Keeping, Caring for, and Discharging the Goods Carried

---

[1] Yang Liangyi, Bills of Lading and Documents, the Publishing House of the China University of Politics and Law, p. 515.

[2] Yang Liangyi, Bills of Lading and Documents, the Publishing House of the China University of Politics and Law, p. 520.

[3] Yang Liangyi, Bills of Lading and Documents, the Publishing House of the China University of Politics and Law, p. 529.

Under Article 3 (2) ofthe Hague and Hague-Visby Rules,

(1) the carrier shall properly and carefully load and handle the goods carried.

(2) the carrier shall properly and carefully stow the goods carried. This stipulation implies that the carrier shall take proper methods of stowing according to the state, weight, price, etc., to put the goods carried in proper places.

(3) the carrier shall properly and carefully carry the goods carried. The carrier has the duty to carry the goods carried directly, promptly and safely to the port of destination.

Material deviation is not allowed. However, Article 4 (4) states: "Any deviation in saving or attempting to save life or property at sea or any reasonable deviation shall not be deemed to be an infringement or breach of this convention or of the contract of carriage, and the carrier shall not be liable for any loss or damage resulting therefrom." According to the cases precedents in the United Kingdom and the United States, if the material deviation is unreasonable, the carrier becomes a virtual insurer of the cargo. When a material deviation occurs, most U. S. courts have held that the carrier cannot claim protection of the $500 per package limitation.

Most courts have also held that stowage of cargo above deck under a clean bill of lading without the consent of the shipper is deemed to be an unreasonable material deviation from the terms of the bill of lading. Accordingly, goods can generally not be stowed above deck, where they are exposed to the weather and seas, unless the bill of lading specifically allows it, or unless the shipper knew that it was the common practice of the carrier to stow the particular type of goods in question above deck.[1]

(4) the carrier shall properly and carefully keep and care for the goods carried.

(5) the carrier shall properly and carefully discharge the goods carried.

E. Carrier's Immunities

Article 4 (2) of the Hague Rules provides: "Neither the carrier nor the ship shall be responsible for loss or damage arising or resulting from (1) act, neglect, or default of the master, mariner, pilot, or the servants of the carrier in the navigation or in the management of the ship; (2) fire, unless caused by the actual fault or privity of the carrier; (3) perils, dangers, and accidents of the sea or other navigable water; (4) act of God; (5) act of war; (6) act of public enemies; (7) arrest or restraint of princes, rules, or people, or seizure under legal process; (8) quarantine restrictions; (9) act or omission of the shipper or owner of the goods, or his agent or representative; (10) strikes or lockouts

---

〔1〕 Richard Schaffer, Beverley Earle, and Filiberto Agusti, International Business Law and Its Environment, West Publishing Company, New York 1996, p. 241.

or stoppage or restraint of labor from whatever cause, whether partial or general; provided that nothing herein contained shall be construed to relieve a carrier from responsibility for the carrier's own acts; (11) riots and civil commotions; (12) saving or attempting to save life or property at sea; (13) wastage in bulk or weight or any other loss or damage arising from inherent defect, quality, or vice of the goods; (14) insufficiency of packing; (15) insufficiency or inadequacy of marks; (16) latent defects not discoverable by due diligence; and (17) any other cause arising without the actual fault and privity of the carrier and without the fault or negligence of the agents or servants of the carrier, but the burden of proof shall be on the person claiming the benefit of this exception to show that neither the actual fault or privity of the carrier nor the fault or neglect of the agents or servants of the carrier contributed to the loss or damage."

A careful reading of the above provisions shows that the Hague and Hague-Visby Rules exempt carriers from almost all liability from damages. Once the goods carried are damaged, carriers can use any of the 17 immunities to excuse his liability. The Hamburg Rules prolongs the carrier' period of responsibility. Article 4 (1), (2) states: "The responsibility of the carrier for the goods under this Convention covers the period during which the carrier is in charge of the goods at the port of loading, during the carriage and at the port of discharge. For the purpose of para. 1 of this Article, the carrier is deemed to be in charge of the goods: (a) from the time he has taken over the goods ... (b) until the time he has delivered the goods ..." The most important modification by the Hamburg Rules is that it has canceled carriers' immunities from the act, neglect, or default of the master, marine, pilot, or the servants of the carrier in the navigation or in the management of the ship.

Case 6-1 Great China Metal Industries Co. Ltd. v. Malaysian International Shipping Corp.

Opinion by Justices Gaudron, Gummow and Hayne

Facts: In 1989, 40 cases of aluminum can body stock in coils were consigned from Sydney to Keelung, Taiwan. The respondent issued a bill of lading dated 5 October 1989, acknowledging receipt of the goods in apparent good order and condition. The vessel named in the bill as the intended vessel was the MV Bunga Seroja. The shipper named in the bill was Strang International Pty. Ltd. ("Strang") as agent for Comalco Aluminium Ltd. Strang packed the containers in which the cargo was shipped. The appellant was named in the bill as "the notify party" and property in the goods duly passed to it.

The bill provided that it should have effect subject to legislation giving effect to the Hague Rules. By the Sea-Carriage of Goods Act 1924 (Commonwealth), the Hague Rules applied to the carriage of the goods. The parties to the bill of lading were deemed by §§4(1) and 9(1) of that statute to have intended to contract according to the Hague Rules.

In the course of its passage across the Great Australian Bight, the vessel encountered heavy weather. That weather had been forecast before the vessel left port. Some of the goods were damaged.

Although, as will appear, it is not determinative of the outcome of the appeal, the question to which submissions primarily were directed is the meaning and effect of Article. IV rule 2(c) of the Hague Rules that:

"Neither the carrier nor the ship shall be responsible for loss or damage arising or resulting from—

...

(c) perils, dangers, and accidents of the sea or other navigable waters ..."

The appellant contended that:

· this exception (the "perils ofthe sea" exception) does not apply if damage to cargoresultsfrom sea and weather conditions which could reasonably be foreseen and guarded against;

· the weather encountered by the Bunga Seroja was foreseen; and

· the statement of Judges Masonand Wilsonin Shipping Corporation of India Ltd. v. Gamlen Chemical Co. (A/Asia) Pty Ltd. 59 that "sea and weather conditions which may reasonably be foreseen and guarded against may constitute a peril of the sea" is wrong and should not be followed.

The appellant pleaded that the respondent had failed to meet its responsibility under Article. III rule 1 of the Hague Rules to exercise, before and at the beginning of the voyage, due diligence to make the ship seaworthy; to properly man, equip, and supply the ship; and to make the holds and all other parts of the ship in which the goods were carried fit and safe for their reception, carriage, and preservation. It also pleaded failure by the respondent to properly and carefully load, handle, stow, carry, keep, care for, and discharge the goods carried (Article III rule 2). By its defense, the respondent relied upon various immunities specified in Article IV rule 2. In particular, the respondent pleaded that it was not responsible for any loss or damage to the goods arising or resulting from perils of the sea and that any damage to the goods resulted or occurred by reason of that matter.

The trial judge (Judge Carruthers) entered judgment for the respondent. His Honor concluded:

"In my view, the [respondent] has established to the requisite degree that the damage to the subject cargo was occasioned by perils of the sea.... In summary, the evidence satisfies me that, bearing in mind the anticipated weather conditions: (i) when the Bunga Seroja sailed from Burnie she was fit in all respects for the voyage; (ii) the [respondent] properly and carefully loaded, handled, stowed, carried, kept, and cared for the subject cargo; and (iii) there was no neglect or default of the master or other servants of the [respondent] in the management of the ship or cargo.

I am satisfied that the damage to the subject cargo was occasioned by perils of the sea, in that, the pounding of the ship by reason of the heavy weather caused the coils within the container to be dislodged and thereby sustain damage."

The New South Wales Court of Appeal dismissed an appeal. The appeal to this Court also should be dismissed.

In understanding the operation of the Hague Rules, there are three important considerations. The rules must be read as a whole, they must be read in the light of the history behind them, and they must be read as a set of rules devised by international agreement for use in contracts that could be governed by any of several different, sometimes radically different, legal systems. It is convenient to begin by touching upon some matters of history.

***Uniform Construction*:**

Because the Hague Rules are intended to apply widely in international trade, it is self-evidently desirable to strive for uniform construction of them. As has been said earlier, the rules seek to allocate risks between cargo and carrier interests and it follows that the allocation of those risks that is made when the rules are construed by national courts should, as far as possible, be uniform. Only then can insurance markets set premiums efficiently and the cost of double insurance be avoided.

In *Gamlen*, Judges Mason and Wilson note that:

there is a difference between the Anglo-Australian conception of "perils of the sea" and the United States-Canadian conception. According to the latter, "perils of the sea" include losses to goods on board which are peculiar to the sea and "are of an extraordinary nature or arise from irresistible force or overwhelming power, and which cannot be guarded against by the ordinary exertions of human skill and prudence." In the United Kingdom and Australia it is not necessary that the losses or the cause of the losses should be "extraordinary." Consequently sea and weather conditions which may reasonably be foreseen and guarded against may constitute a peril of the sea.

When reference is made to occurrences identified as "extraordinary," the question arises as to the nature of the relativity which is contemplated. Thus it has been said that the events which occurred "may be considered extraordinary as compared with an even voyage upon a placid sea; and yet [they] may be an entirely ordinary occurrence as compared with transportation by sea generally."

It may be that the difference between Anglo-Australian and American-Canadian construction of the "perils of the sea" exception is less than might appear from reference to cases such as The Giulia or The Rosalia—both decisions of the [United States] Second Circuit Court of Appeals. In The Rosalia a peril of the sea was described as "something so catastrophic as to triumph over those safeguards by which skillful and vigilant seamen usually bring ship and cargo to port in safety." More recent authority in the United States has, perhaps, placed less emphasis on whether what happened was extraordinary and catastrophic. But whether or not that is an accurate reflection of more recent developments, there is great force in what Judge Learned Hand said in *Philippine Sugar Centrals Agency v. Kokusai Kisen Kabushiki Kaisha*.

The phrase, "perils of the sea," has at times been treated as though its meaning were esoteric: Judge Hough's vivid language in The Rosalia ... has perhaps given currency to the notion. That meant nothing more, however, than that the weather encountered must be too much for a well-found vessel to withstand.... The standard of seaworthiness, like so many other legal standards, must always be uncertain, for the law cannot fix in advance those precautions in hull and gear which will be necessary to meet the manifold dangers of the sea. That Judge Hough meant no more than this in The Rosalia ... is shown by his reference to the definition in The Warren Adams ... as the equivalent of what he said. That definition was as follows: "That term may be defined as denoting 'all marine casualties resulting from the violent action of the elements, as distinguished from their natural, silent influence.'" It would be too much to hope that The Rosalia ... will not continue to be cited for more than this, but it would be gratifying if it were not.

...

Thus there are statements to be found in the United States authorities that a "perils of the sea" exception may apply even if the weather encountered was no more than expected. Nor should statements made in the many English cases dealing with perils of the sea be read divorced from their context. Some can, we think, be seen as no more than decisions about particular facts. Others examine questions of onus of proof and concurrent causation, which do not arise in this case. [For example, in the "Xantho" Lord Herschell drew a distinction] between perils of the sea and other losses of which the sea is the immediate cause. He said:

I think it clear that the term "perils of the sea" does not cover every accident or casualty which may happen to the subject-matter of the insurance on the sea. It must be a peril "of" the sea. Again, it is well settled that it is not every loss or damage of which the sea is the immediate cause that is covered by these words. They do not protect, for example, against that natural and inevitable action of the winds and waves, which results in what may be described as wear and tear. There must be some casualty, something which could not be foreseen as one of the necessary incidents of the adventure.

The distinction drawn by his Lordship is important and must be borne in mind when considering the operation of the "perils of the sea" exception.... Many other cases were mentioned in argument or can be found in the books. We think it desirable to touch briefly on only three other streams of authority. First, it seems that in German law, a peril of the sea need not be an extraordinary event and that a storm of a certain force is regarded as a peril of the sea. Similarly, in French law a peril of the sea need not be "unforeseeable and insurmountable." Finally, the Supreme Court of Canada held in *Goodfellow Lumber Sales v. Verreault* that:

... even if the loss is occasioned by Perils of the sea, the ship owner is nevertheless liable if he failed to exercise due diligence to make the ship seaworthy at the beginning of the voyage and that unseaworthiness was a decisive cause of the loss.

How then are these disparate streams of authority to be brought together? In our view one must begin by recognizing that the inquiry is, in large part, a factual inquiry—is the carrier immune in respect of what otherwise would be its failure to discharge its responsibilities under Art. III because the loss or damage to the goods arose or resulted from a cause which brings the carrier within the immunity conferred by Article. IV, rule 2. ?

If cargo has been lost or damaged and if the vessel was seaworthy, properly manned, equipped, and supplied, what led to the loss or damage? Did it arise or result from want of proper stowing (Article. III, rule 2)? Did it arise from the "act, neglect or default of the master ... or the servants of the carrier in the navigation, or in the management of the ship" (Article. IV, rule 2(a))? Or, did it result from some other cause peculiar to the sea? The last is a peril of the sea.

In *Gamlen*, Judges Mason and Wilson said that "sea and weather conditions which may reasonably be foreseen and guarded against may constitute a peril of the sea." The fact that the sea and weather conditions that were encountered could reasonably be foreseen, or were actually forecast, may be important in deciding issues like an issue of alleged want of seaworthiness of the vessel, an alleged default of the master in navigation or management, or an alleged want of proper stowage.... But if it is necessary to consider the "perils of the sea" exception, the fact that the conditions that were encountered could reasonably be expected or were forecast should not be taken to conclude that question.... Such an approach, even if it is different from the American and Canadian approach, better reflects the history of the rules, their international origins, and is the better construction of the rules as a whole.

The Present Appeal:

In the present case, the trial judge held that there was no breach of Art. III, rule 1 or rule 2. That is, the trial judge rejected the contentions that due diligence had not been exercised to make the ship seaworthy, to properly man, equip, and supply the ship and to "make the holds ... and all other parts of the ship in which goods are carried, fit and safe for their reception, carriage and preservation." Indeed the trial judge found that in fact the vessel was fit in all respects for the voyage when it left port, [and that the goods had been properly stowed...]

It was submitted by the appellant that the master should not have left port or should have diverted so as to avoid the weather which was forecast. The former contention appears not to have been made at trial. The latter was, but was rejected. The trial judge, having heard the evidence of experts called by both parties, said that he was "unable to conclude that any deficiencies in the conduct of the ship and her cargo by [the ship's master] have been demonstrated." There is no basis for departing from that finding. Once it was made, the trial judge's conclusion that there was no neglect or default of the master or other servants of the carrier in the management of the ship or cargo was inevitable. To the extent that the appellant now seeks to expand its contention to include the proposition that the vessel should not have left port, it is enough to say that, if the judge's finding does not meet the contention, it is a contention that could be made only with evidence to support it and there was none.

...

The failure of the submissions by the appellant makes it unnecessary to consider grounds urged in support of the decision of the Court of Appeal by the respondent in its Notice of Contention.

The appeal should be dismissed with costs.

Casepoint: This case turned on the interpretation of the phrase "perils of the sea." This term is one of the exceptions mentioned in the Hague Rules, which protect the carrier from liability when goods are damaged because of perils of the sea. The court noted that there was some difference in interpretation of this phrase in England and Australia compared to interpretations in the United States and Canada (which appear to require that the peril be something extraordinary). However, the court found that the differences were not as large as some had argued, that Germany and France had viewed the phrase in the same way as England and Australia, and that the need to interpret the phrase in a uniform way was important. In conclusion, the court ruled that where there was no negligence on the part of the carrier and the goods had been properly loaded and stowed, that the damage caused by the rough voyage was one of the perils of the sea. [1]

F. Delayed Bills of Lading

A bill of lading is the representation and symbol of the goods to which it refers. In the case The "Houda" (1994) 2 Lloyd's Rep. 541, Neil pointed: "The case for the owners is based on the general principle that once a bill of lading has been issued only a holder of the bill can demand delivery of the goods at the port of discharge. It is because of the existence of this principle that a bill of lading can be used as a document of title so that the transfer of the document transfers also the right to demand the cargo from the ship at discharge." [2] Carke also said in the case "Sormovskiy 3608" (1994) 2 Lloyd's Rep. 266: "It makes commercial sense to have a simple rule that in the absence of an express term of the contract the master must only deliver the cargo to the holder of the bill of lading who presents it to him."

Clearly, according to laws and international trade customs, a carrier has the duty to hand over the goods to the holder of original bill of lading. However, due to the fact that unforeseen things often change irregularly in international trade practices, a carrier upon the arrival of the goods at destination cannot find the holder of original bill of lading, and thus occurs the delivery of the goods without the bill of lading, taking the delivery against indemnity, or even frauds.

---

[1] Ray August, Don Mayer and Michael Bixby, International Business Law, Six Edition, Pearson Education Limited, 2013, p. 635.

[2] Yang Liangyi, Bills of Lading and Documents, the Publishing House of the China University of Politics and Law, 2001, p. 83.

1. Delivery of Goods without the Bill of Lading

This means that a carrier has delivered the goods to the consignee without original bill of lading, either due to the fact that the bill of lading is delayed or stolen or lost. The well-known lawyer Yang Liangyi warns that shipowner or master must bear in mind that they must not deliver the goods without the bill of lading, otherwise, they cannot exempt from the liability.[1]

2. Taking Delivery against Indemnity

Taking delivery against indemnity is a usual custom in trade practices, Clarke said: "In trades where it is difficult or impossible for the bills of lading to arrive at the discharge port in time the problem is met by including a contractual term requiring the master to deliver the cargo against a letter of indemnity or bank guarantee." Leggatt also said: "In practice, if the bill of lading is not available, delivery is effected against an indemnity."

Although delivery against an indemnity is a usual practice in trade, it has evoked much controversy over its nature and whether the shipowner is bound to accept an indemnity among judges and legal experts. According to Article 17 of the Hamburg Rules, the shipper is deemed to have guaranteed to the carrier the accuracy of particulars relating to the general nature of the goods, their marks, number, weight and quantity as furnished by him for insertion in the bill of lading. Such a letter of guarantee or agreement is valid as against the shipper unless the carrier or the person intends to defraud a third party, including a consignee, who acts in reliance on the description of the goods in the bill of lading. Obviously, this provision is consistent with actual trade practices.

G. Frauds on Bills of Lading

In recent years occur more and more maritime frauds of which frauds on bills of lading injure the international tradeseriously as cancers. Frauds on bills of lading refer to false bills of lading, antedated bills of lading, advanced bills of lading and clean bills of lading issued through indemnity.

1. False Bills of Lading (伪造提单)

False bills of lading refer to the bills of lading issued but with the goods not yet shipped. As we have discussed, a bill of lading is a carrier's receipt of the goods. Article 3 (3) of the Hague Rules states that after receiving the goods into his charge the carrier or the master or agent of the carrier shall, on demand of the shipper, issue to the shipper a bill of lading. ... Obviously, false bills of lading are void and constitute tort.

---

[1] Yang Liangyi, Bills of Lading and Documents, the Publishing House of the China University of Politics and Law, 2001, p. 84.

2. Antedated Bills of Lading (倒签提单)

Antedated bills of lading means the bills of lading issued after the goods have been shipped but with the date earlier than actual shipping date. The carrier issues an antedated bill of lading mostly because the banks accept only "on board bills of lading or clean bills" for payment under a letter of credit. If the seller shipped the goods later than the contracted date that was indicated in the bill of lading, there would be discrepancy among the documents, and the bank is entitled to reject the payment.

False and antedated bills of lading are all frauds. In the case SCB v. PNSC (1998) 1 Lloyd's Rep. 684 Cresswell said: "Antedated and false bills of lading are a cancer in international trade. A bill of lading is issued in international trade with the purpose that it should be relied upon by those whose hands it properly comes—consignees, bankers and endorsees. A bank, which receives a bill of lading signed by or on behalf of a shipowner (as one of the documents presented under a letter of credit), relied upon the veracity and authenticity of the bill. Honest commerce requires that those who put bills of lading into circulation do so only where the bill of lading, as far as they know, represents the true facts."[1]

3. Advanced Bills of Lading (预借提单)

Advanced bills of lading means a bill of lading issued under requirement of a seller by a carrier who is already in management of the goods but not yet shipped it, or who is shipping the goods but not finished yet. Advanced bills of lading and antedated bills of lading all constitute fraud.

4. Clean Bills of Lading Issued through Indemnity.

A clean bill of lading proves that the goods shipped have suffered no apparent or outside damage and there does not seem to be any defect in the packing. An unclean bill of lading or foul bill of lading is generally marked "Insufficiently packed", "Covers old and stained", "...packages in damaged condition", "...cartons wet stained", etc. these unclean bills of lading are not acceptable to the banks for negotiation under a letter of credit. In order to obtain a clean bill of lading for timely payment, the seller usually requires the carrier to issue a clean bill of lading against an indemnity.

III. Marine Cargo Insurance

Insurance provides a pool or fund into which the many contribute and out of which the few who suffer loss are compensated. Insurers frequently re-insure a portion of the

[1] Yang Liangyi, Bills of Lading and Documents, the Publishing House of the China University of Politics and Law, 2001, p. 785.

"risk" they have accepted. The insurance of large "risks" is spread directly or indirectly over a large number of insurance or re-insurance companies or underwrites. In international trade, the transportation of goods from the seller to the buyer is generally over a long distance by air, by land or by sea and has to go through the procedures of loading, unloading and storing. During this process, the potential for damages and loss to goods, in comparison with land and air transportation, is tremendous. In order to protect the goods against possible loss in case of such perils, the buyer or seller before the transportation of the goods usually applies to an insurance company for insurance covering the goods in transit.

A. Marine Insurance Policies and Certificates

In an export transaction, the terms of the contract of sale provide normally whether the costs of marine insurance shall be borne by the seller or by the buyer. If the goods are sold on FOB terms these costs have to be paid by the buyer and that is even true if the FOB seller, by request of the buyer, has taken out the policy on behalf of the buyer. If the goods are sold on CIF terms, it is the duty of the seller to take out the policy and pay the costs of insurance.

The marine insurance policies or certificates form part of the shipping documents. Regard shall in particular be had to floating policy, open cover policy and blanket policy.

Floating policy is of great importance for export trade. It is, in fact, a convenient method of insurance goods where a number of similar export transactions are intended, e. g. where the insured has to supply an overseas importer under an exclusive sales agreement or maintains permanent sales representatives or subsidiary companies abroad. A floating policy covers the shipments, as soon as they are made, under previous arrangement between the insured and the insurance company and particulars of the shipment may be supplied to the insurance company later on.

Open cover policy is similar to floating policy. While a floating policy is usually limited to 12 months, the open cover may be limited in time or may be permanent. Where the open cover is perpetual in character, a clause is inserted enabling both parties to give notice of cancellation of the cover within a stated time, e. g. thirty days or three months.

Blanket policy usually provides that the insured need not advise the insurer of the individual shipments and that a lump sum premium—instead of a premium at several rates—shall cover all shipments. In the case of a floating policy or open cover the insured has normally to make declarations of the individual shipments falling under these insurances to the insurer. This is inconvenient to the exporter and requires an excessive amount of labour and costs where the various consignments are of small value or the voyage is of short duration. In these cases the blanket policy is a better choice.

B. Perils and Losses

Goods during transportation on sea and in the course of loading and unloading might meet various kinds of perils and the goods might suffer loss of one kind or another.

In marine insurance, perils are generally of two kinds:

1. Perils

(1) Perils of the sea. This include natural calamities and fortuitous accidents, such as weather, thunder and lightning, tidal wave, earthquake, floods, ship stranded, striking upon the rocks, ship sinking, ship collision, colliding with icebergs, fire, explosion, etc.

(2) Extraneous risks. This cover theft, rain, shortage, leakage, breakage, dampness, etc. they may include special risks, such as war risks, strikes, non-delivery of cargo, refusal to receive cargo, etc.

2. Losses

Losses fall into two main classes: total loss and partial loss.

(1) Total loss. This loss can either be actual total loss(实际全损) where vessel or cargo are totally and irretrievably lost, or constructive total loss(推定全损) in a case where the ship or the goods have been abandoned because the cost of salvage or recovery would have been out of proportion to the value.

(2) Partial loss. This means the loss to the goods is only partial. In case of partial loss a fine distinction is drawn between particular average and general average. In marine insurance *average* has an entirely different meaning from its normal usage and it means loss or damage to the goods in the course of sea transportation due to natural calamities and accidents and extraneous risks.

(a) Particular average (单独海损) is a partial loss to the insured cargo and the loss must be borne by the owner of this individual consignment.

(b) General average (共同海损) is a loss that results when extraordinary expenses or losses are incurred in saving the vessel or its cargo from danger at sea. This ancient principle of maritime law, which was developed long before insurance was available, spreads the risk of a disaster at sea by making all parties to the voyage contribute to any loss incurred. Under this rule, if A's cargo is damaged or "sacrificed" in the process of saving the ship, and B's cargo is saved as a result, B or its insurer must contribute to A for the loss. A's claim is a general average. In other words, the owner of the cargo that was sacrificed would have a general average claim for contribution against the owner of the cargo that was saved. For example, when fire threatens an entire ship, and certain cargo is damaged by water in putting the fire out, the owners of all of the cargo must contribute to the loss of the cargo that was damaged by the water. The owners of cargo that is thrown overboard to save a sinking ship may have a claim against those whose cargo was thereby saved. General average claims are typically covered by marine insurance.

In order to prove a general average claim, the claimant must show that (1) the ship, cargo, and crew were threatened by a common danger; (2) the danger was real and substantial; and (3) the cargo or ship was voluntarily sacrificed for the benefit of both, or extraordinary expenses were incurred to avert a common peril.

A person seeking to claim a general average contribution from other parties must show (1) that the loss was incurred to benefit everyone and (2) that the person making the claim was not responsible for causing the danger. For example, a shipping company cannot claim general average when it has hire tugs to refloat a ship that ran aground because of the captain's faulty navigation.

The set of standardized rules on general average is the *York-Atwerp Rules*, an effort to develop commonly accepted principles of general average started in England as early as 1860, with work on the rules being completed in 1890. Following World War II, an international effort to achieve universally accepted general average rules resulted in the revised York-Antwerp Rules of 1950. The 1950 rules have achieved widespread acceptance by the maritime industry. The rules are not the subject of treaty or convention, and have not been enacted into national laws. They traditionally have become a part of the contract of carriage because their provisions are generally incorporated into all modern bills of lading.

C. Insurance Cover

According to the stipulations of the People's Insurance Company of China, the following basic insurance covers are available in marine insurance:

1. Free From Particular Average Insurance (FPA)(平安险)

Under *free from particular average insurance* the insurance company will be responsible to pay claims for total or constructive total losses suffered by the whole lot of cargoes during transportation due to such natural calamities as vile weather, thunder and lightning, tidal wave, earthquakes, and floods, or for total or partial losses due to the ship or carrier being on fire, stranded, sinking, colliding or meeting other fortuitous accidents.

2. With Particular Average Insurance (WPA)(水渍险)

The cover of this insurance is more extensive. The insurer is liable, in addition to the total or constructive total losses covered by FPA insurance, also for the partial losses of the insured goods due to the risks caused by natural calamities mentioned under FPA insurance.

3. All Risks Insurance (一切险)

Among the three kinds of basic insurance, under an "all risks" policy the goods are insured against all risks, e. g. from natural calamities, fortuitous accidents at sea, or general extraneous risks, irrespective of percentage of loss, total or partial. A natural deterioration of perishable goods, delay, loss or damage caused by inherent vice or nature of the subject matter are not covered.

■ Notes

deviation 绕航,指船舶在海上驶离了正常的航线。绕航一般分为合理绕航和不合理绕航。合理绕航,指为了躲避海上风险,救助或者企图救助人命或者财产,到中途港紧急补给等。不合理绕航包括将偷渡者遣回原地、在合理的绕航后迟延返回正常航线等。根据相关规定,承运人对由于绕航所造成的损失承担责任。

ordinary course of business 正常交易过程。排除低于生产成本的销售费用、一般费用及管理费用所进行的亏本销售,也不包括交易主体之间存在某种关联关系(如母公司与子公司的关系)。

bona fide purchaser 善意购买者。

diligentia (diligence) 勤谨。该概念源于罗马法,有最高勤谨和普通勤谨之分,主要用来确定当事人是否存在疏忽责任。

burden of proof 举证责任。

negotiable instrument 流通票据。

■ Important Legal English Usages

impose 征税,强加(负担,任务)。例如,to impose duties on tobacco (对烟草征税)。

注意该词与下列同义词的区别:

levy 也有征税之意,但主要指征收关税。例如,to levy tariffs on imports (征收关税)。

defects 缺陷,主要指产品方面的缺陷。

modify 修改,变更,更改。例如,to modify the terms of a contract (修改合同条款)。

注意该词与下列同义词的区别:

rectify 也有修改之意,但主要指纠正,改正。例如,He shall be ordered to rectify within a limited period of time and imposed administrative sanctions by the relevant authorities (有关主管部门将命令其限期改正,并给予行政处分)。

■ Review Questions

1. Outline and discuss the main differences between "voyage charterparties" and "time charterparties."
2. Define a bill of lading and state its main features.
3. Explain, giving examples where possible, the immunities of a carrier under the Hague

Rules.

4. Under what circumstances will there be delayed bills of lading? How to resolve the problems caused by delayed bills of lading?
5. Explain briefly the causes of frauds in bills of lading and discuss possible ways to resolve their relevant problems, giving three examples based on arbitration and court practices.
6. Briefly describe the reforms on the nature of bills of lading.
7. What are the new developments of the Hamburg Rules? Give two examples.
8. Briefly define particular average and general average.
9. Briefly describe the differences between "free from particular average insurance", "with particular average insurance" and "all risks insurance".
10. New York Merchandising Company (NYMCO) imported goods produced by C-ART in Hong Kong. The goods were shipped on the Hong Kong Island Lines (carrier). The parties prior course of dealings had been for the carrier to release the goods to NYMCO on its presentation of a "bank guarantee." These bank guarantees released the carrier from liability for any misdelivery. On this occasion, however, the carrier released the goods upon NYMCO's corporate guarantee of payment. Soon thereafter, NYMCO filed for bankruptcy. C-ART sued the carrier to recover the money owed for the goods. The carrier argued that it was not liable for misdelivery because NYMCO had good title to the goods from the time they were shipped in Hong Kong. Do you agree with this argument? The carrier also claims that the bills of lading are not valid because the importer NYMCO was insolvent. What is wrong with this argument?

7 Chapter Seven Finance of International Trade

■ 导读

本章讲授的是国际贸易的付款方式,主要包括汇票的基本知识、托收、信用证、福费廷及保理等。众所周知,货物买卖中,卖方出售货物的目的是及时有效地获取货款,买方的目的是及时有效的获得货物。最使卖方致命的是交货后得不到货款,俗称"货款两空",使买方致命的是付款后得不到货物。因此,本章内容对买卖双方都是至关重要的。本章的重点是托收和信用证。托收虽然有较大的风险,但由于它具有收款快、成本低的优点,一直被国外中小企业所青睐。信用证虽有时间长、成本高等缺点,但是它相对其他付款方式风险较小,一直被我国商人所信赖。由于信用证近年来在国外用得越来越少,福费廷和保理的使用越来越广泛,而且我国一些银行也逐渐开始了这方面的业务,本章对福费廷和保理也进行了简要介绍,并结合我国商人的实际做法进行了分析,以启发我国商人大胆使用不同付款方式,提高经济效益。

Chapter Four discussed the law governing contracts for the sale of goods and the obligations of sellers and buyers. Chapter Six described how the parties can define bills of lading and transfer risks of goods in transit to the insurer. This chapter examines how the international banking system is used to move money from one party in a transaction to another—how sellers collect for their shipments and how buyers remit payments for their purchases. It also addresses how banks guarantee that sellers will be paid for their goods through the use of bank letters of credit and how they provide commercial financing for the international sale. Keep in mind that most of the concepts covered here apply not just to collect money for the sale of goods, but are equally applicable to many different types of international transactions involving the movement of money internationally and the use of banks to provide an assurance of contractual commitments.

I. The Bill of Exchange

A. Origin of Bills of Exchange

The origin of the bill of exchange lies in the history of the merchants and traders of fourteenth and fifteenth century Europe. As merchants visited the markets of distant cities to buy and sell their wares, they sought a safer means of transferring their gold or money than by carrying it in their caravans. It might have worked like this: Assume merchant A delivered goods to merchant B in a distant city, who became indebted to A for the amount of the purchase. Later merchant A desires to purchase goods from merchant C. Merchant A could pay merchant C for the goods with a written piece of paper—an order—addressed by A to B to pay that money to C. Of course, merchant B was probably wealthy and respected in the trade—one whose credit was highly regarded. Merchant C could present the written order to B for payment immediately, or if it wished, it could simply ask B to sign (or "accept") the order for future payment. The written order to pay thus became an *acceptance*. With the acceptance in hand, merchant C could purchase new wares from yet another merchant, and use the acceptance in payment. Eventually, merchants turned to wealthy families, Italian banking societies, or medieval bankers spread throughout Europe, to transfer money over great distances by issuing payment orders to their correspondents living in distant cities. As merchants recognized that these orders could be bought and sold, the concept of negotiability evolved and negotiable instruments were born. At first English law did not recognize the validity of negotiable instruments. But merchants accepted them as substitutes for money, and they were enforceable in the merchant's private courts under the Law Merchant. As their importance and use evolved, so did their validity and treatment under the law. They became formally recognized by statute in England in 1822 in the *English Bills of Exchange Act* and in the United States in 1866 in the *Uniform Negotiable Instruments Law*.

B. The Law Governing Bills of Exchange

Until the middle of the seventeenth century, bills of exchange were governed by a single international law, the *lex mercatoria*. In the seventeenth century, however, the rise of national laws brought about differences in the rules governing bills of exchange. The French bill of exchange came to be governed by the *Savary Code* of 1673, the *Perfect Tradesman*, and the works of Jousse. In England, the courts created a case law that reflected the practice in English banks. At the end of the nineteenth century, the *lex mercatoria* was codifed in England in the *Bills of Exchange Act* (BEA) of 1882. In 1896, in the United States, the National Conference on Commissioners of Uniform Laws drafted a Uniform Negotiable Instrument Law (UNIL), which was largely based on the BEA. Then, in the 1940s, the UNIL was modernized and integrated into the more comprehensive Uniform Commercial Code.

On the European continent, there were calls throughout the latter half of the nineteenth century for the creation of an international negotiable instruments law. Finally, in 1907, a conference convened at The Hague to draw up a convention. A draft was agreed to in 1912, but World War I interrupted ratification. The League of Nations then organized a series of conferences to update the 1912 draft. In 1930, three Geneva Conventions on the Unification of the Law Relating to Bills of Exchange (ULB) were signed. The following year, two additional Geneva Conventions on Unification of the Law Relating to Checks (ULC) were also signed. Within 15 years, the ULB and ULC had been ratified by most continental European countries, and today they serve as the standard laws governing bills of exchange and checks in virtually every nation, with the exception of the Anglo-American common law countries. [1]

Chinese merchants began to use bills of exchange (which was customarily called "Feiqian") as early as in Tang Dynasty, and the bills became poplar in Ming Dynasty. In the late Qing Dynasty, western banking system was transplanted in China, and the first Law of Negotiable Instrument came into being. This Law of Negotiable Instrument was abolished along with the founding of the People's Republic of China and the falling of the Guomintang Government. The present Law of the People's Republic of China on Negotiable Instruments (hereafter called "China Negotiable Instrument Law") was adopted at the 13th Meeting of the Standing Committee of the Eighth National People's Congress on May 10, 1995, and amended on August 28, 2004.

C. Types of Bills of Exchange

Under Article 19 of China Negotiable Instrument Law, a bill of exchange is a negotiable instrument, signed and issued by the drawer, who authorizes the drawee to pay unconditionally a sum certain in money to the payee or the holder at sight or on a specific date. According to most laws, the common types of bills of exchange are as follows:

1. Clean Bill and Documentary Bill

A bill of exchange is called a clean bill when no shipping documents are accompanied with it; on the other hand, if the bill of exchange is accompanied by shipping documents (chiefly bill of lading, invoice, insurance policy, etc.), the bill is called a documentary bill. In international trade, most bills of exchange are documentary bills of exchange.

2. Sight (or Demand) Bill and Time (or Usance) Bill

According to the time of payment, a bill of exchange may be either a sight (or demand) bill or a time (or usance) bill. If the drawee is required to pay the bill on demand or at sight, the bill is called a sight bill. If the drawee is required to pay the bill at a later date, the bill is called a time or usance bill. It requires acceptance before payment.

3. Commercial Bill and Bankers' Bill

If the drawer is a commercial firm the bill is called a commercial bill; when the drawer is a bank, the bill is called a bankers' bill.

---

[1] Ray August, International Business Law, Higher Education Press, 2002, p. 645.

4. Commercial Acceptance Bill and Bankers' Acceptance Bill

In time or usance commercial bills, when the drawer is a commercial firm and the drawee is another commercial firm, the bill after acceptance by the commercial firm or the drawee is called a commercial acceptance bill; when the drawer is a commercial firm or a bank and the drawee is a bank, the bill after acceptance by the bank or the drawee is called a bankers' acceptance bill.

D. General Requirements and Rights of the Holder in Due Course

We turn now to a discussion of the requirements that must be met for the possessor of a negotiable instrument to qualify as holder in due course.

A holder in due course of a negotiable instrument gets special rights. Normally, the transferee of an instrument—like the assignee of a contract—gets only those rights in the instrument that are held by the person from whom he got the instrument. But a holder in due course can get better rights. A holder in due course takes it free from most disputes that might arise between the drawer and drawee—the original parties to the underlying transaction. The most common type of dispute that might arise is breach of contract. This rule ensures the free transferability of commercial paper in international commerce. A financial institution can discount an international draft without fear that it will be caught up in the middle of a breach of contract action between buyer and seller. If a draft did not come with this protection, banks might not be so willing to finance international sales.

1. General Requirements

In order to become a holder in due course, a person who takes a negotiable instrument must be a holder, under Article 3 – 302 of UCC, and take the instrument for value, in good faith, without notice that it is overdue or has been dishonoured or that there is any uncured default with respect to payment of another instrument issued as part of the same series, without notice that the instrument contains an unauthorized signature or has been altered, without notice of any claim of a property or possessory interest in it, and without notice that any party has any defense against it or claim in recoupment to it. In addition, the revision to Article 3 requires "that the instrument when issued or negotiated to the holder does not bear such apparent evidence of forgery or alteration or is not otherwise so irregular or incomplete as to call into question its authenticity."

(1) Holder. This means a person must have possession of an instrument that is either payable to "bearer" or that is payable to him.

(2) Value. To qualify as a holder in due course of a negotiable instrument, a person must give value for it. Value is not identical to simple consideration. Under the provisions of the Revised Article 3, a holder takes for value if: (a) the agreed-upon promise of performance has been performed—for example, if the instrument was given in exchange

for a promise to deliver a refrigerator and the refrigerator has been delivered; (b) he acquires a security interest in, or a lien on, the instrument; (c) he takes the instrument in payment of, or as security for, an antecedent claim; (d) he gives a negotiable instrument for it; or (e) he makes an irrevocable commitment to a third person. Thus, a person who gets a check as a gift or merely makes an executory promise in return for a check has not given value for it and cannot qualify as a holder in due course.

(3) Good faith. To qualify as a holder in due course of negotiable instrument, a person must take it in good faith, which means that the person obtained it honestly and in the observance of reasonable commercial standards of fair dealing. If a person obtains a check by trickery or with knowledge that it has been stolen, the person has not obtained the check in good faith and cannot be a holder in due course. A person who pays too little for an instrument, perhaps because she suspects that something may be wrong with the way it was obtained, may have trouble meeting the good faith test.

(4) Overdue or dishonoured. In order to qualify as a holder in due course, a person must take a negotiable instrument before he has notice that it either is overdue or has been dishonored. The reason for this is that one should perform obligations when they are due. If a negotiable instrument is not paid when it is due, the UCC considers the person taking it to be on notice that there may be defenses to the payment of it.

(5) Notice of unauthorized signature or alteration. This means a holder who has notice that an instrument contains an unauthorized signature or has been altered cannot qualify as a holder in due course of the instrument.

(6) Notice of claims. If a person taking a negotiable instrument is on notice of an adverse claim to the instrument by someone else or that someone is seeking to rescind a prior negotiation of the instrument, the current holder cannot qualify as a holder in due course.

(7) Notice of defences and claims in recoupment. To qualify asa holder in due course, a person must also acquire a negotiable instrument without notice that any party to it has any defenses or claims in recoupment. Potential defenses include infancy, duress, fraud, and failure of consideration. Thus, if a person knows that a signature on the instrument was obtained by fraud, misrepresentation, or duress, the person cannot be a holder in due course.

A claim in recoupment is a claim of the obligor against the original payee of the instrument. The claim must arise from the transaction that gave rise to the instrument.

(8) Irregular and incomplete instruments. A person cannot be a holder in due course of a negotiable instrument if, when she takes it, the instrument is irregular or some important or material term is blank.

2. Rights of A holder in Due Course

The Revision Article 3 of the UCC establishes four categories of claims and defences. They are real defences—which go to the validity of the instrument; Personal defences—which generally arise out of the transaction that gave rise to the instrument; Claims to an instrument—which generally concern property or possesory rights in an instrument or its proceeds; Claims in recoupment—which also arise out the transaction that gave rise to the instrument.

(1) Real defences. Real defences can be used as reasons against payment of a negotiable instrument to any holder, including a holder in due course (or a person who has the rights of a holder in due course). Real defences include:

(a) Minority or infancy that under state law makes the instrument void or voidable. For example, if a person of 17, signs a promissory note as maker, he can use his lack of capacity to contract as a defence against paying it even to a holder in due course.

(b) Incapacity that under state law makes the instrument void. For example, if a person has been declared mentally incompetent by a court, then the person has a real defence if state law declares all contracts entered into by the person after the adjudication of incompetency to be void.

(c) Duress that voids or nullifies the obligation of a party liable to pay the instrument.

(d) Illegality that under state law renders the obligation void. For example, in some states in the United States, checks and notes given in payment or gambling debts are void.

(e) Fraud in the essence.

(f) Discharge in bankruptcy proceeding. For example, if the maker of a promissory note has had the debt discharged in a bankruptcy proceeding, she no longer is liable on it and has a real defence against payment.

(2) Personal defences. These are legal reasons for avoiding or reducing liability of a person who is liable on a negotiable instrument. Personal defences include:

(a) Lack or failure of consideration.

(b) Breach of contract, including breach of warranty.

(c) Fraud in the inducement of any underlying contract.

(d) Incapacity to the extent that state law makes the obligation voidable, as opposed to void.

(e) Illegality, duress, unauthorized completion or alteration, and nonissuance of the instrument.

(f) Modification of the obligation by a separate agreement.

(g) Payment that violates a restrictiveendorsement.

(3) Claims to the instrument. This includes a claim to ownership of the instrument,

a lien on the instrument, and for rescission of an indorsement.

(4) Claims in recoupment. This is not actually a defence to an instrument but rather an offset to liability. For example, Adams purchases a new automobile from Dealership, giving it a note for the balance of the purchase price beyond her down payment. After accepting delivery, she discovers a breach of warranty that the dealer fails to remedy. If Dealer has sold the note to a bank that subsequently seeks payment on the note from Adams, she has a claim in recoupment for breach of warranty. If the bank is a holder in due course, the claim in recoupment cannot be asserted against it. However, if the bank is not a holder in due course, then Adams can assert the claim in recoupment to reduce the amount owing on the instrument at the time the action is brought against her on the note. [1]

E. Common Procedures in Handling Bills of Exchange

A person who signs an instrument has a contractual obligation to make payment. For makers, drawees, and accommodation parties, this obligation is "primary"; that is, they must make payment on presentment of the instrument. If it is other than a demand instrument, it must be presented on the day it is due. If it is a demand instrument, it must be presented within a reasonable time after it was signed. In view of the great importance of bills of exchange in international trade, most countries lay great emphasis on the procedures in handling a bill of exchange.

1. Drawing

Drawing means the act of the drawer in filling up the bill of exchange with particulars as to the name of the drawee (or the payer), the amount payable, the date of payment and them name of the payee and after signature the drawer may present the bill to the drawee through the medium of the payee or a banker.

2. Presentation

Presentation means the act of the holder of the bill of exchange in presenting the bill to the drawee asking the latter either to pay or to accept the bill. The drawee's receiving or seeing the bill is called 'Sight'. If the bill is a sight or demand bill, the drawee has to pay the amount at once; if it is a usance or time bill the drawee has to make his acceptance and pay the amount on the date due.

3. Acceptance (承兑)

Acceptance means the act of the drawee to show his responsibility by accepting the usance bill for payment at a fixed future date by writing the word "Accepted" marking the

[1] James Barnes, Terry More Head Dworkin and Eric L. Richards, Law For Business, Irwin Chicago, 1996, p. 688.

date of acceptance and signing on the face of the bill. The drawee after making the acceptance is called the acceptor and is responsible to pay the amount on the due date of the usance bill.

4. Endorsement (背书)

A bill of exchange is a negotiable instrument, and is circulative or transferable in the international money market. In the case of "to order" bills of exchange, endorsement is the procedure of negotiation or transfer by the payee by signing his name on the back of the bill, either blank endorsed which makes the bill payable to bearer or holder, or endorsed with the name of the transferee and his order, who is called the endorsee. After endorsement and delivery of the bill to the endorsee, the right of receiving the amount is transferred to the endorsee or the holder in due course. The bill can therefore be negotiated or transferred many times after such endorsements.

5. Payment

Immediate payment will be made by the drawee on presentation by the holder in due course if the bill of exchange is at sight or on demand without the necessity of acceptance. If it is a usance or time bill, the drawee will accept it and pay the amount on due date.

6. Protesting

When a bill has been duly presented for acceptance or payment and the acceptance or payment has been refused, the bill is said to be dishonoured for non-acceptance or non-payment. Upon dishonour the holder has an immediate right of action against all parties (including endorsers) to the bill. The holder must normally give a formal notice of dishonour to all the parties he wishes to make liable.

II. Collection of Documentary Bills through Banks

Normally, the buyer does not remit the purchase price, but allows the exporter to draw a bill of exchange, with or without documents attached on him. In such a case, the exporter asks his bank to arrange for the acceptance or payment of the bill overseas, and the bank will carry out his task through its own branch office abroad or a correspondent bank. This procedure is termed as collection of proceeds of sale.

Under collection, the seller makes instructions to the bank to present for acceptance or for payment a documentary bill. They have to be precise and complete and to deal with the various contingencies which may arise in the course of their execution. The bank asks its customers to issue instruction on a "documentary bill lodgment form" which is worded as a questionnaire and designed to obtain instructions for all eventualities.

A. Types of Collection

In practice, collection is of two types:

1. Documents against Acceptance (D/A)

D/A means the documents shall be delivered to the buyer on acceptance of the bill. In other words, the buyer can obtain the documents and the possession of the goods without paying the price. This is rather risk to the seller if the seller knows nothing about the trustworthiness of the buyer.

Clearly, this mode of payment can be used only in the case where the seller knows the buyer well and the deal is small.

2. Documents against Payment (D/P)

This means the documents shall be delivered to the buyer on actual payment of the bill. In other words, the buyer must first pay the price, and then he can obtain the documents for the goods delivered. Comparatively, this is a safer mode payment for the seller.

In addition, the seller may instruct the bank whether the documents shall be handed to a referee in case of need and what the powers of the referee are; whether the buyer shall be allowed a rebate for payment before maturity; and, if the documents are not taken up, whether the goods are to be warehoused and what insurance is to be effected. The lodgment form further requires the exporter to give precise instructions relating to the noting or protect by notary public at the payer's residence if the bill is dishonoured by non-acceptance or non-payment.

B. Advantages of Collection

Chinese merchants for many years do not like collection for fear that foreign merchants may possibly cheat them. However, in recent years, more and more foreigners especially household merchants are getting interested in collection. This is because collection has some noticeable advantages in comparison with other modes of payment in international trade. Collection is a quick and time-saving mode of payment. Also, parties that use collection do not need to pay high expenses, make tremendous deposit in the bank in advance as required in a transaction by letter of credit. We can reasonably predict that, along with the improvement of trustworthiness created by the development of economic globalisation, collection will become favourite mode of payment in China's foreign trade.

III. Letters of Credit (L/C)

Unlike most domestic sales transactions, in a sale of goods across national borders the exporter-seller and importer-buyer may not have previously dealt with one another; or each may know nothing about the other, or the other's national legal system. Seller does not know: (1) whether buyer is creditworthy or trustworthy; (2) whether information received on these subjects from buyer's associates is reliable; (3) whether exchange controls will hinder movement of the payment funds; (4) how great is the exchange risk if payment in buyer's currency is permitted, and (5) what delays may be involved in receiving unencumbered funds from buyer.

On the other hand, buyer does not know: (1) whether seller can be trusted to ship the goods if buyer prepays; (2) whether the goods shipped will be of the quantity and quality contracted for; (3) whether the goods will be shipped by an appropriate carrier and properly insured; (4) whether the goods may be damaged in transit; (5) whether seller will furnish to buyer sufficient ownership documentation covering the goods to allow buyer to claim them from the customs officials; (6) whether seller will provide the documentation necessary to satisfy export control regulations and import customs and valuation regulations; (7) what delays may be involved in receiving unencumbered possession and use of the goods in the buyer-importer's location.

Where the parties are strangers, these risks are significant, possibly overwhelming. Since they operate at a distance from each other, seller and buyer cannot concurrently exchange the goods for the payment funds *without the help of third parties*. The documentary sale, involving the use of a letter of credit, illustrates how these potentially large risks can be distributed to third parties who have special knowledge, can properly evaluate each risk assumed, and thereby can reduce the transaction risks to insignificance.

The third party intermediaries enlisted are banks and at least one carrier. In order to assure payment, what seller wants is a letter of credit. A letter of credit is a contract—a promise by a bank (usually buyer's bank) that it will pay to seller the amount of the contract price. The bank's promise is conditioned upon seller's presenting evidence that the goods have been shipped via carrier to arrive in buyer's port, along with any other documents required by the contract for the sale of goods.[1]

A. Law Applicable to Letters of Credit

Letters of credit are recognized in all legal systems of the world. In the United States, the law governing letters of credit has been codified in Article 5 of the UCC. But perhaps the most important rules affecting letters of credit are not law at all, but a privately developed set of guidelines based on the customs and commonly accepted practices of merchants and bankers, known as the *Uniform Customs and Practice for Documentary Credits*. The *Uniform Customs and Practice for Documentary Credits* (hereafter called UCP 500) is a document that international bankers know well. It is a set of standardized rules for issuing

[1] Folson, Michael Wallace Gordon, John A. Spanogle, Jr. International Business Transaction, Publishing House of the People's University of China, 2001, p. 142.

and handling letters of credit, drafted and published by the *International Chamber of Commerce* (which also publishes Incoterms) with the assistance of the international banking community. The UCP establishes the legal format of letters of credit, sets out rules by which banks process letter of credit transactions, and defines the rights and responsibilities of all parties to the credit. The UCP was first introduced in the early 1930s, with the latest revision (UCP 500) published in 1993. The UCP 500 is in use in virtually every nation of the world. All banks in China use it in their international business transactions.

B. Types of Letters of Credit

The following types of bankers' letters of credit are customary:

1. Confirmed Letters of Credit

For the most part, a letter of credit will serve to adequately assure payment of the seller's drafts. In certain instances, however, the credit of the issuing bank may be insufficient to assure payment. This lack of assurance may occur when shipments are exported to countries that have shortages of foreign currencies, large foreign debts, and a poor balance of payments record. In such a situation, government currency restrictions imposed between the time the contract is agreed to and the time the drafts are tendered for payment could prevent the issuing bank from honouring its letter of credit in dollars. A U. S. seller may want to include as part of the sales contract that the buyer will furnish a letter of credit confirmed by a bank in the United States.

Sellers have other reasons for insisting on a confirmed credit. In some instances, the seller may be unsure of the soundness of the buyer's bank and wants the backing of some reputable national bank on the letter of credit. Additionally, should legal action ever be necessary to collect on a credit, a seller can much more easily sue a national confirming bank than a foreign bank in foreign courts.

2. Standby Letters of Credit (备用信用证)

The standby letter of credit can be used to guarantee that a party will fulfil obligations under a service contract, construction contract, or sales contract. Standby letters of credit can also be used to insure the repayment of a loan. Suppose, for example, that a subsidiary of a U. S. company operating in Latin American borrows money from a local bank. The bank can require a standby letter of credit from a U. S. bank that would allow it to draw against the credit should the subsidiary default on its obligation.

Most standby credits today are used, however, not in sale-of-goods transactions, but as guaranties of performance under consulting and performance contracts. In such a case, the standby credit is issued to guarantee performance of the account party in favour of the beneficiary, the one to whom performance was due. For example, if a firm promises to perform architectural or engineering services related to a major public works project, a standby credit would guarantee its performance to the government that contracted for the architectural or engineering services. Payments under standby credits, however, are usually not due upon receipt of the same type of documentation as would be involved in a sale of goods case. Instead, payments are often required to be made upon the issuing bank's receipt of a signed statement by the beneficiary that such sums are currently due and payable. As such, standby payments are usually payable on the beneficiary's allegation that performance is due.

3. Transferable Letters of Credit

A transferable credit is one which specifically authorizes the beneficiary to transfer part or the whole of the benefit of the credit to someone else. Thus a buying agent abroad can arrange the purchase of goods on behalf of his principal on the footing that the principal opens a transferable credit in favour of the agent and the agent transfers the benefit of the credit to the supplier of the goods.

4. Revolving Letters of Credit

A revolving credit is one where the amount is renewed or reinstated without amending the credit. It revolves in relation to time or amount. In case a credit revolves in relation to time, e.g., one that is available for up to U.S. $ 10,000 per month during a fixed period of time, say, six months, the credit is automatically available for U.S. $ 10,000 each month irrespective of whether any sum was drawn in the previous month. A credit of this kind can be cumulative or non-cumulative.

5. Red Clauses in Credits

The red clause is a financing tool for smaller sellers who need capital to produce the products to be shipped under a letter of credit. A red clause in a letter of credit is a promise by the issuing bank to reimburse the seller's bank for loans made to the seller. The loan, then, is really an advance on the credit. Loans can be used only for purchasing raw materials or for covering the costs of manufacturing or shipping of the goods described in the credit. Ultimately, the liability will fall on the buyer if the seller defaults on shipment or repayment of the amounts taken under the credit. This form of financing is very risky for the buyer and its bank.

C. The Stages of Arranging and Advising A Letter of Credit

When payment under a bank's letter of credit is arranged, four stages can normally be distinguished:

1. The exporter and the overseas buyer agree in the contract of sale that payment shall be made under a letter of credit.

2. The overseas buyer instructs a bank at his place of residence (known as the "originating bank") to make available a credit for another country's exporter on the terms

agreed upon in the contract of sale.

3. The originating bank arranges with a bank at the residence of the exporter (known as the "advising bank") to negotiate, accept or pay the exporter's draft upon delivery of the shipping documents by the seller.

4. The advising bank advises the exporter that it will negotiate, accept, or pay his draft upon delivery of the shipping documents.

The parties relating to a letter of credit are named as follows:

1. The applicant (generally the buyer or importer) to the bank to issue the letter of credit.

2. The originating bank or opening bank or issuing bank, who is the bank receiving the application from the applicant to issue the letter of credit and will be responsible for payment.

3. The advising bank or correspondent bank at the place where the exporter is located and may usually be the branch of the issuing bank or its correspondent.

4. The beneficiary who is empowered to use the letter of credit and is usually the exporter.

5. The negotiating bank ready to accept or discount the documentary bill by the beneficiary under the letter of credit.

6. The paying bank who is the bank responsible for payment mentioned in the letter of credit. It is usually the issuing bank or it may be another bank appointed by the issuing bank according to the stipulation in the letter of credit.

D. Independence Principles and Rule of Strict Compliance

There are two basic principles of the letter of credit rules promulgated by the UCP 500:

1. Independence Principle

Independence principle means that the banks' obligations under the letter of credit are independent of the buyer's and seller's obligations under the contract for the sale of goods. Article 4 of the UCP 500 states that "in credit operations all parties concerned deal with documents, and not with goods, services and/or other performances to which the documents may relate." Indeed, the obligation of the issuing bank to honour the beneficiary's draft under a letter of credit is totally independent of the contract of sale between the buyer and the seller. Also, Article 14 requires that the issuing bank "determine on the basis of the documents alone whether or not they appear on their face to be in compliance with the terms and conditions of the credit." As long as the documents are in apparent good order, appear valid on their face, and correspond to the terms of the L/C, the bank must honour the beneficiary's draft, and will be able to seek reimbursement from its customer, the buyer, regardless of the quality or condition, or even the existence, of the goods. That's to say, the banks deal only with documents, and not with performance of the underlying sales contract. That the goods might have gone to the bottom of the ocean during their voyage is irrelevant to the bank's obligation. The bank has not obligation to check the quality or condition of the goods, nor to investigate rumours about them. The UCP does not require the bank to examine any documents not called for in the L/C.

2. Rule of Strict Compliance

The most important rule of bank's examination of the documents is the *rule of strict compliance* (严格相符原则). In the case of Equitable Trust Co. of New York v. Dawson Partners Ltd. (1926) 27 Lloyd's Rep. 49, Sumner said: "It is both common ground and common sense that in such a transaction the accepting bank can only claim indemnity if the conditions on which it is authorised to accept are in the matter of the accompanying documents strictly observed. There is no room for documents which are almost the same, or which will do just as well ..."〔1〕According to this rule, the terms of the documents presented to the issuing bank must strictly conform to the requirements of the letter of credit. When a document contains language or terms different from the L/C, or some other apparent irregularity, it is said to contain a *discrepancy*. Documents that do not conform are *discrepant*. This does not mean that every "i" must be dotted and every "t" crossed. (As one court stated, it's not a discrepancy if Smith is spelled "Smithh") Some typographical errors are excusable, of course. But the thrust of the rule is that every provision of the bill of lading, commercial invoice, insurance policy, and other required shipping documents must match the letter of credit. Even a small discrepancy can cause the bank to reject the documents. If the issuing bank buys documents that contain a discrepancy, then the bank cannot seek reimbursement from the account party, its customer.

E. Fraud Exception in Letter of Credit Transaction

In recent years, there are more and more frauds in international business transaction, which hinder the international trade seriously. For example, in 1997, Hong Kong suffered a loss of Hong Kong $1.1 billion caused by fraud of which 19 cases were related to letters of credit. However, in 1998, the loss amounted to 2.4 billion of which 24 cases were related to letters of credit.〔2〕

---

〔1〕 Yang Liangyi, Letters of Credit, Publishing House of the China University of Politics and Law, 1998, p. 117.

〔2〕 Jiang Zuoli, International Business Law, Shanghai People Publishing House, 2003, p. 310.

The chief reason for the more frauds in letter of credit transactions is the independence principle and rule of strict compliance. The independence principle promotes the utility of the letter of credit transaction, by offering certainty of payment to the beneficiary who complies with a credit's requirements. According to these principles, banks deal exclusively with documents. They are not responsible to verify whether the goods supplied actually agree with those specified in the credit, nor liable for differences between the goods invoiced and those actually delivered, nor answerable to the buyer's complaints about these differences. Also, the banks assume no responsibility of the authenticity, form or validity of the documents. These principles suggest that the issuing bank must pay, regardless of any underlying fraud. This makes it possible that a seller delivers mislabelled goods to a carrier to obtain the documents it needs to collect payment against a letter of credit, or even makes forged or fraudulent documents in order to cheat a buyer of the payment.

The doctrine of fraud exception means that even if the documents delivered by the beneficiary are in strict compliance with a letter of credit, if a bank or applicant shows definite proof that the beneficiary has made forged documents, the bank has the right to reject payment, and the applicant is entitled to require the court to issue injunction against payment of the beneficiary.

The doctrine that there is a "fraud exception" to the "independence principle" seems to be generally recognized. However, there is still a significant debate about how broad and extensive the fraud exception should be.

As the UCP 500 has no specific provisions on the fraud exception, national courts of many countries began to "fill the gaps." The principle underlying this approach is that the courts will not allow their process to be used by a dishonest person to carry out a fraud.

1. The American Courts

In the case Sztejn v. J. Henry Schroeder Banking Corp. Justice Shientag pointed that where the seller's fraud has been called to the bank's attention before the drafts and documents have been presented for payment, the principle of "the independence of the bank's obligation under the letter of credit" should not be extended to protect the unscrupulous seller (see the next case).

According to Shientag's comment in the next case, the requirements of fraud exception are:

(1) a buyer shall prove that a seller has frauded; (2) a bank has the obligation to dishonour the payment only the bank knows the fraud before honours the draft; (3) if a bank has already honoured the draft when it knows the fraud, the bank is exempted if it has exercised due diligence. In other words, in the case where even the documents are

forged, the bank shall be protected.

Due attention must be paid to the Revised Article 5 of the UCC. In this article there is a series of limitations on the availability of the fraud exception for use by the beneficiary. The first limitation is that the fraud must be "material," but material is not defined. Second, the account party must present sufficient evidence of fraud or forgery, not merely allegations of it. Third, all the procedural requirements for injunctive or other relief must be met. Fourth, the relief can be denied if third parties are not "adequately protected," and no relief will be granted if a confirming or advising bank has paid funds to the beneficiary.

Case 7 -1 Sztejn v. Henry Schroeder Banking Corp.

United States, New York County Supreme Court, Special Terms, 1941.
New York Supplement, Second Series, Vol. 31, p. 631 (1941)

Facts: Transea traders in India contracted to sell hot bristles to Sztejn, the plaintiff. At the request of Sztejn, the J. Henry Schroeder Banking Corp. (Schroeder), the defendant, issued an irrevocable letter of credit in favor of Transea covering the shipment of the hot bristles and payable upon presentation of certain documents, including a maritime bill of lading. Transea allegedly filled 50 cases with cow hair and other rubbish and delivered these to the carrier in order to obtain the required bill of lading. This bill, along with the other required documents, and a draft payable to Transea, were presented to Schroeder by the Chartered Bank of India, acting as an agent for Transea. Before Schroeder could pay on the credit, Sztejn brought this action against Schroeder to enjoin it from doing so. Schroeder asked the court to dismiss the case.

Issue: Should the court dismiss the case?

Decision: No! Justice Shientag stated that one of the chief purposes of the letter of credit is to furnish the seller with a ready means of obtaining prompt payment for his merchandise. It would be most unfortunate interference with business transactions if a bank before honoring drafts drawn upon it was obliged or even allowed to go behind the documents, at the request of the buyer and enter into controversies between the buyer and the seller regarding the quality of the merchandise shipped.... Of course, the application of this doctrine presupposes that the documents accompanying the draft are genuine and conform in terms to the requirements of the letter of credit.

However, I believe that a different situation is presented in the instant action. This is not a controversy between the buyer and seller concerning a mere breach of warranty regarding the quality of the merchandise; on the present motion, it must be assumed that the seller has intentionally failed to ship any goods ordered by the buyer. In such a situation, where the seller's fraud has been called to the bank's attention before the drafts and documents have been presented for payment, the principle of independence of the bank's obligations under the letter of credit should not be extended to protect the unscrupulous seller. It is true that even though the documents are forged or fraudulent, if the issuing bank has already paid the draft before receiving notice of the seller's fraud, it will be protected if it exercised reasonable diligence before making such payment. However, in the instant action Schroeder has received notice of Transea's active fraud before it accepted or paid the draft....

Although tour courts have used broad language to the effect that a letter of credit is independent of the primary contract between the seller and buyer, that language was used in cases concerning alleged breaches of warranty; no case has been brought to my attention on this point involving an intentional fraud on the part of the seller which was brought to the bank's notice with the request that it withhold payment of the draft on this account. The distinction between a breach of warranty and active fraud on the court has stated: "Obviously, when the issuer of a letter of credit knows that a document, although correct in form, is, in point of fact, false or illegal, he cannot be called upon to recognize such a document as complying with the terms of a letter of credit," ...

While the primary factor in the issuance of the letter of credit is the credit standing of the buyer, the security afforded by the merchandise is also taken into account. In fact, the letter of credit requires a bill of lading made out to the order of the bank and not the buyer. Although the bank is not interested in the exact detailed performance of the sales contract, it is vitally interested in assuring itself that there are some goods represented by the documents.

Accordingly, the defendant's motion to dismiss... is denied. [1]

2. The English Courts

The English courts have recognized the "fraud exception," based upon the persuasive precedent of the American cases. However, the House of Lords, while recognizing the basic fraud concept, refused to extend it to protect the buyer when the fraud was committed by a third party without seller's knowledge. In the case United City Merchants

---

〔1〕 Ray August, Don Mayer and Michael Bixby: International Business Law, Pearson Education Limited, 2013, p. 695.

(Investments) Ltd. V. Royal Bank of Canada (The American Accord), 1983 A. C. 168, the credit requires loading by May 15 and the bill of lading shows loading on the 16th, the bank must dishonour. On the other hand, the credit requires loading on May 15, and bank knows that the beneficiary has altered a document in a non-apparent manner, the bank must dishonour. However, where the credit requires loading by May 15, and bank knows that a freight forwarder has altered a document in a non-apparent manner, the bank must honour the credit. In conclusion, the House of Lords held that the bank must honour the draft. Diplock explained: "To this general statement of principle as to the contractual obligations of the confirming bank to the seller, there is one established exception: that is, where the seller, for the purpose of drawing on the credit, fraudulently presents to the confirming bank documents that contain, expressly or by implication, material representations of fact that to his knowledge are untrue".

In conclusion, under the precedents of cases in English courts the requirements of fraud exception are:

(1) There is sufficient proof that documents are forged or fraudulent.

(2) Seller/beneficiary intends to cheat holder of the documents. [1]

3. The International Chamber of Commerce

The opinion of the International Chamber of Commerce plays an important role in international trade. The following paragraph explains its view: "The Commission expressed its opinion that the negotiating bank passing forward what proved to be a forged bill of lading was protected by Article 9 (of UCP) unless it was itself a party to the fraud, or it had knowledge of the fraud prior to presentation of the document, or unless it had failed to exercised reasonable care, e. g. if the forgery were apparent 'on the face' of the document. The Commission noted that this was in line with various court rulings."

It is clear that the International Chamber of Commerce is consistent with court of rulings of some countries, and does not allow their process to be used by a dishonest person to carry out a fraud.

4. The Chinese Courts

China does not have particular provisions on the fraud exception of letter of credit transaction, but the common ground and sense can be found from relevant laws and interpretations. However, the Chinese courts deal with this problem with their own characteristics: in the case of fraud, the courts can preserve measures to protect the innocent buyer; if the draft is already accepted by a bank, the court, holding that the

---

[1] Yang Liangyi, Letters of Credit, Publishing House of the China University of Politics and Law, 1998, p. 181.

letter of credit relationship has now already turned into instrumental relationship, cannot freeze the draft so as to protect the negotiability of the instrument.

IV. UCP 600

UCP 600 as the latest version of the rules that govern letters of credit transactions worldwide, is approved by the ICC Commission on Banking Technique and Practice on 25 October 2006, and the rules have been effective since 1 July 2007. There are several significant differences exist between UCP 600 and UCP 500. Some of these differences are as follows:

1. The number of articles has been reduced from 49 to 39 in UCP 600, because some articles of no real significance have been cancelled, such as "revocable letter of credit", the requirement of "complete and precise", "incomplete or unclear instructions".

2. In order to reach a standard meaning of terms used in the rules and prevent unnecessary repetitions two new articles have been added to the UCP 600. These newly added articles are Article 2 "Definitions" and Article 3 "Interpretations". These articles bring more clarity and precision in the rules: for example, there is a definitive description of negotiation as "purchase" of drafts of documents, and honor means: to pay at sight is the credit is available by sight payment, to incur a deferred payment undertaking and pay at maturity if the credit is available by deferred payment, to accept a bill of exchange ("draft") drawn by the beneficiary and pay at maturity if the credit is available by acceptance.

3. Practices in trade and banking are easier because the added provisions regarding the obligations of all parties involved are more specific and excisable.

On the other hand, UCP 600 still has some deficiency which has to be improved further. For example, UCP 600 says that advising bank means the bank that advises the credit at the request of the issuing bank. This definition is vague because it does not tell what to advise, how to advise, when to advise, and to whom to advise. The more complete and clearer definition would be that advising bank means a bank, usually domiciled in the beneficiary's country and which is correspondent bank of the issuing bank that advises, at the request of the issuing bank, to the beneficiary the apparent authenticity of the credit when it receives it, without the obligation to honor it.

V. Uniform Rules for Forfaiting

Among the many techniques of export finance (documentary credits, export factoring, barter, compensation trade etc), forfaiting (福费廷) is perhaps the least known method. However, as the international exports of more and more countries are developing rapidly in recent decade, it has become of growing interest to some industrial sectors of export-oriented countries and to their financial institutions. As a matter of fact, it seems that the forfait market was born in Switzerland, in Zurich, in connection with the sale of US grain to some East European countries. The US exporter did not want, or was not able, to provide the importer with the necessary medium-term supplier credit out of his own funds, whereas the East European countries needed such credit. The banks were unable to fill the gap and to provide the necessary financing for the transaction. But a small number of Zurich financial companies could. They were specialized in countertrade and barter between Eastern and Western Europe and thus were in the unique position of being able to assess the risks involved in the contemplated sale. The Swiss financial houses accepted to purchase the promissory notes or bills of exchange given as payment by the importer and, after having discounted them at a rather large premium, could provide the US exporter with the cash he wanted. Today, it is obviously very difficult to make a fair estimate of the real importance of forfaiting in international trade but even if it is hard to quantify, one can safely say that it is a technique which has now come out of the dark corner of international capital markets and which is no longer regarded as finance of last resort, as probably was the case a number of years ago.

There is no doubt that forfaiting as a financial technique for exports is becoming more important to China's open-door policy. Unfortunately, forfaiting remains a relatively little-known technique in China. One explanation could be that forfaiting was originally a high risk, high return business and Chinese businessmen comparatively prefer to low-risk business and even disregard high returns. Considering that today's competition in international business is much greater, the appreciation of country risks less haphazard and the extraordinary development in Chinese economy needs new financial methods on the part of the Chinese importers, this part addresses forfaiting briefly to encourage the Chinese businessmen to use it and avoid the legal hazards. Due to the failure of a recognized definition and universally accepted practices, this introduction is generally based on Uniform Rules for Forfaiting (URF 800, 2012) drafted jointly by the Banking Commission of the International Chamber of Commerce (ICC) and the International Forfaiting Association (IFA).

A. Definition

Forfaiting is a technique mostly used in connection with export transactions. The importer typically needs capital goods but is unable to pay for them, or to find adequate local financing. The exporter is willing to deliver the goods but cannot provide the importer with the required medium-term supplier credit out of his own funds; the exporter in fact wants the cash immediately. Because of the difficulty in finding adequate financing, the importer is prepared to bear financing costs which can be higher than the costs of other more common but, to him, unavailable financing techniques. Confronted with this situation, the exporter would typically sell to a forfaiter the bills of exchange that he has accepted from the importer in payment for the goods that he will deliver. The seller of the bill, the exporter in other words, wishes to pass on the responsibility for collection of the bills to the forfaiter in exchange for immediate cash payment, at a discount.

Forfaiting has been defined as follows: "the purchase of obligations falling at some future date, arising from deliveries of goods and services-mostly export transactions-without recourse to any previous holder of the obligation. [1]

Generally, forfaiting has the following legal features:

1. Forfaiting by Legal Nature is a Transaction of Documents

In a forfaiting transaction, the exporter (the initial seller) must deliver the required documents to the forfeiter and then lose the right of collecting payment from the buyer and does not need to bear any risks therein. Moreover, the forfeiter is entitled to the payment from the buyer and also liable to the risks arising from the buyer, guarantee and even political and exchange rate. Therefore, the forfeiter is a buyer, rather than an agent or middleman.

2. Forfaiting is a Financing Method without Recourse

"Without recourse" as the most essential characteristics of forfaiting transaction refers to the right of claim for payment to all parties (including endorsers) to the bill of exchange that the forfeiter must give up in case that the bill is dishonored. The general rule is that, the seller of a bill protects himself from any recourse, whatever the cause. It is, indeed, the very idea of the forfaiting business, that the seller should be freed from any responsibility as to collection problems and related risks and costs.

A distinctive feature of forfaiting is that the financing is usually expressed to be without recourse. The attraction of forfaiting to the exporter is that the uncertainty of the credit risk posed by the importer is avoided as the cash proceeds from the discounting of the paper are substituted for the deferred payment obligation. But it is only when a sale of a forfait paper is without recourse that the credit-risk is laid off and the contingent liability is off the exporter's books.

Article 4 of URF provides: (a) On the settlement date, the seller sells to the buyer and the buyer purchases from the seller the payment claim without recourse. The buyer will have no claim against the seller or any prior seller for the non-payment of any amount

[1] Export Financing, Part II forfaiting C. Gm&r, Finanz AG Zurich, 1978.

due in respect of the payment claim except as provided under Article 13 or Article 4b. (b) If the seller is an obligor under the payment claim or any credit support document, nothing in these rules will affect the seller's obligations in its capacity as obligor.

3. Bills of Exchange in a Forfaiting Transaction are Usually Guaranteed by well-known Banks in the Importer's Country

Since the purchaser of "A forfeit" bills typically accepts to take the risk and the responsibility of collection, without any recourse towards the seller of the paper, he usually requires (because he cannot easily determine the credit worthiness of the importer) that the bills be guaranteed by a reputable bank in the importer's country, and that this bank issue on a separate document an unconditional and irrevocable guarantee in a form acceptable to the forfaiter. This bank guarantee is of the utmost importance to the forfaiter, since it is the only guarantee on which he can safely rely in the event of non payment by the obligor. In passing, one should say that in a typical forfaiting transaction very little is committed in writing, because the principal instrument is either a bill of exchange or a promissory note, and if there is anything in writing it usually concerns either the quotation given by the bank for the discounting of the paper or the acceptance by the exporter of these terms or questions pertaining to the transfer of funds and the settlement date.

Generally, three means of guarantee are employed in forfaiting transaction: aval (the bank writes on the accepted bills Per Aval (包付) and signature and seal to pay unconditionally), demand guarantee (the bank issues guarantee in writing on condition that the exporter delivers the required documents) and standby L/C.

4. Multiple Legal Relationships are Involved in a Forfeiting Transaction

Jurisprudentially, the relationships between all the parties in a complete forfeiting transaction are expressed with different ones: a buying and selling relationship between seller and buyer, a credit assignment relationship between exporter and forfaiter, and a guarantee relationship between importer, bank and exporter. Correspondently, law of negotiable instruments and law of guarantee are the most significant law for forfaiting transaction.

B. Advantages of A Forfaiting for Exporters, Forfaiters and Importers

1. Advantages for Exporters

(1) Exporters obtain medium and long term export finance to meet the need of accommodation of funds. This undoubtedly can improve the capacity and competitiveness of Chinese corporations for exports.

(2) As forfaiting is finance "without recourse", exporters are free from credit risks, state risks, interest rate risk and exchange rate risk. This is helpful to Chinese exporters of

large and advanced machine equipments required by the "One Belt One Road" proposal.

(3) Exporters do not need to deal with possible problems of managing collection of payment.

(4) Chinese exporters can timely handle the verification of export tax rebates because Chinese exports' loans without recourse are treated as export earnings under China's export exchange control regulations. This can avoid large funds occupied on tax.

2. Advantages for Forfaiters

(1) Forfaiters do not need to bear high risks because the bills of exchange under forfaiting are guarantee by reputable banks. As a result, Chinese banks can improve their asset structures for economic efficiency.

(2) Bills of exchange under forfaiting transaction can be negotiable in the second market. If forfaiters get into fund-flow difficulties or high risks, they can transfer or discount the bills to take funds.

(3) A forfaiting transaction usually requires more simple and definite documents, and thus produces higher financing efficiency. What is more, in the process of managing forfaiting transaction, a bank also does new businesses such as negotiable payment under letter of credit and collection, driving the development of other trade finance businesses and provide new opportunities of financial corporation of Chinese banks with foreign banks.

3. Advantages for Importers

As time bills of exchange are employed in a forfaiting transaction, an importer does not need to effect immediate payment, offering advantages of medium and long term loans to an importer and reducing the financial costs in comparison with national loans.

C. Operational Procedures of Arranging A Forfaiting Transaction

1. The exporter must, in accordance with the negotiation with the importer, find a forfeiter. Generally, the forfeiter has to know more about the goods for sale, importer, the guarantor bank, date of shipment and the interest rate that the importer intends to accept. Then, the forfeiter must give an offer to the exporter covering discount charge and other expenses.

2. The importer applies a local bank for guarantee. Upon receiving the offer, the bank has to first take into consideration its indebted structure, the importer, etc. and then decide the banking expenses. The importer also must inform timely the exporter of its arrangement of guarantee. The forfaiting agreement must be concluded after the conclusion of the contract of sale between the exporter and the importer.

3. The exporter delivers the goods and presents the required documents to sell the payment claim. The exporter first must deliver the goods, and then submit the documents

to the bank and the importer. The importer must hand over the bill of exchange or promissory note to the bank for guarantee.

4. The importer must send back the guaranteed bills to the exporter. The exporter discounts, in accordance with the forfaiting agreement, the documents of creditor's right "without recourse" to the forfeiter, and thus obtains cash income. And then, the exporter does not assume any liability the holder of bills. However, if the exporter presented unsatisfactory bill or note, he must be liable for damages of the forfeiter. Similarly, if the forfeiter fails to provide the contracted funds, he must compensate the exporter for the damages arising from his arrangement of finance.

5. The forfaiter requests the importer for payment when the bill falls due. In the case of delayed payment or failure to pay, the forfaiter has to bear relevant losses. If the payment is effected on account by the guarantor bank, the bank can claim for reimbursement from the importer.

6. The forfaiter can also sell the certificate creditor right in the secondary market before the bill falls due. Article 2 of URF provides that the secondary market means the market where the payment claim is purchased by the buyer from the primary forfaiter or another seller. Forfeiters may, under the state's management and guarantor bank's creditworthiness, reduce their risks by means of operation in the secondary market.

D. Avoiding of the Legal Hazards of Forfaiting

Forfaiting, the financing of exports on credit, is on the increase in recent decades. But the legal problems and risks (including interest rate risk, rate of exchange risk, credit risk and state risk) are complex and have never been judicially considered. Those participating in a forfait market for the first time have no previous experience and are more likely to find themselves in dispute. As forfeiting is originated from legal and financial practices by foreigners, Chinese businessmen may be unfamiliar with it, and should therefore bear the following points in mind so as to avoid the legal hazards of forfeiting as much as possible.

1. The exporter and importer should work with care to choose reputable banks. The exporter must work carefully to choose a bank with rich experience of managing forfeiting transaction and international reputation. The legal implications of a forfaiting transaction must be analyzed in terms of the bill of exchange or promissory note that the exporter receives from the importer, and the contract between the exporter and its bank. The bill or note will give rise to contractual obligations between the acceptor or promisee (as the case may be), drawer or promisee, and the guarantor. The liability of the promissor or acceptor may be governed by a different law from that governing the rights and obligations of the guarantor, depending on the place of issue of the paper, and where it was avalised.

Under the contract between the exporter and its bank, the exporter agrees to discount the paper to the bank. This contract may be contained in a commitment letter, subsequently accepted by the exporter, or in a series of letters or telexes between the two, each communication containing some of the terms of the overall contract which will normally be expressed to be without recourse to the exporter. The paper may subsequently be on-traded many times: on each occasion, a separate contract will arise.

It should be emphasized that a reliably guarantor bank is even more important both to the exporter and the importer. For instance, difficulties may arise if a bank finds itself dealing with a small branch or a subsidiary of another bank, or the subsidiary of a large exporter. Different legal systems take different views of group liability. Some regard each subsidiary as an independent legal entity. In others, the group is viewed as a whole. Under English law, the branches of a bank together with its head office consistute one legal entity. The liability of any branch is that of the bank as a whole. The position is not necessarily the same in the case of a subsidiary or where a branch of a bank is established under a legal system with no equivalent concept of overall bank liability. A practical precaution is to ensure that the head office of the entity concerned is aware of the transaction and has confirmed that the transaction is binding on it. This is also a prudent step where a bank finds itself dealing with a small and unknown entity in relation to the size of the transaction.

Another thing that must be stressed is that the exporter should make a reasonable choice between bills of exchange and promissory notes. In practice, therefore, the great majority of forfaitable obligations take the form either of promissory notes issued by the obligor in favour of the beneficiary, or bills of exchange drawn on the obligor by the beneficiary and accepted by the obligor. The promissory note and bill of exchange make it possible for a forfaiting transaction to be carried out with great speed, since these are instruments well known in the market and covered by the 1930 Geneva convention on commercial bills. For the exporter, the choice of instruments is obviously a matter of great importance. There is, indeed, as you well know, a significant legal difference between a promissory note and a bill of exchange as far as the exporter is concerned. Being the drawer of a bill of exchange, the exporter cannot entirely free himself from any liability regarding the bill, simply by adding the "without recourse" clause in his endorsement of the bill. The promissory note is, therefore, preferred from the point of view of the exporter since, with the inclusion of the non-recourse clause in his endorsement of the promissory note, the exporter effectively frees himself of any liability in connection with the said note. In theory, one could imagine that this distinction is not all that important if the exporter discounts the bill of exchange with a reputable forfaiter, since the forfaiter undertakes in writing not to take proceedings against the drawer of the bill of exchange in the event of non-payment on the part of the importer/acceptor. Problems might, however, arise with this non-recourse agreement in the event the bills are sold in the secondary market.

2. Banks should also take reasonable care to find bona fide exporter and importer. As mentioned above, a distinctive feature of forfaiting is that the financing is usually expressed to be without recourse. The attraction of forfaiting to the exporter is that the uncertainty of the credit risk posed by the importer is avoided as the cash proceeds from the discounting of the paper are substituted for the deferred payment obligation. But it is only when a sale of a forfait paper is without recourse that the credit-risk is laid off and the contingent liability is off the exporter's books.

It also must be stressed that the "without recourse" clause, however, cannot be and has never been understood as freeing the seller from absolutely any and every responsibility and liability in connection with the bills sold. Indeed, whenever the holder of a bill sells it 'without recourse' to a forfaiter, he implicitly represents to the purchaser that he is selling a valid bill, validly guaranteed or avalised. The seller is not, therefore, protected in cases of misrepresentation on his part, that is to say in cases where he pretends to sell something different from what he actually sells. The point is to understand what we mean by the seller's responsibility of selling a valid bill, validly guaranteed. Does it simply mean that the seller has to sell bills evidencing a valid claim, relating to a bona fide transaction, or does it also require that the seller sell bills which are valid from a formal point of view.

In addition, banks should possess a sound knowledge of the law relating to negotiable instruments in the jurisdictions in which they will be dealing, as well as a reasonable knowledge of the general contractual principles applying in those jurisdictions. Banks trading in paper should ensure that they purchase and sell, wherever possible, subject to the same law. Standard form documentation vetted by their banks' lawyers should be used.

E. A Typical Forfaiting Transaction

Mr Frick, a partner of the Swiss firm Frick & Schwarz, specialized in the manufacture of turbines, has been in contact for many years with a company in Ciaoland, Newlipurdam Company (Newco). Frick & Schwarz and Newco have done business on many occasions in the past and Mr Frick has just received a telex from Mr Purnag, director of Newco, asking him to submit an offer for the manufacture and delivery of turbines which Newco would need for a new project on the Dai river. Mr Frick is known to be a serious businessman, very competent in his field and his firm Frick & Schwarz enjoys a good reputation in the market. After having submitted offers to Newco and after a few meetings between Mr Frick and Mr Purnag, it appeared that Frick & Schwarz could manufacture and deliver the turbines required by Newco on time and according to the particular specifications. At an advanced stage of the negotiations, Mr Frick arrived in Ciaoland from Zurich in order to discuss the final details of the transaction and, more importantly, its financing aspect, which, according to the most recent telex from Mr Purnag, seemed somewhat of a problem, since Newco had been unable to obtain the medium-term credit that it was hoping to receive from the local government. Mr Frick and Mr Purnag met for a few days to discuss this problem and since it clearly appeared that Newco could not obtain from its bankers the medium-term foreign-currency financing that it needed, it was agreed that Mr Frick would go back to his Swiss bank, with which he was already in discussion about the Newco business, and see whether satisfactory financing could be arranged. It was now the end of April and the whole thing became quite urgent since delivery was to take place in early June. Upon the recommendation of his banker, Mr Frick had taken the precaution of mentioning to Mr Purnag that if Frick & Schwarz were to provide Newco with the necessary financing, it would only be possible if Newco were prepared to pay the necessary expenses and fees related thereto and provided that Newco could secure a suitable guarantee from a local bank. Mr Purnag, who was only too happy to think that the transaction might, after all, be possible, replied that Newco would pay all the costs reasonably related to such financing and that it would not be a problem for the company to obtain from its local bankers the sort of guarantee needed. Newco, indeed, enjoyed a long-standing and satisfactory relationship with First Ciaoland Bank Limited which had in fact already expressed its willingness to guarantee the transaction.

Back in Zurich, Mr Frick met with his partner Mr Schwarz, who in the meantime had been trying to obtain state-guaranteed credit for the transaction, but all to no avail; both partners then decided that, since the company was not able to provide the medium-term supplier credit necessary to Newco, they would have to approach local banks to see whether one of them would be able to arrange the sort of financing needed. An appointment was made for May 15 with Herr Schmidt of Industrie Kommerz Bank Eidgendssische, in Zurich (hereinafter "IKE Bank") to discuss the matter. Mr Frick explained the situation and the needs of Newco which had expressed the wish to spread the cost of the turbines over the working life of the investment. Mr Schmidt concluded the meeting by saying that IKE Bank was in principle able and willing to arrange forfaiting terms, i. e. fixed rate financing without recourse to the exporter (Frick & Schwarz). Mr Schmidt declared, however, that the crucial element in placing the paper in the market would be the quality of the guarantee provided by the importer's local bank. Mr Frick told Mr Schmidt that First Ciaoland Bank Limited, an important local bank in Ciaoland, had agreed, in principle, to provide the necessary guarantee to the satisfaction, at least so Mr Frick thought, of IKE Bank. On May 16, Mr Frick telexed to Mr Purnag to inform him of the meeting with IKE Bank, stressing once again the importance of the guarantee to be delivered by First Ciaoland Bank Limited. Mr Purnag was quite excited at the news and a meeting was fixed with Mr Frick, Mr Purnag and the local Ciaoland bankers on May 20 in Ciaoland. The discussion between Mr Frick and Mr Purnag proceeded quite swiftly. Mr Frick had, by that time, received confirmation from IKE bank (with which he had remained regularly in contact) that the financing could indeed be arranged, provided that the importer, Newco, could secure a satisfactory guarantee from First Ciaoland Bank Limited in two forms, namely an aval on the bills which would have to be issued, and a guarantee on a separate document. First Ciaoland Bank Limited agreed to these requirements, after having in turn secured a lien on some of Newco's assets. It was decided that Newco would pay to Frick & Schwarz US $ 600,000 cash upon delivery of the first turbines in June, with the rest of the purchase price to be paid in the form often bills of exchange, each of a value of US $ 500,000. Mr Frick and Mr Purnag then proceeded to draw up these bills of exchange, which matured at 6 – month intervals beginning on July 1st of the same year. The bills of exchange were standard in form and content. The bills were signed by Mr Frick and Mr Purnag and duly avalised by Mr Zu, the officer of First Ciaoland Bank with whom all these negotiations had taken place. There was a last-minute problem, however, when Mr Zu refused to sign the text of the guarantee which had been drafted by Newco's lawyers in accordance with the requirement of IKE Bank in Zurich. Mr Zu indicated that his bank had never agreed to give a guarantee to the Swiss Bank and that he had always understood that the guarantee would be given to Frick & Schwarz as exporter of the goods in question. After a rather agitated telephone conference between Mr Zu, Mr Schmidt of IKE Bank and Mr Frick and Mr Purnag, it was finally decided that IKE Bank would be satisfied if Ciaoland Bank issued a guarantee in favour of Frick & Schwarz, provided, however, that this guarantee was fully negotiable and indicated expressly that First Ciaoland Bank undertook to pay any successor or assignee of Frick & Schwarz. Newco's lawyers amended the text of the guarantee accordingly and Mr Zu signed it for First Ciaoland Bank Limited.

It was late Friday evening May 25 and Messrs Zu, Frick and Purnag decided to have a good meal to celebrate the conclusion of the transaction, together with the officers and lawyers of Newco who had in the meantime arranged all the various contracts and documents pertaining to the delivery of the turbines to Newco. Mr Frick was extremely pleased with this operation since it meant an important order for his company at a time when business was difficult. It was not too long ago, in January of the same year, that he and his partner had sat together to try to find a solution to the rather strained financial situation of their company. This new business would now provide the company with the cash needed and allow it to weather out the difficult months ahead. In short, this contract meant that Frick & Schwarz would not have to reduce their payroll, as had been sadly contemplated a few months ago. Mr Frick then enjoyed a Saturday excursion in Ciaoland with his friends and returned to Zurich, after a two-day stop-over in the region to visit other customers. On Wednesday, Mr Frick was back at IKE Bank sitting with Mr Schmidt, who had been very active during the past ten days, trying to place the paper that he knew Mr Frick would bring back from Ciaoland. He had found three institutions willing to take this paper, the Syndicated Bank Limited, Sudinvestverein and Holsoa Finanz AG, all three in Zurich. The Syndicated Bank Limited and Holsoa Finanz AG had agreed to take six of the ten bills of exchange, while Sudinvestverein had agreed to take the remaining four. Sudinvestverein, however, had expressly made its agreement to take the paper contingent upon its being provided with a certificate evidencing that the goods had been shipped or with a copy of the bills of lading for the first shipment of turbines which was to take place on June 1. In view of the importance of the transaction, however, and because of the excellent reputation of Frick & Schwarz, Sudinvestverein agreed that the payment would be made immediately to Frick & Schwarz, but under reserve of the presentation of the above-mentioned document, it being understood that the firm would submit the necessary documentation to Sudinvestverein within the next few days. After having duly endorsed the ten bills with the mention "without recourse" and after having received confirmation from his bank that the discounted amount of the bills, i. e. US $3,500,000, had been received on Frick & Schwarz's account with their bank, Mr Frick handed over the bills to the representatives of Syndicated Bank Limited, Sudinvestverein and Holsoa Finanz AG. (The 3.5 million dollars represented the price of the turbines to be exported, since the pricing of the contract had taken into account the discount of the bills). He also handed over First Ciaoland Bank's guarantee of which he had been prudent enough to request several original copies.

At this stage of the transaction, there were only happy people around the table, namely the firm Frick & Schwarz who had received in cash US $3,500,000 (although under reserve on the part of Sudinvestverein), Newco who had been able eventually to get the financing it was seeking, and the takers of the bills who had secured a good profit on the transaction. IKE Bank had only acted as a broker in placing the business with the takers and were at no risk, at least so they thought, not having provided the cash and not holding the bills.[1]

VI. International Factoring

A. Definition and Historical Development

International factoring (国际保理) is one of the most popular modes of payment in foreign countries, however, there is no authoritative definition to its nature till today. Under the UNIDROIT Convention on International Factoring, Ottwa, 28 May, 1988, "factoring contract" is defined as a contract concluded between one party (supplier) and another party (the factor) pursuant to which: (1) the supplier may or will assign to the factor receivables arising from contracts of sale of goods made between the supplier and its customers (debtors) other than those for the sale of goods bought primarily for their personal, family or household use; (2) the factor is to perform at least two of the following functions: (a) finance for the supplier, including loans and advance payment; (b) maintenance of accounts (ledgering) relating to the receivables; (c) collection of receivables; (d) protection against default in payment by debtors; (3) notice of the assignment of the receivables is to be given to debtors.

Factoring has its seeds in the Industrial Revolution, when the textile mills in the north of England, exporting to North America, appointed agents, or "factors" to sell their products and to get the money for them and sent it back. In times, these factors became more involved with their customers in America than with their principals in Britain. They built up intrinsic knowledge of the companies to which they were selling. Then they expanded their services in providing collection, bookkeeping for clients' accounts receivable, discounting factored receivables, guaranteeing the payment of their clients' sales to their customers and purchasing their invoices without recourse.

With the advent of textile mills in the United States, factors began to perform these services domestically. However, as time went on, the selling function was performed by the mills themselves and this service disappeared as a service of the factoring industry. Although the development of the factoring was primarily in textiles and related trades, there has been a mounting diversification and a growing volume of industries using the factoring services during the last two decades. It was estimated that that in 1980, the worldwide factoring volume amounted to 53 billion U. S. dollars, consisting of domestic factoring 49. 1 billion and international trade factoring 3. 9 billion. By 1991, there are more than 600 companies providing factoring services in the world, and the worldwide factoring volume reached 260 billion U. S. dollars.

---

[1] Edmond Tavernier, Legal Aspects of Forfaiting, 11 Int'l Bus. Law. (1983)25.

As there are differences in factoring transactions in different countries, some special organizations in the world work hard for the purpose of unification and harmonization of factoring transactions between different companies. The most important three organizations are Factors Chain International and International Factors. Because these are non-governmental organizations, their rules become effective only upon the agreement of parties. In view of this customs character of these rules, recognising the importance of adopting uniform rules to provide a legal framework that will facilitate international factoring, the UNIDROIT, after a period of ten years of drafting, passed *Convention on International Factoring* in Ottwa, 28 May 1988 (hereafter called "UNIDROIT Factoring Convention"). Because the UNIDROIT is an inter-governmental organization of a number of member countries, the UNITROIT Factoring Convention is playing a significant role in the development of international trade.

B. Obligations of the Parties

In a factoring transaction, the parties involved are: the supplier (the exporter or the seller), the factor (the company providing factoring services), the debtor (the importer or the buyer). Under the UNIDROIT Factoring Convention, their respective obligations are:

1. The Obligations of the Supplier

(1) The supplier shall sign a factoring contract with the factor, according to which the supplier shall assign his existing or future receivables to the factor.

(2) The supplier shall take the receivables returned by the factor. When the debtor rejects payment due to the supplier's failure to perform sales contract, these receivables are considered as bad debts, and the factor has recourse on it.

(3) The supplier shall pay contracted interests and related expenses to the factor.

2. The Obligations of the Factor

(1) The factor shall provide credit investigation on the debtor.

(2) The factor shall provide trade financing if required by the supplier.

(3) The factor shall provide maintenance of the sales ledger for the supplier.

(4) The factor shall provide full protection against bad debts. As long as the factor controls the supplier's sale within a limit appropriate for the buyer's creditworthiness, the factor can remove risk of bad debts caused by the debtor's law of creditworthiness. However, the factor does not provide compensation caused by the supplier's failure to perform sales contract, such as late delivery, delivery of non-conforming goods.

C. Advantages of International Factoring for Chinese Merchants

In 1992, Bank of China began to undertake international factoring services in China, and Bank of Communications started the international factoring services in 1994.

Regretfully, the fact that only two banks in China provide these services fails to match China's important trade position in the world. According to the statistics of the United Nations, transactions by letter of credit nowadays only take a proportion of 18% in international trade, and international factoring is becoming an increasingly important mode of payment. Trade volume by international factoring in 1998 in China was only 20 million U. S dollars, a proportion of less than 0.01% of China's export volume. [1] This clearly suggests that international factoring in China need to develop significantly for the further promotion of China's foreign trade.

1. Advantages for Chinese Exporters

(1) Factors shall evaluate the creditworthiness of the buyer so that the exporter does not need to spend money on credit investigations. In practice, factors usually make thousands of credit investigations every month, have files immediately available on hundreds of thousands of customers, and subscribe to services providing immediate access to credit information on their customers. The credit investigation has one of the four following outcomes:

(a) Approval of a line of credit: a credit line is established with a limit appropriate for the customer's creditworthiness. The exporter can, without further inquiry and in accordance with the sales contract, ship goods to the customer, provided the total amount of accounts receivables outstanding does not exceed the line of credit. The factor agrees to purchase all receivables from the customer, within the established limit.

(b) Approval of specific invoice: The factor agrees to purchase the specific receivables represented by the approved invoices.

(c) Declination: If the factor judges the credit standing of the customer to be an unacceptable risk, it will not purchase receivable to be collected from that customer. The exporter has the option of completing the sales and shipping the goods at his own risk, or requiring the customer to provide a letter of credit.

(d) Limited approval: If the factor judges the customer to be marginally creditworthy or has insufficient information to make a fully informed judgement, it may, sometimes, agree to purchase the receivable, limiting its obligation to the exporter to a lesser amount.

It must be pointed out here that disputes arising from non-delivery, damaged goods, inferior quality, wrong quantities or any other failure of the exporter to provide goods to the customer as agreed, must be resolved directly between the exporter and its customer.

(2) The exporter can obtain more than 80% trade financing at the time of assigning

---

[1] Jiang Zuoli, International Business Law, Shanghai People Publishing House, 2003, p. 329.

the receivables to a factor after shipment.

(3) So long as the exporter performs the contract, the factor must effect payment. That's to say, when the buyer fails to pay due to financial inability or when a late payment exists, the factor will pay the exporter.

(4) Of the letter of credit transactions in China about 80% have discrepancies which are often misused by dishonest foreign merchants as excuses for dishonour. However, in international factoring there are no special requirements of documents, and this is more helpful for safe payment.

(5) International factoring is a trade accounting tool, what is more important, factors are obligated to manage receivables for the exporter. This is particularly important to the small Chinese firms which often lack enough skilful staff and international trade experiences.

2. Advantages for the Chinese Importers

(1) The importer in international factoring can save a big sum required as deposit and other expenses in letter of credit transactions.

(2) International factoring is a type of transaction on credit, thus it is in fact a credit loan to the importer.

■ Notes

the League of Nations 国际联盟。第一次世界大战后成立的国际组织，也称"国际联合会"。根据 1919 年巴黎和会上通过的《国际联盟盟约》，该组织于 1920 年 1 月成立。美国为倡议者之一，后因国会未批准而未参加。国际联盟标榜以"促进国际合作，维持国际和平与安全"为目的，实际上在当时成为帝国主义列强巩固第一次世界大战后形成的凡尔赛体系的工具。主要机构有大会、行政院、秘书处，附设国际法庭、国际劳工局等。总部在日内瓦。第二次世界大战爆发后无形中瓦解，1946 年正式宣告解散。

International Chamber of Commerce 国际商会。工商业企业家以个人或团体名义所组成的国际性组织。1920 年 3 月在巴黎成立。会员分团体会员和赞助会员两种：前者为各国工商业联合会，后者为工商企业和企业家个人。在纽约、日内瓦设有联络处，总部在巴黎。

document against payment D/P 付款交单，指出口人的交单是以进口人的付款为条件。即出口人发货后，取得转运单据，委托银行办理托收，并在托收委托书中指示银行，只有在进口人付全货款后，才能把转运单据交给进口人。

document against acceptance D/A 承兑交单，指出口人的交单以进口人在汇票上承兑为条件。即出口人在转运货物后开具远期汇票，连同货运单据，通过银行向进口人提示，进口人承兑汇票后，代收银行即将货运单据交给进口人。在汇票到期时，方履行付款义务。也就是说，与付款交单相比，出口人交出了物权凭证，其收款的保障依赖进口人的信用，一旦进口人到期不付款,出口人便会遭到货物与货款全部落空的损失。因此,出口人对接受这种方式,一般采用很慎重的态度。

■ Important Legal English Usages

merchant 商人。主要用在法律和商业文书、法规中,比较正式。例如,merchant flag(商船旗),merchant laws(商人法), merchant's court (商事法庭)。

注意该词与下列近义词的区别:

(1)businessman 是口语词,不太正式。

(2)dealer 主要指经销商,商行。

(3)trader 主要指手工业者,经销商等。

due 适当的,所有的,正当的。例如,due course of law (due process, due process of law)(正当法律程序),due diligence (适当的注意)。He asserted that there was no conflict between the censorship law and a due regard for civil liberties (他断言在检查制度与适当尊重公民自由权之间没有冲突)。

forged 伪造的。主要指假冒签字。有时也指伪造其他东西。例如,a forged endorsement on the traveller's cheque (旅游支票上的伪造签名)。

注意该词与下列近义词在用法上的区别:

(1)fake:指某物不是真的。例如,a fake telegram (伪造的电报), a fake picture (一幅临摹的画)。

(2)false:指某物与真的很像,但不一定用作"冒充、欺骗"。false teeth (假牙), false diamonds (人造的宝石)。

(3)counterfeit:指伪造的东西看上去像真的一样,以便能欺骗别人。例如,counterfeit money (假钱), counterfeit diamonds (仿造的珠宝)。

(4)imitation:伪造的,仿造的,冒充的。用作形容词时与 fake 相同。例如,shoes made of imitation leather (人造革造的鞋), imitation pearls(人造的珍珠)。

proof (口头或书面)证明,证据。主要用于证明有罪或身份,使用面较窄。例如,proof beyond a reasonable (确凿的证明), proof of status (身份证明), proof to the contrary (反证)。

注意该词与下列近义词在用法上的区别:

(1)evidence:证据证明,作证。最普通的用词,指证人的各种形式的证词,以及与诉讼有关的所有事实和实物。日常用法指对任何事物区别真与假、对与错的证明。例如,Running away was evidence of his guilt (逃跑是他犯罪的证据). Scholars have been able o unearth some evidence as to the true authorship of the book(学者们已能够发现,谁是此书的真正作者的一些证据)。

(2)testimony:主要指被认为知道案情的证人所说的任何供词。例如,A witness gave testimony that the accused was drunk (一个证人作证说被告确实醉了)。

(3)affidavit:法律用语,指未经对方询问而自动提出的、法庭可以接受的证词。例如,

to swear an affidavit（立口供书）。

（4）deposition：法律用语，指经宣誓后，对法庭正式询问所作的口头答复，加以笔录而成。例如，The deposition of the last witness convicted the accused man（最后一个证人的证词证实了被告有罪）。

■ Review Questions

1. Briefly define"a bill of exchange" and state its main features.
2. What is meant by the term"holder in due course"? And outline its general requirements and rights.
3. Under what circumstance can D/P and D/A be used to promote trade?
4. Define"a standby letter of credit" and identify the circumstances where it can be used in international trade practices.
5. Explain, giving examples where possible, the principle of independence and the rule of strict compliance.
6. Outline and discuss the causes of fraud in letter of credit and state the rationality of doctrine of fraud exception.
7. State briefly the historical development of international factoring.
8. Discuss the advantages and disadvantages of international factoring to Chinese merchants.
9. Habib Bank issued a letter of credit on the instructions of its account party calling for the payment of drafts upon the presentation of documents showing shipment by a certain date. The bank examined the documents and paid the beneficiary's draft. The account party refused to take the documents and reimburse the bank because the shipping date was incorrectly stated in the documents. The bank sued the beneficiary for a return of its money for presenting nonconforming documents. The bank brought its action under the UCP 500. The beneficiary claims that under the UCP the bank was precluded from complaining about the discrepancies because the bank had failed to object to the documents in a timely fashion. UCP 500, Article 14, states that an issuing or nominated bank must notify the beneficiary (or another bank from which it is receiving the documents) of the rejection without delay but no later than the close of the seventh banking day following the day of receipt of the documents. Judgment for whom and why?[1]

---

[1] Richard Schaffer, Beverley Earle and Filiberto Agusti, International Business Law and Its Environment, West Publishing Company, 1996, p. 289.

10. Your firm has contracted to purchase silk from overseas suppliers on letter of credit terms. After contracting, before presentment of the seller's documents, some developing countries expand their production and flood the market with raw silk. The price of silk plummets on world market. Comment on whether you should try to find a minor discrepancy in the documents to justify rejecting the documents. Is it ethical for a buyer to reject documents presented under a letter of credit that contains only a minor discrepancy between the documents and the credit? Do the reasons matter? Does it matter that the buyer may know that the shipment actually conforms to the requirements of the contract and of the letter of credit?

8

Chapter Eight

China Partnership Enterprise Law

■ 导读

本章讲授的是我国合伙企业法,主要包括合伙企业的设立、合伙人的权利义务、赔偿责任及合伙企业的清算等内容。本章的设立主要基于以下考虑:一是国外合伙企业作为一种企业经营模式早已被广泛采用,相关的法律已臻完善;二是随着我国对外开放的深入,《合伙企业法》经过修订后,已经逐渐成熟。特别是,随着"一带一路"倡议的快速实施,越来越多的外资会加速进入我国,合伙企业作为重要的中外合作经营的模式必然会发挥重要的作用。如果读者认真研习我国的《合伙企业法》,必定有助于吸引外资和提高管理合伙企业的技能,促进我国对外开放的更快发展。

This chapter examines the partnership form of business organization and relevant legal issues under the Partnership Enterprise Law of the Peoples' Republic of China on (hereafter called "China Partnership Enterprise Law"). It addresses the conditions for the establishment of a partnership enterprise, rights and duties of a partner, legal liabilities in the process of management of a partnership enterprise.

Ⅰ. Definition and Creation of a Partnership

A. Definition

The basic concept of partnership (合伙) is as ancient as the history of collective human activity. Partnerships were known in ancient Babylonia, ancient Greece, and the Roman Empire. Hammurabi's Code of 2300 B. C. regulated partnerships. The definition of a partnership in the 6th century Justinian Code of the Roman Empire does not differ materially from that in our laws today. During the Middle Ages, much trade between nations was carried on by partnerships.

By the close of the 17th century, the partnership was recognized in the English common law. When the United States became an independent nation and adopted the English common law in 1776, the English law of partnerships became a part of American law. In the early part of the 19th century, the partnership became the most important form of association in the United States.

Today, the American common law of partnership has been largely replaced by statutory law. Every state has a statute on partnership law. The Uniform Partnership Act (UPA) of 1914 is the law in about 40 states and the District of Columbia. The UPA is a model partnership statute that is the product of the National Conference of Commissioners on Uniform State Laws, a group of practicing lawyers, judges, and law professors. The aims of the UPA are to codify partnership law in one document, to make that law more nearly consistent with itself, and to attain uniformity throughout the country. A Revised Uniform Partnership Act (RUPA) was proposed in 1992 and amended in 1994. The RUPA has been heavily criticized for changing partnership rules protecting creditors of partnerships. [1] Most people are surprised to discover that there are amazingly few legal formalities involved in creating a partnership. In fact, a court may find two persons to be partners even though neither had the specific intent to create a partnership. This is because no express agreement is necessary to create a partnership. All that is required is that the parties intended to have the relationship that the law defines as a partnership. The UPA simply defines a partnership as an "association of two or more persons to carry on as co-owners a business for profit." If the definition is satisfied, then the courts will treat those involved as partners.

Under Article 2 of the China Partnership Enterprise Law (which was adopted at the 24th Meeting of the Standing Committee of the Eighth National People's Congress on February 23, 1997, and amended in 2006), partnership enterprise refers to the general partnership enterprises and limited liability partnership enterprises which are established within China by natural persons, legal persons and other organizations in accordance with the law. A general partnership enterprise may be formed by general partners. The partners shall bear unlimited joint and several liabilities for the debts of the partnership enterprise. If this Law has any special provisions on the way in which the general partners shall bear liabilities, these special provisions shall prevail. A limited liability partnership enterprise shall be formed by general partners and limited partners. The general partners shall bear unlimited joint and several liabilities for the debts of the limited liability partnership enterprise. The limited partners bear the liabilities for its debts to the extent of their capital contributions.

Clearly, the definition of a partnership is made under Chinese law together with the main characteristics of a partnership such as all the partners shall conclude a partnership agreement, all partners shall make joint capital contributions, conduct business jointly, bear unlimited joint and several liabilities for debts of the partnership enterprise.

---

[1] Jane P. Mallor, A. James Barnes, Thomas Bowers, Michael J. Phillips, and Arlen W. Langvardt, Business Law and the Regulatory Environment, Irwin McGraw Hill Boston, 1998, p. 750.

B. Establishment of a Partnership Enterprise

To establish a partnership enterprise, the following conditions shall be satisfied: (1) having 2 or more partners. If the partners are natural persons, they shall have complete civil capacity; (2) having a written partnership agreement; (3) having capital contributions subscribed to or actually paid by the partners; (4) having a name and a production and business operation place for the partnership enterprise; and (5) other conditions as provided for by laws and administrative regulations (Article 14).

In order to facilitate the creation of a partnership, Article 9 provides that the applicant shall submit to the enterprise registration organ a registration application, partnership agreement, identity certificates of the partners and other documents. If the business scope of a partnership enterprise contains any item which is subject to approval prior to registration under a law or administrative regulation, such business shall be subject to approval in accordance with the law and the approval document shall be submitted at the time of registration.

1. Capital Contributions

According to Article 16, a partner may make capital contributions in money, in kind, or intellectual property right, land use right or other properties, or labor services. Where a partner intends to make capital contributions in kind, intellectual property right, land use right and other properties, of which the price should be assessed, the price may be determined by all partners through negotiation or may assessed by the statutory assessment institution entrusted by all partners. Where a partner makes capital contributions by labor services, the assessment method shall be determined by all partners and shall be stated in a partnership agreement.

A partner shall perform the capital contribution obligation according to the way and amount of capital contribution and the time limit for payment as stipulated in the partnership agreement. For the capital contributions in non-monetary properties for which the formalities for the transfer of property right shall be gone through under any law or administrative regulation, the partner shall go through the said formalities (Article 17).

2. Carrying on a Business

Any trade, occupation, or profession may qualify as a business. Carrying on a business usually requires a series of transactions conducted over a period of time. For example, a group of farmers that buys supplies in quantity to get lower prices is not carrying on a business but only part of one. If the group buys harvesting equipment with which it intends to harvest crops for others for a fee for many years, it is carrying on a business.

II. Property of a Partnership Enterprise

Under Articles 20 and 21, all the capital contributions made by partners, the proceeds and other properties acquired in the name of a partnership shall be the properties of the partnership enterprise. Prior to the liquidation of a partnership enterprise, no partner may request for dividing the properties of the partnership enterprise, unless it is otherwise provided for in this Law. If the partners privately transfer or dispose of the properties of a partnership enterprise prior to liquidation, the partnership enterprise shall not challenge any bona fide third party. Unless it is otherwise provided for in the partnership agreement, when a partner assigns its entire or partial share of properties of a partnership enterprise, it (he) shall acquire the unanimous consent of all other partners. In the case of assignment of a partner's entire or partial share of properties of a partnership enterprise to another partner, the other partners shall be informed of this assignment (Article 22).

Clearly, Partnership property is held by the partners as tenants in partnership. Partners have no separate interest in partnership property. They have no right to sell, mortgage, or devise to an heir any individual item of the firm's property. A partner has a right to take possession of the firm's property for partnership purposes but not for personal use. For example, if you are a partner, you have no right to use the firm's automobile for your vacation. Permission of a majority of the partners would be required. You may, however, without special permission, drive the car to the bank to deposit the firm's receipts.

Ⅲ. Partners' Rights and Duties

Article 26 addresses partners' rights and duties where the partners enjoy equal rights to the execution of partnership affairs. According to the stipulations of the partnership agreement or upon decision of all partners, one or several partners may be authorized to execute the partnership affairs on behalf of the partnership enterprise. Where a legal person partner or any other organization partner executes the partnership affairs, the representative whom it authorizes shall execute the partnership affairs.

It should be noted that partners must observe the duty of loyalty and good faith. Article 32 further provides that no partner may, solely or jointly with others, operate any business competing with this partnership enterprise. Unless it is otherwise stipulated in the partnership agreement or unless it is unanimously consented by all partners, no partner may have any transaction with this partnership enterprise. No partner may engage in any activity which may impair the interests of this partnership enterprise.

Not only partners be honest but they also must not permit self-interest to come before duty to the partnership. Partners may buy from or sell to the partnership. However, if they do, they must make full disclosure of any facts relevant to the deals that are not known to the other partners. Partners may not make secret profits from their position as members of a partnership.

In the absence of a contrary understanding, each partner owes a duty to devote full time and his or her best efforts to the affairs of the partnership. A partner must not engage in activities that are in competition with or otherwise likely to injure the partnership. For example, suppose you join with a friend in forming a real estate brokerage partnership. If your partner accepts commissions, he is in breach of his obligations based on duty of loyalty and good faith.

IV. Profits and Loss

Under the provisions of Article 33, the distribution of profits or sharing of losses of the partnership enterprise shall follow the stipulations of the partnership agreement. If it is not stipulated or not expressly stipulated in the partnership agreement, a decision shall be made by the partners through negotiation. In case the negotiations fail, the distribution of profits or sharing of losses shall be made in proportion to the actual capital contributions made by the partners. If it is unable to determine the proportions of capital contributions, the profits or losses shall be distributed or shared equally by the partners. It shall not be stipulated in any partnership agreement that all profits will be distributed to some of the partners or that some partners will bear all losses.

As to the debts of a partnership enterprise, Article 42 further stipulates that if the partners' own properties are insufficient to pay off its debt irrelevant to the partnership enterprise, this partner may use the proceeds, which it (he) acquires from the partnership enterprise, to pay for the debt. The creditor may also plead the people's court to enforce the repayment of the debt by the said partners' property share in the partnership enterprise according to the law.

When the court enforces the repayment of the debt by the said partners' property share, it shall send a notice to all partners. The other partners have the preemptive right to the property share of the said partner. If the other partners do not purchase it, nor consent to assign it to others, a withdrawal settlement shall be made for this partner in accordance with Article 51 of this Law, or a settlement shall be made to decrease the property share of this partner correspondingly.

V. Admission to and Withdrawal from a Partnership Enterprise

The admission of a new partner shall, unless it is otherwise stipulated in the partnership agreement, be subject to a unanimous consent of all partners, and for which a written agreement shall be concluded. When concluding an agreement on the admission to the partnership, the original partners shall faithfully inform the new partners of the business operation and financial status of the original partnership enterprise (Article 43).

Article 44 provides that a new partner admitted to a partnership enterprise shall enjoy the same rights and bear the same liabilities as the original partners. If the partnership agreement stipulates otherwise, the said agreement shall prevail. A new partner shall bear joint and several liabilities for the debts of the partnership enterprise incurred before it is admitted to a partnership enterprise.

The withdrawal from a partnership enterprise is addressed by Article 45 where the term of operation of a partnership business has been set in the partnership agreement, a partner may, during the period of existence thereof, withdraw from partnership in any of the following cases: (1) any cause for withdrawal from partnership as stipulated in the partnership agreement occurs; (2) all partners agree to the withdrawal; (3) any cause to make the said partner difficult to remain in the partnership occurs; or (4) other partners seriously violate their obligations as stipulated in the partnership agreement.

Besides, under Article 48, any partner is under any of the following circumstances, the said partner shall be deemed to have withdrawn naturally from the partnership: (1) a natural person partner is deceased or declared deceased according to law; (2) it (he) is insolvent; (3) a partner as a legal person or any other organization whose business license is revoked, or who is ordered to close up for revocation, or who is declared bankrupt; (4) a partner loses the relevant qualifications as required by law or as stipulated in the partnership agreement; or (5) a partner's entire property share in the partnership business has been executed by the people's court. For a partner who is determined as a person without civil capacity or with limited civil capacity according to law, he may be changed into a limited partner upon unanimous consent of the other parties and the general partnership enterprise shall be changed into a limited partnership enterprise in pursuance of law. For failure of unanimous consent of the other partners, this partner without civil capacity or with limited civil capacity shall withdraw from the partnership. The withdrawal from partnership shall be take effect on the date when it is actually made.

VI. Limited Partnership Enterprises

A limited liability partnership enterprise shall be formed by general partners and limited partners. The general partners shall bear unlimited joint and several liabilities for the debts of the limited liability partnership enterprise. The limited partners bear the liabilities for its debts to the extent of their capital contributions.

Under Article 61, a limited partnership enterprise shall be established by not less than 2 but not more than 50 partners, unless it is otherwise provided by law. A limited partnership enterprise shall have at least one general partner.

The capital contributions of partners are addressed by Article 64, a limited partner may make capital contributions in money, in kind, or intellectual property right, land use right or other properties. And no limited partner may make capital contributions in labor services. Article 65 further stipulates that a limited partner shall make full payment of the capital contributions within the time limit as stipulated in the partnership agreement. If it fails to do so, it shall be obliged to make up the payment and shall bear the liabilities for breach of contract to the other partners.

According to Article 74, if the limited partner's own properties are insufficient to pay off his debt irrelevant to the partnership enterprise, this partner may use the proceeds which he acquires from the limited partnership enterprise to pay for the debt. The creditor may also plead the people's court to enforce the repayment of the debt with the said limited partner's property share in the partnership enterprise according to the law. When the people's court enforces the repayment of the debt with the said limited partner's property share, it shall send a notice to all partners. The other partners have the preemptive right to the property share of the said partner under the same conditions.

Under the provisions of Article 81, after a limited partner withdraws from the partnership, it (he) shall, to the extent of the properties it (he) takes back from the limited partnership enterprise at the time of withdrawal, bear the liabilities for the debts incurred to the limited partnership enterprise prior to its (his) withdrawal.

VII. Dissolution and Liquidation

Dissolution occurs when any partner ceases to be associated in the carrying on of the business. However, a partner's demand for dissolution does not automatically terminate the partnership business. Instead, it may be carried on by the remaining partners through a continuation. The dissolution and liquidation of partnership enterprises are mainly addressed by Articles 85 – 92.

Under Article 85, partnership enterprise shall be dissolved under any of the following circumstances: (1) the term of partnership expires and the partners decide not to operate it any longer; (2) any of the dissolution causes as stipulated in the partnership agreement occurs; (3) all partners make a decision to dissolve it; (4) 30 days have lapsed since the number of partners fails to reach the quorum; (5) the partnership aim as stipulated in the partnership agreement has been realized or is unable to be realized; (6) its business license is revoked, or it is ordered to close up or to be revoked; or (7) other reasons as provided for by any law or administrative regulation.

Under the provisions of Article 86, when a partnership is dissolved, it shall be liquidated by liquidators. All partners shall act as liquidators. Upon consent of more than half of all partners, one or several partners or third persons may, after the occurrence of the cause for the dissolution of the partnership enterprise, be designated or entrusted to act as liquidators. With 15 days after the occurrence of the cause for the dissolution of the partnership enterprise, the partners or other interest parties may apply to the people's court to designate liquidators.

Article 88 provides that the liquidators shall, within 10 days after a decision of dissolution is made, inform the creditors of the relevant matters and publish an announcement on a newspaper within 60 days. A creditor shall, within 30 days from the day when it receives a notice or within 45 days from the announcement date if it fails to receive a notice, declare its credits to the liquidators.

When a creditor declares its credits, it shall state the relevant matters of the credits and provide supporting materials. The liquidators shall record the credits.

During the process of liquidation, the partnership enterprise still exists but it shall not carry out any business activities irrelevant to the liquidation.

In order to make sure that the partnership enterprise fulfills the social responsibility, Article 89 stipulates that after paying off the liquidation expenses, wages of employees, social insurance premiums and legal indemnities, the outstanding taxes and the debts with the properties of the partnership enterprise, the residual properties may be distributed in accordance with Paragraph1of Article 33 of this Law.

According Articles 90 - 92, after the liquidation is ended, the liquidators shall prepare a liquidation report. Within 15 days after the liquidation report is affixed with the signatures and seals of all partners, it shall be submitted to the enterprise registration organ for deregistration of the partnership enterprise. After the deregistration of a partnership enterprise, the former general partners shall still bear joint and several liabilities for the debts incurred during the existence period of the partnership enterprise.

Where a partnership enterprise is unable to meet its mature debts, the creditors may apply to the people's court for bankruptcy liquidation or may demand the general partners to make repayments. Where a partnership enterprise is declared bankrupt, the general partners shall still bear joint and several liabilities for the debts of the partnership enterprise.

VIII. Legal Liabilities

The legal liabilities of partners fall within Articles 93 - 106. Anyone who obtains the registration of a partnership enterprise by violating this Law, such as providing false documents or taking other fraudulent means, shall be ordered to make a correction by the enterprise registration organ and shall be fined not less than 5,000 yuan but not more than 50,000 yuan. If the circumstance is serious, the enterprise registration shall be revoked and a fine of not less than 50,000 yuan but not more than 200,000 yuan shall be given. Article 94 provides that where a partnership enterprise fails to indicate his name with the words "general partnership" or "special partnership" or "limited partnership" as in violation of this Law, it shall be ordered to make a correction by the enterprise registration organ and shall be fined not less than 2,000 yuan but not more than 10,000 yuan. According to Article 95, anyone who has not obtained a business license but is engaging in partnership business operations in the name of a partnership enterprise or branch of a partnership enterprise as in violation of this Law shall be ordered to stop such business operations by the enterprise registration organ and shall be fined not less than 5,000 yuan but not more than 50,000 yuan. Where a partnership enterprise fails to modify the registration for the change of any registration item as in violation of this Law, it shall be ordered to go through the registration formalities. If it fails to do so, it shall be fined not less than 2,000 yuan but not more than 20,000 yuan.

Where any registration item of a partnership enterprise changes, if the partners executing the partnership affairs fail to timely go through the registration modification formalities, it shall compensate for any loss incurred therefrom to the partnership enterprise, other partners or bona fide third persons.

Under the provisions of the following articles, partners shall bear the civil compensation liabilities: where any partner executing the partnership affairs or any practitioner of a partnership enterprise, by taking the advantage of his position, usurps any benefit which should attribute to the partnership enterprise, occupy any property of the partnership enterprise by other illegal means, it (he) shall return the benefit or property to the partnership enterprise. If its (his) act causes any loss to the partnership enterprise or to other partners, it (he) shall bear the compensation liabilities.

Where any partner, with no unanimous consent of all partners, handles by himself any affair which shall be subject to the unanimous consent of all partners under this Law or according to this partnership agreement, if his (its) act causes any loss to the partnership enterprise or to other partners, it (he) shall bear compensation liabilities. Where any partner, who does not have the power to execute the affairs of the partnership affairs, illegally executes such affairs, if its (his) act causes any losses to the partnership enterprise or to other partners, it (he) shall bear compensation liabilities.

Article 99 further stipulates that where any partner engages in any business competing with this partnership enterprise or makes transactions with this partnership enterprise as in violation of the provisions of this Law or the stipulations of the partnership agreement, the relevant proceeds shall attribute to the partnership enterprise. If any loss is caused to the partnership enterprise or to other partners, it (he) shall bear compensation liabilities.

According to other articles, partners shall bear compensation liabilities under the circumstances such as concealing or transferring any property of a partnership enterprise, or making any false record in the balance sheet or in the property list, or distributing properties prior to the settlement of debts, and breach of the agreement of partnership.

The methods of disputes settlement are addressed by Article 103: where there is any dispute between the partners over the execution of the partnership agreement, the partners may settle it through negotiations or mediation. If they are unwilling or fail to settle it through negotiations or medication, they may apply to the arbitration institution for arbitration according to the arbitration clause in the partnership agreement or under the written arbitration agreement concluded afterwards. If there is no arbitration clause in the partnership agreement and if they fail to reach any written arbitration agreement afterwards, they may initiate a lawsuit in the people's court.

■ Notes

partnership 合伙。合伙是两个或两个以上的合伙人为经营共同事业,共同出资、共享利润而组成的企业。在大陆法系国家,合伙分为“民事合伙”和“商事合伙”,分别适用民法典和商法典或有关的商事法规。两者的主要区别是,商事合伙必须是达到一定经营规模并专门从事营利性活动的合伙企业。

Justinian Code 优士丁尼法典。该法典指由罗马皇帝优士丁尼(Justinianus)指定的十人编纂的帝国法律汇编。该法典为《民法大全》(Corpus Juris Civilis)的第一部分,共分 12 编。其中所确立的许多原则(特别是民法)和制度,依然为现在许多国家所普遍继承。

good faith 诚信。诚实信用在拉丁文中用 bona fides 表示,法文中是 bonne foi, 英文中是 good faith, 德文中是 true und glauben, 日文中是“信义诚实”。上述外文一般在中文中译成“善意”。现代民法中的诚实信用之义主要源于罗马法中的 bona fides,上述德文、英文及日文中诚实信用也是承袭 bona fides 之意。优士丁尼皇帝曾将著名罗马法学家乌尔比安提出的法的准则表述为:“法的准则是,诚实生活,不犯他人,各得其所。”我国学者对诚实信用原则的含义虽有争议,但一般认为,诚实信用原则就是要求民事主体在民事活动中维持双方的利益平衡以及当事人利益与社会利益平衡的立法者意志。概言之,诚实信用原则就是立法者实现上述三方利益平衡的要求,目的在于保持社会稳定与和谐的发展。三方利益平衡是这一原则实现的结果,当事人以诚实、善意的态度行使权利、履行义务,法官根据公平正义进行创造性的司法活动,是达到这一结果的手段。诚实信用原则在两个方面发挥作用:首先,它是当事人进行民事活动时必须具备诚实、善意的内心状态的要求，对当事人进行民事活动起着指导作用；其次，诚实信用原则是对法官衡平权的授予。[1]

在国际商事交易中，诚实信用原则早已成为各国普遍认可的重要原则。例如，人们普遍认为，诚实信用原则应贯穿于从合同谈判开始直到交易完成时为止。例如，一方当事人无意与对方成交，却为了刺探对方情报或获得秘密技术或获得专有技术之目的与对方进行商务谈判，而一旦达到目的，就终止与对方谈判而不与对方成交。再如，一方当事人声称要购买对方的货物，向对方索取样品。而一旦得到样品，就立即部署其工厂开始大规模生产，并不购买对方的货物。这些显然都违背了诚实信用原则。

■ Important Legal English Usages

employ 雇用，租用，强调受雇者虽为薪金而工作，但工作相当固定且有相当尊严。例如，The factory employed 600 hands（工厂雇用了 600 名员工）。

注意与下列近义词在用法上的区别：

(1) hire：雇用，使用，强调主要为薪金而工作。例如，She hired a man to mow the lawn（她雇了一男人修整草坪）。

(2) engage：雇用，可与 hire 换用，特指雇用专业人员。例如，He engaged a lawyer to argue his case in court（他请了一名律师在法庭上为他辩护）。

lawyer 律师，法律代理人，法学家。该词是对律师的通称，指取得律师许可证开业的人。其职责是接受诉讼案件、讲解法律或出庭辩护。例如，His parents intend to make a lawyer of him（他父母想让他当律师）。

注意与下列同义词在用法上的区别：

(1) advocate：律师，辩护人。该词特指苏格兰等以罗马法律为基本法的国家和特别法庭的律师。例如，He hired the best advocate he could find to represent him in court（他聘请了所能聘到的最好的律师，为他出庭辩护）。

(2) attorney：律师，代理人。该词在美国用作律师，相当于英国的"solicitor"。例如，a letter of attorney（委托他人代理的委托书）。

(3) barrister：律师。该词主要用于英国，指有资格出席高等法庭的律师，而不是被告所聘的一般辩护律师。例如，The jury had heard counsel on both sides, the barristers for the prosecution and the defense（陪审团已听了原告及被告双方辩护律师的意见）。

(4) counsel：律师。主要指辩护律师。例如，After consulting with counsel, the defendant changed his plea（经与辩护律师磋商后，被告改变了他的抗辩）。

(5) solicitor：律师。指英国的初级律师，在美国指在政府部门或一城市中负责法律事务的司法官员。

responsible 尽责的，应负责任的。该词是最常用的词。例如，The judge was pondering over

[1] 彭万林：《民法学》，中国政法大学出版社 1997 年版，第 48 页。

whom to hold responsible for the accident（法官在考虑谁应对这一事故负责）。

注意同下列近义词的区别。

liable for 有责任的，应受惩罚的。指让谁负责，也指应负法律责任或受罚。例如，Laws hold the driver liable for any injury to his passengers（法律认为司机因其乘客受伤而应受处罚）。再如，Is a man liable for his wife's debts in your country（在你们国家里一个男人要对他的妻子的债务负责吗）？

objective 目的，目标，方法。法律英语中用得较多，有时也用在军事方面。例如，This law is formulated for the objective of protecting the lawful rights and interests of parties to economic contracts（制定本法的目的是保护经济合同当事人的合法权益）。

注意与下列近义词在用法上的区别：

（1）purpose：目的，宗旨。常指为达某一目的，经过深思熟虑后而采取果断行动。例如，The "taxable income" for purposes of levying the local income tax mentioned in Article 4 of the Tax Law shall be the same as the taxable income mentioned in Article 3 of the Tax Law（《税法》第 4 条所说征收地方所得税的应纳税的所得额，与《税法》第 3 条所说的应纳税的所得额相同）。

（2）aim：目的，目标。指人实现一般的目的或目标。例如，He has a noble aim（他有一个崇高的目的）。

（3）end：目的，目标。强调实现的最终目标。例如，The happiness of the people is the end of government（人民幸福是政府之目标）。

（4）goal：目标，目的。指要实现远大的目标和目的，同 purpose 意思相近。例如，The purpose of a tutorial system was to let each student realize his own educational goal（导师制的目的是让每一个学生都能实现自己的求学目标）。

（5）grounds：基础，理由（法律上常用复数）。例如，ground of action（诉讼理由，诉讼基础事实）The Italians rejected his complaints on the grounds that such sales were no threat to his country（意大利人以这种销售不会对他的国家构成威胁为理由，拒绝了他的指控）；There are no grounds for anxiety（没有为此担心的理由）。

Review Questions

1. Define "partnership" and identify its main features.
2. Briefly describe the rights and duties of a partner, giving two examples.
3. Under what circumstances will a partnership be terminated?
4. What are the conditions for the establishment of a partnership enterprise?
5. Briefly describe the rights and duties of partners in dissolution and liquidation of partnership enterprise.
6. List briefly the circumstances under which a partner shall bear compensation liabilities, giving examples where possible.

9 Chapter Nine China Company Law

■ 导读

本章讲授的是中国公司法,主要包括公司的历史发展及性质、股东的权利与义务、公司的管理及公司的结算等。我国自对外开放以来,大量的外资进入我国,主要通过公司的企业模式促进了我国经济的发展,也使外商收益颇丰。随着我国对外开放的进一步深化和提速,毫无疑问,公司的作用会日趋重要。建议读者耐心地通读本章内容,为进一步促进我国的招商引资工作做好准备。

The modern corporation has facilitated the rapid economic development of the last 150 years by permitting businesses to attain economies of scale. Businesses organized as corporations can attain such economies because they have a greater capacity to raise capital than do other business forms. This capital raising advantage is ensured by corporation law, which allows persons to invest their money in a corporation and become owners without imposing unlimited liability or management responsibilities on themselves. Many people are willing to invest their savings in a large, risky business if they have limited liability and no management responsibilities. Far fewer are willing to invest in a partnership or other business form in which owners have unlimited liability and management duties.

I. History and Nature of Corporations

Although modern corporation law emerged only in the last 150 years, ancestors of the modern corporation existed in the times of Hammurabi, ancient Greece, and the Roman Empire. As early as 1248 in France, privileges of incorporation were given to mercantile ventures to encourage investment for the benefit of society. In England, the corporate form was used extensively before the 16th century.

In England, the famous British trading companies—such as the Massachusetts Bay Company—were the forerunners of the modern corporation. The British government gave these companies monopolies in trade and granted them powers to govern in the areas they colonized. They were permitted to operate as corporations due to the benefits they would confer on the British Empire, such as the development of natural resources.

Although these trading companies were among the few corporations of the time whose owners were granted limited liability, they sought corporate status primarily because the government granted them monopolies and governmental powers.

Beginning in 1776, corporation law in the United States evolved independently of English corporation law. Early American corporations received special charters from state legislatures. These charters were granted one at a time by special action of the legislatures; few special charters were granted. In the late 18th century, general incorporation statutes emerged in the United States. Initially, these statutes permitted incorporation only for limited purposes beneficial to the public, such as operating toll bridges and water systems. Incorporation was still viewed as a privilege, and many restrictions were placed on corporations: incorporation was permitted for only short periods of time; and ownership of real and personal property was often restricted. During the last 150 years, such restrictive provisions have disappeared in most states.

In the early part of the nineteenth century, business in the United States tended to be local in nature and of primary concern to individual states. Corporations during this period were usually created for public or near public purposes—e. g. to build canals, bridges, or toll roads—and often enjoyed some monopoly privileges.

Beginning roughly at the turn of the 20th century, several states systematically began to seek to attract corporations to incorporate or reincorporate in their states. Statutes were amended to simplify procedures and make the applicable rules more attractive, particularly for large corporations doing business in most or all of the states. In 1950, a committee of the American Bar Association developed and maintained the Model Business Corporation Act (MBCA), which was influential in the development of state incorporation statutes in some thirty states. MBCA largely builds on the provisions of the older MBCA, but adopts innovative provisions in a number of areas and effects a considerable simplification of language in many provisions.

In China, the modern company law originated from the Commercial Laws of The Emperor granted Da Qing (1903) which was chiefly modelled on western laws in the later Qing Dynasty, aiming to promote the national commerce. In 1914, the General Principles of Merchants and Company Regulations were promulgated. In 1929, the Principles of Company Law was issued and put into force in July, 1931. This Principles of Company Law was the first modern company law in China, and has played an important role in regulating companies and promoting economic development at that time. This law has been revised several times in the period of Guomintang Government, and the revision in 1946 enlarged the law into 10 chapters, 361 articles.

The Company Law of the People's Republic of China (China Company Law) became effective in July of 1994 as the first piece of national company legislation promulgated in China, since the founding of the People's Republic of China in 1949. China Company Law was amended for the first time in accordance with the Decision of the 13th Session of the Standing Committee of the Ninth People's Congress on Revising the Company Law of the People's Republic of China dated December 25, 1999, and then amended in 2004, 2005, 2013 and 2018 (New China Company Law). After many times amendments, there can be no doubt that current China Company Law is a very comprehensive body of law and an amazing step by the Chinese government toward conforming Chinese business organizations to international standards in order to meet the needs of establishing a modern enterprise system, to standardize the organization and activities of companies, to protect the legitimate rights and interests of companies, shareholders and creditors, to maintain socio economic order and to promote the development of the socialist market economy, motivated by the further open-door policies of the government, particularly the rapid fulfillment of the proposals of "One Belt and One Road" and "A Community with A Shared Future for Mankind".

II. Purposes of China Company Law

There are many reasons why China has decided to enact a national company law. The ultimate ideological goal of the company law is to unite Western capitalist corporate structures with existing Chinese enterprises while concurrently retaining and promoting the "socialist market economy." However, this ideological goal does not envision a replacement of the state sector by private enterprises. Instead, the pragmatic purpose of the company law is to allow the government to remove itself from the micro-management of enterprises. By removing itself from the day-to-day affairs of a corporation, the government hopes enterprises will become more productive and efficient by the ensuing competition. The competitive enterprises are to then develop and mature, while the means of production remain safely in the hands of the people, who are represented by the Chinese government. In short, with the company law the government hopes market discipline will force Chinese enterprises to become more productive and efficient. However, the government intends the private sector to only be a supplement to the state sector. The second goal of the company law is promote the development of small private enterprises. This new legislation seeks to provide, for the first time, a firm legal basis for the establishment and operation of any company in accordance with the principles of the socialist market economy.

III. Basic Categories of Company Organs

New China Company Law contains 13 chapters and 218 articles. It is one of the largest statutes enacted in China. According to the "structure" of the Law, there are four basic categories of corporate organs in any Chinese Company Limited by Shares: the board of shareholders, the board of directors and the manager and the supervisory committee.

A. Board of Shareholders

The board of shareholders of a limited liability company shall consist of all its shareholders. The board of shareholders is the highest authoritative body of the company and shall exercise its functions and powers in accordance with the Law (Article 36). Article 37 provides that the board of shareholders shall exercise the following functions and powers: (1) determine the company's operational guidelines and investment plans; (2) elect and replace non-employee representative directors and supervisors and determine matters relating to their remunerations; (3) deliberate on and approve reports of the board of directors; (4) deliberate on and approve reports of the board of supervisors or of the supervisor(s); (5) deliberate on and approve annual budgets and final accounts of the company; (6) deliberate on and approve the company's profit distribution plans and loss recovery plans; (7) make resolutions on any increase or reduction of the company's registered capital; (8) make resolutions on the issuance of corporate bonds; (9) make resolutions on any combination, division, dissolution, liquidation or transformation of the company; (10) revise the articles of association of the company; and (11) any other function or power specified in the articles of association.

In respect of any of the matters listed in the preceding paragraph, where the shareholders have unanimously agreed in writing, a decision may be made directly without convening a meeting of the board of shareholders and the decision document shall bear the signatures or seals of all the shareholders.

Under Articles 38 and 39, the first meeting of the board of shareholders shall be convened and presided over by the shareholder with the largest capital contribution, and shall exercise its functions and powers in accordance with the Law. Meetings of the board of shareholders shall be classified into regular meetings and interim meetings. Regular meetings shall be held on time as prescribed in the company's articles of association. An interim meeting shall be held where it is proposed by shareholders representing one tenth or more of the voting rights, by one third or more of the directors or by the board of supervisors or, where there is no board of supervisors, by a supervisor of the company.

In sum, the shareholders of Chinese companies actually exercise considerable control over a company. Most significantly, the New China Company Law requires that many crucial decisions be made only at shareholders' meetings. For example, the shareholders must decide the company's operational principles and investment plans. Further, the shareholders must approve extraordinary matters, such as corporate merger, division, transformation, dissolution and liquidation.

B. Board of Directors and Managers

According to Article 108, a joint stock limited company shall establish the board of directors, members of which shall range from five to nineteen. The board of directors may include employee representatives. Employee representatives who serve as board directors shall be democratically elected through the employee representatives' assembly, the employees' assembly or otherwise. The provisions of Article 45 of the Law on the term of office of the directors of a limited liability company shall apply to the directors of a joint stock limited company. The provisions of Article 46 of the Law on the functions and powers of the board of directors of a limited liability company shall apply to the board of directors of a joint stock limited company.

The board of directors shall elect a chairman and may elect a deputy chairman. The chairman and deputy chairman shall be elected by a majority of directors. The chairman of the board of directors shall call and preside over the meetings of the board of directors and monitor the implementation of resolutions of the board of directors. The deputy chairman shall assist the chairman in his responsibilities and shall perform the chairman's duties in the event that the chairman is unable or fails to perform his duties. Where the deputy chairman of the board of directors is unable or fails to perform his duties as described in this paragraph, a director nominated by a majority of directors shall perform those duties (Article 109).

Under Article 110, the board of directors shall convene no less than two meetings per year and shall notify all directors and supervisors no less than ten days in advance of the meeting. A proposal to hold an interim meeting of the board of directors may be put forward by shareholders representing one tenth or more of the voting rights, or by one third or more of the directors or supervisors. The chairman of the board of directors shall, within ten days of receiving such a proposal, call and preside over a meeting of the board of directors. Where the board of directors holds an interim meeting, it may separately decide the method of and time limit applicable to notifications about meetings of the board of directors.

Article 112 provides that directors shall attend meetings of the board of directors in person. Where any director is unable to attend the meeting for any reason, he may issue a written proxy appointing another director to attend the meeting on his behalf and stating the scope of his authorization. The board of directors shall take minutes of decisions made on matters discussed at its meetings, which shall be signed by directors present. Directors shall be responsible for resolutions of the board of directors. Where a resolution of the board of directors violates any law, administrative regulation, articles of association, or any resolution of the general meeting and causes any serious loss to the company, the directors who participated in adopting the resolution shall compensate the company. Where a director is proven to have raised an objection to the relevant resolution and his objection is recorded in the minutes, the director may be exempted from liability.

All directors are liable for action taken that violates law, statutory regulations or the company's articles of association. An individual director may avoid such liability if they dissent with respect to the decision that led to the particular offence. Apart from the violation of the law or company policy, there is another condition that must be fulfilled in order to sue directors, namely, damage of the company ... as to result in the company incurring serious losses. What are "serious losses"? Certainly these are, above all, financial losses. Although not expressly provided, Article 118 para 3 must be interpreted to cover duties of reasonable care and diligence. However even if Article 118 para 3 covers the duty of care, the Law clearly limits the liability of directors to decisions they make in violation of law, statutory regulations or the company's articles of association.

Under the provisions of Article 113, a joint stock limited company shall have a manager, who shall be appointed or dismissed by the board of directors. The provisions of Article 49 of the Law on the functions and powers of the manager of a limited liability company shall apply to the manager of a joint stock limited company.

C. Board of Supervisors

Article 117 provides that a joint stock limited company shall have the board of supervisors comprised of no less than three members. The board of supervisors shall include shareholders' representatives and an appropriate proportion of employee representatives. The proportion of employee representatives shall be specified in the articles of association but in any event shall account for no less than one third of the supervisors appointed. Employee representatives who serve as members of the board of supervisors shall be democratically elected through the employee representatives' assembly, the employees' assembly or otherwise.

The board of supervisors shall have one chairman and may have a deputy chairman. The chairman and deputy chairman shall elected by a majority of supervisors. The chairman of the board of supervisors shall call and preside over meetings of the board of supervisors. Where the chairman of the board of supervisors is unable or fails to perform his duties, the deputy chairman of the board of supervisors shall call and preside over meetings of the board of supervisors. Where the deputy chairman of the board of supervisors is unable or fails to perform his duties, a supervisor nominated by a majority of supervisors shall call and preside over meetings of the board of supervisors.

No director or senior officer of a company may concurrently act as one of its supervisors. The provisions of Article 52 of the Law on the term of office of the supervisors of a limited liability company shall apply to the supervisors of a joint stock limited company. The provisions of Articles 53 and 54 of the Law on the functions and powers of the board of supervisors of a limited liability company shall apply to the board of supervisors of a joint stock limited company.

All necessary expenses incurred by the board of supervisors in exercising its functions and powers shall be borne by the company.

D. The Two Boards' Duties of Fidelity and Due Diligence

1. Duties of Fidelity and Due Diligence

Article 147 states that the directors, supervisors and senior officers of a company shall comply with laws, administrative regulations, and the articles of association and shall owe duties of fidelity and due diligence to the company. No director, supervisor or senior officer may take any bribe or other illegal gain by taking advantage of his position or misappropriate company assets for personal use. Hence, directors, supervisors, and general managers must perform their duties sincerely and diligently with loyalty and honesty.

In order to help to understand and interpret the duties of fidelity and due diligence, Article 148 gives a specific list of activities which are forbidden under the Law: (1) misappropriate company funds; (2) divert company funds into an account held in his own name or in the name of any other individual; (3) loan company funds or provide any guaranty to any other person by using company property in violation of the articles of association without first obtaining the consent of the board of shareholders, the general meeting or the board of directors; (4) become a party to any contract or business dealings with the company in violation of the articles of association without first obtaining the consent of the board of shareholders or the general meeting; (5) seek business opportunities for himself or for any other person by taking advantage of his position, or operate on his own behalf or on behalf of any other person any business similar in nature to that of the company, without first obtaining the consent of the board of shareholders or the general meeting; (6) personally accept any commission on any transaction to which the company is a party; (7) unlawfully disclose confidential company information; or (8) act in any way that is inconsistent with his duty of fidelity to the company.

Although Article 147 covers the duty of fidelity and due diligence, the Law clearly limits the liability of directors to decisions they make "in violation of law, statutory regulations or the company's articles of association." Thus if the decision itself is not illegal, but the directors failed to exercise this duty, they are, in any case, free from any personal liability. [1]

Unlike the American corporation law, the Chinese Law expressly provides certain basic requirements for corporate fiduciaries, and the legal requirements are expressed in negative forms, preventing certain categories of people from becoming corporate fiduciaries. These requirements provide the minimum standard so that articles of incorporation or by-laws can stipulate more detailed qualification requirements.

Besides, some vagueness still exists. For example, the Law fails to explain what fidelity and due diligence means. Most commentators seem to assume that fidelity and due diligence is a prescription that corresponds to American law's duties of loyalty, good faith, and care. In the United States, the duty of care for directors and corporate managers is generally thought to require a mixture of four different duties. First, there is the "duty of inquiry... or the duty to follow up reasonably on information that should raise concern." Second, there is "the duty to employ a reasonable decision-making process when making corporate decisions." Third, there is the duty to make decisions that are reasonable. Finally, there is "the duty to supervise or monitor the conduct of the corporation's business." There are additional examples of the vagueness under the duty of loyalty. First, the Company Law lacks an explanation of "compensation liability." Because one of the purposes of the Company Law is to allow foreign investors to develop more confidence in the internal governance of Chinese corporations, this vagueness is counterproductive. [2]

2. Legal Remedies for Improper Acts of Directors and Senior Management

The New China Company Law provides a clear set of procedures for shareholder action and specific authority to appeal to the courts to resolve such matters. Article 151 provides where a director or senior officer falls into the circumstance as specified in Article 149 of the Law, any shareholder or group of shareholders of the limited liability company or joint stock limited company concerned who has or have held 1% or more of the shares in the company for 180 consecutive days or more may make a written request to the board of supervisors or to the supervisor(s) of a limited liability company with no board of supervisors to initiate a legal action in the people's court against the relevant director or senior officer. Where any supervisor falls into the circumstance as specified in Article 149 of the Law, the aforesaid shareholder(s) may make a written request to the board of directors or to the acting director of a limited liability company with no board of directors

[1] Philippe Giocca, the Organization of Companies Limited by Shares under the Company Law of the People's Republic of China, 6 Int'l. Trade & Bus. L. Ann, 2001, pp. 287, 296.

[2] John D. Osgathorpe, A Critical Survey of the People's Republic of China's New Company Law, 6 Ind. Int'l & Comp. L. Rev., 1996, pp. 493, 507.

to initiate a legal action in the people's court.

Where any board of supervisors, any supervisor of a limited liability company with no board of supervisors, or any board of directors or acting director refuses to initiate a legal action after receiving a written request described in the preceding paragraph, or fails to initiate a legal action within 30 days of receiving the request, or if, in the event of any urgent situation in which failing to initiate a legal action forthwith will cause irreparable damage to the interests of the company, the shareholder(s) described in the preceding paragraph may initiate a legal action in the people's court in his or their own name(s).

Where the legitimate rights and interests of a company are damaged and the company thereby suffers any loss, the shareholder(s) described in Paragraph 1 of this article may initiate a legal action in the people's court in accordance with the provisions of the preceding two paragraphs.

Under the provisions of Article 152, if any director or senior officer damages the shareholders' interests by violating any law, administrative regulation, or the articles of association, the shareholders may initiate a legal action in the people's court. Clearly, Under the New China Company Law, the court system is intended to be the final authority for protection of shareholder rights and for ensuring that companies comply both with government regulations and with the provisions of their articles of association. These provisions in the New Company Law further underline the importance of the articles of association in governing the company and in protecting shareholder rights.

IV. Abuse of Shareholder Rights and Piercing the Corporate Veil

A corporation is a legal entity separate from its shareholders. Corporation law erects an imaginary wall between a corporation and its shareholders that protects shareholders from liability for a corporation's actions. Once shareholders have made their promised capital contributions to the corporation, they have no further financial liability. This means that contracts of a corporation are not contracts of its shareholders, and debts of a corporation are not debts of its shareholders.

Nonetheless, in order to prevent the abuse of shareholder rights so as to protect both the company and third party creditors, corporate law provides that shareholders must exercise their rights in accordance with the law, the regulations, and the company articles of association. The shareholder must not abuse the independent legal person status of the company or his own limited liability rights in a manner that harms the interests of the company or its other shareholders or creditors. Courts will sometimes ignore the separateness of a corporation and its shareholders by Piercing the Corporate Veil. The primary consequence of piercing the corporate veil is that a corporation's shareholders may lose their limited liability.

The concept of piercing the corporate veil is a longstanding feature of the corporate law of capitalist economies. An important corporate form in such economies is the limited liability corporation (LLC), a key attribute of which is that shareholders are not personally liable for corporate debts in excess of their investment in the LLC. Creditors seeking payment of debts or tort victims seeking redress generally can reach only the corporation's assets, not those of its shareholders. At times, however, courts ignore this corporate fiction and treat a corporation's debt as the debt of the corporation's shareholders. In doing so, courts "pierce the corporate veil."

Prior to 2006, China's veil-piercing doctrine operated in a state of uncertainty. Not until the 1990s, with the rise of the LLC as a corporate form in China, did the notion of a corporate veil become important. In 1994, Chinese law formally recognized LLCs as "legal person[s]" with shareholder liability limited to the extent of the shareholder's "capital contributions" or "shareholdings." However, the 1994 Company Law did not grant Chinese courts the right to pierce the corporate veil. Nor did any other statute confer such power. As a result, most Chinese commentators agreed that China's law did not include piercing the corporate veil. This all changed with the 2006 revisions to China Company Law. Article 20 of the law states: "Where any of the shareholders of a company evades the payment of its debts by abusing the independent status of juridical persons or the shareholder's limited liabilities, and thus seriously damages the interests of any creditors, it shall bear joint liabilities for the debts of the company." In addition, Article 64 provides a veil-piercing provision relevant to single shareholder LLCs. It states: "If the shareholder of a one-person limited liability company is unable to prove that the property of the one-person limited liability company is independent from his own property, he shall bear joint liabilities for the debts of the company."

However, Articles 20 and 64 are only partially successful due to shortcomings such as that the 2006 Company Law provides insufficient guidance to courts about how to proceed with analyzing a veil-piercing case, and that the Law's scope is unclear, or otherwise, too narrowly constrained. These defects mean that considerable uncertainty remains for those who invest in or lend to LLCs. In addition, the extent of the judiciary's power to pierce the corporate veil, as well as limitations on this power, remain less than clear.

Article 20 of the New China Company Law improved the regulation of former edition stating that the shareholders of a company shall abide by laws, administrative regulations and articles of association and exercise shareholders' rights in accordance with the law. They shall neither damage the interests of the company or other shareholders by abusing shareholders' rights nor damage the interests of any creditor of the company by abusing the company's independent status as a legal person or the limited liability of shareholders. Any shareholder of a company who causes any loss to the company or to other shareholders by abusing shareholders' rights shall be liable for compensation in accordance with the law. Where any of the shareholders of a company evades the payment of debts by abusing the company's independent status as a legal person or the limited liability of shareholders, thereby seriously damaging the interests of any creditor of the company, it shall be jointly and severally liable for the debts of the company.

Obviously, the New China Company Law enhanced the provisions of shareholders' liability for the debts of the company, however the uncertainty still exists due to the lack of guidance of the Supreme People's Court (SPC) on the judicial practices and limited scope of application of the provisions.

V. Special Provisions on Single Shareholder Limited Liability Company

The New China Company Law allows natural persons or legal persons to form single shareholder limited liability companies (Articles 57 – 63). Under the Old Company Law, a limited liability company was required to have two or more shareholders. In contrast, the new statute provides for a simplified management structure appropriate to single shareholder entities. However, in order to prevent abuse of the corporate structure in single shareholder companies, the New Company Law provides for a number of restrictions: Article 57 states the term "single shareholder limited liability company" refers to a limited liability company with only one natural or legal person as a shareholder. Under Article 58, any natural person may only establish one single shareholder limited liability company. Such single shareholder limited liability company shall not establish a new single shareholder limited liability company. The company registration and business license of a single shareholder limited liability company shall both clearly indicate whether the company is funded by a natural or legal person (Article 59). Article 60 provides that the articles of association of a single shareholder limited liability company shall be formulated by the shareholder. Article 61 further states that a single shareholder limited liability company shall have no board of shareholders. Where the shareholder makes a decision on any of the matters listed in Paragraph 1 of Article 37 of the Law, it shall be recorded in writing, signed by the shareholder and kept in the company. With regard to the shareholder limited liability, Article 63 stipulates that where the shareholder of a single shareholder limited liability company is unable to prove that the property of the company is independent of the shareholder's own property, the shareholder shall be jointly and severally liable for the debts of the company.

These single shareholder provisions illustrate the manner in which the New China

Company Law attempts to balance the benefits of limited liability status to potential investors while still providing protection to creditors.

VI. Limitations on Third Party Loans and Guarantees

Unrestricted debt guarantees to unrelated companies were a major problem under the former company law system. Large companies that appear to be financially solvent are often actually insolvent because they used their profits to acquire unrelated companies or to guarantee the debts of companies related only through the private financial interests of directors, officers, or controlling shareholders. To the detriment of legitimate creditors, the extent of such loans, guarantees, and other security arrangements are oftentimes not exposed until bankruptcy or insolvency proceedings are commenced. Articles 15 and 16 of the New Company Law seek to remedy this. Article 15 permits a company to invest in another company, but prohibits it from doing so in a manner such that it becomes jointly liable for the debts of the other company. Article 16 provides additional rules concerning the providing of investment or debt guarantees to third party companies: where a company intends to invest in any other enterprise or provide a guaranty for any other person, a resolution shall be passed, pursuant to the company's articles of association, by the company's board of directors, board of shareholders or general meeting. Where the articles of association prescribe any limit on the total amount of investments or guaranties allowed, or on the amount of a single investment or guaranty allowed, the said total amount or amount shall not exceed the limits prescribed.

Where a company intends to provide a guaranty for any shareholder or actual controller of the company, a resolution shall be passed by the board of shareholders or general meeting. No shareholder referred to in the preceding paragraph or under the control of the actual controller referred to in the preceding paragraph shall participate in voting on any matter described in the preceding paragraph. Any such resolution shall be passed by a majority vote from the other shareholders attending the meeting.

VII. Corporate Combination and Division; Increase and Reduction of Registered Capital

Under the provisions of Articles 172 – 179, a corporate combination may be effected by merger or consolidation. In the case of a merger, one company absorbs another company and the company that has been absorbed is dissolved; in case of a consolidation, two or more companies combine to establish a new company, and the existing companies are dissolved. To carry out a corporate combination, parties to the combination shall conclude an agreement with each other and formulate balance sheets and schedules of assets. The parties to a combination shall, within ten days of making the resolution on combination, notify their respective creditors and, within 30 days, make a public announcement in a newspaper. Any creditor may, within 30 days of receiving the said notice or, in the event that the creditor does not receive such a notice, within 45 days as of the issuance of the said public announcement, require the company to repay its debts in full or to provide a corresponding guaranty.

In any corporate combination, the claims and debts of the parties to the combination shall be succeeded by the company that survives the combination, or by the newly-established company in case of a consolidation.

Article 176 states that unless otherwise agreed by the company and its creditors in any written agreement regarding the repayment of company debts concluded prior to any division, the companies that result from the division shall be jointly and severally liable for the existing debts of the company. Where a company finds it necessary to reduce its registered capital, it must prepare its balance sheet and schedule of assets. The company shall, within ten days of the date on which it decides to reduce its registered capital, notify its creditors and make a public announcement about the proposed reduction in capital in a newspaper within 30 days of the date on which it decides to reduce its registered capital. Any creditor shall, within 30 days of receipt of such a notice or, where it does not receive a notice, within 45 days of the date of the public announcement, be entitled to require the company to repay its debt in full or to provide a corresponding guaranty.

Article 178 provides that where a limited liability company increases its registered capital, the subscription by shareholders for the amount of the increase shall be governed by the relevant provisions of the Law regarding capital contributions in the establishment of a limited liability company. Where a joint stock limited company issues new stock to increase its registered capital, shareholder subscriptions for new stock shall be governed by the relevant provisions of the Law regarding stock purchases in the establishment of a joint stock limited company.

Article 179 further stipulates that where, as a result of any corporate combination or division to which a company is a party, any of the company's registered details change, the company shall amend its registered details with the company registration authority. In the event that any company that is a party to a combination or division is dissolved, it shall be deregistered in accordance with the law. In the event that any new company results from any combination or division, it shall comply with the procedures for establishment of a company as provided by law. Where a company increases or reduces its registered capital, the company shall handle relevant procedures for change with the company's registration authority in accordance with the law.

VIII. Company Dissolutions and Liquidations

A company can be terminated through either dissolution by agreement or involuntary dissolution. If the articles of company provide for limited rather than an indefinite life, the company automatically terminates at the end of the designated time. A company can also be terminated by a majority of the shareholders if the company has not begun business or issued any shares. The MBCA authorizes the board of directors to propose dissolution and hold a shareholders' meeting. Dissolution results if a majority of the shareholders entitled to vote do so in favour of the proposal. Involuntary dissolution refers to the dissolution by a judgment of a court. Under MBCA, grounds for dissolution include failure to pay the annual franchise tax and failure to file the company's annual report with the Secretary of State. Failure to appoint or maintain a registered agent in the state is also grounds for dissolution.

A shareholder may ask a court to dissolve a corporation. The MBCA allows this where the directors are in conflict, their deadlock cannot be broken by the shareholders, and the company faces ruin as a result if directors are acting illegally or are being very unfair to shareholders, a court may dissolve the company. Misapplication or waste of corporate assets is also a basis for dissolution. Finally, a creditor may be able to convince a court to dissolve a corporation if it is insolvent and cannot pay its debts.

Articles 180 – 190 of the New China Company Law regulate company dissolution and liquidations. According to Article 180, A company may be dissolved where: (1) its term of business operation as prescribed in the articles of association expires or any dissolution event as prescribed in the articles of association of the company occurs; (2) the board of shareholders or the general meeting resolves to dissolve the company; (3) dissolution of the company is necessary due to any combination or division to which the company is a party; (4) its business license is revoked or it is ordered to close down or be dissolved in accordance with the law; or (5) the people's court makes an order for dissolution of the company in accordance with Article 183 of the Law.

Article 181 provides that if any of the circumstances prescribed in Item 1 of Article 180 of the Law occurs, a company may nevertheless continue in existence by amending its articles of association. Any amendment to the articles of association in accordance with the provisions of the preceding paragraph shall be subject to the consent of shareholders representing two thirds or more of the voting rights in case of a limited liability company, or to the consent of two thirds or more of the voting rights of shareholders who attend the relevant general meeting in case of a joint stock limited company.

Where any company encounters serious difficulties in its operations or management that will lead to significant shareholder losses if they persist and the situation cannot be resolved by any other means, shareholders representing 10% or more of the voting rights of all shareholders may petition the people's court to dissolve the company (Article 182).

Under Article 184, a liquidation group shall be formed to exercise the following functions and powers during the course of the liquidation: (1) liquidate the company's assets and produce a balance sheet and schedule of assets; (2) notify the company's creditors by way of notice or public announcement; (3) manage and clear the remaining business of the company; (4) pay outstanding taxes and any tax liability incurred in the course of the liquidation; (5) pay the company's accounts payable and recover its accounts receivable; (6) dispose of the company's residual assets; and (7) represent the company in any civil litigation to which it is a party. Article 185 further states that a liquidation group shall, within ten days of its formation, notify the company's creditors of its formation, and shall make a public announcement in a newspaper on the formation of a liquidation group within 60 days of its formation. Any creditor shall, within 30 days of receipt of a notice or within 45 days of the public announcement in the event that the relevant creditor does not receive a notice, make a claim to the liquidation group on the debt owed to it/him. In making a claim for any debt outstanding, a creditor shall describe the relevant details and provide supporting evidence. The liquidation group shall record all debts claimed. The liquidation group may not repay any creditor during the debt claim period.

According to Article 186, a liquidation group shall, after liquidating the assets of the company and producing a balance sheet and schedule of assets, draft a liquidation plan and present it to the board of shareholders or the general meeting or to the people's court for confirmation. Any remaining assets after payment of liquidation expenses, employee wages, social insurance premiums and statutory indemnity premiums, outstanding taxes and outstanding debts may, in case of a limited liability company, be distributed to shareholders on a pro rata basis in accordance with the respective proportion of capital contributed by each shareholder or, in case of a joint stock limited company, distributed on a pro rata basis in accordance with the respective proportion of stock held by each shareholder. A company in liquidation shall continue in existence during the course of the liquidation but may not conduct any new business unconnected with the liquidation. No company assets may be distributed to any shareholder before being applied as described in the previous paragraph.

Under the provisions of Articles 187 - 189, where, after liquidating the assets of a company and formulating a balance sheet and schedule of assets, a liquidation group finds that the company's assets are insufficient to meet its obligations in full, it shall file a bankruptcy petition with the people's court. Where the people's court declares the company bankrupt, the liquidation group shall hand over administration of the liquidation to the people's court. On completion of any company liquidation, the liquidation group shall draft a liquidation report and submit it to the board of shareholders or the general meeting or to the people's court for confirmation, and shall submit it to the company registration authority to apply for the cancellation of the registration of the company. The liquidation group shall also make a public announcement about the fact that the company has been terminated.

Article 189 addresses the duties of the members of a liquidation group, stating that the members shall, during the course of liquidation, carry out their duties and perform their obligations in accordance with the law. No member of a liquidation group may take advantage of his position to take any bribe or any other unlawful payment, nor may he misappropriate any company asset. Any member of a liquidation group who causes any loss to the company or to any of its creditors either intentionally or due to his gross negligence shall be liable to compensate the affected party.

Case 9 – 1 Videology Ltd v. Videology Inc ("Inc")

MLCBI 16(3); 17; 20; 21 United Kingdom: England and Wales High Court of Justice, Chancery Division 16 August 2018

Facts: Recognition and relief were sought under the Cross-Border Insolvency Regulations 2006 [enacting the UNCITRAL Model Law on Cross-Border Insolvency ("MLCBI" of "the Model Law") in Great Britain] regarding Chapter 11 proceedings commenced in the United States in relation to Videology Inc ("Inc."), a company incorporated in the United States and its wholly-owned subsidiary, Videology Ltd. ("the company"), a company incorporated in the United Kingdom.

The Company forms part of a larger corporate group ("the Group") of which Inc. is the parent company. The Group provides video advertising software which connects television and video viewing to media behaviour information and thus provides insight to clients on how to improve the effectiveness of video advertising campaigns (the "Video Advertising Software"). The evidence suggested that this technology is unique to the Group and was developed by Inc. to fill a gap in the advertising and media market. The intellectual property rights in the Video Advertising Software are owned by Inc. and licensed to the Company. The Group as a whole has an extensive client base, with over 4,000 active users, including some of the biggest names on both the supply and demand side of the market.

The Company was formed to establish and increase the Group's business in the UK and in Europe, the Middle East and Africa. It operates from leased premises in London. The business conducted by the Company using the Video Advertising Software accounts for a substantial proportion of the Group's revenue and accounts receivable.

The advanced television market is still relatively new, and in the early days of its business, the Group required substantial resources to get the Video Advertising Software onto the market. Initially, the Group focussed on online video sales using third-party data (the "Legacy Business"). However, as time progressed, the Legacy Business faced substantial competition.

In 2015, the Group launched its 'Core Use' business, which enabled its clients to utilise the Group's technology for their advertising strategies (the "Core Use Business"). The Core Use Business has enjoyed strong growth since its launch, with 29% revenue growth in the first year, 27% in the second year and approximately 60% growth expected through the current year. However, the transition from the Legacy Business to the Core Use Business utilised substantial capital resources. This led the Group to pursue additional funding and from about 2014 to engage LUMA Partners, an investment bank focused on digital media and marketing, to provide advice and assistance in finding potential partners and purchasers for its business. These efforts were increased in Spring 2017 when the Group's financial difficulties worsened. LUMA and the Group contacted 27 potential financing partners. Five of these potential partners progressed to the due diligence stage of negotiations with the Group, but the negotiations foundered at the end of 2017 and ultimately no transaction was concluded. One of the reasons cited for the failure of such negotiations was the complex capital and debt structure of the Group.

Earlier this year, the lack of available capital led to the Group's largest client placing a temporary hold on payments. In turn this caused the Group's secured lenders to call a default under the Group's loan agreements, to seize control of the Group's operating bank accounts and significantly to restrict the Group's access to cash. This had a serious adverse effect on the Company.

On 10 May 2018, Inc. and certain of its subsidiaries, including the Company, filed voluntary petitions under Chapter 11 in the United States Bankruptcy Court for the District of Delaware. The purpose of the Chapter 11 proceedings was for the companies concerned to obtain protection from action by individual creditors, to stabilise their current operations and thereby to preserve value, to restructure their balance sheets, and in due course to effect a co-ordinated sale of the Group's business and assets.

Under Article 2 (i) of the Model Law, a foreign proceeding means, "a collective judicial or administrative proceeding in a foreign State, including an interim proceeding, pursuant to a law relating to insolvency in which proceeding the assets and affairs of the debtor are subject to control or supervision by a foreign court, for the purpose of reorganisation or liquidation."

That plainly includes proceedings in the US under Chapter 11.

Article 17(2) of the Model Law provides that a foreign proceeding shall be recognised, "(a) as a foreign main proceeding if it is taking place in the State where the debtor has the centre of its main interests; or (b) as a foreign non-main proceeding if the debtor has an establishment within the meaning of sub-paragraph (e) of Article 2 in the foreign State."

The High Court held that the centre of main interests (COMI) of Inc was indeed in the United States. It therefore recognized the Chapter 11 proceeding in relation to Inc as foreign main proceeding and made an order for a modified regime providing for a stay of individual actions, proceedings and execution against it. However, the court rejected the argument that the COMI of the company was also in the United States. Instead, the court found that the presumption that the place of incorporation of the company (the United Kingdom) is the COMI was not rebutted. The company's main assets were in the United Kingdom, it conducted the majority of its business in the United Kingdom using local employees and its contracts referred to English law and jurisdiction, factors that were ascertainable to its creditors. Additionally, a loan agreement in relation to the company stated that its COMI is in England.

Decision: Thus, the court held that the company's COMI was the United Kingdom and rejected the application to recognize the Chapter 11 proceeding regarding this company as foreign main proceedings. However, the court concluded that the connections with the United States justified recognition of the proceeding as foreign non-main proceeding, on the basis of the presence of an establishment. The court also granted discretionary relief in relation to this proceeding pursuant to Article 21 MLCBI, protecting the company from creditors' claims and entrusting the realization and distribution of the company's assets to the supervision of the United States court in the Chapter 11 process. The court noted that in the circumstances, it will be in the benefit of the creditors if a coordinated sale is pursued in the United States through the Chapter 11 process, which provides adequate protection to the interests of the company's creditors.[1]

■ Notes

piercing the corporate veil 揭开公司面纱理论。一般情况下,公司制度中的股东仅承担有限责任的规定,减轻了股东的责任,有利于众多的股东投资于公司,使公司的发展产生了根本性的变化。但是,在现实的商业活动中,处在公司身后的股东以及同样承担有限责任的公司管理层在其自身利益的驱动下,往往利用公司的法人地位进行各种规避法律甚至违法的行为。对公司承担有限责任的上述行为人,有可能以法人的外壳来从事违反公平、公正和正义原则的活动,甚至以违法的行为为其私利服务。因此,在英美国家法院的许多案件中,为了追求公平正义、维护社会利益,常常会拒绝承认一个合法成立的公司的独立法人地位,直接探究公司与股东的真实关系。这种不考虑或忽略公司独立存在特征的做法,称为"揭开公司面纱理论"。依据该理论,如果法庭认为成立公司的目的在于利用公司作为手段,从事妨碍社会利益、欺诈或逃避个人责任的活动,法院将不考虑公司的法人资格,直接追究股东或其他行为人的民事责任。

limited liability company 有限责任公司。英国的 private company 和美国的 close corporation 也近似于这类公司。我国传统上使用的英文是"closely held corporation"。这类公司的股东人数较少,不发行股票,股份不得随意转让,股东对公司承担有限责任。与此相近的是"publicly held corporation"(股份有限公司),指全部资本划分成等额的股份,其股份以股票形式依法公开发行和自由转让的一种公司企业形式。股份有限公司最本质的特征就是其股票是公开发行和自由转让的。

■ Important Legal English Usages

subject to 从属的,须依照的,易受……影响的。例如,If the goods are subject to rapid deterioration or their preservation would involve unreasonable expense, a party who is bound to preserve the goods in accordance with Article 85 or 86 must take reasonable measures to sell them(如果货物是易腐烂的或对其保存需要不合理的费用,依据本法第 85 或 86 条有义务保存货物一方须采取合理措施予以销售)。

status 地位,资格,身份。指任何非限定性的地位、资格或身份。例如,status quo(事物的现状),status civitatis(市民权),status of member(成员资格)。

注意与下列近义词在用法上的区别:

(1)position:位置,职位,地位。该词是最通俗、最常用的。指位置、工作职位、地位等。例如,families of wealth and position(有钱又有地位的家庭),a scholar of

[1] https://1. next. westlaw. com/Browse/Home/InternationalMaterials/UnitedKingdom160/UnitedKingdomCases? transitionType=Default&contextData=(sc. Default), visit on 12 January, 2020.

unimpeachable position in the academic world(在学术界很有声望的一位学者)。

(2)rank：官阶，地位，等级，品位，阶层。主要指等级阶层给予某人的具体头衔。例如，A duke is a man of rank（公爵是显贵之人）。

(3)standing：地位，名声，身份。该词的意义比 position 模糊，指在等级秩序中的地位。例如，He is in good standing(他有好名声)。

sue 请求，起诉，提起民事诉讼。例如，sue for a breach of promise（为违约起诉），sue out a pardon（诉求赦免），sue for a divorce(诉请离婚)。

注意与下列近义词在用法上的区别：

(1)plead：为(案件)辩护，以……作为案辩，以……为理由。例如，plead for the accused（为被告辩护），plead guilty（认罪），plead innocence（无罪申诉）。

(2)bring an action(lawsuit or suit)against somebody：对某人起诉。

(3)appeal：上诉。例如，appeal against a legal decision（提起上诉），appeal committee（上诉委员会），appeal for redress of a wrong（申诉以求平反），appeal from Philip drunk to Philip sober（提起上诉，请求复审）。

lessen 减少。常用语，可指数量、程度、分量或势力的减少。例如，lessen production costs（降低生产成本），lessen the differences between the city and the countryside（缩小城乡差别）。

注意与下列近义词在用法上的区别：

(1)reduce：减少，指尺寸、数量、程度、强度、可能性等的减少。例如，reduce a price（减价），reduction at discretion（酌量减轻），reduction of punishment（减刑）。

(2)decrease：指数目逐渐减少。例如，The number of nations allied with us decreased as the war continued（随着战争的结束，和我们结盟的国家数目减少了）。

(3)dwindle：缩小，减小，衰弱。主要指程度的减小和有价值东西的减小，含有诗意或悲哀的色彩。例如，His health dwindled slowly day by day（他的健康渐渐衰弱下来）。

■ Review Questions

1. Outline and discuss the history and nature of corporations.
2. Explain, giving examples where possible, the main features of corporation in contrast to partnership.
3. Explain the doctrine of "piercing the corporate veil" and analyze its possible application in China.
4. Discuss briefly the purposes of China company law, giving some examples.
5. Under what circumstances will a shareholders' meeting be held?
6. Briefly describe the liabilities of shareholders, giving examples where possible.
7. List and explain the duties of directors in accordance with the New China Company Law.

8. Explainthe main functions and powers of the board of supervisors of a limited liability company.
9. Discuss the legal remedies for improper acts of directors and senior management, giving examples.
10. What do you think of the limitations on third party loans and guarantees?
11. Do you think it is right that shareholders of corporations have no liability for the obligations of their corporation once they have paid their promised capital contribution? What benefits does society receive from extending such a privilege to shareholders? What detriments does society suffer?
12. Should company law absolutely prevent CEO domination of a company or merely allow shareholders to restrict CEO power if shareholders choose? Why do shareholders invest in a company in which the CEO dominates the company? Why don't shareholders elect directors who control the CEO?

10 Chapter Ten Foreign Investment Law of China

■ 导读

本章讲授我国于2020年1月生效的《外商投资法》。首先,简要介绍我国对外开放以来颁布的吸引外资的三大外资企业法(即《中外合资经营企业法》、《中外合作经营企业法》及《外资企业法》),并分析了存在的主要缺陷。其次,本章结合我国将继续深化和加快对外开放的战略决策及建设"一带一路"和"人类命运共同体"倡议的快速实施,介绍了我国新外商投资法的基本内容和重要的意义。本书设置这一章的目的是让我国学生了解我国政府对外开放的政策及相关法律,积极向外商介绍我国外商投资法,为我国的招商引资作出贡献。

Foreign investment enterprises in China refers to the Chinese Foreign Contractual Joint Ventures, Chinese Foreign Equity Joint Ventures and Foreign Capital Enterprises, which are customarily called also "Three Capital Enterprises" (三资企业). The law of foreign investment enterprises in China means the rules and norms that govern the establishment, management, dissolution and termination, and dispute settlement of the foreign investment enterprises. This law also includes all the agreements related to foreign investment enterprises between China and foreign governments or WTO members, and other rules and norms. Although this legal regime does inevitably have so many defects, it has contributed absolutely to the rapid growth of foreign direct investment into China: by the end of 2018, about 960,000 foreign-invested enterprises had been set up in China, with the accumulated foreign direct investment exceeding 2.1 trillion U.S. dollars. Foreign direct investment into China has ranked first among developing countries for 27 consecutive years, according to the United Nations Conference on Trade and Development (UNCTAD). Its large population and immense commercial opportunities make China one of the most important, if not the key, destination for foreign direct investment in the world. The economic potential of the Chinese market is undeniable, and it has become a magnet for foreign investors.

In order to promote the deeper and more extensive opening up in China under the incentives of "the One Belt and One Road" and the "A Community of Shared Future for Mankind" proposals, China's national legislature passed the Foreign Investment Law of the People's Republic of China (the New Foreign Investment Law) as a unified foreign investment law at the closing meeting of the second session of the 13th National People's Congress on March 15, 2019, which will become effective on January 1, 2020. The law aims to improve the transparency of foreign investment policies and ensure domestic and foreign enterprises are subject to a unified set of rules and compete on a level playing field.

I. Sources of Foreign Investment Law of China

The Chinese central government comprises several different levels of law-making bodies. The National People's Congress (NPC) operates as the most powerful legislative body in the central government of China. Responsibilities of the NPC include supervising the enforcement of the Constitution, amending the Constitution, enacting laws, and other important powers. In addition to the NPC, the Chinese law-making branch also includes the NPC Standing Committee, which is the permanent body of the NPC. The NPC Standing Committee, like the NPC, may enact laws; however, they must be other than the basic laws which should be enacted by the National People's Congress. Another primary source of law in China is the Supreme People's Court (SPC), which is the highest judicial organ in China. SPC interpretations of law are binding on the lower courts, but they are restricted to "clarifying and strengthening laws," as the NPC and the Standing Committee are responsible for interpreting statutes and the Constitution.

There are also secondary law-making bodies in China, which include the State Council as an administrative body elected by the NPC which has the power to pass administrative rules and regulations. The State Council is considered both legislative and executive in its power. Additionally, the many ministries, bureaus, and other administrative bodies supervised by the State Council are also granted certain law-making powers and may issue compulsory directives and rules. Secondary law-making bodies also exist in China, which include the State Council as an administrative body elected by the NPC, which has the power to pass administrative rules and regulations. The State Council is considered both legislative and executive in its power. Additionally, the many ministries, bureaus, and other administrative bodies supervised by the State Council are also granted certain law-making powers and may issue compulsory directives and rules. Besides, with the approval of the State Council, the provincial people's congresses may also enact certain laws to promote local economic and cultural growth.

In order to attract and protect foreign investment China's legislature and central government have tried best in passing legislation. As early as 1979 the National Peoples' Congress adopted the first foreign investment law, i. e., the Law of the People's Republic of China on Chinese-Foreign Equity Joint Venture (hereafter called China Equity Joint

Ventures Law), which was later amended by the National Peoples' Congress in 1990, 2001 and 2016 so as to meet the demand of the fast changing transitional economy, and especially China's access to WTO. For the sake of putting it into practice, the State Council formulated the Implementing Regulations for China Equity Joint Venture Law in 1983 and amended in 1986, 1987, 2001, 2011 and 2014. In order to determine the ratio between the registered capital and the total investment the State Administration of Industry and Commerce issued the Interim Provision on the Ratio between the Registered Capital and the Total Investment in China equity joint ventures in 1987. In the area of Sino foreign contractual joint ventures the National Peoples' Congress adopted the Law of the Peoples' Republic of China on Chinese-Foreign Contractual Joint Venture (hereafter called China Contractual Joint Venture Law) on 13 April 1988 which was amended in 2000 and 2016. The State Council approved and the former Ministry of Foreign Trade and Economic Cooperation issued the Detailed Rules for China Contractual Joint Venture Law in 1995 which was amended in 2014 and 2017. In the area of wholly foreign investment the National Peoples' Congress adopted the Law of the Peoples' Republic of China on Foreign Capital Enterprises on 12 April 1986 which was amended in 2000 and 2016. The former Ministry of Foreign Trade and Economic Cooperation issued the Detailed Rules for the Law of the People's Republic of China on Wholly Foreignowned Enterprises (hereafter called China Foreign Capital Enterprises Law) in 1990 which was amended in 2001 and 2014.

In addition, the State Council formulated the Encouragement of Foreign Investment Regulations on 11 October 1986 granting the foreign investment enterprises various preferential treatments. In 1990 the State Council formulated the Regulations for Encouraging Investment by Overseas Chinese and Hong Kong and Macau Compatriots. On 5 March 1994 the Standing Committee of the National People's Congress adopted the Taiwanese Compatriots Investment Protection Law and the State Council issued the Detailed Rules for this law on 23 December 1999. In order to guide the investment direction the State Council approved the Interim Provisions for Guiding the Direction of Foreign Investment as early as 1995 which was replaced by the Provisions for Guiding the Direction of Foreign Investment issued by the State Council. Besides, there are numerous regulations and rules on other forms of foreign investment and preferential treatments for foreign investment enterprises issued by the central government departments and local governments.

II. Major Forms of Foreign Investment

China has turned its attention to securing active participation in international business transactions since 1979. The scale and speed at which foreign investments are expanding is unprecedented in the history of China. The most common vehicles for absorbing foreign direct investment are: Chinese equity joint ventures (中外合资经营企业), Chinese contractual joint ventures (中外合作经营企业), foreign capital enterprises(中国外资企业), limited liability companies, companies limited by shares, bartering and the assembling of imported components, and other forms of co-operative arrangements. But the major foreign investment vehicles are the first three, each having its own governing law and implementing rules.

A. Chinese Foreign Equity Joint Venture

Article 4 of the China Equity Joint Ventures Law(《中外合资经营企业法》) states: "An equity joint venture shall take the form of limited liability company." This indicates that an equity joint venture is a legal person, and has its own independent property. The parties to the venture shall share the profits, risks and losses in proportion to their contributions to the registered capital. On the other hand, any party shall not assign its registered capital without the consent of the other parties to the venture. An equity joint venture, the most important legal characteristics of the venture, means that the profits and losses are distributed between the parties in proportion to their respective equity interests in the venture. This characteristic distinguishes it from a contractual joint venture.

Registered capital of a joint venture, according to the provisions of law, refers to the capital registered in the authority in charge of registration. Article 5 of the China Equity Joint Venture Law states: "the parties to an equity joint venture may make their investment in cash, in kind or in industrial property rights, etc." In cases where physical goods, industrial property rights and proprietary technology are used as investments at the evaluated price, the investor shall present valid document attesting their proprietary rights and their right of disposal. If the investment is in the form of buildings, premises, equipment or other materials, industrial property rights or proprietary technology, the prices shall be determined through consultation by the parties to the joint venture on the basis of fairness and reasonableness, or they shall be evaluated by a third party accepted and invited by the parties to the joint venture.

The machinery, equipment or other materials, industrial property rights or proprietary technology contributed by foreign joint venturer as investment shall be submitted to the examining and approving authorities for approval, which shall be indispensable to the production of the joint venture. The price fixed shall not be higher than the current international market price for similar equipment or materials. In the case where a foreign joint venturer contributes technology and equipment, these technology and equipment must be really advanced technology and equipment that suit China's need.

Article 5 further provides: "The technology and equipment contributed by a foreign joint venturer as its investment must be really advanced technology and equipment that suit China's needs. In case of losses caused by a foreign joint venturer in its practising deception through the intentional provision of outdated technology and equipment, it shall compensate for the losses."

B. Chinese Contractual Joint Ventures

The China Contractual Joint Venture Law(《中外合作经营企业法》) is a very flexible foreign investment enterprises where Chinese and foreign venturers have more contractual freedom to structure cooperation. It is a joint venture between Chinese and foreign venturers where the profits and losses are distributed between the parties in accordance with the specific provisions in the contract, not necessarily in proportion to their respective equity interests in the China Contractual Joint Venture. China Contractual Joint Ventures include those having acquired the status of Chinese legal persons and those not having acquired the status of Chinese legal persons in accordance with China Contractual Joint Venture Law. In establishing a contractual joint venture, the Chinese and foreign parties shall, in accordance with the provisions of the China Contractual Joint Venture Law, prescribe in their contractual joint venture contract such matters as the investment of conditions for cooperation, the distribution of earnings or products, the sharing of risks and losses, the manners of operation and management and the ownership of the property at the time of the termination of the contractual joint venture. China Contractual Joint Ventures shall develop their own business freely in accordance with the China Contractual Joint Venture Law and conduct operational and managerial activities within the scope of the approved agreements, contracts and articles of association of the contractual joint ventures without any interference from any organizations or individuals. The Chinese government shall protect the lawful rights and interests of the contractual joint ventures and of the Chinese and foreign parties.

The Chinese and foreign parties shall share earnings or products, undertake risks and losses in accordance with the agreements prescribed in the contractual joint venture contract. They may distribute the earnings by distributing the profit, distributing the products or by other means as decided through consultation by all parties to the contractual joint venture. Where earnings are distributed through the method distributing the products or other methods, the amount of tax to be paid shall be calculated in accordance with the relevant regulations of the tax law.

In the case where all the fixed assets of the contractual joint venture shall, according to the contract, be returned gratis to the Chinese party, the foreign party may, in the course of the venture's operation, apply to recover the investment ahead of time in the following ways: (1) On the basis of distribution according to the investment or conditions for cooperation contributed, it may be agreed in the contract of the contractual joint venture to increase the foreign party's proportion in the distribution of earnings; (2) Upon examination and approval of the financial and tax authorities in accordance with the relevant State tax provision, the foreign party may recover its investment prior to the payment of income tax; (3) Other methods of recovering investment which have been approved by the financial and tax authorities and the examination and approval authorities.

C. China Foreign Capital Enterprises

China Foreign Capital Enterprises Law (《外资企业法》) refer to those enterprises established in China by foreign investors, exclusively with their own capital, in accordance with relevant Chinese laws. The term does include branches set up in China by foreign enterprises and other foreign economic organizations. The investments of a foreign investor in China, the profits it earns and its other lawful rights and interests are protected by Chinese law. On the other hand, enterprises with foreign capital must abide by Chinese laws and regulations and must not engage in many activities detrimental to China's public interest. The State shall not nationalize or requisition any enterprise with foreign capital. Under special circumstances, when public interest requires, enterprises with foreign capital may be requisitioned by legal procedures and appropriate compensation shall be made.

Under the relevant law, China foreign capital enterprise shall be a limited liability company. With approval, the enterprises may also take any other liability form. The liability of the foreign investor to the enterprise shall be limited to the amount of investment subscribed and contributed to the enterprise by the investor.

In case that foreign investors intend to use industrial property rights and proprietary technology, being assigned a fixed price, as their investment, the said industrial property rights and proprietary technology must meet the requirement that such industrial property rights or proprietary technology must belong to the foreign investor itself. The assigning of a fixed price for the aforesaid industrial property rights and proprietary technology shall be in conformity with the general pricing principles of the international market, and the amount of pricing thereof shall not exceed 20% of the registered capital of the foreign capital enterprise.

The enterprise is expected to be either technologically advanced or export-orientated. In fact these are prerequisite conditions for the establishment of a China foreign capital enterprise. It must be using advanced technology and equipment, or developing new products and saving energy and raw materials, and it must also be able either to upgrade existing products or produce better goods to substitute for hitherto imported products. Also, it needs to export at least 50% of its products every year and maintain a foreign exchange balance or surplus. However, in practice, if the enterprise fulfils substantively one of the technologically advanced or export-orientated conditions, the enterprise is likely to gain approval. The establishment of a China foreign capital enterprise is prohibited in a number of sectors, now listed in the Guiding Catalogue of Industries for Foreign Investment. Enterprise autonomy is a critical issue for foreign investors in China. A China foreign capital enterprise can provide a more flexible and faster management decision making process, and a better level of protection for the knowhow which the foreign investor intends to transfer to the enterprise. But there are disadvantages, for it is usually more difficult to establish the necessary connections with the local authorities due to the absence of a Chinese partner. [1]

III. Chinese Preferences Drawing Foreign Investment

China began to offer preferences to encourage foreign investment in 1979. However, as the "Open Door" swung wider and the scope of foreign investment grew in amount and sophistication, the preferential terms offered to draw potential foreign investors also grew. The current incentive system consists of a myriad of incentives offered by both the central and local governments. The goals of the incentive system are: to improve the investment environment and better absorb foreign investment, to attract advanced technology, to increase foreign exchange and currency reserves, to raise the quality of products and increase exports, and to develop the national economy. These goals are not unique to the incentive system, but form an ideological basis underlying China's economic policy. Additionally, the government pursues means outside the incentive system for their achievement.

A. Structure of the Incentive System

The Chinese Constitution allocates power to formulate economic policy throughout the legislative and executive branches. People's Congresses constitute the legislative branch at both the national and local levels of government. The executive branch is represented by the State Council at the national level and by People's Governments at the local levels. The Ministers who partially compose the State Council have overall responsibility for ministries and commissions under their charge. Parallel administrative and legislative bodies exist in the autonomous regions, which are allowed to engage in limited self-

---

[1] Li Meiqin, Attracting Foreign Investment into the PRC the Enactment of Foreign Investment Laws, Singapore Journal of International & Comparative Law, 2000(4), pp. 159, 170.

government under the terms of the Constitution.

The State Council is the real actor in formulating economic policy for the country has actively undertaken the responsibility of regulating foreign investment in China by promulgating laws and regulations pertaining to joint ventures, currency exchange regulations and banking, preferential taxes in special investment areas, and encouraging foreign investment. Besides issuing laws and regulations, the State Council may formulate policy and submit it to the National People's Congress (NPC) or the Standing Committee for approval and enactment. State Council laws usually announce the main provisions of government programs, leaving the ministries to implement these laws nationally. Increasingly, however, local governments exercise foreign trade authority, adapting programs to local conditions.

At and above the county level, local people's congresses have the power to examine and approve plans for social and economic development including the power to examine and report on their implementation. Regulations formulated by the local people's congresses are more specific about the terms under which incentive schemes operate. While central government organs direct the creation of particular programs, they have allowed local people's congresses to decide the best means of implementation in their region. For example, after the State Council enacted the Investment Encouragement Provisions in 1986, so many local provincial congresses, particularly by provinces along China's southeast coast, promised to greatly expand upon the incentives offered by the State Council. Regulations promulgated in Guangdong, Fujian, and Zhejiang provinces extend to issues concerning land use, labor management, accounting systems and personnel movement. Local regulations may also address organization, location and longevity of investment. Often, these regulations establish a government commission or corporation responsible for overseeing foreign trade in the region as well as implementing and enforcing the regulations. These regulations may also address the termination of trade, disbursement of assets and the bankruptcy of a foreign partner. The regulations promulgated by a local people's congress may greatly affect the terms of trade and the extent of incentives offered to attract foreign investment.

Besides, local people's governments represent the executive branch and operate under the State Council. They work primarily as administrative bodies regarding the incentive system: implementing provisions promulgated by the local people's congress, and adapting State Council regulations to local conditions. They also offer and promote local projects for foreign investment. Many acts of local people's governments merely implement regulations that carry out the directives of higher legislative bodies. These local administrative bodies approve and control proposed projects and work closely with foreign investors to assist the success of these enterprises. Regulations enacted by local people's governments also set fees and fines, and articulate definitions, qualifications and procedures. Finally, local people's governments encourage investment by suggesting specific projects. For example, the Shanghai Foreign Investment Commission publishes a booklet listing such projects. Organized by industry, the book names the desired project, production scale, desired technology, form of joint venture, the Chinese partner and an individual to contact. Obviously, while the role of local people's governments is administrative, as the branch of government most closely involved with foreign investors, their policies greatly affect the foreign investment environment.

It should be noted that China has five autonomous regions: Guangxi, Ningxia, Xizang (Tibet), Xinjiang and Nei Menggu (Inner Mongolia) which are granted by the central government to enact substantial incentive programs to attract foreign investment. Incentives offered in the autonomous regions include reduction or elimination of income taxes and land use fees, as well as promises of mammoth infrastructure improvements.

B. Types of Incentives

The special incentives offered to attract foreign investment include two broad categories. First, industry-based incentives apply to enterprises involved in a certain type of activity, regardless of location. Industry-based incentives apply to two specific types of foreign investment enterprises: product export enterprises (export enterprises) and technologically advanced enterprises. By granting special treatment to such entities, national and local governments place particular emphasis on the goal of attracting advanced technology. Chinese laws and regulations generally address treatment of these enterprises simultaneously. However, since these two types of enterprises are often subject to different requirements and treatment, they are discussed separately.

Export enterprises initially enjoy the same tax treatment afforded foreign investment enterprises under the Unified Tax Law enacted in 1991. When the period of tax exemption under that law expires, export enterprises continue to pay only 50% of the income tax otherwise due, so long as 70% of their production in a given year is for export. In certain special development areas, where the income tax rate is 15%, export enterprises enjoy a further reduction, paying only 10% annual income tax if they meet the 70% export test just mentioned. A technologically advanced enterprise possesses advanced technology supplied by a foreign investor. The enterprise uses this technology to develop new products or upgrade and replace existing products, thus generating foreign exchange through export or achieving import substitution. Like export enterprises, technologically advanced enterprises continue to receive preferential tax treatment beyond that provided under the 1991 Tax Law.

Second, geographically based incentives apply to all foreign investment enterprises located in a particular development zone. In addition to these two categories, other policies can also act as incentives. Such preferences apply to foreign investment enterprises located within specifically targeted development zones. The first development zones were the special economic zones (SEZs) established in 1979 in Guangdong and Fujian provinces in Southern China. Later, the central government approved similar provisions in fourteen coastal cities. Numerous other types of zones have also emerged. This has created some confusion about which areas are open to foreign investment and what incentives to expect. Each type of development zone established by the central government offers certain incentives. Local governments may offer additional preferences and the zone itself may issue further regulations. [1]

What is more exciting is that China began to set up free trade zones as new incentives to attract foreign investment in recent years: China launched its first free trade zone in Shanghai in 2013, and in late 2014, Tianjin, Fujian and Guangdong were approved to set up the second group of free trade zones. On April 1, 2019, other seven new zones in the provinces of Liaoning, Zhejiang, Henan, Hubei, Sichuan and Shaanxi as well as Chongqing Municipality were set up, bringing the total across the country to 11. "Negative list" were introduced in the free trade zones, which specified the investment sectors off-limits to foreign investors and allowed industries not on the list to follow the same new investment rules as domestic firms.

IV. Chinese Domestic Laws Protecting Foreign Investors

With a view to attracting foreign investment, expanding international economic cooperation and technological exchange, China provides the following investment guarantees:

A. Appropriate Compensation for Nationalization and Requisition

Nationalization(国有化) refers to acquisition by a state of property previously held by private persons or companies usually in exchange for some consideration. India's constitution provides only that no person shall be deprived of his property cannot be expropriated except by the authority of law. The German constitution requires that a taking be in the public interest and pursuant of the law. Mexico's constitution says that private property cannot be expropriated except for a public use and upon payment of compensation. The constitutions of Argentina, Iraq, Malaysia, the Philippines, the

---

[1] Stella J. Edens, A Survey of Foreign Investment Incentives in the People's Republic China, 2 Willametre Bulletin of Int'l law& policy, 1994, pp. 39, 46 – 52.

Sudan all say that a taking must be in the public interest, by means of a law or procedures established by law, and that "fair", "just", or "adequate" compensation must be provided.

The guarantees found in the legislation especially in foreign investment laws tend to be both more detailed and more extensive than those found in constitutions. For example, Indonesia's Foreign Capital Investment law provides that compensation should be mutually agreed upon in accordance with international law and that any disagreements shall be resolved by binding arbitration. Article 2 of the China Equity Joint Ventures Law states: "the State shall not nationalize or requisition any equity joint venture. Under special circumstances, when public interests require, equity joint ventures may be requisitioned by following legal procedures and appropriate compensation shall be made." Article 5 of the China Foreign Capital Enterprises Law also provides: "The State does not nationalize or requisition any enterprise with foreign capital. However, under special circumstances when public interests require, enterprises with foreign capital may be requisitioned through legal procedures and appropriate compensation shall be made."

The expression "social and public interest under special circumstances" is broad and vague. There is no reference to the scope and exact meaning of "social and public interest" or of "special circumstances". It is both political and economic. The matter is left to the government's absolute discretion. Nevertheless, an insufficient undertaking is better than nothing. It also indicates the Chinese Government's intention to provide better conditions and a better environment for foreign investors.

It is clear that the stipulations of the Chinese laws provide better guarantees to foreign capital than many countries in the world.

B. Repatriation Guarantee

The most common repatriation guarantees relate to the right of foreign investors to remit profits and investment capital to their home country in the event of the partial or complete termination of their enterprise. Less common are guarantees relating to the repatriation of other kinds of current income (such as royalties, licensing fees, and fees for managerial and other services) and to the remittance of the principal and interest from loans. [1]

In many countries, monetary remittances abroad are subject to a variety of restrictions. For example, the Chilean Foreign Investment Statute of 1977 does not allow capital to be transferred abroad until 3 years after it is first brought into the country. Net income, however, can be remitted at any time. South Korea's Foreign Capital

[1] Ray August, International Business Law, Higher Education Press, 2002, p. 266.

Inducement Law forbids the repatriation of capital for 2 years following the start up of an enterprise.

Article 19 of the Law of the People's Republic of China on Wholly Foreign-owned Enterprises states: "The foreign investor may remit abroad the profits that are lawfully earned from an enterprise with its investment, as well as other lawful earnings and any funds remaining after the enterprise is liquidated. Wages, salaries and other legitimate income earned by foreign employees in an enterprise with foreign capital may be remitted abroad after the payment of individual income tax in accordance with law." Articles 11 and 12 of the China Equity Joint Ventures Law states: "The net profit which a foreign joint venturer receives as its share after performing its obligations under the laws, and the agreements or the contract, the funds it receives upon the expiration of the venture's term of operation or the suspension thereof, and its other funds may be remitted abroad in accordance with foreign exchange control regulations and in the currency or currencies specified in the contract concerning the equity joint venture.

A foreign joint venturer shall be encouraged to deposit in the Bank of China the foreign exchange which it is entitled to remit abroad.

The wages, salaries or other legitimate income earned by a foreign worker or staff member of an equity joint venture, after payment of the individual income tax under the Tax Laws of the People's Republic of China, may be remitted abroad in accordance with foreign exchange control regulations."

Article 22 of the China Contractual Joint Ventures Law also provides: "After the foreign party has fulfilled its obligations under the law and the contractual joint venture contract, the profits it receives as its share, its other legitimate income and the funds it receives as its share upon the termination of the venture, may be remitted abroad according to law. The wages, salaries or other legitimate income earned by the foreign staff and workers of contractual joint ventures, after the payment of the individual income tax according to law, may be remitted abroad."

Comparatively, the Chinese laws have almost no restrictions on monetary remittances abroad by foreign investors. Therefore, foreign investors' capital, profits, dividends are protected in China.

C. Non-discriminatory Treatment

Non-discriminatory treatment means the assurance of a host government that foreign investors will be treated in the same way as local investors. Many countries either in their constitutions or foreign investment laws provide equality of treatment to foreign investors. For example, the Argentine Foreign Investment Law of 1977 promises that the foreign investors have the same rights and obligations that the constitution and national laws grant to national investors, subject to any qualifications in that law and to rules provided by special and promotion statutes. Brazil's Foreign Capital Investment Law states that foreign capital is to receive the same treatment before the law as that accorded Brazilian capital under similar situations, and that any discrimination not specifically provided for in the law is prohibited.

Chinese laws also provide equal treatment to foreign investors, what is more, the "Three Capital Enterprises" may, in accordance with provisions of the relevant laws and administrative rules and regulations of the State on taxation, enjoy preferential treatment of tax reductions or exemptions. Clearly, Chinese laws provide super-national treatment to foreign investors.

D. Stabilization Guarantee

Chinese government has promised several times to the world that China's policies of opening to the outside world, and attracting foreign investment will not change. Thus, Chinese government has already created a stabilization environment for foreign investors.

It is an indisputable fact that the Chinese government has made tremendous progresses in drawing foreign investment into the Chinese market which has contributed so much to the growth of the Chinese economy. However, it is also true that the Chinese Government still needs to improve its legal regime of foreign investment and policies to meet the rapid rising of China. For instance, the Chinese government has primarily focused its attention on taxation incentives and has neglected other crucial factors such as access to the Chinese market and the removal of legal barriers due to the conflicts of different laws relating to foreign investment. From the viewpoint of foreign investors, the new market and the unified law would be more attractive. In addition, infrastructure, human resources and other relevant factors which affect the operation and management of joint ventures are also crucial. [1]

V. Dispute Settlement for Foreign Investors

As in any commercial relationship, disputes are bound to arise from time to time in the course of foreign investment in China. The increase of foreign investment in China has also increased the number of disputes, and due to the different political system and traditional cultures, the Chinese way of business dispute settlement has its own characteristics. Although China is open to the outside world for many years, the traditional Chinese notions towards resolving conflicts still influence society. Unlike the

---

[1] Yi Yi Wu, Joint Venture Law of the People's Republic of China, 7 Corp. & Bus. L. J. 15, 1994, pp. 15, 47.

Western model of dispute resolution, litigation in China is usually avoided at all costs. Instead, the Confucian ideal of maintaining "harmony" usually leads the parties to seek amiable consultation, mediation or arbitration rather than resorting to a lawsuit. Mediation, arbitration, and litigation are all methods of dispute resolution with Chinese entities, but those that involve "amiable consultation" are the most favored. Arbitration is the preferred and most popular method in China for both foreign investors, who are often uncertain about litigating in Chinese courts, and the Chinese counterparts, usually the party more inclined to the process of "friendly consultation" when faced with a business dispute. As a foreign investor, resolving business disputes in China presents several issues and potential pitfalls, and it is important that some means for resolving disputes be mutually agreed upon before commencing the business relationship. The advantages and disadvantages of choosing either to arbitrate a dispute before an arbitration commission or to litigate in Chinese courts revolve around issues of neutrality, the expertise involved in making that determination, and award enforcement.

The relevant Laws contain provisions relating to dispute settlement. The provisions on dispute settlement fall within the ambit of procedural law and form are an integral part of foreign investment legislation. The aim is to achieve fair, expeditious and efficient settlement of disputes; to protect the legal rights and interests of foreign investors; to foster co-operation between Chinese Foreign parties; and maintain a good investment climate in China.

A. Guiding Principles

China as a socialist state and with a broad and profound traditional culture differing from the Western cultures claims the following guiding principles for settlement of disputes between foreign investors and Chinese counterparts.

1. Maintaining the Sovereignty of China

It is a cardinal principle that the settlement of investment disputes and protection of investors' rights and interests is achieved without affecting the sovereignty of the China. China maintains the position that, if litigation occurs in a foreign investment project, the Chinese courts are the sole forum for their settlement. The governing law for Chinese foreign joint venture contracts is always Chinese law. Parties to such contracts are not able to choose foreign law. However, Article 128 of the Contract Law of the People's Republic of China provides: "Where the parties do not wish to, or are unable to, resolve such dispute through settlement or mediation, the dispute may be submitted to the relevant arbitration institution for arbitration in accordance with the arbitration agreement between the parties. Parties to a foreign related contract may apply to a Chinese arbitration institution or another arbitration institution for arbitration. Where the parties did not conclude an arbitration agreement, or the arbitration agreement is invalid, either party may bring a suit to the People's Court."

2. Guaranteeing Legal Protection for Foreign Investors

To ensure that the rights and interests of foreign investors are adequately protected, China has enacted comprehensive laws, offering foreign investors a variety of methods to settle their disputes. A right to legal recourse is regarded as vital for the protection of legal rights and interests. Under all of China's laws relating to foreign investment, when a dispute arises, a foreign investor possess the right to request that the Chinese party settle the dispute by consultation, mediation or arbitration in accordance with the relevant written agreement. In the absence of a written agreement on arbitration, the foreign party can bring a suit in a Chinese court.

3. Encouraging Dispute Settlement through Amiable Methods to Guarantee A Harmonized Cooperation and Mutual Profits

The broad and profound Chinese traditional cultures are known as one based on peace and harmonization, and thus encourages dispute settlement through friendly methods instead of lawsuits. Instead of insisting on his own interests, the Confucian should willingly accept any infringement on his rights in order to achieve harmony in the society. For example, the Chinese businessman would take it as an indication that the parties did not trust each other if they were to bring in lawyers during the process of FDI negotiations. Other traditional philosophies in China, such as Buddhism and Taoism, also follow these traditional ideas have carried through to the various methods of resolving business disputes. As a result, instead of litigation, the Chinese prefer one of four methods of settlement. In order of preference they are: "friendly negotiations", consultation [friendly negotiations assisted by the China International Economic and Trade Arbitration Commission (CIETAC)], conciliation or mediation (negotiations with non-binding recommendations given by the CIETAC or some other party), or arbitration. Although the Chinese will use the above methods of dispute settlement, very few cases actually go to a final arbitral award.

The Chinese are willing to take the time and expense involved in what have often become long and drawn out negotiations, since such settlement allows the parties to reach an agreement without either side being declared right or wrong by a third party. They prefer to settle disputes within the context of building a mutually beneficial long-term relationship. They seek compromise solutions reached through friendly negotiation as opposed to settlements reached through the more adversarial posture found in formal arbitration. In short, the Chinese desire reconciliation reached in such a manner that the business relationship is allowed to continue in a cooperative spirit. It is not uncommon to find that disputes which arise in the sale of goods are settled by one party giving the other a better deal in a later transaction. [1] In one word, the Chinese prefer the settlement of disputes in a family atmosphere where brothers or sisters sit together to resolve misunderstandings so that both parties will achieve greater gains in the future businesses.

B. Methods of Dispute Settlement

1. Friendly Negotiations

Friendly negotiations are conducted directly between the parties to a dispute, either by correspondence or in person in China. This method of negotiation was utilized in a 1975 United States China grain transaction. A dispute arose when the Chinese cancelled two orders for approximately one million tons of American wheat and 233,000 bales of cotton. After friendly negotiations, an amicable settlement was reached when the Chinese agreed to pay the difference between the contract price and the much lower market prices prevailing when the contract was cancelled. This remedy was the same as that which would have been reached under the Uniform Commercial Code in the United States. By negotiating the settlement, the time and expense of litigation was avoided. Experiences in China show that a large number of disputes have been settled through friendly negotiations because this method has advantages of low cost of resolution and friendly atmosphere for both parties' future cooperation.

2. Consultation

In case a settlement cannot be reached through friendly negotiations, one or both parties may request the assistance of the CIETAC. Once assistance is requested, the CIETAC will begin its own fact finding process. Both parties will be asked to submit an analysis of their positions (by correspondence or in person), along with all relevant documents and other pertinent information. The CIETAC may also conduct its own investigation, getting information from other sources in China or abroad. All information obtained will be disclosed to both parties in order to attempt reconciliation. After the fact-finding process is completed, the parties will be helped in analyzing the facts. The strengths and weaknesses of each position will be pointed out to them, and both will be asked to reconsider their positions in order to negotiate a friendly settlement. If no agreement is reached, the process will be repeated again, with the typical case requiring about six months to settle.

---

[1] Kewin K. Maher, Foreign Investment in the People's Republic of China: Compensation Trade, Joint Ventures, Industrial Property Protection and Dispute Settlement, 10 Ga. J. Int'l & Comp. L., 1980, pp. 233, 261.

3. Conciliation or Mediation

If negotiations or consultation fail to achieve a settlement, the parties may then ask the CIETAC to make nonbinding recommendations. If not satisfied with the recommendations, the parties may continue their negotiations or proceed to arbitration. Conciliation is a natural outgrowth of consultation. The CIETAC will already be familiar with the case, from its extensive fact-finding and analysis in consultation, when conciliation becomes necessary.

Generally, parties must follow a few basic tenets to initiate conciliation or mediation. For example, under the CIETAC, the following guidelines exist: (1) there must be rules that both parties are willing to accept; (2) mediation is conducted by the CIETAC to ascertain the facts and distinguish right from wrong on questions under dispute; (3) mediation is to lead both parties to a form of compromise; (4) the parties decide on the choice of law provisions to be completely recognized and enforceable; (5) international practices can be used and are generally honored; and (6) if an agreement cannot be reached or mediation cannot be continued, mediation will be terminated and an examination and oral hearings can take place in accordance with arbitration rules and standards. Mediation can be conducted prior to arbitration under the CIETAC rules in several ways. Under CIETAC, mediation includes face to-face discussions, discussions over the telephone, and discussions by mail or email. Also, the parties can request that two members of an informal CIETAC mediation panel speak with each side separately, thus being a conduit for compromise.

In summary, the Chinese do not place priority on contractual specificities, but on other social precepts such as mutual benefit, social harmony and long-term objectives as their guiding principles in observing the spirit of the transaction. Although China is a member of the International Centre for Settlement of Investment Disputes (ICSID) and has ratified the United Nations Convention on the Recognition and Enforcement of Foreign Arbitral Awards (the New York Convention), the Chinese place a strong emphasis on resolving disputes through these informal and amiable methods of dispute settlement primarily because Chinese culture and attitudes favor harmony and good relationships between people and enterprises and most Chinese would prefer a compromise reached by themselves to a decision imposed by another. As the Chinese traditional cultures are accepted by more and more countries in the current world, it is easily predicable that friendly negotiation, consultation, and conciliation with non-binding recommendations from the CIETAC will continue as the predominate means of resolving disputes both in China and abroad.

4. Arbitration

If the parties are unable to settle their dispute through friendly negotiation, consultation, conciliation or mediation, arbitration is naturally the next step in the process. Even though the Chinese prefer these informal methods of dispute settlement, arbitration has become, over the last two decades, a mainstream form of dispute resolution in China and the primary way to resolve international commercial disputes. Many international investors view this as a way to get around China's problematic court system. Nonetheless, an arbitration clause in a foreign investment agreement creates a contractual obligation to submit any disputes to an impartial tribunal chosen by the parties. Thus, international commercial arbitration, with regard to Chinese foreign investment disputes, has very appealing qualities, such as procedural fairness, party autonomy in choosing the arbitration rules, neutrality, efficiency and cost effectiveness, arbitrator competence, and binding awards for the parties to enforce. [1]

The Arbitration Law of the People's Republic of China (Arbitration Law) was adopted on August 31, 1994, amended in 2009 and 2017, to promote the fair resolution of disputes and specifies the procedures for arbitration in China. In addition to the Arbitration Law, the Law of Civil Procedure of the People's Republic of China (CPL) adopted in 1991 and amended in 2007, 2012 and 2017, contains regulations that govern arbitrations in China. Moreover, each arbitration commission may have its own rules. However, the Arbitration Law takes precedence over other laws regarding arbitration in China.

In order for the foreign investor to bring a dispute to arbitration, there must be an arbitration agreement, or arbitration clause, written into the parties' contract. The arbitration agreement must contain all of the following elements to be valid. First, "an expressed intent to request arbitration must be noted in the arbitration clause." Second, the "items for arbitration" must be mentioned. Finally, "the chosen arbitration commission" must be indicated specifically. As with choosing the arbitration commission, the party who negotiates the most favorable arbitration clause usually depends on the relative bargaining strength of the parties. The arbitration clause is independent of the contract and any "changes to, rescission, termination or invalidity of the contract" will not affect the arbitration clause's validity. However, there are certain circumstances that may invalidate an arbitration clause, such as coercion, of which the foreign investor must be aware. Both enterprise are affected in certain strategic aspects of arbitration, such as the

[1] George O. White, Navigating the Cultural Malaise: Foreign Direct Investment Dispute Resolution in the People's Republic of China, 5 Tenn. J. Bus. L. 2003, pp. 55, 67.

arbitration commission chosen, the composition of the arbitration panel, and award enforcement options.

As noted earlier, although most Chinese contracts contain arbitration clauses, very few cases of formal arbitration have actually taken place. The question for the potential investor, then, is to what extent formal arbitration can be expected to play a role in future dispute settlements. Of course, the tremendous cultural incentive to use friendly negotiations, consultation and conciliation will remain. Therefore, the mere inclusion of an arbitration clause should not be taken to mean that disputes will be arbitrated.

As to the enforcement of foreign arbitral awards, China ratified the New York Convention on 2 December 1986, seeking to reassure foreign investors whose arbitral awards are obtained in countries outside China that such awards will be recognized and enforced in China.

In summary, it seems that in order to reach satisfactory solutions to contract disputes, the foreign investor in China must follow the old adage, "When in Rome, do as the Romans." This will mean learning to handle problems within the context of the overall business relationship, and learning to rely on friendly negotiations, consultation and conciliation as the primary modes of reaching settlements. This should be beneficial to the investor in the long run in terms of developing a good working relationship with the Chinese partner and building an enterprise which is mutually beneficial to both partners. Attempts to force the Chinese into American-style adjudicatory proceedings should be avoided, if for no other reason than that it would be culturally offensive.

5. Litigation

Litigation is the last resort to dispute settlement in China. Both foreign enterprises and Chinese counterparts have the "same ability" to bring an action in Chinese court, although it is not the most favorable dispute resolution method. However, in the past several decades, the number of civil cases in Chinese courts has increased despite the aversion to conflict. The adversarial system, judicial precedent, and the jury system are frequently absent in Chinese courts. Instead, the Chinese judicial system is based on the "inquisitorial model," where the judge takes an active role in the fact finding process without the use of a jury.

In addition, problems with enforcement of legal judgments continue to plague China. When the losing party to a judgment refuses to comply with a judgment handed down by a people's court, the procedure begins with filing a petition in a people's court. An "enforcement officer" handles the enforcement of the judgment, and then notifies the nonpayer and directs it to comply with the judgment. If the debtor still does not obey the judgment, the enforcement officer may explore other enforcement devices to compel the debtor to satisfy the judgment. However, it is difficult to enforce legal judgments in China. Much of the resistance to complying with legal judgments is due to local protectionism for local industries and businesses, low legal quality of judges and civilians.

Overall, among the advantages of arbitration over litigation in court is that arbitration is usually confidential and more impartial. Arbitration tends to be less adversarial than litigation, so the future of the business relationship can be protected. Also, the expertise of the arbitrators is an attractive characteristic of arbitration compared to litigation in Chinese courts. An indication of this expertise is illustrated by the CIETAC requirement that each arbitrator display "professional knowledge of law, economy and trade, science and technology or maritime affairs, and... working experience."

VI. Defects of the Chinese Legal System of Foreign Investment

China began to open the door to foreign countries and has made foreign investment, especially the attraction of direct foreign investment, a matter of national priority since then. Consequently, attractive and preferential schemes have been introduced to encourage foreign investment, to improve the investment climate, to increase investors' confidence and generally to expedite the integration of the PRC into the global economy. As the Chinese open door policy accompanied accordingly with a legal system under the leadership of the Chinese Communist Party has been successfully implemented, foreign investment has contributed enormously to the rapid development of Chinese economy. By the end of 2018, about 960,000 foreign-invested enterprises had been set up in China, with the accumulated foreign direct investment exceeding 2.1 trillion U.S. dollars. Foreign direct investment into China has ranked first among developing countries for 27 consecutive years and also first in the world since 2018 (surpassed America in that year), according to the United Nations Conference on Trade and Development (UNCTAD). Of the 500 largest multinational corporations, more than 400 of them have invested in China. This has been honored as an economic miracle by many foreign countries. However, well frankly, due to the Chinese unique political and economic systems and especially the demands of the construction of the "One Belt and One Road" and "A Community with A Shared Future for Humanity" under the unexpectedly fast development of economic and legal globalization, the defects and negative effects of such a legislation model began to appear more and more obviously. For instance, the different provisions concerning taxation, foreign currency, import and export etc. make the domestic enterprises at a disadvantage, which drives some domestic enterprises to sham joint ventures by means of fraud, and meanwhile such unequal legal stipulations also dampened down the enthusiasm of foreign investors. Equal competition is the basic principle of market economy, but the two-track legislation model make domestic and foreign enterprises at unequal positions, which not only weakens the competitiveness of domestic enterprises, but also affects the investment confidence of foreign investors because it is counter to the WTO law.

A. Imperfect Legislative Regime of Foreign Investment

Just as the Chinese economy has undergone a long and complicate process from planned economy to social market economy, the foreign investment legislation also has experienced a process from different rules regulating national and foreign investment to unified laws accordingly. At the very beginning, China's foreign investment legislation rooted in the thoughtful idea of reforming the national economic system with the purpose to burst the bonds set by the planned economic system with the market factors. As the market economy began to develop deeply and fast, the legislation of foreign investments became more market-orientated resulting from balancing the approaches and functions of the market and planning in the national economic system. In other words, the significance of planning is fading while that of the market is prospering. The major changes in foreign investment legislation in this period the provisions incompatible to the market in the three basic laws regulating foreign investments were revised and several regulations were repealed.

Although the contents of foreign investment law have been greatly improved, the multiple layers of legislation for foreign investment still fail to meet the demands of market economy.

1. Multiple Layers of Legislature Inevitably Leading to Various Legal Issues

The laws, regulations and the Detailed Rules and local regulations and rules are usually issues by the National People's Congress and the NPC Standing Committee, the State Council and its ministries, and local people's congresses and governments, resulting natural in a complicated mixtures of laws and regulations of which numerous conflicts or rules arise. First, even though after several amendments, the three basic laws regulating foreign investments in China still overlap each other without sufficient coordination. By taking a close look at these three basic laws, it can be found that more than half of the articles resemble, even though there are only 16 articles, 24 articles and 27 articles in content respectively. Furthermore, there are inconsistencies even in the overlapped articles between these three laws. For instance, provisions regarding the time limitations of the examination and approval are different, which may cause unequal treatment among different legal forms of foreign-invested enterprises. Besides, the repetition is also wasting legislative and judicial resources since it makes the application of these laws more difficult and confusing. Second, due to the poor legislative techniques adopted to draft these three basic laws regulating foreign investment, the necessary provisions were absent, which rendered excessive legislative power and the fragmentation of legislative authority. All these laws and regulations regarding foreign investments made the system of foreign investment laws too complicated and confusing to comply with for foreign investors.

2. Two-track Legislative Model Counter to Market Economy

The two-track legislative model, where domestic enterprises and foreign enterprises are subject to total different laws and regulations respectively, is caused by the particular social environment pertaining to the early period of China's opening-up and reform. China takes socialist public ownership as its economic foundation, where state-owned enterprises and collective enterprises occupy a domination position. However, the opening-up and reform policy also requests the state to encourage and protect the development of private economy. This mixture of different ownerships constitutes the basis of China's economic legislation. Accordingly China adopted a legal system for foreign investment independent of that for domestic investment, which caused the aforesaid two-track legislation system. Laws for domestic enterprises, like "State-owned Industrial Enterprise Law", "Interim Regulations on Private Enterprises", "Regulations on Urban Collective Enterprises", "Regulations on Rural Collective Enterprises", "Individual Sole Proprietorship Enterprise Law" etc., do not apply to foreign-invested enterprises. Similarly, the legal provisions on issues concerning foreign-invested enterprises, like the establishment, corporate forms, administrative management, taxation, and foreign currency etc. do not apply to domestic enterprises. Such legislation based on the particular social environment and conditions of that period was suitable to China's national situation thereof and it played an important role in promoting China's opening-up and reform with regards to attracting foreign investment and safeguarding national interests.

However, alone with the deepening of China's economic restructuring, especially the establishment of market economy, the defects and negative effects of such a legislation model began to appear more and more obviously. For instance, the different provisions concerning taxation, foreign currency, import and export etc. make the domestic enterprises at a disadvantage, which drives some domestic enterprises to sham joint ventures by means of fraud, and meanwhile such unequal legal stipulations also dampened down the enthusiasm of foreign investors. Equal competition is the basic principle of market economy, but the two-track legislation model make domestic and foreign enterprises at unequal positions, which not only weakens the competitiveness of domestic enterprises, but also affects the investment confidence of foreign investors because it is counter to the requirements of national treatment.

B. Inconsistency with the WTO Law

In the 1990s, China further improved its investment environment by enacting laws that would speed up integration into global economies. Although China is still not a member of the WTO, it was hoped that enactment and enforcement of these laws will soon lead to membership.

The WTO does not contain an investment agreement commonly found in many of the bilateral investment agreements, nor does it embody such features as a mechanism allowing private investors direct access to an international dispute settlement mechanism, which is common in bilateral investment agreements. As a result of the Uruguay Round negotiations, however, the WTO began to embody various investment-related rules. The General Agreement on Trade in Services (GATS), the Agreement on Trade-Related Aspects of Intellectual Property Rights (TRIPS Agreement) and the Agreement on Trade-Related Investment Measures (TRIMs) contain such provisions. More importantly, all these WTO Agreements containing investment rules put important obligations, based on the fundamental principles, on WTO Member governments with regards to the treatment of foreign nationals or companies within their territories. These include: non-discrimination (MFN treatment and national treatment), freer trade, predictable policies and encouragement of competition. In other words, WTO Members should renounce unreasonable measures that contravene the principles established within the WTO framework and should promptly announce trade-related investment laws and policies.

1. China's WTO Commitments Relating Foreign Investment

In order to join the WTO, China made substantial commitments relating to the admission and operation of foreign investment which were specified primarily in the bilateral agreements with the United States and the European Union and later reflected in the Accession Protocol on China's accession to the WTO. With regard to admission, China's commitments cover nearly all major sectors and, within reasonable time periods (ranging from immediately upon accession to within five years after accession), it will eliminate most foreign equity restrictions in nearly all sectors. Industries that have been closed to foreign investment, such as telecommunications and securities, will be opened to foreign investment; some industries where foreign investment has had to be approved on a trial basis, such as banking and retailing, will allow foreign participation in principle; industries where foreign investment has had to form a joint venture with government-approved Chinese partners, such as accountancy, will be opened for greater foreign participation.

With respect to the operational environment of foreign investment enterprises, China has made commitments to comply fully with the TRIMs Agreement upon accession to the

WTO, without recourse to Article 5 thereof. It will only impose, apply or enforce laws, regulations or measures relating to the transfer of technology, production processes or other proprietary knowledge to an individual or enterprise in its territory that are not inconsistent with the TRIPs Agreement and the TRIMs Agreement. Accordingly, China promised to eliminate trade-balancing requirements, local-content requirements and export-performance requirements. Moreover, it has made commitments not to enforce the terms of contracts containing such requirements. The allocation of or permission for rights for importation and investment will not be conditional upon performance requirements set by national or sub-national authorities or subject to secondary conditions covering, for example, the conduct of research, the provision of offsets or other forms of industrial compensation, including specified types or volumes of business opportunities, the use of local inputs or the transfer of technology. Permission to invest, import licenses, quotas and tariff-rate quotas will be granted without regard to the existence of competing Chinese domestic suppliers.

China has also committed itself to improving transparency and law enforcement. In respect to transparency, China undertook that only those laws, regulations and other measures pertaining to or affecting trade in goods, services, trade-related intellectual property rights or the control of foreign exchange that were published and readily available to other WTO Members, individuals and enterprises should be enforced. In addition, China shall make available to WTO Members, upon request, all laws, regulations and other measures pertaining to or affecting trade in goods or services, trade-related intellectual property rights or the control of foreign exchange before such measures are implemented or enforced.

As for law enforcement, China confirmed that the provisions of the WTO Agreements, as well as the Accession Protocol, would be applied uniformly throughout its customs territory, including in special economic zones and other areas where special regimes for tariffs, taxes and regulations were established, and at all levels of government, and that it would, upon accession, establish a mechanism under which individuals and enterprises can bring to the attention of the national authorities cases of non-uniform application of the trade regime. China's local regulations, rules and other measures of local governments at the sub-national level shall conform to the obligations undertaken in the WTO Agreement and the Accession Protocol. Moreover, according to the Accession Protocol, the administrative law would be improved to such an extent that judicial review of administrative acts and judicial independence would be established in many fields. Thus, law enforcement by administrations can be expected to be more formal and standardized.

2. Rooms for Further Improvement

After China's accession into the WTO, China has acted in accordance with its commitments to lift restrictions on the entry and operation of foreign investment by adjusting its industrial policies and removing such requirements as, for example, local content and forced technology transfer, from relevant laws and regulations. The Chinese government has also replaced the Provisional Guidelines and the Provisional Catalogue with the new Regulations on Foreign Investment Guidelines (Guidelines) and the Catalogue of Industries for Guiding Foreign Investment (Catalogue). The objectives of the revisions were to ensure compliance with the commitments China made concerning market access or, precisely, to remove those clauses that contravene WTO rules, on the one hand, and to pave the way for the Chinese government to create a more liberalized investment environment for foreign investment enterprises, on the other. Nonetheless, certain heritages of the transition economy are still perceptible in the lingering industrial policies, and still exist many defects with regard to the WTO law and China's commitments. First, the foreign investment enterprises and the Chinese counterparts are still treated more or less differently in income tax, import tax, etc, countering to the WTO's principle of national treatment. Second, some laws and regulations governing foreign investment are not completely publicized due to the decentralized legislative models, and the judicial interpretations are not all open to foreign investment enterprises. This is inconsistent with the WTO's principle of transparency. Third, the restrictions of the foreign investment laws are not in conformity with the WTO's rules of general elimination of quantitative restrictions. Undoubtedly, the Chinese legislature needs to remove these barriers so as to create a fair competitive environment for foreign investment enterprises.

C. Inefficiency of Dispute Settlement for Foreign Investment Enterprises

As mentioned above, the dispute settlement for foreign investment enterprises is characterized with high preference for friendly and methods such as friendly negotiation, consultation, conciliation or mediation and arbitration. These flexible methods can certainly contribute to the friendly cooperation and mutual benefits, but there are still rooms for further improvement. First, the Chinese government should strive to further strengthen the rule of law sense and neutrality of mediators or arbitrators who possibly indulge in the local protectionism and disregard idea of rule of law. For instance, reforms should be carried out on the transparency of arbitral procedures. Second, enforcement of arbitral awards and court decisions should be guaranteed. Article 63 of the Arbitration Law governs enforcement of arbitral awards for the domestic entity. It stipulates that under the circumstances of the Law of Civil Procedure of the People's Republic of China

(CPL), the court may not enforce the award against the losing party. In a domestic dispute, which includes the foreign investment enterprises, if a party fails to abide by the arbitral award, the winning party must apply to the people's court to enforce the award. However, it is usually difficult for judges to enforce awards in such circumstances. Significantly, the court may not only review the procedure carried out by the arbitration commission, but also the substantive legal issues of the case when deciding whether to enforce the award. The fact that a Chinese court may review a case on the merits seriously weakens the effect of finality of an arbitral award for the foreign investment enterprises. On the other hand, for the foreign enterprise, which is considered a dispute involving a foreign element, challenges to the arbitral award are governed by Article 260 of the CPL which sets forth the circumstances for invalidating or setting aside an arbitration award for "disputes involving foreigners." Refusal of the courts to enforce a foreign arbitral award is based on procedural errors in the arbitration process, rather than a review of the substantive issues of the dispute. In addition, as opposed to domestic arbitration, if the foreign investor arbitrates a dispute through CIETAC or another international arbitration commission and loses, the Chinese party may apply to enforce the award in the foreigner's country whereas local protectionism and nationalism may possibly weigh against foreign applicants seeking enforcement in China. This makes it difficult for the losing party to secure its assets. Besides, as with domestic and international enforcement applications, a people's court shall decide not to enforce an arbitration ruling which it deems contrary to "social and public interests." The social and public interests that would cause an award not to be enforced are not defined in the law. In addition, decisions to enforce or refuse to enforce an award cannot be appealed.

VII. The Foreign Investment Law of the People's Republic of China

The National People's Congress adopted the New Foreign Investment Law on 15 March, 2019 and the Rules for the Implementation of the New Foreign Investment Law on 31 December, 2019 and these two laws came into force on January 1, 2020. Correspondingly, with unified provisions for the entry, promotion, protection and management of foreign investment, it is a new and fundamental law for China's foreign investment. The New Foreign Investment Law as a landmark in the legislative history of foreign investment in China aims to improve the transparency of foreign investment policies and ensure domestic and foreign enterprises are subject to a unified set of rules and compete on a level playing field. The new law shows China's will and determination to follow through with reform and opening up in a new historical context. It is a full testament to China's determination and confidence in opening wider to the outside world and promoting foreign investment in the new era.

A. A Unified Law to Replace the Three Existing Foreign Investment Laws

There are serious criticisms for many years on the multiple layers of legislature and decentralized laws and regulation leading to numerous conflicts and confusions to both foreign and Chinese investment enterprises. One of the objectives of the New Foreign Investment Law is to unify the existing different laws to establish and improves a mechanism for foreign investment promotion, and creates a stable, transparent, predictable and fair market environment (Article 3). That's say, after taking effect, the unified law will replace the three existing laws on Chinese-foreign equity joint ventures, wholly foreign-owned enterprises and Chinese-foreign contractual joint ventures (Article 42).

As to the organizational forms, institutional frameworks, and standards of conduct laws of foreign investment enterprises, the New Foreign Investment Law provides explicitly that laws including the Company Law of the People's Republic of China and the Law of the People's Republic of China on Partnership Enterprise govern the foreign investment enterprises' "organizational forms, institutional frameworks, and standards of conduct." (Article 31) Article 32 requires foreign investment enterprises to comply with the applicable rules on "labor protection and social insurance." And under Article 33, foreign investors that "merge with or acquire mainland Chinese enterprises" or otherwise participate in concentration of undertakings must submit to anti-monopoly review under the Chinese Anti-Monopoly Law.

It is also worth mentioning that the New Foreign Investment Law provides a five-year transition period, that is, a foreign-invested enterprise already established in accordance with the previous three laws can maintain its original organization form (such as wholly foreign-owned, Chinese-foreign equity joint venture or Chinese-foreign co-operative joint venture) within five years after the new law comes into force in 2020 (Article 42). To ensure the smooth transition of the five-year period, the New Foreign Investment Law further authorizes the State Council of China to formulate specific rules to regulate the organization form of foreign-invested enterprises within such transition period.

Quite a number of foreign and Chinese investment enterprises complain about the different treatment offered to investment enterprises even after China's accession to the WTO. The New Foreign Investment Law also aims to guarantee national treatment to all investment enterprises equally. Article 4 provides that the State maintains a system of pre-entry national treatment plus a negative list management for foreign investment. The pre-entry national treatment mentioned in the preceding paragraph refers to the treatment given to foreign investors and their investment at the stage of investment admission no less than that to domestic investors and their investments; In other words, China will treat foreign investment no less favorably than domestic investment during the "investment access stage" including the "establishment, acquisition, expansion, and such other stages of an enterprise"—unless the negative list provides otherwise. The so-called negative list refers to the special management measures that are adopted for the admission of foreign investment in specific areas. The State gives national treatment to foreign investment outside the negative list.

In 2015, the Negative List was first trialed in four Free Trade Zones of China. In 2018, the Pre-establishment National Treatment Plus Negative List scheme was adopted in the first draft and became a highlight in the Foreign Investment Law of China. This is a systematic modification following the publishing of Negative List on June 26, 2018, conductive to a better convergence of different foreign investment laws and regulations. The key industries encouraged opening-up include modern agriculture, advanced manufacturing, high-technology, modern service industries etc., among which the automotive manufacturing, software and information technology services industries have a relatively higher degree of openness.

To explain more specifically, Chapter II sets out a list of policy measures for promoting foreign investment. Under this Chapter, China will treat foreign and domestic investments equally with respect to the application of business development policies (Article 9), formulation of standards and application of compulsory standards (Article 15), and government procurement (Article 16). In addition, the government will consult foreign investment enterprises when formulating rules on foreign investment (Article 10); will promptly make public legal documents or judicial rulings related to foreign investment (Id.); will provide counseling and services on a range of topics to foreign investors and foreign investment enterprises (Article 11); and will publish foreign investment guidelines for their convenience (Article 19); Foreign-invested enterprises participate in government procurement activities through fair competition (Article 16); foreign-invested enterprises can finance through public offerings of stocks, securities including bonds and other means (Article 17) and etc.

Obviously, the national treatment provided for in the New Foreign Investment Law for the first time in the legislative history of foreign investment laws contributes to the opening of more industries to foreign investment and also shows China's will and determination to follow the established open-door policy.

B. Strengthening of Rule of Law

The progresses of Chinese rule of law construction has been extensively recognized abroad in recent years, however, the current existing three foreign investment laws in

China have often criticized with dominance by political control of the Chinese central government. [1] Undoubtedly, compared with current three foreign investment laws, the New Foreign Investment Law is known with the strengthening of rule of law. For example, the most important change is that this New Foreign Investment Law provides that all acts relating investment such as establishment, tax, organization of enterprises, management and protection by the Chinese government should be fulfilled "according to the laws", "complying with the laws", "pursuant to the legal authorities and procedures" etc. Though such provisions are mostly made to legal principles, and some of them are more or less ambiguous, it demonstrates the attitude and determination of Chinese government to protect foreign investors' interests from a legal perspective, which is aimed to enhance the confidence and sense of belonging for foreign investors to enter China.

Just as President Xi Jinping stressed in his speech at the 2019 Spring Festival Reception, the Reform and Opening-up policy has come to a new era and will be further deepened. The boost of foreign investment legislation not only shows China's emphasis on promoting foreign investment and protecting the interest of foreign investment, but also reflects China's determination and courage to deepen the opening-up. As the new fundamental law of foreign investment, the New Foreign Investment Law is expected to further guide, promote and standardize the foreign investment in China. As a result, it will further facilitate legalization and internationalization of China as well as create a healthy, fair and efficient business environment.

■ Notes

law of Three Capital Enterprises 三资企业法。主要指我国对外开放初期,针对我国的具体情形和吸引外资的需要,先后制定的《中外合资经营企业法》、《中外合作经营企业法》及《外资企业法》。三资企业法的实施成功吸引了大量外资,为我国的经济崛起作出了较大的贡献。然而,随着经济全球化的快速发展,WTO 法的要求及我国决定进一步深入对外开放战略的实施,三资企业法存在的缺陷逐渐显现,不能适应我国经济发展的需要。因此,我国于 2020 年生效的新外商投资法将三资企业法统一起来,有助于为外商投资企业提供更自由、开放及安全的投资环境,促进我国经济的快速发展。

two-track legislative model 双轨立法模式。这里指我国在对外开放初期,针对当时的经济及立法状况,对内资和外资进行不同立法的模式。该模式的优点是保证了我国政府干预外资的灵活性,缺点是法出多门,适用混乱,也存在违法 WTO 国民待遇原则的嫌疑。我国新《外商投资法》2020 年生效后,我国的外商投资法就统一了。

---

[1] Jessica Zone Renwald, Foreign Investment Law in the People's Republic of China: What to Expect from Enterprise Establishment to Dspute Resolution, 16 Ind. Int'l & Comp. L. Rev., 2006, pp. 453, 491.

negative list 负面清单。负面清单是发达国家早已广泛采用的政府管理投资的模式,指政府规定哪些经济领域不开放,除了清单上的禁区,其他行业、领域和经济活动都许可。例如,负面清单管理模式在外商投资领域的运用,即凡是与外资的国民待遇、最惠国待遇不符的管理措施,或业绩要求、高管要求等方面的管理措施以清单方式列明。显然,这种管理模式遵循的是"法无禁止皆可为"的逻辑,自然会产生向外商开放更多领域的效果。我国政府曾在一些自贸区招商引资中尝试过这种模式,取得了较好的效果。2020 年生效的外商投资法已经纳入了该模式,彰显了我国政府进一步对外开放决心和自信。

■ Important Legal English Usages

establish 建立,设立。例如,The case established an important legal principle(该案例创立了一个重要的法律原则)。The company was established in 1860(这家公司创立于 1860 年)。

注意下列几个近义词的用法:

(1)set up:开办,设立,创办。与 establish 相比,该词主要用于商业上创办公司、商铺及企业等,较少用于法律。例如,The group plans to set up an import business(该集团计划创办一家进口公司)。After the war, she set up shop in a quiet Yorkshire town(战后,她在约克郡的一个安静小镇上开了一家店)。

(2)found:创立,创办。该词通常用被动语态,主要用于创立政治组织、公司及学校等。例如,The newspaper was founded in 1909(这家报纸创办于 1909 年)。Shandong University was founded in 1901(山东大学创办于 1901 年)。

enterprise 企业,公司。与 company, firm 及 business 相比,多用于规模较大,专业较强的企业或公司。Euro Disney is a much smaller enterprise than its American counterparts(比起美国迪士尼来说,欧洲迪士尼是家小得多的公司)。

注意下列几个近义词的用法:

(1)company:公司。多用于泛指以营利为目的的营销公司。例如,Johnson joined the company in 1992(约翰逊 1992 年加入了这家公司)。a local/multinational company(本地/跨国公司)。

(2)firm:公司,事务所,商行。例如,a law firm(律师事务所),a firm of accountants(会计师事务所), an engineering firm(工程公司)。

(3)business:工商企业,公司,商店,营业所。该词常指一个人或几个人所拥有并经营的小企业。例如,a small family business(小型家族企业)。Mathew's little shop has turned into a thriving business(马修的小店变成了兴隆的商行)。

improve 提高,改进,改善,增进。该词多用于人民生活品质和环境的改善。例如,Our main objective is to improve educational standards(我们的主要目的是提高教育水平)。The investment environment in China has greatly improved(中国的投资环境已经得到了极大的改善)。

注意下列几个近义词的用法:

(1)enhance:增强,促进,提高。与 improve 相比,该词也可以用于提高人们生活质量和效率方面,但该词的用法并不广泛。例如,The measures taken should considerably enhance the residents' quality of life(采取的措施应该明显提高居民的生活质量)。to enhance economic efficiency and development(提高经济效益和促进经济发展)。

(2)boost:增强,提高。与上述动词相比,该词更多用于数量的增加。例如,Their share price climbed again today, boosted by rising sales(销售额的增加使他们的股票价格今天再次攀升)。

(3)increase:增加,增长。该词主要用于数量的增长,比 boost 用的更广泛。例如,Our costs increased dramatically over the last decade(我们的成本在过去 10 年中急剧增长)。An increasing number of people are choosing not to have children(越来越多的人选择不要孩子)。

legitimate 公正合理的,合法的。例如,It is legitimate to ask questions about a politician's personal life(询问政治家的私人生活状况是完全合乎情理的)。Are the premises being used for legitimate purposes?(这些底盘被用于正当商业目的了吗?)。a legitimate child(婚生的孩子)。

注意下列几个近义词的用法:

(1) legal:法律的,合法的。例如,to seek legal advice before signing the contract(签订合同前找律师咨询)。The driver's blood-alcohol level was three times the legal limit(这位司机血液里的酒精含量是法定限量的 3 倍)。legal action(法律行动)。legal right/requirement(法律权利/要求)。

(2)lawful:依法的,合法的。例如,lawful activities(合法活动)。a lawful marriage(合法婚姻)。lawful ownership(合法所有权)。

这三个词都用来指合法的行为、权利等,但细细揣摩,它们之间的含义和用法仍存在区别。lawful 主要用于正式的场合,且强调的是某行为或权利不违法。legal 强调的是与法律有关的规定、要求或法律许可的事务,所修饰的名词不同。legitimate 除了有合法的含义外,更强调事务的公正合理性,常用于学术文献中。

可见,这几个词在含义和用法上不易准确掌握。建议读者在学习中多读多想,细细品味,才能得其要领,做到熟能生巧。

settlement (纠纷)解决,(法院)裁决。例如,He got the flat as part of their divorce settlement(作为离婚裁决的一部分,他得到了那套公寓)。an out-of-court settlement(庭外和解)。

注意该词与 resolution 的区别:这两个词可以互用,但比较来看,resolution 多用于政治、外交等方面的争端,settlement 则常用于法律纠纷。例如,Both countries called for the peaceful resolution of the border dispute(两国都呼吁和平解决边界争端)。Diplomats are hoping for a speedy resolution to the crisis(外交官们希望尽快解决危机)。

conciliation (安抚性)调解,调停争端。例如,The disputes can be settled by conciliation(该争端可以通过调解解决)。

注意该词与 mediation 的区别:这两个词都指争端双方在中立第三方的协助下解决争端,因此可以互用。但是,这两个词仍存在细微差别:conciliation 下的中立第三方发挥的作用较大,如第三方不仅会就纠纷解决提出具体建议,还常常提出具有拘束力的解决方案;resolution 下的第三方一般仅仅提出纠纷解决建议,如果纠纷不能解决,只能寻求其他方式,如仲裁或诉讼等。

■ Review Questions

1. What is meant by the term "limited liability company" under Chinese laws?
2. Describe briefly the defects of the current legislative system of foreign investment.
3. Compare and contrast the methods of dispute settlement such as negotiation, consultation, conciliation, arbitration and litigation.
4. Outline the main measures by the Chinese government to guarantee the protection foreign investment, giving some examples if possible.
5. Define the "negative list" and explain its significance for China's open door policies.
6. Identify the main improvements of the New Foreign Investment Law compared with the current foreign investment enterprise law.
7. Please make a comment on China's measures of strengthening the rule of law for foreign investment, giving some examples.
8. Discuss briefly the future development of China's foreign investment law.

11 Chapter Eleven Intellectual Property Right Law

■ 导读

本章讲授的是知识产权法，主要包括版权、专利、商标及专有技术、国际上相关规定及国际许可证协议等内容。随着我国的经济发展，知识产权变得越来越重要，也成为我国企业与外国企业纠纷的重要领域之一。因此，希望读者将其作为重点研习，一是可以学到相关学科知识，二是可以提高知识产权方面法律英语水平，对将来处理涉外业务至关重要。

A growing method of doing business abroad is, after the Second World War, to transfer intellectual property rights (IPRs), technological know-how or artistic work—to a foreign business in exchange for a fee or other form of remuneration. Similarly, the tremendous achievements in technological and economic development of China benefit a great deal from the transfer of foreign countries' IPRs to China as an important part of China's open door policies. This chapter discusses copyrights, patents, trademarks, know-how, international legal systems and relevant major issues in transfer of IPRs.

I. The Creation of Intellectual Property Rights

The realm of information that can be owned, assigned, and licensed is as broad as human inventiveness and imagination. Such information can involve either statutory or nonstatutory rights. The former includes copyrights, patents, and trademarks. The latter includes "know-how."[1]

A. Copyrights

As the word suggests, copyright is the right to prevent others from copying, or reproducing one's work. Copyright is a right that arises automatically upon the creation of a work that qualifies for copyright protection. There is registration process. This means that there is no registration certificate to prove ownership or copyright. To prove

---

[1] Know-how is a word of American origin that has now been adopted as a term of art in many languages (Ray August, Don Mayer and Michael Bixby, International Business Law, Pearson Education Limited, 2013, p. 490.)

ownership, the author will need to produce original and, preferably, dated evidence of the creation of the work and proof of authorship. The author will also need to show that he is a qualifying person or that the work was first published in a country.

Copyright has its root in the fifteenth century. The Duke of Milan issued the first known copyright—a grant of the exclusive right to print a work—in 1481 to the printer of a local history. Similar grants were given to other printers in Germany, France, Italy, and Spain at about the same time. In 1556, a system of registration of books with the Stationers' Company was established to offer protection for authors. This optional registration system is still available, though rarely used. If an author registered a book with the Stationers' Company, it gave her a perpetual right to reproduce the book and, consequently, prevent reproduction by anyone else. In 1734, the Engravings Copyright Act was passed, which gave copyright protection to engravings. Similar status appeared in Spain in 1764, in the United States in 1790, in revolutionary France in 1791, and in the German Confederation in 1837. In 1886, 10 countries, including Belgium, Britain, France, Germany, Italy, Spain, and Switzerland, signed the Berne Convention—by far the most influential international copyright convention—at Berne, Switzerland. This convention followed the Continental European model, requiring signatory states to impose minimal formalities and to protect both pecuniary and more rights. Today, most of the nations of the world have ratified the Berne Convention.

Intellectual property is divided, for the purposes of study (and for establishing legal rights), into two principal branches: artistic property and industrial property. Artistic property encompasses artistic, literary, and musical works. These are protected, in most countries, by copyrights and neighbouring rights. Industrial property is itself divided into two categories: inventions and trademarks. Inventions include both useful products and useful manufacturing processes. They are protected in a variety of ways, the most common protection being in the form of patents, petty patents, and inventors' certificates. Trademarks include "true" trademarks, trade names, service marks, collective marks, and certification marks. All of these are markings that identify the ownership rights of manufacturers, merchants, and service establishments. They are protected by trademark laws.

1. Literary Works

Under the Copyright, Designs and Patent Act 1988 in the England, literary works refers to "any work, other than a dramatic or musical work, which is written, spoken or sung". The Act goes on to say that this includes a table or compilation, a computer program and preparatory design material for a computer program and a database.

2. Dramatic Works

Original dramatic works in England are not defined but are said to include a "work of dance or mime". The courts have expanded on the statutory provision by deciding that the word 'dramatic' requires an element of performance accompanied by action.

3. Musical Works

An original musical work is defined as "a work consisting of music, exclusive of any words or action intended to be sung, spoken or performed with the music". Presumably, it would qualify if it has been performed in public, recorded on a sound recording or broadcast to provide pleasure or entertainment. Therefore, the musical work must be recorded in some fixed form for copyright to subsist.

4. Artistic Work

Artistic works are defined as being "a graphic work, photograph, sculpture or collage irrespective of artistic quality, a work of architecture being a building or a model for a building or a work of artistic craftsmanship". "Graphic work" is further defined as including "any painting, drawing, diagram, map, chart or plan and any engraving, etching, lithograph, wood cut or similar work". [1]

Article 3 of Copyright Law of the People's Republic of China provides that the term "works" in this law includes, among other things, works of literature, art, natural sciences, social sciences, engineering and technology, which are created in any of the following form: (1) written works; (2) oral works; (3) musical, dramatic, quyi, choreographic and acrobatic works; (4) works of fine arts and architecture; (5) photographic works; (6) cinematographic works and works created by a process analogous to cinematography; (7) graphic works such as drawings of engineering designs and product designs, maps and sketches, and model works; (8) computer software; and (9) other works as provided for in laws and administrative regulations. [2]

Under the law and regulations in China, these works should satisfy three requirements: (1) they should be the expression of ideas or feelings; (2) they should be original; and (3) they should be able to be reproduced in material form. Oral works can receive copyright protection because they can be reproduced by writing or recording.

---

[1] Tina Hart & Linda Fazzani, Intellectual Property Law, Law Press China, 2003, p. 147.

[2] Copyright Law of the People's Republic of China was adopted at the 15th Meeting of the Standing Committee of the Seventh National People's Congress on September 7, 1990, and amended according to the Decision on Revising the Copyright Law of the People's Republic of China made at the 24th Meeting of the Standing Committee of the Ninth National People's Congress on October 27, 2001. The Implementing Regulations of Copyright Law was formulated by the State Council in 2002.

B. Patents

A patent is "a statutory privilege granted by the government to inventors, and to others deriving their rights from the inventor, for a fixed period of years, to exclude other persons from manufacturing, using or selling a patented product or from utilizing a patented method or process."[1] This means that the patentee has the legal right to stop others producing the patented goods or applying the patented process by suing for infringement. The grant of a patent is, therefore, the grant of a monopoly right for a specified period.

Patents were originally granted by the Crown exercising its Royal Prerogative. Letters Patent were a royal proclamation that the bearer had the Crown's authority to do whatever had been authorised within the Letters. The earliest record of a granted patent dates from 1331, to a Flemish weaver who wanted to practice his trade in England. Most of the patents granted at this time were to encourage trade in general rather than new inventions.

In modern society, several reasons have been given to justify the granting of patents. First of all, in obtaining a patent, the patentee has publicised her invention. Whereas others cannot use the patent during the patent period, they can certainly look at the details and learn from the technological advances made. The grant of the patent is the reward for sharing knowledge regarding new inventions. Second, the inventor who is rewarded in this way may be encouraged to make other useful inventions. The patent is thus an incentive to be more creative. A third possible justification for patents is that, as new products are invented, this stimulates the economy as there are more products for consumers to buy.

The patentee will have often spent a great deal of money on research and development of the product in question. Having the monopoly for a limited period allows her to recoup that investment before others come onto the market to compete. Further, without the grant of a patent, others who have not had to invest in research and development would be able to copy the invention, produce it more cheaply and still make a profit, thereby depriving the inventor of the ability to recoup her investment. To ensure that the patentee uses her monopoly only for legitimate purpose of recouping her investment, and not for the purpose of purely blocking out competition, there is provision for compulsory licenses to be granted if the patentee has not commercially exploited the patent after a certain period.

---

[1] Ray August, Don Mayer and Michael Bixby, International Business Law, Pearson Education Limited, 2002, p. 505.

1. Patentability

Patents are granted only for inventions which fulfil certain criteria. The invention must be one which, under the Act in England, is accorded patent protection; it must be new and it must involve an inventive step.

(1) Novelty. An invention must be "new" to be patentable. It is new (or "novel") if it does not form part of the state of the art at the priority date. The state of art comprises all matter (whether a product, a process, information about either, or anything else) which has at any time before that date, been made available to the public anywhere in the world by written or oral description, by use or in any other way. Where the art is a crowded one, two or more inventors may arrive at the invention at the same time and each file patent applications. To avoid the grant of a patent to two patentees, the earlier application is deemed to be part of the prior art when considering the novelty of the later application.

(2) Inventive step. Even after satisfying the test of novelty, the application must involve an inventive step. This means that it must move the science on and not be merely something that would be 'obvious' to anyone skilled in the art if they had put their mind to it.

This is based on the philosophy, similar to that in novelty, that the public should not be prevented from doing anything that is merely an obvious extension or workshop variation of what was already known. Unlike novelty, it is possible to make a 'mosaic' of documents or information, in other words, put together documents or pockets of separately available information and claim that the invention is obvious. However, the documents must be in the same field, and the 'mosaic' will only establish prima facie obviousness. It is still possible to argue that the combination of the documents has resulted in an unexpected technical advantage and that there has, therefore, been an inventive step.

An invention is taken to involve an inventive step if it is not obvious to a person skilled in the art having regard to the prior art, other than co-pending patent applications which are deemed to be prior art for the purpose of testing for novelty only. Whether an invention is obvious is the most litigious question of all, as a patentee will not defend his patent if shown a clear anticipation. It is the "nearly but not quite" piece of prior art that is the most troublesome. The issue is particularly difficult to resolve as it is often fought years after the invention was made and the benefit of hindsight must somehow be discounted.

The test is directed to a hypothetical addressee: the man skilled in the art. He has been described as "a skilled technician who is well acquainted with workshop technique and who has carefully read all the relevant literature. He is supposed to have an unlimited capacity to assimilate the contents of, it may be, scores of specifications but to be incapable of a scintilla of invention."[1]

The court must decide the question of obviousness having been instructed in the state of the art at the priority date of the patent by technical evidence.

2. Duration of Patents

With the coming into force of the TRIPS Agreement on January 1, 1995, the minimum term of protection for patents has now been set at 20 years for WTO member states. Previously, the terms that countries had established varied widely, ranging from 3 to 26 years (including extensions). The uniformity provided by the new 20-year standard should greatly encourage inventors, who will now be able to exploit their inventions much more widely and for an overall longer period than they were able to do in the past.[2]

3. Non-patentability

Under the Patent Law of the People's Republic of China, two types of invention-creation cannot receive patent protection: (1) illegal invention-creation; and (2) non-patentable subject matters. The illegal invention-creations cannot receive patent protection since its purpose is against the law, the public policy, or detrimental to public interests. The non-patentable subject matters comprise: (a) scientific discoveries; (b) rules and methods of mental activities; (c) methods of diagnosis or treatment of disease; (d) animal and plant varieties; (e) substances obtained by means of nuclear fission. However, the process used to produce the varieties of animal or plant is patentable.

C. Trademarks

1. Functions of Trademarks

A trade mark can be described as a sign or symbol placed on, or used in relation to, one trader's goods or services to distinguish them from similar relation to, one trader's goods or services supplied by other traders. Section 1 of the Trade Marks Act 1994 in England defines a trade mark as any sign capable of being represented graphically which distinguishes the goods or services of one business from those of another.

A trade mark may satisfy a number of functions. Its main function is indicated in the definition given above, namely, to differentiate one trader's goods or services from those of another. As mass production and self-service in the wholesale and retail markets have replaced limited product ranges and personal service, the trade mark allows the consumer

---

[1] Clive. M. Schmitthoff, David A. G. Sarre, Mercantile Law, London Stevens & Sons, 1984, p. 610.

[2] Ray August, Don Mayer and Michael Bixby, International Business Law, Pearson Education Limited, 2002, p. 512.

to distinguish between similar products.

A good trade mark can be essential tool for selling goods. As such, it is invaluable to the producer. In a market swamped by competing goods, the trade mark is a shorthand description for the product. Without a trade mark it would be necessary, each time a purchase is contemplated, to compare products by reference to ingredients, function and consumer experiences, which would be very long-winded. The trade mark is useful to the consumer as she will choose goods based on personal or vicarious experiences of a product and the trade mark allows easy identification of the product which previously gave satisfaction, thus leading to repeat purchases. This leads to another possible function of the trade mark: its guarantee function. Once a customer has tried a product with a particular name and found it satisfactory, repeat purchases of goods bearing that name will guarantee repetition of that satisfaction.

Equally, where a consumer has had a bad experience with a product, the trade mark can act as a warning against further purchases. Traders thus have an interesting protecting the good name of their mark by only attaching it to quality goods. Provided that the mark is imbued with this good reputation, the trader can use it to increase and generate sales by investing in promotions and advertising, and by using the mark.

2. Conditions for Registration of Trademarks

Under the Trade Marks Act 1994 in England, the mark must be: capable of being represented graphically, and capable of distinguishing one trader's products from those of others.

(1) Graphic representation. The objective here is to make it possible for interested parties to judge the monopoly given. Words and symbols will pose no problems and a three-dimensional shape can be represented by a two-dimensional drawing. At present, it is clear that whatever the trade mark, its representation must fit into an 8 cm by 8 cm box on the application form.

(2) Capable of distinguishing. Article 9 of the Trademark Law of the People's Republic of China provides: "A trademark submitted for registration shall bear noticeable characteristics and be readily distinguishable, and it may not conflict with the legitimate rights obtained by others earlier."

3. Absolute Grounds for Refusal of Application

Under the 1994 Act in England, an application of trademark is refused due to the following grounds: (1) signs which do not represent the mark graphically such as sounds, smells; (2) trademarks devoid of any distinctive character; (3) trademarks that consist exclusively of signs or indications which may serve, in trade, to designate the kind, quality, quantity, intended purpose, value, geographical origin, the time of production of goods, or of rendering of services, or other characteristics of goods or services; (4) trademarks that consist exclusively of signs or indications which have become customary in the current language, or in the bona fide and established practices of the trade; (5) trademarks offending public morally and good taste; (6) trademarks prohibited by enactments and emblems; (7) bad faith applications.

Articles 10 and 11 of the Trademark Law of the People's Republic of China have similar provisions.

4. Rights of the Trademark Owner

Section 9 of the 1994 Act confirms the trade mark owner's exclusive rights. Exercise of those rights by anyone else, without his consent, amounts to infringement. In the case of co-owners, each owner is entitled to exercise the exclusive rights in relation to the trade mark without the other co-owner's consent. However, all co-owners must consent to the exercise of those rights by a third party. The rights of the owner date from the filing date of the trade mark application, but an action for infringement cannot be commenced until the registration has been granted. Section 14 provides the owner with the authority to sue, based purely upon ownership of the registered trade mark. Unlike passing off, there is no need to establish trade use of reputation.

Under the Trademark Law of the People's Republic of China, the trademark owner enjoys the following rights: (1) He is entitled to exclusively use the registered trademark; (2) He is entitled to assign the registered trademark according to applicable laws; (3) He is entitled to authorize other people to use his own registered trademark according to applicable laws and to supervise the quality of the goods on which the registered trademark is used by the license; and (4) He also enjoys the right to be protected when the right to exclusive use of the registered trademark is infringed.

5. Obligations of the Trademark Owner

Under relevant Chinese laws, the trademark owner shall bear the following obligations: (1) When he applies for trademark registration and conduct other trademark matters, he shall pay fees, according to the relevant provisions of the Administrative Department for Industry and Commerce of the State Council. (2) He shall not alter any word or design, alphabet, figure, three-dimensional graph or combination thereof, of the registered trademark without authorization; he shall not change his name, address or any other registered matters concerning the registered trademark without authorization, he shall not assign the registered trademark without authorization. (3) He shall practically use his registered trademark, namely he shall not stop using the registered trademark for three consecutive years. (4) He shall guarantee the quality of the goods on which his registered trademark or trademark is used.

D. Know-how

Know-how is practical expertise acquired from study, training, and experience. It has been defined as factual knowledge, not capable of separate description but which, when used in an accumulated form, after being acquired as a result of trial and error, gives to the one acquiring it an ability to produce something which he otherwise would not have known to produce with the same accuracy of precision found necessary for commercial success.

Know-how differs from patent in that: (1) Patent is protected generally by specific statutory enactments, while know-how is protected by contract, tort, and other basic legal principles. (2) Patent has to be open to everyone, but know-how is kept secret and usually protected by trade secrecy laws. (3) Patent must subject to examination and approval by authorities, therefore is advanced technique. While Know-how is a type of technique mostly based on long experiment and experiences, and it is more practical. (4) The validity of patent is limited by time and area, while know-how is always valid so long as it is kept secret.

Internationally, the Agreement on Trade-Related Aspects of Intellectual Property Rights requires WTO member states to protect what the Agreement calls "undisclosed information." That is, natural and legal persons must be given the legal means to prevent information from being disclosed to, acquired by, or used by others without their consent in a manner contrary to honest commercial practice. The information, however, must (1) be secret, (2) have commercial value because it is a secret, and (3) have been reasonably protected from disclosure by its owner. [1]

II. International Provisions

Intellectual property rights are protected and regulated internationally both by bilateral treaties and multilateral conventions. Bilateral treaties were the original means of preventing illegal copying, and they were once quite commonplace. With the growing popularity of multilateral conventions in the mid-nineteenth century, their use has diminished. Today, most bilateral intellectual property treaties are used by states that are not parties to the multilateral conventions.

Nevertheless, multilateral treaties nowadays regulate most matters relating to intellectual property rights. Most of the conventions are administered by the World Intellectual Property Organization (WIPO) and the Council for Trade-Related Aspects on

---

〔1〕 Ray August, Don Mayer and Michael Bixby, International Business Law, Pearson Education Limited, 2002, p. 524.

Intellectual Property Rights.

A. Comprehensive Agreements

The principal comprehensive agreement establishing general intellectual property obligations for most of the world's states is the Agreement on Trade-Related Aspects of Intellectual Property Rights (TRIPS Agreement).

The purpose of the TRIPS Agreement is to create a multilateral and comprehensive set of rights and obligations governing the international trade in intellectual property. As a consequence, the TRIPS Agreement establishes a common minimum of protection for intellectual property rights applicable within all the WTO member states.

The TRIPS Agreement extends the basic principles of the General Agreement on Tariffs and Trade (GATT) to the field of international intellectual property rights. The national treatment principle requires each member state to extend to nationals of other members treatment no less favourable than that which it gives its own nationals regarding protection of intellectual property. The transparency principle requires member states to publish and notify the Council for TRIPS of all relevant laws, regulations and the like and to respond to requests from other members for information.

Comparatively, the TRIPS Agreement is unique in including a provision requiring most-favoured-nation treatment for such property. Under this provision, "any advantage, favour, privilege, or immunity granted by a member to the nationals of any other country (whether or not it is a WTO member) shall be accorded immediately and unconditionally to the nationals of all other members." Read together with the national treatment provision and the transparency provision, this requires each member state to treat the nationals of other member states as least as well (and possibly better) than it treats its own nationals.

B. Artistic Property Agreements

The main international agreements dealing with artistic property are the following conventions:

1. Berne Convention

Berne Convention(伯尔尼公约) for the Protection of Literary and Artistic Works (Berne Convention), adopted in Paris in 1886, came into force in 1887. The original text of the Convention established procedures for its revision, and revisions have been regularly made: in Paris in 1896, Berlin in 1908, Berne in 1914, Rome in 1928, Brussels in 1948, Stockholm in 1967, and Paris in 1971. The latest revision was made on October 2, 1979, but it is customarily called as "Paris Convention 1971". China acceded Berne Convention on July 1, 1992, and it came into effect to China on October 15 of the same year.

Berne Convention is, as the first world multilateral convention in copyright, the most influential copyright convention. Its basic principles are: (1) National treatment. This requires each member state to extend to nationals of other member states treatment no less favourable than that which it gives its own nationals. (2) Nonconditional protection. This requires that the member states must provide protection without any formalities. (3) Protection independent of protection in the country of origin. This allows authors who are nationals of nonmember states to obtain protection within the Berne Union by publishing their works in a member state. (4) Common rules. This establishes minimum standards for granting copyrights common to all member states.

2. Rome Convention

The International Convention for the Protection of Performers, Producers of Phonograms, and Broadcasting Organizations (Rome Convention) was agreed to in 1961. The draft for the Convention was prepared by a joint committee of experts appointed by the Berne Union, UNESCO, and the International Labor Organization. The Convention, accordingly, attempts to balance the interests of performers, producers of phonograms, and broadcasting organizations. Rome Convention was put into effect in 1964, only the countries which are members of Berne Convention or World Copyright Treaty are entitled to accede it. However, China is not a member of it.

3. Phonogram Piracy Convention

Because Rome Convention is too strict with conditions of becoming its members, and is unable to protect phonograms well, Phonogram Piracy Convention, a new convention especially for the protection of phonograms, was made under the charge of the WIPO. The Convention for the Protection of Producers of Phonograms against Unauthorized Duplication of Their Phonograms (Phonogram Piracy Convention) was signed in 1971 at Geneva. China acceded the Convention on April 18, 1973, and it became effective to China on April 30, 1993.

This convention provides that member states must protect producers of phonograms from the unauthorized reproduction and importation of their works for a period of not less than 20 years.

C. Industrial Property Agreements

The principal international conventions concerned with industrial property are the International Convention for the Protection of Industrial Property, the Treaty on Intellectual Property in Respect of Integrated Circuits, the Madrid Agreement for the Repression of False or Deceptive Indications of Sources of Goods, the Patent Cooperation Treaty, and the Trademark Law Treaty.

1. Paris Convention

Drafted in 1880, the International Convention for the Protection of Industrial Property (Paris Convention) (巴黎公约) was ratified by 11 states in 1883 and came into effect in 1884. The Convention establishes a "union" of states responsible for protecting industrial property rights among the members' duties is the obligation to participate in regular revisions. Revision conferences to expand the coverage of the Convention have been held regularly: in Rome 1886, Madrid in 1890 and 1891, Brussels in 1897 and 1900, Washington in 1911, The Hague in 1925, London in 1934, Lisbon 1958, and Stockholm in 1967, as amended on September 28, 1979. China became a member of this Convention on March 19, 1985, and made reservation to Article 28 of this Convention.

Paris Convention is not only the first world multilateral convention on copyright, but also the most influential one to other conventions. In this connection, Paris Convention's basic principles and contents are of significantly directive functions to other conventions.

Paris Convention has 30 articles of which Articles 1 – 12 are regarded the core of the Convention because they provide to all the countries of the Union common principles and minimum requirements of protection in their respective national laws.

(1) Scope of industrial property. Article 1 of the Convention provides that the protection of industrial property has as its object patents, utility models, industrial designs, trademarks, service marks, trade names, indications of source or appellations of origin, and the repression of unfair competition. Industrial property shall be understood in the broadest sense and shall apply not only to industry and commerce proper, but likewise to agricultural and extractive industries and to all manufactured or natural products, for example, wines, grain, tobacco leaf, fruit, cattle, minerals, mineral waters, beer, flowers, and flour. Patents shall include the various kinds of industrial patents recognized by the laws of the countries of the Union, such as patents of importation, patents of improvement, patents and certificates of addition, etc.

(2) National treatment. Article 2 of the Convention states that national treatment for nationals of any country of the Union shall, as regards the protection of industrial property, enjoy in all the other countries of the Union the advantages that their respective laws now grant, or may hereafter grant, to nationals; all without prejudice to the rights specially provided for by this Convention. Consequently, they shall have the same protection as the latter, and the same legal remedy against any infringement of their rights, provided that the conditions and formalities imposed upon nationals are complied with. However, no requirement as to domicile or establishment in the country where protection is claimed may be imposed upon nationals of countries of the Union for the enjoyment of any industrial property rights.

(3) Right of priority. The right of priority gives an applicant who has filed for protection in one member country a grace period of 12 months in which to file in another member state, which then must treat the application as if it were fled on the same day as the original application. Article 4, as the most essential article in this Convention, states:

(a) Scope of application of right of priority. Any person who has duly filed an application for a patent, or for the registration of a utility model, or of an industrial design, or of a trademark, in one of the countries of the Union, or his successor in title, shall enjoy, for the purpose of filing in the other countries, a right of priority during the periods hereinafter fixed. Clearly, right of priority does not apply to business reputation, name of origin and service marks.

(b) Scope of applicant for right of priority and prerequisite to application. Article 4 provides that any filing that is equivalent to a regular national filing under the domestic legislation of any country of the Union or under bilateral or multilateral treaties concluded between countries of the Union shall be recognized as giving rise to the right of priority. Clearly, the prerequisite to application is the applicant has submitted filing in a member of the Convention.

(c) The periods of priority. Article 4 provides that the periods of priority referred to above shall be twelve months for patents and utility models, and six months for industrial designs and trademarks.

(4) Principles of Independence of Patents and Copyrights. Principle of independence of patent means that patents applied for in the various countries of the Union by nationals of countries of the Union shall be independent of patents obtained for the same invention in other countries, whether members of the Union or not.

Principles of independence of copyrights means that an application for the registration of a mark filed by a national of a country of the Union in any country of the Union may not be refused, nor may a registration be invalidated, on the ground that filing, registration, or renewal, has not been effected in the country of origin.

(5) Special provisions of patent.

(a) Importation of patented products. Article 5 of the Convention states that importation by the patentee into the country where the patent has been granted of articles manufactured in any of the countries of the Union shall not entail forfeiture of the patent.

(b) Compulsory licenses. Each country of the Union shall have the right to take legislative measures providing for the grant of compulsory licenses to prevent the abuses which might result from the exercise of the exclusive rights conferred by the patent, for example, failure to work. Forfeiture of the patent shall not be provided for except in cases where the grant of compulsory licenses would not have been sufficient to prevent the said abuses. No proceedings for the forfeiture or revocation of a patent may be instituted before the expiration of two years from the grant of the first compulsory license.

Article 5 further provides that a compulsory license may not be applied for on the ground of failure to work or insufficient working before the expiration of a period of four years from the date of filing of the patent application or three years from the date of the grant of the patent, whichever period expires last; it shall be refused if the patentee justifies his inaction by legitimate reasons. Such a compulsory license shall be non-exclusive and shall not be transferable, even in the form of the grant of a sub-license, except with that part of the enterprise or goodwill which exploits such license.

(6) Special provisions of trademarks.

(a) Well-known trademarks(驰名商标). Article 6 of the Convention provides that the countries of the Union undertake, ex officio if their legislation so permits, or at the request of an interested party, to refuse or to cancel the registration, and to prohibit the use, of a trademark which constitutes a reproduction, an imitation, or a translation, liable to create confusion, of a mark considered by the competent authority of the country of registration or use to be well known in that country as being already the mark of a person entitled to the benefits of this Convention and used for identical or similar goods. These provisions shall also apply when the essential part of the mark constitutes a reproduction of any such well-known mark or an imitation liable to create confusion therewith.

A period of at least five years from the date of registration shall be allowed for requesting the cancellation of such a mark. The countries of the Union may provide for a period within which the prohibition of use must be requested.

(b) Protection of marks registered in one country of the Union in the other countries of the Union. Under Article 6, every trademark duly registered in the country of origin shall be accepted for filing and protected as is in the other countries of the Union, subject to the reservations indicated in this Article. Such countries may, before proceeding to final registration, require the production of a certificate of registration in the country of origin, issued by the competent authority. No authentication shall be required for this certificate.

2. Patent Co-operation Treaty

The Patent Co-operation Treaty, agreed to in 1970, is administered by the World Intellectual Property Organization in Geneva. The objective behind the system is to eliminate the need to make applications in a number of countries. A national of a member state can file an 'International Patent Application' in a given patent office, designating the countries in which she is seeking registration. This has the effect of filing the application in both the first country and also in the designated countries. The application is then transmitted to an International Searching Authority which will do the prior art search and transmit the results to the individual patent offices of the designated states. From that stage, the further prosecution in each country is dealt with by the local patent office in accordance with its normal procedure.

Currently, the Patent Co-operation Treaty is not yet in force.

3. Madrid Agreement

In 1891, the Madrid Agreement (马德里协定) was implemented to simplify the procedure for filing trade mark registrations in many countries. Up until that point, anyone wanting to obtain trade mark registrations in, say, ten countries, had to file ten separate applications at the ten separate national trade mark registries in accordance with the ten different procedural requirements.

The Madrid Agreement allows anyone established or domiciled in a Madrid Agreement country, with a trade mark registration in his or her country of establishment of domicile, to file one international application that can be extended to one or more other Madrid Agreement countries as specified. The central international application is filed with WIPO in Geneva, designating to which countries it is to be extended. WIPO then takes responsibility for passing the application on to each of the designated national laws and procedures of each country.

The Madrid Agreement was revised several times, and the latest revision was made in 1979. China acceded the Madrid Agreement on July 14, 1989, and it came into force to China on October 4 of the same year.

(1) Base registration. In order to be able to file an international application with WIPO under the Madrid Agreement, an applicant must have an existing registration of the trade mark in its 'home country'. 'Home country' means the country where the trade mark owner is a national, or is domiciled, or has a real and effective industrial or commercial establishment.

This requirement has favored trade mark owners of countries which have less stringent examination procedures (for example, countries with so-called deposit systems, where there is little or no examination of prior rights).

(2) Examination period. Under the Madrid Agreement, once an international application has been filed by WIPO at each designated national registry, each registry has 12 months within which to raise an objection. If no objection is raised in that period, the application will automatically proceed to registration. Article 30 of the Trademark Law of the People's Republic of China provides that any person may, within three months from the date a trademark is announced, raised an objection to the trademark that has undergone preliminary examination and obtained approval. Where no objection is raised at the expiration of the time limit, the trademark shall be registered upon approval, a

trademark registration certificate shall be issued, and the matter shall be announced.

4. Trademark Law Treaty

The Trademark Law Treaty, adopted in 1994, is meant to simplify both national and regional trademark registration systems by establishing common minimum rules. In addition, the term for renewal of a trademark is set at 10 years.

III. International Licensing Agreement

This section concerns the most common form of lawful international technology transfer—patent and knowhow licensing. In practices, this mostly refers to the international licensing agreement.

International patent and knowhow licensing is the most critical form of technology transfer to third world development. From the owner's standpoint, it presents an alternative to and sometimes a first step towards foreign investment. Such licensing involves a transfer of patent rights or knowhow in return for payments, usually termed royalties. Unlike foreign investment, licensing does not have to involve a capital investment in a host jurisdiction. However, licensing of patents and knowhow is not without legal risks.

From the licensee's standpoint, their industries in less-developed nations are typically in great need of technological know-how. This significant research and development that leads to technological innovation is generally the product of substantial capital investment, long lead times, and a strong educational infrastructure. Less-developed countries have a great shortage of these commodities. To industrialize, developing countries must rely on important technology. The Japanese success in the period after World War II is largely attributable to an ability to cause the transfer of technology. On the other hand, there is the risk that the licensed technology may be old or obsolete, not "state of the art." Goods produced under old technology will be hard to export and convey a certain "second class" status. Also, excessive royalties may threaten the economic viability of the licensee and drain hard currencies from the country. The licensee typically is not in a sufficiently powerful position to bargain away restrictive features of standard international licenses. For all these reasons, and more, third world countries frequently regulate patent and knowhow licensing agreements. Such law is found in the Brazilian Normative Act No. 17 (1976) and the Mexican Technology Transfer Law (1982) (repealed 1991), among others. Royalty levels will be limited, certain clauses prohibited and the desirability of the technology evaluated.

China has, since the implementation of its open-door policies, transferred a variety of technologies from developed countries, which has pushed forward significantly the economic development. However, due to the lack of international laws governing the affairs of transfer of technology, different understandings of technology and legal systems, etc, there often arise disputes on international transfer of technology. The experience and practices of transfer of technology suggest that a good contract of transfer of technology is most essential to successful transfer of technology.

A. Characteristics of International Licensing Agreement

In today's transfer of technology, licensing is used most extensively. Licensing is a grant of license by the owner of the IPR that permits the other party to use the relevant right. Comparatively, an international licensing agreement has the following characteristics:

1. An International Licensing Agreement Transfers the Right of Use

Under an international licensing agreement the right of using the IPR is transferred to foreign country rather than the ownership.

2. An International Licensing Agreement is Limited by Time and Particular Areas

In almost every country in the current world, a restriction on the territorial scope granted in the license of statutory right (i. e., a patent, trademark, or copyright) is treated as a normal incidence of that right.

3. An International Licensing Agreement is More Complex

An international licensing agreement usually has complex contents because most of the agreements are mixed with sale of machines, contracting engineering, equity joint venture, contractual joint venture, compensation trade, cooperation production, consultation services, etc.

4. An International Licensing Agreement is an Onerous Contract.

B. Major Issues in International Licensing Agreement

Just as mentioned above, an international licensing agreement usually has quite a number of clauses of which many are so controversial that they often cause disputes. Some of the major issues are:

1. Confidentiality and Improvements

When the licensed IPR is technology that is protected primarily by trade secret procedures rather than patent law, another key license provision will be the clause setting forth the licensee's obligation to keep the licensed technology confidential so that third parties cannot exploit the technology or compromise its protected status. The licensee often will try to limit the length of the period during which it must maintain confidentiality, while the licensor's interest is to preserve confidentiality as long as the anticipated useful life of the trade secret.

With respect to confidentiality, the parties will also usually bargain over ownership and use rights in the event that the licensee, with or without licensor assistance, develops improvements in the licensed technology or creates new inventions based on that technology. Reasoning that the licensee would not have had the opportunity to develop these useful technologies without the know-how supplied by the licensor, the licensor may seek a grant back to itself of ownership in or, at a minimum, the right to use—often without compensation—such new technology. In addition, the parties often bargain over whether the licensor shall be obligated to disclose to the licensee, and allow the use of, improvements made by the licensor.

The parties also bargain concerning the period of time curing which the licensee may exploit the licensed IPR, what events may cause the license to be terminated shot of the normal license period, and the rights of the licensee, if any, with respect to the IPR after the agreement has expired or terminated.

Also, in the contract permitting use of the IPR, the licensor will try to be sure that the licensee agrees not to use the IPR in competition with the licensor or to disclose it to a potential competitor. The licensee, on the other hand, will try to keep royalties low and minimize or abbreviate the noncompetition/ nondisclosure provisions.

2. Export Restrictions

A licensor often uses export restrictions to limit partially, or entirely, the rights of a licensee to export goods from the territory where the licensee or its production facilities are located, for fear that the products made by the licensed technology may be competitive to the licensor. Most countries, as a general rule, prohibit export restrictions.

3. Sales and Distribution Arrangements

A sales or distribution arrangement limits a licensee's freedom to organize its distribution system independently of the licensor. Developing countries usually prohibit any interference by the licensor in the licensee's distribution system, while developed countries only prohibit those exclusive sales arrangements that tend to allocate or monopolize markets.

4. Price-Fixing

A price-fixing clause requires a licensee to sell products at a price specified by the licensor. It may specify either maximum or minimum prices. It may be restricted to the technology or goods being licensed, or it may cover other products as well. It may apply only to the price charged by the licensee, or it may extend to the prices charged by retailers who purchase the goods from a wholesaler-licensee.

Most countries prohibit all forms of price-fixing.

5. Noncompetition Clauses

Noncompetition clauses forbid a licensee from entering into agreements to acquire or distributetechnologies or products that compete with ones furnished or designated by the licensor. Direct prohibitions may include an understanding that the licensee is not to manufacture or sell competing technologies, or that the license is to terminate the use of particular technologies or terminate the manufacture and distribution of particular products. Indirect prohibitions may require the licensee not to cooperate with a competing business or not to pay higher royalties of competing products.

In general, noncompetition clauses are prohibited in all countries. Only a few counties allow them under exceptional circumstances.

6. Tying Clauses

A tying clause (搭售) is a provision that requires a licensee to acquire or use, separately from the technology wanted, additional goods (such as raw materials, intermediate products, machines, or additional technology) or designated personnel either from the licensor or from a source named by the licensor. In other words, the acquisition of these additional goods or services is a prerequisite to obtaining the technology license.

In general, tying clauses are illegal in virtually every country. Most countries, however, provide for exemptions in varying degrees. The most common exemption is granted on the grounds that a tie-in is necessary to protect quality standards or to protect the goodwill of a trademark. Other exemptions allow tie-ins if the licensee is not charged an excessive price, if the licensee is free to terminate the tie-in arrangements at any time, or if the licensee is allowed to terminate the clause as soon as a dependable local source of supply can be found.

7. Restrictions that Apply after the Expiration of IPRS

Countries generally hold that payment obligations or restrictions based on statutory intellectual property rights must terminate when the statutory right expires. However, restrictions often arise in connection with the expiration of statutory rights involving package licenses. Package licensing is the transfer of multiple statutory rights under a single license. Generally, if the licensing agreement was entered into voluntarily by both sides and the payment obligations do not extend beyond that of the last-to-expire statutory right, these agreements will be enforceable. On the other hand, if the licensee was at an economic disadvantage and given only the option of taking or leaving the arrangement, it will commonly be found to be illegal as a form of statutory misuse.

Concerning restrictions and payment obligations in connection with nonstatutory rights, in particular secret know-how, there are several differing approaches. In Germany, for example, a licensor may not enforce payment obligations or other restrictions once the know-how has lost its secret character or becomes economically worthless or technically outdated. In some developing countries, such as Brazil, national legislation prohibits any restriction on the free use of know-how once a "reasonable" period has lapsed following the transfer of the technology.

8. Restrictions that Apply after the Expiration of the Licensing Agreement

Licensing agreements may impose obligations on the licensee that continue even after the expiration of the license. Common examples include noncompetition agreements, limitations on the right to carry out research and development activities related to the technology transferred by the licensor, and, in particular, the obligation to keep secret and not make use of confidential information after the licensing arrangement expires.

Some countries such as Germany, the United States allow licensors to impose most types of reasonable restrictions. However, some other countries such as Brazil, Mexico, Venezuela hold that a former licensee is free to use or dispose of the statutory property rights or secret know-how once the licensing agreement terminates. [1]

Most of the above-mentioned practices are known as restrictive business practices. In accordance with the Administrative Regulations of the People's Republic of China on Contracts Involving the Import of Technology (promulgated by the State Council on May 24, 1985), without special approval of the examining and approving agency the contract must not include the following restrictive items: (1) a demand that the recipient accept items that have nothing to do with the technology to be imported, such as unnecessary technology, technological service, raw materials, equipment or products; (2) restrictions on the recipient's buying freely from different sources raw materials, spare and component parts or equipment; (3) restrictions on the recipient's developing and improving the imported technology; (4) refusal to allow the recipient to obtain from other sources similar technology or competitive technology of the same type; (5) unequal bases for the parties' exchange of improved technology; (6) a limit on the number, assortment or selling price of the products the recipient will produce with the technology to be imported; (7) unreasonable restrictions on the recipient's sales channels or export market; (8) refusal to allow the recipient to continue using the imported technology after expiration of the contract period; (9) a demand that the recipient pay for a bear responsibility for an unemployed or invalid patent.

■ Notes

knowhow 专有技术,也可译成技术诀窍或技术秘密。目前国际上对专有技术尚无统一的定义,一般认为专有技术是指生产所必需的秘密技术情报,包括知识、经验、数据公式、配

---

[1] Ray August, Don Mayer, and Michael Bixby, International Business Law, Pearson Education Limited, 2002, p.553.

方、图纸、技术记录、操作手册、材料清单、样品样机等。一般地说,专有技术是经过较长时间的积累过程才形成的。它不仅已经在工业上实施,而且也能使实施者取得一定的经济效益。但专有技术不是工业产权,不受工业产权法律的保护。别人可能有同样的或类似的专有技术在使用,只要专有技术是合法取得的,任何人都无权加以分析干涉。此外,专利等的内容是公开的,而专有技术的内容则是保密的。

international licensing trade 国际许可证贸易。国际许可证贸易是国际技术转让中最重要、最常用的方式。它是一国的技术拥有方允许另一国的技术需求方在一定条件下使用其技术,进行产品的生产和销售的一种商业性交易。就其性质而言,许可证贸易是技术使用权的一种转让,也就是说,技术所有权没有转让,被许可方所取得的只是技术的使用权,许可方并不因为许可别人使用而失去对技术的权利。所以它与技术所有权(如专利所有权)的转让是不同的。

■ Important Legal English Usages

specific 明确的,具体的。例如,A proposal for concluding a contract addressed to one or more specific persons constitutes an offer if it is sufficiently definite and indicates the intention of the offeror to be bound in case of acceptance(向一个或一个以上特定的人提出的订立合同的建议,如果十分确定并且表明要约人在得到接受时承受约束的意旨,即构成要约)。

注意该词与下列近义词在用法上的区别:

(1) definite:明确的,确切的。(见上例)

(2) explicit:明晰的,明确的。例如,He gave us explicit instructions(他给我们作了详细明确的指示)。

(3) express:明确的,明白的。例如,an express provision(明文规定)。

(4) unequivocal:明确的,不含糊的,与 definite 一样,指决定性的选择,以及有真实性和任何无误解可能的言词。例如,A definite agreement made in bad faith would not be unequivocal(以欺诈为手段达成的所谓明确协议不会是很明确的)。

(5) unconditional:无条件的,无限的,多作为协议、买卖合同的用语。例如,an unconditional guarantee(一项不符任何条件的保证)。

distinguish 区别,识别,辨别。着重指察觉差异所需要的技能。例如,I can distinguish right from wrong(我能明辨是非)。

注意该词与下列近义词在用法上的区别:

(1) discriminate:区别,辨别。主要指看出和评价几个相似的东西中的差别。例如,He can distinguish the real antique from the imitation(他能辨别古董的真品和赝品)。

(2) differentiate:区分,区别。指能看出不同于其他事物的特性,与 distinguish 形成明显的对比,该词着重区分轻微的差别。例如,Can you differentiate this kind of rose from the others(你能区分这种玫瑰和其他种玫瑰吗)?

(3) discern:辨别,辨明。属于一般用语,强调具有准确的洞察力。例如,They discerned clearly the faint trail of clues that led to the identity of the murderer(他们辨明了这

些线索上的蛛丝马迹去查明凶杀）。

because of　因为，由于。属于一般用语。例如，Because of gravity, water flows on the earth's surface（由于地心引力，水在地球表面上流动）。

注意下列近义词的用法：

（1）due to：因为，由于。主要指不好的原因。例如，About the change of weather, there are many complications due to such factors as land and sea distributions, manmade atmospheric pollution, etc.（关于天气的变化，有许多复杂情况是由于陆地和海洋的分布、人为的大气污染等诸因素造成的）。

（2）owing to：因为，由于。用法上与 due to 相近。例如，These errors are owing to sheer carelessness（这些错误纯系/由于粗心造成的）。

■ Review Questions

1. Explain the rationality and justification of intellectual property law, giving examples where possible.
2. List and explain briefly the contents of copyright.
3. Define 'patent' under Chinese laws and state briefly its historical background.
4. Your client has developed a chemical compound to produce a fat bursting drug. She would like to apply for a patent. Advise her of the procedure and the costs involved according to Chinese laws.
5. What is the best way to achieve international protection for a patent?
6. Outline all the possible functions of a trademark.
7. List the activities that amount to trademark infringement, giving examples where possible.
8. List and explain the international provisions on the protection of intellectual property rights.
9. Define 'international licensing agreement' and list its main features.
10. Outline and discuss the major issues in international licensing agreement.

12 Chapter Twelve GATT and WTO Law

■ 导读

本章讲授的是关贸总协定和世界贸易组织法(WTO),主要包括关贸总协定的建立、基本原则、世界贸易组织产生的背景、法律结构及争端解决机制等内容。我国自进入世界贸易组织以来,经济发展取得了令世人瞩目的成就。同时,我国的相关法律也得到了较大的完善,进一步地融入世界先进的法律制度。因此,设置本章的目的是丰富读者的世界贸易组织法律知识,拥护国家的对外开放政策,支持我国政府在当前WTO改革中的立场和建议,维持世界多边贸易法律体系。

The Great Depression of the 1930s in western countries showed what can happen when nations try to isolate themselves economically and politically from the world solely for their own economic interests. Also, three decades of open-doorexperiences of China illustrate clearly that no countries can benefit more under policies of isolationism and protectionism. The fact that China has been in WTO for more than two years shows that China's strategic policy to participate in the economic globalization is unprecedently correct and far-reaching, and will speed up China's process to a modernized country.

I. The Founding of GATT

A. Trade Barriers

A trade barrier is any impediment to trade in goods or services. An import trade barrier is any impediment, direct or indirect, to the entrance or sale of imported goods or services existing in the country of importation.

All countries have trade barriers to regulate imports. Nations impose import trade barriers for many economic and political reasons, such as collection of revenue, regulation of import competition, retaliation against foreign government trade barriers, implementation of foreign policy, implementation of national economic policies, protection of the national defense, protection of natural resources or of the environment, protection of public health, safety and morals, and plant and animal life, etc. Import trade barriers can take many different forms and are usually classified as either tariff barriers or nontariff barriers.

1. Tariffs

The most common device for regulating imports is the tariff or import duty. A tariff is a tax levied on goods by the country of importation. It is usually computed either as a percentage of value (ad valorem tariffs) or on the basis of physical units (specific tariffs). Tariffs are generally considered to be one of the least restrictive types of trade barriers. Comparatively, nontariff barriers are much more restrictive to free trade.

2. Nontariff Barriers to Trade

Nontariff barriers to trade are any impediment to trade other than tariffs. They include quotas, embargoes, import licensing schemes, etc.

(1) Quotas and quantitative restrictions. A quota is a quantitative restriction on imports. They can be based either on the value of goods or on quantity. The quota can also be expressed as a percentage share of the domestic market for that product. Quotas can be placed on all goods of a particular kind coming from all countries, a group of countries, or one country.

Quotas work more quickly in restricting imports. A country, which experiences a domestic economic crisis caused by excessive imports can use quotas immediately to restore economic equilibrium. Also, government policy makers can more easily assess the potential impact of a quota than of a tariff, because no one can predict with absolute certainty what the economic effect of a tariff will be. Another advantage is that quotas can either be applied across the board to all imports from a particular nation or be applied to the products of several nations.

(2) Embargoes. Even more restrictive than the quota is the embargo. An embargo can be either a complete ban on trade with a certain foreign nation or a ban on the sale or transfer of specific products or technology. For example, in recent years, the United States has imposed embargoes on Cuba, Iran, Iraq, North Korea, Libya, and a few other countries.

(3) Import licensing schemes. Some of the most insidious indirect barriers to trade are import licensing schemes and customs procedures. Some government requires importers to apply for permission to import products, subject to meeting many complex and often discriminatory requirements. The licensing is often expensive and time consuming. For instance, an importer may have to make a deposit of foreign exchange in order to get the license, or the license may be based on a discriminatory quota system.

B. Trade Liberalization through Cooperation

Most nations have come to realize that trade barriers are damages to the international economy and ultimately to their own. Moreover, they have realized that if they restrict the products of their trading partners in order to protect one segment or sector of their economy, then another sector will suffer. Therefore, beginning in 1934, nations embarked on a long road to improve the world trade environment. At first, negotiations based on reciprocity resulted in mutual tariff reductions. After World War II national leaders and policy makers stressed a more international view of the world's economy. At the same time, the United Nations and other new international organizations were born. Led by the United States, other nations embraced free trade and open market policies. Their efforts to establish new "rules of the game" for conducting their trade relations resulted in the creation of an international legal system to handle trade matters, complete with international law, dispute settlement mechanisms, and agreed-upon codes for regulating trade. This system is based on the General Agreement on Tariffs and Trade (GATT).

GATT provides an organized global structure to improve the economic, political, and legal climate for trade, investment, and development. Its primary goal is to achieve distortion-free trade through the removal of artificial barriers and restrictions imposed by self-serving national governments. The GATT system includes an international legal system with rules, a mechanism for interpreting those rules, and a procedure for resolving disputes under them.

GATT rules are created by international agreement and become guiding principles of international trade law, upon which a WTO member nation's own trade regulations are to be based. In theory, the GATT legal system exists side by side with the domestic legal systems of sovereign nations, GATT anticipates that national legislatures and government agencies will comply with GATT's principles in setting tariffs and regulating imports.

C. Scope and Coverage of GATT 1947 and GATT 1994

The rules of GATT 1947 applied only to trade in goods. Because most of the major trading nations of the world have been members, GATT has controlled more than 80 percent of the world's trade in goods. GATT 1947 was successful in reducing tariffs and nontariff barriers to trade worldwide. However, nations encountered many trade issues over which GATT had no responsibility. Trade in services, such as banking or insurance, was specifically excluded from GATT 1947. It also failed to regulate agricultural trade, an area of constant dispute between nations. Trade in textiles and apparel was also not covered because of the politically sensitive nature of these industries. Because GATT 1947 only dealt with trade in goods, it did little or nothing to protect intellectual property rights, such as copyrights and trademarks. Finally, the dispute settlement process set up under GATT 1947, used to resolve trade conflicts between countries, was filled with loopholes and was often ineffective.[1]

---

〔1〕 Richard Schaffer, Beverley Earle, and iliberto Agusti, International Business Law and Its Environment, West Publishing Company, 1996, p. 335.

GATT 1994 is much broader in scope and coverage than the original agreement, and addresses many of the latter's limitations. In addition to the original provisions of GATT 1947, GATT 1994 includes the following multilateral trade agreements on specific issues such as agreement on agriculture, agreement on the application of sanitary and phytosanitary measures, agreement on textiles and clothing, agreement on technical barriers to trade, agreement on trade-related investment measures, agreement on subsidies and countervailing measures, etc.

II. Major Principles of GATT 1994

GATT 1994 continues four basic principles of international trade law carried out by GATT 1947.

A. Multilateral Trade Negotiations

Under the rules of GATT, nations will meet periodically to reduce tariffs and nontariff barriers to trade. Since 1947 the GATT organization has served to bring member nations together to negotiate tariff reductions and the opening of markets. Under the auspices the GATT, the contracting parties have completed eight major rounds, or multilateral negotiating sessions: (1) Geneva, Switzerland, in 1947, (2) Annecy, France, in 1948, (3) Torquay, England, in 1956, (4) Geneva, Switzerland, in 1956, (5) Dillon Round, 1960 - 1961, (6) Kennedy Round, 1964 - 1967, (7) Tokyo Round, 1973 - 1979, (8) Uruguay Round, 1986 - 1994.

Under Article 2 of GATT, all member nations shall cooperate in lowering tariffs through negotiations. In a tariff concession, one country promises not to levy a tariff on a given product at a level higher than agreed upon. In essence, each country makes a concession to the products of the other country and receives reciprocal treatment. This process does not set the same tariff rate on a particular product for every nation, but determines a tariff rate that is said to be bound. The rates are arrived at through compromise, and these concessions are recorded in tariff schedules, which are detailed product-by-product listings of all tariff obligations for a particular nation.

In the early rounds, countries negotiated on a product-by-product basis by simply presenting lists of tariff reductions that they desired from other countries, who submitted requests for concessions that they wanted in return. The Kennedy Round resulted in even larger across-the-board tariff cuts, particularly in manufactured goods, averaging nearly 40 percent reductions and covering $40 billion in trade. More than 60 nations participated in the Kennedy Round.

By the 1970s, GATT's efforts had proven so successful that tariffs ceased to be the world's greatest barrier to trade in goods. Indeed, without GATT, decades of bilateral negotiations may have been necessary to achieve the reductions that multilateral negotiations reached within a few years. In the Tokyo Round more than 100 participating nations agreed to tariff cuts averaging 34 percent and covering $300 billion in trade, which effectively lowered the average level of tariffs to about 5 percent. [1]

During the Uruguay Round, the United States adopted a zero-for-zero tariff reduction policy. Each nation's tariff schedules deposited with the WTO reflect the new rates. Many member nations have agreed to negotiate additional market access agreements in future WTO negotiations on a zero-for-zero basis.

B. Most-favored-nation Treatment

The guiding concept of trade liberalization under GATT is that of nondiscrimination, which is mostly illustrated by Most-favored-nation principle(MFN)(最惠国待遇原则). MFN principles (Article 1 of GATT) require that any trade advantage or privilege granted by one GATT member to the goods of another member should be granted to all. Any tariff, tax, or other restriction on imports should be applied equally to products, without regard to origination. Because the products of all MFN countries are treated equally, products shipped from both economically powerful countries and small countries will be treated the same in the foreign market.

1. Unconditional MFN Treatment

Unconditional MFN trade requires that when a nation extends some privilege or right to one of its trading partners, such as a reduced tariff rate, that privilege automatically becomes applicable to all other trading partners. So, if nation A negotiates a reduced tariff rate on a particular product imported from nation B, that new rate becomes applicable to like products imported from MFN nation C and from all nations that have MFN status with the importing country. Unconditionally treatment is granted merely because nation C's product is "entitled" to be treated equally and without discrimination, and does not require further concessions to be in effect.

2. Conditional MFN Treatment

Conditional treatment requires that a trading partner give something in return for a tariff concession. Conditional MFN trade was used by the United States in its first trade pact made in 1778 with France and through the end of World War I. Then the United States found out that conditional MFN trade allowed other countries to discriminate against U. S exports, and the practice was phased out. MFN trade today is unconditional.

MFN treatment for imported goods greatly influences trade flows between nations. If

---

[1] Richard Schaffer, Beverley Earle, and Filiberto Agusti, International Business Law and Its Environment, West Publishing Company, 1996, p. 344.

a country's products do not qualify for MFN tariff rates in an importing nation, then it may not be economically practical to import those products at all. The importer may actually have to find substitute products in some other country that is an MFN trading partner.

3. MFN Exceptions

The GATT provides for trade relationships that may be even more favorable than MFN treatment. These include free-trade areas (e. g. the North American Free Trade Agreement) and common markets (e. g. the European Union). GATT also provides for special trade "preferences" for developing countries under which their products qualify for better-than-MFN treatment.

C. National Treatment

The national treatment(国民待遇原则) provisions of GATT are intended to ensure that imported products will not be subjected to discriminatory treatment under the laws of the importing nation. Under Articles Ⅲ, imported products must not be regulated, taxed, or otherwise treated differently from domestic goods once they enter a nation's stream of commerce. GATT Article Ⅲ: 2 provides that imports shall not be subject to internal taxes or charges in excess of those applied to like domestic products. The even broader provisions of Article Ⅲ: 4 state that imported products shall be given treatment no less favourable than that accorded to like products of national origin in respect of all laws, regulations, and requirements affecting their internal sale. This provision has been interpreted as prohibiting discrimination against imports resulting from a wide range of nontariff barriers to trade, including discriminatory customs procedures, government procurement policies, and product standards.

D. Tariff-based Import Restriction

GATT's founders sought a multilateral approach to the elimination of restrictive trade barriers. They selected a tariff-based approach that had two fundamental goals. First, GATT members were to engage in regular negotiations designed to systematically reduce import duties. Second, tariffs were to be the only form of import protection permitted by GATT. Specifically, GATT prohibited the use of non-tariff barriers, such as quotas and quantitative restrictions to trade. As will be seen later, however, there are numerous exceptions to this policy.

The result of Uruguay Round are the individual countries commitments on specific categories of goods and services, including commitments to cut down and bind their customs duty rates on imports of goods. On some cases, tariffs are being cut to zero. There is also a significant increase in the number of bound tariffs, i. e. duty rates that are committed in the WTO are difficult to raise. The tariff cuts of developed countries are for the most part being phased in over five years from 1 January 1995. The result is a 40% cut in their tariffs on industrial products, from an average of 6.3% to 3.8%, and the average tariffs rates for developing countries have been reduced to 12.3%. There will be further more bindings in this area. Developed governments increased the number of imports whose tariff rates are bound, from 78% of products lines to 99%. For developing countries the increase of bound tariff rate was considerable: from 21% to 73%.

III. The World Trade Organization (WTO)

On January 1, 1995, the World Trade Organization (WTO) replaced the original GATT organization. It provides an umbrella organization that sets the rules by which nations regulate trade in manufactured goods, services (including banking, insurance, tourism and telecommunications), intellectual property, textiles and clothing, and agricultural products. The role of the WTO is to facilitate international cooperation to open markets, provide a forum for future trade negotiations between members, and provide a forum for the settlement of trade disputes. The WTO will have a stature equal to that of the IMF or World Bank, and will cooperate with those agencies on economic matters. The WTO's membership includes those countries that previously belonged to GATT, and will eventually be open to other countries, if accepted by a two-thirds majority vote of the members. Now, WTO has 164 members.

A. The WTO and the Economic Globalization

In today's world, the term "economic globalization" has acquired considerable emotive force. Economic globalization is a historical process, the result of human innovation and technological progress. It refers to the increasing integration of economies around the world, particularly through trade and financial flows. The term sometimes also refers to the movement of people (labor) and knowledge (technology) across international borders.

In recent decades, driven by thetelecommunications revolution, the global economy is like a speeding train that keeps getting faster, says Thomas Friedman, the New York Times foreign policy columnist. "What's worse," Friedman writes, "no one can slow the train down, because the world economy today is just like the internet: everybody is connected but nobody is in charge." Truly, the economic globalization is beneficial to wealthy nations, on the other hand, it has increased the gap between rich and poor nations. According to the United Nations Development Program, "the income gap between the richest fifth of the world's people and the poorest fifth, measured by average national income per head, increased from 30 to one in 1960 to 74 to on in 1997." Nearly 90% of all economic activity takes place in the rich nations where only 20% of the world's population lives.

Inequality is also growing within nations, and globalization is a key factor. *Forbes* reports that the richest 400 Americans now control more than $1 trillion in personal wealth. The Economic Policy Institute concludes that globalization and related shifts from industrial to service employment account for about one-third of the growth in U. S. wage inequality over the past generation.

Also, without rules in place that created enforceable procedures to protect workers interests, the environment, and human interests that do not appear on corporate balance sheets, the globaleconomy runs like a race to the bottom for the vast majority of people in the United States and throughout the world.

Clearly, the global economy is out of control. One organization is needed to be in charge of the global economy. The World Trade Organization where the rules of the global economy are set, is just such a crucial institution.

It is at the WTO where the people in charge of the global economy set the rules for what can be protected, what can be regulated, and what punishments can be imposed on whoever breaks the rules.

B. Legal Structure of the WTO

The WTO now has 145 members, accounting for over 90% of world trade. The WTO's top level decision-making body is the Ministerial Conference, made up of high-ranking representatives from all WTO member countries, which meets at least once every two years to direct the polices, activities, and future direction of the WTO. The Ministerial Conference appoints the WTO Director-General and specifies his or her duties. The work of the Director-General is supported by the WTO Secretariat staff. Beneath the Ministerial Conference is the General Council, made up of representatives of each nation and responsible for overall supervision of the WTO's activities. The General Council also oversees the work of the lower councils, which carry out the work of the WTO in specialized areas. At the next level, the Goods Council, Services Council and Intellectual Property Council report to the General Council. There are also in WTO numerous specialized committees, working groups and working parties to deal with the individual agreements and other areas such as the environment, development, membership applications and regional trade agreements.

The Secretariat's main duties are to supply technical support for the various councils and committees and the ministerial conferences, to provide technical assistance for developing countries, to analyze world trade, and to explain WTO affairs to the public and media. The Secretariat also provides some forms of legal assistance in the dispute settlement process and advises governments wishing to become members of the WTO.

C. WTO Antidumping Agreement

1. The Economics of Dumping

In importing, dumping is the unfair trade practice of selling products in a foreign country for less than the price charged for the same or comparable goods in the producer's home market. It is a form of price discrimination causing injury to domestic competitors through artificially low prices against which domestic producers cannot compete at a profitable level. GATT has prohibited dumping since 1947, and virtually all developed nations have statutes, patterned after GATT, that permit the importing country to impose antidumping duties on dumped products to offset the unfair law price and to prevent injury to a domestic producer. The United States, the European Union, Canada, and Australia, Japan and China all have antidumping laws. Partly due to the rising of trade protectionism in developed countries, antidumping laws are used more frequently than any other trade law in developed countries. Since China's entrance to WTO, China has been the area that suffers the most from antidumping suits by other countries.

Dumping is a hot controversial issue among economists. Supporters hold that dumping is often intended to drive competitors out of business so that the dumping firms will ultimately be free to raise their prices to monopoly levels. Some economists point out that dumping is not always predatory, but may be related to market conditions. An exporting firm may not be able to command the same prices from foreign buyers as in its domestic market, where it has brand-name recognition and greater market.

Critics of antidumping laws claim that they injure consumers by "fixing prices" at high levels. Once the prices rise for imported products, domestic manufacturers follow suit by raising their prices as well. They cite the fact that antidumping laws are designed to correct an unfair trade practice and not to protect domestic companies.

2. Determination of Dumping under GATT 1994 Antidumping Agreement

The GATT provisions on dumping are found in GATT 1994 Article VI and in Agreement on Implementation of Article VI of the General Agreement on the Tariff and Trade 1994 (hereafter called "the 1994 *Antidumping Agreement*"). Earlier GATT codes on dumping merely condemned dumping as injurious to competition; however, the 1994 rules are more explicit. The 1994 agreement provides complex rules for determining when dumping has occurred and for resolving dumping disputes.

GATT requires that an importing country resort to antidumping duties only after conducting a formal investigation to determine both the amount of the dumping and the extent of material injury. In these generally administrative agency proceedings, the United States International Trade Administration (ITA) of the U.S Department of Commerce determines the amount of the dumping and the International Trade Commission (ITC) determines the extent of the injury.

Under Articles 2 – 12 of the Regulations of the People's Republic of China on Antidumping (hereafter called "the Antidumping Regulation of China"), China may adopt anti-dumping measures if imported products are dumped onto the domestic market and cause or threaten to cause material injury to corresponding established domestic industries or create material obstacles to the establishment of corresponding domestic industries. Though the former MOFTEC and the State Economic and Trade Commission were consolidated into one single ministry, i. e. Ministry of Commerce (MOC) in March 2003, the Antidumping Regulation of China accorded them different responsibility in anti-dumping investigation, i. e. (1) the MOFTEC is empowered to investigate and ascertain the issue of dumping, (2) the State Economic and Trade Commission is empowered to investigate and ascertain the issue of injury on domestic industry. [1]

(1) Calculating the dumping margin. GATT 1994 states that dumping is the sale of a product in a foreign country at "less than normal value." The U. S. statute refers to a sale below normal value as a sale "for less than fair value." A sale at less than normal value occurs where the export price is less than the normal value of the product in the exporting or producing country. This price differential is known as the *dumping margin*. When dumping causes or threatens material injury to domestic producers of like products, the importing nation may equalize the price differential by imposing an additional tariff, above the normal tariff charged for that product. These antidumping duties are assessed in an amount equal to the dumping margin. Thus, if a Chinese company sells a widget in China at $100, and sells the same widget in the United States at $80, then the dumping margin is $20 and an antidumping duty of $20 can be imposed on the imported widget.

(2) Calculating the export price. The export price is the price at which a product is sold to an unaffiliated or unrelated buyer in the importing country. A constructed export price is used when the exporter and importer are related companies or the product price is "hidden" in some other type of compensatory arrangement.

(3) Calculating the normal value of like products in the exporting or producing country. Normal value is the price at which like products are sold in the exporting or producing country for consumption, in the ordinary course of business, and at the same level of trade—in other words, comparing wholesale sale to wholesale sale, or retail to retail—as the dumped product. If insufficient quantities of like products are sold in the

[1] Regulations of the People's Republic of China on Anti-dumping was adopted at the 46th Executive Meeting of the State Council on October 31, 2001, promulgated by Decree No. 328 of the State Council of the People's Republic of China on November 26, 2001, and effective as of January 1, 2002. This is chiefly patterned on the 1994 Antidumping Agreement of the WTO.

exporting country with which to make a fair comparison, then normal value is calculated on the basis of sales to third countries, or on the basis of a constructed value. Constructed value is calculated on the basis of what it might actually cost to produce the product in the exporting country, plus a reasonable profit.

The dumping margin can be calculated either by comparing average prices (average normal value) for comparable goods sold in the exporting or producing country with average export prices, or by comparing prices in individual transactions. For purposes of calculating the dumping margin, price and cost information can be used from records kept by the producers or exporters under investigation, provided their records follow generally accepted accounting principles.

The Antidumping Regulation of China has the similar provisions on the determination of normal value: (a) if products identical with or similar to the imported product have comparable prices in the exporting countries' marketplace, such comparable prices are the normal value; (b) if products identical with or similar to the imported product do not have comparable prices in the exporting country's marketplace, or their price and sales volume do not permit a proper comparison, the normal value is either the comparable price of identical or similar products exported to the third country, or the production cost of identical or similar products plus reasonable expenses and profit; (c) if they are not imported directly from the country of origin the comparable prices at which the products are sold from the country of export are the normal value. However if they are merely transshipped through the country of export, or are not produced in the country of export, or there is no comparable price for them in the country export, the comparable prices in the country of origin may be applied.

(4) Determination of injury. A determination of injury for purposes of Article VI of GATT 1994 shall be based on positive evidence and involve an objective examination of both (a) the volume of the dumped imports and the effect of the dumped imports on prices in the domestic market for like products, and (b) the consequent impact of these imports on domestic producers of such products.

With regard to the volume of the dumped imports, the investigating authorities shall consider whether there has been significant increase in dumped imports, either in absolute terms of relative to production or consumptionin the importing Member.

The examination of the impact of the dumped imports on the domestic industry concerned shall include an evaluation of all relevant economic factors and indices having a bearing on the state of the industry, including actual and potential decline in sales, profits, output, market share, productivity, return on investments, or utilization of capacity; factors affecting domestic prices; the magnitude of the margin of dumping; actual and potential negative effects on cash flow, inventories, employment, wages, growth, ability to raise capital or investments.

A determination of a threat or material injury shall be based on facts and not merely on allegation, conjecture or remote possibility. The change in circumstances which would create a situation in which the dumping would cause injury must be clearly foreseen and imminent. [1]

With respect to cases where injury is threatened by dumped imports, the application of anti-dumping measures shall be considered and decided with special care.

3. Application of Antidumping Measures

If the dumping margin is below two percent of the value of the products, the dumping is considered de minimis and no duties are imposed. Any antidumping duties that are imposed may not exceed the calculated dumping margin, and they must be imposed on all imports of the dumped products that cause injury, from all sources without discrimination. According to the 1994 Antidumping Agreement, antidumping duties are divided into provisional duty and antidumping duty.

There are three types of antidumping measures: provisional measures, price undertakings and antidumping duties.

Provisional measures may be applied only if: (a) an investigation has been initiated in accordance with the provisions of Article 5, a public notice has been given to that effect and interested parties have been given adequate opportunities to submit information and make comments; (b) a preliminary affirmative determination has been made of dumping and consequent injury to a domestic industry; and (c) the authorities concerned judge such measures necessary to prevent injury being caused during the investigation.

Provisional measures may take the form of a provisional duty or, preferably, a security-by cash deposit or bond-equal to the amount of the anti-dumping duty provisionally estimated, being not greater than the provisionally estimated margin of dumping. Provisional measures shall not be applied sooner than 60 days from the date of initiation of the investigation. Also, the application of provisional measures shall be limited to as short a period as possible, not exceeding four months or, on decision of the authorities concerned, upon request by exporters representing a significant percentage of the trade involved, to a period not exceeding six months. When authorities, in the course of an investigation, examine whether a duty lower than the margin of dumping would be sufficient to remove injury, these periods may be six and nine months, respectively.

---

[1] One example, though not an exclusive one, is that there is convincing reason to believe that there will be, in the near future, substantially increased importation of the product at dumped prices.

A price undertaking is a voluntary action of the foreign exporter or producer to raise prices so as to eliminate the dumping margin. If the price undertaking is satisfactory, the dumping proceeding may be terminated, and no antidumping duties need be imposed.

The antidumping duties apply if the final ruling establishes the existence of dumping and of the resultant injury to domestic industry. The importer of the dumped product is the antidumping taxpayer. The duration of such antidumping duties is subject to the five years time limit which may be extended depending on the review decision. However, if the final ruling is negative, any cash deposit made during the period of the application of provisional measures must be refunded and any bonds released.

The provisions of the Antidumping Regulation of China are much similar to that of the 1994 Antidumping Agreement of the WTO.

IV. WTO Dispute Settlement Procedures

Like GATT 1947, GATT 1994 envisions that one nation will not take unilateral retaliatory action against another nation in a trade dispute, but that the parties will rely on GATT dispute settlement procedures to avert a trade war. GATT's dispute settlement procedures are a quasi-judicial process for resolving trade disputes when attempts by the countries involved to reach a settlement become deadlocked. This process is intended to resolve conflicts before "trade wars" erupt.

A. Deficiencies in the GATT 1947 Dispute Process

Under GATT 1947, the countries involved in a trade dispute could request that their case be referred to a GATT Dispute Resolution Panel, GATT panels were composed of representatives from member nations, chosen for their expertise in particular fields or industries and supported by specializedinvestigating committees. These panels worked to reach a negotiated settlement through "consultation." If that failed, the panel (专家小组) could hear arguments on the legality of the actions of the offending nations. Ultimately the panel decision, or ruling, would be issued in the form of a written report. If the complaining nation was successful in proving that some trade barrier or other action of the offending nations violated the GATT agreement, the panel would issue a ruling of nullification and impairment.

Several problems grew out of GATT 1947. Because of nations' inability to strictly enforce GATT rulings against each other, a GATT panel proved to be more of a political forum than a legal one. This aspect of GATT is not likely to change since many of the issues addressed have tremendous political ramifications. Other problems characterized the GATT 1947 dispute settlement process. First, the GATT process was slow. A legal process that takes months or years to resolve a case is totally ineffective in disputes over seasonal imports that might be awaiting delivery. Also, the parties often used the negotiation process only as a delaying tactic. No appeals process provided review of the panel's written report as is allowed with a court of law. Moreover, without sheriffs and marshals to carry out its decisions as with courts of law, GATT's enforcement process was weak. Once, a remedy was suggested by the Council, GATT could do little to assure compliance. Basically, the process worked only when the parties wanted it to. Under GATT 1947, panel decisions did not have the force of international or domestic law. Decisions did not acquire legal effect until they were adopted by the GATT Council of Ministers. Either party could "block" or veto a panel's decision before it was sent to the Council

B. WTO Dispute Settlement Procedures

Under GATT 1994 the dispute settlement process has been strengthened and the deficiencies remedied. The WTO is given far more authority in handling trade disputes than the former GATT organization had. And individual countries can no longer block panel decisions from going into force. Among the most important changes are new procedures and timetables to assure prompt handling of disputes. The following provisions are expressed in the WTO *Understanding on Rules and Procedures Governing the Settlement of Disputes* (DSU).

1. Compulsory Consultation

Under Article 4 of DSU, each Member undertakes to accord sympathetic consideration to and afford adequate opportunity for consultation regarding any representations made by another Member concerning measures affecting the operation of any covered agreement taken within the territory of the former. In other words, each member is obligated to undertake consultation to settle their dispute rather than direct panel.

This Article further states that if a request for consultations is made pursuant to a covered agreement, the Member to which the request is made shall, unless otherwise mutually agreed, reply to the request within 10 days after the date of its receipt and shall enter into consultations in good faith within a period of no more than 30 days after the date of receipt of the request, with a view to reaching a mutually satisfactory solution. If the Member does not respond within 10 days after the date of receipt of the request, or does not enter into consultations within a period of no more than 30 days, or a period otherwise mutually agreed, after the date of receipt of the request, then the Member that requested the holding of consultations may proceed directly to request the establishment of a panel.

2. Panels

If the consultations fail to settle a dispute within 60 days after the date of receipt of the request for consultations, the complaining party may request the establishment of a panel. The complaining party may request a panel during the 60-day period if the consulting parties jointly consider that consultations have failed to settle the dispute. In cases of urgency, including those which concern perishable goods, the parties to the dispute, panels and the Appellate Body shall make every effort to accelerate the proceedings to the greatest extent possible.

The function of panels is to assist the dispute settlement body (DSB)(争端解决机构) in discharging its responsibilities under this DSU and the covered agreements. Accordingly, a panel should make an objective assessment of the matter before it, including an objective assessment of the facts of the case and the applicability of and conformity with the relevant covered agreements, and make such other findings as will assist the DSB in making the recommendations or in giving the rulings provided for in the covered agreements. Panels should consult regularly with the parties to the dispute and give them adequate opportunity to develop a mutually satisfactory solution.

3. Appellate Review

Under Article 17 of DSU, DSB shall establish a standing appellate body composed of seven persons three of whom shall serve on any one case. They may uphold, modify, or reverse a panel decision. People serving on the Appellate Body will be chosen by the DSB on the basis of their expertise in law and international trade to serve for four-year terms. Appeals are limited to issues of law covered in the panel report and legal interpretations considered by the panel. The appellate report is final unless the DSB rejects it by consensus vote within 30 days.

4. Compensation and the Suspension of Concessions

If the panel report finds that the offending party has violated a GATT agreement, the DSB can recommend ways for the offending party to come into compliance. The offending party has 30 days in which to state how it plans to comply with the panels ' ruling. Compliance must be within a reasonable time. If no immediate solution is available, the offending party can voluntarily make compensatory adjustments to the complaining party as a temporary measure.

If no settlement is reached, or if the trade violation is not removed, the panel may authorize the complaining party to impose a retaliatory trade sanction against the offending party by withdrawing or suspending a concession. The retaliation can be divided into two:

(a) Parallel retaliation. This means that the sanction should be imposed on the same type of goods from the same type of industry or economic sector.

(b) Cross-sector retaliation or cross-agreement retaliation. Article 22 of DSU provides that if the complaining party considers that it is not practicable of effective to suspend concessions or other obligations with respect to the same sectors, it may seek to suspend concessions or other obligations in other sectors under the same agreement. Also, if the complaining party considers that it is not practicable or effective to suspend concessions or other obligations with respect to other sectors under the same agreement, and that the circumstances are serious enough, it may seek to suspend concessions or other obligations under another covered agreement.

Sanctions should be in an amount equal to the impact that the nullification and impairment had on the complaining party. Sanctions are to be temporary and in force only until the offending party's violation is removed.

5. The WTO and the Developing Countries

The World Trade Organization has been progressing with more and more substantial difficulties currently, mainly because most of the developing countries complain that WTO is not fair and they do not benefit from it as much as expected. It is true that WTO was initiated by the industrial countries, as a result, its theoretical framework is based on the western legal ideas partial to the powerful countries and the WTO rules are not beneficial to the disadvantaged developing countries. For example, no priority has ever been given to ensuring that rules are consistent with the development needs of poorer countries and to helping developing countries implement WTO obligations and no binding commitment by industrial countries to abolish export subsidies and nontariff barriers and to reduce most-favored-nation tariffs on labor-intensive products from the developing countries.

It is true that there are more than 140 rules in WTO agreements that granted special and differential treatment (SDT) to the developing countries as a result of the persistent efforts by the developing countries, however, the developed countries in recent years headed by the United States have been trying to invalidate the SDT, with the excuse that more and more developing countries should graduate from the SDT because their economies have developed so rapidly in recent years. Consequently, the SDT system as a symbol of global substantive justice is at risk now.

Therefore, all developing countries must work together to make greater efforts to improve the current theoretical framework and rules of the WTO.

Case 12-1 European Communities (Respondent) —Definitive Anti Dumping Measure on Certain Iron or Steel Fasteners from China (Complainant)

DS397, 31 July 2009. Adopted on 12 February 2016

Facts: On 31 July 2009, China requested consultations with the European

Communities concerning Article 9(5) of Council Regulation (EC) No. 384/96 (the EC's Basic AntiDumping Regulation) which provides that in case of imports from non-market economy countries, the duty shall be specified for the supplying country concerned and not for each supplier and that an individual duty will only be specified for exporters that demonstrate that they fulfil the criteria listed in that provision.

According to China, Article 9(5) of the Basic Anti-Dumping Regulation is inconsistent, as such, with the European Communities' obligations under: (1) Article XVI:4 of the WTO Agreement; (2) Articles I:1, VI:1, and X:3(a) of the GATT 1994; and (3) Articles 6.10, 9.2, 9.3, 9.4, 12.2.2 and 18.4 of the Anti-Dumping Agreement.

China also requests consultations regarding Council Regulation (EC) No 91/2009 imposing definitive anti-dumping duties on imports of certain iron or steel fasteners originating in the People's Republic of China. China considers that the imposition of definitive anti-dumping duties on imports of certain iron or steel fasteners originating in the People's Republic of China is inconsistent with the European Communities' obligations under: (1) Articles VI and X:3(a) of the GATT 1994; (2) Articles 1, 2.1, 2.2.2.4, 2.6, 3.1, 3.2, 3.4, 3.5, 4.1, 5.4, 6.1, 6.2, 6.4, 6.5, 6.10, 9.2, 9.4 and 17.6(i) of the Anti-Dumping Agreement; as well as (3) Part I, paragraph 15 of China's Protocol of Accession. In addition, China also refers to Articles 9.3 and 12.2.2 of the Anti-Dumping Agreement.

China claims that the European Communities acted inconsistently with various procedural obligations in the AntiDumping Agreement. China also claims that the European Communities has acted inconsistently with its obligations under the Anti-Dumping Agreement, the GATT 1994, and the Protocol of Accession through the application of Article 9(5) of the Basic Anti-Dumping Regulation in this investigation as well as decisions and determinations made in the investigation relating to, inter alia, the scope of the like product, the extent of the domestic industry, the conduct of the injury analysis and the lack of price comparability adjustments made in the calculation of the anti-dumping margin.

On 3 December 2010, the panel report was circulated to Members.

The Key Contents of the Panel Report: The Panel found that Article 9(5) of the Basic Regulation was inconsistent with Articles 6.10, 9.2 and 18.4 of the AD Agreement, Article I:1 of the GATT 1994 and Article XVI:4 of the WTO Agreement because, with respect to producers from non-market economy countries, the individual treatment test embodied in this provision conditioned the calculation of individual dumping margins and the imposition of individual duties on the fulfilment of certain criteria.

The Panel also found that the application of Article 9 (5) of the Basic Regulation in the fasteners investigation was inconsistent with AD Agreement Articles 6. 10 and 9. 2. The Panel also found that the EU investigating authorities acted inconsistently with AD Agreement Articles 3. 1 and 3. 2 with respect to the consideration of the volume of dumped imports; AD Agreement Articles 3. 1 and 3. 5 with respect to the causation analysis; AD Agreement Articles 6. 4 and 6. 2 with respect to aspects of the normal value determination; AD Agreement Article 6. 5. 1 with respect to non-confidential versions of questionnaire responses of two European producers and AD Agreement Article 6. 5 with respect to confidential treatment of information in the questionnaire response of an Indian producer; and AD Agreement Article 6. 5 with respect to the confidential treatment of the Eurostat data on total EU production of fasteners.

The Panel rejected China's claims with respect to the standing determination; definition of domestic industry; product under consideration; dumping determination; price undercutting determination; treatment of imports from non-sampled producers; consideration of the consequent impact of dumped imports on the domestic industry; non-disclosure of the identity of the complainants and the supporters of the complaint; confidential treatment of the Eurostat data on total EU production of fasteners; procedural aspects of the domestic industry definition; and the amount of time provided for responses to requests for information.

The Panel found that China's claims concerning the definition of like product; alleged non-disclosure of aspects of the normal value determination; and the procedural aspects of the domestic industry definition were not within its terms of reference and declined to make findings on these claims. Further, it applied judicial economy with respect to some of China's claims regarding the Basic Regulation and the Definitive Regulation.

The Panel recommended that the DSB request the European Union to bring its measures into conformity with its obligations under the WTO Agreement. The Panel declined to make a suggestion on how the DSB recommendations and rulings may be implemented by the European Union.

On 25 March 2011, the European Union notified the DSB of its decision to appeal to the Appellate Body certain issues of law covered in the panel report and certain legal interpretations developed by the Panel. On 30 March 2011, China notified the DSB of its decision to appeal to the Appellate Body certain issues of law covered in the panel report and certain legal interpretations developed by the Panel.

On 15 July 2011, the Appellate Body report was circulated to Members.

China's Main Claims: China's claim with respect to the treatment of certain information as confidential. China claimed that the Commission acted inconsistently with Article 6.5 of the AD Agreement by treating as confidential the information submitted by an analogue country producer regarding the list and characteristics of its products. China asserted that this information was neither by nature confidential nor was it submitted on a confidential basis and that no good cause was shown for its confidential treatment. It also claimed that, should the Panel disagree with that assertion, the EU violated Article 6.5.1 of the AD Agreement by failing to require that producer to provide a non-confidential summary of that information. The Panel found that the Commission failed to act consistently with Article 6.5 of the AD Agreement by treating as confidential the information submitted by that producer and that accordingly, it need not make a finding with respect to China's claim under Article 6.5.1 of the AD Agreement.

China's claim regarding interested parties' rights to have access to information and defend their interests. China claimed that by failing to provide the Chinese producers with the information regarding the list and characteristics of the products sold by the analogue country producer and which were used in the determination of the normal value, the EU violated its obligations under Article 6.4 of the AD Agreement. It argued that by failing to provide such an opportunity, the EU also violated Article 6.2 of the AD Agreement. First, China contended that the violation of Article 6.4 also led to a violation of Article 6.2. Second, China maintained that, even if there was no violation of Article 6.4, the EU has in any case violated Article 6.2 by not allowing the Chinese producers to access information needed for the defence of their interests. China also claimed that the EU violated Article 6.1.2 of the AD Agreement as it did not provide the Chinese producers with prompt access to such information. The Panel concluded that the Commission violated Article 6.4 of the AD Agreement by failing to provide the Chinese producers with timely opportunities to see the information on the list and characteristics of the products, which was not confidential and was relevant to the presentation of the Chinese producers' cases and used by the Commission. The Panel also found that by not allowing the Chinese producers to have access to the information on the file regarding the list and characteristics of the products, the Commission also violated Article 6.2. In addition, the Panel found that China has not shown that the EU violated Article 6.1.2 of the AD Agreement by not making the analogue country's producer's information promptly available to the Chinese producers.

China's claim with respect to the Commission's failure to provide information to enable Chinese exporters to request adjustments. China argued that by failing to provide the Chinese producers/exporters with the information concerning the characteristics of the products sold by the analogue country producer, the Commission violated Article 2.4 of the AD Agreement. It also submitted that the Commission imposed an undue burden on the Chinese producers by rejecting their requests for adjustments on the grounds that they were not based on evidence. The Panel concluded that the Commission violated Article 2.4 of the AD Agreement by failing to provide the Chinese producers with information regarding the characteristics of the analogue country producer's products that were used in determining normal values in the review investigation.

China's claim with respect to failure to ensure that price comparisons were made on the basis of same types of fasteners. China submitted that the EU acted inconsistently with Article 2.4 of the AD Agreement by failing to ensure that the export price of standard fasteners sold by Chinese producers to the EU was compared to the normal value of standard fasteners sold by the analogue country producer, in the calculation of the dumping margins for the Chinese producers. China also requested the Panel to exercise its fact-seeking power under Article 13 of the DSU to request the EU to provide a copy of the analogue country producer's information used to distinguish between standard and special fasteners and to verify the accuracy of the split made by that producer. The Panel rejected China's claim under Article 2.4 of the AD Agreement and considered making a request under Article 13 of the DSU unnecessary in its evaluation of China's claim.

China's claim with respect to the Commission's failure to make adjustments for differences that affect price comparability. China asserted that the EU acted inconsistently with Article 2.4 of the AD Agreement by failing to make adjustments for certain factors that affected price comparability. Specifically, China took issue with three differences that allegedly affected price comparability and that were not taken into account by the Commission: (i) differences in taxation, (ii) differences in physical characteristics, and (iii) certain other differences. The Panel rejected China's argument that the Commission violated Article 2.4 of the AD Agreement.

China's claim with respect to the Commission's failure to take into account all comparable export transactions. China argued that, in calculating the dumping margins in the review investigation, the Commission left out the export transactions for which there was no match in the analogue country producer's sales. China contended that by failing to take into account all comparable export transactions, the Commission acted inconsistently with the obligation to conduct a fair comparison between the normal value and the export price as required by Article 2.4 of the AD Agreement. It further submitted that the comparison made by the Commission resulted in a presumption of dumping for those export transactions that were not used in the dumping determination and thus, such comparison must be considered as failing to meet the requirement of a fair comparison. The Panel concluded that the Commission violated Article 2.4.2 of the AD Agreement by not taking into consideration, in its dumping determinations, Chinese producers' export models that did not match any of the models sold by the analogue country producer. The Panel exercised judicial economy with respect to the consequential claim under Article 2.4 of the AD Agreement.

China's claim with respect to the definition of domestic industry. China recalled that, in the original investigation, the Commission excluded from the domestic industry European producers that did not express willingness to be part of the injury sample. In the original dispute, the Appellate Body found that excluding domestic producers from the definition of domestic industry on the basis of this self-selection gave rise to a material risk of distortion in defining that industry, and that the original panel had erred in finding that the Commission's domestic industry definition was not inconsistent with Article 4.1 of the AD Agreement. Finally, China contended that the EU acted inconsistently with Article 3.1 of the AD Agreement because the Commission's injury determination in the review investigation was based on a wrongly-defined domestic industry.

The Panel found that by defining the domestic industry on the basis of domestic producers that came forward in response to a notice of initiation which stated that only those producers willing to be included in the injury sample would be considered introduced a material risk of distortion to the IA's injury analysis that would necessarily render the resulting injury determination inconsistent with the obligation to make an objective injury analysis based on positive evidence laid down in Article 3.1 of the AD Agreement. It also concluded that the Commission's injury determination, based on the data obtained from a wrongly-defined domestic industry, was inconsistent with Article 3.1 of the AD Agreement.

On 9 September 2015, the European Union notified the DSB of its decision to appeal to the Appellate Body certain issues of law covered in the panel report and certain legal interpretations developed by the Panel. On 14 September 2015, China notified the DSB of its decision to cross-appeal.

On 18 January 2016, the compliance Appellate Body report was circulated to Members.

The Key Contents of the Appellate Body Report: The Appellate Body dismissed the European Union's claims on appeal that the Panel erred in finding that China's claims under Articles 6.5, 6.5.1, 6.4, 6.2,6.1.2, 2.4, 4.1, and 3.1 of the Anti-Dumping Agreement fell within its terms of reference under Article 21.5 of the DSU.

The Appellate Body found that the claims under Articles 6.5 and 6.5.1 raised by China in the compliance proceedings were not the same claims China had raised under these provisions and that were dismissed in the original proceedings. Moreover, the Appellate Body found that the claims raised by China in these compliance proceedings under Articles 6.4,6.2,6.1.2, 2.4, 4.1, and 3.1 were not claims that China could have raised, but did not raise, in the original proceedings. Accordingly, the Appellate Body upheld the Panel's finding that China's claims under Articles 6.5,6.5.1,6.4,6.2,6.1.2,2.4,4.1, and 3.1 were within the Panel's terms of reference.

The Appellate Body found that the Panel did not err in finding that, as a consequence of acting inconsistently with Article 6.4, the European Union also acted inconsistently with Article 6.2 of the Anti-Dumping Agreement in the review investigation. The Appellate Body, thus, upheld the Panel's overall finding that the European Union acted inconsistently with Articles 6.4 and 6.2 in the review investigation.

Article 2.4 of the Anti-Dumping Agreement requires investigating authorities to make a fair comparison between export price and normal value, and to make due allowance for differences which affect price comparability. The Appellate Body found that the Panel erred in concluding that the Commission, solely because the analogue country methodology was used in the review investigation, was not required to consider making adjustments for differences in: (i) taxation; and (ii) costs relating to access to raw materials, use of self-generated electricity, efficiency in raw-material consumption, efficiency in electricity consumption, and productivity per employee. The Appellate Body considered that an investigating authority has to take steps to achieve clarity as to the adjustment claimed, and determine whether, on its merits, the adjustment is warranted because it reflects a difference affecting price comparability or whether it would lead to adjusting back to costs or prices that were found to be distorted in the exporting country.

On the basis of the foregoing, the Appellate Body reversed the Panel's finding that the European Union did not act inconsistently with Article 2. 4 because the Commission's determination did not reflect an adequate examination of whether the Chinese producers' requests for adjustments for differences in taxation and the other costs at issue were warranted or whether they would have the effect of reintroducing distorted costs or prices in the normal value component of the comparison. Instead, the Appellate Body found that the European Union acted inconsistently with Article 2.4 with respect to these two types of differences.

Article 2. 4. 2 of the Anti-Dumping Agreement requires investigating authorities using the weighted average-to-weighted average methodology to establish margins of dumping on the basis of the comparison of "all comparable export transactions". The Appellate Body recalled that when making the dumping calculations based on the weighted average-to-weighted average methodology, the Commission excluded the transactions of certain models of fasteners exported by the Chinese producers that did not match with models of fasteners produced by the analogue country producer, Pooja Forge. The Appellate Body agreed with the Panel that this approach was inconsistent with the requirements of Article 2. 4. 2 of the Anti-Dumping Agreement to establish dumping margins on the basis of a comparison of "all comparable export transactions". The Appellate Body considered that Article 2. 4. 2 requires a comparison of all models of the investigated producers that fall within the definition of like product. The Appellate Body, therefore, upheld the Panel's finding that the European Union acted inconsistently with this provision.

Articles 4. 1 and 3. 1 of the Anti-Dumping Agreement requires investigating authorities to define the "domestic industry" on the basis of the domestic producers as a whole of the like products under investigation, or those whose collective output constitutes a "major proportion" of the total domestic production. The Appellate Body found that by relying on the original Notice of Initiation, which stated that only those producers willing to be included in the injury sample would be considered as cooperating and thus part of the domestic industry, the Commission introduced a material risk of distortion in the industry definition and in the injury determination. The Appellate Body, therefore, upheld the Panel's finding that the European Union acted inconsistently with Article 4. 1 of the AntiDumping Agreement.

The Appellate Body further found that a domestic industry definition based on a self-selection that introduces a material risk of distortion to the investigating authority's injury analysis would necessarily render the resulting injury determination inconsistent with the obligation to make an objective injury analysis based on positive evidence as laid down in Article 3. 1 of the Anti-Dumping Agreement. The Appellate Body, therefore, upheld the Panel's finding that the Commission's injury determination was inconsistent with this provision.

At its meeting on 12 February 2016, the DSB adopted the Article 21.5 Appellate Body report and panel report, as modified by the Appellate Body report. [1]

■ Notes

import quota 进口配额。限制外国商品输入的一种办法。对于某种商品在一定期间的进口数量或金额加以规定,超过部分不准进口。有的国家为了实行差别待遇,除规定总的进口配额外,还对各出口国分别规定不同的国别配额。有的国家还将征收关税与进口配额结合起来,在配额以内征收较低的关税,超过配额征收较高的关税,称为"关税配额"。以上均属于非关税壁垒。

most-favored-nation principle 最惠国待遇原则。1994 年的《关税与贸易总协定》(GATT 1994)第 1 条"普遍最惠国待遇"第 1 款规定:"在对进口或出口、有关进口或出口产品的国际支付转移所征收的关税和费用方面,在征收此类关税和费用的方法方面,在有关进口和出口的全部规章手续方面,以及在第 3 条第 2 款和第 4 款所指的所有事项方面,任何缔约方给予来自或运往任何其他国家任何产品的利益、优惠、特权或豁免应立即无条件地给予来自或运往所有其他缔约方领土的同类产品。"该款对最惠国待遇作了一个完整表述,也是最具权威性的规定。该款的真实含义和目的是阻止"特惠协定"的蔓延,禁止优待某些国家、歧视其他国家的差别措施,将所有成员方置于"平等"地位,保证贸易机会均等,在同等条件下自由竞争,以推动世界生产的扩大和贸易增长。然而,由于经济地位和实力差别,它对于落后的发展中国家来说,实际上是很不公平的,在某种意义上可以说世贸组织在消除贸易歧视方面还远未成功。

clearly foreseen and imminent "可预见"和"迫在眉睫"。一般认为,这是指进口国工业尚未受到实际损害,只是若不采取措施阻止进口产品继续倾销,进口国工业的损害将"可预见"和"迫在眉睫"产生的情形。1994 年的《关税与交易总协定》规定了以下基本原则:第一,要以事实为依据。第二,必须是"清楚地可预见"(clearly foreseen),并且是"迫在眉睫"(clearly imminent)。还必须特别"小心谨慎"(with special care)。同时还要考虑下面四个因素:(1)倾销产品是否正以极大的增长比例进入进口国国内市场,并有持续增长的趋势。(2)进口国国内市场同类产品的价格是否有被抑制的明显迹象,从而导致进口需求的增长。(3)出口商能完全自由处理即将发生大量增长的情况,说明倾销产品向该国国内市场大量出口增长的可能存在,但要考虑其他市场的吸收能力。(4)涉讼出口产品的库存情况。

---

[1] https://www/wto. org/english/tratop_e/dispu-e/cases_ds397_e. htm. visit on 2 January, 2020.

Important Legal English Usages

harm 伤害,损坏,害处。主要指伤及一个人或其心志、健康、权利、事业等,使其产生痛苦,造成损失或其他不幸。例如,An unkind and untrue story harmed his reputation(恶意捏造的故事损害了他的名誉)。

注意该词与下列近义词在用法上的区别:

(1)damage:损害,法律上常指赔偿费,损害赔偿等。例如,to claim damages(诉求赔偿损失)。

(2)hurt:损害,伤害。最通俗的用词。Dirty oil can hurt a car's engine(脏油会损害汽车的引擎)。

(3)impair:损害,伤害。表示借削弱力量或价值以造成伤害。例如,Poor eating habits impair health(不良的进食习惯危害身体)。

(4)injure:伤害,损害。法律上指伤害行为、违法行为、不法伤害等。例如,material injury(严重伤害)。

Review Questions

1. Briefly explain the historical development of GATT.
2. List and explain trade barriers, giving examples where possible.
3. Do you agree to the idea that trade liberalization promotes economic globalisation? Explain.
4. List and explain major principles of GATT 1994.
5. Outline and discuss the advantages and disadvantages of the economic globalisation, giving examples.
6. Explain and discuss national treatment in GATT 1994 and its practice in China.
7. Define 'dumping' in the WTO law and discuss China's counter-measures against antidumping suits of other WTO members under the WTO antidumping agreement.
8. Compare and contrast the dispute settlement procedures in the GATT 1947 and WTO, giving two examples based on the judgments of DSB.
9. One of the central obligations of WTO membership is a limit on tariffs on particular goods according to a nation's tariff commitments. If a member does not abide by its agreement, can another WTO member unilaterally raise its agreed-upon tariff? Describe the dispute settlement mechanism in the WTO. Reports of the dispute settlement panels are available in WTO website.

13 Chapter Thirteen The Law of Agency

■ 导读

本章讲授的是代理法，主要包括代理的概念、代理人及本人的义务、代理的终结、第三人与代理人及本人的关系等。代理人能使本人“分身有术”，极大地提高本人的工作效率，自然成为国外商人开拓市场最重要的方法之一。国外商界有谚：“宁要第一流的代理，第二流的市场，不要第一流的市场，第二流的代理”。遗憾的是，我国至今仍缺乏与国际接轨的代理法，限制了我国商人拓展国外市场的视野和能力。因此，代理法在国际商事中处于极为重要的地位，对我国法律人来说，必须高度重视。由于国外代理法的一些理念与我国商人的传统习惯存在冲突，建议读者重视本章内容，认真研习。如果与国际商务实践结合起来，自然会收到事半功倍的效果。

Sole proprietors seldom have enough time or expertise to perform all the necessary duties of their business. Therefore, growing firms must usually hire employees and retain outside consultants. As artificial entities, corporations can conduct business only through agents, giving most managers some authority to contract with suppliers, customers, and employees. Because agents have widely varying levels of authority, it is a fundamental managerial concern to know precisely when an agent becomes authorized and how to limit agents' powers. A proliferation of agents can expect liability. Additionally, managers need to understand the extent of their personal agency responsibilities to their employer.

An agency is a relationship between two persons. Either can be natural human beings, artificial entities, or a combination of natural and artificial persons. An agency is defined as a fiduciary relationship that results when one person, the principal, consents that another person, the agent, shall act on behalf of the principal. The agent must also consent to the agency and thereby becomes subject to the principal's control. Agents are usually employees appointed by the principal/employer. However, all employees may not be agents if they have no authority to contract for or change the employer's legal relationships.

I. Creation of Agency

A. Formation

An agency(代理) arises whenever the principal and agent consent that the agent may act for the principal. An agency is often created by an employment contract in which both principal and agent consent that the agent is authorized to act for the principal and the contract states a purpose for the agency. In most instances, such employment contracts may be expressed either orally or in writing. Written contracts are advisable even if the law does not require them. The parties are more likely to consider the potential pitfalls of their arrangement when forced to prepare a written contract.

B. Capacity

Contract law requires that all contracting parties have contractual capacity. The law protects certain incapacitated persons who are typically underage, drunken, drugged, or insane, considering them incapable of giving genuine contractual consent. In the agency setting, this rule requires that the principal have contractual capacity before becoming irrevocably bound in a contract negotiated by the agent. However, an agent need not have contractual capacity so long as the agent has the minimum ability to act for another person. For example, very young or mentally incompetent persons may be incompetent to act as agents particularly if they cannot understand the consequences of the transaction. By contrast, teenagers are minors with no contractual capacity but are nevertheless generally qualified to act as agents.

C. Nondelegable Duties

Principals generally may delegate any act to an agent. However, the principal's performance may be required in certain instances, effectively prohibiting the agent's performance of such personal duties. Under contract law, a personal service, contract is nondelegable without the permission of the party expecting performance. Additionally, society has an interest in verifying the principal's identity, so an agent may not sign a testator's will, attest to another person's statements under oath, or cast the principal's vote in a public election.

II. Duties of Agent and Principal

A. Duties of Agent to Principal

The law of agency provides an efficient set of rights and duties between the principal and the agent. These are derived from centuries of experience. Agency law holds the agent to significant responsibilities to balance the significant powers conferred by the principal. The principal also has significant responsibility when employing agents.

Freedom of contract gives the parties great latitude to add, subtract, or change the rights and duties implied by law.

1. Fiduciary Duty of Loyalty

The agent owes a fiduciary duty of good faith and utmost loyalty to the principal. The agent must conduct the principal's business with integrity. Therefore, the agent may not have any adverse personal financial interest in the principal's transactions during the agency. Some aspects of this duty persist even after the agency is terminated. Although the duty of loyalty may seem vague, it becomes more precise as it is applied to more specific situations. The fiduciary duty is a most basic ethical matter applicable to nearly all persons in business and government.

(1) Conflicts of interest. The ancient proviso that no person can serve two masters is at the heart of the prohibition against an agent simultaneously serving two principals in the same transaction. This would be a dual or double agency, and the agent would be unable to serve either principal fully. If the agent negotiates gains for one principal, the gains necessarily come as losses to the other. Also, dual agents are often given confidential information by either or both principals concerning key terms and the principal's willingness to sell or buy at the maximum or minimum price stated.

Conflicts of interest are not always so obvious. Sometimes a full-time agent for one party may be paid a secret bribe, gratuity, gift, or kickback by the other party. The law presumes these payments exert some influence on the agents' judgment and thereby harm the principal.

(2) Self-dealing. Self-dealing is another type of unethical conflict of interest in which the agent's own personal financial interests directly conflict with the principal's financial interests. Agents may not have any undisclosed, unapproved personal financial interest in a transaction in which the principal has a financial interest. The self-dealing prohibition also requires agents to refrain from competing directly with the principal while the agency is in effect. Most firms' employees are prohibited from working for competing firms or personally competing against the principal during their employment.

(3) Confidentiality. Confidentiality becomes necessary because principals often provide confidential information to their agents for the effective conduct of the principal's business. The agent would be ineffective without knowing special facts about the principal's trade secrets, business plans, financial plans, customer lists, sales tactics, manufacturing technologies, and/or new product information. The principal intends this information to be used only to further the principal's business.

The principal has a property right in information produced by all its employees and agents. Generalized knowledge of a trade or profession that the agent gains while in the principal's service is not the principal's exclusive property. Any intellectual property produced by the agent during employment may be used by either party after the agency is terminated unless otherwise provided by contract.

2. Duty of Care

Agents must use reasonable skill and care in conducting the principals' business. They must use all the skill they possess plus any skills the agent claims and any additional skills specified in the employment contract. It is probably unethical for an agent to claim skills he or she does not really possess. Such false bravado is often the basis for liability and ethical abuse.

Professional agents such as accountants, brokers, or attorneys must exercise skill equal to other similar professionals in that region. However, the law does not imply that the agent guarantees success unless the agent specifically makes that promise. However, when an agent's negligent performance causes damage to the principal, liability questions arise. An agent may be released from liability for negligence in the employment contract.

3. Obedience

Agents must generally obey any reasonable directions the principal provides that will impact the principal's business. Even agents given broad discretion must obey the principal's directives. Of course, an agent need not obey orders that are illegal, immoral, or unreasonable. The agent may in good faith interpret vague commands or be disobedient during an emergency if obedience would damage the principal. However, in an emergency during which the principal is unavailable for consultation, the agent could disobey the principal's directive and do as the emergency requires in good faith.

4. Accounting

The agent's fiduciary duty requires that all property and funds belonging to the principal be accounted for adequately. This is the duty to account or provide an accounting. It requires the agent to keep accurate records and keep the agent's individual property separate from the principal's property. Upon demand, the agent must produce accurate records of receipts and disbursements to the principal. Any commingling of funds belonging to the principal and agent makes it difficult to determine the true ownership. Commingling is a fundamental ethical abuse discovered among professional agents such as accountants, real estate brokers, investment professionals, and attorneys.

5. Communication

Agents must communicate to the principal all relevant information and notices they receive in the course of performing the principal's business. Agents are often the principal's most visible communicator because they regularly receive or provide information to third parties about the principal's business. It is probably unethical for an agent to withhold information from the principal either in sympathy for the third party or to conceal the agent's poor performance.

An agent authorized to transact the principal's business generally has authority to receive information from third parties. When third parties provide information to the agent, the law presumes the agent will comply with the duty to communicate. Knowledge or notice received by the agent is therefore imputed to the principal. After the third party gives notice to the agent, the third party is relieved from repeating the communication to the principal or to any other agent who might later replace the original agent. The principal and agent are treated as one party after information is communicated to the agent.

B. Duties of Principal to Agent

Under the common law, the following duties are generally imposed on the principal:

1. Duty to Compensate

Normally, a duty to pay the agent is implied unless special circumstances or the relationship of the parties suggest that a gratuitous agency was intended. The agency agreement should specify the amount of compensation for the agent and when it has been earned. Many disputes arise because no clear agreement has been reached. In the absence of agreement, the agent is entitled to the customary or reasonable value of the services performed. Custom is sometimes quite clear. For example, in most communities, real estate brokers all charge the same commission rate. If there is no clear custom and the amount is in dispute, expert witnesses may testify as to what a reasonable amount would be.

(1) Contingent compensation. Compensation is often made contingent on results. Sales agents are frequently paid an agreed-on percentage of the value of the sales they make. Stockbrokers are also usually paid on a commission basis. Lawyers in the United States, especially when serving plaintiffs in tort actions such as automobile claims, often agree to contingent fees. If they win the case for the plaintiff, they get some share (often one-third) of the recovery. The plaintiff has only expenses and court costs to pay if there is no recovery.

An agent is entitled to be paid if the agreed-on result is obtained even though the principal does not benefit. It is common to give agents who are compensated on a commission basis a monthly or weekly "draw" against commissions to be earned. This gives the agent money for living expenses. At some longer interval, such as quarterly or once a year, the agent is paid the amount by which the commissions exceed the draw.

(2) Procuring cause. Generally, agents do not receive commissions on transactions that occur after termination of the agency relationship. However, when an agent was the

primary factor in a purchase or sale, the procuring cause rule may entitle the procuring agent to her commission regardless of who eventually completes the sale. This rule is designed to permit agents to collect commissions on sales completed after termination of the agency relationship if the sale primarily resulted from the agent's efforts. Without the rule, the principal easily could escape paying the agent's commissions while enjoying the fruits of her labours.

Case 13 – 1 Willis v. Champlain Cable Corp.

748 P. 2d 621 (Sup. Ct. Wash. 1988)

Facts: Willis was employed to find buyers for Haveg Industries' wire products. His agency contract permitted either party to terminate the agreement on 30 days' notice. In the event of such a termination, the agreement entitled Willis to commissions only on orders accepted by Haveg up to and including the termination date. During his employment, Willis convinced Boeing Company to choose Haveg's product as its general-purpose wire. However, before Boeing made anyorders, Haveg terminated Willis's contract. Boeing's first major order did not occur until more than a year and a half after this termination and the company continued to make major purchases during the next five years. Willis argued that Haveg terminated him in bad faith in order to avoid paying his commissions on the Boeing orders. He sued Haveg to recover his commissions on all purchases made by Boeing during the five years following his termination.

Issue: Is Willis entitled to the commissions as the procuring cause of the orders?

Decision: No. The right to commissions is dependent on the terms of the contract. Here, the contract between Haveg and Willis is clear and unambiguous regarding the payment of commissions. While the procuring cause rule has been construed to permit terminated agents to recover commissions for services that already have been performed, it should not override a written contract that provides the manner by which termination can be effected as well as how commissions will be awarded after termination. [1]

2. Duty to Reimburse and Indemnify

Sometimes agents make advances from their own funds in conducting the principal's

---

〔1〕 A. James Barnes, Terry Morehead Dworkin, and Eric L. Richards, Law for Business, Irwin Chicago, 1997, p. 346.

business. If the agent is acting within the scope of her authority, the principal has a duty to reimburse the agent for expenses incurred for the principal. Also, if the agent suffers losses while acting for the principal within the scope of the agent's authority, the principal has a duty to indemnify the agent. For example, suppose David is a salesperson for a company. He is in Chicago when he is asked to go to a foreign trade show. He uses his own funds to pay workers to set up the company's booth at the show. The company has a duty to reimburse him for his expenses.

However, if some fault of the agent causes a loss, the principal will not be required to indemnify the agent for the amount of the loss. And, of course, the principal is not liable for unauthorized expenses incurred by the agent.

3. Duty to Keep Accounts

The principal has a duty to keep records from which the compensation due the agent can be determined. This duty is reinforced by tax laws that require such recordkeeping. For example, an employer must keep and make available to a salesperson a record of the sales on which commissions have been earned.

III. Termination of an Agency

A. Act of the Parties

Principals or agents may personally or jointly terminate agencies either through provisions in the agency employment contract or by their own, unilateral actions. Terminations by virtue of contract provisions can include the accomplishment of the contract purpose, the happening of an event, or the lapse of a prescribed time period. The parties may agree in a later contract to rescind the agency employment contract, the principal may revoke the agency authority, or the agent may renounce authority.

1. Accomplishment of Contract Purpose/Occurrence of Events

Where the agency relationship has a single purpose or is intended to accomplish only one event, the agency is automatically terminated with the accomplishment of the event. For example, after Petty's successful collection suit against a defaulting debtor, the attorney's contract for legal services typically terminates.

2. Lapse of Time

After the passage of a specified number of days, months, or years, a contractual provision may specify termination. An agency or employment contract terminates by its own terms when the specified time period lapses.

3. Mutual Agreement

As a consensual or contractual relationship, an agency gives the parties the power to rescind the consent or contract. A mutual agreement by both the principal and the agent relieves them both of future performance obligations. However, the mutual rescission contract must also relieve the parties of their past responsibilities or they will remain liable for them. For example, an agent may remain liable for damages due to disloyal acts before the rescission. Similarly, the principal must make payments of any unpaid compensation, indemnity, or reimbursement that is still due to the agent for services performed before mutual rescission.

4. Unilateral Termination: Revocation or Renunciation

Except where an agency is irrevocable or coupled with an interest, either party can unilaterally terminate the agency. However, the right to terminate may be limited by contractual terms. The principal's unilateral termination is referred to as a revocation. The agent's unilateral termination is a renunciation of the authority. Damages may be due to the innocent party if the terminating party has no right to terminate.

B. Operation of Law

Under certain circumstances, the agency employment contract may be automatically terminated. Most parties would want the agency to terminate if significant events occur that frustrate the agency's purpose. In these situations, contracts with an unexpired term or unfulfilled purpose are terminated by operation of law and neither party is liable for wrongful termination of future service.

1. Incapacity, Bankruptcy, Death

An agency is such a personal relationship that the death or insanity of either party terminates the agent's authority. The agent's authority is also terminated automatically if the principal goes bankrupt, because this severely limits the principal's ability to conduct business through the agent's new contracts in the future. By contrast, the agent's bankruptcy terminates authority only if the agent's solvency is necessary to effectively represent the principal.

2. Illegality

An agency will automatically terminate if its objective becomes illegal. As under contract law, the law presumes the principal would prefer termination of the agent's authority if the business activity becomes illegal. The same holds true where the principal's business must be conducted under a professional license.

3. Impossibility or Impracticality

Where an agent's authority is limited to contracts involving a particular subject matter, the agent's authority automatically terminates if the subject matter is destroyed. Also, an agency automatically terminates by operation of law if war breaks out between the different nations of the principal and the agent. If both principal and agent are citizens of the same nation, a war terminates authority only if the business activity becomes illegal, unexpectedly impractical, or hazardous.

In unusual situations, the agent's authority is terminated by operation of the law if performance becomes impractical or there is such a significant change in business conditions that reasonable parties would expect authority to terminate. For example, a farmer had authorized an agent to sell the farm and soon thereafter oil was discovered under the farmland, the agent's authority would automatically terminate by operation of law because an oil discovery constitutes a significant change in business conditions.

C. Post-Termination Relationship

The termination of an agent's authority by an act of the parties or operation of law does not terminate all of the parties' duties to each other or toward third parties. After the agency has terminated, the agent's fiduciary duty may continue, the principal's duty to compensate or facilitate the agent's removal of property may continue, the principal may be required to give notice of termination to third parties, and either the principal or agent may still be responsible for torts committed to third party.

IV. Third Party Relations of the Principal and the Agent

The actions of agents are involved in the conduct of nearly all businesses and most activities of governments and unincorporated associations. An understanding of how an agent's activities impact the principal is fundamental to the manager's effective use of agents.

A. Contract Liability of the Principal

The effectiveness of using agents to conduct business is largely dependent on the agent's authority. Contracts enforceable against the principal result when agent is authorized to conduct preliminary negotiations, make offers or counteroffers, and/or accept third parties' offers. The principal's contract liability is derived from three basic forms of authority: actual authority (express and implied), apparent authority, and ratification.

1. Express Authority

Actual authority is composed of express authority and implied authority. An agent is authorized by the principal's directions, written or oral, to negotiate contracts or to otherwise have an effect on the principal's legal relationships. Express authority is often granted in a document such as an employment contract, a resolution of the board of directors, an advisory memorandum, or a special document known as a power of attorney (授权书). Additionally, the corporation's bylaws typically grant express authority to the president, and sometimes to other officers, to take actions affecting the corporation's legal relationships.

2. Implied Authority

Implied authority includes additional authority that an agent may reasonably assume exists to implement the express authority. There can be no implied authority unless first there is express authority upon which to base the implied authority(默示授权)。

Most often, a principal expressly grants an actual express authority. This is so general that it fails to itemize the specifics of the agent's powers, particularly in unusual or unforeseen situations. Most principals and agents expect that the agent will fill in the details with reasonable actions that carry out the principal's main objective.

An agent generally has implied authority to make contracts reasonably necessary to conduct the business in the customary fashion. The apartment superintendent would usually have authority to do any of the acts listed above but not the authority to make capital improvements. Implied authority generally does not include the power to borrow money, issue negotiable instruments, sell capital assets, or create a security interest on the principal's property. These latter actions are more extraordinary, so they are implied only if the nature of the principal's business suggests that the agent should do them.

(1) Course of conduct. Business customs are precedents followed in commercial settings. Customs create expectations among commercial parties as they deal through agents. Business customs differ among industries and within an industry among geographic regions. Third parties who deal through another firm's agent may usually presume the agent has a level of authority similar to most agents in that region and industry. Customs developed between the principal and a third party are called a course of conduct. Customs developed in an entire industry or a region are recognized as a usage of trade.

(2) Emergencies. In some instances, if it is necessary for an agent to use implied authority in unforeseen situations such as where the agent's employment contract fails to specify how the agent should react in an emergency. In an emergency, unless specifically limited, the agent has additional authority reasonably necessary to prevent the principal from sustaining substantial losses. For example, in one case, a train owned by the principal railroad injured a passenger. The railroad's stationmaster transported the injured passenger to a physician for treatment. The passenger's legs were amputated and the passenger sued the railroad. Although the railroad denied liability, the court held that its agent, the stationmaster, had implied authority arising from an emergency to secure the aid of a physician.〔1〕

(3) Apparent Authority and Estoppel. In some situations, an agent's powers are expanded neither by agreement with the principal nor by custom or emergency. Under the doctrine of apparent authority of ostensible authority (表见授权), authority may be created or expanded when the principal causes third parties to reasonably believe the agent

---

〔1〕 Elliot I. Klayman, John W. Bagby, and Nan S. Ellis, Business Law, Irwin Boston, 1994, p. 723.

has authority. Even a volunteer nonagent may be authorized if the principal holds out the purported agent as having authority. In such cases, the agent has this power to contract but has no legal right to affect the principal's legal relationships.

Where a principal's words or inaction makes it appear to reasonably acting third parties that the purported agent has authority, the agent will be authorized. This holding-out is effective to authorize the agent but only in contracts with third parties who are aware of the principal's holding-out.

Agents may also be empowered by a theory similar to apparent authority. This doctrine of estoppel applies where the principal's words, conduct, or lack of action makes it appear to reasonable third parties that the purported agent has authority. For estoppel to apply, the third party must know of the principal's representations and change his or her position in reliance on these appearances. Estoppel requires proof that the third party took some action in reliance on the principal's representations.

(4) Secret Limitations. The doctrine of apparent authority or inherent authority may apply where an agent is clothed with apparent general authority but the principal has secretly specified limitations on the agent's authority. In such situations, if a third party can reasonably infer the agent could have authority to do a particular act, then the secret limitation is ineffective if the third party is unaware and the contracts negotiated by that agent are nevertheless enforceable.

3. Ratification

Ratification (追认) is the principal's adoption of the agent's previously unauthorized act. Ratification arises in two general situations: (a) an agent exceeds the limited authority granted, or (b) a nonagent purports to act as agent for another. In these situations, a principal may supply the needed authority afterwards.

Authority by ratification is actually a legal fiction because the third party is bound to a contract made when the agent had no authority. For example, if an unauthorized agent negotiates a contract on July 1 and the principal ratifies the contract on July 15, after ratification, the law presumes the transaction was originally authorized on July 1. The principal's retroactive authorization is effective only when the requirements for ratification are satisfied. First, the agent's action must be one that the principal could have done lawfully. Second, the purported agent's act must be intended to benefit the principal. Third, the third party must have a reasonable belief that the agent is authorized to act for the principal's benefit. Fourth, the principal may ratify an act only if the principal has full knowledge of the facts and circumstances. Finally, a ratification is effective only if the principal approves the entire transaction, not just the most favourable parts. Ratification of a portion of the agent's contract is ineffective.

4. Third Party's Duty to Determine Authority

Usually, a third party cannot simply rely on the agent's claim of authority to represent a principal. Principals are not liable on contracts negotiated by an unauthorized agent unless an apparent authority or ratification occurs. This usually means that third parties must inquire into the agent's authority or run the risk that the agent is unauthorized and the contract will be unenforceable.

B. Contract Liability of the Agent

The agent's contract liability is determined largely by analysing the same authorization questions discussed above in the principal's contract liability. The primary inquiry is whether the agent had authority to contract for the principal. The next inquiry may focus on the agent's implied warranty of authority. Regardless of these inquires, the agent may separately assume liability apart from the principal's liability. A few limited circumstances give the third party a choice to hold either the principal or the agent liable.

1. Conduit Theory

In most situations, the agent acts primarily to extend the principal's reach by directly affecting the principal's business. Most agents do not want personal liability on contracts negotiated for the principal. Usually, all three parties—principal, agent, and third party—fully understand that the agent assumes only a representative status. The conduit theory explains how authorized agents avoid contract liability to the third party. When the principal authorizes an agent to negotiate contracts, the agent simply acts as a conduit through whom the principal communicates with third parties. For example, when a corporate purchasing agent negotiates contracts with a supplier to acquire component parts, only the purchasing corporation and the outside supplier are bound together in contract. The purchasing agent will have not personal contract liability because the agent acts only as a conduit through whom communications flow between the supplier and the customer. Typically, none of the three parties expects the agent to be liable if the customer corporation fails to pay its bill. The purchasing agent usually has no rights against the supplier should it fail to make timely and conforming deliveries. The following sections discuss the agent's liability under the conduit theory and limited exceptions when the agent has personal liability.

2. Unauthorized Contracts

Usually, agents expect third parties to believe that the agent works for an existing principal, and the principal authorized the agent to act. If the principal truly exists and has authorized the agent's conduct, the third party suffers no harm. However, if the agent is unauthorized or no principal exists, the third party may suffer damage. Therefore, the law usually gives the third party a remedy against the agent if there is no principal or the agent is unauthorized. Similar problems arise if an agent exceeds a limited grant of authority.

(1) Implied warranty of authority. A person who professes to act as agent, but has no authority from the alleged principal or has exceeded his authority, is liable in an action for breach of warranty of authority at the suit of the party with whom he professed to make the contract. The action is based, not on the original contract, but on the implied representation by the agent that he had authority to make the original contract. Remember the following points: (a) The action can only be brought by the third party, not by the principal. (b) The agent is liable whether he has acted fraudulently or innocently, and even if his authority has been terminated, without his knowledge, by death or mental disorder of the principal. (c) The agent is not liable if his lack of authority was known to the third party, or if it was known that he did not warrant his authority or if the contract excludes his liability. (d) If the principal gives ambiguous instructions and the agent acts on them bona fide and in a reasonable way, he will not be liable in an action for breach of warranty of authority even if he has interpreted them wrongly. (e) The agent warrants his authority not only when he purports to contract on behalf of another but also when, purporting to act as an agent, he induces a third party to enter into any transaction with him on the faith of such agency. (f) The measure of damages for breach of warranty of authority is the actual loss sustained.

Most of laws of agency in civil law countries provide that a principal is not liable for the contract made by an agent on behalf of the principal before ratification. Whether or not the agent is liable to the third party depends on the knowledge of the third party. That's to say, the agent is liable when the third party knew that the agent had no authority at the conclusion of the contract.

(2) Nonexistent principal. Agents are typically liable whenever they purport to act for a principal who does not actually exist at the time of negotiations. Of course, in such situations, the purported agent is not actually an agent at all but only claims to be an agent. This situation is known as a nonexistent principal situation.

3. Authorized Contracts

In most situations, the third party knows that the agent is merely a representative of known principal. Commonly, the third party is interested in contracting through the agent because of the principal's reputation for reliable service and/or quality products. Many agents use letterhead, brochures, business cards, or verbal representations identifying the principal to take advantage of the principal's goodwill and reputation. However, in limited situations, the principal or agent may find it advantageous not to reveal the principal's identity. The third party's knowledge about the principal's existence or identity may take three forms: disclosed principal, partially disclosed principal, and undisclosed principal.

(1) Disclosed principal. A principal whose existence and identity are known to the third party is a disclosed principal. In this case the agent incurs neither rights nor liabilities under the contract. However, there are exceptions to this rule: (a) Where the agent executes a deed in his own name he is liable on the deed. (b) Where the agent signs a bill of exchange in his own name without indicating that he has signed as agent, he is liable on the bill. (c) Where the agent is in fact the principal but contracts as agent he is liable on the contract and can enforce it. (d) Where the custom of a trade makes the agent liable.

(2) Partially disclosed principal. In this case the agent discloses the existence, but not the name, of his principal. As the agent expressly contracts as agent, he cannot be personally liable on the contract.

If, however, the agent does not, on the face of the contract, show that he is merely an agent, he will incur personal liability, and the third party may sue either him or his principal at his option. Furthermore, an agent who contracts in his own name but has failed to indicate clearly that he is doing so in his capacity of agent might not cease to be contractually bound even if it is proved that the other knew, when the contract was made, that he was acting as agent.

(3) Undisclosed principal. Both the identity and existence of an undisclosed principal is unknown by the third party. In this case the agent discloses neither the existence nor the identity of the principal; he contracts with the third party as if he were the principal. Here: (a) the undisclosed principal has the right to intervene and claim, and if necessary sue, the third party directly. If he makes use of this right, he renders himself personally liable to the third party; and (b) the third party, after having discovered the principal, has an option. He may elect to hold liable and sue either the principal or the agent.

If the third party unequivocally elects to hold either the principal or the agent liable he cannot afterwards change his mind and sue the other. Commencement of proceedings against either is prima facie evidence of such election, but if that evidence is rebutted this does not bar subsequent proceedings against the other.

4. Election Between Principal or Agent Liability

The third party's expectations are protected by the election doctrine. The principal is bound in contract to the third party even though the principal's existence and identity are undisclosed so long as the agent is authorized. To protect the third party's expectations, the third party may elect to hold either the principal or the agent liable for breach of contract. However, the third party may not hold both principal and agent liable. This rule has caused some procedural difficulties because initially, the third party only knows the agent's identity. To further protect the third party, courts typically permit the third party to add or substitute the principal to the suit after the principal is identified. However, when the third party learns of the principal's identity and takes the suit to judgment, the suit itself constitutes an election and the third party is barred from later suit the other party.

Under the laws of agency of civil law countries, a principal in indirect agency cannot directly hold the third party liable only in accordance with the contract made by the agent and the third party. That's to say, only in the case where the agent signs another contract with the principal and transfers the right by the former contract, can the principal hold the third party liable. Namely, there must be two contracts. While under the common law, the undisclosed principal has the right to directly hold the third party liable for breach of contract, and the third party can directly sue the principal upon finding the undisclosed principal.

Case13 - 2 Eazy Electronics & Technology, LLC., et al, (Plaintiffs) v. LG Electronics, INC., et al, (Defendants)

United States District Court, D. Puerto Rico, 2016

CIVIL NO. 16 - 1830 (GAG)

Facts: Eazy Electronics & Technology, LLC and Billy Medina - Torres (collectively "Plaintiffs") filed the present action against LG Electronics, Inc., LG Electronics Miami, Inc. and LG Electronics Panama, S. A. (collectively "Defendants") seeking the redress of injuries suffered as a result of the Defendants' alleged failure to abide by the terms of an agency contract entered into by the parties. Defendants responded requesting this Court to enter an order compelling arbitration pursuant to the Federal Arbitration Act ("FAA"), given that the same contract which Plaintiffs allege that the Defendants have breached includes an arbitration clause that covers the claims set forth in the Complaint. After considering the parties' filings and applicable law, the Court GRANTS Defendants' Motion to Dismiss and Compel Arbitration.

Co-plaintiff Eazy Electronics & Technology, LLC ("Eazy Electronics") is a company headquartered in San Juan, Puerto Rico which offers repair services to manufacturers and distributors of electronic equipment. The company also sells electronic products to businesses in Puerto Rico's hospitality industry. Co-plaintiff Billy Medina-Torres is the principal officer of Eazy Electronics.

Co-defendant LG Electronics, Inc. ("LG Electronics") is a corporation organized under the laws of the Republic of Korea with headquarters located in Seoul, South Korea. LG Electronics, Inc. is an affiliate of co-defendants LG

Electronics Miami, Inc. ("LG Miami") and LG Electronics Panama, S. A. ("LG Panama"). Several years ago, Eazy Electronics and LG Electronics Alabama, Inc. ("LG Alabama") executed a service agreement under which Eazy Electronics would provide warranty services to customers of LG products in Puerto Rico. For approximately four years, Eazy Electronics claims to have enjoyed a mutually beneficial relationship with LG Alabama and LG USA, Inc., and the responsibilities related to the sale of LG products in Puerto Rico were transferred from LG Alabama to LG Miami.

Afterwards, officials from LG Electronics and LG Miami—seeking to grow their presence in Puerto Rico's market—contacted and met with Medina-Torres. Effective on June 10, 2012, LG Electronics, Inc. and Medina Torres—on behalf of Eazy Electronics—established a Non-Exclusive Agency Agreement ("Agency Agreement") where Eazy Electronics agreed to serve as LG Electronics, Inc.'s non-exclusive agent in Puerto Rico. The stated purpose of the agreement was for Eazy Electronics to assist and promote LG Electronics, Inc.'s sales activities within Puerto Rico.

On or about April of 2013, Eazy Electronics and LG Miami subscribed a Master Supply Agreement ("Supply Agreement") under which LG Miami would provide LG products to Eazy Electronics for resale in Puerto Rico. Additionally, in July 2013, Eazy Electronics and LG Panama signed a Non-Exclusive Technical Service Agreement ("Service Agreement") where Eazy Electronics agreed to provide LG Panama the warranty and repair services that it previously provided for LG Alabama.

Plaintiffs filed the present suit on April 27, 2016. In the Complaint, Plaintiffs allege that they provided information related to Eazy Electronics' clients to representatives of LG Miami that directly resulted in new sales for LG Electronics and LG Miami. Plaintiffs also claim that they provided leads and referrals that resulted in additional sales to Defendants. However, Plaintiffs allege that after they shared this information, and provided such leads and referrals, Defendants opted to sell directly to Eazy Electronics' clients without compensating Plaintiffs. Furthermore, Plaintiffs add that Defendants also hired a third party, POS Caribbean, to perform the warranty and repair services that Eazy Electronics provides.

Plaintiffs claim that these actions violate Puerto Rico's Sales Representative Act, and breach several contracts established between Defendants and Eazy Electronics. Plaintiffs further add that Defendants caused them substantial damages by incurring in deceit, bad faith and breach of fiduciary duties in the performance of the Agency Agreement. Last, Plaintiffs assert that Defendants' employment of POS Caribbean tortuously interferes with Eazy Electronics' contractual rights.

Defendants filed a Motion to Dismiss and Compel Arbitration. They contend that the Agency Agreement contains a compulsory arbitration clause that applies to all of the Plaintiffs' claims. Defendants argue that the FAA and the Convention on the Recognition and Enforcement of Foreign Arbitral Awards, as adopted in Chapter Two of the FAA, require the enforcement of the arbitration clause that was contractually agreed upon by the parties. Defendants also assert that, even if the tortious interference claim presented by Plaintiffs is not covered by the arbitration clause in the Agency Agreement, this Court should dismiss the claim for failure to state a claim upon which relief may be granted and for failure to join a required party.

Plaintiffs opposed Defendant's motion, arguing that the arbitration clause contained in the Agency Agreement should not be enforced by this Court because it is contrary to the public policy recognized by the Puerto Rico Supreme Court. Plaintiffs also argue that the arbitration clause is unconscionable and thus invalid under the FAA. Furthermore, they contend that the arbitration clause and the Agency Agreement's "waiver of discovery clause" infringe upon essential attributes of arbitration proceedings and should be invalidated by this Court for those reasons as well.

Defendants replied, averring that the FAA preempts any state law or court decision inconsistent with its terms. Moreover, Defendants also assert that Plaintiffs' argument to the effect that the arbitration clause is unconscionable and invalid under the Federal Arbitration Act misconstrues applicable case law and does not represent a valid contractual defense under Puerto Rico law.

Plaintiffs filed a sur-reply in which they rehashed the arguments presented in their opposition to the motion to dismiss and countered that unconscionability is a valid contractual defense under Puerto Ricolaw. (Docket No. 17 at 3.)

Standard of Review: Under the FAA, If suit is brought in a U. S. Court with regards to a claim which according to an arbitration agreement should be referred to arbitration, the Court must, upon request to that effect by one of the parties, stay the action until arbitration has concluded. In order to obtain an order compelling arbitration, the party seeking the order, must establish that a valid agreement to arbitrate exists, that the movant is entitled to invoke the arbitration clause, that the other party is bound by that clause, and that the claim asserted comes within the clause's scope.

Under Rules 12(b)(1) and 12(b)(6), a defendant may move to dismiss an action against him for lack of federal subject-matter jurisdiction or for failure to state a claim upon which relief can be granted. When considering a motion to dismiss, the court must decide whether the complaint alleges enough facts to "raise a right to relief above the speculative level." The court accepts as true all well-pleaded facts and draws all reasonable inferences in the plaintiff's favor. However, "the tenet that a court must accept as true all of the allegations contained in a complaint is inapplicable to legal conclusions." "Threadbare recitals of the elements of a cause of action, supported by mere conclusory statements, do not suffice." "Where the well-pleaded facts do not permit the court to infer more than the mere possibility of misconduct, the complaint has alleged—but it has not 'shown'—'that the pleader is entitled to relief.'"

***Discussion*:**

A. The Federal Arbitration Act

A party seeking to compel arbitration under the FAA must demonstrate "(1) that a valid agreement to arbitrate exists, (2) that the movant is entitled to invoke the arbitration clause, (3) that the other party is bound by that clause, and that (4) the claim asserted comes within the clause's scope."

Section two of the FAA provides that: "A written provision in ... a contract evidencing a transaction involving commerce to settle by arbitration a controversy thereafter arising out of such contract ... shall be valid, irrevocable, and enforceable, save upon such grounds as exist at law or in equity for the revocation of any contract." Federal policy strongly favors arbitration over litigation, so long as an agreement to arbitrate exists in the first place. Thus, "there is a presumption of arbitrability in the sense that 'an order to arbitrate the particular grievance should not be denied unless it may be said with positive assurance that the arbitration clause is not susceptible of an interpretation that covers the asserted dispute.'" "By its terms, the Act leaves no place for the exercise of discretion by a district court, but instead mandates that district courts shall direct the parties to proceed to arbitration on issues as to which an arbitration agreement has been signed."

B. The Convention on the Recognition and Enforcement of Foreign Arbitral Awards

The Supreme Court has recognized that the "emphatic" federal policy favoring arbitration "applies with special force" in international commercial transactions, at least since the United States adopted the Convention on the

Recognition and Enforcement of Foreign Arbitral Awards, September 30, 1970, and amended the FAA to include the Convention's terms. The main goal of the Convention—and its adoption by the United States—was to "encourage the recognition and enforcement of commercial arbitration agreements in international contracts and to unify the standards by which agreements to arbitrate are observed and arbitral awards are enforced in the signatory countries."

C. Agreement to Arbitrate Under the Convention

1. Written Agreement to Arbitrate the Disputes between the Parties

Before enforcing an agreement to arbitrate under the Convention, the first issue that must be resolved by this Court is whether there is a written agreement to arbitrate the disputes between the parties. As discussed in the first part of this opinion, the Complaint raises four claims against the Defendants: (1) constructive or *de facto* termination of the Agency Agreement under Puerto Rico's Sales Representative Act; (2) bad faith and breach of fiduciary duties in the performance of the Agency Agreement; and (3) tortious interference with the Agency Agreement.

2. Signatory to the Convention

The next step in the Ledee four-part inquiry is to determine whether the Agency Agreement provides for arbitration in the territory of a country that is a signatory to the Convention. As discussed above, the arbitration clause of the Agency Agreement calls for the arbitration proceedings to be conducted in Seoul, Republic of Korea. The Republic of Korea is a signatory to the Convention.

3. Commercial Relationship

The agreement to arbitrate must arise out of a commercial relationship, contractual or not. The purpose of the Agency Agreement was to appoint Eazy Electronics as LG Electronics' "agent to assist and promote its sales activities" in Puerto Rico. Therefore, the Agency Agreement arises out of a legal relationship that is clearly commercial in nature.

4. Foreign Citizen or State

The last question that must be answered is whether one of the parties to the agreement to arbitrate is a foreign citizen or whether the commercial relationship between the parties has a reasonable connection with a foreign state. The parties to the Agency Agreement are LG Electronics and Billy Medina, on behalf of Eazy Electronics. LG Electronics, Inc. is a corporation organized pursuant to the laws of, and headquartered in, the Republic of Korea. Hence, a party to the Agency Agreement is a foreign citizen.

Considering that all four questions have been resolved in the affirmative, this court must compel arbitration unless the arbitration clause of the Agency Agreement is found to be "'null and void, inoperative or incapable of being performed'." Although the Plaintiffs have not explicitly presented such an argument, they have challenged the validity and enforceability of the arbitration clause. The Court will thus proceed to determine whether the Plaintiffs' thesis on the enforceability of the clause renders it null and void, inoperative or incapable of being performed under the Convention.

D. Enforceability of an Agreement to Arbitrate under the Convention

In their Opposition to Motion to Dismiss Plaintiffs raise two arguments against enforcement of the Agency Agreement's arbitration clause. First, Plaintiffs contend that the arbitration clause of the Agency Agreement should not be enforced because it is contrary to public policy pursuant to the forum selection test set forth by the Puerto Rico Supreme Court. Second, Plaintiffs contend that the Agency Agreement's requirement to arbitrate in the Republic of Korea is unconscionable and, as such, should be invalidated. We address these arguments in turn.

1. Forum-selection Test and the Convention

Plaintiffs hinge their unenforceability argument on inconvenience grounds: "Defendants imposition of an arbitration clause requiring that disputes be heard by an arbitration panel in the Republic of Korea is, on its face not merely inconvenient to Plaintiffs but it practically deprives Plaintiffs from its day in court." Plaintiffs further add that "forcing an individually owned small Puerto Rico business operator like plaintiffs Eazy Electronics to seek redress for the injuries and damages suffered in Puerto Rico in a distant foreign country is unreasonable, inequitable and unfair."

Defendants counter that any reference to the forum-selection test just described "as a way to circumvent the application of the arbitration clause according to its own terms is improper and irrelevant." Defendants support their argument in the FAA and the "strong federal policy favoring arbitration" which "preempts any Statelaw to the contrary, such as the standard adopted in [Ramallo.]"

The standard used to determine the enforceability of forum-selection clauses is broader than the "null and void" standard recognized in Ledee. Since we have already determined that the arbitration clause of the Agency Agreement is an agreement to arbitrate under the Convention, Ledee's heightened standard controls.

Plaintiffs' argument under Ramallo is inapposite because even if this Court were to agree that having to pursue their claims against the Defendants in the Republic of Korea would be gravely inconvenient to the point of practical impossibility, this conclusion would not be enough to invalidate an agreement to arbitrate under the Convention. As the First Circuit held in Ledee, once a district court performs the relevant four-question limited inquiry, and resolves all four questions in the affirmative, "it must order arbitration unless it finds the agreement 'null and void, inoperative or incapable of being performed'." This disposition "must be interpreted to encompass only those situations—such as fraud, mistake, duress, and waiver—that can be applied neutrally on an international scale." Grave inconvenience due to the distance between the arbitration forum and the principal place of business of one of the parties is not one of those situations that may be applied neutrally on an international scale, especially when the arbitration forum is where the headquarters of one of the parties is located. Furthermore, such an argument would be contrary to the goals behind the adoption of the Convention in the United States, which were to "encourage the recognition and enforcement of commercial arbitration agreements in international contracts and to unify the standards by which agreements to arbitrate are observed and arbitral awards are enforced in the signatory countries." Simply put, allowing a party to a valid arbitration agreement to escape a freely-assumed duty, based solely on the distance of the chosen forum, contravenes the text and purpose of the Convention.

2. Unconscionability

Plaintiffs also argue that the arbitration clause of the Agency Agreement should not be enforced because it is unconscionable. Plaintiffs contend that the clause is invalid under section 2 of the FAA which states that an arbitration clause is valid, irrevocable, and enforceable "save upon such grounds as exist at law or in equity for the revocation of any contract." Generally, unconscionability is one of those grounds that exist at law or in equity for the revocation of any contract.

Plaintiffs' argument, however, ultimately misses the mark, given First Circuit precedent. In Ledee, the parties seeking to avoid the enforcement of an arbitration agreement argued that the clause was contrary to Puerto Rico's Dealer Act, and the public policy behind the statute. Just as Plaintiffs contend in this case, the appellants in Ledee argued that section 2 of the FAA allows for the invalidation of the arbitration clause that they had agreed to since there were, allegedly, grounds at law or in equity to set aside the clause.

As an agreement to arbitrate under the Convention, the arbitration clause of the Agency Agreement must be enforced by this court unless the clause is found to be "null and void, inoperative or incapable of being performed." This phrase has been interpreted by the First Circuit "to encompass only those situations-such as fraud, mistake, duress, and waiver-that can be applied neutrally on an international scale." It is under this standard that we must evaluate Plaintiffs' arguments.

Plaintiffs also contend that they were unaware that they agreed to arbitrate their claims in the Republic of Korea. (Docket No. 11 at 7.) This assertion, by itself, is insufficient to challenge the validity of the clause. Finally, Plaintiffs argue that the contract is substantively unconscionable due to the hardship that having to litigate its claims in the Republic of Korea would impose on a company of its size. We already rejected a very similar argument in our forum-selection test discussion and find no reason to reach a different result here, given that, even if Plaintiffs were successful in proving procedural and substantive unconscionability, unconscionability is not a defense that may be effectively applied neutrally on an international scale.

In sum, Plaintiffs' have failed to show the arbitration clause of the Agency Agreement is "null and void, inoperative or incapable of being performed." Accordingly, the Court must order the Plaintiffs to arbitrate their claims against the Defendant in accordance with the terms of the Agency Agreement. ("Enforcing arbitration clauses under the New York Convention is an obligation, not a matter committed to district court discretion").

Conclusion: For the foregoing reasons, the Court GRANTS Defendants' Motion to Dismiss and Compel arbitration at Docket No. 8. Plaintiff's claims against Defendants are hereby dismissed as the claims must proceed to arbitration.

SO ORDERED. [1]

■ Notes

ratification 追认的代理。如果代理人未经授权或者超出了授权的范围而以本人的名义同第三人订立了合同,这个合同对本人是没有拘束力的。但是,本人可以在事后批准或承认这个合同,这种行动就叫作追认。追认的效果就是使该合同对本人具有拘束力,如同本人授权代理人替他订立了该合同一样。

breach of implied warranty of authority 违反有代理权的默示担保。按照英美法的解释,当代理人同第三人订立合同时,代理人对第三人有一项默示的担保,即保证他是有代理权的。因此,如果某人冒充是别人的代理人,但实际上并没有得到本人的授权,或者是超出了授权范围行事,则与其订立合同的第三人就可以以其违反有代理权的默示担保对他提起诉讼,该冒牌的代理人或越权的代理人就须对第三人承担责任。

---

〔1〕 https://1. next. westlaw. com/Browse/Home/ArbitrationMaterials/ArbitrationCases? transitionType = Default&ContextData = (sc. Default), visit on 12 January, 2020.

■ Important Legal English Usages

perform 履行，执行。法律上主要指履行义务。例如，performance of bond（履约保证书）；performance of a contract（履行合同）。与此相关的词有 carry out，该词强调履行或执行的权威性。例如，to carry out a death sentence（执行死刑）。

obey 服从，顺从，遵守。是通常词，主要指服从指挥、命令、禁令等。例如，to obey the order of commander（服从指挥员的命令）。与该词同义的有 abide by，该词主要指服从法律。例如，to abide by the law（服从法律）。

■ Review Questions

1. Outline the ways in which an agency can be created. Include examples for each of the ways indicated.
2. Why is it important to determine whether an agent is acting with authority? In your answer, use at lease one case reference and give an explanation of the difference between actual and apparent authority.
3. Explain the main ways in which an agency can be ratified, giving two examples.
4. What rights does an agent have against a principal?
5. Explain briefly the circumstances that would cause an agent to be liable to the party meant to be contracting with the principal.
6. How can the principal and/or agent cause an agency to end?
7. List and explain the duties of the principal and/or agent, giving examples where possible.
8. Why is the post-termination relationship important?
9. Define 'conduit theory' and state its main features.
10. Tadlock was a tenant on Lest's farm. Without any authorization from Lest, Tadlock ordered a new irrigation pump for the farm from Killinger. Tadlock told Killinger that he was Lest's tenant and that he had authority to purchase a new pump on Lest's behalf. Killinger then installed a new pump and billed Lest for $2,048. Lest denied liability on this bill, claiming that Tadlock 's purchase was unauthorized. Tadlock did not have actual authority to purchase the pump, but was his statement to Killinger enough to give him apparent authority to make the purchase?

14 Chapter Fourteen International Commercial Dispute Settlement

■ 导读

本章讲授的是国际商事纠纷解决，主要包括司法解决、非司法方法解决及商事仲裁等内容。实际上，只要人们之间有经济来往，就必然会有纠纷。近年来，我国的涉外经济纠纷越来越多，不少企业因此遭受重大损失。原因在于：一方面，一些不法外商企图谋取不法利益；另一方面，我国不少企业初次从事国际贸易，缺乏足够的贸易经验，对相关法律一知半解。因此，希望读者将本章作为重点进行研习，做到防患于未然。即使面对不法外商的指控，也能在法庭上运用自如、据理力争，确保自己的合法权益。

The resolution of international commercial disputes among people who are citizens of different countries, with business deals that span continents and cultures, can be fraught with difficulty and uncertainty due to the significant differences in legal systems, cultures, politics, national policies of economic development. In addition, these problems also make resolution more time-consuming and costly. During the resolution of international commercial disputes usually arise the following questions: (1) Should the parties settle, litigate, mediate, or arbitrate? (2) Where should the dispute be settled? (3) Which law applies to the transaction? Chinese law? French law? CISG or other international conventions? (4) If a resolution (a settlement, a verdict, or a judgment) is reached, how will it be enforced?

This chapter examines these questions in settlement of international commercial disputes.

I. Settlement of Disputes through Municipal Courts

Municipal courts are often called upon to settle international disputes. Usually, a lawsuit will not proceed if the court does not have jurisdiction.

A. Jurisdiction and Venue

Jurisdiction(管辖权) means the "power to hear," the "legal right by which judges exercise their authority" or "competence". Jurisdiction refers to "a court's power to decide a case or issue a decree, or a geographic area within which political or judicial authority may be exercised."[1] In the United States, jurisdiction is defined by the U. S. Constitution as well as by various statutes.

Venue is sometimes confused with jurisdiction, but it means the appropriate geographical location of the court with jurisdiction. For example, in the United States, several federal district courts may have jurisdiction over a suit, but venue might be proper in only one of them.

1. Conflicts of Jurisdiction

Internationally, there are no universally accepted rules regarding jurisdiction of a particular court over the parties or subject matter of a dispute. Thus, then a dispute arises out of an international transaction, the parties to that dispute, if they seek litigation, are capable of bringing an action on that dispute in the courts of many different countries. Further, the substantive rules that may be used to resolve the dispute may be different in the different courts. Even the choice of law rules may be different, producing divergent result which depends only upon the court selected to hear the litigation, attempting to obtain such a tactical advantage through court selection is international "forum shopping," and creates uncertainty in the resolution of disputes under the transaction. The causes for these conflict of jurisdiction are the doctrine of in personam and in rem. According to the doctrine of in personam[2] jurisdiction in international law, a state of sovereignty has jurisdiction on matters relating to a natural or juridical person physically present within the forum state. Natural persons subject to in personam jurisdiction include nationals of the forum state, individuals physically present within the state, individuals domiciled in the state, and individuals who consent to such jurisdiction. However, under the doctrine of in rem[3] jurisdiction, the state has the power to determine the ownership rights of persons as to property located within the territory of the forum state. This clearly illustrates that a state has jurisdiction on all the foreign nationals and things within the territory of the state, on the other hand, on its nationals in foreign countries. Hence, there arise again conflicts of jurisdiction on the international commercial cases.

2. Choice of Forum Clauses

Choice of forum clause(选择法院条款) is a way by the parties to avoid conflicts of jurisdiction. It fixes in advance where the case will be heard, thus reducing the forum shopping by parties' lawyers. In western countries, any attempt by private parties to control jurisdiction used to be viewed with hostility by the courts as an effort to usurp their

---

[1] Bryan A. Garner, Black's Law Dictionary, St. Paul, Minn., 1999, p. 855.

[2] Latin: "against the person."

[3] Latin: "against the thing."

authority. The realities of the international marketplace, however, and the recognition of the importance of reducing uncertainty, and thereby lessening risk and cost, have persuaded many courts to accept choice of forum clauses. During the initial drafting of the contract the parties should decide which court shall have jurisdiction, and then specify that court in a Forum Selection Clause. That Clause should both specify the court which has jurisdiction and state that that court has exclusive jurisdiction to preclude other courts from entertaining the case.

Most often, a court of the third country is chosen as the forum by the parties. However, this cannot absolutely insure that the court chosen will accept the choice of forum clauses. Usually, a court applies the following principles to resist application of choice of forum clauses:

(1) Forum Non Conveniens. [1] This doctrine refers to an appropriate forum—even though competent under the law—may divest itself of jurisdiction if, for the convenience of the litigants and the witnesses, it appears that the action should proceed in another forum in which the action might originally have been brought. Forum non conveniens allows a court to exercise its discretion to avoid the oppression or vexation that might result from automatically honouring plaintiff's forum choice. However, dismissal on the basis of forum non conveniens also requires that there be an alternative forum in which the suit can be prosecuted. It must appear that jurisdiction over all parties can be secured and that complete relief can be obtained in the supposedly more convenient court. Further, in at least some states, it has been held that the doctrine cannot be successfully invoked when the plaintiff is resident of the forum state since, effectively, one of the functions of the state courts is to provide a tribunal in which their residents can obtain an adjudication of their grievances. But in most instances a balancing of the convenience to all the parties will be considered and no one factor will preclude a forum non conveniens dismissal, as long as another forum is available. [2]

This following case exemplifies its application.

Case 14 – 1 In Re Union Carbide Corporation Gas Plant Disaster at Bhopal

09 F. 2d 195 (1987) United States Court of Appeals (2d Cir.)

Facts: This case arose out of what has been considered the most devastating industrial disaster in history—the deaths of thousands of persons (estimates range from 2000 to 4000) and injuries of several hundred thousand caused by the release

[1] Latin: "inconvenient forum."

[2] Bryan A. Garner, Black's Law Dictionary, St. Paul, Minn., 1999, p. 665.

of lethal gas known as methyl lisocyanate from a chemical plant operated by Union Carbide India Limited (UCIL) in Bhopal, India, in 1984. The accident occurred in the night of December 2, 1984, when winds blew the deadly gas from the plant operated by UCIL into densely occupied parts of the city of Bhopal. UCIL is incorporated under the laws of India. Fifty-one percent of its stock is owned by Union Carbide Corporation (UCC), a U. S. corporation, 22 percent is owned or controlled by the government of India, and the balance is held by approximately 23,500 Indian citizens. The stock is publicly traded on the Bombay Stock Exchange. The company is engaged in the manufacture of a variety of products, including chemicals, plastics, fertilizers, and insecticides, at 14 plants in India and employs more than 9,000 Indian citizens. Approximately 650 people are employed at the Bhopal plant. It is managed and operated entirely by Indian citizens. All products produced at Bhopal are sold in India. The operations of the plant were regulated by more than two dozen Indian governmental agencies.

Four days after the accident, the first of some 145 actions in federal district courts in the United States was commenced on behalf of victims. In the meantime, India enacted the Bhopal Gas Leak Disaster Act, granting to its government (the Union of India[UOI]), the exclusive right to represent the victims in India or elsewhere. In April 1985, the Indian government filed a complaint in the Southern District of New York on behalf of all of the victims. India's decision to bring suit in the United States was attributed to the fact that although nearly 6,500 lawsuits had been instituted by victims in India against UCIL, the Indian courts did not have jurisdiction over UCC, the parent company. UCC contended that the actions are properly tried in the courts of India on the doctrine of *forum non conveniens*. The district court dismissed the action on the condition that UCC submit to the jurisdiction of the Indian courts and that UCC agree to satisfy any judgment taken against it in the courts of India.

Issue: Did the courts of India have the jurisdiction over the case?

Decision: Yes! According to Mansfield, Circuit Judge, the plaintiffs seek to prove that the accident was caused by negligence on the part of UCC in originally contributing to the design of the plant and its provision for storage of excessive amounts of the gas at the plant. As Judge Keenan found, however, UCC's participation was limited, and its involvement in plant operations terminated long before the accident.... The preliminary process design information furnished by UCC could not have been used to construct the plant. Construction required the detailed process design and engineering data prepared by hundreds of Indian engineers, process designers, and subcontractors. During the ten years spent constructing the plant, its design and configuration underwent many changes.

The vital parts of the Bhopal plant, including its storage tank, monitoring instrumentation, and vent gas scrubber, were manufactured by Indians in India. Although some 40 UCIL employees were given some safety training at UCC's plant in West Virginia, they represented a small fraction of the Bhopal plant's employees. The vast majority of plant employees were selected and trained by UCIL in Bhopal. The manual for start-up of the Bhopal plant was prepared by Indians employed by UCIL.

In short, the plant has been constructed and managed by Indians in India. No Americans were employed at the plant at the time of the accident. In the five years from 1980 to 1984, although more than 1,000 Indians were employed in the plant, only one American was employed there and he left in 1982. No Americans visited the plant for more than one year prior to the accident, and during the five-year period before the accident the communications between the plant and the United States were almost nonexistent.

The vast majority of material witnesses and documentary proof bearing on causation of and liability for the accident is located in India, not the United States, and would be more accessible to an Indian court than to a United States court. The records are almost entirely in Hindi or other Indian languages, understandable to an Indian court without translation. The witnesses for most part do not speak English but Indian languages understood by an Indian court but not by an American court. These witnesses could be required to appear in an Indian court but not in a court of the United States.

Although witnesses in the United States could not be subpoenaed to appear in India, they are comparatively few in number and most are employed by UCC, which, as a party, would produce them in India, with lower overall transportation costs than if the parties were to attempt to bring hundreds of Indian witnessed to the United States. Lastly, Judge Keenan properly concluded that an Indian court would be in a better position to direct and supervise a viewing of the Bhopal plant, which was sealed after the accident. Such a viewing could be of help to a court in determining liability issues.

After a thorough review, the district court concluded that the public interest concerns, like the private ones, also weigh heavily in favor of India as the situs for trial and disposition of the cases. The accident and all relevant events occurred in India. The victims, over 200,000 in number, are citizens of India and located there. The witnesses are almost entirely Indian citizens. The Union of India has a greater interest than does the United States in facilitating the trial and adjudication of the victims' claims.

India's interest is increased by the fact that it has for years treated UCIL as an Indian national, subjecting it to intensive regulations and governmental supervision of the construction, development, and operation of the Bhopal plant, its emissions, water and air pollution, and safety precautions. Numerous Indian government officials have regularly conducted on-site inspections of the plant and approved its machinery and equipment, including its facilities for storage of the lethal methyl isocyanate gas that escaped and caused the disaster giving rise to the claims. Thus India has considered the plant to be an Indian one and the disaster to be an Indian problem. It therefore has a deep interest in ensuring compliance with its safety standards. Moreover, plaintiffs have conceded that in view of India's strong interest and its greater contacts with the plant, its operations, its employees, and victims of the accident, the law of India, as the place where the tort occupied, will undoubtedly govern.

The district court's dismissal of the actions against Union Carbide Corporation is upheld. The doctrine of *forum non conveniens* is a rule of U. S. law, which states that where a case is properly heard in more than one court, it should be heard by the one that is most convenient. Given the facts of this case, the courts of India are the more convenient forum.

In 1989 the Supreme Court of India approved a settlement fund of $470 million to compensate the victims of the disaster. [1]

(2) Minimum contacts(最低联系原则). This legal doctrine requires that before a person or a company is brought before a court, it must have had minimum contracts with the forum. This requirement is based on the premise that bringing an individual or corporation before a court when the "person" has never had "legal" contact with that place would be unfair. This concept has important implications as to when a company has had sufficient contacts that it can be brought before a particular court on a tort, contract, or statutory claim.

3. Choice of Law Clauses

Because the validity of a contractual Forum Selection Clause may turn on its validity

---

[1] Richard Schaffer, Beverley Earle and Filiberto Agusti, International Business Law and Its Environment, West Publishing Company, 1996, pp. 24 – 26.

under the law which governs the contract, the validity of the Choice of Law Clause assumes an added importance. Generally, in common law and European civil law jurisdictions, parties may choose the law which they wish to govern their contract relationship, as long as the law chosen is that of a place which has a substantial relationship to the parties and to the international business transaction, and is not contrary to a strong public policy of the place where suit is brought.

In the United States, the UCC (§1 - 105) permits the parties to choose the law governing the contract, as long as the transaction bears "a reasonable relation" to the jurisdiction providing the governing law. Thus, "party autonomy"(当事人意思自治) is permissible, but only within "reasonable" limits. Likewise, Article 6 of the CISG, when applicable, permits the parties to "derogate," or choose some other law to govern the contract, without limitation. Thus, the CISG permits unlimited party autonomy. In the EU, the 1980 Convention on the Law Applicable to Contractual Obligations (Article 3) also allows unlimited party autonomy. In sum, the legislative trend seems to favour fewer limits on party autonomy, and none in international transactions.

However, courts can still refuse to enforce a Choice of Law Clause on the grounds of public policy. In countries taking their legal heritage from Roman Law, laws expressing strong public policy may be called Jus cogens(强行法)[1] rules of law, the operation of which parties may not contract away. These mandatory rules which are used to limit party autonomy may be either statutory or judicially-created, and will vary from country to country. Thus, they can create legal problems as to whether the parties may submit different aspects of a contract to different laws, or whether the courts of one country should recognize and apply the mandatory rules of a different country, regardless of the contract's Choice of Law Clause.

4. Relevant Provisions of Chinese Laws

In accordance with the General Principles of Civil Law of the People's Republic of China, Civil Procedure Law of the People's Republic of China and other relevant laws, jurisdiction on international commercial cases in China are decided as follows:

(1) The Chinese law shall be applied to all the cases on which Chinese courts have exclusive jurisdiction. For example, real estate within the territory of China, contracts for Chinese-foreign equity joint ventures, or Chinese-foreign contractual joint ventures, of Chinese-foreign cooperative exploration and development of the natural resources in the People's Republic of China shall fall under the jurisdiction of Chinese courts.

(2) In the case of international commercial contracts, if parties fail to make a choice,

[1] Latin: "mandatory laws."

the law of the county to which the contract is most closely connected shall be applied.

If any international treaty concluded or acceded to by the People's Republic of China contains provisions differing from those in the civil laws of the People's Republic of China, the provisions of the international treaty shall apply, unless the provisions are ones on which the People's Republic of China has announced reservations.

Article 142 of Civil Procedure Law of the People's Republic of China further states that international practice may be applied to matters for which neither the law of the People's Republic of China nor any international treaty concluded or acceded to by the People's Republic of China has any provisions.

B. Enforcement of Foreign Judgment

In accordance with general principles of international law, judgments of one country's courts are enforceable only within its territory. In other words, courts of foreign nations are not obligated to enforce the judgments of foreign courts under international law, except for the binding of international conventions or bilateral agreement on reciprocal recognition and enforcement. Even one country under international conventions or bilateral agreement on reciprocal recognition and enforcement has obligation to enforce foreign judgments, all countries usually require that the foreign judgments must be final and under its examination and approval. Grounds for non recognition includes lack of due process, fraud, violation of public policy, lack of jurisdiction over the parties, lack of notice, original forum was seriously inconvenient, and the original proceeding contravened a predispute agreement, etc. For example, the Restatement (third) of Foreign Relations Law of the United States provides that a court in the United States may not recognize a judgment of the court of a foreign state if:

(1) the judgment was rendered under a judicial system that does not provide impartial tribunals or procedures compatible with due process of law; or

(2) the court that rendered the judgment did not have jurisdiction over the defendant in accordance with the law of the rendering state and with the rules set forth in Section 421.

The Restatement further provides that a court in the United States need not recognize a judgment of the court of a foreign state if:

(1) the court that rendered the judgment did not have jurisdiction of the subject matter of the action;

(2) the defendant did not receive notice of the proceedings in sufficient time to enable him to defend;

(3) the judgment was obtained by fraud;

(4) the cause of action on which the judgment was based, or the judgment itself, is

repugnant to the public policy of the United States or of the State where recognition is sought;

(5) the judgment conflicts with another final judgment that is entitled to recognition; or

(6) the proceeding in the foreign court was contrary to an agreement between the parties to submit the controversy on which the judgment is based to another forum.

Under Civil Procedure Law of the People's Republic of China, if a legally effective judgment or written order made by a foreign court requires recognition and enforcement by a people's court of the People's Republic of China, the party concerned may directly apply for recognition and enforcement to the intermediate people's court of the People's Republic of China which has jurisdiction. The foreign court may also, in accordance with the provisions of the international treaties concluded or acceded to by that foreign country and the People's Republic of China or with the principle of reciprocity, request recognition and enforcement by a people's court.

In the case of an application or request for recognition and enforcement of a legally effective judgment or written order of a foreign court, the people's court shall, after examining it in accordance with the international treaties concluded or acceded to by the People's Republic of China or with the principle of reciprocity and arriving at the conclusion that it does not contradict the basic principles of the law of the People's Republic of China nor violates State sovereignty, security and social and public interest of the country, recognize the validity of the judgment or written order, and, if required, issue a writ of execution to enforce it in accordance with the relevant provisions of this Law; if the application or request contradicts the basic principles of the law of the People's Republic of China or violates State sovereignty, security and social and public interest of the country, the people's court shall not recognize and enforce it.

II. International Tribunals

This section discusses the International Court of Justice, the International Center for the Settlement of Investment Disputes, and dispute resolution panel of the WTO.

A. International Court of Justice

The International Court of Justice (ICJ) was created in 1945 as one of the organs of the United Nations. It was modelled on the Permanent Court of International Justice (PCOJ), which functioned as an organ of the League of Nations (国际联盟) from 1920 to 1939. The United Nations Charter declares that all the member states of the UN are automatically parties to the Statute of the International Court of Justice, which is included as an annex to the Charter. Nonmembers may adhere to the Statute, but to do so they must agree to respect the Court's decisions and to help cover the Court's expenses. [1]

1. Contentious Jurisdiction (诉讼管辖)

Before the ICJ can hear a contentious case, all of the state parties to the proceeding must have recognized the Court's jurisdiction. This is usually done in two ways: one is parties to an existing dispute negotiate a special agreement to let the ICJ decide the case, the other way is these agreements are made permanent by being included in a bilateral treaty.

2. Advisory Jurisdiction (咨询管辖)

Advisory jurisdiction refers to the power of the ICJ to give opinions about issues of international law at the request of the United Nations of one of its specialized agencies.

3. Judgments

If the parties to a dispute neither withdraw its suit nor have reached a settlement, the Court will deliver a judgment. In accordance with Article 59 of the Statute of the International Court of Justice, the decision of the Court has no binding force except between the parties and in respect of that particular case. And the judgment is final and without appeal.

Generally, most states have voluntarily complied with the judgment handed down by the Court. However, there are a few exceptions. For example, Albania refused to pay the damages awarded the United Kingdom by the Court for the injuries suffered by the United Kingdom's ships in the Corfu Channel in 1946. [2]

B. International Center for the Settlement of Investment Disputes

The International Center for the Settlement of Investment Disputes (ICSID) (解决投资争议国际中心) was created in 1965 at a conference in Washington, D. C., sponsored by the International Bank for Reconstruction and Development (popularly known as the World Bank). The underlying purpose of ICSID is to encourage private investment in underdeveloped countries. Many individuals and businesses had been reluctant to make investments, fearing they would be expropriated. To calm this fear, the World Bank drafted the Convention on the Settlement of Investment Disputes between States and Nationals of Other States (the Washington Convention), creating ICSID to provide a reliable mechanism for impartially resolving disputes between an investor and the country of investment.

In comparison to other international tribunals, the ICSID has some obvious characteristics: (1) The ICSID is a perfect international legal person. Thus, the ICSID

---

[1] Ray August, International Business Law, Higher Education Press, 2002, p. 111.

[2] Ray August, International Business Law, Higher Education Press, 2002, p. 118.

has contractual capacity to sue and be sued. (2) The ICSID has jurisdiction on the dispute only between the host state and the investor. (3) The investor and the host state must both consent to the ICSID jurisdiction. That's to say, if the proper consent has been given to establish an ICSID tribunal, then the tribunal can be set up even when the host state or the investor refuses to participate. Also, once consent has been given, it cannot be unilaterally withdrawn. A state party cannot withdraw by filling a later reservation to the Convention or even by denouncing the Convention. [1]

WTO Dispute Settlement Procedures has been already discussed in previous chapters.

III. Alternative Dispute Resolution

It is known to all that litigation as a means of settling disputes presents a number of problems at the international level. Consequently, many parties are turning to other ways of resolving problems; those methods are known collectively as alternative dispute resolution (ADR)(非司法方法). One of the most popular form of ADR is arbitration, which can be defined as "the submission for determination of the disputed matter to private unofficial persons selected in a manner provided by law or agreement." Other methods of ADR are negotiation, mediation, Mini-trial, etc.

A. Negotiation

Negotiation is the process of reaching an agreement by discussion. Despite its simplicity, negotiation is an important tool in the process of dispute settlement, and undoubtedly the one most commonly relied on. It is used not merely to resolve disputes but to prevent them from arising in the first place and to lay the groundwork for other forms of dispute settlement.

B. Mediation

Mediation involves the use of a third party who transmits and interprets the proposals of the principal parties and sometimes advances independent proposals. The terms "mediation" and "conciliation" are sometimes used as if they are interchangeable, and there is no general agreement as how they should be defined. However, in the international field a mediator is usually taken to be a person accepted by the parties whose role is to help them reach an agreed settlement. He will see each party privately and listen to their respective viewpoints. He will try to make sure that each party understands the other's point of view. He will also try to bring the parties together in order that they may themselves achieve a compromise solution. A conciliator performs a different function, in that he will himself draw

[1] Ray August, International Business Law, Higher Education Press, 2002, p. 127.

up and propose the terms of an agreement designed to represent what is, in his view, a fair compromise of a dispute, after having discussed the case with the parties.

Mediation and conciliation differ from arbitration in that they do not result in a binding or enforceable award. A mediator cannot compel the parties to reach a settlement; and a conciliator has no power to impose his award on the parties. If the party seeking a decision on their dispute, as opposed to a negotiated settlement, then mediation or conciliation is not for them.

Mediation and conciliation are long-established methods of resolving disputes, are now assuming increasing importance as a way of settling private commercial disputes in many countries in the world. In other words, mediation as a means to resolve international commercial disputes is in its very early stages. For example, The American Arbitration Association (AAA) began a program years ago in which a case manager would call the lawyers for the parties in new arbitration and then suggest mediation. By the year 2000, the AAA was doing perhaps 150 or so commercial mediations.

Internationally, the International Chamber of Commerce (ICC) has rules for the longest time that were called the "Rules for Conciliation and Arbitration." The ICC, as of July 1, 2001, published "ADR Rules" intended to replace the old rules. The ICC, in February 2007, hosted its Second Annual International Mediation Competition in Paris. The ICC's goal, obviously, is to promote the use of mediation to resolve cross-border disputes. In 2002, UNCITRAL adopted a Model Law on International Commercial Conciliation. Conciliation is defined in Article 1(3) as "a process whether referred to by the expression conciliation, mediation or an expression of similar import, whereby parties request a third person or persons to assist them in their attempt to reach an amicable settlement of their dispute."

What is more important is that the Chinese traditional cultures characterized with and known as harmonization internationally has a long history of settlement of disputes by mediation. In the practice of China International Economic and Trade Arbitration Commission (CIETAC), it is quite common and even expected that the arbitrator of the chair of the panel will, at some point in the proceedings, become a facilitator for the parties. That is, the arbitrator will actually recommend a settlement by mediation, and that the parties will often agree. This eliminates the risk of one of the parties "losing face"—a serious cultural taboo—and resolves the case after the merits have been fairly presented. [1] We can reasonably predict that, as a result of the rapid recognition of the

[1] Arthur W. Rovine, Contemporary Issues in International Arbitration and Mediation, Martinus Nijhoff Poblishers, 2007, p. 285.

Chinese traditional cultures internationally, there will be explosive growth of international mediation sooner.

Case 14－2 CHINA MEDIA EXPRESS HOLDINGS, INC., BY Karl BARTH as Receiver (Plaintiff) v. NEXUS EXECUTIVE RISKS, LTD., Torus Insurance (UK) Limited; AIG Insurance Hong Kong Limited, American Home Assurance Company; China Pacific Insurance Co. (H. K.), Ltd., and China Ping An Insurance (Hong Kong) Co. Ltd., (Defendants).

United States District Court, S. D. New York.
182 F. Supp. 3d 42, 04/25/2016

Facts: CME, a Delaware corporation with its principal place of business in Hong Kong, was created in 2009 through a "reverse merger" of a Chinese firm with a publicly traded company in the United States. After the completion of the reverse merger, CME was the defendant in a series of lawsuits and administrative proceedings alleging accounting fraud and securities fraud. One of those actions was a 2011 class action suit brought by CME's investors before this Court ("Securities Class Action,") alleging violations of federal securities law based on misstatements in public filings and press releases prior to a steep decline in CME's share prices in early 2011. After CME's counsel withdrew from representing CME in the Securities Class Action due to non-payment in the amount of $535.5 million was entered against CME pursuant to Rule 55(b)(2) of the Federal Rules of Civil Procedure. Further judgments were entered against CME in the other matters, including a $40 million arbitration award issued in a Hong Kong arbitration filed by investor Starr Investments Cayman II, Inc. and a $49 million penalty in a SEC administrative proceeding and civil lawsuit. The Court subsequently appointed Barth to serve as CME's receiver for the limited purpose of marshaling CME's assets. Barth's responsibilities include "the filing of litigation or arbitration that may be necessary to enforce CME's rights under [its] insurance policies."

From October 16, 2010 to October 15, 2011—the period in which the Securities Class Action and other related actions arose—CME maintained several layers of liability insurance. CME's insurance consisted of: (1) a primary directors and officers liability insurance policy ("Primary Policy") with a limit of $5 million in coverage written by Torus Insurance UK ("Torus") and Starr Underwriting Agents Ltd. ("Starr") (together with Torus, the "Primary

Insurers"); (2) the Excess Policy written by American Home's Hong Kong Branch with a $5 million limit in losses exceeding the coverage provided by the Primary Policy; and (3) the Second Excess Policy written by the Second Excess Insurers with a $10 million limit in losses exceeding the coverage provided by the Primary and Excess Policies, 60 percent of which would be paid by China Pacific and 40 percent of which would be paid by China Ping An. Each policy was negotiated and executed through CME's insurance broker, which was also based in Hong Kong. The Excess Policy and Second Excess Policy were subject to all material terms and conditions of the Primary Policy, including the Primary Insurers' obligations to fund the defense of covered claims against CME and to pay judgments against CME in excess of the Primary Policy's retention.

The Primary Policy, Excess Policy, and Second Excess Policy all contain dispute resolution provisions mandating dispute resolution via mediation or arbitration.

After the Securities Class Action was filed, CME informed the Primary Insurers and requested that they advance CME's defense costs. The Primary Insurers acknowledged their coverage obligations subject to a reservation of rights and requested further information from CME but ultimately refused to advance defense costs or indemnify CME for any judgment on the grounds of breach of warranty or fraudulent misrepresentation. American Home and the Second Excess Insurers adopted the coverage positions asserted by the Primary Insurers and declined to advance CME's defense costs.

The Court's Prior Findings on Arbitration: In his capacity as Receiver, Barth made a demand on the Primary Insurers, American Home, and the Second Excess Insurers for payment under the insurance policies. After receiving Barth's demand, the Primary Insurers filed a demand for arbitration in Hong Kong on August 13, 2015 seeking a declaration that CME was not due coverage because of breach of warranty and other coverage defenses. Barth moved the Court to enjoin the Hong Kong arbitration because the insurers had not sought prior leave of the Court to commence arbitration naming the court-appointed receiver. Barth additionally requested an order enjoining all future litigation or arbitration, arguing that such an order was necessary to permit him to preserve CME's assets.

The Court granted Barth's motion to enjoin the arbitration on October 21, 2015 but denied the request for an anti-litigation injunction. The Court observed that if a binding agreement to arbitrate exists, the Federal Arbitration Act ("FAA"), and the Convention on the Recognition and Enforcement of Foreign

Arbitral Awards would require the Court to grant leave to arbitrate if properly requested. In the October 21 Order, the Court ordered the Receiver to show cause why the Court should not grant the Primary Insurers leave to file an arbitration in Hong Kong to determine coverage under the Primary Policy. To avoid duplicative resolution of claims, upon the filing of the instant Complaint on October 26, 2015, the Court entered an Order in that case reserving decision on whether to grant leave for the Primary Insurers to file arbitration "until the Court has had the opportunity to review the answer or motion to dismiss" in the instant action.

On October 29, 2015, CME, through its Receiver, reached a settlement with Starr under which Starr paid $1.65 million to settle insurance claims against it arising from the Securities Class Action. On December 16, 2015, CME, through its Receiver, reached a settlement with Torus under which Torus paid $1.65 million to settle insurance claims against it arising from the Securities Class Action. Accordingly, the Complaint was dismissed as to the Primary Insurers.

In the instant Complaint, the Receiver argues that Defendant Insurers' failure to fund CME's defense in the Securities Class Action and related matters, and its refusal to indemnify CME for judgments in those matters, constituted a breach of CME's contract for insurance coverage with the Defendant Insurers. The Receiver seeks damages for breach of contract as well as consequential damages sustained as a result of Defendant Insurers' failure to advance CME's defense costs and indemnify CME for the $535.5 million default judgment in the Securities Class Action, the $40 million arbitration award and the $49 million SEC penalty.

Defendant Insurers filed the Motions in lieu of answers, seeking to dismiss the Complaint pursuant to Rule 12 of the Federal Rules of Civil Procedure. Defendant Insurers argue that the Receiver's claims are subject to the dispute resolution provisions in the Excess Policy and Second Excess Policy, both of which mandate mediation and arbitration in Hong Kong. According to Defendants, the Receiver's breach of contract claims fall within the plain language of the arbitration provisions and therefore must be mediated and potentially arbitrated. Defendants further argue that the Complaint should be dismissed on grounds of *forum non conveniens* grounds because the dispute resolution clauses in both policies specify Hong Kong as the proper forum.

Legal Analysis: The Federal Arbitration Act ("FAA") governs whether the Court must compel arbitration. ("A written provision in ... a contract evidencing a transaction involving commerce to settle by arbitration a controversy thereafter arising out of such contract or transaction ... shall be valid, irrevocable, and enforceable ..."). The Court finds that the arbitration clauses in the Excess Policy and the Second Excess Policy are broad. Here, the Court finds that the factual allegations supporting CME's claims are within the scope of the arbitration clauses, because they clearly touch matters covered by the Excess Policy and Second Excess Policy. CME specifically alleges that "Defendants' failure to advance CME's defense costs, failure to indemnify CME ... and wrongful denials of coverage for CME's claims, without any basis, constituted breaches of their contractual obligations under their respective insurance policies." The Complaint alleges that the Defendants adopted the coverage denials asserted by the Primary Insurers, who "had no intention of fulfilling their contractual obligations."

The Receiver argues that CME's claims do not fall within the scope of the dispute resolution provisions in the Excess Policy and Second Excess Policy because they arise from CME's alleged pre-contract nondisclosures and therefore do not involve the "ongoing performance of the Policy." Although the Receiver now reframes CME's cause of action as one implicating fraud in the inducement, the factual allegations in the Complaint tell a different story: the Complaint states that CME's insurers refused to defend and indemnify CME according to the insurance policies, after which CME's insurers defended their refusal by asserting CME's breach of contractual representations and pointing to applicable policy exclusions, including a provision excluding "any Claim ... brought about or contributed by ... the deliberately fraudulent or criminal acts of any Insureds."

At each stage, CME's claims and the Defendant Insurers' defenses alike are expressly premised on a breach of the insurance policies, which define the coverage obligations of the insurers and the contractual duties of the insured. The claims involve the "construction of the contract" and "the parties' rights and obligations under it." It is not a close question as to whether CME's claims "touch matters" covered by the Excess Policy and Second Excess Policy. The claims go to the heart of the contract's terms and are therefore within the purview of the arbitration clauses in those policies.

Convention on Recognition and Enforcement of Foreign Arbitral Awards: Because of the international character of the transactions underlying the Complaint, arbitration of this dispute is further compelled by the Convention on the Recognition and Enforcement of Foreign Arbitral Awards ("Convention"), which provides common standards for the recognition of arbitration agreements made in international commerce. The Convention is incorporated into the FAA.

In accordance with such policy, the Convention mandates arbitration where four factors are satisfied: (1) there must be a written agreement; (2) it must provide for arbitration in the territory of a signatory of the convention; (3) the subject matter must be commercial; and (4) the agreement cannot be entirely domestic in scope.

Each of these factors is satisfied in this case, just as each was satisfied in the October 21 Order addressing the Primary Insurers' proposed anti-litigation order. First, the Excess Policy and Second Excess Policy both contain written agreements to arbitrate. The Excess Policy provides that, after attempts at mediation, any dispute "arising out of this Policy" between CME and American Home "shall be referred to and determined and resolved by arbitration at HKIAC." The Second Excess Policy provides that after mediation attempts, any dispute "regarding any aspect of the operation of this Policy" between CME and China Pacific "shall be resolved by arbitration in the jurisdiction in Hong Kong." Second, both policies provide for arbitration in Hong Kong, which is a signatory to the Convention. Third, the subject matter of both agreements to arbitrate are clearly commercial in nature. Finally, the contractual agreements at issue here are not "wholly domestic" in scope: they were formed in Hong Kong, issued by Hong Kong-based companies, and contemplate the application of Hong Kong law in dispute resolution proceedings.

The Court finds that the Receiver has offered no new information that would compel a finding regarding the applicability of the Convention different from that made in the October 21 Order. Accordingly, the Court is persuaded that under the FAA and the Convention, the dispute resolution clauses contained in the Excess Policy and the Second Excess Policy require the arbitration of CME's dispute with Defendant Insurers.

Dismissal of the Action: Both American Home and the Second Excess Insurers request that the Court dismiss, not stay, CME's claims pending arbitration. The FAA directs the district court, "on application of one of the parties," to enter a stay in a case where the asserted claims are "referable to arbitration." The Court has determined that all of CME's claims must be submitted to arbitration.

Order: For the reasons stated above, it is hereby

ORDERED that the motion of defendant American Home Assurance Company to compel arbitration is GRANTED; and it is further

ORDERED that the motion of defendants China Pacific Insurance Co.

(H. K.), Ltd. and China Ping An Insurance (Hong Kong) Co. Ltd. to compel arbitration is GRANTED; and it is further

ORDERED that all claims brought by plaintiff China Media Express Holdings, Inc. are stayed against all defendants pending arbitration; and it is further

ORDERED that leave is granted to defendants American Home Assurance Company, China Pacific Insurance Co. (H. K.), Ltd., and China Ping An Insurance (Hong Kong) Co. Ltd. to file arbitration in Hong Kong against China Media Express Holdings, Inc. by and through Court-appointed Receiver Karl Barth to determine coverage under any applicable insurance policies.

SO ORDERED. [1]

C. Mini-trial

There are many varieties of "mini-trial" but the underlying concept is basically the same. A third party (sometimes called a "neutral adviser") and a senior member of management from each of the disputing parties form a mini-trial panel. The parties meet to agree the ground rules of the process, which will concentrate primarily on a severe limitation of the number of documents to be disclosed and on the time to be taken by each party in preparing its brief and presenting its case.

On the date appointed for the hearing each party makes a presentation of its case. Following this hearing the management representatives of each party meet by themselves to try to agree upon a settlement. If so requested, the neutral adviser will give an oral opinion on the likely outcome if the case were to go to trial. Following this, the parties may again attempt to negotiate a settlement. The proceedings, which are sometimes described as a "compromise negotiation," are confidential and may not be referred to in any subsequent litigation; however, evidence that would otherwise be admissible or discoverable is not rendered inadmissible or non-discoverable as a result of its presentation or use at a mini-trial.

ADR is a new way of resolving international commercial disputes, and it has some advantages such as bigger reduction of time and expense than conventional methods of resolving disputes, such as litigation, arbitration. However, ADR still has certain limits: (1) ADR is likely to work better where the parties and the mediator have the same or a similar national background. Thus, the scope of ADR is rather limited. (2) The aim of

---

[1] https://1.next.westlaw.com/Link/Document/FullText?findType=Y&serNum=2029962500&pubNum=0004637&originatingDoc=I59b6f810135511e6a3c8ab9852eeabcd&refType=RP&originationContext=document&transitionType=DocumentItem&contextData=(sc.Search), visit on 12 January, 2020.

ADR is compromise and there are some disputes which cannot, or should not be, be compromised. For example, the interpretation of a clause in a standard-form contract of insurance or banking, may affect hundreds or thousands of other contracts, and compromise on this interpretation can hardly reached. (3) There are cases where one party is wholly right and the other is holly wrong. Why should the party which is wholly right take 50 per cent, or less of its entitlement? Humanity's sense of justice (and injustice) is strong, therefore this is perhaps a moral rather than a material point. Obviously, it is unwise to go too far to create a situation to "do a deal", regardless humanity's natural sense to pursue justice and equality. (4) One party may find it better to delay and not agree to any meaningful resolution of the dispute, this will add to the delay and expenses of reaching a resolution of the dispute. [1]

IV. Commercial Arbitration

Uncertainty about identity of the country and the court in which a dispute may be heard, about procedural and substantive rules to be applied, about the degree of publicity to be given the proceedings and the judgment, about the time needed to settle a dispute, and about the efficacy which may be given to a resulting judgment all have combined to make arbitration the preferred mechanism for solving international commercial disputes. Some Western European countries long have been accustomed to arbitration. For example, the London Court of Arbitration, a private arbitration institution, has existed since 1892. The United States has had a Federal Arbitration Act since 1947. Arbitration is also favoured in Asian countries. For example, the China International Economic and Trade Arbitration Commission (CIETAC) and the Chinese Maritime Arbitration Commission (MAC) are becoming increasingly important in settlement of international commercial disputes in the world. Also, the Japan Commercial Arbitration Association has been active since 1953.

Historically, arbitration provisions appeared in Treaties of Friendship, Commerce and Navigation of which the purpose is to ensure the enforcement of arbitration clauses in commercial contracts between nationals of the Contracting States to the treaty. The treaty provisions also required the courts of each Contracting State to enforce the awards of arbitral tribunals rendered under such arbitration clauses, even though the place of arbitration is not located within the Contracting States and the arbitrators are not nationals of the Contracting States.

---

[1] Alan Redfern and Martin Hunter, Law and Practice of International Commercial Arbitration, Sweet & Maxwell, 1991, p. 35.

A. Definition and Special Features

International commercial arbitrations take place daily in different parts of the world. Usually they proceed in accordance with rules agreed by the parties or laid down by the arbitral tribunal without obvious reference to any outside system of law. Arbitration is a method of dispute resolution involving one or more neutral third parties who are usually agreed to by the disputing parties and whose decision is binding. [1]

In international business practices most disputes are resolved by arbitration, if the parties themselves are unable to reach an agreement. Arbitration in contrast with litigation has a number of special features.

1. Arbitration is a Private Process

Arbitration is a private process, an advantage in the eyes of those who do not want details of their quarrels to be disclosed in open court, with the possibility of further publication elsewhere.

2. Arbitration Offers the Parties the Opportunity to Choose their Own Judge

Under arbitration rules the parties usually have the right to choose their own judge, in a way which is not usually possible in court proceedings. One or more arbitrators may be chosen for their special skill and expertise in commercial law, civil engineering or some other relevant discipline. An experienced arbitral tribunal of this kind should be able to grasp quickly the salient issues of fact or law in dispute and so save the parties both time and money, as well as offering them the prospect of a sensible award.

3. There is Continuity in Arbitration

As the arbitral tribunal is appointed to deal with one particular case, the arbitrators follow this case from the beginning to the end, unlike a judge who often makes his appearance when all the pleadings and relevant documents of its role enables an arbitral tribunal to get to know the parties, their advisers and the case as it develops through the pleadings. This is useful for the parties to save expenses and time.

4. Arbitration is in Principle more Flexible, Adaptable and Efficient than Litigation

A trial before a national court must be conducted in accordance with the rules of that court. These rules are usually detailed and will have been established over a long period. They must be capable of dealing with many different kinds of cases. They may well be unsuitable for the trial of commercial disputes. In arbitral proceedings, it should be possible to tailor the rules to fit the particular case which is being arbitrated. For example, the parties may agree to limit the extent of disclosure of documents; to submit evidence in writing; to impose time limits on the length of speeches.

---

[1] Bryan A. Garner, Black's Law Dictionary, St. Paul, Minn. ,1999,p. 100.

Arbitration also has obvious disadvantages: a major weakness of the arbitral process is its limited powers. For example, if it becomes necessary for an arbitral tribunal to take coercive action, such action must usually be taken indirectly, through the machinery of the local courts, rather than directly, as a judge himself can do.

Another perceived drawback ofthe arbitral process lies in the fact that, in general, it is not possible to bring multi-party disputes together before the same arbitral tribunal. [1]

B. The Applicable Procedure Law

In practice, any international arbitration is a forensic minefield. During its course, as many as five or six different national systems of law, or legal rules, may come into play. It would be too much to expect that there will be no material difference between them. On the contrary, the potential for conflict is great—whether it concerns capacity to arbitrate, constitution of an arbitral tribunal, time limits for commencing proceedings, interest on awards or some other aspect of the arbitral process.

It is a feature of international commercial arbitration that it usually takes place in a country which is "neutral" in the sense that it is not the place of business or residence of the parties to the dispute. This means that, in practice, the law which governs the arbitration is likely to be different from the law which governs the substantive matters in dispute.

With regard to the determination of the applicable procedure law for a case, there are usually two important principles:

1. The Lex Arbitri

The doctrine of Lex Arbitri (仲裁地法) means that the proceedings of arbitration are regulated by the law of the place in which the arbitration takes place. This doctrine is a traditional way to determine the procedure law for an arbitral case. This theory has influenced the wording of international conventions from the Geneva Protocol of 1923 to the New York Convention of 1958. The Geneva Protocol states: "The arbitral procedure, including the constitution of the arbitral tribunal, shall be governed by the will of the parties and by the law of the country in whose territory the arbitration takes place." [2]

Clearly, the choice of a particular place of arbitration may have important and unintended consequences if the law of that place confers powers on the courts or the arbitrators not expected by the parties.

---

[1] Alan Redfern and Martin Hunter, Law and Practice of International Commercial Arbitration, Sweet & Maxwell, 1991, p. 25.

[2] Alan Redfern and Martin Hunter, Law and Practice of International Commercial Arbitration, Sweet & Maxwell, 1991, p. 81.

2. The Doctrine of Delocalised Arbitration(非地方化仲裁理论)

The doctrine of lex arbitri has been based on two propositions. The first is that an international commercial arbitration is itself governed by law; the second is that this governing law is that of the state in which the arbitration takes place. It is plain that a court is governed by the law of the country in which it sits. In the same way an arbitral tribunal is governed by the law of the country in which it sits. Although an arbitral tribunal is not a court, in this respect at least its position is analogous to that of a court.

However, in recent years, it has become fashionable to seek to detach international commercial arbitrations from control by the law of the place in which they are held. Such "detached" arbitrations go by many names. They are called "supra-national," "transnational" or even "expatriate." They are said to be "denationalised." More poetically, they are referred to as "floating" arbitrations resulting in so-called "floating awards (浮动裁决)."

There are several reasons for the delocalisation of international commercial arbitration. The first reason is that as a matter of principle, international commercial arbitrations should not be subject to legal controls which vary considerably from country to country and which indeed, in some countries, may be wholly unsuited to the modern practice of international commercial arbitration. This theory clearly reflects an understandable desire for uniformity in the regulation of international commercial arbitration. The second reason is that a law of arbitration is merely a set of procedural rules and that, in an international commercial arbitration, these rules may be made by the parties themselves or by the arbitral tribunal on their behalf. The third reason is that any legal control of the arbitral process ought not to come from the place in which the arbitration is held but from the country in which enforcement of the award is sought.

Obviously, the intention underlying the delocalisation theory is to grant freedom to international commercial arbitration from the constraints of different national legal systems, and so make the place of arbitration a matter of no legal significance. An arbitral tribunal would not need to be concerned with the law of the place in which the arbitration was being held; all that it would need to do would be to comply with the requirements of international public order so as to insure the international acceptability of its award.

The delocalisation theory is now said to apply to all international commercial arbitrations, irrespective of whether or not a state is a party. In support of this view, it is pointed out that the place in which an international commercial arbitration is held is often a matter of chance. The choice of place of arbitration by the parties, or by an arbitral institution, is generally guided by the desire to find a country which is neutral, and which is convenient.

C. The Applicable Substantive Law

When questions of procedure have been settled, the principal task of the arbitral tribunal is to establish the material facts of the dispute. It does this by examining the agreement between the parties, considering other relevant documents, and by hearing witnesses if necessary. The arbitral tribunal then builds its award on this foundation of facts, making its decision either on the basis of what it considers to be fair and reasonable or, more usually, on the basis of law.

Usually, changes in the law applicable to the contract may bring about changes in the contract itself. Therefore, it is not enough to know what agreement the parties have made, and it is essential to know what law is applicable to that agreement. In a purely domestic contract, the applicable law will usually be that of the country concerned. If a Chinese woman purchases a dress in a Beijing boutique, Chinese law will be the applicable or proper law of that contract; equally, American law will be applicable or proper law when an American man buys a bottle of whisky in New York. Yet further complexity is inevitable when the contract is in respect of an international transaction. There may then be two or more different national systems of law capable of qualifying as the proper law〔1〕 of the contract; and these different national systems may contain contradictory rules of law on the particular point or points in issue.

In practice of international commercial transactions, there are several methods of choosing proper law.

1. Major Methods of Choosing Proper Law(实体法)

The autonomy of the parties. There is a principle of law which is generally accepted, and which directs international commercial arbitrators to the correct choice of the law applicable to an international commercial contract. This is the principle of the autonomy of the parties. By this is meant the freedom of the parties to choose for themselves the law applicable to their contract.

The doctrine of party autonomy, which was first developed by academic writers and then adopted by national courts, has gained extensive acceptance in national systems of law. Despite their differences, common law, civil law and socialist countries have all equally been affected by the movement towards the rule allowing the parties to choose the law to govern their contractual relations. It is the result of separate, contemporaneous and pragmatic evolutions within the various national systems of conflict of laws.〔2〕

---

〔1〕 Proper law means "the substantive law that, under the principles of conflicts of law, governs a transaction." (See Bryan A. Garner, Black's Law Dictionary, St. Paul, Minn. ,1999 ,p. 1232.)

〔2〕 Alan Redfern and Martin Hunter, Law and Practice of International Commercial Arbitration, Sweet & Maxwell,1991 ,p. 98.

This doctrine is also extensively used in international conventions. For instance, the Rome Convention (signed on June 19, 1980, by the Member States of the Europe Economic Community) which is applicable to contractual obligations accepts the choice of applicable law by the parties in the exercise of their autonomous will as a basic principle. Article 33 (1) states: "The arbitral tribunal shall apply the law designated by the parties as applicable to the substance of the dispute."

Among the rules of arbitral institutions, the Article 17 of the ICC Arbitration Rules provides:

"The parties shall be free to agree upon the rules of law to be applied by the Arbitral Tribunal to the merits of the dispute. In the absence of any such agreement, the Arbitral Tribunal shall apply the rules of law which it determines to be appropriate." Article 28 (1) of the UNCITRAL Model Law provides: "The arbitral tribunal shall decide the dispute in accordance with such rules of law as are chosen by the parties as applicable to the substance of the dispute. Any designation of the law or legal system of a given State shall be construed, unless otherwise expressed, as directly referring to the substantive law of that State and not to its conflict of laws rules."

These examples indicate clearly that there is a striking unanimity on the rule of party autonomy. Indeed it is one of the few principles of law which appears to be of general, if not universal, application in the field of international commercial arbitration, although some conflicts of law systems require some restrictions. For instance, the Rome Convention requires that the choice shall be bona fide, no offence against public policy, and a connection between the law chosen and the transaction itself.

The international arbitral tribunal chooses the proper law. Conflict of law rules differ from one country to another. A judge or arbitral tribunal in one country may select the applicable law by reference to the place where the contract was made, whereas in another country it may be selected by reference to the law with which the contract has the closest. In the context of international commercial arbitration, this is plainly unsatisfactory; the seat of the arbitration is usually chosen for reasons other than the conflict rules of the forum. Here, the question is that is an international arbitral tribunal bound to follow the conflict of law rules of the country in which it has its seat? Modern tendency is that more and more advocates hold that an international arbitral tribunal is not obliged to follow the conflict of laws rules of the country in which the arbitration has its seat.

Some international conventions support this new doctrine. The Article 42 (1) Washington Convention states that in the absence of any choice of the applicable law by the parties the arbitral tribunal must apply the law of the contracting state which is a party to the dispute, together with such rules of international law as may be applicable. The provision of the European Convention of 1961 is more close to the new doctrine by stating that failing any indication by the parties as to the applicable law, the arbitrators shall apply the proper law under the rules of conflict that the arbitration deems applicable. [1] A similar approach is adopted in the UNCTRAL Arbitration Rules, of which Article 33 provides that failing any designation of the applicable law by the parties, the arbitral tribunal shall apply "the law determined by the conflict of laws rules which it considers applicable." The UNCITRAL Model Law adopts the same terminology in Article 28 (2). Clearly, the intention of these provisions is that the arbitral tribunal should be given almost complete freedom to choose the applicable law in the absence of any choice of law by the parties.

2. Laws to be possibly Chosen as Applicable Law

Subject only to the qualifications of bona fides and of no public policy objection, the parties have the right to choose the law applicable to the dispute. The question which then arises is what system of law should the parties choose as the law applicable to the dispute? Is their choice limited to the choice of a national system of law or may it extend beyond this, perhaps to rules of law such as those of the law merchant? This section examines these issues.

(1) National law. In most cases, parties who choose a law to govern their contract, or any subsequent dispute between them, will choose an autonomous system of law. This may be a national law. There is much sense in such a choice of law. First, a national law is usually complete legal system. It is not merely a set of general principles or of isolated legal rules. It is an inter-connecting, inter-dependent collection of laws, regulations and ordinances, enacted by or on behalf of the state and interpreted and applied by the courts. It is complete legal system which should be inherently capable or providing an answer to any legal question which might be posed. Second, a national system of law will be a known and existing system, capable of reasonably accurate interpretation by experienced practitioners. Furthermore, a national system of law provides a known legal standard, against which the rights and responsibilities of the parties can be measured. In the event of a dispute, the parties can be advised with reasonable confidence as to their legal position; or, at the very least, they can be given a broad indication of their chances success or failure.

Experience indicates that the choice of a suitable system of national law is the choice most commonly made in international commercial contracts. However, there are still objections to the choice of a national system of law: inadequacy, unsuitability for

[1] European Convention of 1961, Article VII.

international trade, national interests, unfair treatment, etc. [1]

(2) Public international law. J. Brierly in his "The Law of Nations" defined the public international law as "the body of rules and principles of action which are binding upon civilized states in their relations with one another." [2] However, public international law in modern times is no longer concerned simply with states. It extends to international organisations such as the United Nations, and even individuals or groups of individuals. Therefore, public international law is capable of applying to commercial contracts, particularly where one of the parties to the contract is itself a state or state entity. There are already some examples of the use of public international law to regulate a primarily commercial relationship in recent decades. [3]

(3) The general principles of law. There are various opinions as to what the general principle of law concept is intended to refer. Some writers regard it as an affirmation of Natural Law concepts, which are deemed to underlie the system of international law, and constitute the method for testing the validity of the positive rules. Other writers, particularly positivists (实证法学家), treat it as a sub-heading under treaty and customary law and incapable of adding anything new to international law unless it reflects the consent of states. Anyway, most writers are prepared to accept that the general principles do constitute a separate source of law but of fairly limited scope, and this is reflected in the decisions of the Permanent Court of International Justice and the International Court of Justice. For instance, the International Court of Justice in the *Corfu Channel* case when referring to circumstantial evidence, pointed out that "this indirect evidence is admitted in all systems of law and its use is recognised by international decision." Five years later in the *Administrative Tribunal* case the Court emphasized: "according to a well-established and generally recognizsed principle of law, a judgment rendered by a judicial body is res judicata and has binding force between the parties to the dispute." [4]

In practice, the general principles of law are frequently referred to in choice of law clauses, whether alone, or in conjunction with some national system of law or as forming

[1] Alan Redfern and Martin Hunter, Law and Practice of International Commercial Arbitration, Sweet & Maxwell, 1991, p. 103.

[2] Barry E. Carter and Phillip R. Trimble, International Law, Little, Brown and Company New York, 1995, p. 2.

[3] Alan Redfern and Martin Hunter, Law and Practice of International Commercial Arbitration, Sweet & Maxwell, 1991, p. 106.

[4] Alan Redfern and Martin Hunter, Law and Practice of International Commercial Arbitration, Sweet & Maxwell, 1991, p. 159.

part of international trade law.

(4) The lex mercatoria. In search for the proper law, it is suggested that the traditional choice of law is out of touch with the realities of modern international trade; and that what is needed is not a particular national system of law, but a modern law merchant. Such a law would meet the requirements of international commerce in much the same way as the lex mercatoria met the requirements of traders living under the Roman Empire; or as enactments of customary law (such as the celebrated *Consulato del Mare*) met the needs of sailors and merchants in the Mediterranean in the fourteenth century. Here the lex mercatoria refers to the modern lex mercatoria that covers much more than traditional lex mercatoria.

In practice, some national courts and international institutions such as the ICC have already made awards based on the new lex mercatoria.

D. Arbitration Agreement and Arbitration Clauses

The agreement to arbitrate is the foundation stone of international commercial arbitration. It serves to evidence the consent of the parties to submit to arbitration; and this consent is indispensable to a process of settling disputes which depends upon the agreement of the parties for its very existence.

There are two basic types of arbitration agreement. The first, and more common, is an agreement to submit future disputes to arbitration; The second is an agreement to submit existing disputes to arbitration; an agreement of this kind is commonly referred to as a "submission to arbitration agreement" or, simply, a "submission agreement."

1. International Standards for Arbitration Agreement and Arbitration Clauses

Under the New York Convention, each contracting state undertakes to recognise and give effect to an arbitration agreement when the following requirements are fulfilled:

(1) The agreement must be in writing. Although in some systems of law no particular form is required for an arbitration agreement, under the more modern international arbitration laws, the requirement that an agreement must be in writing has been preserved. For instance, the UNCITRAL Model Law states that the arbitration agreement shall be in writing. An agreement is in writing if it is contained in a document signed by the parties or in an exchange of letters, telex, telegrams or other means of telecommunication which provide a record of the agreement, or in an exchange of statements of claim and defence in which the existence of an agreement is alleged by one party and not denied by another. The reference in a contract to a document containing an arbitration clause constitutes an arbitration agreement provided that the contract is in writing and the reference is such as to make that clause part of the contract. The Netherlands Arbitration Act 1986 requires that the arbitration agreement shall be proven

by an instrument in writing expressly or impliedly accepted by the parties.

(2) There must be distinction between existing disputes and future disputes. This is important because certain states, notably in the Middle East, do not recognise the validity of an agreement to refer future disputes to arbitration.

(3) Arbitrability. This relates to public policy limitations upon arbitration as a method of settling disputes. Each state may decide, in accordance with its own economic and society policy, which matters may be settled by arbitration and which may not. If the arbitration agreement covers matters incapable of being settled by arbitration, under the law of the agreement or under the law of the place of arbitration, the agreement is ineffective since it will be unenforceable.

(4) Validity. This requirement means that an international effective arbitration agreement should be valid under the law to which the parties have subjected it or, failing any indication thereon, under the law of the country where the award was made.

The validity of an arbitration agreement is of crucial importance.

2. Scope of the Arbitration Agreement

Usually, the arbitration agreement should have the following contents:

(1) The parties' intention to settle a particular dispute through arbitration.

(2) The scope of the arbitration. The arbitrator will look at the proper law of the arbitration agreement to decide whether the wording of the clause covers the dispute which is sought to be arbitrated.

(3) The Arbitral institution. There is no shortage of arbitral institution across the globe today, thus the arbitration agreement should make a choice of arbitration agreement. In order to choose a satisfied arbitral institution for proper resolution, there are usually four criteria for careful consideration: (a) it must have a set of rules which are both fair and effective; (b) it must have an experienced and competent staff; (c) It must be wholly independent in the way in which it is established and operated; (d) It must be able to offer an acceptable assurance of permanence.

(4) Arbitral procedure rules.

(5) Selection of arbitrators—a minimum number of three may be required, and an odd number usually is required.

(6) Payment of arbitrator fees.

(7) Nature of the proceedings—in China arbitration proceedings are public, while in other countries they are private.

(8) Ex aequo et bono (公平合理原则). In some countries, the arbitrators may not decide a dispute ex aequo et bono unless the parties empower the arbitrators to act on that basis.

(9) Validity of the award.

3. Major Implications in Arbitration Agreement

Commercial experience indicates that some important provisions are usually implied in every arbitration agreement unless a contrary intention is expressed therein:

(1) If no other mode of reference is provided, the reference shall be to a single arbitrator.

(2) If the reference is to two arbitrators, the two arbitrators shall appoint an umpire immediately after they are themselves appointed.

(3) If the arbitrators have delivered to any party to the submission or to the umpire a notice in writing, stating that they cannot agree, the umpire may forthwith enter on the reference in lieu of the arbitrators.

(4) The parties to the reference, and all persons claiming through them respectively, shall, subject to any legal objection, submit to be examined by the arbitrators or umpire, on oath or affirmation, in relation to the matters in dispute and shall subject as aforesaid, produce before the arbitrators or umpire all books, deeds, papers, accounts, writings and documents within their possession or power respectively which may be required or called for, and do all other things which during the proceedings on the reference the arbitrators or umpire may require.

(5) The witnesses on the reference shall, at the discretion of the arbitrators or umpire, be examined on oath or affirmation.

(6) The award to be made by the arbitrators or umpire shall be final and binding on the parties and the persons claiming under them respectively.

(7) The costs of the reference and award shall be in the discretion of the arbitrators or umpire who may direct to and by whom and in what manner those costs or any part thereof shall be paid, and may tax or settle the amount of costs to be paid or any part thereof and may award costs to be paid as between solicitor and client.

(8) The arbitrators or umpire shall have the same power as the court to order specific performance of any contract other than a contract relating to land or any interest in land.

(9) The arbitrators or umpire may, if they think fit, make an interim award.

4. Three Examples of Arbitration Clauses

(1) This contract shall be governed by and construed in accordance with the United Nations Convention on Contracts for the International Sale of Goods 1980 and any dispute arising out of and in connection to this contract, and the breach, termination or invalidity thereof, shall be settled amicably through negotiation. In case no settlement can be reached through negotiation, the case shall then be submitted to arbitration. The

location of arbitration shall be in the country of domicile of defendant. If in China, the arbitration shall be conducted by the China International Economic and Trade Arbitration Commission of the China Council for the Promotion of International Trade, Beijing for arbitration in accordance with its Rules of Arbitration (1998). The arbitral award is final and binding upon both parties. The arbitration expenses shall be borne by the losing party unless otherwise awarded by the arbitration organization.

(2) This charter shall be governed by and construed in accordance with English law and any dispute arising out of this charter shall be referred to arbitration in London in accordance with the Arbitration Acts 1950 and 1979 or any statutory modification or re-enactment thereof for the time being in force, one arbitrator being appointed by each party. On the receipt by one party of the nomination on writing of the other party's arbitrator, that party shall appoint their arbitrator within fourteen days, failing which the decision of the single Arbitrator appointed shall apply. If two arbitrators properly appointed shall not agree, they shall appoint an umpire whose decision will be final. [1]

(3) This contract shall be governed by and construed in accordance with the United Nations Convention on Contracts for the International Sale of Goods 1980 and any dispute arising out of and in connection to this contract, and the breach, termination or invalidity thereof, shall be settled amicably through negotiation. In case no settlement can be reached through negotiation, the case shall then be submitted to the China International Economic and Trade Arbitration Commission of the China Council for the Promotion of International Trade, Beijing for arbitration in accordance with its Rules of Arbitration (1998). The arbitral award is final and binding upon both parties.

E. Recognition and Enforcement of Awards

A party who succeeds in an international commercial arbitration expects the award to be performed without delay. The purpose of arbitration, unlike conciliation and most other methods of alternative disputed resolution, is to arrive at a binding decision on the dispute between the parties. It is an implied term of every arbitration agreement that the parties will carry out the award.

Experience indicates that most arbitral awards are in fact carried out voluntarily. However, unlike a court of law, an arbitral tribunal has no role to play in the enforcement of its decision. Once the award has been rendered, the arbitral tribunal usually has nothing more to do with the dispute, because its work is done. If the losing party fails to carry out the arbitral award, the winning party may apply to the court for an order that

[1] Yang Liangyi, International Commercial Arbitration, Publishing House of the China University of politics and Law, 1997, p. 115.

the bank accounts or other assets of the losing party be seized to satisfy the award of the arbitral tribunal. The mechanisms for such court proceedings vary from country to country. However, the effect of the international conventions, culminating in the 1958 United Nations Convention on the Recognition and Enforcement of Foreign Arbitral Awards (the New York Convention).

The New York Convention is a considerable improvement upon the Geneva Convention of 1927, since it provides for a much more simple and effective method of obtaining recognition and enforcement of foreign awards. The New York Convention has been praised in glowing terms. It has been described as "the single most important pillar on which the edifice of international arbitration rests." Further, it has been said that the Convention "perhaps could lay claim to be the most effective instance of international legislation in the entire history of commercial law." [1]

Under the opening article, an award made in any state (even if that state were not a party to the New York Convention) would be recognised and enforced by any other state which was a party to the Convention, so long as the award satisfied the basic conditions set down in the Convention. However, Article 1 (3) of the Convention allows states which adhere to the Convention to make two reservations: reciprocity and commercial relationships.

Reciprocity means that any state may, on the basis of reciprocity, declare that it will apply the Convention to the recognition and enforcement of awards made only in the territory of another contracting state. Commercial relationships of the Convention entitles a contracting state to declare that it will only apply the Convention to differences arising out of legal relationships, whether contractual or not. The effect of this reservation, like the reservation as to reciprocity, is to narrow the field of application of the New York Convention.

1. Formalities for Recognition and Enforcement

The New York Convention provides for both recognition and enforcement of awards to which the Convention applies. So far as recognition is concerned, a state bound by the Convention undertakes to respect the binding effect of awards to which the convention applies. So far as enforcement is concerned, a state which is a party to the Convention undertakes to enforce awards to which the Convention applies, in accordance with its local procedural rules.

The formalities required for obtaining recognition and enforcement of awards to

---

[1] Alan Redfern and Martin Hunter, Law and Practice of International Commercial Arbitration, Sweet & Maxwell, 1991, p. 457.

which the New York Convention applies are simple. The party seeking such recognition and enforcement is merely required to product to the relevant court: the award, and the arbitration agreement under which it was made.

2. Grounds for Refusal(拒绝理由)

In accordance with the New York Convention, the losing party may raise seven different grounds on which recognition and enforcement of an award may be refused at the request of the party against whom it is sought.

(1) Incapacity of the parties or invalidity of the arbitration agreement.

(2) Denial of a fair hearing. To succeed on this ground, it must be shown that: "The party against whom the award is invoked was not given proper notice of the appointment of the arbitrator or of the arbitration proceedings or was otherwise unable to present his case." [1]

(3) Excess of authority of lack of jurisdiction. To succeed on this ground, it must be shown that: "The award deals with a difference not contemplated by or not falling within the terms of the submission to arbitration, or it contains decisions on matters beyond the scope of the submission to arbitration, provided that, if the decision on matters submitted to arbitration can be separated from those not so submitted to arbitration may be recognised and enforced." [2]

(4) Procedural irregularities. To succeed on this ground, it must be shown that the composition of the arbitral authority or the arbitral procedure was not in accordance with the agreement of the parties, or failing such agreement was not in accordance with the law of the country where the arbitration took place.

(5) Invalid award. To succeed on this ground, it must be shown that the award has not yet become binding on the parties, or has been set aside or suspended by competent authority of the country in which or under thc law of which, that award was made.

(6) Arbitrability. Recognition and enforcement of an award may be refused if the court finds that the subject-matter of the difference is not capable of settlement by arbitration under the law of that country.

(7) Public policy. Recognition and enforcement of an award may be refused if the court finds that the recognition or enforcement of the award would be contrary to the public policy of that country.

In recent years, courts in western countries tend to explain more strictly public policy as a ground for refusal of recognition and enforcement of foreign arbitral awards. For

---

[1] The New York Convention, Article V. 1. (b).

[2] The New York Convention, Article V. 1. (c).

instance, in the case of *Parsons & Whittemore Overseas Co., Inc. v. Societe General de l' Industrie du Papier (RAKTA)*, the District Court for the District of New York was confronted by an argument that recognition and enforcement of an award should be refused on the grounds that diplomatic relations between Egypt (the defendant's state) and the United States had been severed. The court rejected this argument and held that the Convention's public policy defence should be construed narrowly; and that enforcement of foreign arbitral awards should only be denied on this basis, "where enforcement would violate the forum's states most basic notions of morality and justice."[1]

Case 14-3 Assam Company India Limited v. Canoro Resources Ltd

2014 BCSC 370

The Supreme Court of British Columbia, Vancouver

Facts: On February 23, 2001 the petitioner ("Assam") entered into a "production sharing contract" with the Indian government with respect to a potential oilfield known as Amguri. In November 2003 Assam was granted an oil lease of the Amguri field by the State of Assam. In May 2004 Assam and the respondent ("Canoro") entered into a joint operating agreement ("JOA") with respect to the Amguri field. Canoro's assigned "participating interest" was 60%. Assam's "participating interest" was 40%. The JOA appointed Canoro as the "operator" of the project until such time as, among other things, it ceased to hold a "participating interest". Article 13 of the JOA addressed the sale, transfer or assignment of either party's "participating interest" and provided for the other party to have a right of first refusal. This right was said to apply "to any sale or assignment of the stock of a Party other than to an Affiliate hereto where the principal or sole asset of such party at the time of such sale is its Participating Interest under the Contract".

Article 18 of the JOA provided for arbitration of any disputes between the parties. That article read as follows: The Parties shall use their best efforts to settle amicably all disputes, differences or claims arising out of or in connection with any of the terms and conditions of this Agreement or concerning the interpretation or performance thereof.

Any dispute, difference or claim arising between the Parties hereunder which cannot be settled amicably may be submitted by any Party to arbitration pursuant to

[1] Alan Redfern and Martin Hunter, Law and Practice of International Commercial Arbitration, Sweet & Maxwell, 1991, p. 464.

Article 18.3. The Arbitral tribunal shall consist of three arbitrators. The Party or Parties instituting the arbitration shall appoint one arbitrator and the Party or Parties responding shall appoint another arbitrator and both Parties shall so advise the other Parties. The two arbitrators appointed by the Parties shall appoint the third arbitrator.

If the two arbitrators appointed by the Parties fail to agree on the appointment of the third arbitrator within thirty (30) days of the appointment of the second arbitrator and if the Parties do not otherwise agree, under the Arbitration and Conciliation Act 1996, the first Party may appoint the third arbitrator who shall not be a national of the country of any Party. If any of the arbitrators fails or is unable to act, his successor shall be appointed in the manner set out in this Article as if he was the first appointment.

The decision of the arbitral tribunal, and, in the case of difference among the arbitrators, the decision of the majority, shall be final and binding upon the Parties.

Prior to submitting a dispute to arbitration, a party may submit the matter for conciliation under the Arbitration and Conciliation Act 1996 as amended or re-enacted from time to time by conciliators to be appointed by mutual agreement of the Parties. If the Parties fail to agree on a conciliator (or conciliators) in accordance with the said rules, the matter may be submitted for arbitration. No arbitration proceedings shall be instituted while conciliation proceedings are pending. The venue of conciliation or arbitration proceedings pursuant to this Article, unless the Parties otherwise agree, shall be in New Delhi and shall be conducted in the English Language. Insofar as practicable, the Parties shall continue to implement the terms of this Agreement notwithstanding the initiation of arbitral proceedings and any pending claim or dispute.

The fees and expenses of conciliator(s) appointed by the Parties shall be borne equally by the contending Parties. Assessment of the costs of arbitration including incidental expenses and liability for the payment thereof shall be at the discretion of the arbitrators.

In April 2010 Canoro entered into an investment agreement with Mass Financial Corp. pursuant to which the latter acquired approximately 18% of the common shares of the former. In July 2010 Mass Financial Corp. acquired further common shares from Canoro thereby bringing its total shareholdings to approximately 53% of the total outstanding shares of Canoro. On April 28, 2010 Assam filed a petition in the High Court of Delhi seeking to restrain Canoro from proceeding with the Mass Financial transactions and claiming that those transactions had resulted or would result in a breach of the production sharing agreement. Canoro's Indian counsel appeared before the court to oppose the petition. On May 18, 2010 the High Court refused to grant the injunction requested by Assam but did issue a *lis pendens* order which allowed the Mass transactions to proceed subject to the findings of an arbitration tribunal should arbitration be pursued by Assam.

On August 19, 2010 Assam invoked the arbitration clause (Article 18) of the JOA and named retired Justice J. K. Mehra as its nominee arbitrator. Canoro nominated its arbitrator, retired Justice A. P. Shah, on September 22, 2010, 34 days after Assam's nomination and within the 45-day requirement stipulated in Article 18.5 of the JOA. Purporting to invoke its rights under Article 18.6 of the JOA, Assam appointed Mr. Lim Kim Jim as the third and presiding arbitrator. That individual is a senior Malaysian barrister based in Kuala Lumpur.

In the meantime, citing a breach of the production sharing contract, on August 27, 2010 the Indian government terminated Canoro's participating interest in the Amguri field. Canoro promptly filed a petition with the High Court of Delhi on August 29, 2010 seeking to restrain that termination, and on August 31, 2010 the High Court granted an interim order restraining the Indian government from terminating or transferring Canoro's interest in the Amguri field.

Canoro disputed the validity of Mr. Lim's appointment as the presiding arbitrator and on December 21, 2010 filed a petition in the Supreme Court of India seeking relief under section 11(6) of that country's *Arbitration & Conciliation Act*, 1996 ("the *Indian Arbitration Act*"). That section (discussed further below) provides that where a party fails to act as required under an arbitration appointment procedure agreed upon by the parties, the other party may request the Chief Justice of India to take "the necessary measure". The petition filed in the Supreme Court of India sets out in detail the basis for Canoro's objection to the validity of Mr. Lim's appointment. It asserts noncompliance with the procedure contemplated by Article 18.6 of the JOA, at least insofar as Canoro's interpretation of that article was concerned. The petition claimed "a plain reading of the article makes it abundantly clear that if the two nominee arbitrators failed to agree on the third presiding arbitrator, the parties may first consult with each other and if after such mutual consultations the parties are still unable to resolve the matter," then a petition to the Chief Justice of India is the next step. It claimed that any entitlement Assam may have had to unilaterally appoint the third arbitrator was "intended to be a last resort" and one not exercisable "unless the alternative procedure contained in the said article is first explored and exhausted". The petition also claimed "deliberate and malicious intent" on Assam's part in refusing to consult with Canoro before "arbitrarily and unilaterally" appointing Mr. Lim.

When the petition first came on for hearing before the Supreme Court of India, the matter was adjourned to permit counsel for the petitioner to circulate a number of judgments which were intended to be cited as part of Canoro's submissions. When the hearing resumed on April 29, 2011, no one appeared on behalf of Canoro. The court issued an order saying, among other things, that dismissing the petition in default would serve no purpose as it would defeat the very purpose of these proceedings for speedy disposal of the matter. However, in the interest of justice, one last adjournment was granted. It was made clear that on the next date of hearing, the matter shall be decided on merits irrespective of whether any of the Counsel or any of the parties are present. The matter was then adjourned to May 6, 2011. On May 6, 2011, counsel appeared for Canoro. Instead of arguing the merits of the case at that time, however, Canoro's counsel made a request to withdraw the petition. The request was granted and the Supreme Court issued an order that "the arbitration petition is dismissed as withdrawn".

In the meantime, the arbitral tribunal was attempting to move matters forward. Canoro had initially protested the validity of Mr. Lim's appointment by letter dated December 6, 2010 and it continued to repeat this objection in its ensuing correspondence to both counsel for Assam as well as the tribunal itself. In one such letter dated May 13, 2011 counsel for Canoro requested that the tribunal "please issue fresh procedural directions after considering the convenience of all concerned, as is the norm. We further request the tribunal to first consider hearing of the 'preliminary issue' and to grant a proper and valid opportunity to our client to be heard in this matter".

The "preliminary issue" referred to, as the letter itself identified, was "the hearing of the question of the validity of the appointment of Mr. Lim as the presiding arbitrator". On July 28, 2011 a new procedural timetable was issued by the tribunal. Among other things, the timetable imposed deadlines in August for the filing of written submissions respecting the "preliminary issues" and scheduled a hearing of those issues for September 13 and 14, 2011. On July 26, 2011 Canoro's counsel wrote a letter to the tribunal advising that they "are no longer going to be representing Canoro Resources Limited in the matter". No reason was given. From that point forward no one appeared on behalf of Canoro in the arbitration proceedings. The tribunal ordered Assam to take out ads in two New Delhi newspapers advising Canoro of, among other things, the hearing scheduled for

September 13 and 14, 2011. It also ordered Assam to serve such notice on Canoro at its offices in Canada and India. All of these steps were taken. The hearing of the "preliminary issues" proceeded on September 13, 2011 in the absence of Canoro. The tribunal decided that Mr. Lim's appointment had been "in strict compliance with the provisions of Article 18.6 of the JOA". The decision was unanimous. On October 24 and 25, 2011, the tribunal held hearings on the merits of Assam's substantive claims in the arbitration. Witnesses were called and oral submissions were made. Further written submissions were ordered and submitted.

The Parties' Positions: Canoro's positions. Canoro invokes subsections 36(1) respecting the appointment of Mr. Lim, the "inability to present their case", and the "improper" composition of the arbitral tribunal. In addition, Canoro asserts that all of these things taken together also support refusing recognition or enforcement of the Award as being contrary to the public policy in British Columbia. In its written submissions Canoro identifies "serious grounds" for refusing recognition/enforcement of the Award as follows: (1) Canoro was not given an opportunity to be heard contrary to the basic principles of natural justice and procedural fairness.... Although Canoro initially participated in the arbitration, they were "forced to withdraw as, given the circumstances surrounding the arbitration, it had no or little chance to receive a fair hearing by the arbitral tribunal"; (2) the composition of the arbitral tribunal was not in accordance with the agreement of the parties.... Assam did not consult as required pursuant to s. 18.6 of the JOA but rather unilaterally appointed the third arbitrator (Mr. Lim) thereby "stacking the deck" in Assam's favor; (3) the arbitral proceeding in India therefore lacked impartiality and fairness; and (4) the Award thus made would be contrary to the public policy in British Columbia.

In addition, Canoro says that the conflicting affidavit evidence filed on behalf of the parties "raises serious and disputed issues of fact and law" warranting a trial including the following: (1) the interpretation of Article 18.6 of the JOA which provides for the process of instituting an arbitration proceeding and constitution of an arbitral tribunal; (2) the interpretation of the *Indian Arbitration Act* as applied to Canoro's objections to the process and constitution of the arbitral tribunal in India; (3) unilateral appointment of the third presiding arbitrator by Assam despite Canoro's objections; (4) the independence and impartiality of the arbitral tribunal; (5) Canoro's incapacity to present its case before the arbitral tribunal.

Assam's positions. Assam's "key points" in reply to Canoro's various objections are that: (1) Canoro voluntarily walked away from both the arbitration and its own legal proceeding before the Supreme Court of India, where all of the above questions were put squarely in issue, and therefore it is not open for them to assert a lack of procedural fairness or, indeed, to re-litigate the same issues in British Columbia. (2) If Canoro is permitted to abandon the arbitration process in India and later raise and re-litigate in another forum (British Columbia) procedural fairness objections to recognition and enforcement of the arbitration award, it would undermine principles of international comity and the very enforcement code prescribed by the 1985 UNCITRAL Model Law on International Commercial Arbitration.

The Honorable Mr. Justice Kent made conclusion on Recognition and Enforcement the following order: (1) Except for the transfer of shares directed pursuant to Article 228(vi) of same, the award of Mr. Lim Kim Jim, Presiding Arbitrator, retired Justice J. K. Mehra, Arbitrator, and retired Justice A. P. Shar, Arbitrator, made in New Delhi, India, on November 21, 2011 (the "Award") shall be recognized as binding and enforceable in British Columbia. (2) The monetary portion of the Award shall carry interest of 12% per annum commencing March 20, 2012 and continuing until the date of payment or recovery as the case may be. (3) The monetary portion of the Award and accrued interest from March 20, 2012 to the date of judgment shall be converted into Canadian currency pursuant to the provisions of the Foreign Money Claims Act, R. S. B. C. 1996, c. 155 and the Foreign Money Claims Regulation, B. C. Reg. 165/96. (4) Judgment based on the Award shall be signed and entered as a judgment of the Supreme Court of British Columbia and is enforceable in British Columbia in the same manner as any other British Columbia judgment of the same effect. (5) If pursuit of the share transfer directed pursuant to Article 228(vi) of the Award is desired and the parties are unable to agree on the mechanism for accomplishing same, Assam may make further application to this Court for approval of alternative mechanisms by which enforcement of this aspect of Award might be accomplished.

F. Enforcement of Foreign Arbitral Awards in the People's Republic of China

1. Implementation of the New York Convention

On 2 December 1986, the 18th Session of the Standing Committee of the Sixth National People's Congress of the People's Republic of China adopted the *Decision of the Standing Committee of the National People's Congress on China Joining the Convention on the Recognition and Enforcement of Foreign Arbitral Awards* within which it was decided that China shall join the 1958 New York Convention. In the meanwhile, two reservations were declared as follows:

(1) The People's Republic of China will apply the Convention to the recognition and enforcement of arbitral awards rendered in the territory of another Contracting State only on the basis of reciprocity (the "reciprocity reservation").

(2) The People's Republic of China will apply the Convention only to disputes which have, according to the laws of the People's Republic of China, been determined as arising out contractual relationship or non-contractual commercial legal relationships (the "commercial" reservation).

Thus the 1958 New York Convention became effective in China on 22 April 1987. These two reservations are explained in the Notice on the Convention by the Supreme People's Court of China on 10 April 1987. China's accession to the Convention is subject to the reciprocity reservation. Accordingly, China will apply the Convention only with respect to arbitral awards made within the territory of another Contracting State. Also, China will apply the Convention only to disputes arising out defined legal relations which are considered to be commercial relations of contractual and non-contractual nature under Chinese law. The phrase "commercial relations of a contractual and non-contractual nature" is defined in the notice as "relations concerning economic rights and obligations arising out of contract, tort or relevant statutory provisions". Examples of such relations provided in the notice include but are not limited to: purchase and sale of goods, lease of property, engineering projects, processing, technology transfer, equity joint venture, cooperative joint venture, exploration and exploitation of natural resources, insurance, borrowing, labor matters, agency, consulting services and the transport of passengers and goods by sea, in civil aviation, by air and by road, as well as products liability, environmental pollution, accidents at sea and disputes over ownership rights, etc. however, the disputes between foreign investors and governments of host countries are excluded from the ambit of application of the Convention by the notice.

2. Relevant Provisions of the Civil Procedure Law of the People's Republic of China

On 9 April 1991, the Fourth session of the Seventh National People's Congress adopted an amended *Civil Procedure Law of the People's Republic of China* (hereafter called "China Civil Procedure Law") (民事诉讼法) which introduces a number of new provisions relating to the enforcement of arbitral awards. On 31 August 1994, the Ninth Session of the Standing Committee of the Eighth National People's Congress of the People's Republic of China adopted the Arbitration Law of the People's Republic of China (hereafter called "China Arbitration Law"). China Arbitration Law basically follows the China Civil Procedure Law in respect of enforcement of awards by merely referring to the relevant provisions embraced in the China Civil Procedure Law.

The China Civil Procedure Law has formulated different treatments for enforcement of Chinese domestic arbitral awards, Chinese foreign-related or international awards and the foreign arbitral awards. Enforcement of foreign arbitration awards that are made in the territory of a foreign country other than China may be pursued according to Article 269 of the China Civil Law which permits the applicant to apply for recognition and enforcement of foreign arbitral awards either by invoking relevant international treaties, or, in the absence of international treaties, by relying on the principle of reciprocity.

In most cases, the enforcement of foreign arbitration award will fall within the domain of the 1958 New York Convention, Article V. However, under the Chinese law, a broader construction on the grounds for denial of enforcement has been put into use, while with respect to the Convention awards, the grounds should be construed narrowly, as it were under the New York Convention.〔1〕

Although enforcement of arbitral awards in China has given rise to special concern of foreigners since China's adoption of the New York Convention,〔2〕a number of foreign arbitral awards have already been enforced by Chinese courts in China. We firmly believe that foreign arbitral awards will, encouraged by China's accession to WTO and the rapid economic development in China, be enforced more and more successfully in China soon.

■ Notes

forum non conveniens 不方便法院理论。通常情况下,在国际民事诉讼活动中,原告可以自由地选择一国法院而提起诉讼,这就有可能选择对自己有利,而对被告不利的法院,从而不能保证争议得到公正、迅速有效的解决。因此,对诉讼同样具有管辖权的法院,可以依职权或根据被告的请求作出自由裁量而拒绝行使管辖权。也就是说,根据该理论,如果法院认为自己在受理某诉讼时具有“严重的不方便”,就可以指示原告去另一个更为方便的法院进行诉讼,从而平衡原告和被告的利益,使争议得到公正而有效的解决。

doctrine of delocalized arbitration 非地方化仲裁理论。该理论主要指当事人可以在其合同中约定,仲裁不依从任何特定的国家的程序法,任何特定国家的冲突法规则,或任何特定法律体系的实体法,以达到当事人意思自治和符合当事人利益的目的。也就是说,仲裁员不必非适用仲裁地的冲突规则,除非他们认为这些冲突规则是合适的。仲裁理论主要包括以下几个方面:首先,充分尊重当事人的意思自治原则。国际商事仲裁与诉讼的本质区别是,当事人在仲裁中享有充分的意思自治权利。既然当事人可以就仲裁涉及的实体

〔1〕 Wang Sheng Chang, Resolving Disputes Through Arbitration in Mainland China, Law Press, 2003, p. 338.

〔2〕 Wang Sheng Chang, Resolving Disputes Through Arbitration in Mainland China, Law Press, 2003, p. 342.

法作出选择,当事人就应该也有权选择仲裁程序法,即仲裁可以在一国境内进行仲裁,但可以不适用该仲裁地国的仲裁法。其次,公正、平等地解决争议是国际商事仲裁中当事人的最主要愿望。这就要求在仲裁中尽量避免可能的干预,例如,组成仲裁庭的仲裁员应分别来自不同的国家,特别是首席仲裁员或独任仲裁员,一般应具有与当事人双方不同的国籍,仲裁所在地应为争议双方所属国以外的国家或地区,那么,当事人也应该有权选择任何国家的仲裁程序法,以排除来自各方可能的干预,确保仲裁裁决的公正性和平等性。采用该理论作出的裁决,通常称为“浮动裁决”(floating awards)。

■ Important Legal English Usage

solve 解答,解决。例如,Knowing certain values enables us to solve the equation(知道某些数值便能使我们解出这道方程)。Computers can solve complicated problems(计算机可以解决复杂的问题)。

注意下列几个近义词的用法:

(1)resolve:决心,分解,解决。例如,alternative dispute resolution(非司法方法)。

(2)settle:解决,决定,结算。法律上用得较多。例如,to settle a dispute(解决纠纷),settlement by arbitration(仲裁解决),settlement of accounts in full(总决算)。

choose 选择,挑选,选定。该词主要强调作出选择的行动,有时也强调最终的决定。例如,choice of jurisdiction(管辖选择),choice of law(法律选择)。

注意下列几个近义词的用法:

(1)cull:拣出,挑出。指从坏的东西中择出好者,从好物中剔除坏者。例如,They are culling the seals(他们保留良种海豹,捕杀劣者)。

(2)elect:选举,作出选择。例如,We elect our school captain by a show of hands(我们用举手表决的方法推选校队队长)。

(3)select:选择,选拔。与 choose 相比,select 强调从数件事物中择取,从两件事物中选择时用 choose。例如,At the beginning of the trial, a great deal of time was spent selecting the jurors(审判开庭之初,大量时间花在选择陪审员这件事上)。

get 得到,获得。该词是最常用语之一,使用很广泛。例如,How can I get a ticket(我怎样才能获得一张票)?

注意与下列近义词在用法上的区别:

(1)obtain:得到,获得。主要强调经过努力,或请求而获得。例如,to obtain confession by compulsion and give it credence(逼供信),to obtain pecuniary advantage by deception(欺诈取得金钱利益)。

(2)gain:获得。强调比 obtain 要更加努力,通常含有努力或通过竞争而获得的优势,胜利的意思。例如,Through technology, science helps man to gain increasing control over his environment（科学通过技术帮助人类获得对环境越来越大的控制能力）。

（3）acquire：获得。主要指凭借自己的工作技术、行动等而获得，含有逐步、缓慢、长期不断的努力而获得的意思。法律上用来表示对领土、财产及国籍等的取得。例如，acquired nationality（取得国籍），acquired rights（取得权利），acquisition and loss of ownership（所有权的取得和丧失）。

procure 获得。该词是正式用语，含有须经过努力和仔细注意而得到的意思。例如，The book is out of print and difficult to procure（那本书已绝版，难以获得）。

■ Review Questions

1. Define jurisdiction and venue, giving at least two examples.
2. Explain minimum contacts. What applications do they have in international disputes?
3. State A sues State B in the International Court of Justice. The ICJ hands down a judgment that is adverse to State B. State B refuses to comply with the judgment. what can State A do to get State B to comply?
4. How is a foreign court judgment usually enforced? Give two examples.
5. Compare and contrast 'negotiation', 'mediation' and 'mini-trial' and list their advantages respectively.
6. Define 'international commercial arbitration' and state its main features.
7. What are the risks associated with and advantages of arbitration? Give two examples.
8. How would a choice of law clause and a clause clearly delineating the power of the arbitrator help to address some of a party's concerns?
9. List and explain the doctrines of choice of procedure and substantive law, giving at least three examples.
10. Describe briefly the scope of an arbitration agreement.
11. How can a company minimize the possibility of coming under a particular court's jurisdiction? Should this issue be a concern to a business?
12. Give two examples to illustrate how foreign arbitral awards are recognized and enforced in China.

Bibliography

1. Alan Redfern and Martin Hunter: Law and Practice of International Commercial Arbitration, Sweet & Maxwell New York,1991.
2. Andreas F. Lowenfeld, International Economic Law, Oxford University Press,2002.
3. Arthor Linton Corbin: Corbin on Contracts, West Publishing Co. ,1952.
4. Arthur W. Rovine, Contemporary Issues in International Arbitration and Mediation, Brill Nijhoff,2014.
5. Barry E. Carter and Phillip R. Trimble, International Law, Little, Brown and Company New York,1995.
6. Blair J. Kolasa, The Legal Environment of Business, Addion-wesley Publishing Company, 1984.
7. Bruce D. Fisher & Michael J. Phillips, The Legal Ethical, and Regulatory Environment of Business, West Publishing Company New York,1995.
8. Cal Zhenshun, ed. , Studies on International Business Law, Law Press,1998.
9. Cao Jianming & Chen Zhidong, ed. , International Economic Law Review, vol. 2, 6,Law Press,2000.
10. Caroyn Hotchkiss, International Law for Business, McGraw-Hill Inc. ,1994.
11. Catharine Titi and Katia Fach Gómez, Mediation in International Commercial and Investment Disputes,Oxford University Press,2019.
12. Chen An ed. , International Economic Law Review, vol. 1, 2, 5,Law Press,1998、1999、2002.
13. Chen An, ed. , International Trade Law,Beijing University Press,2000.
14. Clive M. Schmitthoff: Commercial Law in a Changing Economic Climate, Second Edition, Sweet & Maxwell, 1981.
15. Clive M. Schmitthoff 's Selected Essays on International Trade Law, Chia-Jui Cheng ed. , Kluwer, 1998.
16. Clive M. Schmitthoff: Merchantile Law, London Stevens & Sons,1984.
17. CM. Bianca & M. J. Bonell: Commentary on the International Sales Law: The 1980 Vienna Sales Convention,1988.
18. E. Allan Farsworth: Contracts, Second Edition, Little, Brown and Company Boston, 1990.

19. Elliot I. Klayman, John W. Bagby and Nan S. Ellis, Irwin's Business Law, Irwin Boston, 1994.
20. Evan McKendrick, Contract Law, Law Press. China, 2003.
21. Feng Datong, ed., International Trade law, Beijing University Press, 1995.
22. Francis D. Rose, Lex Mercatoria, MPG Books London, 2000.
23. Gary B. Born, Interantional Arbitration: Law and Practice, Wolters Kluwer, 2016.
24. Giuditta Cordero-Moss, International Commercial Contracts and the Applicable Law, Cambridge University Press, 2011.
25. Han Jian, Theories and Practice of Modern International Commercial Arbitration Law, Law Press. China, 2000.
26. Houston Putnam Lawry, Critical Documents Sourcebook Annonated: International Commercial Law and Arbitration, 1991.
27. Jane P. Mallor, A. James Barnes, Thomas Bowers, Michael J. Phillips, Arlen W. Langvardt: Business Law and the Regulatory Environment, McGraw-Hill New York, 1998.
28. J. Honnold: Uniform Law for International Sales under the 1980 United Nations Convention, 1982.
29. Jiang Zuoli, International Business Law, Shanghai People Press, 2003.
30. Liang Huixing, ed., Civil and Commercial Law Review, vol. 2, 8, 10, 13, Law Press. China, 1994、1997、1998、1999.
31. John H. Jackson, The Jurisprudence of GATT & the WTO, Higher Education Press, 2002.
32. Li Wei, Comment of the United Nations Convention on Contracts of International Sale of Goods, Law Press. China, 2002.
33. Mauro Rubino-Sammartano, International Arbitration Law and Practice, Citic Publishing House, 2003.
34. Michael Joachim Bonell, An International Restatement of Contract Law, 2nd ed. Irvington-on-Hudson, New York, 1997.
35. Ralph H. Folsom, Michael Wallace Gordon, and John A Spanogle, Jr, International Business Transactions, Press of China People University, 2001.
36. Ray August: International Business Law, Second Edition, Prentice Hall, New Jersey, 2013.
37. Richard Schaffer, Beverley Earle, Filiberto Agusti: International Business Law And Its Environment, West Publishing Company, 1996.
38. Robert N. Corley, O. Lee Reed, Peter J. Shedd and Jere W Morehead, The Legal and Regulatory Environment of Business, McGraw-Hill. Inc. New York, 1996.
39. Robert W. Hamilton, The Law of Corporations, Law Press. China, 1999.
40. Shen Muzhu, Studies on International Trade Law, Law Press. China, 2002.

41. Shen Sibao, International Business Law, Press of University of International Economics and Trade, 2003.
42. Song Hong, Recognition and Enforcement of International Business Commercial Awards, Law Press. China, 2000.
43. Stephen Judge: Business Law, Palgrave MacMillan Law Masters, Law Press. China, 2003.
44. Sun Nanshen, WTO Rules and Chinese Economic Law on Foreign Business, Law Press. China, 2001.
45. Tina Hart and Linda Fazzani, Intellectual Property Law, Law Press. China, 2003.
46. Wang Shengchang, Resolving Disputes Through Arbitration in Mainland China, Law Press. China, 2003.
47. Wayne Pendleton & Roger Vickery, Australian Business Law, Prentice Hall Sydney, 1998.
48. Wei Runqun & ChenXin, Law and Practice of Sea Cargo Insurance, China Finance Press, 2001.
49. Xing Haibao, Law of Bills of Lading, Law Press. China, 1999.
50. Yang Liangyi, Rules of International Business, Press of China University of Politics and Law, 2000.
51. Yang Liangyi, Letters of Credit, Press of China University of Politics and Law, 1998.
52. Zhou Ruiqi, Wang Xiaoou and Xu Yuefang, International Trade Practice, University of International Business and Economic Press, 2016.
53. Zhu Yikun, Concise Chinese Law, Law Press. China, 2003.